BOHDAN ?

The Ukrainian
Resurgence

HURST & COMPANY, LONDON

Published in the United Kingdom by
C. Hurst & Co. (Publishers) Ltd.,
38 King Street, London WC2E 8JZ
© Bohdan Nahaylo, 1999
All rights reserved.
Printed in Malaysia

ISBNs
1-85065-169-8 (cased)
1-85065-168-X (paper)

CONTENTS

v

MAPS

ILLUSTRATIONS

between pages 240 and 241

PREFACE

Ukraine's re-emergence from political oblivion and its achievement of independence were major historical events which changed the map of Europe and altered international relations generally. They were the decisive factor which scuttled schemes to preserve the Soviet Union in a revamped form and which precipitated its demise. The Ukrainian resurgence also defined the arrangement which replaced the Soviet Union – the Commonwealth of Independent States (CIS) – as a loose association of independent states, rather than a supranational entity. Since then, Ukraine's determination to stick to its chosen path of independence has thwarted efforts to promote the political and military integration of the CIS into a new bloc, facilitated NATO's enlargement in the east, and transformed the fledgling state into one of Europe's pivots.

Just as in 1917-20, when attempts to establish an independent Ukrainian state were met with scepticism or outright hostility, so Ukraine's reassertion of its desire for sovereignty and independence took many by surprise and the initial reaction was ambivalent. Indeed, the very idea of Ukraine as a distinct nation and country did not fit into traditional political and historiographical schemes. This stemmed largely from the erroneous but widespread tendency to regard Russia and the Soviet Union as one and the same thing and the failure to understand the actual nature of the multinational former Soviet empire. The basic lack of knowledge about Ukrainian history and culture, resulting in the belief or assumption that the Ukrainians are simply Russians who speak a different dialect, also did not help. As Norman Davies noted in his ground-breaking comprehensive history of Europe, 'the best thing to do with such an embarrassing nation', which refused to disappear meekly under both tsarist and Soviet domination, 'was to pretend that it didn't exist'.[1]

In reality, throughout most of the twentieth century, Ukraine remained Europe's largest nation to have been denied the right to

[1] Norman Davies, *Europe: A History*, Oxford and New York, 1996, p. 41.

xi

national self-determination. While externally its fate passed largely unnoticed, some of the more astute observers drew attention to its predicament. As far back as the late 1950s, the incisive scholar of Communism, Milovan Djilas, asked in his celebrated *The New Class:* 'Who knows anything nowadays about Ukrainian writers and political figures? What has happened to that nation, which is the same size as France, and was once the most advanced nation in Russia [that is, the Russian Empire]?'[2] More than a decade later, after the Soviet invasion of Czechoslovakia, the Czech writer Milan Kundera, while reflecting on the erasure of historical memory, noted poignantly in his *The Book of Laughter and Forgetting*: 'Over the past five decades forty million Ukrainian have been quietly vanishing from the world without the world paying heed.'

Ukraine was the Soviet Union's most important non-Russian republic and, in order to ensure that it remained docile, as in the tsarist era, Ukrainian national aspirations were ruthlessly suppressed. The republic was closely integrated into the centralized Soviet political and economic system and its proclaimed sovereignty remained a legal fiction. In addition to the political absorption and Sovietization which accompanied it, the Ukrainians were also confronted with official policies promoting cultural assimilation, denationalization and Russification. Although the Ukrainians were by far the largest non-Russian nation in the Soviet Union, they were, together with the Belarusians, linguistically and culturally the closest to the Russians; therefore, they were particularly vulnerable to Russification through the erosion of their native language and sense of national history, as well as suppression of their national churches. Furthermore, in the post-war period, Russians continued flooding into Ukraine; by 1989 they formed a huge 11-million-strong minority in the republic, and today they are the largest Russian group living outside of Russia proper. This unabated inflow and the restrictions on the development of Ukrainian national institutions perpetuated the sharp regional differences, which for various historical reasons distinguished the more nationally assertive Western Ukraine from the Russified Eastern part of the country, hindering national integration and the completion of the processes of modern nation- and state-building.

How then, after being seemingly written off so long ago, did

---

[2] Milovan Djilas, *The New Class*, New York, 1957, p. 102.

Ukraine manage in a relatively short time, and without bloodshed, to reassert itself? How did the process of revival begin, who led it, and how did it develop into a powerful movement for national renewal and emancipation? What obstacles and weaknesses faced this drive during the period of *glasnost, perestroika* and imperial decay, which external factors influenced and inspired it, and how did the movement eventually succeed? Were the Ukrainians simply beneficiaries of the collapse of the Soviet system, to what extent did they actually have to struggle to achieve their freedom, and how did they contribute to the dissolution of the USSR? These are some of the key questions addressed in this book.

This account would have been incomplete without some attempt to examine the nature of the new independent Ukrainian state, its viability and prospects. The last chapters of the book, therefore, chart the first five or so years of independence and explore how Ukraine has coped with the new challenges and opportunities which the change in its status has brought. They describe how, in the face of economic crisis, internal divisions and friction with Russia, Ukraine consolidated independence, grappled with the problems of transition to democracy and a market economy, and, while preoccupied with state-building, sought greater security for itself within the new Europe.

In tracing Ukraine's road to independence and beyond, an attempt has been made to situate the country's political evolution in a wider historical and geopolitical context. Continuities between the Ukrainian past and present have been indicated, the benefits and costs of Soviet rule considered, and the significance of Ukraine as a regional and international factor, even when not an independent actor, highlighted.

By examining Soviet nationalities policy towards Ukraine and describing how the Soviet Union's decline and disintegration were experienced in its most significant and, at that time, also politically most loyal (at least as far as the local Communist leadership was concerned) non-Russian republic, this book also offers additional insights into the nature and collapse of the Soviet Union. By also focusing on the question of Ukrainian-Russian relations, both on the bilateral plane and within the CIS, and examining Ukraine's attitude towards its other neighbours and the West, the study is also intended to contribute to a better understanding of the post Soviet set-up in the CIS and Eastern and Central Europe.

I began writing this book shortly after Ukraine became independent and initially wanted to chronicle how this had come about
while the events were still fresh in the mind. As someone who had
closely followed these developments, I was aware that I was well
placed to attempt such a study, and the cartons of research material
I had accumulated seemed to beg to be processed and made sense
of.

From the very outset of my academic and professional career, I
had been particularly interested in human rights issues and the
nationalities question in the Soviet Union. As a post-graduate
student at the London School of Economics and Political Science,
I was fortunate to have as my mentors Peter Reddaway and Leonard
Schapiro, who already in the mid-1970s were prepared to support
what was then still a rather unconventional research topic in the area
of Soviet studies – a case study of Ukraine under Shelest. After my
academic studies, from 1978 to 1982 I was Amnesty International's
Researcher on the Soviet Union and afterwards wrote extensively
for the British and American press on Soviet affairs. Eventually, in
1990, together with the late Victor Swoboda who taught at London
University's School of Slavonic and Eastern European Studies, I
published a comprehensive history of the nationalities problem in
the Soviet Union.[3] Writing in late 1989, I concluded with the
observation that 'genuine democratization and the preservation of
empire, however disguised, are incompatible', and predicted that
among the likely scenarios for the 1990s was 'the gradual break-up
of the empire' and 'the creation of some sort of Soviet Commonwealth'. As is known, though, the rapidity of the dissolution of the
'immovable Union' during the next two years took everyone by
surprise, observers and direct participants in the process alike.

Meanwhile, from 1984, I worked as a research analyst for Radio
Free Europe/Radio Liberty (RFE/RL) in Munich, specializing in
Soviet foreign policy and nationalities issues generally and Ukraine
in particular. RFE/RL, an American-financed radio station, control
of which had been taken over in the early 1970s from the CIA by
the US Congress, not only broadcast uncensored information each
day to the peoples of Eastern and Central Europe and the Soviet
Union in their own languages, but also had a renowned research

---

[3] Bohdan Nahaylo and Victor Swoboda, *Soviet Disunion: A History of the
Nationalities Problem in the USSR*, London and New York, 1990.

department, complete with impressive archives, a media-monitoring network and regular analytical publications. At RFE/RL, with its unrivalled publicly-accessible collections of newspapers, journals, books and unofficial writings or *samizdat* from Eastern Europe and the Soviet Union, and rich pool of specialists, I was able to develop my knowledge and understanding of the Soviet Union, and build up my own personal records and expertise on the subjects of particular interest to me.

In May 1989 I was privileged to be appointed Director of the Ukrainian Service of RFE/RL, a position I continued in until September 1991. This meant that during the crucial period from when the cracks in the Soviet edifice had just begun to appear to when Ukraine and other non-Russian republics had declared their independence, I was entrusted with responsibility for supervising the preparation of a daily three-hour programme which, because of the limitations of *glasnost*, was eagerly listened to by millions in Ukraine and the eastern Ukrainian diaspora from Poland, Czecho-slovakia and Romania to Almaty and Vladivostok. The challenge for me and my team was to provide a programme corresponding to the needs of those exciting but still uncertain times, offering timely and balanced news, current affairs and analysis, supplemented with coverage of historical, cultural and religious themes, as well as information about the Ukrainian diaspora. Gradually, as demo-cratization continued to make headway, I was able to establish (telephone) contact with, and eventually meet and interview, many of the leading and less well-known Ukrainian political and cultural figures. In the summer of 1990 I finally made the first of my many visits to Ukraine.

After independence was declared, I returned to analytical research and till the spring of 1994 was an Assistant Director at the RFE/RL Research Institute. I was responsible for coverage of the inde-pendent non-Russian states which had emerged as a result of the collapse of the Soviet Union. It was during this time, in early 1992 to be precise, that with the encouragement of my publisher, Chris-topher Hurst, I began work on this book. Initially it was to have been a brief account of how Ukraine had become independent.[4]

---

[4] This initial effort was published in the form of a brief report by the Royal Institute of International Affairs, which, in places, I have drawn on. See Bohdan Nahaylo, *The New Ukraine*, London, 1992.

But as I began to examine the research material I had collected and tried to fill gaps in it, started interviewing some of the many contacts I had established in Ukraine, and realized just how little scholarly literature had actually been produced about modern Ukraine, I decided to invest the time and effort in producing a more substantial study – one which in fact could serve as a surrogate concise political history of modern Ukraine and offer a tentative picture of the new independent Ukrainian state.

Thus, the book turned out to be longer and more detailed than I had anticipated when I took on the project. I also changed jobs in May 1994 and moved to Geneva, where my new responsibilities for the UN High Commissioner for Refugees left me little spare time after work in which to write. Consequently, with the generous understanding of my publisher, the completion date was pushed back by several years until 1998. If this book helps to fill a void in the literature, chronicles some of what might otherwise be forgotten about an extraordinary period, stimulates interest, discussion and further research, and serves as a rough but useful map for other scholars, the investment will have been worthwhile.

In the book I have used the Ukrainian forms for the names of places and individuals (unless they are Russians). Although, for example, the capital of Ukraine, Kyiv, is still generally referred to in English-language sources in its Russian form as Kiev, the time has come to acknowledge the profound political changes that have taken place during the 1990s and to begin using the Ukrainian name for the city, as the United Nations and OSCE already do. After all, depending on who ruled over Ukraine, the city was variously known as Kijow (Polish) and Kiev (Russian). Today, in independent Ukraine, the official name of the capital is finally Ukrainian, just as the city formerly known as Lwow, Lemberg and Lvov is now Lviv and Odessa is Odesa. This 'nativization' of the names of cities is of course by no means peculiar to the Ukrainians and should not be dismissed out of hand as a manifestation of nationalism: it is a feature of post-Soviet decolonization, i.e. part of the undoing of the previous imperialism. Moldova's Kishinev has become Chisinau, Kazakhstan's Almata, Alma-Aty, and Kyrgyzstan's Frunze, Bishkek. Having got used to the change at China's request of Peking to Beijing, or of Rhodesia's Salisbury to Zimbabwe's Harare, is it really asking too much to show greater sensitivity in switching to the native, as opposed to externally imposed, names of places and individuals, even if up till now they have been the accepted 'English' forms?

Following from this, I have also used the names for the countries which were formally Soviet 'Union republics' as they are now reflected in the new post-Soviet independent states; for example, Belarus rather than Belorussia, and Moldova rather than Moldavia. For the sake of simplifying things, I have also omitted soft signs in my transliteration from Ukrainian and Russian.

As I have indicated, this book does not claim to provide a definitive account of a complex and very recent period, but rather to sketch the main political contours and provide an introductory survey or guide for readers of all kinds. I have therefore approached the topic as both a historian and an informed journalist, hoping to have found an acceptable balance between the descriptive and the analytical. The chronological narrative draws on a wide variety of sources, including numerous interviews with key political and cultural figures, the Soviet, Ukrainian and Western media, *samizdat*, the best of Western analysis and the first publications in Ukraine to deal with the very recent past.

Over the years, it has been my good fortune to meet many individuals who helped develop my interest in, and enrich my knowledge about, contemporary Ukraine. From among them, I would like to thank the following for their help and support, whether wittingly or unwittingly provided, and especially those with whom I was able to discuss at various times topics and themes dealt with in this book, or who helped me obtain material I was searching for. They include Mykhailo Dobriansky, Yaroslav Rozumny, the late Borys Lewytzky, the late Viktor Swoboda, Anatol Kaminsky, Leonid Plyushch, Nadia Svitlychna, Vitalii Korotych, Roman Solchanyk, Frank Sysyn, Roman Szporluk, Adrian Karatnycky, Nadia Diuk, Alexander Motyl, Ivan Myhul, Zenon Kohut, Bohdan Bociurkiw, Petro Potichnyj, Orest Subtelny, David Marples, Bohdan Osadchuk, Yaroslav Pelenski, Bohdan Hawrylyshyn, Serhii Naboka, Taras Kuzio, Mykola Ryabchuk, Mykola Zhulynsky, Les Tanyuk, Vyacheslav Bryukhovetsky, Vyacheslav Pikhovshek, Ihor Markov, Ihor Hryniv, Taras Stetskiv, Ihor Derkach, Vitalii Portnikov, Yurii Pakhomov, Valerii Smolii, Yurii Shapoval, Serhii Marchenko, Yaroslav Koval, Nadir Bekirov, Artur Bilous and Anatolii Rusnachenko.

I am grateful to the many individuals who agreed to be interviewed by me for the purposes of this book and provided me with valuable insights, clues and explanations. They include Ivan Drach, Serhii Holovaty, Bohdan Horyn, Ivan Kuras, Anatolii Matviyenko, Pavlo Movchan, Dmytro Pavlychko, Mykola Shulha, Hryhorii Syvokin, Yurii Tymchenko, Vitalii Vrublevsky, Yurii Yelchenko and Oleksandr Yemets. A few, especially officials, preferred not to be identified.

Naturally, special thanks are owed to former colleagues and staff at RFE/RL in Munich for the stimulating discussions, helping to locate research material and providing a valuable comparative perspective. Here I would like to mention especially Roman Solchanyk, whose readiness to share his knowledge and materials was, whether he knew it or not, an important source of support, and my debt to his writings is apparent from the footnotes. Enders Wimbush, David Marples, Vladimir Socor, Toomas Ilves, John Lepingwell, Ivan Hvat, Chrystyna Lapychak, Andrii and Iwanka Rebet, Volodymyr Hanyk, Lida Holvaty, Garik Superfin and Inna Burgher also helped at different times and in various ways. From outside RFE/RL, Steve Larrabee, Sherman Garnett and John Morrison were generous in sharing their interpretation of developments in Ukraine with me.

The long narrative needed maps and photographs to assist the reader to understand better the geography and spirit of the events being described and I would like to thank all those who helped in this respect. The maps were prepared by Helena Bray and Yves Bouchardy in Geneva on the basis of earlier drafts made by John Richmond in Munich or derived from products by American Digital Cartography.

For the photographs I have to thank Vitalii Vozyanov, the Director of the Ukrainian National News Agency, Ukrinform, who gave permission for me to use photographs from its archives, and Serhii Marchenko, one of the leading contemporary photographic chroniclers of Ukraine's past and its recent resurgence, whose creative work I have admired for years. Serhii Spasokukotsky also provided a selection of photos for me choose from. I would also like to express my gratitude to Joseanne Umpleby for her help in designing the cover of the book from photographs by Serhii Marchenko.

Of course none of those whose assistance I have acknowledged above is responsible in any way for any errors, factual or interpretive, that I may have made in this book and for any imprecision and inconsistency discovered by the reader. There are no research assistants to blame and the index was also my own doing.

The book was written by me in my private scholarly capacity: the views and conclusions presented in it are mine alone and do not purport to represent the views of any organisation with which I have been, or am, professionally associated.

Finally, a special word of thanks to those whose interest and support helped the project through the years of research and writing. Christopher Hurst had the vision and understanding to ask me to write a book on Ukraine several years before I actually agreed and when an independent Ukraine still seemed, as Rosa Luxemburg once put it, to be the dream of coffee house politicians. In Michael Dwyer, Director at Hurst Publishers, I discovered an exemplary partner, a firm but tolerant manager, who is genuinely interested in the themes he proposes and commissions.

Needless to say, the one individual who witnessed the conception, long pregnancy, labour pains and birth of this book was my wife Tamara Tarnawska. Her steady support and readiness to discuss various parts of the work in progress deserve a special '*dyakuyu!*' (thank you in Ukrainian). Her son Alex and my children Emma and Maksym also had to put up with the project's encroachments on the time I could spend with them and I hope that in return they will glance through this book one day and find things of interest. I cannot omit a mention of our cats, Jimmy, Smoky, Toffee and Kyi, who took turns in keeping me company at all hours in my study during the long periods of solitude and who infrequently either 'helped' rearrange my papers or served as splendid paperweights. If only this book could also have nine lives....

Ferney-Voltaire   Bohdan Nahaylo
September 1998

1

HISTORICAL BACKGROUND

Ukraine's long and turbulent history has been marked by devastation, suppression and discontinuity, the absence of any lasting independent statehood, and the division of ethnically Ukrainian lands among foreign conquerors and more powerful neighbours. Located at the former crossroads between Europe and Asia, where the Orthodox, Catholic and Muslim worlds confronted one another, this rich and fertile land was for centuries a magnet for invaders and colonizers, including Tatars, Poles, Turks, Russians and Germans. Over the ages Ukraine's history was rewritten by its foreign rulers in accordance with their own political and imperial interests, thus obscuring the story and aspirations of one of Europe's largest nations. Indeed, having remained a submerged nation for so long, Ukraine's resurgence during the final years of the USSR's existence was to take many by surprise and not only to alter the political geography of Europe but also to challenge the traditional ways of looking at Russia and Eastern Europe.

Early history

The Ukrainians, like the Russians and Belarusians, belong to the eastern branch of the Slavs. All three trace their historical ancestry to the state of Kyivan (Kievan) Rus, which arose in the ninth century and developed into a vast and powerful realm. The centre of this conglomerate of diverse territories and principalities was Kyiv and the area around it, that is, the heartland of present-day Ukraine. Kyivan Rus adopted Christianity from Byzantium in 988, along with Old Church Slavonic, with its Cyrillic script, which became the liturgical and literary language. The Kyivan state's famed 'golden domed' capital flourished as a jewel of East Slavonic culture and its rulers formed dynastic links with many

1

of medieval Europe's royal families as far away as France and Norway. But hardly had Kyivan Rus reached its apogee in the first half of the eleventh century under Volodymyr (Vladimir in Russian) the Great and Yaroslav the Wise when external and internal factors began to weaken it. Under constant pressure in the south and east from incursions by various nomadic peoples, the state's unity was undermined by feuding among the principalities and internecine struggles for the Kyivan throne. The Kyivan realm was transformed into a loose dynastic confederation and powerful new regional centres began to emerge. Furthermore, the establishment of new international trade routes which bypassed Kyiv brought economic problems and stagnation. By the time that Moscow, the future centre of the Russian Muscovite state, was first mentioned in a chronicle in 1147, the process of political fragmentation was well advanced and Kyiv's primacy was fading. When in 1169, Andrei Bogolyubsky, the ruler of the north-eastern territories of Vladimir-Suzdal (from which the Muscovite principality was to emerge in the fourteenth century) sacked and plundered Kyiv, he spurned the old capital as his seat, preferring to build up a new power centre in Vladimir.

Kyiv did not regain its former importance and in 1240 the city fell to the Mongols. The Mongol invasion destroyed the fragile remnants of Kyivan Rus and precipitated the trend towards separate development among the eastern Slavs. In the western part of present-day Ukraine, however, the principalities of Galicia and Volhynia managed to hold out for another century and kept alive the Kyivan heritage until they were absorbed by Poland and Lithuania. The latter subsequently also extended its rule to Kyiv. After the union of Poland and Lithuania in 1569, virtually all ethnically Ukrainian lands came under Polish rule. During this period, the Ukrainians (and Belarusians) were usually referred to as Ruthenians (derived from the Latin for Rus), and the Russians as Muscovites.

In the Polish-Lithuanian Commonwealth, the Ukrainian Orthodox nobility was pressured to adapt to Polish ways and to adopt Catholicism, the peasantry was driven into serfdom, and Ukrainian lands were colonized by Polish or Polonized magnates. In the sixteenth century, though, the Ukrainian Cossacks began to emerge as a significant military force, posing a considerable challenge for the Polish state. Initially composed of runaway peasants and frontiersmen, they established an autonomous stronghold on the lower Dnieper (Dnipro), or Zaporozhya as the area came to be called, in the no-man's land between Poland, the Crimean Tatar Khanate and Muscovy, and developed into a Ukrainian martial brotherhood. The Cossacks acted as a bulwark against the marauding Tatars from the south who treated the Ukrainian areas as a source of plunder and slaves. Unruly and rebellious as they were for the Polish authorities, the Cossacks were legendary warriors and were frequently used by the Polish state in military campaigns and to defend its borders.

In the early part of the seventeenth century, under the leadership of Petro Konashevych-Sahaidachny, the Ukrainian Cossacks became the champions of Ukrainian Orthodoxy and culture, both of which began to experience a revival at this time. Kyiv once again became a centre of culture and learning, proud of the Ukrainian Orthodox tradition inherited from Kyivan Rus, but receptive to Western influences. Ironically, this religious and cultural recovery was stimulated by a split in the Ukrainian Orthodox Church and the religious polemics that followed it. The rupture occurred in 1596 when, as a result of the Union of Brest, some Ukrainian Orthodox leaders entered into a union with Rome to form the Uniate (or Ukrainian Greek Catholic, as it was later known) Church, which was allowed to retain its traditional Orthodox liturgy and Eastern (Greek) rites.

Poland's inconsistent policy towards the Ukrainian Cossacks and reluctance to recognize the rights which they claimed generated numerous revolts and increased the Cossacks' identification with the plight of the peasantry and the Ukrainian Orthodox cause. In 1648, under their elected leader, or *hetman*, Bohdan Khmelnytsky, they launched an uprising against the Poles (the Uniates and Jews were regarded as auxiliaries of the Poles and thus were also targets) that turned into a war of liberation and culminated in the establishment of a quasi-military independent Ukrainian Cossack state. Although Khmelnytsky won a series of impressive military victories, his search for a reliable ally against the Poles led him to conclude a treaty in 1654 in Pereyaslav with the Muscovite state. The hetman acted in the belief that the Orthodox tsar would respect the fullest autonomy of the Ukrainian Cossack state which he had created, but was to die three years later bitterly disappointed. The Muscovites not only broke their word by coming to terms with the Poles and subsequently partitioning Ukraine[1] with them, but also set about reducing Ukrainian self-rule.

Khmelnytsky's successor, Ivan Vyhovsky, reached an accommodation with the Poles in 1658 – the Treaty of Hadyach – which provided for the recognition of an autonomous Ukrainian principality as a third and equal partner in the Polish-Lithuanian Commonwealth. But shortly after defeating a Muscovite army that same year at Konotop, Vyhovsky was forced to resign by a rebellion of his officers opposed to the Hadyach compromise. A period known as 'the Ruin' began. The Cossack state split along the Dnieper River into two rival parts, with the pro-Muscovite forces on the left bank and the pro-Polish on the right bank, each with their own hetman. In 1667, the Poles and Russians concluded the Treaty of Andrusovo which formalized the *de facto* partition of Ukraine.

The hetman of Right-Bank Ukraine, Petro Doroshenko, however, sought to reunite Cossack Ukraine with the help of the Ottoman Porte and there followed over a decade of wars, with Ottoman-Ukrainian Cossack armies fighting first against the Poles and then against the Muscovites and Left-Bank Cossacks. After much devastation and loss of life, the attempt to establish a Ukrainian Cossack state under the protection of the Turks ended in failure. Between 1681 and 1686, Ukraine was again divided up among Muscovy, Poland and the Ottoman Empire (which added the southern part of Right-Bank Ukraine to Crimea and the Black Sea coast, which were already under its control).

The last attempt during the Cossack era to establish an independent Ukrainian state occurred at the beginning of the eighteenth century. It was made by the hetman of Left-Bank Ukraine, Ivan Mazepa, who was a great patron of Ukrainian religious and cultural institutions. Mazepa provided Peter I with considerable Ukrainian help in his campaigns during the 1690s against the Crimean Tatars and the Turks, but the increasing burden which the tsar's subsequent war against the Swedes for control of the Baltic Sea coast placed on the Ukrainians, as well as the continuing reduction of Ukrainian

---

[1] The term Ukraine (Ukraina) first appeared in a twelfth-century Kyivan chronicle and meant a 'borderland' or 'country'. In the late sixteenth and during the seventeenth centuries, it was used to denote the middle Dnieper region, which was identified with Ukrainian Cossackdom. By the middle of the seventeenth century it had become a name for all the lands embraced by the Ukrainian Cossack movement.

autonomy, led Mazepa to switch sides. His attempt to throw off
Muscovite domination by siding with Sweden's Charles XII during
the Great Northern War ended in disaster: Peter the Great's victory
over the Swedes and their Ukrainian allies at Poltava in 1709 sealed
the fate of Ukraine and marked the emergence of Muscovy – or
Russia as it was now to be called – as a major European power.

Ukrainians played no small role in the 'Europeanization' and
development of Petrine Russia and the Russian Empire. While
representatives of Ukraine's first political emigration, led by
Mazepa's former chancellor Pylyp Orlyk, vainly sought international support for the Ukrainian cause, and Ukraine's political and
cultural rights were being further reduced (in 1720 Peter I forbade
the publication of all books in Ukrainian except those dealing with
religious themes), higher clergy, scholars and cultural figures were
recruited from Ukraine to serve St Petersburg; they supplied Russia
with many of its leading religious and cultural figures, such as Feofan
Prokopovych, Stefan Yavorsky, Maksym Berezovsky and Dmytro
Bortnyansky. This 'brain drain' was facilitated by the fact that in
1686 the Ukrainian Orthodox Church had been brought under the
control of the Muscovite Patriarchate. The Ukrainian Cossacks were
also to play an important role in Catherine II's wars against the
Crimean Tatar Khanate and the Turks, which resulted in Russia's
annexation of Crimea in 1783 and conquest of the northern coast
of the Black Sea.

Gradually, Ukrainian institutions were abolished and replaced by
a Russian imperial administration, and the Ukrainian Cossack gentry
and clergy were assimilated. The last vestiges of Ukrainian autonomy
were eliminated under Catherine II and in 1775 the Zaporozhyan
Cossack fortified base, or Sich, was destroyed in a surprise attack by
Russian troops returning from the Turkish front. Evidently, now
that Russia had defeated the Turks, the Zaporozhyans had outlived
their usefulness and St Petersburg regarded their Sich as a potential
centre of rebellion and an obstacle to the imperial colonization of
the newly acquired Black Sea hinterlands, which were named New
Russia (Novorossiya). The Ukrainians were thereby effectively
reduced to a peasant nation. Their land was treated as a mere
province and was referred to as 'Little Russia' (Malorossiya).

During the eighteenth century in Polish-ruled Right-Bank Ukraine there were numerous popular rebellions, in which the
peasantry was led by rebels known as *haidamaky* and Zaporozhyan

Cossacks. The largest of these occurred in 1734, 1750 and in 1768; they were crushed with the assistance of Russian forces. By the end of the eighteenth century, though, with the decline of Poland and the partitioning of its territories among Russia, Prussia and Austria, most Ukrainian lands ended up under Russian rule, with the exception of the Ukrainian parts of Galicia and Bukovyna, which were annexed by Austria. During the first half of the nineteenth century, though, the Polish influence in Right-Bank Ukraine and in Kyiv itself was to remain considerable and in fact Polish insurrectionism led the Russian imperial authorities to step up their efforts to Russify this area.

The making of modern Ukraine

As Russia expanded southward to the shores of the Black Sea, the tsarist state's policies of Russification, centralization and the imposition of serfdom weakened the Ukrainian sense of identity and led to a sharp drop in the level of literacy. Nevertheless, in the nineteenth century, under the influence of Romanticism, a Ukrainian cultural revival got underway. In 1847 the first modern Ukrainian political organization, the secret Society of Saints Cyril and Methodius, which was formed in Kyiv by young, patriotically minded intellectuals espousing Christian democratic ideals and the principle of equality between the Slavic peoples, was uncovered by the tsarist secret police. The promoters of modern Ukrainian nationhood, the most notable of whom was the poet Taras Shevchenko (1814-61), were imprisoned, exiled, or denounced as 'Mazepists' and 'separatists'. The tsarist authorities also continued to issue restrictions that virtually banned the use of the Ukrainian language. The official position was summed up by the Russian Minister of the Interior, Count Petr Valuev, who declared in 1863 that the Ukrainian language 'never existed, does not exist and shall never exist', maintaining that the 'Little Russian dialect' was but 'bad Russian spoilt by Polish influences'.

Towards the end of the nineteenth century a new generation of nationally conscious Ukrainian activists appeared who were committed to obtaining political freedom and social justice for their people. In 1900, the first Ukrainian political party – the Revolutionary Ukrainian Party – was formed in Russian-ruled Ukraine in Kharkiv, but had to operate underground. Only after the Russian

Revolution of 1905 was there a brief respite which allowed the burgeoning Ukrainian national movement to surface. Ukrainian newspapers, cultural and educational societies and cooperatives proliferated, and the Ukrainian faction in the Russian parliament, or Duma, unsuccessfully pressed for greater autonomy for Ukraine and the Ukrainization of education. As the post-revolutionary wave of reaction set in, though, Ukrainian political parties were driven underground and the tsarist government renewed its campaign against Ukrainian 'separatism'. Furthermore, the chauvinistic Russian monarchist movement known as the Black Hundreds also established branches in Ukraine and openly pursued its anti-Semitic and anti-Ukrainian activity.

In the final decades of the nineteenth century the shortage of land drove more and more Ukrainians eastward in search of a better life. By 1914 an estimated 2 million Ukrainians had migrated to Siberia and Russian-ruled Central Asia. Of these, about half a million settled in Russia's Far East and 800,000 in Kazakhstan. Another 2 million Ukrainians had settled in the North Caucasus, mainly in the Kuban and Stavropol areas.

Political conditions for the Ukrainians under Austrian rule were more favourable and in the nineteenth century their national consciousness and political activity progressively developed. Here, the Ukrainian Catholic Church played an important role as a custodian and reviver of national identity. In Galicia, however, the Ukrainian national movement was confronted by Poles intent on restoring their state with its former imperial boundaries. As early as 1848, when, during Europe's 'Spring of Nations', Galicia's Ukrainians made their debut as an organized political force at the Slavonic Congress in Prague, they demanded the administrative division of Galicia into a Polish western part and eastern Ukrainian one. Subsequently, there were growing contacts and cooperation between Galician Ukrainians and 'Dnieper' (or Eastern) Ukrainians for whom Galicia served as a sanctuary from tsarist persecution and a base where their works could be published.

During the second half of the nineteenth century, the Galician Ukrainians stepped up their struggle for territorial autonomy and by the turn of the century some of their new political parties, inspired by the outstanding Eastern Ukrainian political thinker, Mykhailo Drahomanov (who was forced into exile by the tsarist authorities in 1876), were advocating the unification of Ukraine and its political independence. The Austrian-ruled Ukrainian lands, however, were impoverished and the social and economic problems facing the Ukrainian peasantry were acute: consequently, between 1890 and 1913 an estimated 750,000 Austro-Hungarians (from Galicia and Transcarpathia) emigrated to the United States, Canada and Brazil, while tens of thousands sought seasonal work in Germany.

At the outbreak of the First World War, Eastern Galicia, whose capital Lviv was still claimed by both Ukrainians and Poles, was a true Ukrainian Piedmont and when Russia's forces initially captured the region the tsarist regime set about suppressing the Ukrainian movement on this territory. After the collapse of Austria-Hungary in 1918, the Galician Ukrainians proclaimed the independent West Ukrainian People's Republic (the ZUNR) and this led to a war with the restored Polish state. After nine months of bitter fighting, Poland eventually managed to impose its rule over Eastern Galicia, or Halychyna, as the Ukrainians called it.

In Russian-ruled Ukraine, the fall of the Romanovs in 1917 found the Ukrainian national movement still relatively weak. After 250 years of Russian rule over large parts of Ukraine, even Russian liberals were often reluctant to recognize a distinct Ukrainian nation, language, culture and history, not to mention the political aspirations that went with them. Indeed, Russian imperial historiography had obfuscated the distinction between Rus and Russia and depicted Kyiv as the 'mother of Russian' cities. For instance, when Russia occupied Eastern Galicia in 1914, the tsarist government referred to it as an 'ancient Russian land' that was being 'reunited for ever with Mother Russia'. Deprived of schools in their own native language, of knowledge about their own history, and of their own cultural and religious institutions, many Ukrainians had come to regard themselves as *malorosy* or Little Russians, in other words as a regional offshoot of the 'Great Russian' people. The problem was exemplified by the case of the Ukrainian Mykola Hohol, who at first intended to dedicate himself to writing a 'history of our beloved, poor Ukraine' (as he put it in a letter in 1833), but who subsequently achieved world fame as the 'Russian' writer Nikolai Gogol.[2] It was thus all the more remarkable that after the overthrow of the tsarist regime the Ukrainian national movement was able to crystallize so

---

[2] See George S.N. Luckyj, *Between Gogol' and Sevcenko: Polarity in the Literary Ukraine: 1798-1847*, Munich, 1971, pp. 109-14.

rapidly and, after initially demanding little more than the Ukrainization of education, the courts and administration, to launch a struggle to achieve independent statehood. In 1917 and early 1918, the Ukrainian Central *Rada* (Council), headed by the eminent historian Mykhailo Hrushevsky, proclaimed first the autonomous and then, as Bolshevik Russia invaded from the north, the independent Ukrainian People's Republic (UNR), which was recognized in the Treaty of Brest-Litovsk by the Central Powers and reluctantly also by Bolshevik Russia. This socialist and democratic Ukrainian government was replaced in April 1918 for a few months by the conservative German-backed regime of 'Hetman' Pavlo Skoropadsky. Subsequently, former leaders of the Central Rada formed a new government known as the Directory which, under the leadership of Symon Petlyura, kept up the fight for Ukrainian independence until 1920.

During these years, Ukraine was engulfed by strife, anarchy and pogroms as Ukrainians, Russians, Germans and Poles, and the 'Blue and Yellows' (Ukrainian nationalists), Reds, Whites and Anarchists battled it out. Pressed from all sides, the Ukrainians put up a spirited fight but could not hold out and effect Ukraine's unification, which was proclaimed by the UNR and ZUNR on 22 January 1919. The following year, in a last desperate attempt, Petlyura formed an alliance with Poland's leader Jozef Pilsudski against Moscow (to the disgust of the leaders of the ZUNR), but the Soviet-Polish War ended in failure and disappointment for the UNR's forces.

Finally then, after three invasions of Ukraine, the Russian Bolshevik forces emerged victorious and established a Soviet Ukrainian state, the Ukrainian Soviet Socialist Republic (SSR). They made Kharkiv, not Kyiv, its capital. The Poles took Eastern Galicia and Volhynia, where over 5 million Ukrainians lived, and the Romanians seized ethnically Ukrainian areas in Bukovyna and Bessarabia, where there were some 750,000 Ukrainians. About 450,000 Carpatho-Ukrainians ended up under Czechoslovak rule.

Further afield, there were of course the large Ukrainian groups which had settled in North and South America, and the new Ukrainian political émigré communities in Prague, Paris and Vienna. In the east, millions of Ukrainians lived in Russia and other parts of the former Russian Empire. In 1917 Ukrainian organizations and newspapers had sprung up in the Russian Far East in Vladivostok and other centres, and subsequently the Ukrainian movement in this region had recognized the UNR. When the Bolsheviks finally established their rule in this region in 1922, they initially suppressed organized Ukrainian life, but later set up a number of Ukrainian 'national districts' where, until the second half of the 1930s, the Ukrainian language was used in schools and administration.

Soviet Ukraine

Although the Ukrainian 'national revolution' of 1917-20 ended in failure, it did not spell the end of the Ukrainian national regeneration. In fact, the armed struggle for national self-determination (some pro-UNR insurgent groups fought on into the 1920s) strengthened the sense of nationhood, something that Lenin and the Bolsheviks were forced to recognize, especially in view of the weakness of their party organization and social base in Ukraine. The Communist Party of Ukraine (CPU), which was formally established in July 1918 in Moscow as a regional sub-unit of the Russian Communist Party, initially numbered less than 5,000 members of whom the majority were non-Ukrainians. Even in 1922, when the CPU had grown to 56,000, the percentage of Ukrainians was only 23%, compared with 54% of Russians, 14% of Jews and 3% of Poles, and almost half of the membership was in the Red Army. Four years later, the first census conducted under Soviet rule revealed that the size of Soviet Ukraine's population was almost 29 million, and that 81% of the population gave their nationality as Ukrainian and 9.2% as Russian. Only 11% of Ukrainians in 1926, however, lived in the cities. In essence then, the Bolsheviks in Ukraine were an alien and urban movement in a country whose population was overwhelmingly Ukrainian and rural.

But from the very outset there was also a Ukrainian 'national Communist' current within the CPU which had unsuccessfully sought to create a Ukrainian Bolshevik party separate from the Russian one; its adherents promoted the ideas of an independent 'Soviet' Ukrainian state and were opposed to Russification and manifestations within the Bolshevik party apparatus of what they openly denounced as 'Great Russian chauvinism'. Although this 'Ukrainian' tendency was strongly opposed by the 'internationalist' elements within the CPU who wanted to secure the victory of the language and culture of 'proletarian Russia' over what they considered to be the backward and 'bourgeois nationalist' values of 'peasant Ukraine', Lenin and the Moscow leadership acknowledged the need for concessions designed to win over both the peasantry and the non-Russians.

In the early 1920s, when the future form of the Soviet multinational state was being decided, Ukrainian Communists also opposed Moscow's centralism and defended their republic's rights. In March 1922, for instance, Lenin expressed his impatience with their tendency to 'edge away from us'.[3] Soon afterwards, when it came to the actual creation of the Soviet Union, the Ukrainians came out strongly against Stalin's 'autonomization' scheme, whereby the non-Russian republics would be transformed into autonomous republics of the Russian Soviet Federative Socialist Republic (RSFSR). Along with the Georgians, they continued to press for the broadest rights for the republics. After Lenin's personal intervention, the new union took the form of a 'voluntary' federation in which the constituent republics were recognized as sovereign and equal states with the right to secede. In March 1923, that is three months after the Union of Soviet Socialist Republics was established, Stalin complained that the 'Ukrainian comrades', headed by the Old Bolshevik, Mykola Skrypnyk, wanted to 'obtain in the definition of the Union something midway between a confederation and a federation, with a leaning towards confederation'.[4]

During the relatively liberal 1920s, when Moscow's nationalities policy was aimed at enabling Soviet rule to 'take root' in the non-Russian republics through a combination of cultural concessions, a repudiation of the imperial Russian legacy, placation of the peasantry and the 'indigenization' of the Party and state structures (through the recruitment of native cadres and promotion of the native language), the Ukrainians had a brief chance to get on with the unfinished business of nation-state building. A crucial aspect of this was the de-Russification of Ukraine's cities and the Ukrainization of education (carried out simultaneously with a major drive to eliminate illiteracy) and of public life, and cultural and religious life. Ukrainization extended even to the Red Army and to the regions outside of Ukraine within the USSR with a large compact Ukrainian population – the Kuban, Kazakhstan and the Far East.

---

[3] V.I. Lenin, *Collected Works*, Moscow, 1966, vol. 33, p. 298.
[4] J.V. Stalin, *Works*, Moscow, 1953, V, p. 343.

In these more auspicious conditions a vibrant cultural revival began, and in a relatively short time the Ukrainians started to come into their own. While Skrypnyk and other Ukrainian Communist leaders sought to give Soviet Ukraine's sovereignty real meaning and to spur on the process of Ukrainization, Hrushevsky and other scholars returned from exile to Soviet Ukraine and contributed to the renaissance in scholarship, especially in Ukrainian studies. Even the tradition of an independent Ukrainian Orthodox Church was revived in the form of the Ukrainian Autocephalous Church, which was created in Kyiv in 1921 and by 1924 had thirty bishops, 1,500 priests and millions of adherents.

Disturbed by the national assertiveness of the Ukrainians and the Western, 'European' orientation of their cultural élite, in 1926 Stalin again inveighed against Ukraine's national Communists. This time he singled out the writer Mykola Khvylovy, who had advanced the cultural slogan 'Away from Moscow', and Ukraine's Commissar for Education, Oleksandr Shumsky, who argued for the right of Ukrainian Communists to run the republic without the supervision of Moscow's non-Ukrainian plenipotentiaries, as for example, the first secretary of the CPU at that time, Lazar Kaganovich. This case, the condemnation of other 'national deviationists' such as the economist Mykola Volobuev (who in 1928 argued that under Soviet rule Ukraine remained an economic colony of Russia, just as it had been under the tsars), and the growing official pressure after 1926 on the Ukrainian Autocephalous Orthodox Church, underlined the strictly limited nature of Moscow's concessions.

While Ukrainization continued to make rapid headway, the Soviet Ukrainian government was careful to respect the rights of the republic's national minorities. Apart from having schools and other cultural facilities in their own language, the minorities were allowed to establish their own 'national soviets' in districts where they formed a majority of the population. Skrypnyk pressed for the similar satisfaction of the national needs of the nearly 8 million Ukrainians who, according to the 1926 Soviet census, lived in other parts of the USSR, mainly in the Russian Federation. He not only criticized the Russian Republic for not doing enough in this respect, but also demanded the transfer to the Ukrainian SSR of those adjacent areas containing Ukrainian majorities.

Beginning in the late 1920s, Stalin abandoned the policy of conciliating the peasantry and, while pursuing his relentless industrialization and collectivization campaigns, also reversed Soviet nationalities policy. While subduing the peasantry, he began purging the non-Russian élites. In Ukraine, a major show trial – the case of the so-called Union for the Liberation of Ukraine (SVU) – was staged in 1930, being its aim to discredit those representatives of the Ukrainian intelligentsia who had supported the UNR. During the next few years, though, it became evident that Stalin was seeking to eliminate the Ukrainians as a political factor. He carried out repeated purges of the Ukrainian cultural and political élite, destroyed the Ukrainian Autocephalous Church, terminated Ukrainization and reverted to Russification. In 1932-3, as if (as many Ukrainians believe) to break the very backbone of their nation, Stalin starved millions of Ukrainian peasants to death as a result of a man-made famine induced by the ruthless imposition of excessive grain quotas on the republic. Skrypnyk and Khvylovy both committed suicide in 1933 as the Soviet Ukraine that they had sought to build was destroyed around them. By 1938, when the young secretary of the Moscow Party organization Nikita Khrushchev was sent to Kyiv (which in 1934 had been made the Ukrainian capital again) to run the decimated CPU, it appeared that Ukraine had once again been reduced to the status of a pacified province.

Between Stalin and Hitler

Meanwhile, during the inter-war period, the Ukrainians in Poland and Romania were denied self-rule and had to endure varying degrees of official intolerance and repression. Nevertheless, Polish-ruled Western Ukraine (the Polish government referred to Eastern Galicia as 'Eastern Little Poland') continued to be a bastion of Ukrainian nationalism. Within the authoritarian limits imposed by the Polish state, the Ukrainians sought to defend their rights and develop their political, cultural, and religious life as best they could through a number of legal Ukrainian political parties, an economic 'self-help' cooperative movement, educational societies, and the Ukrainian Catholic and Ukrainian Orthodox Churches. There was also more militant resistance to the Poles led by the underground Organization of Ukrainian Nationalists (OUN), which adopted an integral nationalist ideology and resorted to terrorist methods. The situation of the Ukrainians in Romania was even more difficult and their cultural, civic and religious life was more restricted. The OUN was also active in Ukrainian areas of Bukovyna.

In August 1939, the two great ideological rivals, the Soviet Union and Nazi Germany, concluded a non-aggression pact which had a secret additional protocol providing for a division of Eastern Europe into Soviet and German 'spheres of influence'. On the basis of the 'Molotov-Ribbentrop Pact', as it was called, after Germany invaded Poland in September 1939, the Red Army 'liberated' the Ukrainian territories in Galicia and Volhynia. The following June, Moscow issued an ultimatum to Romania after which Soviet forces took control of the Ukrainian territories held by Bucharest and also the remainder of Bessarabia, where a Moldovan Soviet Socialist Republic was established. In the newly acquired Ukrainian lands, the Soviet authorities combined Ukrainization, designed to win over the bulk of the Ukrainian population, with Sovietization, political repression and mass deportations.

During the inter-war period, the Ukrainians in Czechoslovakia enjoyed more liberal conditions, and here the Ukrainian national movement made considerable headway. In 1938, after the process of Czechoslovakia's dismemberment had begun, Transcarpathia, or Carpatho-Ukraine, received autonomy. Confronted by Hungary's claims to this territory, and unable to join with other parts of Ukraine, the Carpatho-Ukrainian government defiantly proclaimed independence in March 1939. After a secret deal between Hitler and Hungary the tiny would-be state was soon overrun by Hungarian troops.

When in June 1941 the Germans invaded the Soviet Union, many Ukrainians naively welcomed them because they hoped for liberation from the Stalinist system. In Lviv, members of the radical faction of the OUN led by Stepan Bandera promptly declared the restoration of Ukraine's statehood only to discover the bitter truth about Nazi intentions in the East. The Nazi invaders imprisoned or shot Ukrainian nationalists and permitted only modest cultural and religious activity; they treated Ukraine as a colony and ruthlessly exploited its resources and population. Over 2 million Ukrainians were deported to Germany for forced labour as *Ostarbeiter*; at the same time, some 3.3 million Soviet prisoners of war – of whom about a third were Ukrainians – perished of hunger and cold in German camps. As elsewhere, Ukraine's Jews were targeted for extermination and about 850,000 of them were killed. Meanwhile, in the south-east of Ukraine, Germany's Romanian allies occupied a large area extending to Odesa (which they called Transnistria) in which they, too, sought to suppress the Ukrainian national movement.

Millions of Ukrainians were involved in the Red Army's defence of the Soviet Union and subsequent defeat of Nazi Germany. In order to win the loyalty of the Ukrainians, Stalin permitted a number of concessions to Ukrainian patriotism, but they proved to be only temporary. In north-western Ukraine, however, by the end of 1942 Ukrainian nationalist resistance to the Germans (and Red partisans) assumed the form of guerrilla warfare waged by the Ukrainian Insurgent Army (UPA). Closely linked with the OUN network, the UPA grew in strength and gradually extended its activity throughout and even beyond Western Ukraine. At the height of its strength in early 1944, the UPA may have had as many as 40,000 fighters.

During the war Ukrainian-Polish rivalry persisted and the massacres which were carried out by both Ukrainian and Polish resistance forces in the areas, mainly in Volhynia, which they contested, were one of the ugly features of the struggle behind German lines. This early example of attempted 'ethnic cleansing' claimed tens of thousands of victims on both sides and was to leave bitter memories among both Poles and Western Ukrainians.

When Soviet forces eventually pushed the Germans out of Ukraine, the UPA and OUN kept up an armed struggle against the reimposition of Soviet rule. This frequently meant that Ukrainians in one uniform fought against their fellow-countrymen wearing a different one, and the Stalinist propaganda machine went all out to depict the insurgents as Nazi henchmen and bandits. The resistance in Western Ukraine was not extinguished until the early 1950s. In order to expedite the Sovietization of this recalcitrant region, as in the Baltic states, the Soviet authorities carried out mass deportations – over 200,000 people were shipped out – and brought in tens of thousands of Russians. In 1946 the Ukrainian Catholic Church was also officially 'liquidated': its hierarchy were imprisoned and some of the terrorized clergy were assembled at the so-called Lviv Sobor (ecclesiastical council) to petition for incorporation into the Russian Orthodox Church. Driven underground, the Ukrainian Catholic Church nevertheless survived as a catacomb church.

In the Second World War, Ukraine lost between 5 to 7 million

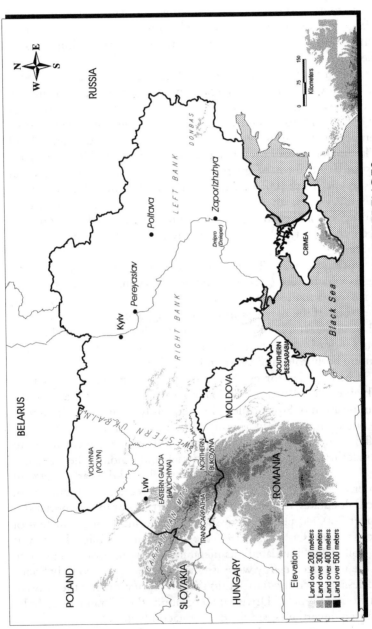

GEOGRAPHICAL AND HISTORIAL REFERENCES

people (the estimates vary) and suffered immense devastation. Ironically, however, the Soviet victory did bring an essential change – the unification of almost all ethnically Ukrainian lands in one, albeit 'Soviet', Ukrainian state. As a result of the Soviet Union's military might, Poland was forced to cede Eastern Galicia and Volhynia, while Romania again parted with Northern Bukovyna and Southern Bessarabia, and Czechoslovakia gave up Transcarpathia.

From a broader historical perspective, the extrication of Western Ukraine from Poland's control was especially important not only because this territorial consolidation facilitated the completion of the process of Ukrainian nation-building, but also because it essentially marked the resolution of the long-standing Ukrainian–Polish conflict. As part of the territorial settlement with the Poles, over 800,000 Poles were resettled from Ukraine to Poland, and about 500,000 Ukrainians transferred from Poland to Ukraine. As late as April 1947, however, as a part of a punitive military operation codenamed 'Wisla', some 130,000 Ukrainians living on the Polish side of the border in a region where the UPA was still active were suddenly rounded up by Polish troops and dispersed throughout the lands which Poland had newly acquired from Germany.

The Soviet victory brought one other significant fillip for Ukraine: for reasons of political expediency, Stalin demanded and obtained a seat for Soviet Ukraine (and Soviet Belarus) in the United Nations. Although in practice this separate membership turned out to be quite fictional, it was the first time since the early 1920s that Ukraine was represented as a state in its own right on the international stage. Meanwhile, the Ukrainian Western diaspora was revitalized and enlarged by the gradual arrival of some 200,000 Ukrainian refugees from the post-war camps for displaced persons in Germany; the vast majority of the Ukrainian *Ostarbeiter* and political refugees who had ended up in Germany and Austria at the end of the war were, however, repatriated to the Soviet Union, where, more often than not, they were punished for their 'betrayal' or 'ideological contamination'.

Any hopes that Ukraine would now be allowed a respite were soon dashed, though, for just as the enormous task of economic reconstruction got under way Stalin launched new campaigns against 'Ukrainian nationalism', and Russification and the extolling of things Russian were stepped up. Between 1946 and 1948 the CPU Central Committee passed no less than eight resolutions concerned with combating 'Ukrainian bourgeois nationalism', the influence of Hrushevsky in the historical sphere being singled out for special attention. In the middle of it all, Stalin sent his veteran troubleshooter Kaganovich to Ukraine to oversee the new witch-hunts, and in 1947 the latter took over for a time from Khrushchev as the Ukrainian Party chief. In July 1951, the general ideological offensive, which by now had made the Jewish intelligentsia a primary target, culminated in *Pravda*'s notorious condemnation of Volodymyr Sosyura's war-time poem 'Love Ukraine', indicating how limited the toleration of even 'Soviet' Ukrainian patriotism had become.[5]

---

[5] *Pravda*, 2 July 1950.

2

UKRAINE IN THE POST-STALIN PERIOD

At the time of Stalin's death in March 1953, only the last flickers of armed resistance in Western Ukraine and the defiance being shown by Ukrainian political prisoners in the Gulag at attested that Ukraine's spirit had not been completely broken. Yet no sooner had the dictator died than his secret police chief Lavrentii Beria demonstrated the political importance of Ukraine: in his abortive bid for power, he made his first moves in this republic, ones which were designed to win Ukrainian support. Among the changes which he engineered was the removal of the leader of the CPU, Leonid Melnikov – a Russian – on the grounds that he had made mistakes in nationalities policy and promoted the Russification of Western Ukraine's institutes of higher education. Melnikov was replaced by Oleksandr Kyrychenko – the first ethnic Ukrainian to head the CPU.

Khrushchev and measured de-Stalinization

After Beria's arrest and execution, Khrushchev, who had largely made his political career in Ukraine, sought to use the republic as a power base and wooed its Party and state apparatus. Significantly, he and others in the post-Stalin Kremlin leadership went to the unusual lengths of in effect offering the Ukrainians the role of the junior partners of the Russians, but only after reaffirming in more precise detail the Stalinist line on how the 'special' Russo-Ukrainian relationship was to be understood. At the end of 1953 Moscow announced that there would be lavish celebrations during 1954 of the tercentenary of the Treaty of Pereyaslav, and at the beginning of the jubilee year the Central Committee of the Communist Party of the Soviet Union (CPSU) issued special 'Theses' for the occasion. In this prescriptive document Ukrainian history was reduced to an age-old longing for 'reunion' with the Russians and Ukrainian patriotism reinterpreted in terms of a commitment to inseparability from, and dependence on, Russia. The following month, as a token of the 'indissoluble' bond between the two peoples, the Ukrainian SSR was handed the Crimean peninsula by the RSFSR. This region had lost its autonomous status within the Russian Federation following Stalin's deportation in 1944 of its Crimean Tatar population (which by that time, as a result of emigration, Slavonic immigration, purges and earlier deportations, had shrunk to about 25% of the peninsula's population), and Russian and Ukrainian migrants were moving in. Crimea's economic dependence on Ukraine, territorial proximity and cultural ties were cited as the reasons for Khrushchev's decision to transfer the peninsula to Ukraine.

What this 'courtship' amounted to in practice was that, for all of Ukraine's supposed sovereignty, Moscow continued to treat the republic as if it were merely an extension of Russia that had preserved its own quaint folk traditions and dialect. Much as imperial St Petersburg had done, it viewed docile Ukrainians as surrogate Russians, nationally minded Ukrainians as 'nationalists', and the stauncher ones as subversive separatists. This attitude was to foster a climate in which, as Ukrainian patriots were to protest over the next three decades, in many parts of Ukraine simply speaking Ukrainian in public was regarded as a manifestation of nationalism. On the other hand, as in tsarist times, compliant Ukrainians prepared to act as latter-day 'Little Russians' could make good careers within the Soviet system. Indeed, under Khrushchev both the size of the CPU and the proportion of Ukrainians within it grew rapidly. Moreover, not only did Ukrainians gradually take over the key leadership positions in the CPU but also quite a number of them were promoted to important posts in Moscow and the Kremlin.

The Twentieth Congress of the CPSU in February 1956, at which Khrushchev caused a sensation by condemning some of Stalin's crimes, seemed to herald better days ahead. The Soviet leader also declared at the congress that 'the petty tutelage of the Union republics' was 'impermissible' and that 'far from erasing national differences' the Party would ensure the 'flourishing' of the cultures of the non-Russian peoples. For a while, Khrushchev's measured de-Stalinization and zig-zags in nationalities policy allowed Ukraine to gain a little control over some parts of its economy and to begin reasserting itself. Moreover, the post-war economic rebuilding and development had restored the republic's economic importance; in 1957, for example, Ukraine supplied almost one-fifth of the USSR's total industrial production. The political thaw also precipitated the emergence of an amorphous cultural self-defence movement led by the Ukrainian cultural intelligentsia and a campaign in defence of the Ukrainian language in the pages of the republic's press.

The scope for action turned out to be rather limited, though, and Khrushchev's selective approach to de-Stalinization did not extend to the rehabilitation of Skrypnyk, Khvylovy and other national Communists, muchless Hrushevsky and Stalin's non-Communist victims. Furthermore, the repercussions in Poland and Hungary of Khrushchev's denigration of Stalin alarmed the Kremlin and in October 1956 the Soviet leadership sent in troops to crush the Hungarian Revolution. This led to a tightening of ideological controls in the Soviet Union and an offensive against 'revisionism'. On 4 December, *Pravda* reported cryptically that two well-known Ukrainian writers and Party members, Vasyl Shvets and Andrii Malyshko, had been censured for making 'utterances of an anti-Party, hooliganish nature aimed at undermining the friendship of the peoples'. It also said that a third writer, Mykyta Shumylo, who in the summer had published an outspoken article in which he invoked Lenin to condemn Russification and defend the Ukrainian language,[1] admitted that he had made 'mistakes' in some of his previous statements.

Hopes that Khrushchev would reduce Russification, continue with his decentralization of the economy, and grant more powers to the republics were soon dashed when, beginning from about 1958, he began to retreat from his more liberal course. Despite considerable opposition from the non-Russian élites, Khrushchev forced through provisions in a new education law which promoted Russification. With non-Russian parents already under increasing pressure to send their children to Russian schools, the law had the effect of depriving the native language of its status as an obligatory subject of study in the Russian-language schools in the non-Russian republics. The implications for Ukraine, with its Russified larger cities and eastern and southern regions, were obvious, and among the Ukrainian officials who opposed the change were the CPU's ideological secretary, Stepan Chervonenko, and the first deputy

---

[1] 'Lyubov do ridnoi movy' [Love for the Native Language], *Zmina*, July 1956.

chairman of the Ukrainian SSR Council of Ministers, Mykhailo
Hrechukha.

In 1958, Khrushchev also launched a major anti-religious campaign which hit Ukraine the hardest: between 1959 and 1964, 3,933
Russian Orthodox churches (the Ukrainian Autocephalous Orthodox and Ukrainian Catholic Churches were still banned) were
closed down.[2] In Western Ukraine, petitions for the legalization of
the Ukrainian Catholic Church inspired by de-Stalinization were
treated as acts of treachery; indeed, in the spring of 1958 the leader
of the Ukrainian Catholic Church, Metropolitan Yosyf Slipy, was
arrested in his place of internal exile, accused of maintaining illegal
contacts with his catacomb Church, and given a further seven years
of imprisonment.[3]

Meanwhile, in the labour camps Ukrainian political prisoners –
largely UPA and OUN members and their sympathizers – played a
leading role in the strikes and uprisings which shook the Gulag after
Stalin's death. Many of the most active Ukrainian prisoners were
not released, or were rearrested soon after being freed. Indeed, with
the Soviet authorities continuing to pursue a tough policy towards
Ukrainian 'nationalists', from the 1950s onwards Ukrainians formed
a disproportionately large proportion of Soviet political prisoners.
In Western Ukraine, the tradition of underground nationalist activity continued and between 1958 and 1962 at least a dozen
clandestine groups are known to have been uncovered. Although
none of these groups used violence, their members were depicted
at closed trials as dangerous terrorists and usually given heavy
sentences including the death penalty.

The best known of these cases involved a group, led by the
lawyers Levko Lukyanenko and Ivan Kandyba, which between
1959 and 1960 had discussed setting up an organization –
provisionally called the Ukrainian Workers' and Peasants' Union
–which would campaign openly and non-violently for Ukraine to
exercise its constitutional right to secede from the USSR. Charged
with treason, Lukyanenko was sentenced to death in May 1961 (his

---

[2] I.P. Merkatun, 'Antyrelihiina kampaniya 50-60-kh rokiv na Ukraini' [The
Anti-Religious Campaign of the 50s and 60s in Ukraine], *Ukrainskyi Istorychnyi
Zhurnal*, no. 10, 1991, p. 75.

[3] Metropolitan Slipy was finally freed in early 1963 and allowed to leave for Rome
after the personal intervention of Pope John XXIII.

sentence was later commuted to fifteen years' imprisonment), while six of his colleagues received terms ranging from ten to fifteen years.

After the Twentieth Party Congress the Khrushchev leadership also did not soften its line towards the large Ukrainian Western diaspora and its anti-Communist leaders. Continuing the Stalinist practice of eliminating political adversaries who were living abroad, the Soviet secret police assassinated two prominent Ukrainian political leaders living in Munich: in 1957 a Soviet agent using a special cyanide-spraying pistol killed Lev Rebet, a moderate nationalist, and two years later the same agent using the same method assassinated the more militant Bandera.

The toughening of the Kremlin's nationalities policy was emphasized at the Twenty-second Congress of the CPSU in October 1961 and reflected in the new Party programme adopted by the congress. Emphasis was switched from allowing the non-Russian cultures to 'flourish' to accelerating their eventual 'fusion' or 'merger'. The new Party programme also stressed the special role and importance assigned to the Russian language, and it even declared that the boundaries between the Union republics were loosing their former significance. After the congress, proponents of the Soviet melting-pot scheme went on the offensive, and the prospect of denationalization and the creation of a Russian-speaking 'homo Sovieticus' generated anxiety and indignation among the non-Russians, and some Russian patriots too. In Ukraine, in February 1963, a conference attended by over 1,000 representatives of the nation's cultural intelligentsia defiantly opposed the new assimilationist course and called on the leadership of the CPU to carry out the Ukrainization of the republic's public, educational and cultural life.

During the early 1960s, the ferment in Ukraine was given fresh impetus by the emergence of a new generation of writers and artists known as the *shestydesyatnyky* or 'Sixtiers', who combined a strong sense of Ukrainian patriotism with a search for new creative forms and values. They included: the poets Ivan Drach, Lina Kostenko and Vasyl Symonenko; the literary critics Ivan Dzyuba, Ivan Svitlychny and Yevhen Sverstyuk; the theatre director Les Tanyuk; the artists Alla Horska and Panas Zalyvakha; and the composer Leonid Hrabovsky. Representatives of this 'new wave' formed an unofficial Club of Creative Youth in Kyiv, which served as a focal point of national dissent until its dispersal in 1963. Its members sought to rediscover and retrieve Ukraine's officially forbidden past, especially the national renaissance of the 1920s, and, in open defiance of the Kremlin's renewed emphasis on assimilation, worked to bring about a new revival. They were also interested in establishing contacts with the large Ukrainian diaspora in the West and in Eastern Europe – in Poland, Czechoslovakia and Romania, from which Ukraine was still effectively sealed off. The bold spirit of the Sixtiers was perhaps best expressed in the powerful publicistic poems of Symonenko, who declared characteristically in one of his verses: 'My people exists! My people will always exist! No one can blot out my people!' The Party's efforts to reassert ideological controls only radicalized the students and young intellectuals: there were more and more protests against Russification and the volume of Ukrainian *samvydav* (or *samizdat* in Russian, that is, uncensored and 'self-published' literature) steadily expanded.

To a considerable extent the growing national ferment in Ukraine also reflected rising social and economic tensions resulting from the rapid urbanization of Ukrainians which was taking place and the simultaneous large in-migration of Russians into the republic, most of whom settled in the cities of the already Russified south-eastern regions. Between the two censuses taken in 1959 and 1970, the Russian population of Ukraine grew by just over 2 million, or by 28.7%, from 7 million to 9.1 million, whereas the number of Ukrainians in the republic increased by only 9.7%, from 32.1 million to 35.3 million. This resulted in a rise in the Russians' share of Ukraine's total population from 16.9% to 19.4%, and a drop in the proportion of Ukrainians from 76.8% to 74.9%. The influx of Russians, who enjoyed the various advantages which the system afforded them as the USSR's 'leading people', hampered the social mobility of Ukrainians, and during the decade they were unable to improve their disadvantaged standing among the students in higher education, the intelligentsia and white-collar occupations. The proportion of Ukrainian students attending the republic's institutes of higher education (*vuzy*) declined steadily from 63.8% in the 1955–6 academic year to 59.9% in 1970. The Ukrainians' share of the republic's intelligentsia and white-collar staff also roughly corresponded to this figure.[4]

[4] On this, see Bohdan Krawchenko, *Social Change and National Consciousness in Twentieth-Century Ukraine*, London, 1985, chapter 5.

The fate of the millions of Ukrainians living outside of Ukraine in Russia and in other parts of the USSR, and of the hundreds of thousands of Ukrainians who during the Khrushchev years left to work in Siberia or the Virgin Lands, was also a cause for serious concern for Ukrainian patriots, all the more so since the Ukrainian government turned a blind eye to this problem. While Russians who moved to Ukraine had no problems with using their language, or with access to Russian-language education and Russian cultural facilities, the Ukrainians outside their republic were, in the words of one prominent dissenter, condemned to 'denationalization and assimilation'. They did not have 'a single Ukrainian newspaper . . . radio program or cultural, educational establishment'.[5]

The trend toward economic recentralization continued and the republican Party bosses were increasingly treated as economic managers whose primary task was to ensure that the plans set by Moscow were met. Even at the highest levels dissent was not tolerated and in June 1963 the relatively new chairman of the Ukrainian Council of Ministers, Volodymyr Shcherbytsky, was abruptly demoted and sent back to work in the provinces for disagreeing with the Soviet leader. Khrushchev often showed little regard for tact and sometimes criticized and embarrassed republican Party leaders in public. For instance, in April 1964, during a visit to Hungary, Khrushchev castigated the recently appointed Ukrainian Party chief Petro Shelest in front of 8,000 workers because a Ukrainian factory had not met its delivery dates. Pointing to the Party boss of the USSR's second most important republic, the Soviet leader declared in his typical boorish style: 'The main criminal is amongst us. Here is Shelest, eating Hungarian goulash, and he does not supply materials in time for this factory.'[6]

Later that year, one of the first Ukrainian *samvydav* protests appeared. It took the form of an appeal from a 'group of Ukrainian communists' to the outside world which claimed that Ukraine, like the other 'sovereign' Union republics, had been transformed into 'a colonial administrative-territorial region' and was being subjected to 'Russification and the colonialist policies of Moscow'. As an example of Ukraine's fictional sovereignty, the document stressed

---

[5] Ivan Dzyuba, *Internationalism or Russification? A Study in the Soviet Nationalities Problem*, London, 1968, p. 109.

[6] Reuter, 8 April 1964.

that in reality Shelest was not able even to authorize the building of an underpass for pedestrians of Kyiv without Moscow's approval.[7]

Shelest and renewed Ukrainian assertiveness

This was the situation in October 1964 when Khrushchev was deposed in a palace coup by his colleagues, including Shelest's predecessor in Kyiv, Mykola Pidhorny (Nikolai Podgorny), who was a member of the CPSU Presidium. The following month, Shelest, who had been the Party boss of Ukraine only since July 1963, but who had backed the plotters, was also made a member of the Presidium, which was now headed by the new leader of the CPSU, Leonid Brezhnev.

Some elements within the CPU, including Shelest, seem to have wanted to take advantage of the changing of the guard in Moscow to promote a more autonomous Ukrainian course. It appears that behind the scenes Ukraine's representatives became more assertive in defending their republic's interests, especially in the economic sphere. As early as June 1965, the Russian *samizdat* journal *Politicheskii dnevnik* (Political diary), whose contributors appeared to have links with circles within the Soviet establishment, reported that: 'According to reports from many comrades, a strengthening of nationalist tendencies in Ukraine is being witnessed.' Not only was this trend visible among the Ukrainian intelligensia (the example of attempts to Ukrainize the republic's film industry was given), but also among some of the republic's state and even Party organs. The journal noted that Moscow's central planners were having problems with Ukrainian administrators, some of whom were openly claiming that Ukraine was being economically exploited by Russia. For instance, one unidentified 'highly placed' official was reported to have declared that Ukraine would have solved its housing problem a long time ago if the republic did not have to contribute so much to the all-Union budget.[8]

According to those who worked with Shelest, the Ukrainian Party leader was himself not afraid of speaking his mind and he developed a reputation for his readiness to stand up to the Kremlin

[7] AS 912. AS = Archiv *samizdata* (*Samizdat* Archive, published by Radio Liberty, Munich).

[8] *Politicheskii dnevnik 1964-1970*, Amsterdam, 1972, pp. 90-1.

leadership. In October 1965, the chairman of the Ukrainian Council of Ministers, Ivan Kazanets, was replaced by Brezhnev's friend and client and Shelest's political rival, Shcherbytsky. Shelest was later to explain that he and Kazanets had worked well together and formed an effective partnership which sought to defend the republic's economic interests. This had resulted in Kazanets and Shelest being criticized at a meeting of the CPSU Presidium: it had been pointed out to the two Ukrainian leaders that Ukraine was better off than the towns in the Moscow region and that they were expected to increase the republic's contribution to the centre. According to Shelest, Brezhnev and another key figure in the new Soviet leadership, Mikhail Suslov, 'wanted to have their own loyal person in the republic and wanted to separate us'. They arranged for Kazanets to be moved to a new position in Moscow, overrode Shelest's choice of Oleksandr Lyashko to replace Kazanets, and secured the important post for their man – Shcherbytsky.[9]

Some of Shelest's team also attempted to reduce the tension in Ukraine by showing more responsiveness to the problems in the sphere of nationalities policy. In August 1965, the republic's minister of higher and secondary specialized education, Yurii Dadenkov, announced far-reaching instructions regarding the Ukrainization of higher education which, if implemented, would have begun to reverse the accelerated Russification of education that Khrushchev had set in motion. The reform, however, generated strong opposition from lecturers who were not proficient in Ukrainian[10] and, according to the dissident journalist and human rights campaigner Vyacheslav Chornovil, was blocked 'by a directive from Moscow'.

Reflecting on this period, Shelest revealed in 1989 how hard-line and chauvinistic members of the post-Khrushchev leadership had actually been in their attitudes towards the non-Russians generally, and Ukraine in particular. Already in the mid-1960s, the CPSU's chief ideologist Suslov and other Russian members of the Presidium began expressing concern about 'manifestations of nationalism' and 'localism' in Ukraine. Suslov 'strongly insisted on the speediest

[9] See Dmytro Tabachnyk's lengthy interview with Shelest in *Kyiv*, no. 10, 1989, pp. 90-110.

[10] Author's interview with Vitalii Vrublevsky, Kyiv, 20 March 1993. Vrublevsky, a Belarusian, worked from 1964 to 1972 in the CPU Central Committee apparatus as a lecturer. See also the interview with Vrublevsky in *Ukraina*, no. 23, 1992, p. 13.

fusion of nations and their languages and cultures' and this was to result in 'repeated clashes' with the Ukrainian Party boss over 'questions of ideology and culture'. As for Brezhnev, at a meeting of the Presidium in the autumn of 1965, he ridiculed the very idea of Ukrainization and described the Ukrainian language as 'pidgin Russian'.[11]

In the same month that the Ukrainian authorities sought to inaugurate a measure of Ukrainization, the new leadership in Moscow demonstrated its intention to 'restore order' by launching an extensive crackdown on Ukrainian national dissent and, two weeks later, arresting the Russian writers, Andrei Sinyavsky and Yulii Daniel. These repressive actions – the first major KGB operation of this sort since Stalin's death – backfired. They not only failed to stifle dissent, but triggered off a public protest campaign which, to the surprise and embarrassment of the authorities, was supported by a number of prominent Ukrainian cultural and scientific figures.

The offensive against Ukrainian national dissent prompted one of the leading representative of the 'Sixtiers', Ivan Dzyuba, to write a penetrating book-length critique of the Soviet nationalities policy aptly entitled *Internationalism or Russification?* in which he set forth Ukrainian grievances and demands. In his classic *samvydav* work, which was addressed to the Party and state leaders of Ukraine, Dzyuba contrasted what Lenin and the Bolsheviks had promised the non-Russians in the early years of Soviet rule with the 'chauvinism, Great-power ideology and Russification' which he argued had characterized Soviet nationalities policy under Stalin and his successors. Recalling the tremendous progress that Ukraine had made in the 1920s during the brief period of Ukrainization, he pointed to the 'crisis' in which his nation now found itself and which was giving 'cause for great alarm'.

> *Territorial unity and sovereignty* are being gradually and progressively lost through mass resettlement . . . of the Ukrainian population in Siberia, Kazakhstan, the North, etc., where it numbers millions but is quickly denationalized; through an organized mass resettlement of Russians in Ukraine . . . and through the doubtful sovereignty of the government of the Ukrainian SSR over the territory of Ukraine. This latter reason,

---

[11] See the interviews with Shelest in *Argumenty i fakty*, no. 2, 1989, and in *Kyiv*, no. 10, 1989.

coupled with excessive centralization and a total subordination to all-Union authorities in Moscow, makes it equally difficult to speak about the *integrity and sovereignty of the economic life* of the Ukrainian nation. *A common historic fate* is also being lost, as the Ukrainian nation is being progressively dispersed over the Soviet Union, and as the sense of the historic national tradition and knowledge of the historical past are gradually being lost due to a total lack of national education in school and society in general. Ukrainian national *culture* is being kept in a rather provincial position and is practically treated as 'second-rate'; its great past achievements are poorly disseminated in society. The Ukrainian language has also been pushed into the background and is not really used in the cities of Ukraine. Finally, during the last decades the Ukrainian nation has virtually been deprived of the natural increase in population which characterizes all present-day nations. As far back as 1913 one would hear about 'the 37 million Ukrainians'. After all . . . the number of Russians has doubled [since 1913] in spite of war losses.[12]

What had emerged, Dzyuba explained, was a 'spontaneous, multiform, widespread, self-originating process of a nation's "self-defence" in the face of a clear prospect of disappearing from the human family'.[13] But the official response had been 'an indefatigable, pitiless and absurd persecution of national cultural life'.[14] Arrests and repression were no solution, he argued; what was needed was a return to a nationalities policy which recognized the equality of all the nations of the USSR, their right to free development and the sovereignty of the Union republics. The starting point, Dzyuba emphasized, however, had to be *hlasnist* (*glasnost* in Russian, i.e. openness) in the sphere of national relations.[15]

The protests in Ukraine failed to make the Kremlin reconsider and during the first half of 1966 sixteen dissenters were convicted behind closed doors of 'anti-Soviet agitation and propaganda' and given sentences of up to six years. The trials provoked further indignation and protest and led activists like Chornovil to pioneer new forms of open and legalistic national dissent in which concerns for human and national rights were interwoven. One of the major

[12] Dzyuba, *Internationalism or Russification?*, pp. 14-15.

[13] *Ibid.*, p. 204.

[14] *Ibid.*, p. 6.

[15] *Ibid.*, p. 213.

problems facing the fledgling Ukrainian human and national rights movement, however, was Ukraine's isolation: it took seven months for news of the 1965 arrests in Ukraine to filter out to the West. In the late 1960s, therefore, Ukrainian dissenters established links with human rights campaigners in Moscow and Ukrainian groups in Eastern Europe and the West. Consequently, by the beginning of the 1970s, by which time the Ukrainian patriotic movement had begun publishing its own *samvydav* journal, *Ukrainskyi visnyk* (The Ukrainian Herald), a steady trickle of information about developments in Ukraine was reaching the West. Moreover, the work of Dzyuba, Chornovil and other Ukrainian dissidents, such as the historian Valentyn Moroz (one of the intellectuals imprisoned after the 1965 crackdown), also found their way to the West and helped to draw attention to the situation in Ukraine.

Significantly, despite the tough action taken against the more outspoken Ukrainian dissenters and the Kremlin's sensitivity to anything that smacked of Ukrainian nationalism, Shelest continued to identify with Ukrainian cultural values and sought to establish a *modus vivendi* with the republic's cultural élite. In November 1966, he addressed the Fifth Congress of the Writers' Union of Ukraine (WUU) and demonstratively pledged the CPU's support for improving the position of the Ukrainian language and culture. Shelest also called on Ukraine's technical and scientific intelligentsia to use the Ukrainian language in their work and, for instance, encouraged the preparation in Ukrainian of the USSR's first encyclopedia of cybernetics. The Ukrainian Party leader was proud of Ukraine's past, especially the period of Ukrainian Cossack statehood, and under him there began a revival of Ukrainian historical studies.

Shelest, a metallurgical engineer by training who was primarily dedicated to economic management, was also eager to stress Ukraine's economic and political importance and the great strides which the republic had made in urbanization, economic development and education. In 1966, for the first time the proportion of Ukraine's urban population exceeded that of the rural population, and by 1970 it had reached 54.5%. As for the republic's economic clout, in 1967 Ukraine produced 55% of the USSR's iron ore, 42% of its steel, 33% of its coal, 30% of its natural gas, 47% of its metallurgical equipment, 22% of its grain, 23% of its meat, 22% of its milk and 58% of its granulated sugar.

Another factor also underlay the new Ukrainian national assertiveness associated with the Shelest period. During the 1960s the size of the CPU continued to expand rapidly, its membership growing from 1.1 million in 1959 to 2.5 million in 1971. The proportion of Ukrainians in the CPU also steadily increased, and in 1968 they made up 65% of the membership (although this was lower than their share of the total population of Ukraine – 74.9% in 1970 – it approximated their still disadvantaged position within the urban and educated sectors of society). Moreover, Ukrainians took over most of the positions in the CPU leadership. In 1971, for example, nine out of the ten full CPU Politburo members were Ukrainians, as well as all five candidate members.

Shelest, however, was no crypto-nationalist, nor, for that matter, closet democrat, as his hawkish stance in 1968 during the events connected with the Prague Spring showed. It is worth noting though that in the spring of 1968, just as he was facing an indirect attack against him from his political adversaries within the CPU, Shelest was confronted with the largest protest yet from the Ukrainian public about the political repression and 'distortion of the nationalities problem' in the republic – an appeal from 139 scientists, writers, artists, students and workers addressed to the Party and state leaders in Moscow. Among the signatories was the historian Mykhailo Braichevsky, who in 1966 had got into trouble at the Institute of History for writing a study entitled 'Pryyednannya chy vozzyednannya?' (Annexation or Reunification?), in which he had challenged the officially prescribed line on the Treaty of Pereyaslav and the history of Ukrainian-Russian relations. By this time, his work was circulating in *samvydav* and providing further ammunition for Ukraine's burgeoning human and national rights movement.

Many Ukrainian intellectuals followed the process of liberalization in neighbouring Czechoslovakia with considerable interest and sympathy, though few dared to speak out openly. In May 1968, the Ukrainian political prisoner Valentyn Moroz, whose writings were vividly describing the mechanics of totalitarianism and Russification and exposing conditions in the Gulag, wrote an appeal to Shelest drawing a parallel between the situation in Czechoslovakia and Ukraine. 'The Communists of Czechoslovakia are demonstrating to the Communists of all countries the necessity of throwing overboard that which had become a ballast and opening the sluices to those forces which guarantee a future', he wrote. 'Will the

Communists of Ukraine succeed, in their own interest, in mastering this lesson?'[16]

Instead, during these crucial months, the Ukrainian Party leader denounced 'reformism and revisionism, whenever and in whatever form they may appear', and called for the closing of Communist ranks against proponents of 'contrived, lifeless "models of socialism", abstract humanism, ideas of so-called "democratization" and 'liberalization" of socialism'.[17] Though twenty years later Shelest was to attempt to 'whitewash' himself, he was one of the Soviet leaders who pressed for the military intervention to crush Czechoslovakia's attempt to build socialism with a human face.[18]

Shelest also adopted an uncompromising position towards, as he put it in early 1968, 'treacherous Ukrainian counter-revolutionary elements' among the émigrés who continued to 'babble on about so-called "independence", [and] about some sort of decline of culture and language'.[19] He also appears to have been a hard-liner on foreign policy issues and remained outspoken in warning about the dangers purportedly posed by 'world imperialism'.

In essence then, Shelest turns out to have been a watered-down version of the national Communists of the 1920s who apparently saw nothing wrong in promoting a sense of 'Soviet' Ukrainian patriotism and defending the interests of Soviet Ukraine while remaining loyal to Moscow and the Soviet federation. Indeed, Shelest was not only proud of his Ukrainian heritage but also sought

[16] See in Yaroslav Bihun (ed.), *Boomerang: The Works of Valentyn Moroz*, Baltimore, 1974, pp. 146-7.

[17] *Pravda Ukrainy*, 6 July 1968.

[18] In an interview published in *Komsomolskaya pravda* on 19 October 1989, Shelest condemned the invasion of Czechoslovakia as a 'negative' and 'damaging' decision and sought to place all the blame on Brezhnev. Former Czechoslovak leaders, however, have portrayed the former Ukrainian Party boss as one of the main hard-liners on the Soviet side. This has also been confirmed by Pavlo Fedchenko, who in 1968 was appointed head of the CPU Central Committee's Cultural Section. He has described how Shelest called the Central Committee secretaries and department heads together and told them that at a meeting with the Czechoslovak leaders in Cierna, Brezhnev 'vacillated' but that he 'had impressed upon them that I and Czechoslovakia are neighbours and that I will not allow the disease to spread to here'. See the discussion with Fedchenko in *Literaturna Ukraina*, 24 September 1992.

[19] See, for instance, his speech at the Kyiv *oblast* Party conference in February 1968; *Pravda Ukrainy*, 17 February 1968.

to protect Ukraine's economic interests and opposed the diversion of funds away from the republic for the development of the Siberian regions. While his role in the political arrests and trials which took place in Ukraine during the time he was the CPU's first secretary is unclear, both he and some of his key officials, such as the republican KGB chief, Vitalii Nikitchenko, and ideological secretary, Fedir Ovcharenko, were generally regarded as being relatively moderate in their approach to national dissent. On being pressed to take tougher action against dissenters such as Dzyuba, Shelest was even reported to have told Ovcharenko's predecessor, Andrii Skaba, that he was not Kaganovich and that these were not the times of Stalin.[20] In short, the Ukrainian Party leader's attitude and forceful personality stimulated the restoration of a sense of national pride and afforded some protection to those dissenters who were prepared to work 'within the system'.

Shelest's removal

Shelest's 'autonomist' course gave rise to concern not only in Moscow but also in some quarters in Ukraine. The CPU was after all by no means monolithic: apart from its large Russian element, it contained a considerable number of Ukrainians who were Russified, or who had a 'Little Russian' mentality, and were hostile to Ukrainian national aspirations. For instance, Yurii Yelchenko, who was the head of the Ukrainian Komsomol from 1960 to 1968, told the author in an interview that he and his colleagues had been 'educated to accept the idea of the indivisibility of the Soviet Union' and the sense of the national factor 'had been diluted in all of us'. Thus 'not everything' that Shelest and his team did in the nationalities sphere 'was understood or accepted' within the CPU.[21] Also, apart from Moscow's continuing emphasis on assimilation, the situation was complicated by the Russian influx into Ukraine and the ensuing competition for jobs, housing and places in higher education between Ukrainians moving into the cities from the villages and the Russian newcomers. There was thus a very large 'Russian' constituency which feared and, under the guise of defending 'internationalism', resisted any moves

---

[20] John Kolasky, *Two Years in Soviet Ukraine*, Toronto, 1970, p. 206.

[21] Author's interview with Yurii Yelchenko, Kyiv, 20 March 1993.

towards Ukrainization.

Perhaps the best example of the kind of problems which Shelest faced from the orthodox 'internationalists' was the case of Valentyn Malanchuk, whom Dzyuba had portrayed in *Internationalism or Russification?* as a zealous Russifier and promoter of 'the national dissolution of Ukraine into Russia'.[22] The son of a Party worker from Eastern Ukraine who had been killed in the Lopatyn district of Western Ukraine by the UPA, Malanchuk is described by those who worked with him as having had a 'pathological' hatred of everything connected with Ukrainian nationalism. He specialized in the study of 'Ukrainian bourgeois nationalism' and, as a Doctor of Historical Sciences and professor, became a leading expert on the nationalities problem, especially in Western Ukraine. After being appointed the ideological secretary in the Lviv region Party organization in 1963, he wrote numerous articles, the purpose of which seemed to be to warn that the nationalities problem in Ukraine was not under control and that the Shelest leadership was not doing enough in this respect. After the crackdown on Ukrainian dissent in the summer of 1965, Malanchuk published an outspoken article in *Pravda* on 16 December of that year which portrayed the ideological situation in the republic, especially in Western Ukraine, as still unsatisfactory and implicitly seemed to criticize the line being taken by Shelest's team. The Ukrainian Party boss apparently realized that Malanchuk was a 'time bomb' that had to be defused. First, in 1967, Malanchuk's wings were partly clipped when he was transferred to Kyiv as the deputy minister for higher and secondary special education. Nevertheless, he continued to cause trouble. Fedchenko recalls that in 1971, for instance, when Shelest authorized the publication of a book about Drahomanov, Malanchuk was quick to fire off a protest to Suslov. Shelest's people therefore sought to discredit the self-appointed ideological watchdog. A special CPU Central Committee team was formed to find 'compromising' evidence against Malanchuk: it was duly discovered in the form of the latter's alleged 'distortions' in his interpretation of the role of certain Ukrainian social democrats. Apparently, there was even talk of having Malanchuk expelled from the Party, but Shelest's fall saved him.[23]

[22] Dzyuba, *Internationalism or Russification?*, pp. 183–6.

[23] Author's interviews with Vrublevsky, Yelchenko, and also Ivan Kuras, Kyiv, 17

The existence of differences within the Ukrainian leadership was confirmed when, in the spring of 1967, the Communist Party of Canada (which contained many Canadians of Ukrainian descent) sent a delegation to investigate the ferment in Ukraine. In its report, which was not published until January 1968, the delegation concluded that the Ukrainian leadership was divided on nationalities policy, especially on how to deal with the language issue and the dissidents. Shelest himself was cited as acknowledging that 'we have had problems, many of them, and we still have problems, but we are overcoming them'. Outlining his position, the Ukrainian Party leader told the Canadian delegation 'emphatically' that 'the development of Communist society must permit the fullest and freest economic and cultural development of each nation'. As for the language question, he declared: 'Yes, some comrades have, on occasion, expressed mistaken ideas about what they call the merging of languages, but only a fool could imagine that there is any possibility of Russian taking over in Ukraine.' The report, however, portrayed, among others, the CPU's conservative ideological secretary Skaba, who had held this key post since 1959 and was detested by the nationally minded intelligentsia, as taking a very different view and displaying indifference to Ukrainian national aspirations and sensitivities. It also noted the 'tendency in some quarters to brand as bourgeois nationalism, or some kind of deviation, demands for the greater use of the Ukrainian language in public institutions', and expressed concern about the recent arrests and trials of Ukrainian intellectuals.[24]

Soon after this embarrassing document was published, Shelest managed to replace Skaba. Although the change was made at a time when, just across the border in Czechoslovakia, the Prague Spring was in full bloom, Shelest appointed a liberal figure, the chemist Ovcharenko, who, just after the Twentieth Congress of the CPSU, had been made head of the CPU Central Committee's Department for Science and Culture, to oversee ideology in Ukraine. Despite

---

March 1993. Kuras, a historian, headed the Social Sciences Sector of the Science and Educational Institutions Department of the CPU Central Committee from the mid-1970s until 1983. See also the above-mentioned interview with Fedchenko in *Literaturna Ukraina*.

[24] See 'Report of Delegation to Ukraine. Central Committee Meeting, September 16, 17 and 18, 1967', *Viewpoint*, 5, no. 1 (January 1968).

Shelest's subsequent tough stance on Czechoslovakia, Ovcharenko did in fact adopt a milder line than his predecessor.

Within the CPU Shelest and his allies were opposed by the powerful Dnipropetrovsk group, which was closely linked with Brezhnev and Shelest's political adversary, Shcherbytsky. The latter had twice headed the Dnipropetrovsk region Party Organization and in the meantime, between 1961 and 1963, had been chairman of the Ukrainian Council of Ministers. In October 1965 Brezhnev had helped him regain this position.[25] In 1968, the Dnipropetrovsk region's Party bosses launched a major implicit attack against Shelest in the form of an unexpected and vitriolic campaign against a new novel called *Sobor* (The Cathedral) by the head of the WUU, Oles Honchar. In it, the writer had painted a candid picture of some of the problems facing Ukrainian society; but he had also defended Ukrainian cultural and historical values and raised environmental issues. It later transpired that in the Kremlin there had been objections to the novel's praise for the Ukrainian Cossack era, or in other words, to Honchar's treatment of Ukrainian history, and that the Dnipropetrovsk region Party boss, Oleksii Vatchenko, had seen the work as a veiled attack against him and his policies. Whether by coincidence or not, the latter fired the opening salvo in the campaign against Honchar at the same plenum of the CPU Central Committee on 29 March at which Skaba was replaced by Ovcharenko.[26]

Increasingly, Ukraine's assertiveness under Shelest and the more tolerant domestic line identified with Ovcharenko appeared to be at variance with the new emphasis in Soviet nationalities policy, which was finally enunciated by Brezhnev at the Twenty-fourth Congress of the CPSU in March 1971. The Soviet leader announced that a 'new historical community of people – the Soviet people', had emerged and that the Party would concentrate on promoting the further 'drawing together' of the nations of the USSR and strengthening the unity and cohesion of the new supranational

---

[25] On relations between Shelest and Shcherbytsky, see the political portrait of the latter by Dmytro Tabachnyk, entitled 'Ostannii z mohikan' [Last of the Mohicans], in *Ranok*, no. 2, 1991, pp. 16-20, no. 3, 1991, pp. 18-21, and no. 5, 1991, pp. 24-8, and a revised enlarged version entitled 'Apostol zastoyu' [Apostle of Stagnation], in *Vitchyzna*, no. 9, 1992, pp. 159-63; no. 10, 1992, pp. 107-13, and no. 11, 1992, pp. 119-23.

[26] On the *Sobor* affair, see Vitalii Koval, *'Sobor' i navkolo Soboru* ['Sobor' and Around Sobor], Kyiv, 1989.

entity. Furthermore, Brezhnev's paean to the 'Great Russian people' and their 'revolutionary energy, selflessness, diligence and profound internationalism', which was reminiscent of the Stalin era, indicated that the Russians would continue to be the first among 'equals'. It was also at this time that the idea of the Soviet economy as an 'integral national-economic complex' was projected with its even greater emphasis on the importance of the role of Moscow and the central planners.

In July 1970, just as a Ukrainian human and national rights movement seemed to be crystallizing, Moscow abruptly replaced Ukraine's KGB chief and Shelest's friend, Nikitchenko, with Vitalii Fedorchuk, who had formerly worked for SMERSH[27] (a division of the Soviet security service which had eliminated opponents to the Soviet government). The resulting tougher line against Ukrainian national dissent was demonstrated in November of that year when the recently freed former political prisoner Moroz was given a new draconian fourteen-year sentence for his protest essays.

Soon afterwards, as if heeding Malanchuk's continuing warnings about the tenacious hold of nationalism in Western Ukraine, a special group was sent to the region by the CPSU Central Committee to investigate the situation. But as Yelchenko, who served as the second secretary in the Lviv region Party organization from 1969 to 1971 told the author, it was clear that the 'brigade' from Moscow had come to 'collect ammunition against Shelest'. On 7 October 1971, the CPSU Central Committee adopted a special resolution criticizing the ideological situation in the Lviv region and calling for a tightening of ideological controls and a 'cultural-educational' offensive against all vestiges of nationalism and religion. Despite this, the following month Shelest is reported to have still managed at a CPSU Central Committee plenum in Moscow to block the removal of his political ally heading the Lviv region Party organization, Vasyl Kutsevol.

In January 1972, however, Fedorchuk used the pretext of the detention of a Ukrainian student from Belgium, who had met with a number of Ukrainian dissenters, to launch a new wave of arrests on a far larger scale than the clampdown of 1965. It soon became clear that this operation represented more than just an attempt to suppress the Ukrainian human and national rights movement. The

---

[27] See the *Ukraina* interview with Vrublevsky, p. 13.

offensive developed into a broad political and cultural purge which also targeted the republic's top Party leadership. Behind the closed doors of a Politburo meeting in Moscow in March, Shelest and the CPU leadership were criticized for 'shortcomings in the internationalist education of the workers, [and their] conciliatory attitude towards manifestations of nationalism'.[28] In May 1972 Shelest was replaced as leader of the CPU by Shcherbytsky and transferred to Moscow to serve as a deputy chairman of the USSR Council of Ministers. During 1972 and 1973 scores of Ukrainian dissidents were arrested and given heavy sentences, or, in some cases, confined in mental hospitals; nationally minded elements of the intelligentsia were purged; and the CPU was thoroughly cleansed of 'national Communists'.

In April 1973 the CPU's theoretical organ *Kommunist Ukrainy* finally revealed publicly what Shelest and his associates were deemed to have been guilty of. Vehemently attacking Shelest's book *Ukraino nasha Radyanska* (Ukraine, Our Soviet Land), which had been published in 1970, it accused the author of 'ideological errors', 'serious mistakes', and 'biased evaluations of important historical matters'. Among other things, Shelest was castigated for 'elements of autarchy'. In other words, acting almost like a latter-day hetman, Shelest had overstepped the mark in his promotion of a Soviet Ukrainian patriotism and defied the CPSU's canons on the treatment of Ukrainian history and the nature of the Russo-Ukrainian relationship.[29] That same month Shelest was dismissed from the Politburo of the CPSU, banned from returning to Ukraine, and for the next fifteen years vanished from sight.

Shcherbytsky and 'normalization'

Although Ukraine had hardly been on the brink of breaking

---

[28] Heorhii Kasyanov, *Nezhodni: ukrainska intelihentsiya v rusi oporu 1960-80-kh rokiv* [Dissenters: the Ukrainian Intelligentsia in the Opposition Movement of the 1960s-1980s], Kyiv, 1995, pp. 132-3.

[29] Both Vrublevsky and Yelchenko, who held important positions under Shcherbytsky, told the author that they consider the charges against Shelest to have been deliberately exaggerated. The day after he became Ukraine's new Party boss, Shcherbytsky asked Vrublevsky, an economist, to become his personal aide. He served Shcherbytsky loyally until the latter's last day in office. Yelchenko was Ukraine's minister of culture from 1971 to 1973. After this, until 1980, he was the head of the CPU Central Committee's Propaganda and Agitation Department.

away, Moscow had decided to intervene to bring the Ukrainians back into line. The wave of arrests was followed by an extensive ideological purge and an intensification of Russification, and Shcherbytsky himself set the new tone by addressing meetings of the CPU in Russian. But the official most directly involved in overseeing the extirpative campaign against Ukrainian 'nationalism' was none other than Malanchuk. Shortly after Shcherbytsky had taken over, Malanchuk had written an 'emotional' letter to the new leader of the CPU describing the attempts Shelest's team had made to discredit him and in effect proposing a programme of struggle against Ukrainian nationalism. According to the historian and CPU Central Committee functionary Ivan Kuras who later saw the letter, Shcherbytsky wrote on it: 'Comrade Malanchuk is a genuine internationalist.' The zealous ideologist was proposed by his patron, Shcherbytsky's ally and member of the Dnipropetrovsk group, the veteran neo-Stalinist CPU apparatchik Ivan Hrushetsky, who in the summer of 1972 was appointed chairman of the Presidium of the Ukrainian Supreme Soviet as the replacement for Ovcharenko; moreover, Malanchuk's candidacy was also strongly supported by Suslov. In October 1972 Malanchuk was appointed the CPU's new ideological secretary.

Under Malanchuk's hard-line stewardship, restrictions on the development of Ukrainian studies, especially historical research and writing, and cultural life generally, were drastically tightened and educational and cultural institutes purged of nationally minded individuals. All this was accompanied by a renewed emphasis on the 'unity' and 'closeness' of the Russians, Ukrainians and Belarusians. In October 1973, Shcherbytsky explained what was expected of his fellow-countrymen. Addressing a meeting of Kyiv University's Party members he declared:

> To be an internationalist means to express feelings of friendship and brotherhood towards all people of our country and, first of all, toward the great Russian people, their culture, their language – the language of the Revolution, of Lenin, the language of international intercourse and unity. To be an internationalist means to lead an uncompromising struggle against nationalism, and in particular against the worst enemy of the Ukrainian people – Ukrainian bourgeois nationalism – and also against international Zionism.[30]

A year later, as if to reinforce the message, Shcherbytsky lashed out in a major article against national communism in both its political and economic forms.[31]

These conditions encouraged the growth of what was later to be referred to in the second half of the 1980s as 'national nihilism', that is, a disdainful and cynical attitude towards one's native language and culture, and a readiness, for opportunistic and mercenary reasons, to go along with Russification and pass oneself off as a 'superinternationalist'.[32] Shcherbytsky exemplified this attitude and even his former personal aide, Vitalii Vrublevsky, though seeking to project a favourable image of his former boss, depicted him in 1992 as a 'product of the system' for whom the Party line was sacred.[33] Consequently, as Honchar was to point out, 'in the 1970s, Ukrainian national schools were closed in their dozens and hundreds, and all this was done in order to flaunt "loyalty", zeal and orthodoxy in one's capacity as an official.'[34]

Despite the devastating blow which it had been dealt, Ukrainian resistance manifested itself again in November 1976 when, inspired by the human rights provisions of the 1975 Helsinki Final Act, ten dissenters, including two well-known writers (Mykola Rudenko and Oles Berdnyk), a former Red Army Major-General (Petro Hryhorenko) and several former political prisoners (including Lukyanenko and Kandyba), set up the Ukrainian Helsinki Monitoring Group. Its goal was to expose human and national rights violations in Ukraine and to reduce the republic's international isolation. During its four-year existence, the group issued numerous documents and appeals, but paid a heavy price for its defiance: over twenty Ukrainian Helsinki monitors were arrested, half of them receiving sentences of ten years or more. The repression only radicalized Ukrainian national dissent and during the 1970s there was a shift away from cultural and largely patriotic protest activity

---

[30] *Pravda Ukrainy*, 5 October 1973.

[31] V. Shcherbitskii, 'Mezhdunarodnoe znachenie opyta natsionalnykh otnoshenii v SSSR' [The International Meaning of the Experience with National Relations in the USSR], *Kommunist*, no. 17, November 1974. See especially pp. 18 and 22.

[32] See, for example, the interview with the Kyrgyz writer Chingiz Aitmatov in *Ogonek*, no. 26, July 1987, pp. 4–9.

[33] See the above-mentioned interview with Vrublevsky in *Ukraina*, pp. 12–14.

[34] *Literaturna Ukraina*, 10 October 1987, p. 3.

to political opposition with more and more Ukrainian dissidents coming out in support of independence.

All this time Moscow was continuing to promote the idea of 'the Soviet people' and it was becoming increasingly clear that the Ukrainian and Belarusians were being moulded to form part of the assimilated Russian-speaking Slavonic core of this entity. In January 1979, for instance, on the occasion of the 325th anniversary of the Treaty of Pereyaslav, Shcherbytsky reiterated the unchanging refrain: 'Indissoluble fraternal union' with Russia, he declared, 'that is how it has been, how it is, and how is will be forever!'[35] The theme of unity in both the past and the present also figured prominently in the preparations for the celebrations in 1982 of the 1500th anniversary of Kyiv (the date seems so have been chosen quite arbitrarily) with the ancient state of Kyivan Rus being depicted more or less as a forerunner of the Soviet Union.

During this bleak period, the Ukrainian philologist Yurii Badzo worked on a mammoth study examining Soviet policy towards Ukraine, entitled 'The Right to Live'. Although the work was confiscated, before he was arrested in April 1979, the author addressed an open letter to the Soviet authorities in which he concluded:

> There is enough evidence to see that my description of the present national predicament of the Ukrainian people as a state of siege possesses not only a metaphorical and ideological import, but also a practical one. The official ideology of the 'internationalization', 'drawing together', and fusion of nations and the historiographic concept of Ukraine leave the Ukrainian people virtually no room for free movement either forward or backward. They block our access to the future and to the past; and the practical creators of this predicament beat over the head anyone who rises above the level of planned extinction, anyone who tries to tell the truth about the reality of the Ukrainian nation, or God forbid, tries to evaluate the overall picture on an 'all-nation', historical scale, according to political criteria.[36]

---

[35] *Radyanska Ukraina*, 31 January 1979.

[36] Iurii Badzo, 'An Open Letter to the Presidium of the Supreme Soviet of the USSR and the Central Committee of the CPSU', Part 2, *Journal of Ukrainian Studies* (Toronto), no. 17 (winter 1984), p. 70.

Badzo's concern for the fate of his nation earned him a twelve-year sentence.

The results of the 1979 census certainly gave nationally minded Ukrainians plenty to worry about. They revealed that since 1970 the Russian population of Ukraine had increased by 1.3 million while the Ukrainian population had risen by only 1.2 million. The proportion of Ukrainians who named Ukrainian as their mother tongue had dropped from 91.4% to 89.1%. This, of course, was only the tip of the iceberg, for although Ukrainians still spoke their native language at home, at work or when conducting official business they switched to Russian, or, as was frequently the case, to *surzhik*, that is, a mixture which was neither Russian nor Ukrainian. A stark example of the way things were going was provided by the data on book and brochure publication in Ukraine during 1984: 72.6% of books and brochures published in the republic during the year were in Russian (in 1979 Russians accounted for 21.1% of Ukraine's population) and 24% in Ukrainian.[37] With Ukrainian also being artificially squeezed out of kindergartens and schools, not to mention science, technology and the economic sphere, the future for the mother tongue seemed bleak. What was also alarming for the long term was the sharp drop in the rate of natural population growth in the republic from 6.4 per 1,000 in 1970 to 3.4 per 1,000 in 1980.

In April 1979, however, Malanchuk was suddenly replaced in circumstances which were hitherto shrouded in secrecy. According to Vrublevsky, Malanchuk's 'ideological maximalism' and seemingly boundless zeal gradually antagonized not only the more docile representatives of the Ukrainian intelligentsia but also leading Party officials and eventually Shcherbytsky himself. Not only did the ideologist virtually set himself up as a law unto himself, preparing 'black lists' and interfering in areas that lay beyond the scope of his duties, but also he was suspected of continuing to act as Suslov's informant. As Vrublevsky points out though, Malanchuk was armed with a seemingly invincible trump card: everything he did was purportedly in the name of internationalism, Soviet patriotism and hostility towards all manifestations of Ukrainian nationalism.

The story of Malanchuk's removal, as related to the author by Vrublevsky, sounds like something out of a political thriller. At the

[37] See Roman Solchanyk, 'Oversight or Disinformation? Language Politics and Book Publication in the Ukraine', RL 69/86, 10 February 1986.

beginning of 1979, a pretext for Malanchuk's dismissal was found: after a tip-off, Vrublevsky confirmed for Shcherbytsky through friends in the Central Committee apparatus in Moscow that Malanchuk, without clearance from the Ukrainian Party leader, was preparing to publish a monograph in Moscow on the nationalities question in Ukraine under the pseudonym V. Yefimov. 'Normalization' in Ukraine, it seems, had not gone far enough for Malanchuk. This information apparently finally convinced Shcherbytsky that Malanchuk was an 'adventurer' who was 'playing for the highest political stakes'. That very night the Ukrainian Party leader made an emergency telephone call to the Kremlin and succeeded in persuading Brezhnev that, regardless of what Suslov might think, Malanchuk had to go. The very next day, Shcherbytsky dictated to Vrublevsky the main theses of a secret letter to members of the CPU Central Committee in which Malanchuk was accused of abuses, of not understanding the Party's nationalities policy properly, and of having alienated the Ukrainian intelligentsia from the Party. A plenum of the CPU Central Committee was promptly convened at which the unsuspecting Malanchuk was fired.

With Malanchuk's departure there was a slight easing up in the cultural sphere, though not in the general Russification drive. As if to indicate that the process of 'normalization', or stamping out of 'Shelestivism', had gone far enough, Shcherbytsky announced a few weeks later that there now existed 'a healthy ideological situation in the republic'.[38] The CPU leadership proceeded to seek a working accommodation with the cultural intelligentsia, but within the new narrower limits, and offered modest concessions in return for the cultural élite's help in rallying the population behind the Party's policies. To make the deal more attractive, additional material incentives were also provided, including awards, apartments, travel and various other perks.

Members of the WUU immediately made use of the opportunity to revive the historical novel and publish a number of important historical documents in their literary journals, such as modern Ukrainian translations of the Rus Primary Chronicle and the Galician-Volhynian Chronicle. At the Eighth Congress of the WUU in April 1981, writers like Dmytro Pavlychko, Ivan Drach, Roman Lubkivsky and Volodymyr Yavorivsky pressed once again

[38] *Radyanska Ukraina*, 8 June 1979.

for more Ukrainian literary journals, bilingual dictionaries, more foreign contacts and travel abroad. In November of that year, the CPU Politburo convened a meeting with representatives of the Ukrainian cultural intelligentsia at which Shcherbytsky appeared to reaffirm that the CPU leadership wanted to maintain a *modus vivendi* with Ukraine's cultural élite.

Malanchuk may have unexpectedly emerged as a problem for Shcherbytsky, but he was apparently not his only one. According to Vrublevsky, the Ukrainian Party leader, though ultra-loyal to Moscow and to the idea of the preservation and strengthening of the Soviet Union, felt in private that he was not always trusted as fully as he should be by the leaders in Moscow, or the 'Moscow *boyars*' as he and his closest aides referred to them behind closed doors. These were years when 'if you didn't praise the Russian elder brother enough in your speeches, eyebrows were immediately raised in Moscow'. At home, Shcherbytsky remained wary of the secret police chief Fedorchuk, who in September 1974 was elevated to candidate membership of the Ukrainian Politburo. Vrublevsky also says that the Ukrainian Party leader 'did not like' the fact that Ivan Sokolov, the Kharkiv region Party boss and an ethnic Russian, was elected second secretary of the CPU Central Committee in February 1976 – the first time since 1949 that this sensitive position was not held by a Ukrainian.

True, Shcherbytsky maintained a close friendship with Brezhnev, who at the end of 1975 apparently failed to persuade the Ukrainian Party leader to agree to replace Aleksei Kosygin as Soviet prime minister. But as Brezhnev's health began to fail in the second half of the 1970s, Shcherbytsky found himself increasingly left out of the Politburo's decision-making and, apparently not wanting to get involved in the 'game-playing and intrigues' going on in Moscow, found himself more and more in the role of a spectator as the power struggle in the Kremlin got under way. For instance, according to Vrublevsky, in 1978 Suslov's choice for the new CPSU Central Committee's secretary for agriculture, Mikhail Gorbachev – the first secretary of the Stavropol *krai*, was chosen in preference to Shcherbytsky's nominee, Fedir Morhun. At the end of the following year, the Ukrainian Party leader was simply asked *pro forma* to endorse the decision to invade Afghanistan after it had already been made by a small inner group led by Soviet Defence Minister Dmitrii Ustinov and Soviet Foreign Minister Andrei Gromyko. In private,

Vrublevsky maintains, Shcherbytsky was opposed to this 'adventure'.

In the economic sphere also Shcherbytsky had soon found himself forced to defend the economic interests of the republic *vis- à-vis* the centre. Of his team, according to Vrublevsky, the head of the Ukrainian State Planning Committee (Derzhplan, Gosplan in Russian), Rozenko, was apparently especially courageous in this respect. Though Shcherbytsky did not display the forcefulness in this area which Shelest had done, his former colleagues stress that he did much to ensure that the food supply and the standard of living remained better and higher in Ukraine during the 1970s and 1980s than in most of Russia's major industrial regions, and to develop the republic's economic and scientific-technological potential.

After Malanchuk's removal, Fedorchuk continued to oversee the Ukrainian KGB and there was no let-up in the suppression of dissent. With the emergence of the Polish independent trade union movement Solidarity in August 1980, the Ukrainian authorities began to show signs of concern about a possible spillover effect from Poland and clearly did not want to leave anything to chance. After all, the first attempt to form an independent trade union in the Soviet Union had been made in 1977 by a miner from the Donbas, Vladimir Klebanov. The republic's ideological apparatus also had to contend with the influence of the Polish Pope, John Paul II, who had been elected in October 1978 and who, unlike his predecessor Paul VI, was determined to speak out in defense of the USSR's Catholics. In October 1982, three priests and two laymen from Western Ukraine announced the formation of an 'Initiative Group' to campaign for the legalization of their outlawed Ukrainian Catholic Church.

The death of the Kremlin's chief ideologist, Suslov, in January 1982 did not bring any significant improvement; soon afterwards Fedorchuk moved to Moscow to take over control of the entire KGB, while the former chief of the Soviet secret police, Yurii Andropov, took over Suslov's responsibilities for ideology in the Central Committee Secretariat. In November of that year Brezhnev died and was replaced as Party leader by Andropov. The latter began by appearing, in his speech in December 1982 on the sixtieth anniversary of the USSR, to rehabilitate the concept of the fusion of nations.[39] During Andropov's brief rule supplementary measures were taken to boost Russification: in Ukraine teachers of Russian

and Russian literature were given a pay rise of 16%. Taking his cue
from Andropov's jubilee speech, in March 1983 Shcherbytsky called
for even greater 'internationalization' and, sounding a familiar note,
warned the cultural intellingentsia about getting carried away with
historical themes. The 'passion' for, and 'idealization' of, 'antiquity',
he stressed were incompatible 'with the objectives of Communist
upbringing'.[40]

After Andropov's death in February 1984 Konstantin Chernenko
took over but he himself lived only for thirteen more months.
Nevertheless, during this period all the signs pointed to a further
toughening of Moscow's policy. Between June and November
1984, leading Russian nationalist writers received prestigious
awards. Towards the end of the year, one of the USSR's most senior
historians, Sergei Tikhvinsky, called for a reassertion of Moscow's
control over the writing of history in the non-Russian republics.
And in the labour camps, conditions became harsher and even
greater pressure was applied to force political prisoners to recant.
During a six-month period in 1984, three Ukrainian dissidents died
in the camps: Oleksii Tykhy, Yurii Lytvyn and Valerii Marchenko.
The only open dissent in Ukraine at this time was the continuing
campaign of the Ukrainian Catholic activists, who in the spring of
1984 began publishing their own *samvydav* journal, *Khronika
Katolytskoi Tserkvy v Ukraini* (A Chronicle of the Catholic Church
in Ukraine). At the end of 1984 and beginning of 1985, two of the
leaders of the Ukrainian Catholics' 'Initiative Group' were arrested.

Stagnation

According to Vrublevsky, Shcherbytsky watched the changes going
on in the Kremlin with growing concern and dismay. Although
within the Politburo he was a respected figure, he continued to
remain aloof from the maneuvering for power. Contrary to what
was supposed by many Western observers at the time, the Kremlin
gerontocracy did not form a united front. Shcherbytsky, for instance,
genuinely mourned the death of Brezhnev and had deep respect
for Andropov. He was also supportive towards Gorbachev, who
had become a full member of the Politburo in 1980 and whom

[39] *Pravda*, 22 December 1982.
[40] *Radyanska Ukraina*, 26 March 1983.

Andropov had taken under his wing. According to Vrublevsky, the relatively young Gorbachev in turn was very respectful towards Shcherbytsky. On the other hand, the Ukrainian Party boss 'detested' the Moscow city Party chief, Viktor Grishin, and was very 'sceptical' about both Chernenko (whom, when the latter was elected Party leader, he saw very much as a compromise figure), and the Leningrad Party boss, Grigorii Romanov, who was Gorbachev's rival. As for other members of the Soviet leadership, the Ukrainian Party leader apparently got on especially well with Petr Masherov, the Belarusian Party first secretary (who was killed in a car crash in 1980) and Kazakhstan's Party boss, Dinmukhamed Kunaev.

The high reputation which Shcherbytsky enjoyed within the CPSU leadership seems to have been based largely on his record of having maintained order in Ukraine. Certainly, with dissent stifled, and Shcherbytsky's team firmly in control, Ukraine in the mid-1980s appeared to be a model of political stability – at least in the old Brezhnevist sense. In actual fact, like the rest of the Soviet Union, it was experiencing a deepening economic and social crisis for which the old methods were no solution. More and more complaints were being officially sounded about excessive bureaucracy, corruption, bad management and falling labour discipline and production.

As throughout the USSR, for the Ukrainian authorities the number one issue was the economy. If for Ukraine the 1960s had been a period of above-Union-average economic growth, the 1970s and early 1980s had brought mounting economic difficulties and deceleration in growth rates. Centralized planning, which meant that Ukraine's economy was run from Moscow to serve the interests of the Soviet empire, had taken its toll. After years of intensive exploitation, with Ukraine's labour resources depleted and energy reserves exceeded, and with Moscow having reduced the level of capital investment, the Ukrainian economy had begun to stagnate. In the industrial sector, many of the plants and much of the machinery was outdated and inefficient; coalmining in the Donbas had become increasingly costly and dangerous; and agriculture was plagued with chronic inefficiency and a shortage of rural labour. Ukraine remained one of the major Soviet military staging areas against the West and a significant portion of its economy was connected with the defence sector. On top of this, the official disregard for environmental issues while economic development was pursued had created serious ecological problems, the full scale of which were not acknowledged in the press. This was particularly so in the case of the development of nuclear energy, which also involved fundamental issues of safety and ultimately also of the republic's right to have some say about what was happening on its territory and about its future well-being.

Although in 1970, Ukraine still had a small energy surplus, the growing energy needs of the republic's heavy industrial complex had made Ukraine increasingly dependent on the import of fuels from Russia and other republics. Moscow, however, was faced with the problem of plugging the energy gap not only in the European part of the USSR but also in Eastern Europe, which relied heavily on the imports of Soviet oil at relatively inexpensive prices. The decline of Ukraine's coal industry and the difficulties and costs of both producing oil in Siberia and shipping it westward had led the Soviet leadership to seek alternative supplies of energy. Nuclear power seemed to offer the solution and in the 1970s the USSR had embarked on the large-scale and increasingly rapid development of nuclear energy. As a voracious consumer of energy and because of its location next to Poland, Czechoslovakia, Hungary and Romania, Ukraine was designated the principal area for nuclear power development.

The first nuclear reactor in Ukraine began operating in 1979 at the Chornobyl (Chernobyl in Russian) power station (which was commissioned in 1971 when Shcherbytsky had been chairman of the Ukrainian Council of Ministers), north of Kyiv; by 1985, nine nuclear power stations or nuclear power and heating plants were either in operation or under construction in Ukraine. The speed and 'shock-work' methods of construction, shortage of skilled labour, chronic supply problems and shoddy construction materials raised questions of safety. But these matters, together with the issue of the seemingly irresponsible siting of some of the nuclear power stations close to major cities, were not a subject for public discussion. As became known much later, some of the republic's leading scientists did express their concern to the Ukrainian Party and state leaders, but to no effect.[41]

---

[41] See some of the letters from the President of the Ukrainian Academy of Sciences, Borys Paton, to Ukrainian leaders written in 1980 and 1981 and other material. *Pravda Ukrainy*, 30 January 1993.

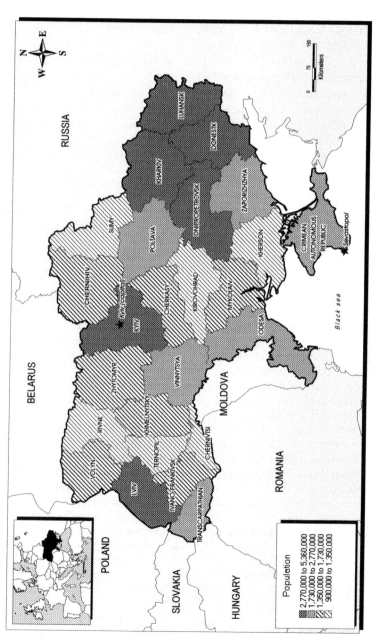

ADMINISTRATIVE DIVISIONS
AND POPULATION

As the economic difficulties mounted, the centre increased its demands of Ukraine and the republican leadership found it even more difficult to defend the republic's interests, though not from any national considerations but rational ones. In fact, those of Shcherbytsky's former colleagues who were interviewed by the author maintain that in reality Ukraine was far more of a colony than was supposed in the West. Yelchenko, for instance, who from 1980 was the first secretary of the Kyiv city Party organization and from 1982 a member of the CPU Politburo, described the atmosphere during the first half of the 1980s to the author as follows:

> Shcherbytsky would return from Moscow and say to us: 'What do they think they're doing. Do they think that they can simply go on demanding more and more from us?' The main part of the Ukrainian Council of Ministers wasted at least 75% of its time and efforts trying to convince Moscow that 'Lads, don't exploit us, don't take it all away, leave us something.' Whenever any of our people returned home with a victory – whether it was the head of the Council of Ministers or one of his deputies, or the head of the Ukrainian Derzhplan, Vitalii Masol – we would carry them on our shoulders. There seems to have been some strange conviction in Moscow that in Ukraine we had it too good, that we were stuffing ourselves. What did this amount to in practice? Take the case of the republic's metallurgical industry. Shcherbytsky campaigned very hard for its modernization. But for the repair and modernization of our metallurgical plants we needed metal. We ourselves produced the metal but didn't have any for repairing our own plants because it was all divided up and distributed by Moscow . . . It was craziness. Everything could have collapsed much earlier, in 1984 or 1985 . . . We needed metal to repair our metal factories but couldn't have any because Moscow thought that it was more important that, say, Kyrgyzia had enough hammers. It was the same with dairy products, meat and grain. Every year it was: 'Give us over three million tons of milk, butter and other dairy products, six hundred thousand tons of meat and 17 million tons of grain!' Such quantities can't just be produced out of thin air, but each year they expected even more and their attitude was one of: we don't care how you do it, even if you perish, just deliver what you're expected to.

It is therefore perhaps not surprising that Shcherbytsky's former colleagues speak very highly of him. They consider him to have been a very capable politician and administrator – a dedicated technocrat who understood the workings of the economy and who got on well with the directors of the republic's large enterprises. With someone else in charge of administering Ukraine during these difficult years, they maintain, the exploitation by the centre would have been much greater and the economic and social conditions in the republic would have deteriorated more markedly. They also claim that, compared to many other high-ranking Soviet officials at that time, Shcherbytsky did not tolerate corruption within his inner circle and was relatively modest when it came to accruing decorations and privileges. But then, as Kuras emphasized to the author, Shcherbytsky's team 'put the interests of production first', above the interests of the individual or society at large. Loyal to the system which had shaped and made them, in serving it they lost sight of both the human factor and the national dimension, which cut them off from their people and their homeland. While the Kremlin's leading figures were absorbed by the protracted struggle for power and the USSR's economic decline, Shcherbytsky and his lieutenants perpetuated and refined the old-style Brezhnevist 'administrative-command system' in Ukraine. In some ways, they grew more orthodox than the centre itself.

At the end of December 1984, the population of the Soviet Union was informed by an ailing Chernenko that the achievement of communism had been put off indefinitely and that the future would consist of 'a historically long period of developed socialism'[42] His heir apparent, Mikhail Gorbachev, told a conference on ideology that same month that the Party's priority was 'the rational distribution of productive forces and their further integration into the overall national complex'. He also accused the West of having stepped up its 'psychological warfare' against the socialist countries and called for an improvement of the Party's ideological work and counter-propaganda, and especially for greater 'ideological vigilance' and 'intolerance of alien views'.[43] Thus, at the time of Chernenko's death in March 1985 there did not seem to be any real grounds to expect changes in Moscow's approach towards Ukraine

---

[42] *Kommunist*, no. 18, December 1984, pp. 3-21.

[43] Radio Moscow and *Pravda*, 11 December 1984. For the full text of this speech, see M.S. Gorbachev, *Zhivoe tvorchestvo naroda*, Moscow, 1984.

and the other non-Russian republics or, for that matter, that official Kyiv would want to alter things.

The Ukrainian Party leader was on one of his rare visits outside of the USSR when Chernenko died: he was heading a delegation from the USSR Supreme Soviet to the United States. Shcherbytsky flew back to Moscow and endorsed a decision which had already been made in his absence – that Gorbachev, whom Gromyko had nominated, would take over as the new Soviet leader. A last-minute attempt by Romanov to block Gorbachev's appointment by proposing Grishin instead was defeated, thereby eclipsing Shcherbytsky's two least popular Politburo colleagues. Although a younger figure had broken the hold of the Kremlin's old guard, Shcherbytsky had no reason to feel that he had anything to fear from Gorbachev. Whatever changes were taking place in the Moscow leadership, with no significant personnel changes having taken place in the CPU leadership since Malanchuk's departure, Shcherbytsky's conservative team appeared solid and self-confident.

3

GORBACHEV, CHORNOBYL AND THE WRITERS' CHALLENGE

Gorbachev takes over but Shcherbytsky remains

After Gorbachev's election as general secretary of the CPSU in March 1985, all the signs seemed to indicate that despite the new, and considerably younger, leader's emphasis on revitalizing the USSR's stagnant economy, as far as the Kremlin's nationalities policy was concerned, it would be a case of more of the same.

What was particularly disconcerting for those Ukrainians who were hoping for change, though, was what occurred when, barely three months after he took over, Gorbachev visited Ukraine. On 25 June, in an extemporaneous conversation with residents of Kyiv that was later shown on Soviet television, Gorbachev, with Shcherbytsky at his side, twice referred to the Soviet Union as 'Russia'. He made matters even worse when he attempted to correct himself by saying: 'Russia – the Soviet Union, I mean – that is what we call it now, and what it is in fact . . .'[1] His general message to the Ukrainian public seemed to be that their 'huge' republic, with its 'more than 50 million inhabitants', would be crucial for the success of overhauling the Soviet economy. Ukraine's contribution, Gorbachev stressed, 'makes itself felt everywhere' and 'if there are any bad things in Ukraine, this also makes itself felt everywhere'.[2]

There was also no hint from Gorbachev that Shcherbytsky or his style of running Ukraine needed changing. In fact, during Gorbachev's visit to Kyiv, two things stood out about the new leader. On the one hand, there was the stark contrast between the vitality of the new man and his old and ailing predecessors; and, on

[1] See Bohdan Nahaylo, 'Gorbachev's Slip of the Tongue in Kiev', RL 221/85, 3 July 1985.
[2] Moscow television, 26 June 1985.

53

the other, how deferential Gorbachev was towards Shcherbytsky.[3] It was almost as if the new leader was looking up to Shcherbytsky as an elder statesman and wanting to show in public that he had the Ukrainian Party boss's full backing. The apparent harmony between the Moscow and Kyiv leaders was demonstrated again on 23 August when *Pravda* carried an article by the CPU's ideological secretary, Oleksandr Kapto, which echoed what Gorbachev had said a few months earlier about ideological tasks. Kapto stressed that as the CPSU prepared for its Twenty-seventh Congress, it was necessary to intensify the struggle against nationalism and the 'malicious propaganda offensive against the gains of developed socialism' purportedly being waged by 'right-wing and left-wing revisionism and foreign bourgeois nationalist, Zionist and clerical centres'. Ukraine's scholars, he noted, had done much in recent years to improve work in this area and were paying special attention to 'criticism of modern bourgeois "Ukrainian studies"'.

When, in October 1985, the draft of the new Party programme was published, it reiterated the Kremlin's commitment to promoting the 'steady drawing together' of the nations of the USSR and solidifying the 'Soviet people'. There was nothing in the document to indicate that the Gorbachev leadership might be prepared to allow some decentralization of economic decision-making to the republics and expansion of their rights.

The policy towards dissent and the treatment of political prisoners remained just as harsh as before. Between April and November 1985, three Ukrainian dissidents – Mykola Horbal, Yosyf Terelya and Petro Ruban – were given sentences of between twelve to fifteen years. Moreover, during the first six months that Gorbachev was in power, the Ukrainian dissidents suffered two other heavy blows: in the summer of 1985, a publication aimed at Ukrainians abroad published what was purportedly a recantation written by the fifty-one-year-old son of the UPA commander Taras Chuprynka, Yurii Shukhevych, who had spent most of his adult life in imprisonment and internal exile;[4] and, on 4 September, the outstanding Ukrainian poet and national rights campaigner Vasyl Stus died in a Soviet labour camp.

Although Gorbachev soon began talking of the need for *glasnost*

---

[3] Author's interview with Kuras.

[4] *Visti z Ukrainy*, no. 28, July 1985.

in public life and the press, and recognition of the 'human factor' in the social and economic spheres, he also made it clear that he was not contemplating inaugurating political liberalization or a new wave of de-Stalinization. In an interview which he gave in February 1986 to the French Communist Party daily *L'Humanité*, which was also reproduced in the Soviet press, he denied that there were any political prisoners in the USSR and branded the most famous of them – Andrei Sakharov – a criminal. When asked whether the 'vestiges of Stalinism' had been overcome in the Soviet Union, he replied: 'Stalinism is a concept thought up by the enemies of communism and widely used to discredit the Soviet Union and socialism as a whole.'[5]

Gorbachev's more dynamic and assertive style of leadership, emphasis on *glasnost* and initial moves to weed out the inefficiency and conservatism associated with the Brezhnev era nevertheless gradually fuelled speculation that Shcherbytsky would be replaced by someone more in the 'Gorbachev mould'. In December, the Moscow Party organization boss Grishin was sacked and the following month Fedorchuk was removed from his position as head of the MVD (Ministry of Internal Affairs). The republican Party congress and the Twenty-seventh Congress of the CPSU were scheduled for February 1986, and the appearance in *Pravda* in mid-January of criticism of local officials in the Kharkiv region and Kyiv seemed to indicate that Shcherbytsky's days were also numbered. Intriguingly, in the middle of January it was also suddenly announced that the CPU's ideological secretary, Kapto, had been appointed ambassador to Cuba.

At the end of the month, however, when the CPU Central Committee held its pre-congress plenum, it became clear that Shcherbytsky would be staying on as the Ukrainian Party leader. Indeed, the pre-congress Party conferences in Ukraine's twenty-five *oblasts*, or regions, as well as of the Kyiv city Party organization, left the leadership of their Party organizations virtually as they were. At the Twenty-seventh Congress of the CPU itself there was plenty of self-criticism in the new Gorbachev style, but the Ukrainian Party organization, now numbering almost 3.1 million members and 105,600 candidates, did not undergo any shake-up. The important vacancy created by Kapto's departure was filled by Volodymyr

[5] *L'Humanité*, 8 February 1986.

Ivashko, a secretary of the Kharkiv region Party committee. While the congress focused most of its attention on economic matters, Shcherbytsky, who again spoke in Russian, also stressed that there could be no let-up in the ideological sphere and reminded the cultural intelligentsia that its function was to contribute to 'the development of the single multinational Socialist culture'. Echoing this, the poet Boris Oliinyk, who was the secretary of the Party organization of the Kyiv branch of the WUU and a good political weather-vane, declared that there could be no 'economizing on ideology' and called for the opening of a museum in Pereyaslav-Khmelnytsky that would 'sanctify' Ukraine's reunification with the Russian brother'.[6]

The first glimmers of glasnost

The Twenty-seventh Congress of the CPSU, at which the new edition of the Party's programme was adopted, did not bring any major changes in the Kremlin's nationalities policy. The only apparent departure from the general line in this sphere was the statement by the new Politburo member, Yegor Ligachev, who had assumed responsibility for ideology, that the Party: 'highly values and supports the upsurge in patriotic feeling, of which we are all aware and the increased public interest in the homeland and the wealth of our age-old, multinational culture'. Ligachev also praised efforts to preserve 'all that is dear to the people's memory' and declared that the Party would not condone 'the neglect of national shrines'.[7]

Initially, however, it appeared that it was mainly the Russians who would be given more freedom to affirm their history and cultural values. Already at the end of 1985, Russian writers were voicing their opposition to the northern (or Siberian) rivers diversion scheme – on which the parched Central Asian republics were depending – as well as their concern for the preservation of Russian culture, historical monuments and Russia's environment. In fact, leading Russian writers began to express their national feeling quite openly. Valentin Rasputin, for instance, declared at the RSFSR Congress of Writers in December 1985: 'There is no life for us, and

---

[6] See *Radyanska Ukraina*, 7, 8 and 9 February 1986.

[7] *Pravda*, 26 February 1986.

we have nothing to say, apart from Russia.'[8] At the beginning of March, the Russian writers won an important victory, for it was announced that the northern rivers diversion scheme had been shelved.

With the Russian cultural intelligentsia becoming the first beneficiary of Gorbachev's relaxation of censorship and loosening of controls in the cultural sphere, some Ukrainian writers sought to circumvent the enduring tight restrictions in Kyiv by turning for help to colleagues in Moscow and Leningrad. At the beginning of 1986, *Literaturnaya gazeta* published an article by the Ukrainian writer Sava Holovinsky, the aim of which seemed to be to remind readers that censorship in Ukraine remained more severe than in the RSFSR. Ukrainian writers, he stressed, still needed special permission from the authorities in Kyiv to publish a work in Moscow in Russian translation if it had not yet been published in Ukrainian.[9]

One book which had been published in Ukrainian, but then 'suppressed', was Honchar's *Sobor*. A symbol of the stifled Ukrainian revival of the 1960s, it had been effectively proscribed now for almost two decades. As Ukrainian writers cautiously began to follow the lead set by Russian intellectuals and probe the new limits, this novel became an early rallying point for them. In the early part of 1986, the editors of the liberal Moscow literary monthly *Druzhba narodov*, the deputy editor of which, Oleksandr Rudenko-Desnyak, was a Ukrainian, helped out by finally obtaining permission to reissue the novel in the Soviet capital in Russian.[10]

By the spring of 1986, the first signs of measured *glasnost* started to become detectable in the Ukrainian press, though it was restricted to the exposure of inefficiency, wastage or corruption. Among them were two candid articles about the serious problems with labour, morale and chronic supply shortages at the Chornobyl nuclear power station. The first, in the March issue of the literary monthly *Vitchyzna* revealed that because of all the difficulties, the plant's chief of construction management had gone to Moscow in 1984 and succeeded in reducing the schedule for the construction of the fifth reactor from three to two years. The second, by Lyubov Kovalevska,

[8] *Literaturnaya gazeta*, 18 December 1985.

[9] · *Ibid.*, 8 January 1986.

[10] The announcement was made by the editor of *Druzhba narodov*, Sergei Baruzdin, in *Kyiv*, no. 1986, p. 6.

which appeared in *Literatuma Ukraina* on 27 March, provided even more disturbing details about 'unsolved' construction problems which had been passed on from one reactor to the next, defective supplies, the disorganization caused by the change in the construction schedule, the demoralization of the work force and shoddy workmanship. The article implicitly made the point that though rapid building methods and improvisation might work elsewhere, they were hardly suited to the construction of nuclear reactors. Kovalevska also reminded readers that by 1988, when its sixth reactor was due to come on line, the Chornobyl atomic power station would be the 'most powerful' in the world.

Of course, Kovalevska's article would not have acquired the significance which it did if the terrible tragedy had not occurred only a few weeks later at Chornobyl. In her warning, she had not been able to question openly the safety of nuclear energy nor raise the issue of the Chornobyl plant's proximity to the Ukrainian capital. This did not mean that people were not concerned about these questions. For instance, Academician Aleksandr Alymov, who had headed the Ukrainian Academy of Sciences' council for the study of Ukraine's productive forces had 'categorically opposed' the building of the Chornobyl nuclear power station, and this was apparently why he had been replaced in 1985.[11] And just before the disaster, on 18 April 1986, the president of the Ukrainian Academy of Sciences, Boris Paton, had proposed that the republic's scientists make a study of safety procedures at nuclear power plants and review how sites for them were selected.[12] Though subsequently it was also claimed that public anxiety about the construction of nuclear power stations already existed at this time in Ukraine,[13] the republic's press did not let on.

In any case, the nuclear power stations in Ukraine were directly subordinated not to Kyiv but to Moscow, in other words, the USSR Ministry of Atomic Energy had more say in these matters than the Ukrainian government. The situation as regards the Chornobyl

[11] Tabachnyk, 'Last of the Mohicans', *Ranok*, no. 5, 1991, pp. 27-8.

[12] See Roman Solchanyk, 'Pre-Chernobyl Premonitions at the Ukrainian Academy of Sciences', RL 343/86, 10 September 1986.

[13] The claim was made by the head of the Cherkasy *oblast* branch of the WUU, Mykola Nehoda. See Paul Quinn-Judge, 'Soviets Feel Nuclear Heat: Work Halted on Ukrainian Nuclear-Power Station', *Christian Science Monitor*, 4 February 1988.

nuclear power plant was subsequently described by Oleksandr Lyashko, who was the chairman of the Ukrainian Council of Ministers at this time. He stressed:

> The plant . . . was not under our control. During the entire fourteen years I worked as the head of the Council of Ministers I visited it only once . . . All the documents concerning the various experiments and tests there . . . did not reach us.[14]

The Chornobyl nuclear disaster and the political fallout

On the night of 26 April 1986, the world's worst nuclear accident occurred at the Chornobyl nuclear power station, situated only 80 miles north of Kyiv, on the border between Ukraine and Belarus. It was three days, and only after the Swedes had registered high levels of radiation from the fallout and protested about Moscow's silence, before the first terse official announcement was made, acknowledging an 'accident' and 'damage' to 'one of the atomic reactors'. The Gorbachev leadership continued to withhold information and sought to minimize the scale of the disaster. At the height of the danger and uncertainty, the May Day celebrations went ahead as usual in Kyiv, with Shcherbytsky and other CPU leaders pretending before tens of thousands that everything was normal. It was only on 8-9 May that full emergency measures were undertaken in Kyiv and not until 14 May that Gorbachev finally made a television address about the disaster, after which more detailed information began to appear.

Initially, two people were said to have been killed outright but the number of victims steadily rose, reaching twenty-six by the end of June, and thirty by the beginning of August. About 135,000 people were evacuated permanently from a 30-kilometre (18-mile) danger zone around Chornobyl, 90,000 of them Ukrainians, and the rest Belarusians. The subsequent temporary evacuation from Kyiv of about 250,000 children, pregnant women and mothers with infants, as well as of many inhabitants from the Gomel region in Belarus, raised the minimal overall figure of evacuees to well over half a million. While it appeared that countless people had been subjected to radiation and faced the threat of radiation-induced

---

[14] See the major interview with Lyashko in *Ukrainska hazeta*, no. 8, 10-23 June 1993.

cancers, the full extent of the damage to health and the environment was something that would take years, and even decades, to assess.

The Chornobyl nuclear disaster became a turning point in more ways than one. After attempting a major cover-up, the Gorbachev leadership was forced to review its policy on handling information and ended up giving fresh impetus to the development of *glasnost.* The accident also raised awareness and concern about environmental issues among the Soviet population. For the non-Russians, it sharpened sensitivities about the extent of Moscow's control over them and the power of the central ministries.

In Ukraine, the accident first traumatized the population and then galvanized it. After the initial confusion and panic, the disaster brought home the extent of the bureaucratic indifference not only of the central ministries but also of the authorities in Kyiv and especially of the servility and self-interest of the latter. The cynical way in which Kyiv's officials had staged the May Day celebrations while secretly evacuating their own children appalled even those who had learned to live with the Shcherbytsky regime.[15] Shcherbytsky's aide recalls that the Ukrainian Party leader had been well aware during the crisis that he could have become a 'national hero' had he put the interests of his people first and 'taken a position at the time which was independent of the centre' – but 'he simply could not rise to this'.[16]

Instead, Chornobyl came to be seen as a great national tragedy for Ukraine and all of its people and, as Roman Szporluk noted, although it was equally so for Belarus, it was only in Ukraine that the population 'reacted to it on a scale commensurate with its importance'. Here, 'writers, artists, scientists and students' viewed it as a 'Ukrainian issue' and it became a point of departure for them,

---

[15] The writer Yurii Pokalchuk echoed a widely held view when he told David Marples in an interview on 27 September 1989: 'Ever since they pressed ahead with the 1986 May Day parade in Kyiv, one week after Chernobyl, I have regarded both Shcherbytsky and Ukrainian president Valentyna Shevchenko [she was the Chairman of the Presidium of the Ukrainian Supreme Soviet at the time] as *ipso facto* criminals.' See Roman Solchanyk (ed.), *Ukraine: From Chernobyl' to Sovereignty: A Collection of Interviews*, London, 1992, p. 31. Independent Ukraine's reformist minister for the environment, Yurii Kostenko, told a Western correspondent that the Chornobyl accident 'shattered my final illusions abut the totalitarian system'. Chrystia Freeland, 'Waiting for the Next Chernobyl', *Financial Times*, 21 April 1993.

[16] *Ukraina* interview with Vrublevsky, p. 14.

inspiring 'what in the end would grow into a popular national movement'.[17] Chornobyl also acquired a broader symbolic meaning for Ukrainians. As Roman Solchanyk explained,

> In the aftermath of the nuclear catastrophe, Ukrainian writers and journalists began to talk in terms of a 'linguistic Chernobyl' or a 'spiritual Chernobyl' when discussing the consequences of the seventy-odd years of the Soviet experiment for the Ukrainian language and culture. In short, for Ukrainians, Chernobyl became identified with the duplicity and failure, indeed the complete bankruptcy, of the Soviet system as a whole.[18]

As the gravity of what had befallen their nation sank in, leading Ukrainian writers began to face up, as Honchar put it, to the 'responsibility' that Chornobyl had placed on them,[19] and began speaking out. This inevitably meant attacking the Shcherbytsky team and its record, albeit only implicitly at first. The first opportunity to do so was at the Ninth Congress of the WUU, which convened in Kyiv on 5 June 1986. It met in the chamber of the Ukrainian Supreme Soviet, in which the Ukrainian quasi-parliament held its sessions. The symbolism is apparent only with the aid of hindsight: delegates to this congress, at which the latest Ukrainian national renewal can be said to have been launched, could hardly have foreseen that in only a few years time some of them would be sitting in the same hall as members of the parliament of an independent Ukraine.

Honchar, the most senior Ukrainian literary figure of the day, set the tone at the congress with his rallying address. In the presence of Shcherbytsky, he reminded the delegates that Gorbachev's new course called for 'principled behaviour, truth and new thinking'. Proceeding in this spirit, he stated that the Chornobyl disaster had 'shaken the world' and there was no pretending that Ukrainian writers, as representatives of their people, could ever look at things in quite the same way. The catastrophe had concentrated their minds

[17] Roman Szporluk, 'National Reawakening: Ukraine and Belorussia', in Uri Ra'anan (ed.), *The Soviet Empire: The Challenge of National and Democratic Movements*, Lexington and Toronto, 1990, pp. 78-9.

[18] See in Solchanyk's introduction to his *Ukraine: From Chernobyl' to Sovereignty*, p. xiii.

[19] See the interview with the Ukrainian writer Yurii Shcherbak conducted by Lyubov Kovalevska in *Literaturnaya gazeta*, 2 September 1987.

and helped them see which values mattered above all. Drawing on the example being set by Russian writers, Honchar maintained that just as it was necessary to protect the natural environment, it was also crucial to safeguard the nation's cultural and linguistic 'environment', or heritage. There would have to be more civic engagement by the writers and they would have to take the fight to the 'philistines' and cynics who had no time for such notions as 'conscience, patriotism or spiritual values' and who considered that the Ukrainian language had 'no future'. The latter had to be told 'that to hold the language of one's people in contempt' means, above all else, to reveal 'one's own narrow-mindedness', and had to be shown that 'having survived all the tsarist bans', the Ukrainian language had and would have a future.

Other writers raised issues as diverse as the damage that had been done to Ukraine's ecology, the sorry state of the Ukrainian theatre and cinema, and the lack of attention being paid to the Ukrainian communities in the Eastern European countries. What was also apparent from some of the speeches was the recognition that, with the relaxation of censorship and the new opportunities which Gorbachev's policy of economic and social 'restructuring' (*perestroika*) seemed to offer, the WUU, with its 1,095 members (two-thirds of whom belonged to the Communist Party) was potentially quite a force. The new spirit that was taking hold of the writers was captured by the poet Dmytro Pavlychko. 'Today, as never before', he told the delegates, the writers needed 'to close ranks and realize that only together, and not individually' could they serve as a 'needed support' for their people and as a source of 'spiritual strength'.[20]

But the highlight of the congress was an explosive speech by Ivan Drach, who brought the delegates to their feet with a devastating indictment of the Soviet system and its consequences for Ukraine. The poet not only blamed the CPU leadership for the Chornobyl disaster, but also reminded delegates that Ukraine had lost more people as a result of Stalin's man-made famine in Ukraine than during the Second World War. He also argued that under Soviet rule Ukraine had been subjected to a policy of virtual ethnocide, and that through forcible Russification, cultural engineering and repression, the nation had suffered a spiritual Chornobyl. Although

---

[20] For details, see *Literaturna Ukraina*, 12 and 19 June 1986.

Literaturna Ukraina provided only a very sanitized version of his speech, which did not reveal its significance, many of Drach's colleagues were later to describe his fiery improvisation as the first trumpet call in the Ukrainian national revolution.[21]

The new boldness of Ukraine's writers was demonstrated later that month by Oliinyk at the Eighth Soviet Writer's Congress in Moscow. The poet, a secretary of the Boards of both the WUU and the Writers' Union of the USSR, a deputy to the Ukrainian Supreme Soviet, and a candidate member of the Central Committee of the CPU, delivered the most forthright speech by a non-Russian representative since Gorbachev had taken over. He informed the gathering that Ukrainian writers had every reason to be concerned about the situation of the Ukrainian language. 'The problem of the native language in the school, in the theatre, in the kindergartens', he argued, 'is already a question of Leninist nationalities policy, and the violation of its principles is very painful.' Rather than blame 'the hand of Moscow', however, Oliinyk denounced 'local, native, home-grown enthusiasts of our political orthodoxy' who as a result of their 'servile psychology', and 'in the name of the Russian people', acted as 'great-state-chauvinists' and Russifiers to the point of 'forgetting who they themselves are'.

Oliinyk also spoke candidly about the lessons of the Chornobyl disaster. With Moscow still apparently determined to push on with its ambitious nuclear energy policy, he argued that the accident demanded from the writers that they 'convince the scientists that sometimes they are confident to the point of cocksureness, seeming to know everything but in reality [knowing] far from everything'. The poet also referred to *Sobor*, noting that it had taken eighteen years to get permission to publish the novel in Russian translation even though, as was now apparent, the novel had raised issues concerning 'the protection of nature, the linguistic environment and memory', as well as the problem of 'careerism', the importance of

---

[21] Author's interview with Dmytro Pavlychko, Kyiv, 23 June 1993. The writer Roman Ivanychuk provides a vivid description of the congress and of Drach's speech in his memoirs. See *Berezil*, no. 1, 1993, pp. 102-7. It is worth noting that even the official 'internal' transcript of Drach's speech, which the author obtained from him in the summer of 1993, was expurgated. According to Pavlychko, the Party authorities subsequently attempted to depict Drach's address as an 'emotional outburst' provoked by the fact that his son Maksym had been one of the medical personnel sent to the Chornobyl disaster area.

which was now acknowledged. Interestingly, *Literaturnaya gazeta* published an expurgated sanitized version of Oliinyk's speech on 2 July, whereas *Literaturna Ukraina* ran it in full on 3 July.

Oliinyk, it should be noted, was a complex and ambiguous character. A quasi-'Sixtier', he was both a Ukrainian patriot and, it seems, a genuine Communist. While remaining to all intents and purposes a conformist, he had nevertheless helped to broaden the cultural thaw that ensued after Malanchuk's removal. He had not been exceptional in following this path: Drach, Pavlychko and many others had done the same. Oliinyk, however, was increasingly to be perceived as wanting to have it both ways: to keep on good terms with the Shcherbytsky regime in Kyiv while at the same time playing up to liberals in Moscow and projecting himself as a radical supporter of restructuring.[22] What was important at this stage, though, was what Oliinyk had begun saying out loud, not his motivation.

The campaign to rehabilitate *Sobor* continued, but in the new defiant tone. In early August, at a meeting of the Kyiv writers' Party organization, the critic Vitalii Koval demanded that those responsible for the 'vulgar interpretation' that had been given to the novel, or who had been accomplices through silence, should be exposed. 'Let's name names', he urged, 'the names of those who simply remained silent at the time, and whose conspiracy of silence brought so much damage to all of literature'.[23] The mounting pressure was successful: the novel was rehabilitated *de facto* and in November the Ukrainian press confirmed that it would be republished in Ukrainian. This was the first battle to be won by the resurgent Ukrainian cultural intelligentsia in its new undeclared struggle with the Shcherbytsky regime.

In the meantime, Moscow carried out an investigation into the causes of the Chornobyl disaster. Evidently not wanting to risk undermining the future of nuclear power in the USSR, it settled on finding a number of scapegoats among fairly low-level Party functionaries, leaving it to the CPU Central Committee to deal with them. The result was that in the summer a number of dismissals were

---

[22] For instance, Yelchenko considers that Oliinyk sought to ingratiate himself with Gorbachev's team, while in Pavlychko's view, the poet and leading Communist representative within the WUU (Drach described him in his speech at the previous WUU Congress as our 'commissar') in fact sought to moderate the attitudes of his literary colleagues.

[23] *Literaturna Ukraina*, 6 August 1986.

made and reprimands issued but the CPU leadership, and the key officials in the Kyiv region and Chornobyl area, escaped any serious consequences. In fact, though from time to time criticism of the work of Ukrainian Party officials was to be voiced in Moscow, Shcherbytsky and the CPU organization continued to run things much as before, paying only lip service to *glasnost* and 'restructuring'.

The writers broaden their campaign

Though Chornobyl had goaded Ukrainian writers into action, this did not mean that they still did not have to contend with the old problems and constraints. It was not only that Shcherbytsky and his 'home-grown' Russifiers remained in place, but also that Moscow itself continued with much of its 'old thinking', and on the very issues that were of such concern to the writers sent mixed, if not discouraging, signals.

During the summer and autumn of 1986, it became increasingly clear that *glasnost* and *perestroika* were not being extended to the area of nationalities policy except in the case of the Russians. While a leading Soviet expert on the nationalities question stressed that there could be no return to the 'indigenization' policies of the 1920s[24] and *Pravda* issued new warnings about 'nationalistic delusions' and 'the role of religion in inflaming nationalistic passions',[25] it was announced that classics of Russian tsarist and imperial historiography were to be published again.[26] A similar double standard was also evident in the official attitude towards the forthcoming millennium in 1988 of the Christianization of Kyivan Rus. Not only had the Russian Orthodox Church been given a complete monopoly on the preparations and celebrations as far back as 1983, but also the jubilee was being depicted as marking a thousand years of 'Russian' history, statehood and culture. No specifically Ukrainian or Belarusian elements were acknowledged; on the contrary, the Ukrainian press stepped up its attacks in this connection against Ukrainian émigrés, the Vatican and Catholic activists in Ukraine. In July, the Russian Orthodox Church held a major international

[24] Eduard Bagramov, in an interview broadcast by Radio Moscow on 13 August 1986.

[25] *Pravda*, 14 August 1986.

[26] Radio Moscow, 6 August 1986.

historical conference in Kyiv which was repeatedly referred to by the official Soviet news agencies in their English-language reports as dealing with the 'Christening of Russia'. The following month, *Radyanska Ukraina* announced that the leading Ukrainian Catholic activist Terelya had recanted and confessed to his 'criminal activities'.[27]

It is therefore not surprising that after the language problem, the next issue which the Ukrainian literati began to raise was that of the erasure of national memory. The Ukrainian scholar Mykola Zhulynsky led the way with an article published in *Literaturna Ukraina* on 18 September 1986 in which he emphasized that the problem 'of the loss of national memory' had become 'especially acute and alarming'. He even introduced a new name for this phenomenon into the Ukrainian language – *mankurtstvo*, from the *mankurts* described by Chingiz Aitmatov in his novel *The Day Lasts More than a Hundred Years*. These were slaves who had been tortured by their captors until they lost all sense of their identity.

With Ukraine's 'official' historians and their monthly journal *Ukrainskyi Istorychnyi Zhurnal* (Ukrainian Historical Journal) still very much under the CPU's strict ideological control, however, it was left to the writers and literary scholars to begin the difficult task of retrieving Ukraine's suppressed history. They began by taking advantage of the relaxation of censorship to begin pushing for the rehabilitation of proscribed Ukrainian literary and cultural figures, and by demanding that the full and uncensored works of Ukrainian literary classics be published. An important role in this process was to be played by the Institute of Literature of the Ukrainian SSR Academy of Sciences, of which Zhulynsky was the deputy director. Pavlychko pointed to the changing atmosphere in this important institute when he announced in *Literaturna Ukraina* on 11 September that its leadership had taken *glasnost* and *perestroika* to heart and decided to throw away their censors' scissors.

As the year drew to a close, the writers broadened their offensive. In November, the tighter censorship and restrictions that had been imposed on Ukrainian cultural life after Shelest's removal were mentioned by Volodymyr Yavorivsky in an article in *Literaturnaya gazeta*. How did one begin assessing the damage that had been caused by Malanchuk (his career was described but he was not actually

[27] *Radyanska Ukraina*, 27 August 1986.

named) and his like, the writer asked.[28] That same month, the Ukrainian writers' weekly discussed the damaging effect of the tsarist edicts banning the Ukrainian language.[29] And on 18 November, at a meeting of the Board of the WUU, the prose writer Volodymyr Drozd made the first of the new calls for a return to the Ukrainization policies of the 1920s. Appeals to respect the Ukrainian language were not enough, he argued. What was needed were 'decisions by the state' which would make the Ukrainian language 'fundamentally indispensable in everyday life, in the theatre, in scholarship and in institutions of higher learning'.[30]

Another sign of the changing times was the return to Kyiv from Moscow of the innovative theatre director Les Tanyuk and his appointment in July as the chief director of the Kyiv Youth Theatre. Over twenty years before Dzyuba had reported in *Internationalism or Russification?* that this talented 'Sixtier' had been 'forced to leave Ukraine'. In an interview which appeared in November, Tanyuk declared not only that he saw himself as a follower of the traditions of the modern Ukrainian theatre that had been founded in the 1920s by the director Les Kurbas and playwright Mykola Kulish – both of whom became victims of the Stalin terror – but also that he wanted the Kyiv Youth Theatre to assume the kind of role which the Club of Creative Youth had played in the early 1960s as a cultural centre 'for the new generation' and all those who wanted 'to think and act in a new way'. The director also revealed that he intended to stage plays based on Honchar's *Sobor* and a work by fellow 'Sixtier' Lina Kostenko set in the Cossack era – *Marusya Churai*.[31] Tanyuk and Drach wasted no time in translating Mikhail Shatrov's powerful play in the new *glasnost* style, 'Dictatorship of Conscience', into Ukrainian, and Tanyuk's première production of it in Kyiv at the beginning of 1987 was a sensation.[32]

The CPU's conservatism comes under fire

The year of Chornobyl ended with a major shock and a pleasant

[28] *Literaturnaya gazeta,* 26 November 1986.

[29] *Literaturna Ukraina,* 6 November 1986.

[30] *Ibid.,* 27 November 1986.

[31] 'Teatr ityme dali' [The Theatre Will Go Further], *Ukraina,* no. 45, 1986, p. 6.

[32] For some of the reactions, see *Literaturna Ukraina,* 5 February 1987.

surprise. In Kazakhstan, ethnic riots erupted after the republic's veteran Party chief Dinmukhamed Kunaev was abruptly replaced on 16 December by a Russian, Gennadii Kolbin. On this occasion the Soviet media seemed to respect the need for *glasnost* by promptly announcing that rioting had occurred in Alma-Ata. But as new conflicting reports began appearing in the Western press about the scale and causes of the unrest, the Gorbachev leadership itself made news: it decided to free Andrei Sakharov from internal exile and, though this only became evident a few weeks later, to begin releasing political prisoners.

During the last few months, Gorbachev had taken the political fight to the strong conservative forces within the CPSU by shifting the emphasis to the need for political reform, or 'democratization', as a precondition for the success of economic restructuring. At the important Central Committee plenum on 27 January 1987, he raised the stakes by proposing the introduction of multiple-candidate balloting for local government positions and multi-candidate, secret balloting for Party posts. But when it came to the Party's nationalities policy, Gorbachev remained intransigent. He declared that the Soviet leadership would remain 'firm and principled'. 'Let those who would like to play on nationalist or chauvinistic prejudices,' he warned, 'entertain no illusions and expect no loosening up'.[33]

At least the cause of *glasnost* and 'democratization' appeared to have been further advanced, even if not as fully as the non-Russians would have liked. This again raised the question of the survival of Shcherbytsky and his team. Early in January, the Ukrainian Party leadership was embarrassed by Moscow's handling of an affair involving the unlawful arrest in July 1986 of a journalist, Viktor Berkhin, by local authorities in Voroshilovhrad. In a brutal style reminiscent of the years when Fedorchuk had headed the KGB in the republic, Berkhin had been detained and mistreated (he died in July 1987, after apparently failing to recover from the ordeal[34]) for exposing the abuse of power and corruption. On the very day that the Ukrainian press published the report of the CPU's investigation into the matter, *Pravda* ran an article by the head of KGB, Viktor

[33] TASS in English, 27 January 1987.

[34] See the report by V. Plekhanov in *Meditsinskaya gazeta*, 16 October 1987, which also revealed that a doctor and his brother had been 'framed' and imprisoned for refusing to consent to a scheme to incriminate Berkhin.

Chebrikov, identifying the main culprit as the regional KGB chief, a fact not admitted in Kyiv's account.[35] This was the first time since the early 1950s that the Soviet secret police had been criticized in the Soviet press and the action was widely interpreted as a calculated blow against the CPU leadership.

The scandal was followed by what appeared to be the beginning of a purge in the CPU. In mid-February, Shcherbytsky himself announced in the pages of *Pravda* that the Party boss of the Voroshilovhrad region had been sacked. The following month, the Party chiefs of the Dnipropetrovsk and Lviv regions, both products of the 'Dnipropetrovsk group', were fired.

The *New York Times* reported on 22 March that the dismissals had been engineered by Gorbachev in an attempt to 'gain control' of the CPU but that the sixty-nine-year-old Ukrainian Party leader, by now the longest serving member of the Politiburo, was 'strenuously' resisting efforts to remove him. The newspaper cited unnamed 'Soviet officials' as reporting that Gorbachev and Shcherbytsky 'had quarrelled' at the January Central Committee plenum and that the Soviet leader had 'made no secret of his desire to remove' the Ukrainian Party boss.[36] When, however, on 24-5 March, the CPU Central Committee held a plenum, Shcherbytsky engaged in a measure of self-criticism, accepting responsibility for the republic's economic problems, but retained his post.

Shedding light on the real situation in the republic, Shcherbytsky admitted at the plenum that 'restructuring' was 'proceeding slowly' in Ukraine and that the main obstacles were 'conservatism, inability, and even unwillingness to work in a new way'. He also acknowledged that 'the main reason' why the three regional Party bosses had been dismissed was 'the absence of genuine democratism and *glasnost*, the absence of criticism and self-criticism'.[37]

The sackings set in motion a number of important personnel changes. In April, Ivashko took over as the Dnipropetrovsk region Party chief and his position as ideological secretary was filled by the Kyiv city Party boss, Yurii Yelchenko. He in turn was replaced by Kostyantyn Masyk. Another CPU Central Committee secretary,

---

[35] *Pravda*, 8 January 1987.

[36] Philip Taubman, 'Gorbachev Encounters Party Resistance in Ukraine', *New York Times*, 22 March 1987.

[37] *Radyanska Ukraina*, 25 March 1987.

Yakiv Pohrebnyak, took over as first secretary of the Lviv region and his place in the Secretariat was filled by Stanislav Hurenko, who was also elected a candidate member of the CPU Politburo. The following month, the republic's KGB chief, Stepan Mukha, was retired and replaced by Mykola Holushko. With Ukraine's economic performance still coming under fire from Moscow,[38] in July there was also a shake-up of the Ukrainian government. A number of key officials were retired, including the chairman of the Council of Ministers, Lyashko, who had held the post for fifteen years. He was replaced by Masol.

The struggle for greater glasnost

During this period, when it did indeed seem as if the Shcherbytsky era in Ukraine was finally coming to an end, the Ukrainian literati kept up their pressure for change. In January 1987, the writers nominated Lina Kostenko for the Shevchenko State Prize for Literature, the republic's most prestigious award. The uncompromising poet had been proposed for the prize in 1981 but, hardly surprisingly in view of the political climate at that time, had not won it. This time she was put forward as a representative of an unvanquished Ukrainian literature and a model for her contemporaries. The article by Anatolii Makarov in *Literaturna Ukraina* nominating her stressed her commitment to 'concepts such as civic conscience, patriotism, devotion to the national cause and to national culture'. The time had come, he argued, 'for precisely such socially active poetry . . . which tells us the truth, no matter how bitter it may be'. The nomination was successful: in early March it was announced that Kostenko had won the award.

Another candid, though indirect, reminder to the literary community about what their role should be was delivered by a senior literary scholar from the Institute of Literature, Hryhorii Syvokin. In a round-table discussion organized in Kyiv in January by three journals and published in April in *Kommunist Ukrainy*, he stressed that literary work had also to be judged from the standpoint of Ukrainian nation-state building. He called for a more purposeful

[38] For example, in May the CPSU Central Committee criticized Ukraine's key ferrous metals industry. Reuter, 17 May 1987.

approach from the cultural intelligentsia aimed at safeguarding and developing 'national' values in a 'wise, tactful and delicate' way.

A good example of this approach was to be set by Ivan Dzyuba, who from about this time began to regain his former authority with his thoughtful contributions to the growing debate about the state of Ukrainian culture. In February, for instance, he added his voice to the calls for the full rehabilitation of leading Ukrainian writers and cultural activists from the nineteenth century and the 1920s; he also mentioned Drahomanov as an example of an important figure whose activity was still distorted.[39] Behind the scenes, other writers and literary scholars began pressing for the rehabilitation of Khvylovy and of Volodymr Vynnychenko, a leading Ukrainian writer, who had also been a prominent political activist and a prime minister during Ukraine's shortlived period of independence.

An important initiative was taken by a group of leading literary critics who in May formed the Creative Association of Critics of the Kyiv Writers' Section. Anxious to adapt literary life to the new conditions, restore the writer's authority and contribute to democratization, they established their own unregimented club for discussion and elected Syvokin, a non-Party member, to head it. Its leadership, or *buro*, included, among others, Dzyuba, Vyacheslav Bryukhovetsky and Mykola Ryabchuk. The Association invited economists, philosophers, historians and culturologists to its monthly discussions on topical themes and thereby created one of the earliest forums for democratically and nationally minded intellectuals. Describing the atmosphere at this time, Syvokin recalls: 'We didn't know where all the changes were leading to and where we would end up. But we knew we had to do something . . . Without our having foreseen it, our initiative turned into a civic action and our meetings became a school for civic and political activity.'[40]

The growing ferment also became visible in other cultural spheres. In May, sharp criticism was voiced at the inaugural congress of theatre workers of some of the 'classics' of Soviet Ukrainian drama and their legacy. The playwright Yaroslav Stelmakh, the son of a

[39] *Literaturna Ukraina*, 26 February 1987.

[40] Author's interview with Hryhorii Syvokin, Kyiv, 19 March 1993. On the Association's activity, see the collection of documents compiled by Syvokin entitled *Avtorytet. Literatura i krytyka v chas perebudovy: Statti, ese, informatsiya* [Authority. Literature and Criticism in the Time of Restructuring: Articles, Essays, Information], Kyiv, 1989.

famous Soviet Ukrainian writer, was the most outspoken. He told
the participants that they had to choose between creating a new
union in which careerists and bureaucrats would predominate, or
breaking with the past and uniting all those who genuinely wanted
the renewal of Ukrainian theatre and culture generally. This was
also echoed by Tanyuk who argued that what was needed was a
transformation of social consciousness, and he called upon his
colleagues to display greater civic courage and truthfulness.[41]
This was still very difficult for many to do, though. Tanyuk
himself pointed out during the above-mentioned round-table discussion published in *Kommunist Ukrainy* that the authorities were
uncooperative, obstructive or openly hostile to attempts to revitalize
and democratize social and national life.[42] In his own case, although
he did manage to transform the Kyiv Youth Theatre into an
important centre of Ukrainian cultural renewal which was supported by 'the flower of the city's creative intelligentsia', he ran up
against considerable opposition from local Komsomol officials and
other conservative elements.[43]

An important new opportunity for promoting Ukrainian cultural
renewal through semi-official channels presented itself, however, at
precisely this time as a result of an all-Union initiative which had
been launched by pro-Gorbachev Russian patriotically minded
intellectuals. This was the creation of a Soviet Cultural Fund, the
aim of which was to promote restructuring in the cultural sphere
and preserve the cultural heritage of the peoples of the Soviet Union.
It was headed by Academician Likhachev, and Gorbachev's wife,
Raisa, was on its board. Realizing the dividends that such a body
could bring them, representatives of the Ukrainian cultural élite lost
no time in offering their support: on 11 April the Ukrainian section
of this new organization – the Ukrainian Cultural Fund – held its
inaugural conference in Kyiv and Oliinyk was elected its head.
During the next months, the Ukrainian Cultural Fund proceeded
to work out its goals and strategy and to establish a republican
network.[44]

---

[41] See the reports on the congress in *Kultura i zhyttya*, 31 May 1987 and in *Teatr*,
no. 10, 1987, pp. 113-17.

[42] *Kommunist Ukrainy*, no. 4, 1987, p. 71.

[43] See Oksana Telenchi, 'Zapytai u svoyei sovisti' [Ask Your Conscience], *Lyudyna
i svit*, January 1988, pp. 43-6.

The fact was that as far as *glasnost* was concerned, because of the different political climates in Moscow and Kyiv, in most respects Ukraine continued to lag behind Russia.[45] Nevertheless, in one especially sensitive area, a Ukrainian newspaper helped to break a taboo. In January 1987, the republican Komsomol daily *Molod Ukrainy* published a letter from the mother of two draftees expressing criticism of the Soviet role in Afghanistan and the way that it was depicted in the Soviet media. On 5 May, the newspaper followed this up with an article by Oleksandr Klymenko which not only confirmed how strongly readers felt on this subject, but also indicated that there was considerable opposition to the war and that the official media were widely mistrusted.

Though Klymenko's article broke new ground, it was itself a good example of selective *glasnost* in practice. It pointed to a problem, described some of its salient features, but stopped far short of telling the full story. Klymenko, however, alluded to the constraints within which even the boldest pioneers of *glasnost* in the official press still had to operate. As he explained to readers:

> Today we no longer remain silent. But, if one is to be frank, we still haven't learned to speak forthrightly. This is clear from our newspaper and your letters. We still look over our shoulder, are frightened, [and] hint at things.[46]

The writers defy the CPU leadership

The writers continued to concentrate on the language issue and, after the boost which Gorbachev had given *glasnost* at the January Central Committee plenum, became more radical. At a meeting in Kyiv on 10 February, they reopened the debate about Thesis 19 of the 1958 Education Law (the provisions of the draft Statute

[44] See the interview with Oliinyk on this subject in *Visti z Ukrainy*, no. 19, May 1987, and his article 'Cultural Fund' in *Ukraine* (Kyiv), no. 1, 1988, pp. 16-17.

[45] Interestingly, the Ukrainian poet and WUU member Vitalii Korotych, who had moved from Kyiv to Moscow in the summer of 1986 to become editor of *Ogonek*, was at this time successfully transforming this formerly conservative weekly into a flagship of *glasnost* and boosting its circulation.

[46] For further details, see Bohdan Nahaylo, 'Ukrainian Mother Protests Soviet Media Coverage of the War in Afghanistan', RL 34/87, 22 January 1987, and 'Ukrainian Mother's Protest Attracts Numerous Letters on the Afghanistan Theme', RL 188/87, 18 May 1987.

on the Secondary Education School had just been published and Section Four of the document continued to give parents the right to decide which language their child was taught in[47]) and demanded that the study of Ukrainian be made obligatory in all of the republic's schools. Honchar pointed out that writers in Belarus, the Baltic republics and Turkmenistan had also launched campaigns in defence of their mother tongue and he attacked the 'falseness and hypocrisy' which called into question 'the need to learn one's native language'. Such a question, he maintained 'cannot arise in any civilized country'.

The problem, the writers emphasized, was not simply the sharp reduction of Ukrainian-language schools. Assimilationist pressure had restricted the 'social functions' of the Ukrainian language and led to a drastic decline in its prestige, especially in the Russified eastern regions of the republic. As Drach put it, the Ukrainian language and literature had 'become a subject for derision and mockery, where gentrified Philistines, with a chauvinistic deviation, hiding behind the shield of pseudo-internationalism, frequently scoff at the roots whence they came'. Another speaker, Pavlychko, warned quite bluntly that unless the official policy towards the non-Russian languages changed, there would soon be 'no friendship of peoples' left in the Soviet Union. 'The unjust, condescending, and thoughtless attitude towards the Ukrainian language' had to be eliminated, he urged, stressing that 'responsibility for learning the native language' had to rest not with parents and pupils, 'but with our state'.[48]

This point was also made in a letter to the education workers' newspaper *Radyanska osvita* from Zhulynsky and three other senior figures at the Institute of Literature, Bryukhovetsky, Vitalii Donchyk and Leonid Novychenko, who proposed that the education law be changed to require all students in the republic 'to study both Ukrainian and Russian with equal respect and dignity'.[49] Their position was supported in letters from readers.

In mid-March, the writer Serhii Plachynda sharpened the debate by publishing an article containing far-reaching proposals on reversing Russification and bolstering the status of the Ukrainian language.

---

[47] See *Radyanska osvita*, 6 February 1987.

[48] *Literaturna Ukraina*, 12 March 1987.

[49] *Radyanska osvita*, 3 April 1987.

He suggested, among other things, that in every non-Russian republic the native language and Russian be designated as 'state languages'. The recognition of Ukrainian as a state language was to become a key demand of the writers, especially after they managed to obtain the first hard data on the existing state of affairs.

At the end of 1986, Drach had called for the creation of a working group to monitor the study of the Ukrainian language and literature in the republic's schools. Such a special permanent commission was set up in February by the Presidium of the Board of the WUU under the chairmanship of Pavlychko. By now the Ukrainian authorities were under pressure to be at least seen to be responding to the writers' campaign and opening some sort of dialogue with them. Both the Ukrainian minister of education, Mykhailo Fomenko, and the official responsible for education in the Ukrainian capital, attended the first meeting of the WUU's new commission; moreover, they provided the kind of information that had hitherto been kept secret. Fomenko revealed that 50.5% of the republic's pupils were being taught in Ukrainian (a drop of about 11.5% since the 1960s) and 48.7% in Russian. In Kyiv, however, the percentage of pupils being taught in Ukrainian was only about 23%, even though the 1979 census had shown that Ukrainians constituted about 68.7% of the city's population and that 52.8% of the inhabitants had named Ukrainian as their native tongue.[50]

This manifestation of 'statistical *glasnost*', welcome as it was, did not mean that the Shcherbytsky leadership was changing its general line. At the beginning of February, for instance, it was announced that the Ukrainian Ministry of Culture had adopted a series of measures designed to promote the further 'internationalization' of Ukrainian youth.[51] Shcherbytsky himself showed no 'new thinking' when he spoke about 'nationalism' and religion on 25 March at the end of the CPU Central Committee plenum. As in the pre-*glasnost* era, he warned against showing any complacency in ideological work, especially when it came to dealing with historical themes and religion, and demanded that 'more consideration' be shown for 'the objective process of internationalization'.[52]

---

[50] *Ibid.*, 9 April 1987. For more details, see Roman Solchanyk, 'Statistical *Glasnost*: Data on Language and Education in Ukraine', RL 152/87, 15 April 1987.

[51] *Kultura i zhyttya*, 1 February 1987.

[52] *Radyanska Ukraina*, 29 March 1987.

This was precisely the time when interest in history, or more precisely, in the forbidden themes, or so-called blank spots or pages, was growing. Not only was the approaching millennium of the Christianization of Kyivan Rus stimulating interest in the past, but also the work that was being done in the West on Stalin's man-made famine in Ukraine in 1933. Listeners in Ukraine to Western radio stations, such as Radio Liberty, could learn about the recent publication in the West of Robert Conquest's book on this subject, *The Harvest of Sorrow*, as well as the study of this tragedy which had been undertaken by a commission appointed by the US Congress. At home, the issue of the famine had been cautiously raised in a story by Vasyl Zakharchenko which had appeared in 1986 but, as Dzyuba pointed out in a review in the March 1987 issue of the literary monthly *Kyiv*, it had left a great deal unsaid. The official line, however, remained that no such famine occurred and that this was all an anti-Soviet fabrication thought up by Ukrainian émigrés and Western anti-Communists.

The frustration with the unforthcoming attitude of the Kyiv authorities was apparent in the unusual step taken by Oliinyk during his next appearance in Moscow at the end of April. Addressing a plenum of the Board of the Soviet Writers' Union, the Ukrainian poet called on 'Russian brothers' to help the Ukrainians restore what he euphemistically called 'Leninist norms' in their republic, in other words to reinstate the principles on which the nationalities policy of the 1920s had been based. The situation had got so bad, he informed the delegates, that in some of Ukraine's regional centres 'the number of Ukrainian schools' was 'approaching zero'. Oliinyk also called for the lifting of the ban on 'most' of the works of Vynnychenko and the publication of Dmytro Yavornytsky's works on the history of the Zaporozhyan Cossacks.[53] Another writer, Oleksandr Pidsukha, lashed out at the 'Little Russian' mentality of Shcherbytsky and his officials in a satirical 'pamphlet' which appeared in May in *Radyanska osvita* only a few days before Shcherbytsky was scheduled to address a congress of the republic's teachers.[54]

At the teachers' congress on 15-16 May, it suddenly seemed as if all the pressure was beginning to have an effect. The minister of

---

[53] *Literaturnaya gazeta*, 6 May 1987.

[54] *Radyanska osvita*, 12 May 1987.

education, Fomenko, surprised the delegates by expressing his support for some of the demands being made by the writers. He acknowledged 'the uneasiness on the part of teachers, writers and the public' about the way in which the Ukrainian language had been effectively downgraded in the republic's educational system and the 'indifferent and irresponsible attitude towards this problem' on the part of some school teachers and local educational authorities. While rejecting the idea of making the study of Ukrainian compulsory, he conceded that proposals about amending Section Four of the Draft Statute on the Secondary General Education School deserved attention. He called on the Soviet Ministry of Education 'to take them into consideration'.

Shcherbytsky's speech, which followed that of Fomenko, however, not only did not mention the protests and demands which the writers were making, or the issues to which the Ukrainian minister of education had devoted his address, but emphasized 'the need for students to further improve their study of the Russian language'. Almost as if they were overruling the minister, the Ukrainian Party leaders insisted that the Soviet authorities had created for each nation 'the most suitable conditions for developing national culture and the national language'.[55]

One other major problem that both the Shcherbytsky leadership and the authorities in Moscow preferred not to address during this period was the growing opposition in Ukraine to the further development of nuclear energy in the republic, a campaign in which the writers were also providing the leadership.

The Chornobyl theme figured prominently in their works and helped shape public opinion on the issue of nuclear power. But there were problems, even for the most prominent of the writers. Oliinyk, for instance, complained in his speech at the plenum of the Board of the Soviet Writers' Union that 'for some months now' he had not managed to get anything published in the central press on the subject of Chornobyl and nuclear power. At the end of March, though, the republic's scientists also took a stand. At a discussion of specialists which had been convened in Kyiv by the authorities, more than sixty of the scientists, from various fields, voted against continuing with the construction of the fifth and sixth reactors at the Chornobyl plant; only two voted for.[56] This was one of the first

[55] *Pravda Ukrainy*, 17 May 1987.

genuine victories for independent public opinion, for in May it was announced that work on the new reactors would stop.

But elsewhere, the Moscow and Kyiv authorities were determined to continue with their ambitious nuclear energy programme. One of the new plants was supposed to be constructed near the city of Chihirin in the Cherkasy region. Not only would the new atomic power station be located in a densely populated area which had a special historical significance for Ukrainians, but also it would stand on the banks of the Dnipro, which is Ukraine's main water supply. Local opposition was supported by leading writers in Kyiv: in June, Honchar condemned the idea of building 'another Chornobyl' on the Dnipro,[57] while Oliinyk pointed out that Ukraine, which comprised 3% of the area of the USSR, already had about 25% of the Soviet Union's reactors located on its territory.[58]

On the eve of a plenum of the Board of the WUU, the CPU's leadership appears to have decided that it was time to draw the line. The occasion was a meeting on 11 June of the Party organization of the Kyiv branch of the WUU. This time, Oliinyk, the overseer of this group, in effect donned his Party uniform and sought to call his colleagues to order. After a few words of warning to younger writers to avoid 'speculative hysteria' when dealing with 'the most sacred things' (as an example, he singled out the iconoclastic speech by Stelmakh at the recent Congress of Theatre Workers) and condemnation of 'demagogues and speculators' who he said were trying to abuse democracy, he turned his attention to the newly formed independent association of Kyivan critics. Oliinyk strongly criticized this group for trying to evade supervision by the Communist Party by failing to set up its own internal Party committee. He also castigated the critics' association for allowing non-writers to attend its discussions. 'What is this', he asked, 'a variant of Hyde Park?' The Party, he stressed, would not allow groups 'using the banner of democratization' to splinter the 'monolithic' and Party-guided unity of the WUU. During this period of 'democratization', the Party's 'leading role', he said, was becoming even more important, and the critics' association would have to have an internal 'Party organization' whether it wanted to or not.

---

[56] *Literaturnaya gazeta*, 27 May 1987.

[57] *Literaturna Ukraina*, 18 June 1987.

[58] *Literaturnaya gazeta*, 1 July 1987.

Ironically, compared to what Oliinyk said, the speech by the new ideological secretary, Yelchenko, in which he set out the CPU leadership's position, actually sounded more moderate. He acknowledged that there had been 'a certain restriction' in the use of the Ukrainian language in recent years and that this was eliciting 'justifiable complaints'. Announcing a number of modest concessions – mainly measures to improve the teaching of the Ukrainian language and literature – he made it clear, however, that the CPU leadership was not prepared to budge on the key questions.[59] 'Whether one likes it or not', he told the writers, the 'spirit' of the provision in the education law giving parents the right to choose the language in which their children were taught was 'democratic'. The CPU leadership, he declared, would not deviate from the principles of 'internationalism' and the general Party line, and remained committed to fostering Russian-Ukrainian bilingualism in the republic. Rejecting the call to make the study of Ukrainian obligatory, Yelchenko did not even address the question of recognizing Ukrainian as a state language.

The ideological secretary also indicated a similar unbending attitude as regards historical research and rehabilitations. Although he stated that the 'practice of administrative bans and voluntaristic

---

[59] Hardly surprisingly, when interviewed by the author in 1993 about the CPU leadership's policy at this time, Yelchenko denied that he, Shcherbytsky, and others, had been hostile or unresponsive to the writers' campaign in defence of the Ukrainian language. The language issue, he acknowledged, had been the 'most acute' question, indeed the 'alpha and omega' in the sphere of nationalities policy and the Party had had to tread carefully. The question was how to solve the language issue in Ukraine 'so that the restoration of the Ukrainian linguistic environment did not cause a social explosion'. Shedding some light on what went on behind the scenes, Yelchenko says that in response to the changing political conditions and pressures, the Shcherbytsky team decided to prepare a 'broad programme to improve the situation of the Ukrainian language'. Responsibility for this task was entrusted to Yelchenko himself and the head of the propaganda and agitation department under him, Leonid Kravchuk. 'Shcherbytsky didn't leave us in peace', Yelchenko claims. 'He kept asking me: "When will you have the draft ready for the Politburo to examine?"' The former ideological secretary also concedes that although a 'programme' of sorts was eventually produced, 'we didn't manage to keep up with the pace of change'. Of course, there was another factor which Yelchenko did not mention. Shcherbytsky's team continued to take its cue from Moscow's general approach to nationalities policy. And, for all of Gorbachev's emphasis on *glasnost* and democratization, there was still no indication of any real restructuring in this crucial sphere.

decisions' was no longer acceptable, he stressed that 'ideological responsibility' and 'Party-mindedness' were still imperative. Yelchenko singled out the cases of Khvylovy and Vynnychenko and emphasized that even the 'uncontroversial works' of these writers had to be approached from this standpoint.[60]

Demonstrating just how much the climate had changed during the last year, the writers refused to accept these limitations. Honchar took the floor after Yelchenko and reiterated that the Education Law was 'anti-democratic' and directed at 'destroying the language of our people'. He also announced that he and a group of his colleagues had appealed to the writers of Russia to support the principle that all pupils have to learn both Russian and their national language in school. This time, *Literaturna Ukraina* published only a short summary of Honchar's response to Yelchenko which did not convey its spirit.[61]

The plenum of the Board of the Writer's Union held on 16 June was largely devoted to the language question and turned into a demonstration of defiance and reviving national assertiveness. In their forthright speeches, most of the writers seemed to be saying that the time had come to dispense with pretenses about internationalism, the equality of the peoples of the USSR and their rights, and to see things as they really were and no longer put up with the injustices and discrepancies. Several of the speakers emphasized, however, that it was crucial that the writers did not limit themselves just to words, but turned to deeds and hard work. 'We are living in truly revolutionary times', Volodymyr Drozd reminded the writers, 'and our descendants will not forgive us if we squander our opportunity'.

The writers raised a broad range of issues that challenged in one way or another the existing state of affairs. For example, implicitly responding to the Russian usurpation of the historical and cultural patrimonies of the Ukrainians and Belarusians,[62] Drozd affirmed the Ukrainians' link with Kyivan Rus and emphasized the need for a

---

[60] *Literaturna Ukraina*, 18 June 1987.

[61] *Ibid*, On Honchar's reaction to Yelchenko's speech, see Vitalii Koval's article on *Sobor* and its author in *Molod Ukrainy*, 2 April 1993.

[62] See, for example, the article by the Russian imperial nationalist Oleg Trubachev in *Pravda* of 27 March 1987 in which the corresponding member of the USSR Academy of Sciences, among other things, insisted that the language and literature of Kyivan Rus be called Russian.

full picture of the Ukrainian nation's cultural and spiritual development over the last thousand years. Drach pushed for the rehabilitation of Khvylovy and also asked why all official efforts were
concentrated on combating 'nationalism' when what was needed,
in his view, was an intensification of the struggle against 'great-state
chauvinism'. Partly answering his own question, he commented
sarcastically that the Ukrainian authorities had gained international
notoriety for their zealous ideological vigilance. 'When fingernails
are being trimmed in Moscow', he declared, 'they chop off fingers
in Kyiv'. Another speaker, Pidsukha, among other things asked why
the Soviet Germans living in the Altai had their own schools, press
and radio while 'the millions of Ukrainians living in the same Altai',
or in the Russian Far East or the Kuban, 'do not have anything'.

The most dramatic moment at the plenum came when Pavlychko
provided the participants with 'catastrophic' new data about the
situation of Ukrainian-language schools in the republic's major
cities. The percentage of Ukrainian schools in Ukraine's regional
centres, he revealed, had been reduced to about 16%, and there were
large cities, such as Voroshilovhrad and Chernihiv, which no longer
had any Ukrainian schools. This, he pointed out, was the result of
twenty-seven years of an education law which, though camouflaged
as democratic, had worked only in one direction – against the native
language. It was also the fault of the 'republican apparatus', which
had been instilled, as Pavlychko put it, with indifference to the
Ukrainian language and fear 'that love of the mother tongue could
be construed – and we've experienced this! – as nationalism'.

Stressing the need for urgent remedial measures, Pavlychko
announced that the newly established Commission for Ties between
the WUU and Educational Institutions had sent a letter to the
Presidium of the Supreme Soviet of the Ukrainian SSR calling on
it to amend both the existing republican educational legislation and
the Draft Statute on the Secondary General Education School in
two crucial respects, so that: the Ministry of Education, and not
parents, determine the language of instruction in schools according
to the national composition of a given region; and, in the Russian-
language schools in the non-Russian republics, the language, literature and history of the titular nation be made obligatory subjects.

Even more significant was the fact that the plenum adopted a
resolution which read not only like the outline of a programme for
Ukrainization, but also like a call for the mobilization of the public.

Demanding 'radical changes in the functioning of the Ukrainian language in the republic's state institutions, scientific and educational establishments and production collectives', the resolution declared that the writers wanted to focus the attention of 'all men of letters and the Ukrainian public generally' on 'the struggle against manifestations of national nihilism' and 'disrespect for the national language and culture'. The writers themselves were urged to support actively the policies of 'restructuring' and to oppose 'stagnationist features in the development of the economy and culture' and combat 'bureaucratism, protectionism and corruption'. Specifically, the resolution charged the leadership of the WUU to appeal to the Presidium of the Ukrainian Supreme Soviet with a request to accord the Ukrainian language the status of a state language within Ukraine and to amend the educational legislation to make the study of the Ukrainian language and literature obligatory in all of the republic's schools. The document also proposed that the WUU take up with the various ministries a variety of fundamental issues, including increasing Ukrainian-language television and radio programming; dubbing foreign films into Ukrainian (this had stopped under Malanchuk in 1974); improving Ukrainian-language training for theatre and cinema workers; and expanding the use of Ukrainian in business and official life.[63]

Following up on the plenum, on 20 June Honchar sent a letter to Gorbachev, along with a copy of the Russian edition of *Sobor*, in which he described the alarming situation into which the Ukrainian language had been forced and the campaign that had been launched in its defence. He stressed that at various recent meetings in which thousands of representatives of the Ukrainian creative intelligentsia had participated, such as the teachers' congress, a session of the Ukrainian Academy of Sciences and the plenum of the WUU, grave concern and dissatisfaction had been expressed. The Ukrainian cultural intelligentsia, he informed Gorbachev, was united in considering that what was needed was 'constitutional protection' for the Ukrainian language and reform of the education law that would make the study of both Russian and Ukrainian compulsory in the republic's schools. Implicitly aiming at the Shcherbytsky regime,

---

[63] *Literaturna Ukraina*, 9 July 1987. For English translations of excerpts from some of the speeches delivered at the plenum, see *Soviet Ukrainian Affairs* (London), no. 3 (1987).

Honchar also argued that the 'continuing discrimination against the Ukrainian language' was linked to the enduring 'stagnation', 'corruption, violations, careerism, bribetaking and other negative features' in Ukraine. The republic's most senior man of letters concluded with a virtual appeal to Gorbachev to intervene by stressing that Ukraine was 'very hopeful of assistance' from the Soviet leader.[64]

Thus, a year after their memorable Ninth Congress, Ukraine's writers passed another milestone: they had defied the CPU leadership and in effect set out an alternative agenda for restructuring and democratization in Ukraine. During the year, the WUU had developed into a forceful patriotic pressure group with its largest section, the Kyiv region branch, acting as a spearhead and the writers' weekly *Literaturna Ukraina* as its mouthpiece. In the absence of independent national institutions or associations, the Ukrainian literary intelligentsia had become the main promoter of *glasnost*, democratization and national renewal in Ukraine. Placing their hopes on Gorbachev and the liberal course which he had ushered in, leading representatives of the Ukrainian literary élite had begun appealing directly to the Soviet leader not to tolerate any further the reactionary Kyiv leadership. But just as the confrontation between the writers and the Shcherbytsky regime was opening up, new independent Ukrainian voices began to be heard.

---

[64] At the time, however, the press did not mention this letter. It was not published until six years later in the above-mentioned article by Koval in *Molod Ukrainy*.

4

THE REBIRTH OF INDEPENDENT PUBLIC
AND CULTURAL LIFE

A number of other developments during the spring and summer
of 1987 helped to revitalize Ukraine's public and cultural life:
Gorbachev's gradual release of political prisoners and the resumption
by some of them of their dissident activity, the appearance throughout the Soviet Union of unofficial, or 'informal' as they were
referred to, clubs and associations, and religious resurgence in
Western Ukraine. Furthermore, by the middle of the year some
non-Russian groups had begun to put *glasnost* and democratization
to the test by organizing large demonstrations and other protests.
Latvian activists led the way with a commemorative march in
Riga on 14 June to honour the victims of the mass deportations
of their countrymen by the Soviet authorities in June 1941; in
July the Crimean Tatars, who had been campaigning since the
1960s to be allowed to return to their homeland in Crimea, held
a series of demonstrations in Moscow; and, on 23 August, in all
three Baltic republics, the anniversary of the Molotov-Ribbentrop
Pact was marked by protests. All this only increased the salience
of the nationalities question.

Although political conditions in Ukraine were not as auspicious
as in Russia's major cities or in the Baltic republics, the more liberal
atmosphere emanating from Moscow also encouraged the mush-
rooming of unofficial groups in the republic. While most of them
seemed to be concerned with pop music or sport, some of the new
associations devoted their attention to the preservation of the
Ukrainian cultural and historical heritage, ecology, and even and the
issues of peace and disarmament. As their activity unfolded and came
under fire from the republican Party authorities, it soon became
apparent that some of them represented not so much a 'counter-
culture' as a 'counter-ideology'.

The Ukrainian Catholics emerge from the underground

At the same time, a wave of religious fervour spread through Western Ukraine. The climate was conducive because not only was the millennium of the Christianization of Kyivan Rus now only a matter of months away, but also the Chornobyl tragedy had created apocalyptic associations in the minds of many people. The name Chornobyl means wormwood in Ukrainian and this happens to be the name of the apocalyptic star mentioned in the Revelation of St John the Divine (8: 10-11). Furthermore, for Ukrainian Catholics 1987 was special: it had been declared a Marian year by the Pope and also, with Gorbachev's freeing of political prisoners and emphasis on democratization, it seemed to offer the prospect of an improvement in the situation of the outlawed Ukrainian Catholic Church.

In April, on the first anniversary of the Chornobyl disaster, a young girl claimed to have seen an apparition of the Virgin Mary by a locked-up Catholic chapel in Hrushiv, near Lviv, which had been built in the nineteenth century on the site of a supposedly miraculous shrine. Reports about recurrent apparitions quickly spread and soon thousands of people were converging each day on Hrushiv. So great were the excitement and curiosity that by September, according to *Moscow News*, 'some half a million people dropped everything and rushed to the place where, as they said, the Virgin Mary had appeared[1] This mass display of religious zeal left the authorities at a loss as how to respond; moreover, both the local and the central Soviet media were forced to acknowledge this phenomenon, which only focused attention on a church which officially no longer existed.

At the height of the interest in the 'Miracle of Hrushiv', some of the leaders of the Ukrainian Catholic Church decided to emerge from the underground in order to give the campaign for the legalization of their church new impetus. Early in 1987 the leadership of the Ukrainian Catholic Church had appealed in vain to the Soviet government and to Gorbachev personally to lift the ban on

[1] *Moscow News*, no. 37, September 1987. On the 'Miracle of Hrushiv', see also Andrew Sorokowski, 'The Apparition at Hrushiv: A Miracle in Western Ukraine?', *The Ukrainian Weekly*, 16 August 1987; 'Our Lady in the Soviet Union', *The Tablet*, 25 July 1987; Felicity Barringer, 'Purported Miracle Focuses on a Non-Existent Church', *New York Times*, 13 October 1987.

their church, without disclosing their identities. The only reply, they claimed, had been an intensification of the harassment of Ukrainian Catholic believers and more attacks on their church in the press.[2] Subsequent calls for the legalization of the Ukrainian Catholic Church by the newly freed political prisoners Vitalii Shevchenko (who also called for the removal of the ban on the Ukrainian Autocephalous Orthodox Church[3]) in May and Stepan Khmara[4] in June also fell on deaf ears. On 4 August, therefore, two clandestine Ukrainian Catholic bishops, twenty-three priests, and a group of 206 monks, nuns and laymen appealed to Pope John Paul II to press Soviet officials for the legalization of the Ukrainian Catholic Church. They declared that:

> In light of restructuring in the USSR and the more favourable circumstances which have arisen, as well as in connection with the jubilee of the millennium of the baptism of Ukraine, we consider it inopportune to remain in the underground.[5]

Three weeks later, some 3,000 Ukrainian Catholics, including Bishop Pavlo Vasylyk, gathered in the village of Zarvarnytsya, in the Ternopil region. The local authorities seemed unsure how to respond, and although police with dogs sought to disperse the gathering, no arrests were made. The Catholics proceeded to form parishes, and here and there priests began to hold religious services in the open. Clearly, this manifestation of the vitality of a church which officially had ceased to exist long ago and which was now demanding quite openly that the official policy towards it be changed was something that required decisions from Moscow. For the time being, though, the Ukrainian authorities refused to register the Catholic parishes and subjected Catholic activists and clergy to petty harassment and small fines. In September, the head

---

[2] See AS 5759: 'The Appeal of the Central Committee of the Ukrainian Catholics in the Catacombs of Ukraine', dated 8 February 1987; and a statement addressed in the early part of 1987 (no date is given) to Gorbachev and the Pope by a group of leading Ukrainian Catholic activists. A copy of the handwritten document exists in the former RFE/RL Samizdat Archive in Munich.

[3] See Shevchenko's open letter to *Izvestiya* in *Soviet Ukrainian Affairs*, no. 1 (1988), pp. 15-16.

[4] AS 6038. Also published in *Russkaya mysl* (Paris), 28 August 1987, p .6.

[5] AS 6097. Also published in Ukrainian in *Ukrainskyi visnyk,* no. 7, (Kyiv-Lviv), 1987; reprinted ed, n.p.: Suchasnist, 1988, pp. 76-7.

of the Committee in Defence of the Ukrainian Catholic Church,
Terelya, was allowed to leave for the West, ostensibly for medical
treatment. His departure, however, did not weaken the movement
for the legalization of the Ukrainian Catholic Church. His successor,
the former political prisoner Ivan Hel, was to prove an effective
leader and good organizer.[6]

In October, the Ukrainian Catholics were given a boost by a deft
move in the Pope's Ostpolitik which placed the Soviet authorities
in an embarrassing situation. Only a month after he had addressed
a synod in Rome of the Ukrainian Catholic hierarchy in the West,
Pope John Paul II arranged a historic reconciliation between the
leaders of the Polish and Ukrainian Catholic Churches. At a
ceremony in Rome on 17 October, the Polish primate, Cardinal
Josef Glemp, emphasized how 'few altars' Ukrainian Catholics had
to worship at in their homeland and invited the head of the
Ukrainian Catholic Church, Cardinal Myroslav Lyubachivsky, and
his bishops to come to Poland the following summer to participate
in the Polish celebrations of the millennium of the Christianization
of Kyivan Rus.[7]

The denial of the basic human rights of Ukrainian Christians did
not square with *glasnost* and democratization, and this was to be
increasingly pointed out not only by the Vatican, but also by
Western politicians and churchmen. For instance, during a pioneering television linkup in October between representatives of the US
Congress and the USSR Supreme Soviet, Senator Daniel Moynihan
raised the issue of the Ukrainian Catholic Church. The reaction,
however, indicated that the Kremlin was not about to change the
traditional policy which had been pursued towards the Ukrainian
'Uniates' by both the tsarist government and Stalin and his successors. On 23 December, *Izvestiya* responded to Senator Moynihan
with an old-style diatribe against the Ukrainian Catholics. The
newspaper denied the existence of a Ukrainian Catholic Church in

[6] On these developments see *Ukrainskyi visnyk*, No. 8 (Kyiv-Lviv), September
1987; reprinted edn, n.p.: External Representation of the Ukrainian Helsinki
Union, 1988; and *Ukrainskyi visnyk* 9-10 (Kyiv-Lviv), October-November 1987;
reprinted, n.p.: External Representation of the Ukrainian Helsinki Union, 1988,
pp. 260-3.

[7] *The Times*, 31 October 1987. For the texts of the statements made by the two
primates, see *Studium Papers* (Ann Arbor, Michigan), XII, no. 2 (April 1988), pp.
43-6.

Ukraine and dismissed its representatives in the West as the successors of the agents of 'the Polish gentry', 'the Austro-Hungarian
monarchy' and the 'Hitlerites', claiming that they were serving
'reactionary imperialist circles'.

Izvestiya's broadside against the Ukrainian Catholics may also
have been prompted by the fact that the Committee in Defence of
the Rights of the Ukrainian Catholic Church had begun collecting
signatures in support of the legalization of their church. On 22
December, Hel and two priests travelled to Moscow to attend an
unofficial human rights seminar and while in the Soviet capital
handed a petition to the USSR Supreme Soviet.[8] The contacts
which the Ukrainian Catholic activists established in Moscow with
Russian Orthodox dissenters also proved useful, and during the next
few months the Russians Alexander Ogorodnikov, Father Georgii
Edelshtein and Vladimir Poresh were to speak out in defence of the
Ukrainian Catholics.

It should be pointed out that apart from the obvious political
reasons why Moscow did not want to lift its ban on a church which
was so closely identified with Ukrainian nationalism, the Russian
Orthodox Church had its own reasons for opposing the legalization
of the Ukrainian Catholic Church. Quite apart from its traditional
antipathy towards the Uniates, the reappearance of the Ukrainian
Catholic Church, or, for that matter, any concessions to a specifically
Ukrainian church, threatened to undermine its position. In fact, of
the close to 7,000 Russian Orthodox churches functioning at this
time in the Soviet Union, over 4,000 were situated in Ukraine.
Moreover, the largest single Russian Orthodox eparchy was Lviv-
Ternopil, which had over 1,000 working churches; but, this was the
heart of the traditionally Catholic Ukraine.[9] In other words, for the
Moscow Patriarchate there were also the questions of status and
prestige, revenues, and the loyalty of clergy and their parishes to
think about.

Unofficial groups in Lviv and Kyiv become catalysts

Whether by coincidence or not, in the same week that some of

---

[8]   Reuter, 22 December 1987.

[9]   See Bohdan Nahaylo, 'Ukrainian Catholic Issue Overshadows Start of Moscow
Patriarchate's Millennial Celebrations', RL 230/88, 6 June 1988.

the Ukrainian Catholic leadership emerged from the underground, newly released political prisoners in Lviv and Kyiv launched attempts to revive independent public life. They formed groups seeking both to extend *glasnost* more fully to the nationalities problem as it existed in Ukraine and to focus the public's attention on the situation in which the Ukrainian nation found itself.

In Lviv, the new circle of activists coalesced around the veteran dissidents Vyacheslav Chornovil and Mykhailo Horyn. On 4 August, Chornovil issued an open letter to Gorbachev announcing the intention of the group, which included Hel, to resume publication of *Ukrainskyi visnyk* (The Ukrainian Herald), or in other words, to renew the Ukrainian campaign for human and national rights that had been suppressed during the 1970s. This thirty-page document was an important programmatic declaration which revealed how Ukraine's latent national-democratic opposition viewed the changes that were taking place in the Soviet Union and how much the writers, who as members of an official union were after all trying to operate within the general limits set if not by Kyiv, then by Moscow, had still left unsaid.

While in principle welcoming Gorbachev's new course, Chornovil began by placing certain things in perspective. He pointed out that for all the Soviet leader's claims, the changes he had inaugurated so far amounted only to a 'revolution in words' because there was still no legal recognition of the right to dissent, no toleration of political opposition, nor any restructuring in the sphere of nationalities policy. Chornovil also reminded the Soviet leader that long before he came to power the 'dissidents' and former political prisoners had been the pioneers of genuine *glasnost* and democratization. They, he maintained, were 'only the tip of the iceberg', the representatives of 'those healthy forces which had resisted stagnation and the bureaucratization of Soviet society and, in the non-Russian republics, also the great-state chauvinistic policies of denationalization'.

Chornovil went on to stress that the same system and people who had once stifled the voices of 'all independent thought' were still in place, except that non-Russian cultural figures, mainly writers, had now been given a licence to speak about the 'depressing situation' of their native language and national culture. But this was a 'superficial' *glasnost*, he argued, for the permitted discussion did not delve into the reasons for this state of affairs and avoided the question of the erosion of the statehood of the supposedly sovereign nations. Chornovil also accused the Soviet leader of avoiding any analysis in his speeches of the issues connected with the national question and of simply repeating the same vague phrases and warnings that had been used since Stalin's time.

As far as the situation in Ukraine was concerned, Chornovil was equally blunt. In the twenty-two years since Dzyuba had completed *Internationalism or Russification?*, he wrote, the situation in the republic had 'significantly worsened thanks to the efforts of Shcherbytsky and Fedorchuk'. Thus, 'many people' in Ukraine were convinced that 'in order for restructuring to reach the republic, the entire Shcherbytsky "team", poisoned by bureaucracy, corruption and chauvinism, should have been removed from leading positions . . . a long time ago'.

As for the Ukrainian writers and their campaign in defence of the Ukrainian language and culture, Chornovil pointed out that they were sticking to the limits of an incomplete *glasnost* and hence were not yet calling things by their real names or addressing the cardinal issues. Was not the fact that at the last writers' plenum not one of the speakers had had 'the courage or decency' to mention 'with / gratitude' the name of Dzyuba, who had dared to tell the truth in the pre-*glasnost* era and paid for it, and who was sitting in the audience, an apt illustration of the state of *glasnost* in Ukraine, Chornovil asked.

The former political prisoner urged Gorbachev to face up to the acuteness and real nature of the national question and not simply accept the assurances of 'some literary half-patriots and half-careerists' that Moscow was not to blame for the problems, that it was all the fault of Russified non-Russians, and that all that was needed was to revoke 'the more abhorrent provisions of Khrushchev's education policy'. The opening of more Ukrainian schools or theatres, which the writers were calling for, would only be a palliative, not a remedy and, in any case, Chornovil stressed, without more fundamental changes in the official policies, this would only antagonize Ukraine's sizable Russian population.

What was needed, Chornovil maintained, was a special plenum of the CPSU Central Committee to discuss the national question with the same courage and openness as economic problems. At this meeting, 'the true situation of the USSR's non-Russians' would have to be examined and the 'fictitious character' of the sovereignty of their republics acknowledged. After this, there would have to be a return to the principles which Lenin had set out for Soviet nationalities policy in the last years of his life and on which the Ukrainization programme of the 1920s had been based. What it boiled down to, Chornovil specified, was that the CPSU leadership would have to recognize that it was essential to broaden the political, economic and cultural rights of the republics and to restore the native language in their official and public life.

In the final part of his letter to Gorbachev, Chornovil pointed out that compared with the progress made in Russia, the process of filling in the blank pages of Ukrainian history had essentially not even begun yet. He added a long list of themes and individuals, beginning with the Ukrainian struggle for independence in the 1917-20 period and ending with the death of Vasyl Stus in 1985, which still remained forbidden topics or were subject to falsification and distortion. Among them he mentioned the UNR, the ZUNR, Hrushevsky, Vynnychenko, Skrypnyk and Khvylovy, the 'executed renaissance of the 1920s', 'the greatest and most infamous blank page in the Soviet history of Ukraine' – the 'genocidal' great famine of 1932-3 – the fate of the Ukrainian Autocephalous Orthodox and Ukrainian Catholic Churches (Chornovil called for the ban on them to be lifted), the armed resistance in Western Ukraine in the 1940s and early 1950s, the 'smothered renaissance' of the 1960s and the suppression of Ukrainian national assertiveness in the 1970s. Chornovil ended by requesting that the body of Stus be allowed to be brought back for reburial in Ukraine and that the poet's confiscated works be returned to his family.[10]

Although Chornovil's demands and proposals stopped well short of calling for independence for Ukraine or even challenging the Communist Party's monopoly on power, they went much further than what the writers had dared to press for. Chornovil's open letter to the Soviet leader represented a manifesto from those indomitable Ukrainian patriots who had refused to give in even during the most difficult years and who, being very sceptical about the 'democratization' that was taking place under Gorbachev, felt they had nothing to lose. Having spent long years in imprisonment, these

---

[10] *Ukrainskyi visnyk*, no.7, pp. 7-25. For an English translation, see Taras Kuzio (ed.), *Dissent in Ukraine Under Gorbachev*, London, Ukrainian Press Agency, 1989, pp. 3-20.

activists had been released but not rehabilitated, and now existed in a legal limbo. Moreover, quite a few Ukrainian political prisoners, such as Lukyanenko and Badzo, had still not been freed or allowed to return to Ukraine from their places of exile.

The letter also indicated the distrust with which the former political prisoners viewed some of the new 'nightingales of restructuring' (as the former journalist Pavlo Skochok dubbed them[11]), especially those like Oliinyk who, as Chornovil pointed out, had once publicly smeared the dissidents. The latter stressed that the official creative unions, like the WUU, were continuing to regard the former political prisoners as *personae non gratae* even though some of their members were now 'repeating from public platforms and in the press' the kind of things 'for which until not long ago we were carted off to labour camps'. Chornovil announced that because of this the newly freed dissident intellectuals were considering forming their own creative circles and publications independent from the official organizations.

That same month, Chornovil and his colleagues went ahead and published a new *samvydav* issue of *Ukrainskyi visnyk*. In October 1987, this circle founded two new groups: an Action Group for the Release of Ukrainian Political Prisoners and a Ukrainian Association of Independent Creative Intelligentsia (UANTI). The former represented the first human rights group to be set up in Ukraine since the Ukrainian Helsinki Monitoring Group was suppressed at the end of the 1970s. It sought to establish ties with human rights activists in other republics, and its first contacts were with similar new groups in Armenia and Georgia. The UANTI aimed to unite writers, poets and artists who had been victims of the cultural purges in Ukraine and who wished to work for the good of Ukrainian culture outside of official institutions.[12]

The authorities responded with old-fashioned denunciations in the official press, and organized special meetings for this purpose at local factories. Much was made, for instance, of the fact that in September Chornovil and Horyn gave a video interview to an

[11] *Ukrainskyi visnyk*, no. 7, p. 52.

[12] For details, see Roman Solchanyk, 'New Human-Rights Group Formed in Ukraine', RL 403/87, 7 October 1987, and Bohdan Nahaylo, 'Ukrainian Association of Independent Creative Intelligentsia Formed', RL 489/87, 25 November 1987.

American-Ukrainian journalist which was 'discovered' and confiscated by the republic's vigilant customs officers.[13] In December, Chornovil and Horyn were prevented from travelling to Moscow to participate in an unofficial human rights seminar.

Chornovil's group, however, was not the only indication of the revival of independent public activity in Lviv. For instance, in September an unofficial peace group – the Lviv Trust Group – held a demonstration in the city in which about thirty people took part. The following month, an important semi-official patriotic association – the 'Tovarystvo Leva', or Lion Society – was formally founded. Its members, mainly young people, including Komsomol members and officials, had begun their activity during the summer of that year by cleaning up the city's famous but long-neglected Lychakivsky cemetery. The Lion Society subsequently concentrated on preserving national traditions and cultural monuments and on local ecological issues.[14] On 30 October it organized a charity concert at which a newly formed group called 'Ne Zhurys' (Don't Worry) made their debut and introduced vital new elements to the burgeoning Ukrainian national renewal – political satire and songs of social and political protest.[15]

Meanwhile in Kyiv, the former political prisoners Serhii Naboka, Leonid Milyavsky and Oles Shevchenko, along with other dissenters, founded a discussion group for nationally minded citizens – the Ukrainian Culturological Club – which became an important vehicle for Ukrainian national dissent. Its inaugural meeting on 6 August on the theme 'Ukrainian Culture: Facade and Reality' drew scores of people. Subsequent meetings dealt with environmental issues, the preservation of historical and cultural monuments, and 'blank pages' in Ukraine's history.

It was the meeting on 4 October which first drew the wrath of the custodians of orthodoxy. At it, Leonid Milyavsky, a young Ukrainian Jew, who had been arrested in 1981 with Naboka and their wives for attempting to set up a democratic club in the

[13] See, for instance, P. Vilkhovy's diatribe against the two in *Radyanska Ukraina*, 13 November 1987.

[14] See Marusia Drohobycky, 'The Lion Society: Profile of a Ukrainian Patriotic "Informal" Group', RL 325/88, 18 July 1988.

[15] See the reports on Ne Zhurys' debut and on the singing 'bards', Andrii Panchyshyn, Viktor Morozov and others, in *Ukrainskyi visnyk*, nos 8-9, pp. 118-21.

Ukrainian capital and posting up leaflets in defence of Ukrainian political prisoners, gave a candid presentation aimed, as he put it, at curing the 'national amnesia, or loss of historical memory' to which the Ukrainians had been subjected. He touched upon numerous sensitive themes, such as Stalin's famine in Ukraine, which he said the whole world now knew about but was still a 'blank page' in the official Soviet history of Ukraine, and the persecution of dissidents. Milyavsky concluded by declaring that the prerequisites for the success of restructuring and society's triumph over the 'anti-democratic' and 'anti- national' 'bureaucratic administrative system' inherited from the Stalin era were 'freedom' and making the authorities publicly accountable to society. At the same meeting, Oles Shevchenko called for monuments to be erected to the victims of Stalin's purges and famine in Ukraine, while another recently released political prisoner, Khmara, decried the fact that on the occasion of the centenary of Stalin's Russian 'henchman' in Ukraine during the 1930s, Pavel Postyshev, who himself later became a victim of Stalin's terror, the Stalinist functionary was being white-washed in the Ukrainian press by 'so-called historians, or more accurately falsifiers of history', while the real history of Ukraine was, 'as in the past', still being approached with 'lies and half-truths'.

The first salvo against the Ukrainian Culturological Club was delivered on 19 October by the Kyiv evening newspaper *Vechirnyi Kyiv*. But the effect was only to draw attention to the club and its activities. The members of the club defended themselves in various statements and letters. Shevchenko, for instance, sent a statement to leading Russian liberal figures and publications in which he asked for support in the name of democracy against the 'conservatives' who had 'transformed Ukraine into a reserve of Brezhnevism'. There was something of a breakthrough in November and December, however, when *Vechirnyi Kyiv* broke with standard practice by also publishing letters which supported the group. From these, and subsequent articles in the newspaper, it was clear that the club enjoyed the backing of at least some members of the Ukrainian intelligentsia who were members of official institutions. Though subjected to heavy fire from the authorities for refusing to abide by 'Soviet' and 'Socialist' values and discipline, the club defiantly continued to test the limits of *glasnost* and to revive national consciousness.[16]

As new unofficial Ukrainian groups and *samvydav* publications continued to appear, there were also indications that, in Western Ukraine at any rate, there also existed a more militant and uncompromising strain of opposition among some young people. In November a Ukrainian newspaper revealed that in the Ternopil region alone two clandestine 'nationalist' youth groups had recently been uncovered. One of them, in Chortkiv, had hoisted the banned blue and yellow flag of independent Ukraine over 'a government building'; the other, in Zbarazh, almost all of whose members 'had a higher education', had been preparing to disseminate 'anti-Soviet leaflets'.[17] During this period *Sobesednik*, the weekly supplement to the all-Union Komsomol daily, *Komsomolskaya pravda*, also published letters from two young Western Ukrainians which attested to the growing boldness of the youth in this region. The author of the first letter asserted his Ukrainian Catholic faith and challenged members of the Komsomol to a public debate, while the other called on the newspaper to take heed of *glasnost*, stop 'singing songs about brotherhood' and begin 'a serious discussion of national problems'.[18]

The widening rift between the writers and the CPU leadership

In the meantime, Ukraine's writers kept up their campaign on a broad front encompassing the language issue, the filling in of the blank pages of Ukrainian history and opposition to the construction of more nuclear reactors in the republic. Responding to the mounting pressure, in August the CPU Central Committee adopted a special resolution on the national question formulated to placate the writers and their allies. The document acknowledged that 'recently, many questions of a national-cultural character' had 'been raised by the public' and that the CPU leadership, the Presidium of the Ukrainian Supreme Soviet and the mass media were receiving

[16] On the Ukrainian Culturological Club, see Bohdan Nahaylo, '"Informal" Ukrainian Culturological Club Under Attack', RL 477/87, 23 November 1987, and 'Informal Ukrainian Culturological Club Helps to Break New Ground for *Glasnost* ', RL 57/88, 8 February 1988.

[17] B. Yefremov, 'Po rizni boky mynuloho' [On Different Sides of the Past], *Kultura i zhyttya*, 22 November 1987, p. 2.

[18] See *Sobesednik*, no. 27, 1987, p. 11, and no. 48, 1987, p. 11.

letters expressing concern about the situation of the Ukrainian language. The actual 'complex of measures' offered in the resolution, however, boiled down to the modest concessions on the language question which Yelchenko had proposed in June.[19]

The following month, the Presidium of the WUU replied with what was in effect a counter-resolution of its own which only highlighted the gap between what the writers were demanding and what the CPU leadership was prepared to offer.[20] The tug of war on the language issue continued with the discussion being taken up in more and more newspapers and journals, and representatives of the CPU being forced to respond.

The writers' campaign against the building of the Chihirin and other new nuclear plants in Ukraine also gathered strength. In August *Literaturna Ukraina* published a protest in the form of a collective letter to the editor signed by seven Ukrainian writers,[21] including the first secretary of the Poltava region Party organization, Fedir Morhun. The latter had recently become something of a maverick and some Western observers viewed him as a potential replacement for Shcherbytsky. The protesters also collected about 6,000 signatures and sent them in October to the Supreme Soviet of the USSR. The following month, work on the Chihirin plant was stopped, but the Ukrainian press kept silent about this.[22]

In October, Honchar delivered his most outspoken speech yet, at a conference in Leningrad, in which he took a frank look at some of the problems troubling the Ukrainian public, ranging from Russification to the 'endless' construction of new atomic reactors and the alarming environmental situation. Now, *Literaturna Ukraina* promptly published the full text while Radio Moscow and *Literaturnaya gazeta* subsequently provided toned-down versions.[23] Honchar, Shcherbak and Drach also proposed the organization of a forum in

[19] *Radyanska Ukraina*, 14 August 1987. See also Roman Solchanyk, 'Ukrainian Party Adopts Program on National Question', RL 350/87, 26 August 1987.

[20] *Literaturna Ukraina*, 7 October 1987.

[21] *Ibid.*, 6 August 1987.

[22] See Bohdan Nahaylo, 'Mounting Opposition in Ukraine to Nuclear Energy', RL Supplement 1/88, 24 February 1988.

[23] *Literaturna Ukraina*, 7 October, 1987. Radio Moscow excerpted the speech on 22 October 1987, and *Literaturnaya gazeta* published its abridged version on 9 December 1987. For a Western reaction to Honchar's speech, see Arnold Beichman, 'Anxieties in Ukraine', *Washington Times*, 1 December 1987.

Kyiv for writers from all over the world at which some of the questions and issues raised by the Chornobyl disaster could be discussed. The idea seems to have been blocked, though.[24]

The writers also started to cooperate more closely with concerned scientists and engineers, who in the summer of 1987 began holding their own meetings and discussions in response to the Soviet Ministry of Atomic Energy's determination to continue with its programme of expanding nuclear energy in Ukraine. In December, *Literaturna Ukraina* and *Radyanska Ukraina* organized a round-table discussion at which the growing solidarity between the writers and the scientists was demonstrated. Drach, who in November had been elected head of the Kyiv section of the WUU, welcomed the example which the president of the Ukrainian Academy of Sciences, Paton, had set with his 'principled position' on the nuclear energy and related ecological issues, and urged the participants that:

> All of us, as one community, should support the position of our leading scientists. Why is our conscience, [our sense of] morality, dormant when these energy units are being forced upon us beyond reasonable limits. . . . It is necessary that everything that is happening, being planned, especially in the field of nuclear energy, should become the subject of the widest possible public discussion, [and] the strictest public control.

Drach went on to announce that the WUU had decided to form an ecological commission, headed by Yurii Shcherbak, which would 'work in close contact with the scientists'.[25] That same month, writers were among the founders of an unofficial 'Green World' ecological association.

Despite the mounting protests, in December three more nuclear reactors were put into operation in the republic, including the third unit at the Chornobyl plant; it was restarted even though, as *Izvestiya* pointed out on 5 December, concern persisted about whether conditions in and around the station could be considered normal and safe. On 3 January, *Radyanska Ukraina* welcomed the starting up of the new reactors, noting that the motto at the builders at the Zaporizhzhya plant was: 'Each year – a new reactor'.

This only cemented the new coalition of writers and scientists. Three weeks later, the writers' weekly published a letter from

[24] See Nahaylo, 'Mounting Opposition'.

[25] *Literaturna Ukraina*, 17 December 1987.

thirteen leading Ukrainian scientists, most of them academicians, explaining in considerable detail why they were opposed to the expansion of nuclear energy in Ukraine and urging the authorities to reassess their policy. The way it was worded, their blistering attack on the Soviet Ministry of Atomic Energy might equally have applied to the Shcherbytsky team. The scientists accused the central ministry of displaying a 'belligerent, bureaucratic' attitude and 'of refusing to submit itself to any restructuring'. They argued that its refusal to take into account public opinion and 'the bitter lessons of Chornobyl' seemed to be dictated by 'the desire to hold on to a system . . . that is slipping out of their hands'. 'But times are changing', the authors stressed, and it was 'not so easy to wave restructuring aside'.[26]

The battle for the recovery of the nation's history and 'rehabilitation' of some of its most prominent figures also intensified. Drach and others had indicated at the June plenum of the Board of the WUU that the writers would not be deterred by Yelchenko's pronouncement on this subject. Among other things which made the position of the CPU leadership increasingly untenable was the fact that the Russians were being allowed to publish historians like Vasilii Klyuchevsky, who, as one Ukrainian author pointed out in an article published in June, were not only not Marxists but were outright imperialists.[27] The situation was aptly described by the American historian Roman Szporluk:

> If Karamzin, the bard of autocracy who in Pushkin's words had sung the praise of 'the charms of the knout' (*prelesti knuta*) is being rehabilitated – and he is being published in hundreds of thousands of copies – then the rehabilitation of Ukrainian historians – many of whom were leftist (populist, socialist, and radical) but had been banned precisely because they were Ukrainians – could not be denied much longer.[28]

For the time being, though, the CPU's overseers of the writing of history seemed determined to act as the defenders of orthodoxy against both Ukrainian critics and the 'revisionists' among the more

[26] *Ibid.*, 21 January 1987.

[27] Fedir Bratyshan, 'Stezhky do dzerel' [Paths to the Sources], *Zhovten*, no. 6, 1987, pp. 121–2.

[28] Roman Szporluk, 'National Reawakening: Ukraine and Belorussia' in Uri Ra'anan (ed.), *The Soviet Empire: The Challenge of National and Democratic Movements*, Lexington and Toronto, 1990, p. 78.

liberal historians in Moscow. In June, the director of the Institute of Party History in Kyiv, Vasyl Yurchuk, declared that there was 'no basis' for re-examining the Party's position towards the likes of Hrushevsky, Vynnychenko and Khvylovy, and went on to criticize two Russian historians: Academician Vladimir Tikhonov, for questioning the necessity of Stalin's 'liquidation of the *kulaks* as a class', and Yurii Afanasev for his description of the 1930s as 'the Stalinist epoch'.[29]

Less than a month after the writers' plenum, Zhulynsky opened an important new series in *Literaturna Ukraina* entitled 'Pages of a Forgotten Heritage', which was devoted to uncovering aspects of Ukraine's submerged history and culture. During the next few months, the newspaper carried articles on Khvylovy[30] and other leading cultural figures of the 1920s. By the end of the year, several important bridgeheads had been established: in December, *Kyiv* published works by Vynnychenko; another literary monthly, *Vitzchyzna*, published a number of Khvylovy's short stories, and *Literaturna Ukraina* of 10 December ran a long piece by a young philologist turned historian, Serhii Bilokin, on Skrypnyk and his cultural policies.

For the first time in an official publication, in November a call was also made to tell the truth about the more recent past, namely the KGB offensive in Ukraine in 1972-3. Demonstrating his talent as a budding publicist, the young literary critic and poet Mykola Ryabchuk insisted in his review of the Russian-language edition of *Sobor* that the purges of those years should be seen for what they really were – 'repressive measures' directed against 'many talented writers and activists in the artistic, cultural and educational fields'. Ryabchuk's pithy review went on to examine the mentality of the bureaucratic class in Ukraine which had found *Sobor* so objectionable and which now, as he suggested, regarded restructuring as nothing more than an exercise in 'window-dressing'.[31]

In the meantime, however, there also appeared the first tentative

---

[29] *Pravda Ukrainy*, 9 June 1987. See also the articles in the same newspaper by V. Melnichenko on 31 July 1987, and by V. Kulchytsky on 11 September 1987.

[30] *Literaturna Ukraina*, 24 September 1987.

[31] Mykola Ryabchuk, 'Sobor u ryshtovannykh' [The Cathedral in Scaffolding], *Sotsialistychna kultura*, no. 11, 1987. The review also appeared in Russian in *Novyi mir*, no. 11, 1987.

signs that some of the official Ukrainian historians favoured a somewhat less rigid approach to the nation's past. In April 1987, *News from Ukraine* carried a candid interview with Kuras, who for the last few years had been the deputy director of the CPU Central Committee's Institute of Party History. He acknowledged that, in dealing with the period 1917–20, Soviet historiography was 'stereotyped, simplified, [and] incomplete' and that instead of trying to 'present our ideological adversaries in a grotesque and caricatural way', historical works should be 'populated with people with all their merits, controversies and shortcomings'.[32] Four months later, the director of the Institute of History, Yurii Kondufor, admitted that 'We know practically nothing or very little about the tragic events in Ukraine in the 1930s, particularly about the famine, and a whole series of other episodes'.[33] And in September, Yurii Shapoval, a senior scholar at the Institute of Party History, admitted that 'the figure of silence' had ruled over Soviet historical research. 'Surely it does no harm', he asked in a newspaper article, 'to raise the question of the famine at the start of the 1930s, of the victims of illegal repression'.[34]

Defending the bastion of stagnation

Any hopes that Shcherbytsky and his team would start giving way a little on the past as they had done on the language issue were dashed, however, by the speeches which the Ukrainian Party leader delivered during the final weeks of 1987 and the first month of 1988. In essence, though, Shcherbytsky adhered to the cautious line on the Soviet past which Gorbachev set out in his eagerly awaited address on 2 November on the occasion of the seventieth anniversary of the Bolshevik revolution. The Soviet leader hardly went beyond what Khrushchev had acknowledged over two decades before, and broke no new ground with respect to the history of relations between Moscow and the non-Russians.[35]

In fact there were disturbing signs at this time that the conservatives in the Soviet leadership, headed by Yegor Ligachev, had

---

[32] *News from Ukraine*, no. 17, April 1987.

[33] *Lyudyna i svit*, no. 8, 1987, p. 24.

[34] *Pravda Ukrainy*, 20 September 1987.

[35] TASS, 2 November 1987.

strengthened their position and forced Gorbachev on to the defensive. News had begun to filter out that at a Central Committee meeting on 21 October the outspoken Moscow Party chief Boris Yeltsin had declared that reform was being blocked by Ligachev and other conservatives and announced his resignation. Yeltsin had also asserted that *perestroika*, as far as the man in street was concerned, seemed to amount only to words, and that a new personality cult was growing up around Gorbachev. Three weeks later, after the rumours about the 'Yeltsin affair' had begun to be confirmed, Gorbachev dismissed the most radical member of his team.[36]

Against this background of increasing drama and turmoil in Moscow around the struggle for reform, Shcherbytsky continued in his role as a staunch defender of the status quo. The thrust of his speech on the anniversary of the Bolshevik Revolution was that whatever 'shortcomings, difficulties and mistakes' had occurred during the years of Soviet rule they could not be allowed to overshadow the 'convincing successes in all areas of economic and cultural construction'. The people, he declared, would 'obviously have to be helped' to assess the past 'correctly'.[37]

A few weeks later, on 12 December, Shcherbytsky elaborated. Addressing a plenum of the Kyiv city Party organization, he acknowledged that the 'interest of the public, and in particular of young people, in questions of culture and our history' was growing, 'especially in connection with the introduction of Christianity in Rus'. Betraying a certain amount of unease about the way things were going, he warned patriotically minded individuals, regardless of whether they were members of unofficial associations (here the Ukrainian Culturological Club seems to have been one of the implicit targets) or official structures, not to overstep the mark. The Ukrainian Party leader clarified the CPU's attitude towards the incipient revival in the republic's public and cultural life with the following warning and instructions:

> It is . . . necessary to take account of the fact that culturological problems often also become the object of political speculation. And now, when many issues are the subject of sharp discussions, informal associations, including ones with dubious platforms,

[36] See John Morrison, *Boris Yeltsin: From Bolshevik to Democrat*, London, 1991, pp. 60-73.

[37] *Radyanska Ukraina*, 6 November 1987.

often take the initiative themselves. There must not be an unprincipled attitude towards instances when some comrades, including Party members, use *glasnost* and the development of democracy as a pretext for misrepresenting tendentiously and in a sensational manner our difficulties and failures [and] individual historical facts without making any constructive proposals. In ideological questions, a wait and see attitude is impermissible . . . Communists, and primarily leaders, must defend the Party line . . . and resolutely combat any attempts to utilize the processes of *glasnost* and *perestroika* for purposes far removed from the tasks of restructuring.[38]

Three weeks later, in a speech on the seventieth anniversary of the Ukrainian SSR, Shcherbytsky seemed to go out of his way to reassert the Party line on one of the major blank spots in modern Ukrainian history – the great famine of 1932-3. Hailing collectivization as a 'turning point of historical significance', he acknowledged that there had been 'violations' and 'distortions' in the implementation of this policy and said that 'an unanticipated drought caused additional problems'. All of this, he maintained, had 'brought serious food problems' and 'famine in a number of rural areas', not only in Ukraine, but also in Russia and Kazakhstan. Without delving into the specifics of the Ukrainian case, Shcherbytsky denounced the 'political speculation' in the West on 'this difficult time'.

Having indicated that no new approach to the famine or to Ukraine's history generally was to be expected, the Ukrainian Party leader nevertheless conceded that there were periods and events that needed 'further study and elaboration'. He announced that the CPU Central Committee had instructed the Institute of Party History and the Institute of History 'to examine and clarify a series of questions and to submit appropriate proposals'.

For a second time that month, Shcherbytsky also warned that there were those who wanted to 'misuse *glasnost* and democracy' and to 'exploit national feeling'. Without providing any concrete examples, he claimed that they were setting themselves up as the only defenders of 'national dignity' and the 'historical heritage', and posing 'virtually as fighters for restructuring'. Although the Ukrainian leader expressed his confidence that 'our people', as he put

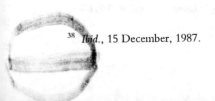

[38] *Ibid.*, 15 December, 1987.

it, 'have a resolute immunity to ideationally alien views', he nevertheless stressed that ideological work needed to be modernized.[39]

There was little evidence that in Ukraine this was being done, though. By now, the acuteness of the multifarious nationalities question in the Soviet Union was becoming more and more evident. In the Baltic republics, the pressure for greater national rights was growing. Here, representatives of the native élites had begun to raise political and economic issues, such as those of sovereignty and republican economic self-management. During the last six months, there had been protests in Armenia, and even in Belarus and Moldova patriotic forces were emerging which were challenging Russification and foreign domination. Yet, for instance, the best that a Ukrainian 'official historian' and 'specialist' on the nationalities question, Larysa Nahorna, could manage in an article in *Radyanska Ukraina* on 22 January 1988, which was billed as a discussion of some of the 'questions of the theory and practice' of 'national relations in the USSR', was to echo Shcherbytsky by asserting that there were 'extremist elements' which were 'openly seeking to exploit *glasnost*' for 'subversive anti-Soviet actions' in order 'to undermine the friendship of nations'. She maintained that: 'In quite a few republics, including Ukraine, attempts are being made behind the cover of informal associations to exploit the lack of proper political education of young people, and to entangle them in the snares of nationalistic fantasies.' Nahorna also repeated another standard warning that hostile foreign forces were seeking to exacerbate and exploit these difficulties, citing as an example the interest shown in the Stalin famine in Ukraine by 'bourgeois Sovietologists' and the US Congress.

In actual fact, at the beginning of 1988, just as it was preparing to hold the Central Committee plenum devoted to the progress of restructuring in Ukraine, the CPU leadership was indeed being subjected to heavy criticism, not from Washington, but from much closer to home. In a sequence reminiscent of the events surrounding the Berkhin affair, on 2 December 1987 *Literaturnaya gazeta* uncovered another scandal in Ukraine pointing to high-level corruption, this time involving the frame-up of a local official in the Ministry of Internal Affairs in Odesa. Early the following month, *Pravda* reported that the CPSU Politburo had criticized the work of

[39] *Ibid.*, 26 December 1987.

the Kyiv city Party Committee and stressed that restructuring had not yet taken hold in the Ukrainian capital.[40] This was seen as an indirect attack on Shcherbytsky and once again fuelled speculation about his replacement.

What was also significant was that on 8 January, the same day as *Pravda*'s swipe against the CPU leadership, Gorbachev held a meeting with representatives of the mass media, cultural unions and ideological institutions at which he seemed to call on supporters of reform not to lose hope but to regroup their forces. Acknowledging that the campaign for restructuring and democratization had come under fire from critics on both the right and the left, he declared that 'to stop now would be disastrous. If we take fright and stop the process we have begun, it would have the most serious consequences, because we simply could not raise our people to such a massive task a second time.' The Soviet leader also indicated that a Party conference scheduled for June 1988, which he had first suggested a year ago as a way of speeding up reform instead of waiting for the next five-yearly Party Congress in 1991, would see a crucial showdown between the forces for change and their conservative opponents. He promised that at the conference, 'questions concerning the democratization of Soviet society will be the main, central problems', adding that they would also include electoral and judicial reform.

As for *glasnost*, Gorbachev stressed that 'If *glasnost*, criticism and democracy are in the interests of socialism and the people, then they have no limits.' Clearly, much depended on how socialism was to be understood, and this in turn was connected with how the Soviet past was viewed. And here too Gorbachev seemed to want to reassure liberal intellectuals that his recent speech on the seventieth anniversary of the Bolshevik Revolution was not a final official version. He told the newspaper editors and cultural figures that the interpretation of the past 'was not something frozen and handed down once and for all time. It will deepen and develop in the course of further research.'[41]

At the plenum of the CPU Central Committee, which was held on 22-3 January, Shcherbytsky and the CPU Politburo faced

---

[40] *Pravda*, 8 January 1988.

[41] TASS, 12 January 1988. The TASS report on the meeting was reprinted in Ukrainian in *Literaturna Ukraina* on 14 January, taking up the first three pages.

unprecedented direct and 'incisive', as *Pravda* called it, criticism. Several of the regional Party bosses, as well as the Party chief of the Kyiv city Party organization, Kostyantyn Masyk, complained that the Politburo had not gone far enough in 'renewing its style of work'. The Lviv region Party leader, Pohrebnyak, suggested that the top CPU leadership was too conservative, remote and out of touch with the real state of things. Addressing the Ukrainian Party leader directly, he stressed: 'Effecting the reorientation of the style of work of the Politburo and Secretariat depends to a considerable degree on you, Volodymyr Vasylovych, as first secretary of the Central Committee.' For his part, Masyk, who spoke as if he represented other delegates, declared that 'In our opinion, when it comes to questions of the development of democratic norms in their work, the Politibuto and ... Comrade Shcherbytsky have something to think about.' Although the latter survived this criticism and once again emerged as Party leader, *Pravda* echoed what Masyk had said, commenting that, 'with regard to developing democratic initiatives', the CPU 'Politburo and the first secretary of the Central Committee' were left with plenty to think about.[42]

Although under fire, and forced once again to engage in self-criticism, Shcherbytsky nevertheless reiterated his general tough line as regards *glasnost* and democratization. He noted that in some newspaper publications and even sometimes in radio and television programmes, there were instances when certain facts had been 'distorted and slanted', the 'ideological criteria' for assessing them ignored, or 'undisguised disinformation' presented unchallenged. *Glasnost*, he stressed, required 'a Party standpoint from journalists and a responsible attitude towards shaping public opinion'. He singled out for criticism both the CPU's ideological secretary, Yelchenko (whom he accused of not displaying sufficient 'initiative and dynamism'), and the head of the Central Committee's department of agitation and propaganda, Leonid Kravchuk (who, he said, would have to analyse these problems more profoundly and provide editors with better 'assistance'). Shcherbytsky also stressed that it was imperative that Party organizations within the republic's creative unions did not permit the 'the broad rights that have now been given the creative unions' to be used 'for the satisfaction of ambitious pretensions, manifestations of cliquishness, not to mention demag-

[42] *Pravda*, 26 January 1988.

ogy and political indifference'. At the same time, he said, the Party would continue to 'react promptly to the enemy's ideological sabotage, including its attempts to use certain unofficial organizations for its purpose'. He notified the plenum that 'active ideological and organizational pressure' was being applied against such groups 'to neutralize the aspirations of demagogues and extremists'.[43]

The fact that Pohrebnyak, Masyk and some others criticized Shcherbytsky at the plenum did not mean that they were necessarily more democratically minded themselves. Pohrebnyak, for instance, who was responsible for the region in which Chornovil's circle and the Ukrainian Catholics were so active, also said in his speech that 'the deepening of democratization and *glasnost*' had activated the CPU's 'ideological opponents'. 'Nationalist and religious propaganda' were on the rise, he complained, and 'all sorts of rabble-rousers and slanderers' had appeared. He also hinted that there could be more trouble in store because in 1989 the fiftieth anniversary of the 'reunification' of Western Ukraine with the Ukrainian SSR would be celebrated. Pohrebnyak urged that those responsible for overseeing ideological work should improve their work and ensure better coordination of counter-propaganda. Masyk was even more categorical here, and accused the ideological apparatus and the republic's media of not doing enough to combat 'manifestations of nationalism, religious extremism and fanaticism, [and] the exploitation for anti-social purposes of all sorts of unofficial groups'. He criticized the ideological cadres for not being aggressive enough in 'defending our class and ideological principles' and demanded that the CPU ideological secretary, Yelchenko, adopt a tougher position.

A good example of such a hard-line position was given by the editor of the workers' daily *Robitnycha hazeta* and head of the still highly conservative Union of Journalists of Ukraine, Mykola Shybyk. Despite his profession, he did not call for the broadening of *glasnost* and democratization, but attacked the 'non-literary' activity of Ukrainian writers. He accused them of having become preoccupied with resolutions and open letters and, especially when they discussed the issue of the Ukrainian language, of offending with their 'excessive, angry tone' and 'lack of objectivity'. Shybyk pointed out that

[43] *Radyanska Ukraina*, 23 January 1988.

this applied even to such highly respected figures as Honchar, and he proposed that some of the writers be called in for a 'discussion' either by the Central Committee, or at least by Yelchenko.

There were, however, a few speeches at the plenum which reflected the growing frustration and anger in society with the Shcherbytsky regime and the policies it was associated with. The president of the Ukrainian Academy of Sciences, Paton, for example, complained that certain republican and central ministries were ignoring the scientific findings and recommendations of the republic's scientists concerning ecological questions, the best use of the republic's water and other natural resources, and the siting and construction in Ukraine of new heavy industrial complexes. The Poltava region Party chief, Morhun, also emphasized the need for greater attention to be paid to ecological problems and urged that the CPU leadership begin repairing part of the colossal damage that had been done to some of Ukraine's most fertile areas through flooding as a result of grandiose but shortsighted irrigation schemes. He also called for radical changes in the policy that had promoted the development of urban centres at the expense of the villages and led to the impoverishment and depopulation of the rural communities. A third speaker, the rector of Kyiv State University, Viktor Skopenko, protested, among other things, about the 'sharp' decline of textbooks and manuals published in Ukrainian, and the failure of the Kyiv city authorities to keep to the approved plans for the expansion of the university. The rector declared that in no other capital of a Union republic did the local authorities display such indifference to the needs of their university as in Kyiv.[44]

The following month brought further disappointment. At a special CPSU Central Committee plenum in Moscow on education on 17-18 February, Gorbachev failed to respond to the calls from the Ukrainians and other non-Russians to bolster the status of their native languages and did not offer anything new in the sphere of nationalities policy. Apart from acknowledging that the national problem was a 'most fundamental and vital issue', the best he could come up with was to admit that the Party leadership should some day hold a special plenum devoted to nationalities policy.[45] Though the Kremlin leadership seemingly preferred to prevaricate in this

---

[44] *Ibid.*, 26 January 1988. The speeches were published in a summarized form.

[45] *Pravda*, 19 February 1988.

crucial area, the eruption of ethnic conflict in the Transcaucasus between Armenians and Azerbaijanis, and the growing national assertiveness of the Baltic élites, demonstrated the perils of continuing to delay dealing with the nationalities question.

5

NATIONAL RENEWAL

Facing up to the enormity of the task

With Shcherbytsky and the CPU leadership clinging to their reactionary positions, the tension in society increased. The forces for change grew stronger and bolder, forcing the defenders of the political status quo even more on the defensive. But the general political situation remained complex because the continuing struggle in Moscow between the conservatives and more liberal elements in the Party periodically seemed to place Gorbachev's new course in jeopardy. Furthermore, despite the flare-up of inter-ethnic strife at the end of February 1988 between Armenians and Azerbaijanis over the disputed territory of Nagornyi-Karabakh, the Gorbachev leadership was still not injecting any new thinking into its nationalities policy.

Although there was more and more talk of a new Ukrainian cultural revival, it was also evident that for many of those involved in bringing about a Ukrainian national regeneration the uncertainty about the scope and duration of *glasnost* and democratization reinforced the feeling that this might be the 'last chance' and the attitude of 'now or never'. Another reason for this was that with the advent of a measure of *glasnost*, the full scale of the damage that had been inflicted on Ukrainian culture and the sense of national identity was being exposed. The picture which was emerging was depressing, to say the least.

The material appearing in the more liberal press – especially in the various literary publications – revealed the virtual destruction of the Ukrainian cinema (in the 1920s Oleksandr Dovzhenko had been hailed as one of the world's best film directors and in the 1960s Ukrainian cinema had experienced a revival), the 'denationalization' of Ukrainian theatre, and the Russified and sorry state of Ukrainian television. On top of this, there were complaints in the press about such basic problems as the lack of typewriters with Ukrainian keyboards, the refusal of post offices in Ukraine to accept telegrams written in Ukrainian, the absence of a single record factory in the republic, the isolation of Ukraine's population from the large Ukrainian diaspora, including from the Ukrainians in the neighbouring 'Socialist' countries of Eastern Europe, and the total lack of any cultural facilities for the millions of Ukrainians living in other parts of the Soviet Union.

The writers themselves had to face up to questions and doubts about the quality and appeal of the Ukrainian literature which they had produced or were producing and the general perspectives for Ukrainian literature, especially in light of the challenge from Russian letters. Korotych, enjoying immense success in Moscow as the liberal editor of the revamped *Ogonek*, triggered off a heated debate on these issues by giving an outspoken interview in January 1988 to a Ukrainian newspaper in which he described contemporary Ukrainian writing as unexciting and unable to match the level being set by, say, leading Belarusian authors. He claimed that after years of complaining about censorship and bans, now that *glasnost* had been ushered in, Ukrainian writers were not coming forward with material they had written 'for the drawer'.[1] Korotych's provocative comments drew an angry response from other Ukrainian writers, who reminded him not only of the trials which Ukrainian literary and cultural life had had to endure, but also of how he had made a career for himself and won numerous awards during 'the years of stagnation'. What moral right, they asked, had he to judge his colleagues.[2]

Considerable attention was focused on the damage done to Ukrainian historical studies and national memory. The numerous blank pages were not restricted to the more recent periods. As the young Kharkiv-based scholar Yurii Isichenko now emphasized in print, 'the first eight centuries' of Ukraine's 'thousand-year-old literature' had been 'crossed out'.[3] Describing what had gone on after Shcherbytsky had replaced Shelest, the historical novelist

[1] *Molod Ukrainy*, 7 January 1988.

[2] See, for instance, the letter by four Ukrainian writers in *Literaturna Ukraina* of 21 January 1988. Just before he had left for Moscow, Korotych had been criticized by Drach at the Ninth Congress of the WUU for his 'demagogic divertissements' in connection with the Chornobyl disaster.

[3] *Prapor* (Kharkiv), no. 2, 1988, p. 169.

Roman Ivanychuk asserted that in 1973 a 'taboo was placed on all Ukrainian historiography and historical novels'.[4] How could one begin talking about national self-respect, the young philosopher and poet Oksana Zabuzhko asked, when there were no courses in 'Ukrainian history' in the schools.[5] In addition to this, the emphasis being placed by the Moscow Patriarchate on the 'Russian' dimension of the millennium of the Christianization of Kyivan Rus, and the enduring ban on the two Ukrainian 'national' churches – Autocephalous Orthodox and Catholic – did not help matters.

Not surprisingly, this impoverishment and provincialization of Ukrainian culture through the erasure of national memory, Russification, isolation from the outside world and the stigma of 'Ukrainian nationalism' had perpetuated 'Little Russianness' and what Dzyuba described as a 'complex of national inferiority' among millions of Ukrainians.[6] Ryabchuk provided a graphic example of this problem. Citing data from a survey recently carried out in the Kirovohrad region in central Ukraine by the republican Institute of Linguistics, he revealed that 68% of the region's urban population spoke Ukrainian at home, 24% spoke it outside the home with friends and colleagues, and only 12% used it for conducting official business. Decades of relentless assimilatory pressure, Ryabchuk pointed out, had subjected not only the Ukrainian language to 'severe erosion', but also national consciousness as such. 'A disdainful nihilistic attitude towards the Ukrainian language, culture, and history', he concluded, had 'become almost the norm for many of our denationalized fellow citizens'.[7]

What all this suggested was that nationally conscious Ukrainians had become a minority among their own people. Not only did many Ukrainians in the Russified southern and eastern regions of Ukraine no longer see any point in seeking a Ukrainian-language education for their children, but also a considerable number of them were even hostile to most things Ukrainian. 'Ukrainophobia among Ukrainians' was how the writer Volodymyr Bazilevsky was to describe the problem.[8] Another writer, Shcherbak, ventured in *Literaturnaya*

---

[4] *Kyiv*, no. 4, 1988, p. 119.

[5] *Prapor*, no. 3, 1988, p. 163.

[6] *Literaturna Ukraina*, 30 June 1988.

[7] *Sotsialistychna kultura*, no. 11, 1988, pp. 30–1.

[8] *Dnipro*, no. 2, 1989, p. 9.

gazeta that the main conflict in Ukraine was not between Ukrainians and 'outsiders', but between Ukrainians and 'Little Russians'.[9]

Assessing the state in which the Ukrainian nation found itself in the late 1980s, Drach concluded that after all the 'bone-breaking blows' that had been inflicted over the decades on its literature, culture and very soul, it was remarkable that it had survived at all.[10] But perhaps the most sober appraisal of the situation was offered by the literary critic Valerii Dyachenko. Unless, on the one hand, broad sectors of Ukrainian society recognized the seriousness of the Ukrainian nation's predicament and the need to withstand denationalization, and on the other, the Ukrainian authorities altered their negative attitude, the efforts of the nationally conscious cultural intelligentsia would resemble the 'work of Sisyphus'. What were needed, he stressed, were 'Heraclean feats' undertaken by a united people.[11]

Dzyuba was more concrete in pointing the way. Returning to some of the issues he had raised over twenty years earlier in *Internationalism or Russification*, he published a seminal article on 24 January 1988 in *Kultura i zhyttya* calling on his compatriots to think harder and more critically in philosophical and sociological terms about what constituted Ukrainian culture and how its structures were interrelated, and to begin conceptualizing it as a complete system. Otherwise, he argued, because of 'missing pieces' or 'links', caused through such factors as a distorted historical perspective and 'blank pages', the lack of contacts with the Ukrainian Western and Eastern diaspora, compartmentalization in the approach of the Cultural Unions, and 'purism assiduously limiting the sphere of Ukrainian cultural phenomena only to that which appears in the Ukrainian language', the notion of Ukrainian national culture would continue to be marred by 'incompleteness', resulting in a perpetuation of a faulty sense of its strengths and weaknesses.

The affirmation of national identity

However difficult, the process of national recovery had nevertheless now begun. Indeed, at the end of 1987 and during the first part

[9] *Literaturnaya gazeta*, 18 January 1989.

[10] *Ukraina*, no. 13, 1988, p. 9.

[11] *Prapor*, no. 5, 1988, pp. 151-70.

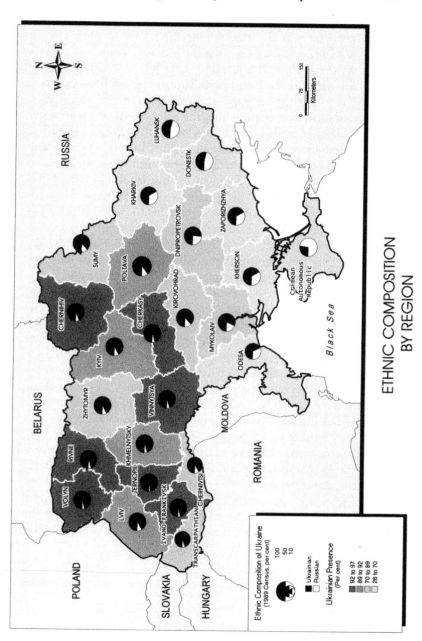

ETHNIC COMPOSITION
BY REGION

of 1988 a new vitality became apparent in Ukrainian cultural and public life. This was also the period when *glasnost*, albeit still far from complete, really began to take hold in Ukraine.

The Ukrainian Cultural Fund had by now established a republican network and with a full-time staff of fifty-nine was seeking to mobilize public support for the preservation of historical and cultural monuments, museums, the preparation of historical and cultural reference books, and efforts generally to revive historical memory and to encourage interest in local history, customs and folklore. Among the tasks which the organization set itself was to seek the return of all items of cultural and historical value which 'for one reason or another' had been removed from Ukraine.[12]

In December and January, the writers held important meetings at which their assessment of Ukraine's experience during seven decades of Soviet rule contrasted sharply with the picture that Shcherbytsky presented. The first, held in the middle of December in Kharkiv, the city which had been the capital of Soviet Ukraine during the dynamic 1920s, was a conference devoted to the theme 'Great October, Restructuring, Literature'. Radio Kyiv's reporter commented that he had never heard such 'forthright, sharp, and constructive' discussions among the literati and that they had focused their attention 'on the most important things' – 'historical truth', the 'revival of national traditions', 'civic consciousness' and the role of the writers in the restructuring process.[13] A few days later, at a joint meeting of the Board of the WUU and the Learned Council of the Institute of Literature to discuss Soviet Ukrainian literature of the 1920s and 1930s, the writers raised to a new level their campaign for the rehabilitation of the architects of the Ukrainian national renaissance of the 1920s. Emphasizing that far from flourishing, as the official line stated, during most of the Soviet period Ukrainian literature and culture had in fact been trammelled, the writers called for a new truthful history of Ukrainian literature and decided to push ahead with the publication of the works of the major literary figures of the 1920s.[14]

[12] Oliinyk, 'Cultural Fund'. For a more detailed description of the work of the Ukrainian Cultural Fund, see the article by B. Bilyashivsky in *Sotsialistychna kultura*, no. 2, 1988, pp. 26-8.

[13] Stanislav Soldatenko, Radio Kyiv, 18 December 1987. For details of the speeches, see *Literaturna Ukraina*, 31 December 1987.

[14] *Literaturna Ukraina*, 21 January 1988.

By focusing on the 1920s the writers not only drew attention to a suppressed heritage but also reopened the main issues of the great political and cultural debate of 1925-8: relations with Russia and Europe, Ukrainization and its tempo and goals, freedom of speech and the principle of free competition between literary groups.[15] All of these questions which had preoccupied the Ukrainian intelligentsia during the 1920s were still very relevant. During February and early March, *Literaturna Ukraina* ran a four-part series by Nataliya Kuzyakina which provided much interesting information about the context in which the literary discussion of the 1920s took place. On 24 May, the Creative Association of Critics of the Kyiv section of the WUU devoted a meeting to this subject which was also given prominent coverage by *Literaturna Ukraina*.[16]

For the writers, however, the 1920s were only the thin end of the wedge in their assault on the CPU's interpretation of Ukrainian history. On 28 January 1988, that is, less than a week after Shcherbytsky had enjoined the Party organizations within the republic's Creative Unions to exercise more control, the deputy secretary of the Party organization of the Kyiv branch of the WUU who, moreover, was responsible for ideological questions, delivered a bombshell. Addressing a meeting of his branch's Party organization on the theme 'The Writer and Restructuring', Oleksa Musiyenko presented a totally different account of the Soviet period from what Shcherbytsky, or for that matter, even Gorbachev, had recently put forward. In fact, what he had to say amounted to the most outspoken and critical speech in living memory from a Ukrainian Communist official. Moreover, in another dramatic sign of the times, the speech did not have to be disseminated in *samvydav* but was reproduced in *Literaturna Ukraina* on 18 February, filling almost two full pages.

Although Musiyenko, a fifty-three-year-old writer from Poltava, did not challenge the Leninist foundations of the Soviet system, his depiction of Stalin and his heirs and the consequences of their policies for Ukraine was boldly unorthodox. Portraying Stalin as a ruthless dictator and 'monster' who began his autocratic ways almost immediately after Lenin's death in 1924, Musiyenko described in

---

[15] On this, see Myroslav Shkandrij, 'The Twenties Revisited', *Soviet Ukrainian Affairs*, no. 4 (1987), pp. 5-7 and 'New Line on Soviet Ukrainian Literature?', *Soviet Ukrainian Affairs*, no. 1 (1988), pp. 2-3.

[16] *Literaturna Ukraina*, 30 June 1988.

graphic detail how he had destroyed the political and cultural élite of the Ukrainian nation and precipitated the 'mass famine' of 1933. The writer also emphasized that Skrypnyk had been one of the first to 'protest openly against the deformation of socialism and the establishment of an autocratic regime', and argued that Stalin had never forgiven the Ukrainian Communist leader for challenging him on the nationalities policy and standing up to him in the name of Leninist principles. Skrypnyk's suicide had been a 'demonstrative protest' and warning against Stalinism. Yet, for some reason, Musiyenko pointed out, Skrypnyk – 'one of Ukraine's foremost sons – and 'a whole legion' of Ukrainian political and culture figures who became victims of the Stalin terror continued to remain discredited nonpersons long after Stalin's death. 'For whom was the silencing, distortion, and even falsification of many pages of our fatherland's history convenient?' the writer asked.

Musiyenko did not limit himself to the Stalin era. He criticized Khrushchev for the inconsistencies and half-measures inherent in the de-Stalinization that he had launched and described him as a crude 'green-eyed product of his times' who attempted to 'ride two horses simultaneously that were pulling in different directions'. As for the Brezhnev years, the writer said that during this period the 'administrative-command structures' that had formed during the Stalin era had been 'renewed, together with the administrative-command style of leadership, [and] the *diktat* of the bureaucratic functionary apparatus'. It became the heyday for all manner of 'lackeys' and 'careerists' as a new 'cult of personality' arose and was emulated by officials at the regional and district levels. Democracy and respect for the law were supplanted by lawlessness, corruption, nepotism, exploitation, a disregard for ecological factors and embezzlement and theft on a grand scale. In such conditions, Musiyenko reminded his colleagues, even such a well-known and respected writer as Honchar was given short shrift for exercising his civic duty as a writer and speaking out. Alluding to the dissidents and political prisoners, Musiyenko also stressed that the stigma of 'bourgeois nationalism' was used as a weapon against those 'who had the natural gift of critical thinking and who were sincerely concerned about the fate of their land and their people'.

Musiyenko concluded his remarkable speech with a series of recommendations to his fellow writers. At this crucial time, he declared, Ukraine's writers were called upon to fulfil their traditional role of serving their nation by becoming 'the mouthpiece of *glasnost*' and implacable opponents of all vestiges of Stalinism. But in order to do this, he stressed, 'we should first cleanse ourselves of the nucleons of slavery that have eaten their way even into the cellular tissue of our bones, of the slime of conscious deception, of fear, servility and a lack of self-esteem'. Musiyenko called on the writers to concentrate on campaigning for the full rehabilitation of all the Ukrainian writers who had become victims of political repression and who had not yet been rehabilitated, and on the removal of all the blank pages in their nation's history. He ended by pointing out that at this time, when all sorts of new unofficial groups were appearing and new creative associations were being formed within the Cultural Unions, there was a danger of the fragmentation of the forces supporting restructuring and democratization: unity and the consolidation of these forces, Musiyenko stressed, was therefore essential.

Musiyenko's speech, with its emphasis on Skrypnyk and his legacy, indicated that despite the political and cultural purges which had been carried out in Ukraine under Shcherbytsky, the tradition of Ukrainian 'national Communism', at least among some of the writers, had lived on. Further evidence of the resilience of this tradition was provided by the publication in January and February of hitherto suppressed autobiographical writings by Volodymyr Sosyura, one of the century's outstanding Ukrainian poets, who had been in Petlyura's army, as a Communist taken part in the literary renaissance of the 1920s, survived severe criticism in the Stalin era and died in official favour in 1965. The newly published poems and autobiographical novel[17] revealed Sosyura's enduring Ukrainian patriotism and his candid views on some of the blank spots in modern Ukrainian history. For instance, Sosyura's autobiographical novel *Tretya rota* (The Third Company) included the following lines which had a special significance in 1988, the year in which the Russian Orthodox Church was laying claim to the entire thousand-year-old heritage dating from the Christianization of Kyivan Rus:

Russian autocracy, having taken as a helper a terrible ally – Orthodoxy – reduced our people (over almost three hundred years) to such a state that it forgot its name (we were forbidden

[17] See *Ukraina*, no. 1, 1988, pp. 7-9, and *Kyiv*, no. 1, 1988, pp. 63-122, and no. 2, 1988, pp. 69-122.

to pray in churches in our own language, not to mention [the ban on Ukrainian in] schools), and when Ukrainians were asked who they were, there was only one terrible response – Orthodox.[18]

The writers' campaign to recover Ukrainian history began to bear fruit in quite a few areas. In the first weeks of 1988, a series of articles appeared about the leading historian of the Ukrainian Cossacks, Yavornytsky, which were soon followed by the serialization in the Lviv literary monthly *Zhovten* of his classic history of the Zaporozhyan Cossacks.[19] Even more encouraging was the first indication that the official attitude towards Hrushevsky was softening, at least in some quarters. On 12 February *Izvestiya* published an article by its Kyiv correspondent announcing that after 'half a century' Hrushevsky's works had become accessible again to scholars in the Ukrainian capital. The article provided a biographical sketch of the historian and a glowing appraisal of his achievements by the directory of the Institute of Archaeology of the Ukrainian Academy of Science, Petro Tolochko.[20]

That some month *Literaturnaya gazeta*'s Kyiv correspondent reported that the process of removing the blank pages in modern Ukrainian history had finally got underway.[21] Indeed, during the next few months, *Literaturna Ukraina* alone was to publish articles on Drahomanov and the national Communists Khvylovy, Shumsky and Yurii Kotsyubynsky.

The growing national assertiveness of the Ukrainian writers, as indeed of the non-Russian literati generally, was demonstrated at the beginning of March at a plenum of the Soviet Writers' Union in Moscow. This time Oliinyk reminded the delegates that 'from the time that the Zaporozhyan Sich was abolished and destroyed by Catherine II until October 1917, Ukrainians, not just on one occasion, have been deprived of the right to be themselves' and were only 'permitted to pass themselves off as Little Russians'. Even now, he pointed out, they were still being subjected to Russification

---

[18] *Kyiv*, no. 2, 1988, p. 107.

[19] See *Ukraina*, nos 1, 2, 4, and 5, 1988, and *Zhovten*, no. 4, 1988.

[20] S. Sikora, 'K chitatelyu cherez polveka' [To the Reader after Half a Century], *Izvestiya*, 12 February 1988.

[21] K. Grigorev, 'Rukopisi ne goryat' [Manuscripts do not Burn], *Literaturnaya gazeta*, 10 February 1988.

under the guise of internationalism. His colleague Lubkivsky also spoke out strongly in defence of the non-Russian languages and condemned the falsification of the histories of the non-Russians and the 'excessive centralization of culture, sciences, education [and] publishing', as well as Moscow's 'unfamiliarity' with the 'values' of the diverse peoples of the USSR.

A new note was also creeping in – open criticism of Russian tutelage and imperial attitudes. In his speech at the plenum, for example, Lubkivsky took the Russian television moderator Genrikh Borovikh to task for being 'tactless' and 'patronizing' in his treatment of problems connected with national relations. He also rebuked an unnamed 'well-known Russian writer and editor of an all-Union journal' for making the 'strange and absurd claim' at the plenum that anti-Russian attitudes were being whipped up in Ukraine. Lubkivsky pointed out that Ukraine had 'from time immemorial' been a 'mother, and not a stepmother' for various ethnic groups and went on to suggest that whereas the rights of the Russians were well catered for, more should be done – as had been the case during the period of Ukrainization – to provide better cultural facilities for some of the other groups, such as Jews, Bulgarians and Czechs. At the same time, however, he emphasized that Ukrainians themselves were forced to campaign in their own homeland to safeguard their own cultural rights and language and to be allowed to establish contacts with the Ukrainian minorities in Eastern Europe.[22]

Ryabchuk, too, came out with another provocative article which appeared in May in *Druzhba narodov*. In it he dealt with the perpetuation of the 'Little Russian image' of Ukrainians in Russian society. He claimed that even well educated Russians 'know practically nothing about Ukraine' and its history and culture. Consequently, as a result of this ignorance and what he called 'the poison' from Russian imperialistic 'propaganda and historiography', on the one hand a stereotype of the Ukrainians as 'Little Russians' persisted, while on the other Ukrainian culture was 'being robbed of such names as [the composers] Vedel, Bortnyansky and Berezovsky, [the painters] Levytsky and Borovykovsky, [the philologist] Potebnya

---

[22] See *Literaturnaya gazeta*, 9 March 1988. The full text of Lubkivsky's speech was published in *Zhovten*, no. 7, 1988, pp. 106–8. On 5 March 1988 *Izvestiya* had also reported that a well-known Russian writer had expressed concern at the plenum that anti-Russian feeling in Ukraine was on the rise.

and [the Orientalist] Krymsky, [the geochemist and mineralogist] Vernadsky and [the aeronautical engineer] Korolev'.

Ryabchuk went on to accuse the Russian intelligentsia of generally being insensitive to, and even disinterested in, the problems and demands of the non-Russians. Citing as an example how the Soviet media had treated the Kazakh protests in Alma-Ata, he emphasized that:

> Scarcely a single Russian took the blame for what happened. And yet the blame was, and is there. It is there because hundreds of thousands of Russians don't know – and don't consider it important to know – the languages of the peoples among whom they live.

It was essential, he argued to change the approach to national relations and base it on 'a cultured appreciation of national sensibilities' and 'respect for everyone'.

During the spring, the 125th anniversary of the birth of the distinguished scientist Volodymyr Vernadsky, whom the world knew primarily as the 'Russian' Vladimir Vernadsky, was celebrated, and provided another occasion for Ukrainians to reclaim more of their suppressed heritage. Ukrainian publications carried hitherto unpublished material revealing Vernadsky (who in fact had been the first president of the Ukrainian Academy of Sciences) to have been a Ukrainian patriot.[23] In particular, the appearance of Vernadsky's essay entitled 'The Ukrainian Question and Russian Public Opinion',[24] which he apparently wrote in 1915, caused quite a stir. In it, Vernadsky had expressed his disappointment with the Russian democratic intelligentsia for its lack of understanding and sympathy for the Ukrainian national movement, or indifference to Ukrainian national grievances and aspirations. The scientist had emphasized that Ukrainians viewed restrictions on their educational and cultural life as 'a crime against universal human rights' and that they were

---

[23] See Olena Apanovych, 'I Iyubov do Ukrainy yednala nas' [And Love for Ukraine United Us], *Literaturna Ukraina*, 10 March 1988, and 'Chytach – Akademik Vernadskyi' [The Reader – Academician Vernadsky], *Vitchyzna*, no. 3, 1988, pp. 194-201. In the latter article, Apanovych emphasized that much of Vernadsky's unpublished writings, such as the diaries which he kept on and off for almost seventy years, had not been accessible to researchers in the archives of the USSR Academy of Sciences where they were kept.

[24] The essay was first published in the Kyiv Komsomol daily, *Moloda hvardiya*, on 12 March 1988; it subsequently also appeared in *Vitchyzna*, no. 6, 1988.

seeking to exercise their 'right to national and cultural self-determination', that is, to 'unhindered activity in the spheres of education, science, literature and public life', the 'Ukrainization of local community and religious life', and 'self-government'.

For readers in 1988, Vernadsky's essay brought home the extent to which after seven decades of Soviet rule, and despite 'Soviet Ukraine's' trappings of sovereign statehood, the Ukrainians were forced to return to essentially the same basic issues as before the collapse of the Russian Empire. This parallel was also apparent from some of the new societies which began to appear in the first half of 1988. Just as in the liberal interlude after 1905 *Prosvita* (Enlightenment) societies had sprung up in Russian-ruled Ukraine to promote Ukrainian cultural self-awareness, so now, ironically, Ukrainian language societies began to be formed to improve the status of the Ukrainian language.

Searching for ways to break the impasse with the authorities on the language issue, in February 1988 the writers supported a proposal by the director of the Institute of Linguistics of the Ukrainian Academy of Sciences, Academician Vitalii Rusanivsky, to establish a 'Ukrainian Language Society'.[25] Behind the scenes, though, the authorities pressured the writers to call it a 'Native Language' rather than 'Ukrainian Language' Society. Nevertheless, that same month, one of the first Ukrainian language societies to be organized was set up in Donetsk.[26] The creation of such societies allowed the writers and other patriotic activists to begin harnessing popular support for the campaign in defence of Ukrainian cultural rights; gradually, it also helped to provide a broader infrastructure for this movement.

With the aim of raising the prestige of the Ukrainian language, the writers also began organizing 'Ukrainian language festivals', the first republican one being held in May in Poltava. These efforts to improve the standing of the Ukrainian language readily found a resonance in Western Ukraine, where the problem was not so serious as elsewhere; therefore, the writers' leaders seem to have consciously focused their attention on central and Eastern Ukraine. In mid-May, the main annual celebrations of the birth of the

---

[25] *Literaturna Ukraina*, 2 February 1988. There was an enthusiastic response to this proposal. See the survey of letters supporting it in *Literaturna Ukraina* of 21 July 1988.

[26] *Silski visti*, 18 February 1988.

Ukrainian national bard Taras Shevchenko were held in Kharkiv; Kirovohrad was chosen to host the second republican Ukrainian language festival in September.

All this, of course, did not pass unnoticed in Moscow, which by now had to contend with similar campaigns by the literary élites in other republics, including Belarus and Moldova, in defence of the native language. Oliinyk was later to reveal, for example, that Honchar's letter to Gorbachev was not ignored and was instrumental in getting the Kremlin to send its representatives to investigate the situation in the republic. He mentions several commissions of the Central Committee of the CPSU which were dispatched to Ukraine, apparently during 1988, and which took a particular interest in the language issue and ecological problems.[27]

Confronted, on the one hand, with the growing strength of the Ukrainian national revival and, on the other, with the Kremlin's acknowledgement that more attention had to be paid to the national question, the Kyiv authorities sought to appear more responsive. In April, the Ukrainian Supreme Soviet established a Commission for Patriotic and Internationalist Education and for Inter-Ethnic Relations.[28] This was hardly a bold move though, for similar commissions had first been set up in Kazakhstan and Latvia a full year earlier. Kravchuk, the ideological official, who was also a deputy in the Supreme Soviet, was made chairman of the commission.

Independent public and religious activity

Meanwhile, independent public and religious life also continued to develop. Undaunted by the old-style attacks on them in the press, Chornovil and Horyn sought to create a new organization which would campaign for human and national rights in the open and base its activity on international human rights norms. At the end of December 1987, they and other members of the editorial board of *The Ukrainian Herald* issued appeals addressed to Western governments and human rights organizations in which they described the harassment to which they were being subjected and

---

[27] See Oliinyk's speech on 1 November 1988 at a meeting of the Communist members of the Kyiv section of the WUU in *Literaturna Ukraina*, 10 November 1988.

[28] *Pravda Ukrainy*, 19 April 1988.

explained that through their journal and other activity they were seeking to revive the Ukrainian Helsinki Monitoring Group.[29]

The following month, two Ukrainian representatives travelled to Yerevan to take part with Armenian and Georgian representatives in a meeting of a newly formed Inter-National Committee in Defence of Political Prisoners. The participants issued statements calling on representatives of other nationalities to join forces with them and proposing a series of 'minimal' reforms designed to foster the overhaul of the official nationalities policy. This meeting and the documents which it produced represented the first attempt outside the camps and prisons by former non-Russian political prisoners to form a common front against Moscow's imperial rule.[30]

A few weeks later, the visit to Kyiv of the British Foreign Secretary Sir Geoffrey Howe provided Ukrainian activists with an important opportunity to expose the limitations of democratization and *glasnost* in Ukraine and to publicize their demands. On 17 February they succeeded in handing an open letter addressed to the British foreign minister to a British journalist who was accompanying him. The document, signed by ten 'representatives of the independent Ukrainian community', including members of the Ukrainian Culturological Club and the editorial board of *The Ukrainian Herald*, invoked the provisions of the Helsinki Final Act and asked for support on such issues as: securing the release of members of the Ukrainian Helsinki Monitoring Group, who were still serving sentences, as well as other Ukrainian prisoners of conscience; removing the ban on the Ukrainian Catholic and Ukrainian Autocephalous Orthodox Churches; guaranteeing genuine freedom of expression in Ukraine and ending the official harassment of unofficial groups and publications; and ensuring conditions for the free development of Ukrainian culture and functioning of the Ukrainian language. Significantly, the signatories also demonstrated that, like the founders of the Ukrainian Helsinki Monitoring Group, they were also anxious to reduce Ukraine's international isolation: they urged the British authorities to consider opening a consulate in Kyiv and inaugurating broadcasts in Ukrainian by the BBC World Service.[31]

---

[29] Ukrainian Press Agency (UPA) Press Releases, no. 6, 22 January 1988, and no. 15, 4 February 1988.

[30] See Bohdan Nahaylo, 'Representatives of Non-Russian National Movements Establish Coordinating Committee', RL 283/88, 22 June 1988.

On the same day Hel brought a new petition to Moscow calling for the legalization of the Ukrainian Catholic Church; it was signed by 5,450 people. Although the Soviet authorities refused to accept it, Hel told the Moscow correspondent of *Il Messagero* that the Ukrainian Catholics would continue gathering signatures and would pass on their demands 'to the Pope through diplomatic channels'. Describing the rapid growth of Ukrainian Catholic activity which was taking place despite harassment by the police, Hel informed the Italian newspaper that in the Lviv region alone there were some 300 Ukrainian Catholic priests and a secret seminary. Three bishops, including the first hierarch of the Ukrainian Catholic Church in Ukraine, Archbishop Volodymyr Sternyuk, had now emerged from the underground while another five were still awaiting more certain times. He also announced that in January the Ukrainian Catholics had begun publishing a new journal – *Khrystiyanskyi holos* (Christian Voice) and that they were preparing for a large-scale celebration in the open in the summer of the millennium of 'Christianity in Ukraine'.[32]

The campaign of the Ukrainian Catholics for the legalization of their church was also beginning to find sympathy and support in the West. On 14 February, Ukrainian Catholics were heartened when, in connection with the millennium of the Christianization of Kyivan Rus, Pope John Paul II addressed a special letter to the Ukrainian Catholic Church praising the courage it had shown in remaining loyal to its faith.[33] What was even more encouraging, though, for Ukrainian Christians generally was that during his visit to Kyiv Sir Geoffrey Howe declared that he looked forward to the day when 'Ukrainian Christians' would be 'enabled to practice their religion with freedom and with pride'.[34]

New unofficial groups and publications, some of which clearly followed the example of the Ukrainian Culturological Club and *The Ukrainian Herald*, continued to appear throughout the republic. In

[31] UPA Press Release, no. 36, 28 February 1988.

[32] *Il Messagero*, 18 February 1988; and UPA Press Release, no. 37, 28 February 1988.

[33] Message *Magnum Baptismi Donum* of the Supreme Pontiff John Paul II to Ukrainian Catholics on the Occasion of the Millennium of the Baptism of Kyivan Rus, Rome, 14 February 1988.

[34] Rupert Cornwell, 'Sir Geoffrey Pleads for Ukrainian Christians', *Independent*, 18 February 1988.

mid-February, *Radyanska Ukraina* commented that 'the politicization of clubs and associations attested to the growth of social activity
among the youth.' It also mentioned, among others, a new society
in Kyiv devoted to the protection of the capital's historic and
architectural monuments called Spadshchyna (Heritage), which it
said had over forty members, and a discussion group at Kyiv
University called Danko.[35] Soon afterwards, university students in
Kyiv formed a society called Hromada (Community), which concerned itself with the defence of Ukrainian historical monuments
and the environment. One of its first actions was to organize a
meeting demanding that the buildings of the celebrated Kyivan
Mohyla Academy be restored and protected, and that a naval
political school be removed from its premises.[36] This issue had been
raised a few months earlier by members of the Ukrainian Culturological Club.

Discussion and debating groups were also springing up in
Ukraine's cities. By the spring of 1988, meetings in Lviv to discuss
political topics were drawing hundreds. At two such gatherings in
March, Mykhailo Horyn argued that 'real democracy is only possible
under a multi-party system' and that 'without economic freedom
there cannot be civil and political freedom'.[37] That same month,
Chornovil and Horyn announced the formation of a human rights
organization, which they called the Ukrainian Helsinki Union
(UHU). In order to emphasize that it was a continuation in a new
form of the Ukrainian Helsinki Monitoring Group, one of the
latter's founding members, Levko Lukyanenko (who was still in
internal exile in the Tomsk region) was named as its head.[38] The
original leader, Rudenko, had left for the West after being freed at
the end of 1987.[39]

---

[35] L. Ostrolutska and M. Doroshenko, 'Formulyary . . . "heformalam"' [Formulas
for "informals"], *Radyanska Ukraina*, 7 February 1988. In fact, 'Danko' was founded
a lot earlier, and its activities had been discussed by S. Pravdenko in *Radyanska
Ukraina* on 5 June 1987.

[36] For details about this society, see Taras Kuzio, 'Unofficial and Semi-Official
Groups and Samizdat Publications in Ukraine' in Romana M. Bahry (ed.), *Echoes
of Glasnost in Soviet Ukraine*, Toronto, 1989, pp. 75–7; and Olena Yashchenko,
'Demokratiya "zadnim chyslom"' [Backdated Democracy], *Molod Ukrainy*, 8
December 1988.

[37] UPA Press Release, no. 71, 21 April 1988.

[38] See Kuzio, 'Unofficial and Semi-Official Groups', p. 68.

The revival of Ukrainian national self-confidence and assertive-ness was also becoming detectable among Ukrainians living beyond the borders of Ukraine in other parts of the Soviet Union. On 3 March 1988, *Literaturna Ukraina* published 'An Appeal to the Citizenry of Ukraine' from fifty-five residents of Leningrad, includ-ing prominent Russians, who announced that they wanted to re-establish the Taras Shevchenko Society (which was first founded in the city in 1898) and to press for the erection of a Shevchenko monument there (such a project had been approved in 1918 but never realized). The following month, Ukrainians in Moscow organized the 'Slavutych' Ukrainian Cultural Society to serve as a focal point for the many Ukrainians residing in the Soviet capital.[40]

While this process of national renewal was getting under way in Ukraine, the general political climate in the Soviet Union remained unsettled. The bloodshed in the Transcaucasus and the ensuing mass protests in Armenia, to which Moscow responded by sending troops into Yerevan on 24 March, was bad enough. But in the middle of it all, on 13 March, while Gorbachev was about to begin a visit to Yugoslavia, *Sovetskaya Rossiya* published the notorious 'open letter' written ostensibly by a certain Nina Andreeva attacking 'left-wing liberal intellectual socialism' and defending Stalin, 'Great Russian national pride', and traditional Soviet values. The Leningrad schoolteacher's letter, which evidently had Ligachev's blessing, was widely interpreted as a rallying call by the conservatives. For almost three weeks it went unchallenged until on 5 April *Pravda* finally denounced it as a 'manifesto of the anti-*perestroika* forces'.

The victory in this particular battle by the reformist forces in Moscow brought little change to Ukraine. If anything, news of the dismissal of Tanyuk from his position at the Kyiv Youth Theatre at the beginning of April suggested that here the clock was being turned back, not forward. On 26 April – the month in which the Ukrainian literary monthly *Vsesvit* became the first publication in the Soviet Union to publish extracts from George Orwell's classic anti-totalitarian novel *1984* – the authorities in Kyiv once again demonstrated their determination not to allow *glasnost* and the

---

[39] See the author's interview with Rudenko taken shortly after his arrival in the West in *Index on Censorship*, no. 5, 1988, pp. 11–13.

[40] See Roman Solchanyk, 'Ukrainians in Moscow and Leningrad Organize', RL 396/88, 5 September 1988.

revival of independent public activity to get out of control. When, on the second anniversary of the Chornobyl nuclear disaster, the Ukrainian Culturological Club attempted to hold a peaceful anti-nuclear demonstration in the centre of the Ukrainian capital, the gathering was roughly dispersed by plainclothes and uniformed police. Seventeen of the approximately fifty participants were detained, and one of them, Oles Shevchenko, was sentenced to fifteen days of so-called administrative arrest. Although the protest was quickly broken up and placards that read 'Nuclear Power Plants Out of Ukraine' and 'Openness and Democracy to the End' ripped from the demonstrators by the police, it marked the first unsanctioned political demonstration in Kyiv since the mid 1960s.[41]

The protest was also an indication of something else. While the demonstration had been going on, the Writers' Union had hosted a public meeting of their own to mark the Chornobyl anniversary. But, as a British professor who was present at it observed, there appeared to be 'some disappointment that the meeting had not been more outspoken', especially as the participants were informed that the police had broken up the protest in the city centre and detained the demonstrators.[42] Clearly, the new independent forces which had appeared in Ukraine during the last months were more radical and militant than the writers, and this only reflected the general tendency towards politicization among the Soviet Union's numerous and multifarious unofficial groups. Now, all of a sudden, it seemed that those who had led the campaign to raise national and social consciousness and defend Ukraine's cultural rights were going to be faced with the choice of either moving with the times or being left behind.

---

[41] AP, 27 April 1988. Although the protesters were branded 'extremists' in the local press, interestingly, the English-language weekly produced by Kyiv for Ukrainians living in the West, *News from Ukraine*, carried an unusually objective account of the demonstration (no. 21, 1988). On this, and the other accounts of the protest, see Roman Solchanyk, 'Soviet Press Reports on Antinuclear Demonstration in Kyiv', RL 249/88, 8 June 1988.

[42] Geoffrey A. Hosking, 'A Public Meeting About Chernobyl; or *Glasnost* in Kyiv', *Index on Censorship*, no. 6, 1988.

6

THE GROWTH OF DEMOCRATIC
OPPOSITION

Baltic echoes

As the crucial Nineteenth Party Conference approached, the political struggle in Moscow intensified. It also raised hopes and further stimulated independent political activity. Throughout the Soviet Union, conservative forces battled to keep the reformists at bay and to prevent the selection of democratically minded delegates to the conference. Indeed, the conservative resistance was so strong that the elections, scheduled for April, were delayed for six weeks. Even then, charges of ballot-rigging abounded, making a mockery of the supposed shift towards more democratic elections. The dissatisfaction with this state of affairs precipitated the first attempts to form mass grass-roots movements for genuine democratization and reform – the so-called popular democratic fronts.

The need for new independent organizations which would mobilize the public behind Gorbachev's restructuring drive was increasingly recognized during the first half of 1988 by leading Russian reformist intellectuals, such as Boris Kurashvili and Tatyana Zaslavskaya. They realized that the reformers in the Party would not be able to defeat the conservatives with the help of the liberal intelligentsia alone, and therefore began calling on the public to lend its support by organizing popular unions, or fronts, to promote restructuring.[1]

Zaslavskaya, interviewed in *Izvestiya* on 4 June, pointed to the example already being set by the Estonians, who were the first to demonstrate how powerful a force for change popular fronts could be. In mid-April, Estonian reformists and nationally minded Com-

---

[1] See Bill Keller, 'Gorbachev Adviser Urges "Popular Front" as Alternative Party', *Washington Post*, 24 May 1988.

128

munist intellectuals announced the formation of an Estonian Popular Front in Support of Restructuring. Carefully avoiding calling itself a political party, it acted as a loyal opposition to the Estonian Communist Party and literally within weeks grew into a mass grass-roots movement for democratization and republican sovereignty. The Lithuanians set up their own popular movement – Sajudis – on 3 June, and later that month the Latvians also began to organize an analogous Latvian Popular Front.

The response in Ukraine to the initial Estonian initiatives in early April was surprisingly prompt. Within weeks of the Council of Estonian Cultural Unions adopting two radical resolutions which, in connection with the forthcoming Nineteenth Party Conference, demanded the decentralization of the USSR and broad political, economic and cultural autonomy for the republics, the Ukrainian cultural workers' weekly *Kultura i zhyttya* suggested on its front page that a similar independent cultural council should be established in Ukraine. The proposal seems to have been quashed behind the scenes, for there was no follow-up to this implicit call to emulate the Estonians. The newspaper also broke new ground by asking readers to comment on the election of delegates to the Party conference and by suggesting that those who were chosen to go to Moscow familiarize themselves with what had appeared in the press on Ukrainian national issues.[2]

By this time, the political ferment throughout the Soviet Union was manifesting itself in a wave of protest meetings and the appearance of the first openly political opposition groups. In the first half of May, representatives from various 'informal groups' met in Moscow to form a united front – the Democratic Union – which they saw as an 'alternative political party' committed to ending the Communist Party's monopoly on power. Though it consisted mainly of Russians, this new coalition also included several representatives from Ukraine. Among other things, the Democratic Union recognized the rights of all nations to self-determination and proposed that the USSR be turned into a democratic confederation. During the second half of the month there were demonstrations about the undemocratic way in which delegates to the Party

---

[2] 'Bilshe demokratii i hlasnosti' [More democracy and openness], *Kultura i zhyttya*, 8 May 1988.

Conference were being selected in cities as far apart as Odesa in Ukraine and Sverdlovsk and Omsk in Russia.

While all this was going on, Ukrainian activists were given an unexpected boost from another quarter. During President Reagan's visit to the Soviet Union, five of them were invited to a reception in Moscow on 28 May given by the American president for Soviet dissidents, and Chornovil ended up sitting next to him. Two days later, in a speech at the Danilovsky Monastery before Russian Orthodox hierarchs, Reagan spoke out in defence of the Ukrainian Catholic and Ukrainian Autocephalous Orthodox Churches.[3] To add to the Moscow Patriarchate's and the Kremlin's discomfort, on 3 June Sakharov publicly condemned the 'archaic' ban on the Ukrainian Catholic Church, pointing out that it damaged the international prestige of the USSR.[4] This, and the absence of Pope John Paul II from the official celebrations of the millennium of the Christianization of Kyivan Rus, drew more international attention to the situation in Ukraine and Ukrainian national aspirations. The first sign that the pressure from both inside and outside Ukraine was having some effect appeared the very next day when the Russian Orthodox Metropolitan of Kyiv and Halychyna, Filaret, an implacable foe of both the Ukrainian Catholic and Autocephalous Orthodox Churches, acknowledged at a press conference in Kyiv that the issue of the Ukrainian Catholic Church was indeed an obstacle to better relations with the Vatican and announced that Russian Orthodox officials would shortly be holding talks on the status of the Ukrainian Catholic Church with representatives of the Vatican.[5]

On 5 June, activists from the Ukrainian Culturological Club held an unofficial commemoration of the religious jubilee in Kyiv by the statue of Saint Volodymyr, who had introduced Christianity to Kyivan Rus. Some 200 people attended and heard renewed calls for religious freedom and for more truthful accounts of Ukraine's history. The meeting was not dispersed.

That same day, however, one of the first demonstrations sanctioned by the authorities was held in the Ukrainian capital by members of the growing 'Green' movement to protest about the

[3] USIS transcript of President Reagan's speech, 30 May 1988.

[4] Reuter, 3 June 1988.

[5] Reuter and AP, 4 June 1988.

felling of trees in the city's Holosiivskiy Wood. The defenders of the environment were joined on their march through the city centre to the First of May Park, where a public meeting took place, by democratically minded individuals and representatives of various informal clubs and societies. The gathering provided an opportunity for the city's diverse unofficial activists to meet and begin forging a coalition. Indeed, it was at this ecological protest that the call for the creation of a 'Popular Union to Support Restructuring', only just delivered by Zaslavkaya in Moscow, was first publicly advocated in the Ukrainian capital.[6]

Four days later, a meeting of representatives of some of the capital's unofficial groups was held at which the 'Popular Union' was launched. Some 500 people are reported to have attended the inaugural meeting.[7] The leaders of the new democratic umbrella organization included Oleksandr Yemets and Oleksandr Zoryanov, both of whom were research workers at an institute of the Ministry of Internal Affairs with the ranks of captain, and Aleksandr Sheikin, who was elected head of the organizing committee. As Yemets put it: 'We were naively romantic in our desire to help Gorbachev in what we saw as a struggle against the conservative bureaucracy.'[8]

On 22 June, the new democratic pressure group held a meeting with several of the officially nominated delegates to the Party conference from Kyiv, including Oliinyk. During the session, which was chaired by Yemets, a lawyer and psychologist by training, delegates were quizzed by the public about their position on a broad range of issues ranging from the status of the Ukrainian language to ecological questions. Speakers called for some delegates to be stripped of their mandates because of their non-democratic attitudes. Thus, for instance, the mayor of Kyiv, Valentyn Zhursky, was criticized for allowing the demonstration on the second anniversary of the Chornobyl disaster to be broken up, and Masyk, the city's Party boss, was castigated for his hostility towards unofficial groups and his advocacy of stricter ideological controls. Interestingly, in the

---

[6] O.V. Haran, *Ubyty Drakona: Z istorii Rukhu ta novykh partii na Ukraini* ' [To Kill the Dragon: From the History of Rukh and New Parties in Ukraine], hereafter referred to as *To Kill the Dragon*, Kyiv, 1993, p. 16; and the author's interview with Oleksandr Yemets, Ebenhausen, Germany, 5 October 1993.

[7] *Russkaya Mysl*, 24 June and 15 July, 1988.

[8] Author's interview with Yemets.

account of this meeting which appeared in *News from Ukraine*, the official newspaper for Ukrainians abroad, it was also revealed that an ecological group had gathered 27,000 signatures for a petition demanding the recall of another delegate, Yurii Kolomiyets, the chairman of the State Agro-Industrial Committee of the Ukrainian SSR.[9] Less than a week later, on the very eve of the opening of the Party Conference, the Popular Union in Support of Restructuring held a small demonstration in central Kyiv during which placards were displayed with slogans such as 'We Trust in the 19th [Party conference] – But for the Last Time!'[10] A similar attempt, but on a more modest scale, to found a 'Democratic Union in Support of Restructuring' was also made at this time in Odesa.

Ten days that shook Lviv

In Lviv, the developments were rather more dramatic and the issue of democratization was intertwined with that of national rights. First, on 11-12 June, leading national rights campaigners from Ukraine, Armenia, Georgia, Lithuania, Latvia and Estonia met in the city and established a Coordinating Committee of the Patriotic Movements of the Peoples of the Soviet Union. Although those who took part in the meeting were primarily advocates of political independence for their respective nations (Chornovil, Mykhailo Horyn and Khmara were the main Ukrainian representatives), the goal of the new body was tactfully toned down to resemble that of the new Baltic popular fronts, namely 'the complete political and economic decentralization of the Soviet Union', and the transformation of the USSR into a 'confederation of separate sovereign states'.[11]

When, on 13 June, the authorities in Lviv attempted to prevent the inaugural meeting of the local Ukrainian Language Society by locking up the hall in which the gathering was to take place, the action backfired on them. Hundreds of indignant people moved to the square in front of the university, in the centre of which stands

---

[9] Andriy Savitsky, 'Informal Meeting Formulates Requests to Delegates', *News from Ukraine*, no. 27, 1988.

[10] Author's interview with Yemets.

[11] See Bohdan Nahaylo, 'Representatives of Non-Russian National Movements Establish Coordinating Committee', RL 283/88, 22 June 1988.

the statue of Western Ukraine's greatest poet and writer, Ivan Franko, and held the first of Ukraine's mass protest meetings. The participants, who were addressed by the former political prisoners Mykhailo Horyn and Iryna Kalynets, as well as representatives of a new generation of activists, such as the engineers Ivan Makar, Yaroslav Putko and Ihor Melnyk, not only elected the leadership of the new local Ukrainian Language Society, but also raised numerous political and cultural issues. Makar, in particular, incensed the authorities by daring to question the official view of the Ukrainian nationalist resistance movement in Western Ukraine of the 1940s and early 1950s as having been made up of despicable bandits and killers. It was time to acknowledge, he argued, that the OUN and UPA had fought against two equal evils, Stalinism and Fascism, and to begin erecting monuments also 'to those who had died in the struggle against Stalinism'. The participants of the meeting decided to send a telegram to Gorbachev protesting about the undemocratic behaviour of the local authorities and to reconvene in the same place on 16 June and to invite delegates to the Nineteenth Party Conference to attend.

Three days later, some seven thousand people turned up at Lviv's second mass political demonstration. The authorities sought to prevent the meeting between the delegates to the Party Conference and the public by organizing a smaller official assembly elsewhere, but the mass meeting summoned the delegates to appear before the people. Several of them, including the first secretary of the Lviv city Party organization, Viktor Volkov, and the renowned physicist, Academician Ihor Yukhnovsky, turned up and faced the crowd: Volkov had quite a difficult time trying to defend the Party's unchanging nationalities policy, while Yukhnovsky's speech, with its emphasis on supporting democratization and Ukrainization, went down very well. In general, though, strong criticism was voiced about both the undemocratic way in which delegates to the Party conference were being chosen and who was being picked to represent Ukraine. Disgust was expressed, for instance, about the choice of Shcherbytsky, Yelchenko, Pohrebnyak and the local KGB chief, Stanislav Malyk, all of whom were accused of having contributed to Russification and repression in Ukraine; the meeting called for the local well-known writers Ivanychuk and Lubkivsky, as well as the head of the Lion Society, Orest Sheika, to take their place. Chornovil, who also spoke, called for genuine elections and demanded that the UHU and other independent public organizations be allowed to put forward their own candidates.

This mass meeting became a political turning point for other reasons too. Makar opened it with a call for the creation of a united front which would take on 'the forces of bureaucratic stagnation'. The proposal met with an enthusiastic response, and later during the meeting the idea of forming a local 'Democratic Front to Support Restructuring' was overwhelmingly endorsed and the draft statutes for such an organization read out. Furthermore, the more radical speakers at the meeting, who apart from Makar and Chornovil included Mykhailo Horyn, his brother Bohdan (who was also a former political prisoner) and Ihor Derkach, a young engineer, in effect proposed an alternative agenda for the delegates going to Moscow. They urged them to raise, among other things, the issues of restoring the sovereign statehood of the USSR's constituent republics, economic decentralization and republican economic self-management, the dissolution of the KGB, the release of the remaining political prisoners and the elevation of Ukrainian to the status of the state language of Ukraine. Before concluding, the assembled decided to call a follow-up meeting on 21 June at the city's main sports stadium for which the embarrassed Volkov reluctantly gave his permission.

The local Party authorities were clearly alarmed by these developments. In Kyiv, too, the events in Lviv and the Ukrainian capital, as well as the news that on 16 June public pressure had finally toppled Estonia's Shcherbytsky – Karl Vaino – must also have set off alarm bells. At any rate, on 17 June Yelchenko arrived in Lviv to take stock of the situation. The following day, the local newspapers carried the first of the predictable denunciations of the meetings and their organizers, depicting Chornovil, Mykhailo Horyn, Makar and several others in the standard fashion as dangerous demagogues and extremists who were attempting to lead the public astray.

On the morning of 21 June, Lviv's residents received leaflets in their mailboxes informing them that new 'temporary regulations' had been introduced concerning the holding of demonstrations and public meetings in the city and urging them not to attend the mass meeting. Nevertheless, an estimated forty to fifty thousand people arrived at the stadium only to find it 'closed for repairs'. Despite demands by officials that the crowd disperse, a huge meeting was held outside the stadium and it was decided to call another public meeting for 7 July. A large group of protesters, some carrying portraits of Gorbachev, subsequently marched through the city and gathered by the statue of Lenin.

Undaunted by this setback and the continuing propaganda campaign in the press against 'nationalist provocateurs', on 23 June some 5,000 people gathered at the city's Lychakivsky cemetery for a memorial service conducted by Ukrainian Catholic priests for the victims of Soviet repression.[12]

Undoubtedly, the public mood in Lviv had undergone a profound change. Fear had receded and a new sense of solidarity and purpose had been demonstrated. Former political prisoners, representatives of the cultural and technical intelligentsia, disaffected but patriotically minded Party members, leaders of the Ukrainian Catholic Church and, significantly, representatives from the national minorities (including democratically oriented Russians and Jews), were forging a coalition – exemplified in the attempt to create a local democratic popular front. Moreover, the demands being made were no longer limited to cultural matters, but were clearly political in nature. The situation in Lviv had come to resemble what was taking place in the Baltic republics, and the question now was whether the new spirit would spread to other parts of Ukraine.

One other development also added piquancy to the situation on the eve of the Party conference – the surprise re-emergence of Shelest after fifteen years of political obscurity. On 23 June, Moscow's *Stroitelnaya gazeta* published an interview with the former Ukrainian Party leader in which the latter criticized Brezhnev, and especially Suslov, but did not explain why he had been ousted and isolated. The reappearance of the octogenarian 'private pensioner' in a positive light became a sword of Damocles hanging over Shcherbytsky, for it appeared that as soon as it were felt in Moscow that the latter had outlived his usefulness, Shelest could be used to discredit him.

---

[12] For details about the 'ten days that shook Lviv', as the editors of *The Ukrainian Herald* put it, see their bulletin *U[krainskyi] V[isnyk]-Ekspres*, no. 8 (Kyiv-Lviv), August 1988, reprinted by the External Representation of the Ukrainian Helsinki Union, New York, 1989.

The Nineteenth Party Conference

The Party Conference, which lasted from 28 June to 1 July and was broadcast live on television, lived up to expectations. Although a majority of the 5,000 or so delegates were probably conservatives, there was a refreshingly candid and unpredictable atmosphere. Hardly surprisingly, the nationalities question figured prominently in the debates. The radical proposals for economic, cultural and political autonomy put forward by the Baltic delegates emboldened representatives from some of the other non-Russian republics to come out with their own demands. Reflecting the pressure that was welling up from below in their republics, quite a few of the republican Party leaders, including the Estonian, Latvian, Lithuanian, Georgian, Azerbaijani, Armenian and Uzbek ones, championed republican and national rights. The result was the most open debate on the nationalities question at any major Party meeting since the 1920s. During it, despite Gorbachev's disappointingly conservative comments on this topic in his opening address, the issue of genuine, as opposed to proclaimed, sovereignty for the republics was pushed to the forefront.

While delegates from the Baltic and Transcaucasian republics pressed for a fundamental review of the relationship between Moscow and the Union republics, Ukraine's main speaker, the CPU Central Committee secretary Borys Kachura, came across as an old-style defender of the 'integral' Union and of the Party's monopoly on power. In fact, his address may well have been intended to sound like a manifesto of the Shcherbytsky team, whose leader was not only present but even chaired one of the sessions at the conference. Pointing to the changing political atmosphere in the Soviet Union and the reduction of fear and apathy, Kachura warned that it was time to take legal measures to ensure that 'speculation around democratization' did not get out of hand. The Party, he declared, would never relinquish its leading role, and this remained an 'axiom'. Going on to attack nationalism, he told the delegates that for 'the Ukrainian people' the 'internationalist brotherhood of the peoples' of the USSR remained 'sacred and unshakable'.

Oliinyk, however, who represented the Boards of the Ukrainian and Soviet Writers' Unions, saved the honour of his countrymen. With the outspokenness that had come to be expected of him when he was delivering a speech in Moscow, the poet raised three of the major issues which were of such great concern to Ukraine's patriots and burgeoning democratic opposition: Stalin's man-made famine, the language question and nuclear power plants. After affirming his pride in his 'motherland' – 'Soviet Ukraine' – and his 'country' – 'the Union of Soviet Socialist Republics' – Oliinyk announced that he had been 'instructed to recommend, to request, that, finally, a "white book" be published' about the crimes of the Stalin era, which would identify those responsible for the terror and the victims. Stressing that since in Ukraine 'persecutions began long before 1937', he added: 'The reasons for the famine of 1933, which extinguished the lives of millions of Ukrainians, need to be made public, and those responsible for this tragedy [should] be identified by name.'

Whatever Shcherbytsky and his colleagues may have thought, according to *Pravda*, the delegates greeted this bold request with applause.[13] It was the first time that the Ukrainian famine had been mentioned in such a way before the assembled Party leadership and in full view of the entire Union.

The poet went on to reiterate that one of the 'burdensome legacies' of the Stalin era was the 'universal' distortion of Lenin's nationalities policy. In Ukraine, he explained, this had meant that the national language was progressively being squeezed out of all aspects of social and political life, schools and higher education. What was needed was an official policy of affirmative action – 'a state-sanctioned programme to create the most favourable conditions for the functioning of the native language in all spheres and at all levels of society, reinforcing theory with laws, right up to prosecuting people who impede the development of national culture.'

Oliinyk then turned to the issue of nuclear energy and announced that he had brought an appeal signed by over 6,000 people asking for a review of Moscow's plans for the expansion of Ukraine's nuclear energy facilities. 'The arrogance and disdain' which some central agencies, and especially the USSR Ministry of Power and Electrification, were showing towards Ukraine, he protested, 'borders not only on some sort of merciless cruelty, but also on an insult to national dignity'. The need for energy was understood well

---

[13] *Pravda*, 2 July 1988.

enough, he explained, but there were 'limits, saturation limits, which it would be simply criminal to exceed'.

The writer finished his speech with a more general proposal. In contrast to Kachura's emphasis on the Party retaining its leading role in society, he suggested that 'the equality of Party and non-Party people in their movement up the hierarchical ladder' be established by law. This would have a 'refreshing effect' and hopefully force out careerists.[14]

The voice of Ukrainian forces supporting democratization was also heard when a Russian delegate read out a telegram that he had received at the conference from Kharkiv University. Grigorii Baklanov, the editor of the all-Union journal *Znamya*, informed the delegates that the message asked whether any of the liberal writers were going to reply to the reactionary views propagated by Andreeva in her infamous letter, or by Yurii Bondarev, the deputy chairman of the Board of the Union of Writers of the RSFSR, in his speech at the conference. Responding to this call from Eastern Ukraine, Baklanov then proceeded to deliver one of the most outspoken speeches at the conference in support of *glasnost* and restructuring.[15]

Undoubtedly, the Nineteenth Party Conference succeeded in conveying the message of change and endorsing reformism, and it can be considered a watershed. Although the various resolutions which were adopted at the conference represented compromises in which high-sounding phrases more often than not were substituted for specifics, the gathering nevertheless paved the way for the inauguration of the 'cardinal reform of the political system' which Gorbachev had called for in his opening address. The conference endorsed the creation of a new Congress of People's Deputies, to be elected the following spring in multi-candidate elections, which in turn would elect a smaller, full-time, two-chamber Supreme Soviet and, by secret ballot, a chairman of this body. Gorbachev made it quite clear that he wanted the chairman of the Supreme Soviet to be a president in all but name and to transfer political power from the Communist Party to revamped elected soviets.

As far as the nationalities question was concerned, the resolution adopted by the conference on this issue, though nowhere near as

[14] *Ibid.*
[15] *Ibid.*

radical as some of the non-Russians delegates would have liked, represented an important step forward. However grudgingly, the Party had finally been forced to acknowledge the need to rectify its nationalities policy and broaden the rights of the non-Russian nations and republics. The resolution recognized that 'within the framework of the restructuring of the political system urgent measures' had to be undertaken to ensure the 'further development and strengthening of the Soviet federation on the basis of democratic principles'. It noted:

> Above all it is a question of the expansion of the rights of the Union republics and autonomous formations . . . decentralization, the transfer to the local level of a number of managerial functions, and the strengthening of their independence [*samostoyatelnost*] and responsibilities in the spheres of the economy, social and cultural development, and environmental protection . . . the idea of the transition of the republics and regions to the principles of cost-accounting . . . merits attention . . . More concern must be shown for the active functioning of national languages in various spheres of state, public, and cultural life. Encouragement must be given to the study of the language of the people whose name a republic bears by citizens of other nationalities residing on its territory, above all by children and young people.[16]

Thus, despite Gorbachev's efforts to keep the nationalities question on hold, powerful, newly released forces were beginning to push things along. *Perestroika* and *glasnost* were beginning to acquire a dynamic of their own.

Hopes raised

With democratization now linked more and more in the minds of non-Russians with the need for a fundamental change in the imperial relationship between Moscow and the republics, the preliminary concessions that had seemingly been won in this respect at the Party Conference raised expectations and spurred on the various national movements.

On 7 July, over 10,000 people gathered in Lviv to launch the city's 'Democratic Front to Promote Restructuring' formally. The

[16] *Ibid*, 5 July 1988.

constituent members of the new coalition included the Ukrainian Helsinki Union, the Native Language Society, the Public Committee of the Ukrainian Catholic Church, the Lion Society, the local Trust Group, the Lviv Political Discussion Group and a newly formed Jewish Cultural Society. The Democratic Front defined its goals as: support for restructuring, raising democratic consciousness among the public, monitoring the observance of democratic procedures and participating in elections.

Once again, however, the officially controlled press not only in Lviv and Kyiv, but also in Moscow, sought to discredit the organizers of the meeting as extremists. On 10 July, for example, the all-Union Komsomol daily, *Komsomolskaya pravda*, did not even mention the creation of the Democratic Front but instead depicted 'Makar and the group of Western-supported, previously convicted "[human] rights defenders"', as crypto-fascists who were really out to achieve the rehabilitation of the 'terrorists' of 'the OUN-UPA Banderist movement'.

In fact, by this time, the leaders of the Ukrainian Helsinki Union (UHU) had elaborated their political platform and on 7 July they issued it in the form of a 'Declaration of Principles'. As before, though, it remained exceedingly difficult for this, and other dissident groups, to make their position known and to refute effectively the accusations being levelled against them in the officially controlled media. Apart from reading between the lines of the official accounts, the public could still only learn about these things either from *samvydav* publications, with their very limited print runs, or from Radio Liberty's Ukrainian and Russian broadcasts, which, despite *glasnost*, the Soviet authorities were still continuing to jam.

The Declaration of Principles drawn up by the leaders of the UHU represented the first attempt to provide a comprehensive programme for the emerging Ukrainian national democratic movement. Indeed, in the preamble, the authors declared that they hoped that the UHU's Declaration of Principles would become 'the basis for uniting democratic forces in the struggle for restructuring society and for human and national rights'. Although, for the purposes of self-protection, they denied that the UHU was a political party, or even a political organization – that is also why they called their document a declaration of principles and not a programme – there was no disguising the fact that that is precisely what the leaders of the UHU were aiming at. The Principles stated quite clearly that the UHU would strive to bring about 'the all-round activation of the popular masses, [and] the development of a mechanism for the participation of the people in the government of the state and for reliable control over the state apparatus', and that it intended to field candidates in forthcoming elections.

Defining the principal task of the UHU as the 'defence of national rights', the document dismissed the sovereignty of the Ukrainian SSR as a legal fiction. It stressed that Ukraine's ruling Party was a mere 'regional subdivision' of the CPSU which, together with the so-called Ukrainian government had 'not been able or wanted' to protect the republic's population over the decades from denationalization, starvation, economic exploitation and 'the artificial transformation' of its 'ethnic composition'. Thus the first of the Basic Principles proposed in the document stated:

> The Ukrainian Helsinki Union considers that the re-establishment of Ukrainian statehood, which today exists only on paper, would be the fundamental basis for guaranteeing the economic, social, cultural, civil and political rights of both the Ukrainian people, and of the national minorities which live on the territory of Ukraine.

Having identified the restoration of genuine sovereign statehood for Ukraine as the UHU's principal goal, the document nevertheless followed the successful example being set by the Baltic Popular Fronts and stopped short of calling for political secession from the USSR. Invoking the calls that had been made at the Nineteenth Party Conference for transforming the Union into a genuine federation, the leaders of the UHU tactfully came out for the replacement of the 'state, centralized to the maximum, which was built by Stalin', by a 'confederation of independent states', adding that a 'federation of sovereign democratic states', with the 'fullest political, economic and cultural decentralization', could serve as a transitional stage to it. In this way, they also marked out the various stages in what they evidently envisioned as being a complex and protracted process of achieving independence.

The Declaration of Principles contained numerous other radical and far-reaching aims. The leaders of the UHU proposed, among other things, that the all-Union and republican constitutions be revised to reflect the ending of the imperial set-up and to take into account international human rights norms; that the new Ukrainian constitution establish Ukrainian citizenship and recognize Ukrainian as the state language of the republic; that the rights of national minorities in Ukraine be fully guaranteed; that the autonomous statehood of Crimea within Ukraine be re-established and the return of Crimean Tatars and others who had been deported from the peninsula be organized (on 9 June 1988 *Pravda* had reported that a special state commission chaired by Soviet head of state Andrei Gromyko had rejected the demands of the Crimean Tatars for the recreation of their autonomous republic in Crimea); and that Ukraine start caring for its large Eastern diaspora and the Ukrainian minorities in Eastern Europe, and begin cooperation with the Western diaspora. As far as the external sphere was concerned, the document also asserted Ukraine's right as a sovereign state to proper representation in the international arena and to establish its own diplomatic contacts.

Other principles included the reduction of military forces to reasonable limits necessary only for defence and that military service be carried out on the territory of the respective republics in republican military formations; that the KGB be dissolved or cease functioning as a political police; that political power be transferred from the Communist Party organs to democratically elected councils; that all political prisoners be freed and repressive legislation repealed; and that full religious freedom be inaugurated. In the economic and social spheres, the document called for a shift towards a market economy; for industry to be restructured to take into account environmental factors; for independent trade unions to be allowed to function; and for the establishment of a 'just system of social security'.[17]

This manifesto was an important landmark in the evolution of Ukrainian political thinking. The broad programme for the achievement of a sovereign Ukrainian state was notable for its practical, tolerant and forward-looking features. The UHU, which was being depicted in the official media as an extremist nationalist organization, was in fact judiciously eschewing any trace of political intolerance and ethnocentrism and instead proposing a concept of an inde-

---

[17] The document is analysed in Anatol Kaminsky, *Na perekhidnomu etapi: 'Hlasnist', 'perebudova' i 'demokratyzatsiya' na Ukraini* [In a Transitional Stage: 'Glasnost', 'Restructuring' and 'Democratization' in Ukraine], Munich, 1990, pp. 321-6; an English translation is provided in Kuzio, *Dissent in Ukraine*, pp. 24-31.

pendent democratic Ukrainian state in which all of its citizens, regardless of their nationality, would feel at home.

Indeed, this, the most radical 'nationalist' group to have emerged so far in Ukraine during the Gorbachev era, issued a special statement on 24 July addressed to the national minorities living in Ukraine. Identifying themselves as 'representatives of the Ukrainian *national democratic movement*', the UHU leaders urged non-Ukrainians not to believe the 'slanderous' attempts of the authorities to depict them as xenophobic ultra-nationalists and to join forces in a common struggle for the improvement of the situation of all of Ukraine's citizens. Reiterating the main planks in their political platform, the UHU's leaders concluded their appeal with the following words: 'We call on you. Ukraine is in peril. But she is not only our motherland, but also yours as well.'[18]

A growing awareness of the need to protect the rights of the Crimean Tatars and other national minorities living in Ukraine while simultaneously pressing for the redress of Ukrainian national grievances was also apparent at the first meeting to be held by Ukrainian writers after the Nineteenth Party Conference – a joint plenum on 12 July of the Board of the WUU and the Board of its Kyiv section. But this was not main feature of the meeting.

Generally encouraged by the results of the conference, the writers delivered their most outspoken criticism so far of the Shcherbytsky regime and the way it was 'hindering' the Ukrainian national renewal. Drach led the attack and implicitly called on Shcherbytsky to resign. In order to repair the colossal damage which had been done to the Ukrainian nation and its 'soul', he argued that enormous measures 'on a state scale' were required. Addressing the Ukrainian Party and state leadership, he declared:

> If any of our leaders do not know how, do not want, or do not have the strength to revive this living soul, if any of them are not prepared to take on the resolution of these painful problems, then let them leave the stage with a firm and confident step. This will indeed be the honourable thing to do in the spirit of restructuring.

Another writer, Oles Lupii, suggested that it was perhaps time

---

[18] For the text of the appeal, see *U[krainski] V[isnyk]-Ekspres,* no. 9 (Kyiv-Lviv), July-August 1988, reprinted by the External Representation of the Ukrainian Helsinki Union, New York, 1988, pp. 17-19.

for Ukrainians to stop 'requesting' and to begin taking more resolute action.

Responding to what had gone on at the Party Conference, the writers supported the idea of transforming the 'multinational Soviet state' into a union of genuinely 'free and equal peoples'. On the other hand, they openly denounced the very notion of a 'Soviet people', which some of the conservative speakers had referred to, and the fact that the term had appeared in the resolution on national relations. They also expressed dismay that the Party Conference had failed to support the view that the study of the native language in the republics, along with that of Russian, be made compulsory.

Inspired by Oliinyk's bold speech at the Party Conference, the writers demanded that a monument be erected for the victims of the Stalin famine in Ukraine and that the archives covering this period be opened. Several writers once again urged that the works of Hrushevsky be republished, with the novelist Pavlo Zahrebelny describing his *Istoriya Ukrainy-Rusy* (History of Ukraine-Rus) as the best there was. This time, however, the writers also stressed that it was time to remove the 'blank spots' from the most recent period of Ukrainian history – the 1970s, or in other words, the Shcherbytsky era. Zahrebelny, for instance, who from 1979 to 1986 had headed the WUU, proposed that the cases of the 'young people, who were accused on the basis of the very things that we are talking about openly today' be reviewed.[19]

Anatolii Makarov had already described in *Literaturna Ukraina* of 19 May 1988 the tragic fate which had befallen a large group of young promising modernist poets who had been prevented from making their contribution to Ukrainian literary life. Furthermore, the Ukrainian Culturological Club and the UANTI had been conducting a campaign for the rehabilitation of Vasy Stus, the poet who had died in a labour camp only three years earlier, and posthumous publication of his works. Several members of the WUU had extended their support to the campaign, including Drach, Pavlychko and Stanislav Telnyuk. The first breakthrough had been achieved when, on 22 June, *Literaturnaya gazeta* had published an article by Yaroslav Melnyk which mentioned Stus. It was to take

---

[19] See *Literaturna Ukraina*, 21 and 28 July, 1988, and Bohdan Nahaylo, 'Ukrainian Writers' Plenum Reveals Growing Frustration and Radicalization', RL 356/88, August 10 1988.

another two months before Danylo Kulynyak managed to do the same in a Ukrainian publication, in his article which appeared in *Molod Ukrainy* on 25 August.[20]

There were other signs that the Shcherbytsky era was coming to an end. Between 14 and 19 July, Dzyuba, the leading Sixtier whom Shelest had defended and Shcherbytsky had imprisoned and forced to recant, was able to publish a series of five major articles dealing with the defence of the Ukrainian language in *Vechirnii Kyiv*. His earlier articles on this theme had elicited scores of letters, and the editor of the newspaper, Vitalii Karpenko, had decided to provide Dzyuba with the opportunity for a thorough discussion of the issue. Dzyuba's reasoned and unemotive approach helped hundreds of thousands of readers in the Ukrainian capital (the mass circulation evening newspaper appeared in Ukrainian and Russian) to understand better the concerns and demands of Ukrainian patriots.

On 21 July, *Literaturna Ukraina* published an article by Bilokin which presented Hrushevsky in a positive light. Two days later, *Molod Ukrainy* ran another piece which broke new ground – an article by the Western Ukrainian poet Rostyslav Bratun in which he touched on several hitherto taboo subjects and thereby presented a different picture of the recent history of Western Ukraine. These included the arrest of Communists by the Soviet authorities after the incorporation of Western Ukraine into the Soviet Union in 1939, the mass execution of political prisoners in Western Ukrainian jails by the Soviet authorities at the outbreak of the Second World War, and the mass repression in the region after the war which accompanied the Soviet campaign against the Ukrainian nationalist resistance. Referring to the situation in Lviv, he assailed the local bureaucrats who remained indifferent to pressing national and ecological issues, and, as an example of the vibrant independent life in the city, he noted that an unofficial Russian group calling itself 'Friends of Ukrainian Art and Culture' had recently appeared, as well as Jewish, Polish and Armenian cultural societies.

Needless to say, the Ukrainian Catholics, too, were heartened by recent events and intensified their campaign for the legalization of their church. On 17 July some 15,000 of them gathered in Zarvarnytsya for the largest of the numerous unofficial celebrations by

[20] See Bohdan Nahaylo, 'Rehabilitation Sought for Victims of Brezhnev's Political and Cultural Repressions in the Ukraine', RL 410/88, 7 September 1988.

Ukrainian Christians of the millennium of the Christianization of their homeland.[21]

Hopes dashed

But just as it seemed that the Nineteenth Party Conference had blown new wind into the sails of the democratic and national movements, matters unexpectedly took a turn for the worse. The first sign of this was on 18 July when, at a meeting of the Presidium of the USSR Supreme Soviet dealing with the continuing crisis in the Transcaucasus, Gorbachev seemed to backtrack. He was shown on Soviet television expressing his annoyance about the tendency of the non-Russians, as he put it, to conclude that 'Moscow is to blame, the centre is to blame'. He also claimed that, 'under the banner of democratization', national movements were exerting 'shameless pressure' on the authorities.

Shcherbytsky, too, took an active part in this meeting and used the occasion to argue the case for toughening policy towards national movements and democratic activists. Although the theme under discussion was the conflict between Armenia and Azerbaijan over Nagornyi-Karabakh, the Ukrainian Party leader might as well have been outlining his understanding of the situation in his own republic. Shcherbytsky claimed that it was 'becoming increasingly obvious' that the people behind the recent events in the Transcaucasus were subversives who sought 'to fan national egoism and aggravate emotions, making them increasingly militant and anti-social – even anti-Soviet'. 'Extremists', he said, were urging the people of Armenia 'to take it upon themselves to change the leadership of the Party' and government of their republic. Ukrainian citizens, especially local Party officials from the Donbas, were asking why such things were being tolerated. Shcherbytsky then issued the following warning:

> We have no right to forget that some people abroad are trying to do everything possible to have what is happening in Transcaucasia now take place on as broad a scale as possible in other parts of our country . . . We cannot allow anyone, no matter who he is, to interpret our democracy as all-per-

---

[21] UPA Press Release, no. 128, 1988.

missiveness and impunity. Otherwise situations like this will arise again and again.[22]

Controls were duly tightened. On 28 July, the USSR Supreme Soviet surreptitiously issued a decree giving sweeping powers to the paramilitary forces of the Ministry of the Interior, empowering them to suppress unauthorized political meetings and demonstrations. Another decree published that same day required all demonstrations to be registered ten days in advance.

In Ukraine, as Shcherbytsky had indicated at the meeting of the Presidium of the Supreme Soviet, the reaction of the authorities to the surge of independent political and religious activity and the continuing peaceful revolution in the/Baltic republics was even greater determination not to allow *glasnost* and democratization to take their course. In fact, they went on the offensive before the decrees were even issued in Moscow. On 23 and 24 July, the media in Lviv announced that criminal proceedings had been initiated against the activists responsible for organizing the Democratic Front. Chornovil, the Horyn brothers, Makar and Putko were singled out. Resorting to threats, administrative detention and the use of force, the authorities sought to prevent any more public unauthorized meetings or religious gatherings from being held. This was demonstrated on 24 July, when the police in Kyiv detained sixteen activists of the Ukrainian Culturological Club who were planning to collect signatures that Sunday for a petition calling for the release of political prisoners. Most of them were driven several dozen kilometres outside of Kyiv and abandoned in the countryside.[23]

In Lviv, the authorities used even tougher methods. Here, on 28 July, a public meeting at which about 1,000 people had gathered was dispersed by force. When, a week later on 4 August, the Democratic Front attempted to hold its next scheduled meeting, the police were sent in with truncheons and dogs and brutally broke up the gathering. The shock and outrage which this caused was conveyed in a press release issued the following day by the UHU. It stated:

The barking of dogs, screaming of children, and pitiful cries of women provided the final brushstrokes to the portrait:

[22] *Pravda*, 20 July 1988.

[23] *Russkaya mysl*, 29 July 1988.

'Democracy and Restructuring Ukrainian Style' . . . Thus, on 4 August 1988, for the first time in many years, blood was spilt on the pavements of Lviv, and together with it fell the last illusions of people who were treated by the authorities as if they were enemies.[24]

It also transpired that on the morning of what the residents of Lviv dubbed as 'Bloody Thursday', Makar had been arrested. He was subsequently charged with 'violating public order'. Makar's colleagues, who immediately began a campaign for his release, described him 'as the first political prisoner of the era of restructuring'.

On 13 August, the Associated Press reported that the Ukrainian Catholic activist Hel had told its representatives that pressure was being stepped up not only on Ukrainian Catholics but 'on the whole of society'. He revealed that the police were disrupting services and imposing heavy fines on participants. Among those who were detained and fined were several Ukrainian Catholic priests.

As the summer continued there were more and more reports about the prevention of meetings and the harassment of dissenters in various parts of the republic, and the official press continued to vilify the leaders of the UHU and Ukrainian Culturological Club. The case of Kyiv's Popular Union in Support of Restructuring was indicative of the general policy. The authorities sought to stifle the new organization by delaying registration of it and other forms of red tape. When, in September, the organization finally obtained permission to hold a meeting, it had to be held behind closed doors in a small hall, and the authorities demanded to receive details of the agenda in advance. According to Yemets, the activists were told by the authorities that they could not hold a rally in the open because stormy winds were expected which could endanger lives. A sympathetic journalist who attended the meeting was led to ask in the pages of the workers' daily:

> As regards public meetings – which have become possible thanks to the process of democratization in society and which reflect the reawakening of people from social slumber – is it necessary for us to fear such manifestations of *hlasnist* and strive in every

[24] See Bohdan Nahaylo, 'Lviv Authorities Resort to Old Methods in Breaking Up Unauthorized Meetings and Religious Services', RL 355/88, 13 August 1988.

way to isolate them, hiding them behind closed doors, from the eyes and ears of uninvolved people?[25]

After such embarrassing questions had been asked in the press,[26] the authorities relented somewhat and allowed the Popular Union to stage a demonstration in the centre of Kyiv on 7 October – Soviet Constitution Day. About two thousand people participated with banners calling for the rule of law. This, however, became the peak of the organization's activities for it was not allowed to hold any more public meetings or demonstrations.[27]

By the use of these tactics, the authorities appeared to succeed for the time being in obstructing the development of the Ukrainian democratic movement and of the popular fronts. Once again, the image of Ukraine as a 'bastion of stagnation' was reinforced. Thus, for instance, when at the end of August, a Spanish newspaper asked Korotych to assess the situation in Ukraine, he summed it up as 'rather sad and anti-democratic'.[28]

Two weeks later, in what appears to have been an 'old-style' attempt to play up the danger of resurgent Ukrainian nationalism in order to justify the hard-line stance of the Shcherbytsky regime, a purported KGB 'triumph' in its war against Ukrainian nationalist émigrés was announced in *Pravda* and subsequently played up in the Soviet media. According to the claims, as a result of a twenty-year-old operation codenamed 'Boomerang', the Ukrainian KGB and its ally, the Polish security services, had infiltrated the largest Ukrainian émigré nationalist group – the Bandera faction of the OUN – and neutralized its 'subversive' activities. Significantly, *Pravda* and other newspaper, laid emphasis on 'the US leadership's support for anti-Socialist and anti-Soviet forces' and warned that young people who participated in unauthorized public meetings were 'playing into the hands of dark forces'. It was also probably not entirely coincidental that this joint Soviet-Polish 'success' was announced the day after the joint Polish-Ukrainian celebration in Czestochowa of the millennium of the Christianization of Kyivan Rus.[29]

---

[25] O. Kuts in *Robitnycha hazeta*, 4 October 1988.

[26] See also *Radyanska osvita*, 30 September 1988.

[27] Haran, *To Kill the Dragon*, pp. 16- 17.

[28] *La Vanguardia*, 28 August 1988.

[29] Pravda, 12 September 1988. For further details, see Bohdan Nahaylo. 'KGB "Success" in War Against Ukrainian Nationalist Emigres', RL 420/88, 15 September 1988.

In the historical sphere, Shcherbytsky's defenders of orthodoxy continued to hinder the efforts of the Ukrainian literary intelligentsia to secure the rehabilitation of Hrushevsky and Drahomanov. On 4 August, *Literaturna Ukraina* unexpectedly ran a piece signed by three authors seeking to discredit Drahomanov, and on 27 August *Radyanska Ukraina* published an article by an official historian in which he labelled Bilokin's recent positive article about Hrushevsky as 'incompetent'. Vitalii Sarbei, a section head at the Institute of History, maintained that despite Hrushevsky's undeniable scholarly achievements 'Soviet historians had no grounds for reviewing their generally critical attitude' towards the historian and his works. This did not stop *Vitchyzna* from beginning to publish Hrushevsky's memoirs in its September issue.

Now that Oliinyk's speech at the Party Conference had made the Shcherbytsky regime's position on the Ukrainian famine untenable, the new line was apparently being drawn at Hrushevsky. On 10 October, at a plenum of the Central Committee of the CPU, the Ukrainian Party leader himself inveighed against *Literaturna Ukraina* for publishing Bilokin's article about Hrushevsky. Shcherbytsky claimed that the newspaper had made a 'deplorable' mistake because Bilokin's article had been 'one-sided' and had sought to 'exonerate' Hrushevsky's 'notorious nationalist positions'.[30]

The CPU's plenum was held less than two weeks after Gorbachev had managed to carry out major changes in the Soviet leadership and have himself elected Chairman of the Supreme Soviet, that is, head of state, in place of Gromyko, who retired. At a Central Committee plenum on 30 September, three other holdovers from the Brezhnev era in the Politburo, Mikhail Solomentsev and non-voting candidate members Vladimir Dolgikh and Pyotr Demichev, were dismissed, while another, Gorbachev's conservative rival, Ligachev, was effectively demoted by being given responsibility for agriculture. Vladimir Kryuchkov now replaced Chebrikov as the head of the KGB and Vadim Medvedev was given responsibility for ideology. Shcherbytsky, however, retained his Politburo seat and thus became the last of the Brezhnevite veterans in the Soviet leadership.

Why was Shcherbytsky still there, was the question that reverberated among supporters of change. A month earlier, Korotych had

[30] *Radyanska Ukraina*, 11 October 1998.

offered an explanation. Gorbachev, he had told a Spanish paper, needed to 'consolidate his strength', and 'the last thing' which he needed was 'a civil war'. Ukraine was a 'very strategic republic' and, in Korotych's view, this was not 'strategically the right time' for Gorbachev 'to tackle the issue of Ukraine'.[31]

Whatever the case, the October plenum of the Central Committee of the CPU, which focused mainly on economic and social issues, confirmed how unyielding the conservative Ukrainian Party leadership remained. Once again there was a measure of self-criticism and plenty of lip-service was paid to the reformist slogans being advocated by Gorbachev's team; and, as before, those genuinely advocating change were depicted as 'demagogues', 'extremists', 'nationalists', or simply 'politically immature' persons. Among other things, Shcherbytsky went out of his way to castigate the writers for indulging, as he put it, in 'demagogic verbiage' at their meeting in July.

Nevertheless, Shcherbytsky sounded an unusually defensive note when he acknowledged that the CPU leadership was now facing up to 'the shortcomings and miscalculations made in the past [which had] reduced in an unjustified way the sphere in which the Ukrainian language was used'. He announced that new efforts were being made to remedy the situation, including the opening of new Ukrainian-language schools, an increase in the number of hours devoted each week in schools to Ukrainian language and literature, more opportunities for learning and using Ukrainian at higher educational institutions, and the creation of a unit at the Dovzhenko Film Studio to dub films in Ukrainian.

The CPU plenum also revealed that despite all the bluster and the use of traditional methods of suppressing dissent, the authorities in Ukraine were increasingly losing control of the situation. Shcherbytsky himself acknowledged that: 'Lately, speculating on the development of the Socialist pluralism of ideas, individuals have begun propagating views that are ideologically hostile to us, instigating, with this aim in mind, various meetings and demonstrations that violate the law.' Although, as he put it, 'as a rule' it was former political prisoners, nationalists and Ukrainian Catholics who were responsible 'for all this', politically naive students, 'especially in Kyiv, Kharkiv and Lviv', were also involved.

[31] *La Vanguardia*, 28 August 1988.

The head of the Ukrainian Komsomol, Valerii Tsybukh, hinted at the scale of the problem. He drew attention to the fact that a process of 'politicization' was taking place among young people, which was leading to 'a pluralism not only of ideas, but also of actions'. Without elaborating, he added:

> It is symptomatic that the number of independent associations of a political orientation has grown sharply. From the Lviv, Zaporizhzhya, Kyiv and other examples we see that various extremist elements sometimes attempt to prod young people, as they say, in the wrong direction.

A good example of what Shcherbytsky and Tsybukh were alarmed about was the activity of the Hromada Society among the students of Kyiv University. By the time of the CPU's plenum, the unofficial group had published three issues of an independent patriotic journal called *Dzvin* (*The Bell*), the third of which, for example, contained among other material a poem by Sosyura about Mazepa (in which the latter was depicted as a Ukrainian national hero), an interview with Chornovil and works by Stus. It also carried an open letter from Hromada to the CPU plenum in which the CPU leadership was held responsible for 'stagnation', Russification and repression in Ukraine and was urged to alter its policies radically and remove Shcherbytsky and his team from power.[32]

But what was probably even more worrying, although Tsybukh did not mention it, was the fact that ferment had also become apparent within the ranks of the Ukrainian Komsomol where the developments in the Baltic republics were also having an effect. For instance, Sheika and other leaders of Lviv's Lion Society who were Komsomol officials sought to develop contacts with the Baltic popular fronts and in October organized a conference in Lviv to which they invited representatives from the Baltic republics. Anxious to prevent ideological contagion, the authorities in Lviv intercepted the Baltic guests on their arrival and sent them back.

In September and October, moreover, the Ukrainian Komsomol daily, *Molod Ukrainy*, underscored its continuing shift towards a more autonomous and liberal position by providing favourable coverage about events in the Baltic republics, including a highly sympathetic report from the inaugural congress on 1 October of the

---

[32] UPA Press Releases, nos 172 and 173, 8 November 1988.

Estonian Popular Front.[33] While the rest of the Ukrainian press remained conspicuously silent about events in the Baltic republics, *Molod Ukrainy*, with its mass circulation of about 600,000 (as compared to *Literaturna Ukraina*'s 71,000 at this time) therefore played an important role in breaking the information blockade being imposed by the authorities in Kyiv.

At the CPU plenum, frustration was in fact expressed by some speakers about the avoidance by the press of the more delicate but pressing issues, 'such as questions connected with political reform, international relations, and the functioning of the Ukrainian language'. Describing the problems in his region, Pohrebnyak, the Lviv region Party boss, appeared to call for a more differentiated approach to ideological work which would take into account the peculiarities of the various regions. To the west of his own fiefdom, the Polish Communist authorities had decided in August to open negotiations with Solidarity. The imposition of martial law had proved unsuccessful and the new wave of industrial strikes in the spring and summer of 1988 had forced the Polish Communist leadership to begin seeking an accommodation with the opposition. Clearly, in addition to what was happening in the Baltic states and Moscow, events just across the border in Poland would also have an influence on Western Ukraine.

Pohrebnyak emphasized that in Western Ukraine, apart from 'extremist manifestations', the 'natural pull towards the Ukrainian culture and language' had to be taken into account. Admitting that there was a shortage of 'highly professional ideological' workers available who were up to the task, he also criticized the press, and especially certain unnamed central newspapers, for displaying 'insufficient judgement and knowledge of the concrete situation and the complex, controversial history of the region'.[34]

As part of a general streamlining of the apparatus of the Central Committee of the CPU and an effort to improve the quality of ideological work, the responsibilities for overseeing agitation and propaganda, science and education, and culture were merged in a revamped Ideological Department, and Kravchuk was appointed to head it. As he was later to reveal, that same month functionaries of

---

[33] See *Molod Ukrainy*, 20 September, and 6 and 20 October, 1988.

[34] For material on the CPU plenum, see *Radyanska Ukraina*, 11,12,13 and 14 October, 1988.

the CPU Central Committee were sent out 'into the field' to get a
better reading of the situation in the regions. Consultative meetings
were then held with representatives of the cultural and scientific
intelligentsia about ways of remedying matters in the sphere of
national cultural policy and thereby hopefully taming the forces that
had been released.[35]

In October, the custodians of ideology also resorted to rather
unusual measures to try and halt the growth of the Ukrainian
Catholic Church. Kravchuk and Yelchenko supported recommendations from M. Kolesnyk, the head of the council on religious affairs
attached to the republican Council of Ministers, that concessions be
made to the Russian Orthodox Church in order to strengthen its
position *vis-à-vis* the Catholics. In a special note for the Ukrainian
leadership, Kolesnyk warned that the Ukrainian Catholic Church
was gaining widespread support in Western Ukraine and that
'recently an obvious alliance has been made between the advocates
of Uniatism and the advocates of Ukrainian nationalism'. As
counter-measures, he proposed: that the registration of Russian
Orthodox religious communities in Western Ukraine should be
facilitated; that conditions for Russian Orthodox priests to conduct
their parish duties be improved; that permission be given for the
opening of a Russian Orthodox monastery at a former Catholic
monastery near the village of Hoshiv in the Ivano-Fankivsk region;
that more places be created in the Russian Orthodox seminary in
Odesa, and training be provided elsewhere, to prepare clergy and
religious activists for work in Western Ukraine; and that assistance
be provided for the publication of Russian Orthodox religious
literature, including a prayer book with a print run of 100,000, in
the Ukrainian language. The state's interference in religious life was
of course a standard feature of Soviet life, but here, as documents
subsequently uncovered in the archives show, the CPU leadership
was cynically using the Ukrainian language as a means to block the
recovery of a Ukrainian church in favour of one identified with
Russia and hostility towards Ukrainian patriotism.[36] Moreover, the

---

[35] See the interview with Kravchuk in *Pravda Ukrainy*, 20 January 1989.

[36] Volodymr Lytvyn, *Politychna Arena Ukrainy: Diiovi osoby ta vykonavtsi* [The
Political Arena of Ukraine: Cast and Performers], Kyiv, 1994, pp. 106–8. Hereafter
referred to as *Political Arena*.

CPU's backing for the Russian Orthodox Church in Western Ukraine could only inflame the situation in this indomitable region.

Even as they revised their strategems, though, the CPU's leaders were overtaken by events. On 1 November, the citizens of Lviv demonstrated just how strong their sense of history and national pride was when some 15,000 of them gathered at the city's Yanivsky cemetery to commemorate the anniversary of the proclamation of the ZUNR and the fallen in the struggle for Ukrainian independence between 1917 and 1920. This time the banned blue and yellow Ukrainian national flag was raised and patriotic songs were sung.[37] That same day in the Ukrainian capital, Ukrainian writers were discussing assuming responsibility for creating a popular movement for democratization and national renewal.

[37] UPA Press Release, no. 188, 11 November 1988.

7

THE BIRTH OF RUKH

The writers launch a new effort to create a popular movement

Despite the Shcherbytsky regime's efforts to stem the tide, under the influence of developments in the Baltic states and Moscow, the amorphous movement in Ukraine for democratization and national renewal continued to gather strength. The turning point came when, in the late autumn, a group of literati in Kyiv decided to revive the idea of forming a popular movement in support of restructuring which would unite all the various disparate groups and organizations that wanted to see meaningful political and economic change.

It appears that after the attempts in Lviv and Kyiv to form democratic fronts had been blocked, it was increasingly realized by democratic activists, including literati, that the writers and their allies in the other cultural unions were the only force with the moral weight and organizational structures which stood a chance of breaking a way out of the impasse. Yemets, for example, recalls that around this time he and his colleagues in the leadership of the Public Union in Support of Restructuring initiated an appeal to the WUU to form a popular front from members of the Union of Cinematographers.[1] Also, apart from the continuing impressive successes of the Baltic Popular Fronts, there was also one other source of encouragement – ironically, the Kremlin's new ideological secretary, Medvedev. Interviewed in October in *Kommunist*, he seemed to welcome the appearance of the popular fronts, adding that to see them 'almost as a threat to the social order' did not correspond with the Party line on 'democratization, *glasnost* and pluralism.'[2]

Drach recalls that the idea of forming a popular front 'hung in

[1] Author's interview with Yemets.
[2] *Kommunist*, no. 17, October 1988, pp. 3-18.

the air'. He himself had travelled in the summer to Italy with two leading Baltic poets, the Latvian Janis Peters and the Lithuanian Algimantis Baltakis, and had had the opportunity to learn directly from them about the role which the writers and cultural unions had played in creating the Baltic popular fronts. Seeking a way to channel a similar initiative through some official structure, during the late summer and autumn further attempts were apparently made behind the scenes by representatives of the Ukrainian cultural élite to hold a joint meeting of the Cultural Unions. The authorities, especially the ideological secretary, Yelchenko, and the Kyiv city Party boss, Masyk, however, knew full well 'what this smelt of' and blocked things.[3]

The two writers who appear to have played a leading role in preparing the ground were Viktor Teren, a member of the Communist Party, and Pavlo Movchan, a non-Communist. On 30 October an informal preliminary meeting was held at the WUU building to discuss forming an Initiative Group. It was attended by about 150 people and chaired by Teren and Movchan. Potential problems emerged when Pavlychko and several others urged a cautious approach by proposing that the entire Party Committee of the Kyiv section of the WUU be included in the Initiative Group, while Movchan maintained that the initiative should be seen as a 'popular' one, and not Party-inspired.

The following day, Pavlychko, Drach and Oliinyk were called in by Yelchenko. According to the latter, he and Kravchuk 'knew immediately what the writer's initiative represented – an attempt to form an organization which would compete with the CPU for political power'. Multi-candidate elections to the new USSR Congress of People's Deputies were scheduled for 26 March and they offered dissenters the first legal opportunity to challenge the CPU's monopoly on power through the ballot-box. Moreover, the components for the nucleus of a broad coalition of democratic forces in which the writers were providing the leadership were fast crystallizing. Numerous branches of the Native Language Society and of the 'Green World' ecological association had been formed and their leaders were planning to hold inaugural republican conferences; the activity of the 'Memorial' group in Moscow, which was dedicated to exposing the crimes of the Stalin era and honouring the victims

---

[3] Author's interview with Ivan Drach, Munich, 28 November 1993.

of Stalinism, had found a resonance in Ukraine and efforts were being made to create a Ukrainian organization by that name; and, of course, the UHU and numerous other unofficial groups were stepping up their challenge to the Shcherbytsky regime. The consolidation of all these elements would make for a powerful political force and pose a formidable challenge to the rule of the CPU. The ideological secretary called on the writers to put their cards on the table and admit what they were really after. Pavlychko, however, apparently sought to reassure him that he and Kravchuk were wrong and simply too conservative. The writers, he explained, simply wanted to help the Party promote restructuring.[4]

On emerging from the meeting, Pavlychko and Drach announced that the Party Committee would form its own Initiative Group.[5] Had Party discipline prevailed? Interestingly, just as the writers were starting their attempt to form a popular movement, the Ukrainian authorities began indicating their readiness to offer more substantial concessions including a compromise on the issue of making Ukrainian the state language of the republic. In fact, in early November, two commissions of the Ukrainian Supreme Soviet held a special hearing on this question at which several writers, including Mushketyk, Drach and Pavlychko were asked to speak. One of the commissions, on education and culture, was headed by Oliinyk, the other, on internationalist education and inter-ethnic relations, by Kravchuk, who also chaired the hearing. The outcome, as *Pravda Ukrainy* reported on 11 November, was that the commissions decided to recommend that the republic's constitution be changed in order to raise the status of Ukrainian to that of the state language, though there was no knowing how long this might take. It is possible, therefore, that this might have influenced Pavlychko's and Drach's initial behaviour.

On 1 November, the initiative was taken a step further at an official meeting of the Communist members of the Kyiv section of the WUU to which non-Communists were also invited. Kravchuk was also present. Teren formally proposed that the writers take the lead in creating a popular front-type organization. He argued that, as far as restructuring was concerned, the republic was lagging

---

[4] Author's interview with Yelchenko.

[5] See Solchanyk's interview with Movchan on the origins of the Popular Movement in *Ukraine: From Chernobyl' to Sovereignty*, pp. 7–8.

behind others and that 'all attempts at democratization are severely punished'. Even the modest measures that had been adopted by the CPU leadership to bolster the position of the Ukrainian language were being sabotaged. In order to change things, it was imperative to consolidate all the various centres of opposition and democracy and he offered as an example the role which the Latvian Writers' Union had played as an initiator and coordinator in the formation of the Latvian Popular Front. The time had come, Teren declared, for Ukraine's writers to follow suit and to form an Initiative Group to create a 'Popular Movement of Ukraine for Restructuring'. The Group's first task would be to draft a programme which could then be published, discussed and fine-tuned at a joint plenum of Ukraine's Cultural Unions. Movchan seconded Teren's proposal. Their initiative seems to have been deliberately played down, however, for, according to *Literaturna Ukraina*'s account of the meeting, the 'Communists unanimously' agreed simply 'on the need to form an initiative group from among the writers to promote restructuring'.[6]

What helped the writers was the fact that after the Nineteenth Party Conference democratization had begun to make itself felt even within the CPU and this, in turn, also affected the make-up of the Party structures within the WUU. At the meeting, Pavlychko and Teren were among those elected to the Party committee of the Kyiv section of the WUU.[7]

Although the writers' initiative generated considerable excitement and discussion among the creative intelligentsia, it was not until 17 November that the public was able to read about it in the pages of *Literaturna Ukraina*. In the meantime, a splendid opportunity presented itself to sound out the citizens of Kyiv about this idea. Concern about the dangers of nuclear energy and industrial pollution had grown even more during the last few weeks as a result of a mysterious disease in the south-western city of Chernivtsi that had caused loss of hair and nervous disorders in scores of children. The Kyiv authorities had permitted the local 'Greens' and other informal groups to hold an outdoor public meeting on 13 November to

---

[6] *Literaturna Ukraina*, 17 November 1988. The newspaper, it turns out, also published a sanitized summary of Teren's speech. A fuller version appeared in *Rozbudova derzhavy*, no. 5, 1993, pp. 23-4.

[7] Author's interview with Drach. On the new composition of the Party committee, see *Literaturna Ukraina*, 3 November 1988.

discuss ecological issues. The meeting drew over 10,000 people and
turned into a huge political demonstration. Among the writers who
addressed the gathering were Pavlychko, Shcherbak, Yavorivsky
and Bratun. They linked the worrying environmental situation in
Ukraine with the republic's lack of sovereignty and its conservative
leadership. Pavlychko, however, was more direct: he openly called
for the formation of a Ukrainian popular front and his proposal drew
enthusiastic support. After hearing other speeches from representatives from Latvia, Lithuania and Armenia, as well as from the
recently freed Makar, the crowd started chanting: 'Popular Front!,
Popular Front!'

During the following fortnight, the general atmosphere in the
Soviet Union was strained by a constitutional crisis precipitated by
Gorbachev's attempts to reassert control over the republics through
amendments to the Soviet constitution. On 16 November, the
Estonian Supreme Soviet defiantly adopted a 'Declaration of
Sovereignty' and asserted its right to veto laws passed in Moscow.
Despite the strong condemnation of this action by Moscow as
'unconstitutional', the Supreme Soviets in Latvia, Lithuania and
Georgia also voiced their objections to what was seen as an unexpected departure by the Gorbachev leadership from the positions
adopted at the Nineteenth Party Conference. The Lithuanian parliament also proclaimed Lithuanian the state language of the republic
and designated the flag and hymn of independent Lithuania as the
official flag and anthem of the Lithuanian SSR.

While the Ukrainian authorities joined in the orchestrated condemnation of Estonia's stand, there were both implicit and explicit
unofficial manifestations of Ukrainian support. For instance, the
UHU, which by now had even formed a group in Moscow,
deplored the position of the Ukrainian Supreme Soviet and on 20
November addressed a statement to the Estonians assuring them that
'the national democratic forces of Ukraine are fully on your side'.
Furthermore, on 24 November, *Literaturna Ukraina* published a
discussion in which three legal experts condemned the proposed
changes to the Soviet constitution and emphasized the need to begin
respecting the proclaimed sovereignty of the Union republics. One
of them, Volodymyr Vasylenko, a professor of juridical sciences of
Kyiv University, reminded Ukrainian readers that, according to the
Nineteenth Party Conference and the democratic principles which
it had upheld, the rights of the Union republics were supposed to

be broadened and not narrowed.

In the meantime, encouraged by the display of public support for the idea of a popular movement, on 23 November a group of writers and literary scholars met in Kyiv to elect a representative Initiative Group. Evidently, by this time, despite pressure from the CPU's ideological officials to make it appear that the initiative to form a popular front had come from the Party organization of the Kyiv section of the WUU, Drach and Pavlychko, at any rate, had accepted the view that the Initiative Group could not be limited to Party members. Representatives of some of Kyiv's unofficial associations were also present. The meeting was chaired by Movchan who told the assembled that there should be no further delay: other republics were watching Ukraine and 'waiting for it to awaken'. According to the record of the meeting, Teren, Zhulynsky, Donchyk, Pavlychko, Drach and several others took part in the discussion. One, a worker, said that hundreds of signatures in support of the idea of forming a Popular Movement for Restructuring had already been collected and he proposed Drach to head the Initiative Group. The meeting elected an Initiative Group led by Drach (his candidature had apparently already been agreed on by the writers), which also included Pavlychko, Telnyuk, Teren, Movchan, Bryukhovetsky, Donchyk, Dzyuba, Syvokin and several others.[8]

After the meeting, Drach, Pavlychko and Mushketyk were once again called in 'for talks' by Yelchenko at which Masyk and Kravchuk were also present. The writers stood their ground and continued to argue that they simply wanted to help the Party by mobilizing popular support for restructuring. In public, Drach also challenged the impression which some newspapers now sought to convey that the idea to create an Initiative Group had come from the writers' Party committee and not the public. In fact, the pressure on Drach and his colleagues only seems to have made them more determined to press on.

At the end of November, the question of creating a popular movement was discussed at a plenum of the Board of the WUU. Shcherbak was among the speakers who brought out the full dramatic significance of the situation. After decades during which it had seemed that 'time had been suspended' indefinitely, he ex-

---

[8] The protocol of the meeting, which was not mentioned in the press, was later also published in *Rozbudova derzhavy*, no. 5, 1993, pp. 24-6.

plained, the 'energy of restructuring and *hlasnist*' had finally
'reawoken us'. Now history, with its perennial hard choices, was
knocking at the door and asking: 'Whose side are you on, Ukrainian
writers?' Having made the choice to defend democracy and their
own people, the writers had to be in the front ranks of the movement
for change. The conservative forces were not about to give in and
the writers knew what they were up against. As Shcherbak put it:

> Even now, in the fourth year of restructuring, we feel the deaf
> unwillingness of officials to face up to the new realities of life.
> We feel their suspicious and hostile glances; we know that the
> civic and publicistic activity of the writers irritates certain people
> and makes them recall the old days nostalgically.[9]

Therefore, Shcherbak and his colleagues argued, the struggle had
to be stepped up. Mushketyk, the head of the WUU, also delivered
a powerful speech in this vein and spoke of the need for 'gigantic
and broad-ranging work' by the writers, including 'political and
democratic actions', to raise the national and political consciousness
of their compatriots. He also renewed the call for a joint meeting
of the republic's cultural unions.

The plenum not only endorsed the idea of creating a popular
movement, but also devoted a special resolution to it which made
it clear that the new organization would be an all-republican one
and that its leadership would not be restricted to Communists. The
plenum resolved:

> To entrust the initiative group of the WUU in support of
> restructuring, which includes members of the Party Committee
> and also writers elected to this group by other organizations,
> to prepare a draft programme of a Popular Movement of Ukraine
> for Restructuring. In doing so, to take into account proposals
> from the regional writers' organizations. To authorize regional
> writers' organizations to take an active part in the work of the
> appropriate initiative groups.

Other resolutions adopted by the plenum called on the Presidium
of Ukraine's Supreme Soviet to expedite the recognition of Ukrainian as the republic's state language; for the WUU to sponsor the
formation of a republican 'Memorial' Society dedicated to inves-
tigating the crimes of the totalitarian era and to help with the

[9] *Literaturna Ukraina*, 15 December 1988.

organization of a republican inaugural conference of the Native Language Society; and, for the resolutions adopted at the ecological meeting on 13 November to be published.[10] One other noteworthy feature was the forthright way in which Drach, Zhulynsky and others now raised the cases of Stus and other writers who had been imprisoned during the Shcherbytsky era.[11]

Faced with this demonstration of collective determination, Kravchuk chose to echo Medvedev and reassured the plenum that the official position on popular fronts was 'absolutely clear: to support popular initiative, everything that helps restructuring'.[12] That very same evening, however, he was shown on Ukrainian television questioning the need for a popular movement. Did Ukraine want the same sort of problems as Estonia, he asked, alluding to the appearance there of the so-called Intermovement (Interdvizhenie, or Internationalist Movement), consisting mainly of Russians and Russian speakers who felt threatened by Estonia's assertion of its sovereignty and national identity.[13]

The writers immediately began to receive support from outside the WUU. The staff of the Institute of Literature promptly voted to back the writers and formed its own Initiative Group to help with the drafting of the programme for the Popular Movement. Various unofficial groups, ranging from the Greens to the branches of the Native Language Society, also extended their support.

A vivid reminder of the difficulties that lay ahead, though, was provided on 10 December when democratic activists in various cities attempted to hold demonstrations to mark Human Rights Day. In Kyiv fifteen activists were detained and the authorities succeeded in preventing any large public protest. In Vinnytsya, the authorities banned the meeting that had been called by the local popular front. But in Lviv, several thousand people nonetheless defied the authorities and turned up for a meeting organized by the UHU.

On 18 December, the UHU's Coordinating Council, consisting of delegates from six cities, met in Kyiv and issued a statement expressing support for efforts to create popular fronts or movements.

[10] *Ibid.*, 8 December, 1988.

[11] *Ibid.*, 22 December 1988.

[12] *Ibid.*

[13] Haran, *To Kill the Dragon*, p. 22.

It stressed that attempts at creating such organizations had already
been made in Kyiv, Lviv, Odesa, Kharkiv, Vinnytsya, Ivano-
Frankivsk and other cities and described the writers' initiative as 'the
latest and most serious attempt'.[14] Nevertheless, it was clear from
the statement that the leaders of the UHU were somewhat uneasy
that the writers were attempting to form a popular movement when
in fact they considered that their own organization, with its Baltic-
front like programme, was best suited for this task and in any case
was already trying to do precisely this. Evidently, the veteran
dissidents and former political prisoners at the head of the UHU
remained sceptical about writer-radicals who were also members of
the Communist Party. What was important, though, was that the
UHU was seen to be endorsing the writers' efforts to create a popular
movement.

The emergence of Kravchuk

While the Initiative Group continued its work, the CPU leadership
held another Central Committee plenum on 12 December at
which important personnel changes were made. Shcherbytsky's
number two man, Oleksii Tytarenko, was retired and in his place
Ivashko was elected the CPU's new second secretary. Clearly,
Ivashko was now the figure to watch as Shcherbytsky's most
likely successor. What was not known on the outside at this time,
however, was whether the fifty-six-year-old Ukrainian Politburo
member, who had trained as an economist at a mining institute
in Kharkiv, was Shcherbytsky's choice or Gorbachev's candidate.
According to Yelchenko, it was the latter. Gorbachev wanted
Ivashko to take over in Ukraine after Shcherbytsky, 'but he had
to work to get him elected'.[15]

It was another senior Party official, though, who was to gain more
and more prominence in the coming months and to establish a
reputation for himself as perhaps the CPU's most capable representative. This was Leonid Kravchuk, the fifty-four-year-old
ideological apparatchik from Volhynia, who too had trained as an
economist. Highly intelligent, crafty and eloquent, he was increasingly used by the CPU leadership to deal with the rebellious

[14] UPA Presss Release, no. 12, 1989.
[15] Author's interview with Yelchenko.

intelligentsia. In the process he developed a style of his own and underwent a certain evolution. Able to reason, argue or deliver warnings with a certain amount of flair, something which few of his Party colleagues possessed, he was gradually to win the respect of many of his political adversaries.

After being appointed head of the CPU Central Committee's Ideological Department, Kravchuk became in effect the Ukrainian Party's spokesman on nationalities policy and the line as regards the democratic opposition, while Yelchenko, the ideological secretary, remained more and more in the background. Kravchuk sought to convey the impression that, just as the Kremlin was now facing up to the need to make adjustments in its nationalities policy, Shcherbytsky's team also recognized that there had been considerable neglect of problems in the national-cultural sphere and that mistakes had been made, especially concerning the narrowing of the use of Ukrainian in the republic, but that the authorities were working to put things right. His general message seemed to be that the CPU was trying to be more responsive to public opinion, whether on the language issue, the rights of national minorities or ecological issues – in other words, that it was heading the process of restructuring and democratization in the republic and there was no need for any other organization to claim this role.[16] At the same time, Kravchuk carefully distinguished between what he depicted as positive forces for change in the republic, that is those organizations and groups, such as the WUU, which were still prepared to accept the leading role of the Party, and the 'political extremists', such as the UHU, which were not. His tactic was to drive a wedge between the 'constructive' moderates whom the CPU hoped to control in some way, and the 'destructive' radicals with whom there could be no compromise.[17]

The new lengths to which the CPU leadership was now prepared to go in order to harness the national revival was revealed on 5 January when the Central Committee published a wide-ranging decree on inter-ethnic relations that was devoted largely to 'expanding the sphere of the use of the Ukrainian language' and 'developing Ukrainian national culture', even if it was on the basis of Ukrainian-Russian bilingualism, 'socialism' and 'internationalism'. Had the

---

[16] See the interview with Kravchuk in *Radyanska Ukraina*, 19 November 1988.

[17] See the interview with Kravchuk in *Pravda Ukrainy*, 20 January 1988.

measures to encourage 'the active use of the Ukrainian language in all spheres of socio-political, public and cultural life' and promote the restoration of some sense of national dignity[18] been proposed a year and a half earlier, they might have placated some of the patriotic activists. But now they were seen as belated concessions being grudgingly made by a regime that had been hostile all along to any Ukrainian national revival and which was finally being forced to give way.

In fact, reminders about the record of the Shcherbytsky team continued to appear in Moscow, as well as Kyiv. In the second half of December, the CPSU's main journal, *Kommunist*, unexpectedly reprinted Dzyuba's article of almost a year before about conceptualizing Ukrainian culture in which he had also described the repressive policies which had been pursued during the Shcherbytsky years.[19] Moreover, the following month the mass circulation all-Union publication *Argumenty i fakty* published another interview with Shelest, who this time confirmed that he had been purged for 'nationalism'.[20]

The CPU leadership had missed the boat in another sense, too: language and cultural issues, though still highly important, had been overtaken by political and economic ones concerning democratization and republican sovereignty. Nonetheless, by giving the go-ahead for the republican inaugural conference of the Ukrainian (or Native, as the authorities still insisted that it be called) Language Society, and bending on the question of making Ukrainian the state language, the Shcherbytsky team still hoped that it would be able to appease the cultural intelligentsia and steer it away from further engagement in the political sphere.

Furthermore, in Western Ukraine, and especially Lviv, the national revival was now beginning to assume openly political forms. In November, the Ukrainian Christian Democratic Front had been formed in the Ivano-Frankivsk region by the former political prisoners and radical UHU members Vasyl and Petro Sichko. It held its inaugural meeting in Lviv on 13 January. Though small, its significance lay in the fact that it was one of the first groups to come out openly for Ukrainian independence.[21] Just over a week later,

---

[18] For the text of the decree, see *Pravda Ukrainy*, 5 January 1989.

[19] *Kommunist*, no. 18, 1988, pp. 51-60.

[20] *Argumenty i fakty*, no. 2, 1989.

the citizens of Lviv defied the authorities to observe an important anniversary. On 22 January 1989, several thousand of them gathered outside the former Ukrainian Catholic Cathedral of St George (Yurii) (which the Russian Orthodox Church had taken over) for a commemorative mass to mark the seventieth anniversary of the proclamation of the unification of Ukraine by the UNR and the ZUNR (and the seventy-first anniversary of the declaration of independence by the UNR).

But in Kyiv, too, more modest attempts were made to mark the anniversary. On that day, the authorities prevented a new opposition political party – the Ukrainian Democratic Union (UDU) – from holding its inaugural congress, which had been scheduled to coincide with the anniversary, and also denied UHU activists permission to hold a commemorative public meeting.[22] The following month, the UDU, which included Milyavsky and many other activists from the Ukrainian Culturological Club (UCC), changed its name to the Ukrainian People's Democratic League (UPDL) and on 12 February its Kyiv regional branch adopted a programme aimed at achieving an independent, democratic Ukraine.[23]

In both Lviv and in Kyiv, then, political organizations more nationalistic than the UHU were appearing whose leaders were either members of the UHU or were supporters of it. With the leadership of the UHU preferring to stick to its tactic of not openly calling for full independence, this trend was soon to lead to trouble and factionalism.

The battle over the Popular Movement's programme

All this time, while playing up the CPU's new responsiveness to cultural problems, the republican press, with the exception of *Literaturna Ukraina*, kept silent about the writers' attempt to form a popular movement. On 15 January, however, Dzyuba was able to promote the idea in the pages of the liberal *Moskovskie novosti*. He argued that such a movement would be 'a logical development' in view of the revival of Ukrainian cultural and public life and the search for solutions to 'general political and socio-economic

---

[21] See UPA Press Release, no. 25, 1989.

[22] See UPA Press Releases, nos 34/1989, and 9/(25 January) 1989.

[23] See UPA Press Release, no. 56 (8 May) 1989.

problems', as well as national-cultural and inter-ethnic ones. The writers and their allies were also fortunate in that their initiative coincided with the end of the Soviet jamming of Radio Liberty's broadcasts to the republics of the Soviet Union. From December 1988 onwards, anyone who tuned in could listen unimpeded to news and political, cultural and religious programmes in their native language. Moreover, a number of courageous activists linked primarily with the UHU and UCC promptly began to provide information by telephone about events in Ukraine which was then beamed back in from Munich throughout the republic. Thus, news about what the writers were attempting and the barriers that were being placed in their way spread rapidly.

The work on preparing a draft programme for the Popular Movement proceeded reasonably quickly. 'Above all, we had as models those programmes with which we were already familiar, the programmes of the Estonian Popular Front, Sajudis, and the Latvian Popular Front', Movchan recalls.[24] The writers in the Initiative Group and their colleagues from the Institute of Literature were helped by a variety of specialists. These included the economists Volodymyr Chernyak and Venyamin Sikora and the young legal specialist Serhii Holovaty. The latter had got involved with the writers and their allies by responding to a report in the press that the Native Language Society was planning to hold an inaugural republican conference and offering his services.[25] Many other supporters of democratization and national renewal did likewise.

Matters came to a head on 31 January when the Initiative Group presented its draft programme to a general meeting of the Kyiv section of the WUU at which Kravchuk was present. Faced with continuing pressure from the Party's ideological officials, on the eve of the gathering the authors of the programme had decided to moderate some of its more radical provisions, namely the right of the republic to veto legislation passed in Moscow which affected it and the principle that all resources and property on the territory of Ukraine were owned by the republic. They had also added a statement conceding recognition of the leading role of the Party. Kravchuk, however, disregarded the changes and proceeded to denounce the original version. He argued that it violated the

---

[24] See Solchanyk's interview with Movchan, *op. cit.*, p. 11.
[25] Author's interview with Serhii Holovaty, Ebenhausen, 23 November 1993.

constitutions of the USSR and the Ukrainian SSR and the Programme of the CPSU. In particular, he attacked the authors of the draft for challenging the Party's right to its leading role, calling for the replacement of the existing political system, and proposing that the Popular Movement become the 'genuine' embodiment of the will of the Ukrainian people. The draft, he maintained, represented a manifesto of political demands and the Popular Movement was proposing itself as a political alternative to the Communist Party. Members of the Party could therefore not take part in such an organization. Who, in any case, Kravchuk asked, gave the writers the right to speak on behalf of the Ukrainian people and to propose such a programme when the CPSU had already initiated a course of political and economic restructuring.

The writers stood their ground and Drach made it clear that they would not be intimidated. In particular, he urged the CPU leadership to be more careful with issuing warnings to Communist Party members not to participate in the Popular Movement – the creation of which, he stressed, had been endorsed by the writers' own Party committee – as this could boomerang on it and lead to the embarrassing exodus of writers from the Party. The only somewhat dissonant note from among the writers was sounded by Shcherbak, who was preparing to stand for election to the new USSR Congress of People's Deputies and, according to some of his colleagues, did not want to spoil his chances by appearing too radical. He felt that the programme was too long and detailed and that parts of it needed to be improved, especially by legal specialists, to make it appear less categorical and confrontational. The writers decided to adopt the draft in principle and asked the editorial team to polish it up and then publish the programme in *Literaturna Ukraina* and, hopefully, other newspapers. In the event of the authorities banning the publication of the programme, Drach called on all of the writers to help disseminate the document independently.[26]

Within the next few days, a major press campaign was launched attacking the writers for their draft programme and repeating the accusations which Kravchuk had made. Although the public had still to see the text of the draft, the offensive against the writers caused

---

[26] For details, see Haran, *To Kill the Dragon*, pp. 23-4, and the articles by V. Desyatnykov in *Radyanska Ukraina*, 7 February, and E. Lohvyn, *Robitnycha hazeta*, 8 February 1989.

a stir and inadvertently revealed that a serious challenge was being
made to the CPU by democratic and patriotic forces whose representatives included Communists and leading cultural figures. The
timing also added to the drama: whether the writers intended it or
not, the fact that they were proposing an alternative programme
only weeks before the multi-candidate elections to the Congress of
People's Deputies were due gave the document the aura of an
election manifesto.

The attacks against the writers only precipitated the consolidation
of the democratic opposition. Drach, Pavlychko and their colleagues
realized that a critical phase had been reached in the long, drawn
out, trial of strength between Shcherbytsky's conservative regime
and the resurgent Ukrainian cultural intelligentsia and that they had
to go for broke. Drach, for instance, decided to try to run for election
in the Ukrainian capital. During these tense days, he and Pavlychko
pressed Kravchuk to allow the draft programme to be published.
'We told him', Pavlychko recalls, 'that if Rukh's [Popular Movement of Ukraine for Restructuring] programme is not published, all
of the members of the Writers' Union who are members of the
Communist Party will leave the Party'.[27] Reluctantly, the CPU
leadership gave way.

But before the draft programme was published, a major event
took place which became a triumph for Ukraine's national
democratic forces: on 11-12 February the inaugural republican
conference of the Native Language Society was held in Kyiv. It
brought together hundreds of delegates from all parts of Ukraine, as
well as Ukrainian communities in the Baltic republics, Eastern
Europe and the West. Ukraine's national minorities were also
represented. What is more, for the first time, leading writers and
cultural figures (Honchar opened the proceedings) shared the stage
with former political prisoners (UHU activist Bohdan Horyn was
elected to the Board of the Society). The Ukrainian Party leadership
came under strong attack – Yelchenko, who was present, was booed
– as did Soviet nationalities policy generally. In particular, the
delegates assailed the notion of bilingualism in Ukrainian and
Russian as a norm and demanded that Ukrainian be made the state
language of the republic without further delay. The delegates
formally named their organization – which at this time had about

---

[27] Author's interview with Pavlychko.

10,000 members – the Ukrainian Language Society and elected Pavlychko to lead it.

The delegates also expressed their wholehearted support for the Popular Movement of Ukraine for Restructuring. Dzyuba compared the campaign being waged against it with the Stalinist tactic of setting the workers against the intelligentsia. For his part Drach, who suspected that the Shcherbytsky leadership hoped that by allowing the creation of a republican Ukrainian Language Society it would blunt the push for the creation of the Popular Movement, was determined not to allow this to happen. He told delegates that the creation of the Ukrainian Language Society was only the first stage in the creation of a broad popular movement and not an end in itself. The conference duly registered its backing for the Popular Movement in its resolutions.

Unexpectedly, outspoken criticism was also voiced at the conference of the Russian Orthodox Church's attitude towards the Ukrainian language and its hostility towards the Ukrainian Autocephalous and Ukrainian Catholic Churches. It was delivered by a young Ukrainian priest ordained in the Russian Orthodox Church, Father Bohdan Mykhailechko. Criticizing Metropolitan Filaret, the Russian Orthodox Exarch for Ukraine, for not having accepted an invitation to attend, he commented: 'This again underlines the attitude of the Russian Orthodox Church towards our language and culture. . . . It is not only the policy of Stalin and of the period of stagnation; it is the policy of Peter I and of other Russian tsars.' His bold stand was strongly supported and, on 15 February, he and four others announced the formation of an 'Initiative Committee for the Restoration of the Ukrainian Autocephalous Orthodox Church'.[28]

The following day, *Literaturna Ukraina* published the draft programme of the Popular Movement of Ukraine for Restructuring, or Rukh (which, like Sajudis, meant 'Movement'), as it was now called for short. Although it did not go quite as far as the programmes of the Baltic popular fronts, or the 'Declaration of Principles' of the UHU, bearing in mind the political conditions existing in Ukraine, it was still a radical document. The preamble

---

[28] See Bohdan Nahaylo, 'Inaugural Conference of Ukrainian Language Society Turns into Major Political Demonstration', *Report on the USSR*, no. 9 (3 March 1989), pp. 20-2, and Haran, *To Kill the Dragon*, pp. 25-7.

reflected the compromises which the authors had made as a result
of pressure from the CPU leadership. It described the new movement as 'a mass, voluntary organization, based on the patriotic
initiative of citizens of Ukraine', to support the 'revolutionary
restructuring initiated by the Party' and the 'fundamental socialist
renewal in all spheres of state, public and economic life' which this
policy entailed. It also acknowledged 'the leading role of the
Communist Party in socialist society'. But the rest of the document
made it quite clear that the new organization, in taking at face value
and supporting the progressive course launched by Gorbachev, was
in fact seeking an end to the traditional authoritarian Soviet political
and economic system which the CPU was still perpetuating in
Ukraine. Indeed, the programme declared that Rukh 'will do its
utmost to dismantle the administrative-bureaucratic system which
was formed during the periods of Stalinism and stagnation'.

Broad in scope, the programme called for fundamental changes
in the political, economic, social, cultural and ecological spheres,
the aim of which was to transform Ukraine into a genuinely
sovereign republic and a law-governed state. Unlike the UHU's
'Declaration of Principles', which had come out for a Soviet
confederation, it envisaged Ukraine within a revamped Soviet
federation based on Leninist principles. Although the document did
not assert outright the republic's right to veto legislation affecting it
which was passed in Moscow, it stressed that the powers of the
Ukrainian and Soviet Supreme Soviets had to be clearly delineated,
that all of the republic's resources, enterprises, and communications
and transport networks were the property of its people and only the
Ukrainian Supreme Soviet had the right to decide how they were
to be used, and that the republic should become economically
sovereign on the basis of republican cost-accounting. The people of
Ukraine, it stated, had the right to determine their own destiny and
Rukh would seek the realization of the republic's proclaimed rights
as a sovereign state.

As for the political reforms which were to transform Ukraine into
a state based on the democratic rule of law, the programme emphasized the following principles: 'the state exists for the people, not
the other way around'; equality before the law; and respect for civil
rights and international democratic norms. It demanded the banning
of persecution on political, racial or religious grounds and of political
censorship and sought the inauguration of freedom of thought,

religion, expression and of information. Stalinist crimes, it added, had to be recognized as crimes against humanity and there could be no statutes of limitation in this regard. The cases of the more recent victims of political persecution had to be reviewed and those responsible for them brought to account.

Indicating the political role that Rukh wanted to assume, the programme insisted that free elections – a particularly sensitive issue at this time – were a precondition for the democratization of society and declared that the new organization intended to 'take an active part in election campaigns and propose its own candidates', and that it would demand the recall of 'idle' deputies, or ones whose activities were considered to be damaging to the people of Ukraine. Rukh would also 'systematically organize public opinion polls and publish their results and introduce proposals on holding referendums'.

In the economic sphere, the programme was rather more vague. It called for the transformation of the Ukrainian economy into a 'genuinely socialist one, free of deformations and distortions', which would be, 'humane . . . ecologically healthy and resource-balanced'. This entailed reducing bureaucratization, centralization and every-thing impeding the gains of the scientific-technical revolution. Furthermore, a 'rational restructuring' of the Ukrainian economy had to be carried out and the priorities in the distribution of capital investments changed. The programme stated that it was 'necessary to switch over from an economy in which the mining and high energy-consuming branches play an excessively vast role', to scien-tifically based 'ecological clean' industries. Turning to agriculture, the programme denounced the 'brutal violence' and damage that forcible collectivization had brought and suggested that economic policy should move some way towards privatization through flexibility with respect to the size of agricultural enterprises and the leasing of land to the rural population 'with rights of inheritance'. In the social sphere, the programme called for the 'humanization of society', an end to the *nomenklatura*'s privileges, greater equality, a struggle against corruption, 'a genuine emancipation of women', and an overhaul of the security and health care systems. The programme also expressed its support for the Green movement and urged the strict legal protection of the environment. It called for a radical review of the nuclear energy programme in Ukraine, the closure of the Chornobyl nuclear power station, as well as stopping the construction of new atomic reactors in the republic.

Last, but certainly not least, the programme addressed the issues connected with nationalities policy, language and culture. Invoking once again 'Leninist principles' in the sphere of nationalities policies, it called for the national rights of the Ukrainian people – including the right to 'state sovereignty' – to be respected, and at the same time extended this principle to all the other nationalities living in Ukraine. Indeed, the programme declared that 'genuine friendship between peoples can only be achieved on the basis of mutual respect for the language, culture, history and traditions of each people'. Thus, it presented the realization of the national rights of the Ukrainians as something that was to be done not at the expense of the other national groups living in the republic, but in tandem with their own national-cultural development. While, on the one hand, stressing that the Ukrainian language should be recognized as the state language in the republic and be made a compulsory subject in Ukraine's educational institutions, and that the revival of 'national dignity [and] historical memory' be officially promoted, it also upheld the right of all the other nationalities in Ukraine, from the Russians to the Crimean Tatars, to have their own schools, newspapers, theatres, and other cultural facilities necessary for their cultural development and well-being. The programme also sought the same for Ukrainians living in other republics of the Soviet Union and maintained that it was the duty of the Ukrainian state to care for their cultural needs.

By referring throughout the document to the 'people of Ukraine', rather than to the 'Ukrainian people', and by naming Rukh itself the 'Popular Movement of Ukraine', rather than the 'Ukrainian Popular Movement,' the authors of the programme emphasized that they were not seeking to mobilize purely ethnic 'Ukrainian' forces, but were seeking to build a broad coalition representing all of Ukraine's inhabitants. In fact, they were projecting an understanding of Ukrainian statehood and citizenship based not on an ethnic principle but a territorial one wherein Ukraine was regarded as a homeland for all of its residents.

Although what Rukh's programme was advocating boiled down to a cross between national Communism and Socialism with a human face, both of these were anathema to the Shcherbytsky regime, and the reaction was predictable enough. Apart from *Literaturna Ukraina*, no other publication published the document and a special appeal which the authors of the programme had addressed to the nationalities of Ukraine explaining Rukh's objectives was not allowed to appear even in this newspaper. Within two days of the programme's publication, a 'collective letter' was published in *Radyanska Ukraina* attacking the programme; it was signed by, among others, three vice-presidents of the Ukrainian Academy of Sciences.[29] It signalled the beginning of a new barrage in the press against Rukh.

The democratic opposition makes headway

Attention now focused on the first multi-candidate elections and the political struggle throughout the Soviet Union between the forces of change and the defenders of the status quo. Although the elections represented a major step forward in the direction of democracy, they were still far from being truly democratic. Their intention, after all, was not to encourage the development of a multi-party system in the Soviet Union, but to enable Gorbachev and his team to establish better control over the reform and modernization process by means of a revamped and 'democratized' CPSU and a new two-tier quasi-parliament, in other words, through the creation of an as yet undetermined form of socialist democracy within a mono-Party system and a unitary USSR. Thus, of the 2,250 seats in the Congress of People's Deputies, only two-thirds were to be filled by popular vote, with 750 being reserved for representatives of 'public and professional organizations', that is, the CPSU and organizations operating under its aegis. Furthermore, the complicated procedures for the nomination and registration of candidates effectively gave local Party officials control over determining who would be allowed to stand for election.

In Ukraine, as elsewhere, the election campaign was heating up. The CPU apparatus was increasing tension by seeking to prevent its critics and opponents from being registered as candidates. In Kyiv, where the political awakening of the public was becoming increasingly apparent, some Rukh leaders and supporters, such as Drach and Yavorivsky, were allowed to stand and thereby afforded the opportunity to promote the Popular Movement at election meetings and in the capital's evening newspaper *Vechirnii Kyiv*.[30] To add to

[29] *Radyanska Ukraina*, 18 February 1988.

the CPU's problems, several leading local Communist Party figures began at this time either to express their support for Rukh, or to dissent from the Shcherbytsky regime's general line. They included Ivan Salii, the first secretary of the Podol district Party organization, Karpenko, the editor of *Vechirnii Kyiv* and Petro Talanchuk, the Rector of the Kyiv Polytechnical Institute, who was running for election.

But in the regions the situation was more difficult. In Lviv, for example, the authorities blocked Bratun's registration, while in nearby Chervonohrad, the former political prisoner Khmara was placed under administrative arrest for fifteen days, ostensibly for organizing an illegal meeting, when in fact he had simply sought to present his platform at a gathering to select candidates.[31] These actions only led to protests, which in Zhytomyr, at least, were successful. Here, the courageous journalist Alla Yaroshynska, who had exposed corruption among the local Party authorities, was registered as a candidate, but only after thousands had come out in support of her. In the Ukrainian capital itself, on 19 February democratic activists began a chain of pre-election demonstrations.[32]

It was in this charged atmosphere that, on 20 February, Gorbachev made a previously unannounced visit to Ukraine. He did little to clear the air, however, for in his numerous comments and statements he once again gave mixed signals. Although he urged the public to remove those who were blocking restructuring, he did not openly criticize Shcherbytsky, who was shown by his side throughout most of the visit. This time, however, the Soviet leader was more tactful as regards Ukrainian national sensibilities. He visited Lviv and met there with representatives of the city's cultural and scientific intelligentsia. At the meeting, the writers Lubkivsky and Roman Fedoriv spoke of the concern for the fate of the Ukrainian language and culture, and a pensioner complained that the history of the Communist Party of Western Ukraine, which had been purged and suppressed during the Stalin era, was still being distorted.[33] Generally though, Gorbachev stayed off the nationalities

[30] See the interviews with Drach and Yavorivsky in *Vechirnii Kyiv* of 6 and 9 March 1989, respectively.

[31] See UPA Press Releases, nos 14/1989; 30/(19 February) 1989; and, 7/(25 January) 1989.

[32] AP, 22 February 1989.

question and restricted himself to statements about the economic importance of Ukraine for the Soviet Union, the need for unity among the peoples of the USSR, especially the Slavs, and to repeating the claim that Ukrainian national culture had flourished under Soviet rule. In Donetsk, though, Gorbachev was put on the spot in front of television cameras by a Donbas miner who castigated the writers for creating a Ukrainian popular front and for, as he implied, their excessive zeal for the Ukrainian language. The Soviet leader evaded committing himself on these issues and instead responded defensively with a rhetorical question: 'Can anyone . . . say that we are indifferent to the fate of the Ukrainian people, to its culture, history, language and literature, and to its intelligentsia?'[34]

At the same meeting in Donetsk, Gorbachev revealed what was probably behind his foray into Ukraine. He openly acknowledged Moscow's concern about the possibility of Ukraine making 'a contribution . . . to all these revolutionary changes of ours . . . in a way not contemplated by restructuring' and about the potential consequences of unrest in the republic. The effects of the conflict in Nagornyi-Karabakh, he stressed, had been felt throughout the Soviet Union. 'You can only imagine what would happen if disruption were to begin in a republic such as Ukraine where . . . 51 million people live', he told miners. Restructuring would fail and the whole fabric of the USSR would come apart. That is why 'at this crucial time', as he acknowledged, 'a close watch' was being kept on the situation in the republic.[35]

Although the media depicted Gorbachev's meetings with residents of Kyiv, Lviv and Donetsk as 'spontaneous' ones, it transpired that they were in fact 'choreographed' by local officials who had carefully selected the people he encountered. Moreover, in both Kyiv and Lviv, the authorities detained a number of local activists during the visit.[36] Nevertheless, in both cities, demonstrations against Shcherbytsky and his methods took place, with hundreds of

---

[33] *Pravda*, 23 February 1989.

[34] Soviet television, 22 February 1989. Interestingly, the comments made by the miner, identified as O. Lyashok, were subsequently toned down in the official TASS account which appeared in the Soviet press.

[35] *Ibid.*

[36] One of Lviv's singing bards, Andrii Panchyshyn, wrote a song satirizing Gorbachev's visit to the city ('Novyna u misti Lvovi' [News in Lviv City]), and it subsequently became popular throughout the republic.

protesters gathering in the Ukrainian capital for several nights running.[37] For all of Gorbachev's continued emphasis on the need for *glasnost*, the Soviet media made no mention of this.

While Gorbachev was actually in Ukraine, on 22 February Yelchenko and Kravchuk jointly submitted a report about Rukh to the CPU's Politburo which also outlined a plan for stifling it. They described Rukh as an attempt to create a political opposition movement which, behind the facade of support for restructuring, was, as they claimed its draft programme indicated, 'nationalistic' and under 'extremist' influence. Political exigencies, they explained, had required that in order to 'expose the real aims' of Rukh *Literaturna Ukraina* had been allowed to publish the draft programme and this had been followed up by a campaign organized with 'the use of all means of propaganda and agitation' to discredit the writers' initiative. The offensive against Rukh would be stepped up with more organized attacks in the media from 'mass public organizations', such as trade unions, the Komsomol, and veterans' and women's organizations, and meetings would be organized in factories to denounce the fledgling movement. If the organizers of Rukh persisted, the Presidium of the Supreme Soviet would rule that the creation of Rukh violated the Soviet and Soviet Ukrainian constitutions. A proposal that Drach, Pavlychko and Bryukhovetsky be called to face workers' meetings in Eastern Ukrainian cities was personally rejected by Shcherbytsky because this could provide them with opportunities to get their message across.[38]

Unexpectedly for the democratic opposition, though, the Soviet leader's visit finished on an encouraging note. The leaders of the WUU, most of whom were also the founders of Rukh, managed, at virtually the last moment before Gorbachev's departure, to obtain a meeting with him. Oliinyk apparently pulled this off because of his good contacts with Raisa Gorbachev. The meeting was held on 24 February in Shcherbytsky's office in the presence of the Soviet Ukrainian leaders. Drach and Pavlychko did not mince their words and, in describing the situation in the republic, castigated Shcherbytsky and his policies. For his part, Gorbachev sought to soothe tempers and promote conciliation between the CPU leadership and

---

[37] David Remnick, 'Activists Arrested in Ukraine before Gorbachev's Arrival', *The Washington Post*, and AP, 22 February 1989.

[38] Lytvyn, *Political Arena*, pp. 118–21.

the writers. On the one hand, quoting Shevchenko and other Ukrainian poets, he assured the writers that he understood and sympathized with their concern for the Ukrainian language and culture, but appealed to them to be patient, to 'understand the complexities of the entire situation', and not to get carried away. It was imperative, he told them, for the Slavonic peoples of the USSR to maintain their unity. On the other hand, after being reassured by Pavlychko that Rukh did not view itself as a new political party, he did not condemn the creation of the Popular Movement. In fact, as Yelchenko recounts, he demonstratively told the CPU's ideological secretary: 'Yura, you have to pay heed to the issues which the writers have raised.' At any rate, the writers emerged from the meeting with the feeling that the Soviet leader had endorsed their efforts and that Shcherbytsky and his lieutenants had been put in their place.[39]

After Gorbachev's visit, however, the struggle between the Shcherbytsky regime and the democratic opposition only intensified. On 27 February, Rukh was denounced at a meeting of the Presidium of the Ukrainian Academy of Sciences by Yelchenko and other speakers and the press kept up its attacks against the Popular Movement. But fear was receding and political protests, mainly connected with the forthcoming elections, were becoming almost daily occurrences, especially in Kyiv and Lviv.

More and more patriotic demonstrations were also taking place. On 26 February, for instance, thousands of people gathered outside St George's Cathedral in Lviv for a requiem service on the 125th anniversary of the death of Shevchenko, which was conducted jointly by a Ukrainian Catholic priest and an Orthodox one who had just broken with the Russian Orthodox Church. On the same day, a large public meeting was held outside Kyiv's Republican Stadium to discuss the defence of the Ukrainian historical and cultural heritage and among the speakers were Drach, Tanyuk, Yavorivsky and Salii.[40] That the national revival was continuing to gather momentum could also be seen from the fact that more and more material was appearing in the Ukrainian press about previously proscribed historical and cultural subjects, including, for instance,

[39] Author's interviews with Yelchenko, Pavlychko and Drach, and AP, 24 February 1989.
[40] Bill Keller, 'In the Ukraine, Nationalism Gains Respect', *New York Times*, 9 March 1989, and UPA Press Release, no. 41, 1989.

the role of Mazepa, the works of Hrushevsky, Vynnychenko, and Khvylovy, and Stalin's terror-famine in Ukraine.

Ukraine's democratic opposition was given a new boost in early March by the inaugural conference in Kyiv of the Ukrainian Memorial Society. It again brought together representatives of the democratic intelligentsia and leaders of Rukh with former political prisoners and representatives of the still outlawed Ukrainian Catholic Church. The conference, in which about 500 people participated, was opened by Oliinyk, and among the activists which the conference elected to lead the new organization were Tanyuk, and the former political prisoners Mykhailo Horyn, Yehven Pronyuk and Ihor Dobroshtan (who had been a leader of an uprising in the Vorkuta labour camps after Stalin's death). During the forthright and broad-ranging discussion, calls were made for, among other things: the opening of the secret police archives; official acknowledgement that the trials of Ukrainian scholars and cultural figures at the end of the 1920s had been deliberately fabricated; the erection of a monument to the victims of Stalin's famine in Ukraine; for the truth to be told about the Bykivnya wood, on the outskirts of Kyiv, and other such sites throughout the republic, where, according to Memorial's supporters, thousands of victims of Stalin's executions were secretly buried in mass graves; for a reappraisal of the struggle which the UPA had waged; for the freeing of all remaining political prisoners; the return to Ukraine for reburial of the remains of Stus, Marchenko, Tykhy and other political prisoners; for an end to the political abuse of psychiatry; and for not only 'moral,' but also material, compensation for the victims of political persecution. Most of these demands, as well as a strong statement of support for Rukh, were incorporated into a programmatic resolution adopted by the conference.

On 5 March, the final day of the conference, Memorial held its first public rally and more than 5,000 people turned up.[41] Thus, within weeks of the creation of a republican Ukrainian Language Society, this patriotic pressure group had been joined by an important new vehicle for setting the historical record straight and exposing the political crimes of the Soviet period.

The CPU leadership fought back and did its best to neutralize

---

[41] See Bohdan Nahaylo, 'Ukrainian "Memorial" Society Confronts Stalinist Heritage in Ukraine', *Report on the USSR*, vol. 1, no. 11 (17 March 1989), pp. 15-18.

the challenges from the democratic opposition. It managed momen-
tarily to stun the leadership of Rukh when, on 8 March, Oliinyk
unexpectedly published a letter in *Radyanska Ukraina* in which he
criticized Drach's version of how the writers' Initiative Group to
create a Popular Movement had been established and Rukh's
programme drafted (the Party Committee, he implied, had been
tricked). In effect, he thereby publicly distanced himself from the
Popular Movement. In Drach's view, the reason for Oliinyk's
volte-face was pressure applied by the authorities on him as a
potential candidate from the Communist Party in the elections.[42]
Movchan, however, suspected that Oliinyk's action was motivated
as 'an attempt to outshine Drach', whose popularity was quickly
growing.[43]

Work on uniting Rukh's supporters and building a genuine
grass-roots movement went on, with Bryukhovetsky playing a
leading role in the organizational work. On 18 March a meeting of
the representatives of some seventy-one diverse groups from Kyiv
and the surrounding region which backed Rukh was held in the
capital and a coordinating council was elected. The respected
philosopher Myroslav Popovych was chosen to head it. His presence
and active role in promoting Rukh – among other things, he ably
defended Rukh in televised debates with Kravchuk – helped to
thwart the CPU's attempts to depict the Popular Movement as an
'extremist' organization and to broaden its appeal.[44]

A week after Rukh established its coordinating council, the
CPU's Ideological Department held a round-table with leading
representatives of Ukraine's cultural intelligentsia. Kravchuk sought
to persuade the cultural intelligentsia to concentrate on cultural
matters and not meddle in politics. Rukh, he claimed, had failed to
win mass support and, holding out the prospect of further cultural
concessions, he invited the cultural élite to assist the CPU in
formulating 'a comprehensive programme for the development of
Ukrainian national culture for the period to the year 2,000'. Drach,
however, countered by asserting that Rukh was in fact gathering
strength and by arguing that cultural work did not preclude involvement in the Popular Movement and its activities. The opponents

[42] Author's interview with Drach.
[43] Solchanyk's interview with Movchan.
[44] See Haran, *To Kill the Dragon*, pp. 37–8.

of Rukh, he declared, were simply 'defending the administrative-command system by whatever means'.[45]

On 28 March, the CPU's Politburo discussed another report on Rukh from Yelchenko and Kravchuk in which the latter two called for an intensification of the struggle against the defiant unofficial formation. They also proposed that the regional, district and city councils begin sending denunciations of Rukh to the Presidium of the republican Supreme Soviet in order to prepare the ground for a ruling that the activities of the organizers of the popular movement were illegal. Interestingly, the record reveals that Valentyna Shevchenko, the chairman of the Presidium, opposed this proposal and therefore in effect vetoed it. Perhaps alluding to this, Shcherbytsky commented that, unlike Kravchuk, not all of the Central Committee's leading officials were pulling their weight in the struggle against the Party's opponents.[46]

[45] For details about the proceedings, see *Pravda Ukrainy*, 30 March 1989, and *Literaturna Ukraina*, 6 April 1989. From the official account of the meeting, it appears that most of the participants, the majority of whom were members of the cultural *nomenklatura*, preferred to play it safe for the time being and not to stick their necks out by coming out in support of Rukh.

[46] Lytvyn, *Political Arena*, pp. 126–31.

8

PSYCHOLOGICAL AND POLITICAL BREAKTHROUGH

Victories in the first multi-candidate elections

The election campaign was now entering its final stages. In Ukraine, many of the new democratic activists cut their political teeth during this bitter struggle and were radicalized by the ruthless methods resorted to by Shcherbytsky's apparatus. In fact, speakers at Memorial's rally had warned the crowd that 'modern' Stalinism lived on in Ukraine and informed it about the detention in Kyiv ten days earlier of four activists who had taken part in a protest against undemocratic practices. In Lviv, the authorities once again began using units of the special riot police to disperse demonstrations, and the brutal way in which a huge unsanctioned pre-election rally was broken up on 12 March generated outrage in the city and led the mayor, Bohdan Kotyk, to defy Party discipline and condemn the violence.

Assessing the general situation, a British correspondent reported from Kyiv that 'the Ukrainian Party machine had clearly been more ruthless than elsewhere' in manipulating the electoral screening process and that 'at least 30% of the Ukrainian candidates, probably the highest percentage' in the USSR, were standing unopposed.[1] In many cases where the CPU machine had ensured that its nominees would stand unopposed, there was little that the democratic activists could do other than to urge voters to cross out the names of the candidates. Shcherbytsky himself eventually did not risk running for election in the Ukrainian capital and instead opted for what was considered a 'safe' constituency in the Dnipropetrovsk region.[2]

[1] Xan Smiley, 'Nationalist Assault Looks Likely to Topple Ukraine "Mafia" Boss', *Daily Telegraph*, 7 March 1989.

[2] Interestingly, Radio Kyiv announced on 12 January 1989 that Shcherbytsky had been nominated as a candidate in the Moskovksky territorial electoral district in

When the voting finally took place the Ukrainian Party apparatus successfully secured the vast majority of the seats for its nominees, although it suffered a number of humiliating shocks. Several senior Party officials who had run unopposed failed to get the necessary number of votes (more than 50% of those cast) to be elected. This happened in the cases of Masyk and Zhursky in Kyiv (where almost 86% of the voters turned out), Pohrebnyak in Lviv (where the UHU had called for a boycott of the elections) and Kachura in Chernivtsi; the first secretaries of the Transcarpathian, Chernihiv and Voroshylovhrad regions were not elected either. Furthermore, although Shcherbytsky was successful, 63,000 of the 240,000 voters in his constituency crossed his name off the ballot. Among the candidates from the democratic camp who won were Shcherbak and Talanchuk in Kyiv, Yaroshynska in Zhytomyr, the scientist Ivan Vakarchuk in Lviv, and the writers Fedoriv in Drohobych and Roman Hromyak in Ternopil. Drach came in second out of six, losing to a celebrated surgeon, Mykola Amosov, who had declared his support for Rukh.

Oliinyk and Honchar also became deputies, though without having had to face the electorate: they were nominated for seats reserved for 'public organizations', in their case, by the CPSU and the Writers' Union of the USSR, respectively. In short, then, the CPU's monopoly on power in the republic had been breached (though far from broken), its reputation further sullied and the entire organization shaken by the unnerving exposure of its latent vulnerability. The election campaign, however, was not yet over: in about one-sixth of the republic's electoral districts new and run-off elections had to be held.

The conservative forces in the CPSU suffered embarrassing upsets in other parts of the USSR, too, but the victories by some of the radicals and reformists was hardly good news for the Gorbachev leadership. In Moscow itself, for instance, Yeltsin, whom the local Party authorities had tried to prevent from running, won a landslide victory, with 5.1 million of the 6.8 million registered voters casting their ballot for him; and, in the Baltic republics, the representatives

Kyiv. The Moscow *samizdat* publication *Ekspress-Khronika* subsequently reported, however, that attempts to nominate Shcherbytsky as a candidate in a Kyiv constituency had run into problems because of opposition both in the Institutes of Cybernetics and of Electrical Welding, which were to have formally proposed his candidature. See *Russkaya mysl*, 27 January 1989.

of the popular fronts swept to victory in a majority of the electoral districts. Although Gorbachev insisted that the results had shown that the USSR did not need a multi-party system, the voting confirmed something rather different: the processes which the Soviet leader had inaugurated were getting out of control.

In Eastern Europe, too, political change was taking place and was to assume an even faster pace. In Poland, the Communist authorities had by now effectively yielded on the sacrosanct principle of the leading role of the Party. In the political compromise finally concluded with Solidarity leader Lech Walesa's Citizens' Committee on 5 April, they agreed to the legalization of Solidarity in exchange for the latter's participation in elections and support for tough economic measures.

As before, despite the continuing push for greater national rights by the non-Russians, the Soviet leadership showed no readiness to overhaul its nationalities policy. Its draft programme for republican autonomy which was unveiled in mid-March had made it abundantly clear that the degree of decentralization was to be kept to a minimum, with the republics being offered only limited control over their budgets and Moscow maintaining control over most heavy industry. Now, despite the excitement generated by the results of the elections, on 8 April Radio Moscow announced that the outgoing Supreme Soviet of the USSR had rejected calls by the non-Russians for a new Union treaty, or, in other words, a new deal for the non-Russians.

The very next day, a tragic development in Georgia sent new shock waves throughout the Soviet Union. Troops armed with sharpened spades and toxic gas were sent in against peaceful nationalist demonstrators in Tbilisi who were demanding independence for their republic: twenty protesters, the majority of them women, were killed. Outraged democratic activists, including Sakharov, condemned the killings and warned that the violent intervention showed how fragile the reform process still was. At one of the protests in Moscow, blue and yellow Ukrainian national flags, carried by members of the UPDL, were first seen in the Soviet capital. The police reacted by arresting the Ukrainian activists.[3]

To add to the consternation of the democratic forces, on the same day as the tragedy in Tbilisi, the Presidium of the USSR Supreme

[3] UPA Press Release, no. 52, 24 April 1989.

Soviet issued a decree designed to strengthen, rather than to moderate, the existing laws against anti-state activities. In connection with this, on 11 April *Pravda* called for tougher action against 'nationalists' and all those who it said were exploiting *perestroika* as an excuse to violate law and order.

The effect of all this was to increase disillusionment with Gorbachev and to convince leaders of the national movements that there was no point in waiting for reform in the sphere of nationalities policy to come from above. Thus, the following month the Baltic popular fronts held their first joint council, at which they rejected the limited economic autonomy scheme which the Kremlin had proposed. Moreover, on 18 May, the Lithuanian Supreme Soviet voted to assert the republic's sovereignty, while its Estonian counterpart passed a series of resolutions affirming the republic's control over its own economy and allowing for, among other things, private ownership of land.

Shaken by the defeats it had sustained in the elections, the CPU sought to take stock of the situation. On 6 April, the Party authorities in the Ukrainian capital held a plenum for this purpose. According to *Vechirnii Kyiv*, the degree of candour, soul-searching and division was unprecedented.[4] Masyk admitted that the Kyiv Party organization had made mistakes, especially by underestimating the 'novelty and complexity of the current electoral campaign'. Nevertheless, he sought to shift the main blame for the results on popular dissatisfaction with the lack of tangible results from Gorbachev's policy of *perestroika*.

One Kyiv district Party boss, Valerii Kiryan from Darnytsya, acknowledged that the CPU had 'lost authority', that 'cases of voluntary resignations from the Party' were becoming more frequent, and that it was 'getting increasingly difficult to recruit cadres for Party work'. Salii went further and expressed what his colleagues were not prepared to admit openly. The 'moment of truth' had arrived, he declared, 'and we can no longer entertain illusions. And the truth is that we have suffered a major political defeat'.[5]

Public attention remained riveted on the new election campaigns in the numerous electoral districts where deputies had not been

[4] *Vechirnii Kyiv*, 10 April 1989.
[5] See Roman Solchanyk, ' "A Serious Political Lesson": Kyiv Party First Secretary Steps Down', *Report on the USSR*, no. 31 (4 August 1989), pp. 28–30.

elected. This time, encouraged by the results of the first round of elections, many more hopefuls put themselves forward as candidates. In some of the electoral districts the authorities gave in and registered all the candidates. By 20 April, Soviet domestic media were reporting that, for instance, in Kyiv sixty-nine candidates, including Pavlychko, Tanyuk, Chernyak, Yavorivsky, Salii and Karpenko were competing for three seats, and in the Dnipropetrovsk region, over fifty candidates for four seats. Some of the liberal Communists who decided to stand for election became even more outspoken. For instance, both Salii and Karpenko openly criticized the lack of democratization and renewal within the CPU, strongly supported Ukrainization, and called for dialogue and cooperation with unofficial groups, instead of confrontation and repression.[6]

Nevertheless, there were still cases where democratic norms were blatantly violated to prevent the registration of 'undesirable' candidates or to hinder their campaigning activity. In Lviv, where the authorities were still smarting from Pohrebnyak's humiliation, Bratun was now reluctantly registered as a candidate, but Drach's candidacy was blocked. The leader of Rukh had been persuaded that he had a better chance of being elected in Lviv than in Kyiv (he was born in the Kyiv region), but though he was nominated by over thirty local factories and enterprises, the Lviv authorities refused to register him as a candidate. On 20 April, Drach's supporters launched mass daily demonstrations to demand his registration. Thousands of people participated in them and workers at a number of enterprises staged warning strikes. These protests, in the same way as the ones before on behalf of Bratun and Khmara, served only to radicalize the Western Ukrainian public and, in Drach's case, also to promote Rukh in a city where the more radical UHU had its base. Meanwhile in the Ukrainian capital, conservative forces sought to discredit Karpenko (whose newspaper *Vechirnii Kyiv* had more than doubled its circulation during the last three years, from 210,000 to 460,000 copies) by accusing him in the pages of the worker's daily *Robitnycha hazeta* and a local newspaper of plagiarism. He fought back, however, and exposed the editor of *Robitnycha hazeta*, Shybyk (who had attacked the writers in 1987), as a conservative *apparatchik* who was hostile to the Ukrainian national revival.[7]

[6] See, for example, their discussion in *Ukraina*, no. 15, 9 April 1989.

[7] See David Marples and Roman Solchanyk, 'Plagiarism and Politics in Kyiv',

While the campaigning for the additional elections, scheduled in Ukraine for 14 May, was taking place, Gorbachev used the results from the voting on 26 March to force a quarter of the voting members of the CPSU Central Committee to resign. Altogether, at the plenum of the CPSU Central Committee, held on 25 April, 110 members of the Central Committee and the Central Auditing Commission announced their retirement, ostensibly because they were pensioners, or because of the poor state of their health. By this skilful manoeuvre Gorbachev managed to remove quite a few, but by no means all, of the conservatives in the Party's ruling bodies.

According to Vrublevsky, this was the moment when Shcherbytsky finally acknowledged that it was time for him to go. Dismayed by what was happening all around him as a result of Gorbachev's policies, the Ukrainian Party leader had been 'deteriorating both psychologically and physically'.[8] At the time of the mass resignation of members of the CPSU Central Committee, Shcherbytsky 'had a talk' with Gorbachev and offered to retire. But the Soviet leader had not accepted his resignation. On returning to Kyiv, Shcherbytsky told Vrublevsky with unconcealed satisfaction that Gorbachev had replied: 'Volodya, I ask you to stay. When the appropriate time comes, I'll let you know.'[9]

Rukh takes hold in Western Ukraine

The public, and for that matter even other members of the CPU leadership, were not aware of Shcherbytsky's offer to resign, and the protests against him and what he represented continued. Once again, as during the previous summer, the citizens of Lviv took the lead. On 26 April, thousands of people attended a public meeting in the city called by local Rukh supporters, Greens and the Lion Society to commemorate the third anniversary of the Chornobyl nuclear disaster. During it, some of the speakers, who included Mayor Kotyk, called for genuine sovereignty for Ukraine;

Report on the USSR (26 June 1989), pp. 17–19.

[8] Vitalii Masol, who was the chairman of the Council of Ministers from 1987 to 1990 confirms this. He writes that during the last years of his life, Shcherbytsky increasingly displayed 'excessive caution, intolerance of even the slightest disagreement [with him], a weakness for praise, and caprice'. See Vitalii Masol, *Upushchenyi Shans* [The Missed Chance], Kyiv, 1993, p. 18.

[9] Author's interview with Vrublevsky.

moreover, as a sign of mourning, the banned Ukrainian national flag with a black ribbon was raised. Within a week, the CPU leadership was embarrassed by demonstrations in Lviv and Chervonohrad during the official May Day celebrations, which were inspired largely by the UHU. In Lviv thousands of supporters of Drach and Rukh, some carrying blue and yellow flags, formed their own column in the official parade and, despite efforts by the police to block their path, managed to make their way past the tribune on which the startled local Party leaders were assembled.[10] This protest marked a turning point: the struggle for democracy and reform, of which Rukh was now the embodiment, had fused – in Western Ukraine at any rate – with the cause of national self-determination and national emancipation.

From now on, the question of restoring Ukraine's suppressed 'national symbols', that is, the blue and yellow flag of independent Ukraine, the national emblem – the 'tryzub' or trident, which had been used by the rulers of Kyivan Rus – and the national anthem, was to become an increasingly important issue. Although the UHU had raised this question in one of its press releases at the end of 1988, it was only now, when the Balts had succeeded in restoring their national flags and the national revival and growth of the democratic opposition in Ukraine had made more progress, that the push for the lifting of the ban on Ukrainian national symbols began in earnest. Two days after the success of the May Day protest, a mass meeting in Lviv adopted a resolution calling on the authorities to recognize and restore Ukrainian national symbols.

The mood in and around Lviv was now such that the local supporters of Rukh were able to proceed with organizing the first regional organization of the Popular Movement. On 7 May, some 200 representatives of various local independent groups, enterprises, and cultural, educational and scientific institutions and organizations participated in the inaugural conference of the Lviv Region Organization of the Popular Movement of Ukraine for Restructuring. It brought together an impressive team of leading local activists and prominent representatives of the region's cultural and scientific intelligentsia, many of whom were members of the Communist Party; they included: the physicists Academician Yukhnovsky and

[10] For accounts of these protests, see the monthly information bulletin issued by the Lion Society, *Postup*, no. 2, May 1989.

Lviv University professor Orest Vlokh, the economist Mykhailo Shvaika, the editor of the local Komsomol daily (*Leninska Molod*) Mykhailo Batih, as well as representatives of the local Russian and Jewish cultural societies. The conference elected, among others, Bratun, Vakarchuk, Vlokh and UHU leader Mykhailo Horyn to head the council of the new organization.

The programmatic declaration issued by the Lviv regional organization of Rukh reflected the radicalization that had taken place over the previous three months. It went a lot further than Rukh's programme, moving closer to the programmes of the Baltic popular fronts, the UHU and UPDL. Not only did it not acknowledge the leading role of the CPSU, it even stressed that it was 'opposed to any monopoly on political power'. Among other more radical demands, the declaration called for a new Union treaty on the basis of a new Union and republican constitutions; the demilitarization of society and for military service by Ukrainian citizens to done on Ukrainian territory; the institution of a citizenship of the Ukrainian SSR; the regulation of the inflow of migrants into the republic; the development of Ukraine's diplomatic representation abroad and of foreign diplomatic representation in the republic; the transfer of political power to freely elected councils of people's deputies at all levels; the recognition of different forms of ownership; the creation of a Ukrainian Olympics Committee and the establishment of direct links between Ukraine and international sports organizations; the restitution of Ukraine's cultural and historical treasures which had been 'removed from Ukraine'; the restoration of Ukrainian national symbols; and 'historical justice' for the Ukrainian Catholic and Ukrainian Autocephalous Orthodox Churches and recognition of them as part of the 'spiritual heritage of the nation'.[11]

In Western Ukraine then, the long-standing efforts to create a popular movement had finally been crowned with success. Significantly, the catalyst had been the political piggyback ride given by Lviv's democratic opposition to the leader of Rukh from Kyiv. 'The struggle to nominate Drach as a candidate for people's deputy', as one local independent publication commented at the time, became 'a lever which raised broad sections of society to conscious

---

[11] For the text of the declaration and details about the inaugural conference of the Lviv Region Organization of Rukh, see the organization's journal *Viche*, no. 1, June 1989, and *Postup*, no. 3, May 1989.

political life' and paved the way for the creation of a regional organization of Rukh. 'Striking changes in the attitudes and psychology of people compared even with the end of 1988' were 'apparent everywhere'. The 'difference between the present and the summer of last year', it noted, was that 'after their victory in the elections of 26 March the people . . . [had] realized their strength and learned to resist the bureaucracy'.[12]

With the Party authorities having decided to block Drach's candidacy at all costs, Bratun's victory in the new elections on 14 May brought some consolation to Lviv's democratic opposition. Elsewhere in Ukraine, two liberal writers who had been blocked from standing in Moscow, Korotych and Yevgenii Yevtushenko, were elected in Kharkiv. Because of the large number of candidates in many electoral districts, quite a few of the results were inconclusive, necessitating run-off elections.

On 16 May, the embattled CPU leadership held a plenum of its Central Committee to assess the situation and, as Shcherbytsky put it, 'to draw lessons from the results of the elections'. Stressing at the very outset of his address that the Party did not intend to relinquish its leading role in society, the Brezhnevite holdover indicated that because of 'the growth and deepening of the restructuring processes' the CPU was having to operate in 'unusual and complex conditions' characterized by 'the unprecedented rise in the civic and political activity of people'. Although he maintained that there was no need to 'dramatize' the situation in the republic, from the picture which he presented, it was clear that the CPU was under siege and was losing ground. 'One cannot help but see', the Ukrainian Party leader acknowledged, 'that nationalist manifestations are at times taking on an aggressive and overtly anti-Soviet character in many regions of the republic'. Ecological questions had acquired 'strongly national overtones', students were continuing to fall under the influence of politically 'dubious' unofficial groups, and 'extremist formations' were attempting to penetrate 'workers' collectives' and establish their cells there. Because of 'growing shortages, inflation and crime' social discontent was growing and, 'under the pretence of criticizing the administrative-command system and struggling against the bureaucracy' all kinds of 'demagogues and extremists' were attacking the Party and its leading role. As if invoking the warning that

[12] *Postup*, no. 4, May 1989, pp. 1-2.

Gorbachev had made in Donetsk, the Ukrainian Party leader declared: 'Our people are seriously concerned and alarmed that the development of events could lead to a situation like that in the Baltic states and Transcaucasia.'

According to Shcherbytsky, during the election campaign the CPU had been confronted by 'overt political opponents with far-reaching goals' and the Party authorities in some areas had been either unprepared or found wanting in facing this challenge from 'political extremism'. He expressed concern that some CPU officials had broken ranks during the election campaign and in effect had sided with the democratic opposition. The Ukrainian Party boss singled out Salii, adding that he and others like him would have to answer for their 'politically immature' behaviour.

Although Shcherbytsky said that there were 'about fifteen groups' that were 'overtly destructive and anti-Socialist in their orientation', he focused on the UHU and Rukh. The former, he claimed, was attempting to 'undermine constitutional laws and order', to rehabilitate the OUN, and 'to develop a broad "national" or, more precisely, nationalist movement for the secession of Ukraine from the USSR'. The growing 'impudence' of the UHU, Shcherbytsky added, had been demonstrated at the May Day protest in Lviv.

In actual fact, the dramatic surge of support for Rukh in Western Ukraine had somewhat eclipsed the UHU, which had done so much to prepare the ground. The leaders of the UHU (which still called itself a federation of human rights organizations, and in April had accepted the UPDL as a collective member) had gradually given up trying to transform their own organization into a broad popular front-type movement; instead, having given their backing to Rukh, they continued to concentrate on building up an organization which increasingly resembled a political party. Internal conflicts between moderates in the leadership and some of the more militant members had also come to a head in the spring, and at a meeting of the UHU's Coordinating Council on 7 May Vasyl Sichko and Ivan Makar had been expelled from the organization. Under criticism from radical nationalists, both in Ukraine and in the West, however, the UHU had, at the same meeting, amended its Declaration of Principles to get around the problem of the compromise over the issue of independence. The change accentuated the UHU's commitment to Ukrainian statehood and to upholding the right of individuals or civic groups to 'promote their ideas regarding statehood in a

constitutional manner, [whether] in the form of a federation, confederation with other nations of the USSR or Europe, as well as full
state independence'.[13]

The Ukrainian Party leader was a little less scathing in his
condemnation of Rukh, which he described as a 'new political
structure', which sought mass support and saw itself as being in
opposition to the Communist Party. Rukh's draft programme, he
warned, was 'imbued with essentially separatist' and 'destructive'
goals and it was no coincidence that 'the UHU and formations
similar to it' had 'hurried to announce' that they were joining the
Popular Movement. All the same, acknowledging that there were
'reasonable people' among the founders and leaders of Rukh who
perhaps had not fully realized the dangers of uniting with 'nationalist
and extremist elements', Shcherbytsky implicitly called on the
moderates and Party members in the Popular Movement to break
with the 'extremists'. In something of a departure for him, he
conceded that the CPU could not simply remain deaf to the myriad
of unofficial associations and that it ought to conduct a dialogue with
them with the aim of 'winning over to its side healthy forces, [and]
directing their initiative into healthy channels'.

Apart from calling on the CPU to close ranks, learn from its
mistakes, and improve its ideological work, especially in the mass
media, the Ukrainian Party leader had little else to say to reassure
the CPU's formidable force of 3,304,000 members and candidate
members. What he did stress, however, was that the CPU had to
ensure that it would be ready for the next stage of the political
struggle – the elections in the near future to the Supreme Soviet of
the Ukrainian SSR and the regional and district councils. Party
committees at all levels were instructed to 'approach this exceptionally important political campaign with a clear understanding of their
tasks and the methods' to be employed. As the first stage in the
preparations, Shcherbytsky announced that the drafting of a new
republican election law had been placed at the top of the CPU's
political agenda.[14]

A few days later, *Pravda Ukrainy* published the text of an interview
which Shcherbytsky had given to the Associated Press over a month

[13] UPA Press Release, no. 63, 12 May 1989.
[14] *Radyanska Ukraina*, 17 May 1989.

earlier. In it, having had adequate time to prepare the answers, he provided a spirited defence of his stewardship in Ukraine and of the supposed progress which restructuring and democratization were making there. As for Rukh, he claimed that the republic's workers had not supported its creation and that this had been demonstrated in the extensive debate in the press about its draft programme.[15]

On 21 May, the final run-off elections brought further blows to the CPU. In Kyiv, two more prominent Rukh supporters, Yavorivsky and Chernyak, were elected, as well as a liberal Communist university lecturer, Valerii Hryshchuk. Furthermore, the following day in the Ukrainian capital, blue and yellow flags first appeared in the crowd during an official outdoor meeting in honour of Shevchenko. Pavlychko, who was on the tribune, recounts that the crowd tried to prevent the police from seizing the students who had raised the national colours and eventually succeeded in securing their release. That memorable day, he says, senior Communist officials throughout Kyiv were stricken by panic as if they were expecting a revolution.[16]

All in all, then, the drawn-out election struggle contributed significantly to the politicization of society and resulted in a psychological and political breakthrough. The size of the protest vote revealed the level of dissatisfaction in the republic not only with declining social and economic conditions but also with the Shcherbytsky regime and what it represented. Although the old order had demonstrated that it still remained powerful, the victories scored by the democratic opposition showed what could be achieved with united action. Democratic candidates had triumphed in Kyiv, while in Lviv resurgent national democratic forces had demonstrated their strength and advanced the national cause. Lviv, moreover, had given its weighty support to Rukh, providing it with a large new and dynamic regional section, and thereby stimulated the symbiosis between Western and central Ukraine. And of course, the elections had resulted in the election of a number of democratic and nationally minded deputies, including Rukh supporters, who, enjoying the authority, exposure and relative

[15] *Pravda Ukrainy*, 21 May 1989.

[16] Author's interview with Pavlychko. For a fuller account of this demonstration see the letter from Teren and five other writers defending the action of the young people who had unfurled the blue and yellow flags in *Vechirnii Kyiv*, 27 May 1989.

immunity that went their new positions, could more effectively carry the fight to their reactionary adversary and publicize the grievances and demands of their compatriots.

The national democratic opposition consolidates

When the Congress of People's Deputies convened on 25 May, it gradually emerged that the size of the reformist contingent from Ukraine was larger than originally thought and not limited to deputies elected in Kyiv and Lviv. Among the new radical or liberal figures were Sergei Konev, a young ethnic Russian doctor from Dnipropetrovsk (elected in Dniprodzerzhynsk), Mykola Kutsenko, a legal specialist from Kremenchuk (elected in Poltava), Vilen Martyrosyan, an ethnic Armenian Red Army colonel based in Rivne, and Yurii Sorochyk, a young veteran of the war in Afghanistan, who had defeated Kotyk in Lviv. Nevertheless, the overwhelming majority of the 262 representatives from Ukraine were nominees of the CPU and, with the division of the deputies at the Congress into republican delegations so as to simplify procedure, the Ukrainian reformists were to find themselves blocked from reaching the rostrum (Bratun voiced a complaint about this on 30 May, but to no avail) and from nomination to the new bicameral Supreme Soviet, the members of which the Congress formally elected. It also turned out that, despite the headway which the reformist forces had made in different parts of the Soviet Union in the elections, most of the deputies elected to the Congress were conservatives who formed, as the radical Moscow historian and deputy Yurii Afanasev labelled them, an 'aggressively obedient' majority representing 'the Brezhnevite-Stalinist apparatus'. Nevertheless, the reformists succeeded in having the proceedings televised live, thereby allowing the population of the Soviet Union to watch events which in fact proved to be even more dramatic than at the Nineteenth Party Conference.

Before leaving for Moscow, the reformist deputies from the Ukrainian capital formed a 'Kyiv's Deputies' Club' along the lines of the analogous 'Moscow Group'. At the Congress, according to Yavorivsky, he, Chernyak, Hryshchuk and other democratically minded deputies from Ukraine immediately found they had common ground with the Lithuanian representatives, next to whom they had been seated, and also some of the reformist deputies from

Moscow. In fact, Konev, who represented a district in the heart of the traditional Brezhnev-Shcherbytsky political stronghold – the Dnipropetrovsk region – made a striking debut on 27 May in which he spoke out in support of Afanasev and the Baltic delegates. During the four years of restructuring, he claimed, the backbone of the administrative-command system had been 'very carefully preserved' and the reforms had been only 'half measures'. The Baltic representatives were being accused of 'separatism and self-isolation' when all they were doing was speaking about republican sovereignty and, despite the opposition of the 'centre', developing their own approach to economic reform. Konev proposed that instead of attacking the Baltic delegates, they should be encouraged to share their ideas with the deputies from the other parts of the Soviet Union.[17] A group of Ukrainian deputies, including Honchar, also addressed a note to the presidium of the Congress condemning the killings of the demonstrators in Tbilisi and expressing sympathy to the Georgian people.[18]

Disappointed by the conservative attitude of the majority, the reformist Ukrainian deputies were forced to watch in disgust as, for instance, on 2 June a delegate from Ukraine, Serhii Chervonopysky, a Komsomol official and Afghan war veteran, launched into a diatribe against Sakharov for daring to criticize the role of the Red Army in Afghanistan, and also when a week later Gorbachev (who had been elected chairman of the new Supreme Soviet on the first day of the Congress) cut short Sakharov's speech just as the latter was about to deal with the nationalities problem. Subsequently, when a new radical faction headed by Sakharov (who had been nominated by the USSR Academy of Sciences) and Yeltsin – the Interregional Group – began to form, the Ukrainian reformists supported it.[19]

Still, quite a few radical deputies, mainly Russians and Balts, did manage to get to the rostrum and to raise a host of sensitive issues, including the question of responsibility for the bloody crackdown

[17] *Izvestiya*, 29 May 1989.

[18] Honchar included the text in his article about the Congress in *Literaturna Ukraina*, 29 June 1989.

[19] Author's telephone interview from Munich with Yavorivsky on 14 June 1989 for Radio Liberty's Ukrainian Service (broadcast on 16 June 1989). A sign of the times, this was the first interview given by a Ukrainian deputy to Radio Liberty, which the official media in Ukraine were still depicting as subversive and nefarious.

in Tbilisi, the role of the CPSU, the powers of the KGB, the violation of democratic norms during the elections, and the consequences of the Molotov-Ribbentrop Pact (a special commission was established to study this problem). Indeed, with protests going on at this time in Georgia, Moldova and Uzbekistan, and the Baltic deputies, including for instance the Lithuanian Party leader Algirdas Brazauskas, and the chairman of the Latvian Supreme Soviet, Anatlolijs Gorbunovs, who had been the Latvian Communist Party's ideological secretary, pressing for the fullest degree of sovereignty for their republics, the nationalities problem figure as one of the main themes in the debates.

From among the Ukrainian delegation, Oliinyk was the only representative who took advantage of his opportunity to address the Congress to raise questions of concern to Ukrainian patriots. After starting by describing Ukraine as 'the most docile and loyal republic', he went on to call for a strengthening of the sovereignty of the republics, for Ukrainian to be made the state language in his republic and for the inauguration of a broad programme of Ukrainization. Stressing that the Ukrainian state should simultaneously encourage the development of the languages of the national minorities, he strongly opposed the idea that Russian should also be made a state language in Ukraine. Just two weeks after he had staunchly defended the good name of the Communist Party at the plenum of the CPU Central Committee, he complained publicly that members of the Ukrainian Language Society were being persecuted by 'bureaucrats actively opposed to restructuring in the sphere of national relations'. Oliinyk also protested against the unchecked powers of all-Union ministries which, he said, were continuing to get away with their abject disregard for the protection of the environment and, in particular, he called for the closure of the Chornobyl nuclear power station.

But the most significant feature about Oliinyk's speech was the important new argument which he presented. As if to emphasize that he was no nationalist, he made it clear that the desire for genuine sovereign statehood was not something that only the non-Russians ought to be thinking about. The Russians, he reminded the Congress, did not have their own Communist Party, Academy of Sciences, or separate seat in the United Nations. This theme was taken up three days later by the Latvian Janis Peters who asked: 'Why is Russia afraid of becoming independent of the all-Union *diktat*.[20] The Estonian deputy Klara Hallik was to go further still and argue that the Russian nation had lost out as a result of the blurring of the distinction between the Russian identity and the all-Union one, and that its national revival was impeded by the perpetuation of 'habits of imperial thinking' and the idea that Russia and Moscow were necessarily somehow not only political and economic, but also cultural, linguistic and religious 'centres' for the USSR's diverse Slavic, Baltic, Turkic, Finno-Ugric and other peoples.[21]

Although the reformist Ukrainians allied themselves with like-minded Russian deputies, some of them were disappointed to discover that their new Russian colleagues did not have much understanding for, or even interest in, the issues connected with nationalities policy which they wanted to raise. Fedoriv, for instance, told a Lviv newspaper that Yeltsin 'practically pays no attention to nationalities' problems' and 'supports [Russian-native-language] bilingualism, not understanding what this means in practice in the republics'.[22] Sakharov was one of the few exceptions, though. In his speech on 9 June he described the USSR as an imperial edifice, the victims of which included both the non-Russian and Russian nations alike, and called for its replacement by a genuine federation of equal states based on a new freely negotiated Union treaty. Although he was forced to break off his address before reaching this section, the full text of his speech was reproduced in numerous independent publications.[23] Moreover, Sakharov was to develop his views on this matter in a interview which *Ogonek* published the following month. By then he was calling for the dismantling of the Soviet Union's 'imperial' structures and the creation of a voluntary confederation in which the non-Russians would be given 'independence to the maximum degree'.[24]

While the Congress was meeting, a group of Ukrainian Catholics who had recently begun a hunger strike on Moscow's Arbat drew the attention of the foreign and Russian press to the continuing lack of religious freedom in Ukraine. The authorities in Ukraine had

---

[20] Moscow television, 30 May, and *Izvestiya*, 2 June 1989.

[21] *Pravda*, 7 June 1989.

[22] *Leninska Molod*, 3 June 1989.

[23] *Holos*, no. 1, 6 August 1989, pp. 2- 3.

[24] *Ogonek*, no. 31, July 1989, pp. 26-7.

remained hostile to the Ukrainian Catholics and, apart from continuing to harass Ukrainian Catholic priests, had exacerbated tensions in Western Ukraine by starting to transfer 'closed' former Uniate churches to Orthodox believers. The preparation of a new Soviet law on freedom of conscience had nevertheless raised hopes that both the Ukrainian Catholic and Ukrainian Autocephalous Orthodox Churches would finally be allowed to exist legally. Speaking at a press conference in Lviv on 10 May in St George's Cathedral and in the presence of senior officials responsible for religious policy in Ukraine, Metropolitan Filaret had, however, dashed them: stressing the need to preserve not only religious 'unity', but also, as he put it, unity 'among all our nations', he had reiterated the Russian Orthodox Church's opposition to the restoration of the two Ukrainian national churches. The legalization of the Uniate Church would lead to religious and inter-ethnic conflict, he maintained and proposed that Ukrainian Catholics who did not want to attend Orthodox services should worship in Roman Catholic (which in practice usually meant Polish) churches. He also claimed that the movement for the restoration of the Ukrainian Autocephalous Orthodox Church was inspired by individuals who wanted to exploit religion for political purposes – 'the separation of Ukraine from the Soviet state.'[25] To protest this attitude, a few days later a delegation of Ukrainian Catholic bishops and clergy travelled to Moscow to hand over to the Soviet authorities yet another petition for the legalization of their church. After their visit, groups of volunteers began the hunger strike protest in the centre of Moscow which was to last for four months.

The Ukrainian Catholics protesting in Moscow received support from sympathetic Ukrainian deputies, including Honchar and the Western Ukrainian representatives, Bratun, Fedoriv and Sorochyk, who raised their case in the pages of the Ukrainian press. A number of liberal Russian Orthodox activists also responded sympathetically, and Sakharov included a call for the legalization of the Ukrainian Catholic Church in his above-mentioned speech. What was also encouraging for the protesters was that on 11 June *Moskovskie novosti*, which had become one of the flagships of *glasnost*, reported on their hunger strike. This publicity elicited an angry reaction from Metropolitan Filaret, prompting the newspaper to provide more

[25] Radio Kyiv, 10 May 1989.

detailed coverage of the issue. At the end of July it was to publish a commentary which for the first time ever in a Soviet newspaper not only told the truth about how the Ukrainian Catholic Church had been forcibly incorporated in the Russian Orthodox Church and its members repressed, but also called for the legalization of the Ukrainian Catholic Church and the restitution of its property, including the Cathedral of St George.[26]

Back in Lviv, the Ukrainian Catholics, and for that matter, the activists seeking to revive the Ukrainian Autocephalous Orthodox Church, received support from the Lviv regional section of Memorial, which held its inaugural conference in the city on 27 May. This gathering, which was followed the next day by a huge public meeting, complete with national flags and a religious service conducted by a Ukrainian Catholic priest, once again attested to the growing civil and national assertiveness in Western Ukraine. Among other things, the resolutions adopted by the conference rejected the distorted official history of the region; supported the Balts in their condemnation of the Molotov-Ribbentrop Pact and its consequences; recognized the union proclaimed by the UNR and ZUNR in January 1919 as 'the actual legal basis' of Ukraine's unification, as opposed to the 'liberation' of Western Ukraine by Soviet troops in 1939 following the Nazi-Soviet agreement; and denounced the bloody repression in Tbilisi as a 'manifestation of Stalinist methods to deal with complex problems of inter-ethnic relations'.[27] Yukhnovsky was elected head of the organization and Chornovil to its council.

In the short period since the founding conference of the republican Memorial organization, the authorities and the official press had been forced to begin acknowledging some of the crimes of the Stalin era that had either been covered up, as in Bykivnya, or blamed on the Nazis, as in Vinnytsya, where, as in Katyn, the German invaders had uncovered the mass graves of thousands of victims of Stalinist terror. More and more such sites were being discovered throughout the republic and the press was providing new information about the liquidation of Ukrainian political and cultural

---

[26] See Bohdan R. Bociurkiw, 'The Ukrainian Catholic Church in the USSR Under Gorbachev', *Problems of Communism*, no. 6 (November-December 1990), p. 10.

[27] *Postup*, no. 6, July 1989, p. 5.

figures and the famine of 1932-3. As far as Western Ukraine was concerned, the emergence of the gruesome details about the scale of Soviet repression in the region, not to mention the now widespread denunciations of the Molotov-Ribbentrop Pact, was not only complicating official preparations for the celebration in September of the fiftieth anniversary of Western Ukraine's incorporation into the Ukrainian SSR, but also making it difficult to dismiss the UPA's and OUN's resistance fighters as fascists and bandits, which the official newspapers were still endeavouring to do.

The authorities were also being forced to respond to the mounting pressure, in Western Ukraine and Kyiv at any rate, for the restoration of Ukrainian national symbols. Towards the end of June, the Supreme Soviet's commission on patriotic and internationalist education and inter-ethnic relations held a special hearing to discuss this issue at which a number of official historians and experts were asked to speak, presumably to give the meeting some semblance of objectivity. In fact, in his concluding remarks, the chairman of the commission, Kravchuk, agreed that the history of Ukraine's national symbols needed further study but stressed that the entire issue was first and foremost a political and ideological one. There was no basis, he declared, for changing the existing state symbols of the Ukrainian SSR, which reflected the socialist choice which the workers of the republic had supposedly made once and for all, that is, the red and sky blue flag, the star and the hammer and sickle. He also reaffirmed the traditional Soviet line on the blue and yellow flag and trident: these 'dirty and bloody symbols' had always been identified with enemies of the Ukrainian people and exploitation. The forces which sought to restore them were nostalgic 'for an independent . . . Ukraine' and by 'choosing the blue and yellow flag' were 'saying openly that they are for breaking away from the Soviet Union'.[28] The commission duly laid down the law and the official press was used to amplify the message: the national symbols were to remain prohibited and more attention was to be devoted to inculcating the youth with socialist and internationalist values.[29]

Yelchenko and Kravchuk also advised the CPU's Politburo not to yield on the issue of the legislation of the Ukrainian Catholic

[28] See the official account of the meeting issued by the Ukrainian state news agency RATAU in *Literaturna Ukraina*, 6 July 1989.
[29] *Radyanska Ukraina*, 7 July 1989.

Church. In a report submitted at the end of June, they supported the position espoused by Metropolitan Filaret, maintaining that the regularization of the Church would provide a legal basis for anti-Soviet and nationalist activity. Revealing the extent of official Kyiv's increased support for the Russian Orthodox Church, they noted that during 1988-9 more than 1,300 religious communities belonging to it had been registered in Ukraine, and close to 1,000 churches and several monasteries in Kyiv, Chernihiv and the Ivano-Frankivsk region transferred to it.[30]

Also at the end of June, the month in which Solidarity had gained 65% of the votes cast in the Polish elections, the CPU Central Committee's ideological commission met to discuss policy towards Rukh and its allies. Although it was chaired by Yelchenko, the tone was set by Kravchuk. His remarks appeared to reflect a certain adjustment to the changing political climate in the USSR as a whole, as demonstrated in the debates at the Congress of People's Deputies in Moscow. Indeed, on 24 June, the CPU's organ *Radyanska Ukraina* had even called its interview about the Congress with Shcherbytsky's new deputy, Ivashko, 'Twelve Days Which Made Us Different'; and, on 1 July, against the background of a new wave of ethnic unrest, this time in Central Asia, Gorbachev was to appear on Soviet television with a warning about the 'tremendous danger' threatening 'the very unity' of the USSR.

Kravchuk emphasized that the main threat facing the CPU was the attempts being made by 'politicized' and 'extremist' groups to 'consolidate' their forces 'under the umbrella' of Rukh. There was danger that 'anti-Soviet' elements might even begin to take control of the Popular Movement. The Party machine, therefore, had to do everything possible to prevent this process. On the one hand, Party committees were to be instructed to cooperate with moderates in Rukh and other independent organizations, and if possible 'steer' them in the right direction, and on the other, to continue exposing and denouncing 'extremist elements'. Outlining the CPU's modified approach to Rukh, Kravchuk announced that the ideological commission had decided that the Party's representatives at all levels should 'explain' to the population that the CPU was not against the Popular Movement as such, but against attempts by anti-Soviet forces to hijack it.[31]

---

[30] Lytvyn, *Political Arena*, pp. 146-8.

The CPU's enduring conservative attitude was a far cry from what was happening in the Baltic republics (or, for that matter, Poland), which were continuing to serve as sources of inspiration for the Ukrainian democratic opposition. In June, the Lithuanian Komsomol declared its independence from the all-Union body and a plenum of the leadership of the Lithuanian Communist Party revealed that the spirit of independence had also taken hold of this organization.

By now, the Baltic republics had also begun to provide valuable technical assistance to the Ukrainian and other national democratic movements. Quite a few of the numerous new independent publications which appeared in Ukraine during the spring and summer of 1989 were printed in the Baltic republics. The Russian-language newspaper of the Latvian Popular Front, *Atmoda*, not only provided sympathetic coverage of the Ukrainian national movement but also served as an invaluable source of information at this time about events in other parts of the Soviet Union. The Baltic republics also served as a haven for non-Russian movements and organizations which were being blocked from holding founding congresses in their own republics by the local authorities. On 24-5 June, for instance, the Belarusian Popular Front held its founding congress in Vilnius and that same weekend the UPDL did likewise in Riga. This set a useful precedent for Rukh and afforded the Ukrainian Popular Movement some leverage with the Party authorities.

On 1 July, the inaugural conference of the Kyiv regional organization of Rukh was finally held. Although spurred on by more radical activists, Popovych and Bryukhovetsky had waited for the right moment. Indeed, Popovych acknowledged that the meeting could have been held sooner in Vilnius, but argued that this would not have had the same effect as convening it in the Ukrainian capital. The two leaders had also rejected the temptation to 'rush things' by turning the inaugural conference of the Kyiv regional organization into the founding congress of the republican organization of Rukh.[32]

What seems to have made the conference possible was the softening in official policy towards Rukh. Whether chastened by the recent election results or simply displaying greater political realism and flexibility, Kravchuk not only attended the conference

[31] *Radyanska Ukraina*, 5 July 1989.

[32] Haran, *To Kill the Dragon*, p. 41.

but also even declared in his speech that he and Drach had 'mutually acknowledged . . . mistakes' they had made in the enduring stand-off between the CPU leadership and Rukh and had now 'found a common language'.[33]

From what went on at the conference, however, there was not much sign of any closer understanding. In essence, Kravchuk again called on Rukh's leadership not to align their movement with 'extremist' organizations. For their part, Drach, Pavlychko, Yavorivsky and other Rukh leaders kept up the attack against the Shcherbytsky regime and its record on a broad range of issues, accusing it, as before, of being anti-democratic, hostile towards restructuring and the Ukrainian national revival, and indifferent to public concern about protection of the environment. Describing the attitude of the Kyiv authorities, Pavlychko, for instance, asserted that they were

> ....trying in all possible ways to salvage the administrative-command system; stir up dissatisfaction with the changes under *perestroika*; frighten the people with the chimera of raging nationalism among the creative intelligentsia; and portray the initiators of Rukh, who are without a doubt honest and brave citizens, as adventurers who are trying to seize power.

Although no new variant of Rukh's draft programme was unveiled at the conference, it was clear that the radicalization of the movement was continuing. Speakers included former political prisoners, UHU leaders and national democratic activists, such as Chornovil, Mykhailo Horyn, Badzo, Naboka and Yehven Sverstyuk, and several UHU members were elected to the organization's new coordinating council. Chornovil, who was given a standing ovation, used the opportunity to reject the label of extremism which the authorities were seeking to pin on the UHU and to denounce the attempts to split Rukh into moderates and radicals. He reminded the delegates of the pioneering work which the UHU had carried out in less auspicious conditions in laying the groundwork for a democratic opposition movement and called on them to oppose the recognition of any 'leading role' for a party which had 'oppressed Ukraine for seventy years'.

Two of the newly elected radical deputies, Yavorivsky and

---

[33] *Robitnycha hazeta*, 8 July 1989.

Konev, delivered outspoken speeches and emerged as Rukh's up
and coming new figures. Yavorivsky began his speech, tongue in
cheek, with the words, 'Dear extremists', and asked 'what kind of
a people' were the Ukrainians if they had to beg 'Leonid
Makarovych Kravchuk, a Ukrainian from Volhynia', that their
native language be made the state language of the republic, or
deprived themselves of a future by meekly allowing such ecological
disasters as Chornobyl and Chernivtsi. The whole problem boiled
down to one thing, he argued: the Ukrainians did not have a real
state or government of their own. As for the CPU, he added
sarcastically, it had demonstrated its independence long ago by
lagging so far behind with the implementation of restructuring. For
his part, Konev drew the delegates' attention to the need for the
democratic forces to be well prepared and organized for the elections
to the Ukrainian Supreme Soviet and local councils – which he
described as 'the decisive stage in the struggle against totalitarianism,
conservatism and national nihilism' – which were scheduled for the
following spring. He also called for changes in Rukh's draft
programme, which he said was obsolete and too ambivalent, adding
that he, for one, could not contemplate joining a movement which
still reverentially recognized the leading role of the Communist
Party. Other speakers, too, many of whom were still members of
the Communist Party, supported the calls for the abandonment of
the clause in the draft programme recognizing the leading role of
the Party and for the establishment of genuine Ukrainian statehood.

Representatives of Sajudis and the Latvian Popular Front were
given an especially warm welcome. When the latter declared that
the Latvians and Ukrainians shared the common goal of achieving
'genuine democracy, a law-governed state and . . . independence'
by following the Polish and Hungarian examples, the delegates
responded with tumultuous applause.

Drach himself seemed eager to infuse his colleagues with the
revived national spirit he had encountered during the election
struggle in Lviv. He spoke forcefully in defence of Ukraine's national
symbols and countered the arguments which had been advanced by
Kravchuk's Supreme Soviet commission that the blue and yellow
colours were associated with enemies of the Soviet state and should
therefore remain banned. Should not then the red Soviet flag be
rejected, Drach asked, because 'so many millions of Ukrainian were
murdered when it was held in the hands of Stalin and Beria'.

Contrasting the CPU's hard-line position with that of the Baltic Communist parties, the fiery poet expressed regret that the CPU had not produced a Brazauskas.

Drach, as well as Chornovil, also raised an issue which had recently galvanized the patriotically minded public. On learning that on 5-9 July 'Rossiya Molodaya,' or 'Young Russia,' the youth branch of the Russian ultra-nationalist organization *Pamyat*, as well as several Soviet 'patriotic' organizations under the aegis of the all-Union Komsomol, were planning to celebrate the 280th anniversary of Peter the Great's victory at Poltava on the site of the battlefield, Rukh and UHU leaders had sought to block this action. They not only urged their supporters to converge on Poltava on that day but also called on the republican authorities not to permit the 'insult' to Ukrainian national feeling. At the conference, both Drach and Chornovil warned, as the former put it, about 'the vitality of great-state chauvinism', and stepped up the pressure on the republican authorities to ban the celebrations. Kravchuk managed to cool emotions somewhat by reassuring the delegates that official Kyiv had 'approached the appropriate Union authorities with a request not to permit the celebration of the 280th anniversary of the Battle of Poltava on Ukrainian territory'.

The conference demonstrated the strong appeal and rapid growth of Rukh. Donchyk informed the delegates that the Kyiv regional organization now had almost 200 groups and thousands of members.[34] Coordinating Councils had also been established in Lviv, Kharkiv, Vinnytsya and Ternopil, and new groups were being formed throughout the republic. The strength of Rukh in the Ukrainian capital was also manifested by the mass rally which the organization held in Kyiv at the end of the conference: it drew over 10,000 people and blue and yellow flags abounded. Accentuating Rukh's recognition of the need to prepare to ensure that democratically minded candidates did well at the next round of elections, the meeting's main slogan was: 'All power to the [popularly elected] councils'. Within a few days, the Coordinating Coun-

---

[34] *Literaturna Ukraina* of 13 July 1989 cites him as giving an improbably high figure of 'not less than 200,000'. But perhaps this was a typo as Serhii Naboka, reporting on the conference for *Atmoda*, gave the more realistic figure of 20,000. See *Atmoda*, 7 August 1989.

cil met and elected an organizing committee headed by Yavorivsky to prepare for the republican inaugural conference of Rukh.[35]

In the meantime, despite Kravchuk's assurances, a new battle of Poltava was fought. On 5 July, a group of about 300 members of 'military-patriotic clubs' arrived in the city from Moscow and after laying wreathes at the graves of Peter the Great's soldiers were sent back home by the police. Groups of Ukrainian activists from various parts of the republic also began arriving, and in most cases, after attempting to stage demonstrations, distribute leaflets, or lay wreathes at the graves of Mazepa's and Swedish soldiers, were detained and expelled from the city. This went on for four days, with groups of Ukrainian activists arriving from Kyiv, Lviv, Kharkiv, Chernihiv, Vinnytsya and Dnipropetrovsk. The outcome was that no significant official, or semi-official, celebrations of Peter the Great's victory were held and that, despite their harassment by the police, Ukrainian patriotic activists were able to present a different interpretation of the Battle of Poltava from the officially prescribed one. Although Memorial was to complain to the authorities about the rough treatment of the Ukrainian demonstrators, overall the action resulted in an important symbolic victory for the Ukrainian national movement.[36]

Another significant success achieved by Ukrainian patriotic forces at this time was the formal acknowledgement by the republican Procuracy and KGB that the case of the Union for the Liberation of Ukraine had been fabricated and that leading members of the national intelligentsia who had been convicted at the subsequent show trial in 1930 ought to be fully rehabilitated.[37]

The miners' revolt

Despite this progress, Rukh and its allies were soon reminded of how much remained to be done. When, in the second half of

---

[35] On the conference, see Roman Solchanyk, 'Constituent Conference of Kyiv Regional Popular Front', *Report on the USSR*, no. 32 (11 August 1989); Haran, *To Kill the Dragon*, pp. 41-2; *Atmoda*, 7 August 1989; and Kaminsky, *In a Transitional Stage*, pp. 183-5 and 191-215.

[36] For very different accounts of what occurred, see *Vilne Slovo* (a Rukh newsletter published in Kyiv), no. 3, July 1989, p. 4, and the diatribe against the Ukrainian activists in *Pravda Ukrainy*, 23 July 1989.

[37] *Pravda Ukrainy*, 23 July 1989.

July, a wave of miners' strikes spread from the Kuzbass in Siberia to the Donbas, the national democratic moment saw just how little influence it had among the workers in the eastern and central regions of Ukraine. The miners treated what few local representatives of the UHU, UPDL or Rukh there were, or who came from other regions of Ukraine to talk to them, with suspicion or hostility; they appeared to have little interest in matters other than the improvement of their social, economic and working conditions. Nevertheless, from the very outset, the authorities both in Kyiv and in Moscow betrayed their concern that the strikes in the Donbas might take on a political dimension: in the very first official report about the start of strikes in this region, TASS conjured up the image of UHU 'extremists' from Western Ukraine stirring up trouble among the miners.[38]

The situation was different, though, in Western Ukraine. Here, some of the miners in the Chervonohrad area, close to the Polish border, were reported to have come out with political demands, including the establishment of an independent trade union of mineworkers with the proposed name of 'Solidarity'. In Pavlohrad, in central Ukraine, the miners also apparently supported the idea of independent trade unions, though here the UHU and Rukh did not play a role.[39]

For ten tense days from 18 to 28 July, strike committees were in control of the Ukrainian coalfields; the miners did not begin returning to work until the Soviet government gave in and agreed to all of their demands, including a considerable degree of autonomy and self-management for the mines. Even then the miners did not disband their strike committees but sought to build regional and an all-Union organizations.

Throughout the main phase of the protests, the strike committees ignored Shcherbytsky and the Ukrainian government and addressed their demands and appeals directly to the Kremlin. In fact, Shcherbytsky's team seems to have been at a loss how to respond to the strikes. Soviet television even implicitly criticized its inaction by asking on 18 July why the Ukrainian government had not begun any negotiations with the miners. Perhaps one of the reasons for this passivity was the fact that Kyiv in reality had very little control over

---

[38] TASS, 17 July 1989.
[39] See UPA Press Release, no. 109, 29 July 1989.

conditions in the Donbas and that the miners in the region had made a perennial source of friction in relations between Moscow and Kyiv their key demand: the allocation of additional funds for the development of the Donbas.

The miners' strikes revealed that the workers, or at any rate the coalminers, were more disciplined and politically resourceful than had been thought and were potentially a very powerful force. Furthermore, the strikes, on the one hand, exposed a fundamental weakness of the Ukrainian national democratic movement – the lack of support, and frequently even of understanding, for it in the heavily Russified, industrialized, south-east, and, on the other, highlighted the disaffection of the working class with the Party which claimed to rule in its name. For Rukh's leaders, who admired the example which Solidarity had set in Poland, this was a missed opportunity to follow the Polish path and reach out to the workers. No attempt seems to have been made to form a body similar to the Polish intellectuals' Workers' Defence Committee (KOR), or even to adopt a clear position on the strikes.[40] The UPDL did produce a leaflet backing the miners, but even if it had been widely distributed among them, the text was probably too radical.[41]

The strikes also showed once again how highly centralized the Soviet economy remained and that, as local officials explained to the strikers, decisions on such matters as the allocation of funds, food supplies and the availability of consumer goods, were still made in Moscow. Hardly surprisingly, therefore, the miners' protests influenced attitudes on the issues of republican economic sovereignty and greater local control of economic decision-making.

Initially, at the Congress of People's Deputes, the Baltic proposals

[40] When asked by the author about this on 6 October 1989 during a discussion recorded in the Munich studios of Radio Liberty, Drach replied: 'As for "Solidarity" and the overall situation in Poland, it is generally understood that this is a link-up of Poland's intelligentsia and workers. It was made possible by the years and years of, perhaps thousand-year-long, nurturing by the Church of this single ethnos, this one Polish stream, and so on. In the current Ukrainian situation, we do not have a comparable variant. We have on the one hand, this plundered, mutilated, downtrodden, chemicalized village that is rising to its feet under very difficult conditions. On the other hand, we have the workers, who in most of Ukraine are Russian-speaking . . . Therefore, the problem of relations with the working people . . . is for us especially complicated and particularly important.' See in Solchanyk, *Ukraine: From Chernobyl' to Sovereignty*, pp. 49–50.

[41] For the text, see *Soviet Ukrainian Affairs*, no. 2 (summer 1989), pp. 28–9.

for economic autonomy had come under heavy fire from the central planners and conservatives. On 8 July, the Western Ukrainian representative Bratun had spoken out in defence of the Baltic scheme. But once the strikes got under way, on 26 July, Anatolii Saunin, a deputy from the Donbas who had been delegated by miners to represent them, hailed the Baltic plan for economic autonomy and republican cost-accounting as a 'revolutionary step in the restructuring of the country's economic mechanism'. When, on 27 July, the Baltic scheme was finally approved, Shcherbak called it a 'historic day'. He told the Congress that he regretted that it had not been Ukraine that had initiated the breakthrough.[42] During the next few weeks, the Party leaders in the Donestk, Voroshylovhrad and Lviv regions were all, in their way, to call for a review of the relations between Moscow and the regions and for economic decentralization.[43]

Cracks in the empire

As the fiftieth anniversary of the Molotov-Ribbentrop Pact approached, developments in the Baltic republics continued to reverberate in other parts of the USSR. On 29 July, Latvia joined Estonia and Lithuania in declaring its sovereignty. A few days later, the Estonian Supreme Soviet approved a controversial new election law setting minimum residence requirements for voters and candidates (two and five years respectively), which triggered off protests by the republic's Russian-speaking population.

Although, as far as the struggle for democracy and national self-determination was concerned, Ukraine still lagged far behind the Baltic republics, Shcherbytsky's team was increasingly anxious about the way things were going in their own republic and sought a firmer approach from the Soviet leadership. On 8 August, Shcherbytsky sent a report on the situation in Ukraine, which had been prepared jointly with Yelchenko and Kravchuk, to the Central Committee of the CPSU. It presented an alarming picture of growing ferment, widespread mass meetings and protests, increasing anti-Russian

---

[42] Radio Moscow, 8, 26 and 27 July 1989.

[43] On the miners' strike in Ukraine and its consequences, see Bohdan Czajkowsky, '"We Want To Live as Human Beings": The Miners' Strike in Ukraine', *Soviet Ukrainian Affairs*, no. 3-4 (1989), pp. 10-16.

sentiment and trouble with Crimean Tatars returning to Crimea and with some of Ukraine's national minorities. 'Nationalists' and 'extremists' were drawing support especially from the creative and scientific intelligentsia and the students, and unless tougher measures were taken the political unrest would increase. Shcherbytsky noted that the republic's capacity to deal with these problems had been weakened because a large contingent of republican MVD troops and militia had been dispatched to trouble spots in other parts of the USSR. He requested that at least half of this contingent be returned to Ukraine, 'first and foremost to the Lviv region'. The Ukrainian Party leader also noted that 'the development of events in Lithuania, Latvia, Estonia, Moldova and several other regions of the country is creating a dangerous precedent for the further activation of anti-Socialist forces in our republic as well'.[44]

While Shcherbytsky waited for a response and *Pravda* was accusing the Balts of 'nationalist hysteria', the Kremlin on 17 August published its 'Platform', 'for improving inter-ethnic relations . . . and renewing nationalities policy', which was to be discussed at a forthcoming special plenum of the CPSU Central Committee. Although the Platform recognized the need to revamp the Soviet federation, the idea of renegotiating the Union treaty was rejected as was that of transforming the existing quasi-federation into a confederation. For all the talk of broadening the rights of the republics, not only was Moscow's predominance over them re-asserted but also the Russian nation was described as the 'consolidating basis of our entire Union', and the concept of a 'Soviet people' was again invoked. Whereas this document recognized the need to bolster the sense of Russian statehood by creating new Russian political, economic, scientific and other institutions, apart from conceding a measure of economic autonomy to the republics via self-accounting and self-financing, it offered little encouragement for non-Russians seeking genuine sovereignty and qualitatively different relations with Moscow. Besides, the principle that each nation of the USSR should have 'the right and real possibility of preserving its independence, uniqueness, culture, traditions and language' was something that had been promised throughout the Soviet period.[45]

Although it was becoming increasingly clear that democratization

---

[44] Lytvyn, *Political Arena*, pp. 151-2.

[45] See *Pravda*, 16 and 17 August 1989.

and the preservation of empire, however disguised, were incompatible, Gorbachev was determined to hold the Soviet Union together and seemed to underestimate the power of the pent-up centrifugal forces which had been released. For all his reformism in other spheres, his thinking on the nationalities question differed little from that of Brezhnev, Suslov and other proponents of the concept of the Soviet people with its Russianized Slavonic core. The chairman of the Ukrainian Council of Ministers at this time, Masol, has given a poignant description of what Gorbachev's real attitude was at this delicate moment.

> I remember how during one of the customary visits of Gorbachev and his family to Crimea for a holiday (it was in the summer of 1989), a discussion started up during dinner about events in the Baltic republics. Mikhail Sergeevich said the following: 'Just think, a group of loudmouths have got together in Lithuania – they'll let off steam for a while and then disperse. The main thing is that Russia, Ukraine and Belarus are united. Then nothing frightens us. We can get by without the Baltic republics or Georgia.'[46]

In fact, events in the Baltic republics were to continue to reverberate far beyond their borders. On the eve of the anniversary of the Molotov-Ribbentrop Pact, a commission of the Lithuanian Supreme Soviet declared the Nazi-Soviet agreement illegal and invalid and the popular fronts of all three Baltic republics issued a joint statement calling on Moscow to do likewise. On 23 August, some one million Balts marked the anniversary by forming a human chain stretching 600 kilometres from Tallinn to Riga and Vilnius. There was also a major demonstration that day by Moldovans in Kishinev (Chisinau). It took place against the background of strikes by Russian-speaking workers who were protesting against moves to make Moldovan the state language in the republic and restore the Latin alphabet. In Kyiv, on 21 August, the UHU and the UPDL organized a demonstration in solidarity with the Balts and Moldovans, the main Ukrainian protests against the consequences of the Molotov-Ribbentrop Pact having been planned for the following month.

While this was going on, the strike committees of the Donetsk, Voroshylovhrad, Dnipropetrovsk and Rostov (in the RSFSR)

---

[46] Masol, *The Missed Chance*, p. 54.

regions convened a meeting on 17 August in Horlivka in the Donbas and set up the Regional Union of Strike Committees of the Donbas. It not only began to sweep aside some of the local Party committees, but also issued a call for a new strike on 1 October because, as it put it, the authorities were not honouring all of their promises and were distorting the miners' demands in the media.[47]

As the summer progressed, the Kyiv Deputies' Group gradually developed into a Ukrainian 'Republican Deputies' Club'. This loose coalition, which was formally established on 12 August, had a nucleus of about twenty-five, but, depending on the issue, could draw on the support of a further two dozen deputies. Its leadership consisted of four joint heads: Yavorivsky, Chernyak, Talanchuk and Arnold Nazarenko, an engineer from Dnipropetrovsk. The group published its own information bulletin, *Holos* (Voice), the first issue of which had been put out by the Kyiv Deputies' Club on 6 August. Among the first priorities of the Republican Deputies' Club was to ensure that the forthcoming elections to the Ukrainian SSR Supreme Soviet and local councils would take place in more democratic conditions than to the Congress of People's Deputies. In fact, the first issue of *Holos* carried a declaration issued by Kyiv independent groups proposing the following basic principles: one man, one vote; direct elections of deputies to the Supreme Soviet on the basis of proportional representation; direct elections of the president of the republic; and multiple candidacies.

The proposed draft law on elections published on 6 August retained a number of undemocratic features favouring the Party apparatus, including the allocation of 25% of the seats to representatives of 'public organizations'. Only three other republics attempted to preserve this conservative prerogative of the ruling party. As before, the proposed law also left the Party-controlled electoral commissions with the power to accept or reject candidates if, in their view, the programmes of the candidates did not accord with the provisions of the constitution of the Ukrainian SSR.

The Republican Deputies' Club responded by issuing a statement signed by thirty-eight members, including two from the Donbas, addressed to all deputies of the Ukrainian Supreme Soviet and representing Ukraine in the Congress of People's Deputies in which

[47] See David Marples, 'Increased Militancy in the Donetsk Coal Basin', *Report on the USSR*, no. 49 (8 December 1989), pp. 11–12.

it described the draft law on elections as anti-democratic and urged that it adhere to the above-mentioned democratic principles, with the addition of depriving the electoral commissions of their political screening role. The reformist Deputies' Club also announced that it would prepare an alternative draft law on elections, and called on the population to demonstrate on 2 September against the officially proposed draft law. It urged the authorities to put the question of the election law to a referendum and warned that in the event of an 'anti-democratic' law being adopted, the Club would call for a boycott of the elections and other forms of civil protest.[48] This outright challenge to the CPU coincided with the formation of a Solidarity-led government in Poland – the first of the Eastern and Central European Communist dominoes to fall.

On the day of protest, tens of thousands turned out in Kyiv, Lviv, Zhytomyr and other cities to support the call by the Republican Deputies' Club, but in many cities and towns, such as Simferopol and Vinnytsya, the authorities banned public meetings. The demonstrators in Lviv, who were supported by the local Komsomol organization, threatened strike action if the alternative draft election law was not published in the press. In Donetsk, the participants in a large public meeting adopted a resolution expressing their 'lack of confidence' in Shcherbytsky and Valentyna Shevchenko, the chairman of the republican Supreme Soviet, for having supervised the preparation of the 'undemocratic' draft election law and also threatening protest action if the Supreme Soviet approved 'anti-democratic' election laws. Moreover, they also called for Article 6 of the USSR Constitution recognizing the leading role of the CPSU to be repealed.[49] With the strike committees consolidating their organization in the Donbas and surrounding areas and beginning to call for new and democratic elections to the local councils, the authorities were thus faced with the prospect that the disaffected workers might give their backing to the campaign which the Republican Deputies' Club had launched, On 7 September, the alternative draft election law appeared in the Lviv Komsomol newspaper *Leninska Molod*, and a week later *Literaturna Ukraina* published it.[50]

[48] *Holos*, no. 2, 20 August 1989, p. 1.

[49] *Holos*, no. 3, 3 September 1989, pp. 1 and 7, and Haran, *To Kill the Dragon*, p. 47.

All this, however, was nowhere near as dramatic as developments in some of the other republics. On 27 August, the Central Committee of the CPSU had issued a stinging attack on the Baltic popular fronts, warning that 'the fate of the Baltic peoples is in serious danger'. In Moldova, the adoption on 1 September of the law making Moldovan the state language further inflamed the situation and intensified the protests in Tiraspol by the 'Edinstvo' (Unity) movement, which like the 'Intermovement' in Estonia, the 'Interfront' in Latvia and the 'Edinstvo' movement in Lithuania, claimed to represent the interests of Russian-speaking residents, but in fact acted as an ultra-loyalist defender of the status quo. And in Azerbaijan, the local popular front had successfully called a general strike, which began on 4 September.

With the Kremlin continuing to issue warnings but seemingly unwilling or unable to do more to control things, it was becoming increasingly difficult for Shcherbytsky's regime to hold the line. The political change emanating from Moscow itself, the continuing pressure on the centre from some of the republics, and the growing strength of democratic opposition and national feeling in Ukraine[51] were forcing official Kyiv to make adjustments, which compared to the official position of only six months or a year before, represented significant concessions. On 5 September TASS reported that the Presidium of the Ukrainian Supreme Soviet had finally published the text of a draft law on languages designating Ukrainian as the state language of the republic. Shortly afterwards, the press also published the draft of a proposed law 'On the General Principles of the Economic Independence of the Ukrainian SSR'.[52] These developments, however, failed to overshadow news of the really critical breakthrough in the republic: behind the scenes, the leadership of Rukh had secured permission to convene its inaugural congress in Kyiv on 8-10 September.

Forced into making this concession by the growing strength of Rukh, threats from its leaders that they would hold their inaugural congress in one of the Baltic republics, and the absence of a firm line

[50] *Literaturna Ukraina*, 14 September 1989.

[51] According to the republican Ministry of Internal Affairs, during the first nine months of 1989 there were 724 mass meetings or demonstrations in Ukraine, 388 of which were not officially sanctioned. *Radyanska Ukraina*, 5 November 1989.

[52] *Pravda Ukrainy*, 7 September 1989.

in Moscow, the CPU leadership still hoped that it could upset this event and exploit it. Briefing the CPU's Politburo on the eve of the congress, Kravchuk emphasized that the CPU was determined to discredit Rukh's meeting. Its plan was to ensure the presence at the congress of representatives from various industrial enterprises, who although they were not delegates, would demand the right to speak and would disrupt proceedings by criticizing Rukh and calling into question the right of those present to represent the population of Ukraine. It was expected that the congress would take place under 'nationalist and separatist slogans', and therefore the official media would be mobilized to attack Rukh for its 'extremism'. Meetings were to be organized throughout the republic to protest against the congress, leading to a statement condemning Rukh issued by the Central Committee of the CPU.[53]

[53] Lytvyn, *Political Arena*, pp. 157-8.

9

THE STRUGGLE FOR DEMOCRACY
AND SOVEREIGNTY

Rukh's inaugural congress

As was to be expected, Rukh's inaugural congress turned into a celebration of the national and political awakening of Ukraine and was a landmark in modern Ukrainian history. Held in the hall of Kyiv's Polytechnical Institute, which was lavishly decorated with Ukrainian national symbols and regional emblems, and with the Ukrainian Zaporozhyan Cossack march sounding as the theme tune, the atmosphere was euphoric. Not since the days of the shortlived independent Ukrainian state seventy years before had Kyiv witnessed such a gathering. The broader international significance of what the congress represented was emphasized by one of the main foreign guests, the Polish historian and veteran Solidarity activist, Adam Michnik. With the 'totalitarian system' in Eastern and Central Europe collapsing and a new European community of free nations appearing in its place, this 'historic day' of 'Ukraine's national rebirth' was important for 'all of Europe', he maintained. Michnik brought the delegates to their feet by calling for closer Polish-Ukrainian cooperation in a 'new common European family' and by finishing his speech with the words: 'Long live a democratic, just, free Ukraine!'

Rukh's growth had been spectacular. According to the data presented at the congress, the Popular Movement's membership had soared to almost 280,000. The congress was attended by 1,109 of the 1,158 elected delegates (some were prevented from participating by local authorities), representing 1,247 groups throughout Ukraine and several in the Baltic republics. The delegates represented a broad cross-section of Ukraine's population and included 994 Ukrainians, 77 Russians, 9 Jews, 6 Poles, 6 Belarusians, 2 Armenians, and representatives of seven other national groups. There was a preponderance of intellectuals and white collar workers, though 109 of the delegates were workers. Although all the regions of Ukraine were represented, almost half of the delegates came from Western Ukraine, some 35% from the central regions, 9% from the southern ones, and less than 6% from Eastern Ukraine. The largest delegations were from the Kyiv region (accounting for 17.71% of the total), Lviv region (14.21%), and Rivne region (10.23%); Party members made up just over 20% of the delegates, and Komsomol members another 2%.

Understandably, the congress saw three days of catharsis, emotions ran high, and many of the speakers treated the congress as a rally rather than as an occasion for offering constructive proposals and identifying and debating concrete tasks. Nevertheless, the overriding theme was the need for unity – political, ethnic and social – and its prerequisites: tolerance and democracy. With Communists and non-Communists, Ukrainian nationalists and representatives of Ukraine's national minorities, Western Ukrainians and Eastern Ukrainians, workers and intellectuals, former political prisoners and representatives of the militia and army all meeting together under one roof and, by and large, finding a common language, the congress demonstrated how much progress Rukh's organizers had made in building a broad coalition. The presence of representatives of the Regional Union of Strike Committees of the Donbas was also an encouraging sign. Faced with such an impressive assembly, the CPU's plan to disrupt proceedings failed.

Although there were calls at the congress for independence, most notably from UHU leaders Lukyanenko and Chornovil, the majority of speakers called for the broadest political and economic sovereignty for Ukraine and for the USSR to be transformed into a confederation. As Pavlychko put it, Rukh rejected the existing 'paper' statehood of Ukraine but was not calling for secession from the USSR. 'We want an independent Ukraine', he declared, 'within a constellation of free states'. This position was reflected in the new, more radical and detailed version of the Popular Movement's programme, which was approved by the congress. It stated that Rukh sought 'the creation of a sovereign Ukrainian state', which would 'build its relations with the other republics of the USSR on the basis of a new Union treaty'. As before, it also committed Rukh to striving for a democratic law-based state, a mixed economy, social justice and ethnic harmony. Recognition of the Party's leading role, however, was dropped.

The congress also adopted a statute and numerous programmatic resolutions and appeals, including ones addressed to all the non-Ukrainians living in the republic, and separate ones appealing for understanding and support from Ukraine's 11-million strong Russian minority, condemning all forms of anti-Semitism, and supporting the national rights of the Crimean Tatars. Pavlychko warned in his speech about the rise of the Interfronts in the Baltic republics and Moldova and the fact that 'the centre', including the all-Union media, seemed to be encouraging these 'chauvinistic' and 'reactionary' movements, and clearly Rukh's leaders were anxious to forestall similar developments in Ukraine. Even Chornovil, one of the most radical figures at the congress, went out of his way to reassure Russians. He explained that he was telling Western Ukrainians not to use the slogan 'Occupiers out!', without qualifying what was meant. If by 'occupiers' was meant those responsible for imposing the control of the central ministries and 'Moscow's imperialism' in Ukraine, then he supported the slogan. But if it meant 'the Russian worker, who not being conscious of his role, ended up here as a result of the Stalin-Suslov policy of intermixing peoples, and whose children have grown up here and have no fatherland other than Ukraine', then he was against it.

Several new themes were raised at the congress which reflected the continuing radicalization of society and the progress of the national revival. One was that of the degree of economic control and 'exploitation' by Moscow. For instance, in addressing the question of economic sovereignty, the economist Mykhailo Shvaika from Lviv claimed that the central ministries controlled enterprises responsible for 95% of the republic's output and the distribution of 90% of the wealth produced in Ukraine. He told delegates that sovereignty was impossible without the creation of Ukrainian financial, monetary and banking systems and the introduction of a national currency. Another was that of the role of the army. The Armenian Colonel Martyrosyan assured delegates that officers such as he would never lead the army against the people. Aleksandr Volkov, a Russian worker from Ivano-Frankivsk and UHU member, who introduced himself as the son of a Red Army officer and the grandson of a tsarist officer, told the congress that only 'an independent, strong Ukraine' would be able to safeguard the rights of all of its citizens. But without the creation of a 'strong Ukrainian national army' the achievement of political independence would be impossible. As a first step, Volkov proposed that Rukh demand that Ukrainian citizens do their military service only 'in Ukraine and in the Black Sea Fleet' and that Ukrainian be the official language used by military units stationed in Ukraine.

Kravchuk represented the CPU leadership at the congress and was given quite a warm welcome. Adopting a moderate tone, he appealed to the delegates not to rush matters, to recognize existing political realities, and to distance themselves from 'extremists'. His arguments failed to make much of an impression and, hardly surprisingly, the congress heard repeated calls for Shcherbytsky to go, including from Salii. In fact, a group of nineteen deputies from the Republican Deputies Club attending the congress issued an open letter to Gorbachev, which was read out to the delegates, in which they accused the Ukrainian Party leader and his team of sabotaging *perestroika* and deliberately destabilizing the situation in the republic through disinformation and by fomenting confrontation between Rukh and its opponents as well as between Ukrainians and non-Ukrainians.[1] Among those who criticized Shcherbytsky at the congress, as well as the attempts to discredit Rukh in the official media, was the deputy head of a Donbas strike committee and Party member Petro Poberezhny.

As at the inaugural conference of the Kyiv regional organization of Rukh, Yavorivsky and Konev delivered two of the best speeches and emerged as the congress' stars. The latter emphasized the critical importance of the forthcoming elections to the republican Supreme Soviet and the local councils and declared that Rukh and its allies had 'no right' to lose them. He told delegates that, apart from keeping up the pressure for a revision of the officially proposed draft law on elections, it was essential that Rukh and its allies made good preparations, such as building up a network of voters' associations that would guard against efforts by the Party apparatus to dominate the local electoral commissions, and establishing a republican committee to coordinate the activity of these associations. Konev also

---

[1] For the text, see *Holos*, no. 4, 17 September 1989. Two other signatories, Yaroshynska and Chelyshev, withdrew their signatures because, as the same issue of *Holos* put it, their constituents did not necessarily support Rukh and its position on the national problem.

warned the delegates to be on their guard against efforts by the Party apparatus to split the opposition into 'patriotic' and 'democratic' camps, or along regional lines, by, for instance, frightening Eastern Ukrainian workers with the blue and yellow colours or the prospect of forcible Ukrainization, or by setting strike committees against Rukh groups; he also called on Rukh to refrain from actions in the east that might antagonize the local population.

These problems were also raised by a representative from the Donbas, S. Furmanyuk, who caused controversy by declaring that the region was not yet ready to accept Ukrainian national symbols and that the workers there 'will not understand us'. Poberezhny, however, offered a somewhat different assessment. He told the delegates that it was not true that the miners had made only economic demands: they wanted better contacts with the intelligentsia, more information about Rukh and to learn about Ukrainian national symbols.[2] Other representatives from the strike committees, however, were less receptive to what they encountered at the congress. According to one from Voroshylovhrad, not enough was said in support of the workers and insufficient attention was paid to economic questions.[3] Indeed, among the resolutions, which included an appeal addressed to personnel in the military, militia and KGB, there was also one addressed to the republics' workers and peasants. Apart, however, from recognizing in very general terms the 'unjust' and 'unbearable' conditions in which the workers found themselves, and calling for unity between the workers and intelligentsia, the resolution failed even to mention the recent miners' strikes.

The congress elected Drach leader of the Popular Movement, Konev, as his first deputy, and Yavorivsky, Mykhailo Horyn and Chernyak as other deputies. Horyn was chosen to head the secretariat and Yavorivsky to lead Rukh's Grand Council. Apart from establishing a new organizational infrastructure, the congress also set up numerous *collegia* and committees to work on a broad range of issues ranging from economic reform to stimulating cultural revival. Overall, whatever its shortcomings, the congress was a major success and, having confirmed the consolidation of the Ukrainian

[2] See Viktor Hrabovsky's report on Rukh's congress in *Literaturna Ukraina*, 14 December 1989.

[3] *Postup*, no. 11, October 1989, p. 2.

national democratic movement in the form of Rukh, marked the opening of a new chapter in the political transformation of modern Ukraine.

Kravchuk's ambiguous role at this time should be mentioned. Pavlychko recalls that Kravchuk's attitude in private, if not in public, had begun to change and that, for instance, behind the scenes, he helped the organizers of the congress deal with some of the technical problems which they had faced, such as arranging hotel accommodation for the delegates.[4] At the congress itself, Pavlychko acknowledged Kravchuk's help and also paid tribute to his position on the draft law on languages, stressing that had it not been for Kravchuk, the draft would be proposing two state languages for the republic – Ukrainian and Russian.[5] For his part, Kravchuk called for an end to confrontation, saying that the CPU wanted to see in Rukh 'its natural and active ally in the cause of renewing society', and was ready to cooperate with 'all progressive forces' that were prepared to work within, as opposed to against, the 'socialist Soviet' system. He concluded his speech at the congress with the declaration: 'I wish the Ukrainian people well, [and wish for] real sovereignty for Ukraine in a friendly family of all peoples and nationalities.'[6]

Kravchuk provided a clue to understanding his behaviour in a candid interview which he gave during the congress to *Postup*. Asked about his 'evolution', he replied that if a politician does not alter his views to take into account changes in the political situation and the balance of political forces, 'he is not a politician'. Citing the example of how Lenin had changed his policies when circumstances demanded it, he argued that politics demand political flexibility and that those who attempt to 'stand still' lose 'touch with real life'. As for Rukh, he predicted that if the movement applied itself to concrete tasks, then 'the people will of course support it'. Among these tasks, he mentioned work in the cultural and environmental spheres and, especially, generating ideas and support for economic reforms and their implementation. Reviewing the years of restructuring, he acknowledged that there had been plenty of proposals,

[4] Author's interview with Pavlychko.

[5] Haran, *To Kill the Dragon*, p. 55.

[6] On Rukh's Congress, see the issues of *Literaturna Ukraina* from 14 September to 14 December 1989; *Suchanist*, no. 12, 1989; Haran, *To Kill the Dragon*, pp. 48–60; Kaminsky, *In a Transitional Stage*, pp. 235–70.

but that no economic progress had been made and that in some respects the situation had deteriorated. Public meetings and talk alone without work, including 'work towards building democracy', would not solve anything. Without a solid economic basis, he asserted, democracy would remain 'a mirage'.[7]

Behind the scenes, though, Kravchuk stuck to his previous 'official' position: on the basis of his report about the congress the Central Committee of the CPU adopted a resolution on 11 September calling on regional Party organizations to step up their activities against Rukh. Local Party bosses were instructed to use 'actively all forms and methods of political struggle'. Rukh was described in the document as aiming to take power by a 'peaceful parliamentary' route and to 'achieve the complete independence of Ukraine'.[8]

Thus, despite Kravchuk's apparent flirtation with Rukh, the general reaction of the Shcherbytsky regime to the congress was prompt and predictable. There were new attacks on Rukh in the republican press, amplified by *Pravda* and TASS,[9] which focused on the influence of 'extremist' elements in the organization. On 14 September *Radyanska Ukraina* published an open letter from a group of representatives of the strike committees in Voroshylovhrad who had attended Rukh's congress in which they praised the movement's programme for its 'democratic, progressive and constructive' features, but condemned the 'nationalism' and 'extremism' which they claimed had been supported by the delegates. They announced that because of this, they had decided to withdraw from the Voroshylovhrad Rukh organization. The following day, thousands of residents of Kyiv found leaflets attacking Rukh in their mailboxes and in newspapers bought in kiosks.

The most direct official response to the congress came a week after its close. On 16 September the Kyiv authorities organized a mass meeting in the Ukrainian capital to denounce the Popular Movement, filling the city's Republican Stadium with thousands of Party and Komsomol members, pensioners, workers and schoolchildren. Speaker after speaker, who included the commander of the Kyiv military district, Lieutenant-General Boris Gromov, ac-

---

[7] *Postup*, no. 11, 1989, pp. 2-3.
[8] Lytvyn, *Political Arena*, pp. 158-9.
[9] *Pravda* and TASS, 15 September 1989.

cused Rukh of having become a forum for forces which wanted to sow inter-ethnic discord. One speaker, a certain G. Mykhailyuk, representing Red Army veterans, even compared Ukrainian national democrats to the Nazis, claiming that they were resorting to the methods used by Goebbels: 'hysteria, lies, demagogy, exploitation of the herd instinct, influencing the immature minds of children'. Yelchenko, whose strident denunciation of Rukh's congress contrasted with Kravchuk's far milder earlier criticisms, warned of the danger of 'counter-revolution' in the republic. The meeting's implicit message, or warning, seemed to be that there was a need for an 'Interfront'-type of organization to combat Rukh. Yavorivksy and Hryshchuk, and to some extent Oliinyk, all of whom also spoke, managed, however, to add a more objective tone to the proceedings.[10]

But even as the Party authorities were attempting to strike back at Rukh, there were new dramatic developments in Western Ukraine. On 17 September – the fiftieth anniversary of the Soviet takeover of Western Ukraine – at least 150,000 Ukrainian Catholics from all over the region joined a procession through Lviv organized by Hel and other activists to demand the legalization of their Church; they then defiantly participated in an open-air Mass.[11] Later that evening, throughout Western Ukraine tens of thousands of people held silent vigils with lighted candles as a sign of mourning on the anniversary of the Molotov-Ribbentrop Pact and what they depicted as the replacement of 'the Polish occupation' of the region by a harsher Soviet one.[12]

A few days later, in Chernivsti, the first republican festival of contemporary Ukrainian song (named 'Chervona Ruta' after a song by the patriotic young Ukrainian composer Volodymyr Ivasyuk, who had been found dead in Lviv in 1979 in mysterious circumstances), further embarrassed the authorities. Bringing together young musicians and singers not only from all over the republic, but also from Eastern Europe and the Western diaspora, it revealed that the

[10] *Radyanska Ukraina*, 17 September 1989.

[11] See, for example, Michael Dobbs, 'Catholic Ukrainians Demand Legalization of Disbanded Church', *Washington Post*, 18 September 1989, and Masha Hamilton, 'Thousands of Ukrainian Catholics Pray in Show of Strength', *Los Angeles Times*, 18 September 1989.

[12] Reuter, 18 September 1989.

national revival had affected the younger generation and that a vibrant new 'Ukrainian' pop culture was developing. Although blue and yellow flags were banned, the youth smuggled them into the concerts and support for Rukh was manifested by both performers and spectators. Efforts by the police and the organizers to control the proceedings only produced protests and strengthened the sense of solidarity. One of the main organizers of the festival was the republican Komsomol, which was by now plagued with internal ferment and declining influence, and the defiant and increasingly patriotic mood of the youth gave the Komsomol's leaders plenty to think about.[13]

Ivashko replaces Shcherbytsky

On 19 September, the long-overdue plenum of the CPSU's Central Committee devoted to the nationalities question was finally held but, as had been expected, no new deal for the Russians was offered. In his report, Gorbachev largely adhered to the Party's previously published 'Platform' on nationalities policy, and the only new element it contained was hardly good news for the non-Russians: the Soviet leader announced that it had become 'expedient to give the Russian language the status of a common state language across the USSR'.[14] During the discussion, Yelchenko stuck to his hard-line position, warning that 'the future of our common home had been put under threat by anti-Soviet forces, nationalists and extremists.'[15]

The plenum did, however, bring one important surprise: on the second day of the meeting, Shcherbytsky and two other members of the Politburo, Viktor Chebrikov and Viktor Nikonov, were unexpectedly retired. With a plenum of the CPU Central Committee scheduled in a few days, Shcherbytsky's seemingly imminent departure from the helm of the Ukrainian Party was cause for jubilation among the democratic opposition in his republic even

---

[13] Video recordings of the concerts in the author's archive. See also the 'indignant' reports about the festival in the main CPU organs, *Pravda Ukrainy*, 7 October 1989, and *Radyanska Ukraina*, 13 October 1989, as well as a more balanced one in *Molod Ukrainy*, 4 October 1989.

[14] *Pravda*, 20 September 1989.

[15] *Ibid.*, 21 September 1989.

though it was by no means certain who would succeed him, and whether a new first secretary would make much of a difference. The two leading contenders appeared to be Ivashko and Kapto.

A week later, Gorbachev flew to Kyiv to oversee the replacement of the seventy-one-year-old apparently ailing Ukrainian Party leader. Nevertheless, at the plenum of the CPU Central Committee, the emphasis seemed to be placed not on making a new start but on continuity. Shcherbytsky was given almost a hero's send off by his colleagues and Gorbachev himself joined in the praise by speaking of the retiree's 'great life', his many years of 'fruitful labour for the good of the Party and the country', and his 'great contribution to the development of the republic', all of which, the Soviet leader declared, 'undoubtedly deserve a positive evaluation'. Only one of the speakers, the director of the Botanical Institute, Academician Kostyantyn Sytnyk, implicitly challenged this view, saying that 'during the last three or four years' things had not gone 'as well as we would have wanted'. This drew an angry rejoinder from Yelchenko who, on behalf of his colleagues in the CPU Central Committee, denied that anything had begun to go amiss in the republic.

Significantly, Gorbachev also revealed in his speech that Shcherbytsky had asked to be allowed to retire during his previous visit to Ukraine because of old age and poor health, but that the Politburo of the CPSU had asked him to stay on until after the election campaign was over. In other words, the Soviet leader acknowledged in so many words that at a very critical moment, when many in the West and in Ukraine too had assumed that Gorbachev the reformer had wanted to get rid of Shcherbytsky – the personification of Brezhnevist stagnation – he had in fact kept the unpopular Ukrainian Party boss on.

The rationale behind this seems to have been that, whatever his faults, for the Kremlin Shcherbytsky remained the best figure for maintaining order in the vitally important Ukraine. In fact, indicating why he had come to Kyiv again for the second time that year, Gorbachev reiterated the crucial importance of Ukraine and the 'great' responsibility which its Party organization bore. 'Without things going well in Ukraine', he reminded the plenum, 'we can hardly expect *perestroika* to succeed in the country.'[16] He also

[16] See the report on the plenum in *Radyanska Ukraina*, 30 September 1989.

repeated this in an interview for *Pravda* published on 30 September, saying: 'If *perestroika* falters in Ukraine, it will falter throughout the entire country.'

From the Kremlin's standpoint, however, things were no longer going so well in Ukraine. It was not only that Rukh had emerged as a major force, which was disquieting enough, but also that the Donbas, a traditional stronghold of the Communist Party in Ukraine, had unexpectedly staged a social revolt and its disaffected miners were threatening to begin new strikes. The traditional methods of maintaining order were no longer appropriate. As if implicitly responding to Shcherbytsky's communication from the previous month, Gorbachev told the plenum: 'If someone thinks that it is possible to control the situation by using old methods of force . . . it is a dangerous mistake.' Either the Party recognized the principles of freedom of thought and action, accepted the idea of political dialogue and cooperation with other social forces, and worked to win public sympathies and support, or it risked becoming 'a secluded force claiming a leading role'. In these circumstances, Shcherbytsky had finally become politically inexpedient, if not obsolete, and expendable.

Gorbachev provided few clues as to which of the two threats – Ukrainian 'nationalism', or the workers' movement – Moscow feared most at this stage. In his address to the plenum, and during his one-day stay in Ukraine, he again stayed off the national question and avoided the issue of Rukh. When asked, though, during one of his walkabouts in the Ukrainian capital, about the Popular Movement, he replied evasively that he welcomed 'healthy' public movements that supported *perestroika* as long as they were not the bearers of 'separatism or nationalism'.[17] On this occasion he did not meet with representatives of the cultural intelligentsia but did find time to talk with a group of miners. While appearing receptive to their concerns, he emphasized just how damaging to the economy strikes were.[18]

In a display of 'democratization', six candidates were initially proposed for Shcherbytsky's post: Ivashko, Hurenko, Kapto, Yelchenko, Masol and Anatolii Korniyenko, who in July had replaced Masyk as the Kyiv city Party boss. The latter three nominees

[17] *Radyanska Ukraina*, 1 October 1989.

[18] TASS, 28 September 1989.

declined to stand and Gorbachev, who personally proposed Ivashko, told the members of the CPU Central Committee that Kapto was not available because he had a 'responsible assignment' from the Soviet Party leadership heading the CPSU's ideological department. In the secret ballot, Ivashko was elected by 136 votes to Hurenko's 43.

The new first secretary of the CPU was born in Poltava and before coming to Kyiv had spent most of his political career in the Kharkiv region. A mining engineer trained in economics, he had served in, among other positions, as a political instructor in Afghanistan in 1980, and as the CPU's ideological secretary in 1986-7. Shcherbytsky described him at the plenum as 'our new right flank' while Ivashko thanked his predecessor for having devoted all his 'exceptional talent, energy and creativity' for the good of the 'Party and the people'.

But in his first speech as republican Party leader, Ivashko indicated that he was more in the mould of his Moscow patron than the former Kyiv boss. Sounding quite outspoken but not confrontational, he acknowledged that 'the pace of renewal in different spheres of the republic's life' was 'clearly unsatisfactory', and that the population was 'dissatisfied with a great number of things'. More would have to be done, he said, to tackle the problems of housing, food shortages, protecting the environment and improving health care. It was imperative for the CPU not to lose the political initiative, and it would have both to improve and democratize its cadres policy and to present a platform to voters at the forthcoming elections which addressed all of the republic's vital needs. Political reform needed to be carried out consistently and the 'socio-political activity of the masses' supported.

Revealing how fast political changes were progressing in the USSR, Ivashko also came out with the kind of statements about republican economic sovereignty that only a few months ago the Baltic representatives at the Congress of People's Deputies had been attacked for but which had gradually become politically acceptable. He told the plenum that a 'key direction' which the CPU ought to follow was 'to secure and put into practice the principles of Ukraine's economic sovereignty' within the all-Union 'integral nationaleconomic complex' and go over to cost-accounting. Moreover, acknowledging that restructuring in Ukraine was developing 'most dynamically' in the 'spiritual sphere', he sounded a note reminiscent of Shelest: the Party had to do 'everything it could', he said, 'to ensure the all-round flourishing of Ukrainian culture' and the satisfaction of the national-cultural needs of the republic's minorities.[19]

Just as the public were reading the speeches delivered at the plenum to find out if Ivashko represented a genuine break with the past, events in Western Ukraine suggested that, despite the change of leadership, the old regime was determined not to give up. On 1 October in Lviv riot police were used to disperse a peaceful demonstration and dozens of people were hurt. The renewed use of force shocked the city's residents: a local strike committee was quickly formed and tens of thousands took part in protests. Moreover, deputies from the city raised the issue in the USSR Supreme Soviet and succeeded in having a special commission appointed to investigate the incident.

Meanwhile, the Ukrainian Catholics were also continuing to organize large rallies to press for the legalization of their Church. The latest was held in Ivano-Frankivsk on 1 October. Support for their campaign was also expressed by the mass circulation Moscow publications, *Ogonek* and *Argumenty i fakty*. As a Western observer noted, these articles 'shattered the pretense of canonicity of the Russian Orthodox Church in Galicia and Transcarpathia and were widely perceived as a sure portent of a policy shift in Moscow'.[20] News that Gorbachev might meet with the Pope during a visit to Rome later in the year also strengthened the belief that legalization could not to put off for much longer.

Although the CPU leadership without Shcherbytsky was trying to put a brave face on things, it was facing enormous difficulties and challenges and being forced not only by developments in Moscow and society at large, but even by forces which had hitherto been considered its allies or extensions, to be more responsive to changes in the political climate.

Right after the CPU Central Committee plenum, on 29-30 September the Central Committee of the Komsomol held its own plenum. Under the leadership of its liberal new first secretary Anatolii Matviyenko, the Komsomol's leadership acknowledged

---

[19] *Radyanska Ukraina*, 30 September 1989.

[20] See Bociurkiw, ' The Ukrainian Catholic Church', p. 11; *Ogonek*, no. 38, 1989; and *Argumenty i Fakty*, 7-13 October, 1989.

that the organization was in a 'crisis', that its membership and prestige were declining and that the organization was threatened with fragmentation and marginalization. It decided to embark on a new heterodox course which amounted to a declaration of autonomy, if not independence, from the CPU. The plenum renounced the Komsomol's traditional claim to a monopoly over the youth movement and, echoing much of what was in Rukh's programme, called, among other things, for the creation of a democratic law-based state, genuine sovereignty for Ukraine within a revamped Soviet federation based on a new Union treaty, republican economic sovereignty, different forms of ownership, fuller information about the workings of government, live radio and television coverage of the sessions of the Ukrainian Supreme Soviet, cooperation with Rukh, and complete freedom of conscience. Furthermore, the plenum also relinquished the Komsomol's claim to the quota of seats allocated to it as a 'public organization' in the Supreme Soviet by the officially proposed draft law on elections. Last but not least, the plenum also adopted a resolution giving a generally positive appraisal of the Chervona Ruta festival and directly criticizing some of the official and semi-official institutions and organizations which had been co-sponsors, such as the Ministry of Culture, for their meagre involvement.[21]

Implicitly distancing himself from what had just happened in Lviv, Ivashko proceeded to try and promote a positive image of himself as a more tolerant, conciliatory and progressive leader and to convey the impression, as he put it, that 'we are entering a new epoch'. During his first days in office, he met with representatives of the cultural intelligentsia, media and Rukh's leader Drach. He told foreign journalists that he had found Drach 'a reasonable person' and that he did not consider Rukh to be dominated by 'nationalists', though the presence of 'extremists' was a problem. As long as the movement did not assume a 'destructive or destabilizing nature', he would be prepared to cooperate with it and would not oppose its registration. He also indicated that he accepted some of the criticisms of the draft law on elections and would go along with some of the proposed changes. The new Party leader was unforthcoming on the issue of the Ukrainian Catholic Church, hinting only that 'a process' was under way. As for the restless miners, he said that he was

---

[21] See the materials on the plenum in *Molod Ukrainy*, 4, 5, and 10 October 1989.

sympathetic to their complaints, but that his 'biggest fear' was of 'a chain reaction'.

Foreign journalists, however, came away not entirely persuaded. David Remnick of the *Washington Post* concluded: 'From his comments, Ivashko made it clear that he would be Moscow's instrument, and not do anything to encourage any permissiveness on his own.' Indeed, Ivashko even told Remnick that 'it was more to the point to speak of similarities' than any differences between himself and Shcherbytsky. 'There should be no illusions', the new Ukrainian Party leader had warned: 'Both Shcherbytsky and I are convinced Communists.'[22]

Still, a difference in style was apparent. Ivashko let journalists know that they would be 'somewhat freer to criticize the Party and its leaders than they were under Shcherbytsky',.[23] and it was not long before the first signs of greater *hlasnist* were appearing. For instance, on 5 October, the CPU's mouthpiece *Radyanska Ukraina* published an article by the young pro-Rukh economist Oleksandr Savchenko criticizing the proposed draft law on the principles of the economic independence of the Ukrainian SSR as being too tame and urging that it be scrapped and replaced by a more radical one. And on 17 October, the eve of the first CPU Central Committee plenum under Ivashko, the same newspaper carried a candid interview with Komsomol leader Matviyenko in which, among other things, he stated outright that communism was no longer a rallying idea either for youth or for society generally.

The more open approach was also displayed in the coverage of the plenum itself, which was supposed to ensure that the Party line on nationalities policy enunciated by the September CPSU Central Committee plenum was adhered to. It revealed that the CPU leadership was not as united as the public had been led to believe under Shcherbytsky and that there were serious problems that had been covered up. Ivashko sought to set the new tone in his report, stressing that the 'style' of the CPU's work would have to change and compromises made as regards the provisions of the draft

---

[22] David Remnick, 'New Party Boss in Ukraine is Clearly no Liberal', *Washington Post*, 5 October 1989. His American colleague, Bill Keller, concurred with this assessment of Ivashko. See his 'Party Chief in Ukraine Offers Lighter Touch', *New York Times*, 8 October 1989.

[23] Keller, *New York Times*, 8 October 1989.

election law. Nevertheless, he also made it quite clear that the forthcoming elections would be a struggle to determine 'in whose hands power would end up' and warned that the CPU was being challenged by 'demagogues' who were calling for a 'return to capitalism, [and] secession from the Soviet Union'. Invoking the CPSU's 'Platform' on nationalities policy, Ivashko called for the strengthening of the sovereignty of the Ukrainian SSR within a revamped Soviet federation, affirmed the inviolability of the territorial integrity of the republic and the republic's right to challenge all-Union laws conflicting with republican ones, and acknowledged the need for 'a new approach' to the idea of 'a citizenship of the Ukrainian SSR'. On the other hand, he condemned the 'revelry of blatantly nationalist elements in Lviv', the 'activation of religious extremists', attempts to rehabilitate the Central Rada and the OUN and UPA, and to foist 'bourgeois nationalist' national symbols on the population of Ukraine.

Other speakers at the plenum, representing the diverse regions, brought out the full complexity of the problems facing the Ukrainian SSR. For instance, Pohrebnyak from the Lviv region called for an understanding of the distinct conditions in Western Ukraine, including the higher level of national consciousness, and the outstanding need to resolve the issue of the Ukrainian Catholic Church and for Ukrainian to be made the state language of the republic. Representatives from the Russified Donbas, Kryvyi Rih and Odesa regions, however, expressed misgivings about the proposed draft law on languages which designated Ukrainian as the republic's state language, the first secretary of the Donetsk region Party organization, Vinnyk, calling for two state languages – Ukrainian and Russian. The representatives from the Donbas also complained that Rukh's activists were becoming a nuisance in the region. The hard-line Odesa region Party boss, Heorhii Kryuchkov – who had attacked Rukh in Gorbachev's presence at the previous CPU Central Committee plenum – called for a tougher line towards the Popular Movement and warned that there were signs of dissatisfaction with the proposed new law on languages among the region's non-Ukrainians. Furthermore, the Crimean regional Party leader, Mykola Bagrov, emphasized the peculiarities of Crimea – the only region of Ukraine with a Russian majority (which was now also faced with the problem of integrating tens of thousands of Crimean Tatars returning to their historic homeland), and in effect served notice of the growing movement among the peninsula's population for broad regional autonomy. The discussion about Crimea's future status and orientation had been stimulated, he said, by the moves to make Ukrainian the state language.

The plenum elected Hurenko as the CPU's second secretary and Kravchuk as a candidate member of the Ukrainian Politburo and a Central Committee secretary. He was given responsibility for ideology, becoming the head of the CPU's Ideological Commission. Mushketyk, the head of the WUU, was also appointed to this commission, while Yelchenko and Vrublevsky were moved to a new Central Committee Commission on Inter-Ethnic Relations, which Yelchenko was put in charge of.[24]

Ukraine's Supreme Soviet makes adjustments

When the eagerly awaited session of the Supreme Soviet of the Ukrainian SSR that was to debate changes to the republic's constitution, the proposed law on languages and the elections opened on 25 October, it was clear that the CPU leadership was going for compromise. Moreover, in an important break with the past and following the example set in Moscow by the coverage of the USSR Supreme Soviet, the proceedings were broadcast live by the republican radio, thus giving Ukraine's residents their first chance to hear the debates for themselves.

In the opening address, the chairman of the Supreme Soviet's Presidium, Shevchenko, acknowledged that the public discussion of the draft electoral law had revealed 'a change in the psychology of the people, [and] their increased activity and national self-awareness'. No less than nine alternative drafts had been submitted to the Supreme Soviet. She announced that, because of the 'negative' public reaction, and foreseeing pre-election district meetings (at which undesirable candidates could be blocked), the provisions allocating a quota of seats to public organizations had been dropped. Shevchenko also confirmed that the general trend towards revamping the system of soviets and enhancing republican sovereignty had also been taken into account: she unveiled a series of major revisions to the republican constitution designed both to broaden the powers

[24] See *Radyanska Ukraina*, 19-21 October 1989.

of the republican Supreme Soviet and to bolster its position *vis-à-vis* Moscow.[25]

Ivashko himself played a refreshingly constructive and conciliatory role. He intervened when the more conservative deputies attempted to prevent reformist deputies to the USSR Congress of People's Deputies, who were present as observers, from participating in the debates. Urging the deputies to avoid confrontation, he appealed to them with the words: 'there is only one way [forward] for us: the consolidation of the entire Ukrainian people for the good and well-being of the Ukrainian people.'

The charged atmosphere at the session was demonstrated by an incident involving the radical deputy to the USSR Congress of People's Deputies, Kutsenko. During one of the breaks, Kryuchkov ripped a blue and yellow national emblem from Kutsenko's tie and caused a scandal. Later, a deputy from Kharkiv protested that Kutsenko had been wearing a 'nationalist' emblem and succeeded in persuading a majority of the deputies to vote for Kutsenko's expulsion from the chamber. When Bratun attempted to protest this action on behalf of the Republican Deputies' Club, he was shouted down.

After heated debate, the proposed laws on the elections and revisions to the constitution were adopted, and the date for the elections to the Supreme Soviet set for 4 March 1990. The new election law was considerably more democratic than the original draft and, depending on the spirit in which it would be observed, foresaw that only candidates advocating the violent overthrow of the Soviet system or inter-ethnic enmity could be barred by the local electoral commissions.[26] One of the members of the Republican Deputies' Club, Shcherbak, welcomed this 'wise compromise' and described the new law as 'one of the most democratic election laws' to have been adopted in the various Soviet republics. For all the residual political intolerance displayed by some of the deputies, he told *Radyanska Ukraina* during the session, there was definitely 'movement forward'.[27]

Although overshadowed at the time by the election and language laws, the changes which were made to the constitution were also

[25] *Ibid.*, 26 October 1989.
[26] *Ibid.*, 1 November 1989.
[27] *Ibid.*, 28 October 1989.

highly significant and marked a major step in the direction of transforming the republican Supreme Soviet (Verkhovna Rada [Supreme Council] in Ukrainian) into the legislature of a sovereign republic and making it function like a proper parliament. The idea of a republican Congress of People's Deputies was rejected and it was decided that the legislature would consist of a streamlined Supreme Council with 450 (that is 200 less than before) directly elected deputies. Although the concept of a popularly elected chairman of the Supreme Council, or 'president', which some democrats had advocated, was also discarded, the role of the chairman, elected by secret ballot by the Supreme Council, was enhanced. The office-holder was now to be the republic's highest official and representative both within the USSR and abroad. The system of permanent parliamentary commissions was also to be overhauled and these bodies given greater responsibility in preparing legislation and approving candidates for government posts.

As Shevchenko herself noted in her address, this was to be 'a qualitatively new Supreme Council, endowed with broad powers'; the changes were designed to create a legal framework which would stimulate the economic development of the republic and strengthen its sovereignty. The Verkhovna Rada now assumed the rights to challenge any all-Union laws if they infringed on the republic's sovereignty and likewise to suspend on the territory of the republic the implementation of any decrees or decisions of the Soviet government which did not conform with Ukrainian laws, and to 'decide questions' connected with the use of the republic's territory and resources. The Supreme Council also asserted its 'exclusive' right to, among other things, 'the formulation of the main directions of the internal and foreign political activity of the Ukrainian SSR' and deciding questions concerning the opening of diplomatic, consular and trade offices abroad representing the republic.[28]

The high point of the session, however, was the adoption of the historic law designating Ukrainian as the state language of the republic. Oliinyk introduced the proposed law and pointed out that it had taken almost seven months of intensive work and extensive debate to prepare an acceptable draft on such a sensitive but cardinal issue. The working group charged with preparing the draft, which had been headed by the director of the republican Institute of

[28] *Ibid.*, 31 October 1989.

Philosophy, Academician Volodymyr Shynkaruk, and included, among others, Oliinyk, Mushketyk, Pavlychko, Dzyuba, Vasylenko and Ivan Tymchenko, a specialist in constitutional law from the Institute for State and Law, had received over 50,000 letters with comments and proposals, and four alternative drafts had been submitted. The draft which had finally been published for public discussion had been the seventeenth version. The key problem had been to devise a compromise whereby the status of the Ukrainian language would be enhanced and legally bolstered without antagonizing the republic's large Russian and Russian-speaking population, thereby avoiding the kind of conflicts that had been generated in the Baltic republics and Moldova by the introduction of new language laws. The working group had rejected the idea of two state languages for the republic – Ukrainian and Russian – which, as Oliinyk acknowledged, 'a considerable number of citizens' had called for, arguing that this would only perpetuate the status quo and put no onus on Russian-speakers to learn Ukrainian. Instead, the proposed law envisaged making Ukrainian a compulsory subject in all schools, but at the same time safeguarding the right of citizens to learn Russian and, where applicable, the languages of a given national minority (that is, in areas where a national minority was 'compactly' settled).

Behind the scenes, Tymchenko played a major role in finalizing the draft and travelled to Russian-speaking areas in the Donbas and the Odesa *oblasts* to gauge what would be acceptable.[29] The compromise formula enshrined in the law was as follows: Ukrainian was recognized as the state language of the Ukrainian SSR; Ukrainian, Russian and 'other languages' were recognized as languages of 'inter-ethnic communication' within the republic; and the Ukrainian SSR safeguarded 'the free use of the Russian language as the language of communication between the nationalities of the USSR'. The very fact that the law was entitled 'On Languages in the Ukrainian SSR' was intended to denote that it was not concerned with Ukrainian alone or aimed against any other ethnic group, and that it recognized the language rights of all Ukraine's nationalities. While inaugurating gradual Ukrainization, it also contained provisions to foster the developments of the languages of the national minorities. The law allowed for a protracted period of from three

---

[29] Author's interview with Ivan Tymchenko, Paris, 22 March 1995.

to ten years for implementation, depending on the sphere and region in which the transition to Ukrainian was to be made, and no specific sanctions were prescribed for violations of the law.

Despite this extremely cautious approach, the passage of the law was far from smooth. Deputies from the Odesa, Kharkiv, Voroshylovhrad, Crimean and Chernihiv regions voiced their concern and called for Russian to have the same status as Ukrainian. They warned of possible inter-ethnic friction, of 'unpleasant consequences' for the 'international' Soviet armed forces stationed in Ukraine, and argued, among other things, that the economic cost of making the transition to Ukrainian as the state language could not be justified at a time of mounting economic difficulty, and that switching over to Ukrainian would impede technical and scientific progress.

Significantly, Oliinyk, Honchar, Pavlychko, Mushketyk and others were joined by Ivashko, Kravchuk, Masol and Valentyna Shevchenko in seeking to allay the fears of the republic's Russian-speakers that they faced forcible Ukrainization and in presenting the case for recognizing Ukrainian as the state language of the 'sovereign' Ukrainian SSR. For instance, Kravchuk stressed the political significance of the law, arguing that it was prompted by the 'complex political situation' and the growing national consciousness and political activity of Ukraine's multinational population. Appealing to the republic's Russian-speaking workers to support the law, he explained that it had been necessitated because of the disregard for 'humanism and justice' in the past which had left the Ukrainian language, and those of the republic's national minorities, 'unwell' and requiring 'treatment' to restore them to health. For his part, Ivashko urged the deputies to cast aside their prejudices and fears, and to show goodwill and understanding. 'Let's live in a civilized way', he proposed, 'so that our Soviet Ukraine flourishes, and its language and culture; and so that no harm is done to anyone, whatever their nationality'.[30]

This was an important turning point, for it marked the first time since the Shelest period that the Party and state leaders of the Ukrainian SSR had come out in defence of Ukrainian national rights. Whether this was out of political expediency rather than

---

[30] For the debate on the law on languages, see *Radyanska Ukraina*, 28, 29 and 31 October 1989.

patriotism was open to question: the main thing, though, was that the same arguments as had been advanced during the 1920s by Skrypnyk, Shumsky and other national Communists were being taken over from Rukh, the Ukrainian Language Society, and other national democratic organizations by the post-Shcherbytsky Kyiv leadership and becoming the new orthodoxy.

After some last minute revisions to the draft, the law on languages was adopted on 28 October.[31] Although it contained numerous loopholes, and failed to provide legal sanctions for violators of the law and to allocate funds for its implementation, it was nevertheless a historic achievement. As various speakers pointed out during the debate in the Verkhovna Rada, the adoption of the law marked the recognition of a fundamental principle (that Ukrainian should be the state language in Ukraine) and right (of the Ukrainian people to their national language, with all that this entailed), something which the Ukrainian national movement had striven for since at least the first decades of the century. Not only was this a matter of national dignity and self-respect: in a broader sense, the struggle for the recognition of Ukrainian as the state language of Ukraine had also been implicitly a struggle for the affirmation of Ukrainian statehood and sovereignty.[32]

The passage of the language and election laws, their shortcomings notwithstanding, signified a notable victory for Ukraine's national democratic forces. The more constructive and conciliatory attitude shown by the post-Shcherbytsky official Ukrainian leadership, and the new emphasis being placed on augmenting republican sovereignty, albeit within a revamped Soviet federation, also seemed to offer the prospect of change for the better. On the other hand, though, the debates in the Supreme Council had highlighted the regional differences in the republic and the latent split between the Ukrainian-and Russian-speaking groups. Moreover, the enduring hostility of conservatives to Rukh and Ukrainian national and cultural symbols, as well as their aversion to the idea of sharing political power, did not bode well for the new election campaign.

---

[31] For the text, see *Radyanska Ukraina*, 1 November 1989. The details of the voting do not appear to have been published.

[32] Author's interview with Pavlychko.

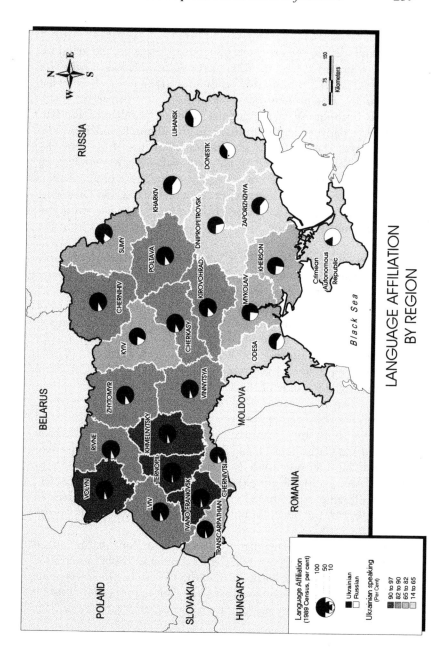

LANGUAGE AFFILIATION
BY REGION

The battle is resumed

Important developments were also taking place in the religious sphere. The revival of the Ukrainian Autocephalous Orthodox Church (UAOC) was by now gathering momentum. Somewhat surprisingly, this process was having its greatest impact in traditionally Catholic Western Ukraine where a number of Russian Orthodox parishes had gone over to this Church and Lviv was emerging as the centre of the revival. The first had been the parish of Sts Peter and Paul in Lviv, which had switched its allegiance to the UAOC on 19 August. On 22 October, Bishop Ioann Bodnarchuk of Zhytomyr broke with the Russian Orthodox Church and became the leader of the UAOC. He was promptly excommunicated by the Holy Synod of the Russian Orthodox Church.

The emergence of the UAOC was a source of concern not only to the Russian Orthodox Church but also the Ukrainian Catholics. Some of the latter began to suspect that the rise of the UAOC in Western Ukraine was being encouraged by the KGB as a means of weakening and blocking the Ukrainian Catholic Church. A three-sided contest for influence and parishes began in the region. On 29 October, the Ukrainian Catholics peacefully took over the Transfiguration church in Lviv which, while St George's Cathedral remained in the hands of the Russian Orthodox Church, was to serve as their main centre. This action, and the emergence of the UAOC, drew a statement of protest from Metropolitan Filaret and the other Russian Orthodox hierarchs in Ukraine. In it they accused the Catholics of using force to seize 'Russian Orthodox' property and condemned Bishop Bodnarchuk's 'violation of Church unity'. Significantly though, the Russian Orthodox leadership in Ukraine also sounded a new concessionary note: it pledged its support for the development of Ukrainian national culture and traditions.[33]

With Gorbachev scheduled to meet with the Pope in the Vatican at the beginning of December, the Ukrainian Catholics intensified their campaign for the legalization of their Church. On 26 November, over 150,000 of them took part in a religious procession through Lviv. At the end of the month, in a move clearly timed to coincide

---

[33] *Radyanska Ukraina*, 19 November 1989.

Petro Shelest. (Ukrinform)

Oles Honchar. (Ukrinform)

Volodymyr Shcherbytsky. (Ukrinform)

Vitalii Malanchuk. (Ukrinform)

Shcherbytsky welcomes Gorbachev to Kyiv, June 1985. (Ukrinform)

Vasyl Stus.

Vyacheslav Chornovil.

Left: Chornobyl, April 1986: the stricken fourth reactor. (Ukrinform)

Below: Children being evacuated from Kyiv after the Chornobyl nuclear disaster. (Ukrinform)

Ivan Drach. (Photo by Serhii
Spasokukotsky)

Dmytro Pavlychko. (Ukrinform)

Borys Oliinyk. (Ukrinform)

Ivan Dzyuba. (Photo by Serhii Marchenko)

Yurii Yelchenko. (Ukrinform)   Leonid Kravchuk. (Ukrinform)

Glasnost Shcherbytsky-style. A protester is seized outside the parliament building.

An unauthorised public meeting in Lviv, 26 February 1989.

The banned blue and yellow national colours appear in Kyiv, 22 May 1989.
(Photo by Serhii Marchenko)

Mykola Zhulynsky. (Photo by Bohdan Nahaylo)

Volodymr Yavorivsky. (Ukrinform)

Ivan Drach addresses Rukh's inaugural congress, September 1989. (Photo by Serhii Marchenko)

Above: Procession for the reburial of Stus, Tykhy and Lytvyn, 19 November 1990. (Photo by Serhii Marchenko)

Right: The human chain from Kyiv to Lviv: the scene in Kyiv, 21 January 1990. (Ukrinform)

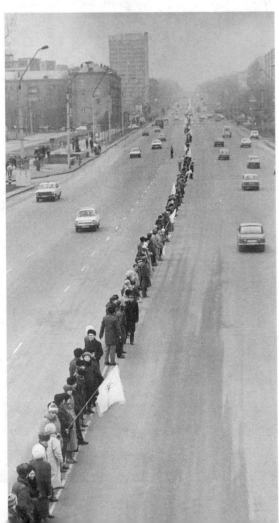

Volodymyr Ivashko. (Ukrinform)

Ihor Yukhnovsky. (Ukrinform)

Democratic deputies confer during a crisis in the parliament, 4 June 1990.
(Photo by Bohdan Nahaylo)

The inaugural meeting of the People's Council, 4 June 1990. (Photo by Bohdan Nahaylo)

National democratic deputies: (*from left to right*) Levko Lukyanenko, Ivan Zayets, Mykhailo Horyn.

Left: Democratic deputies Bohdan Horyn (*left*) and Serhii Holovaty (*right*) at celebrations after the adoption of the Declaration of State Sovereignty, 16 July 1990. (Photo by Serhii Spasokukotsky)

Below: Jubilation as the blue and yellow flag is raised at Kyiv City Hall, 20 July 1990. (Ukrinform)

Confrontation outside the Verkhovna Rada, October 1990. (Photo by Serhii Spasokukotsky)

The student hunger strike protest in central Kyiv, October 1990. (Ukrinform)

Yes to independence: a rally in Kyiv in support of Lithuania's bid for independence. (Photo by Serhii Marchenko)

A relieved gathering in Kyiv welcomes news of the failure of the attempted coup in Moscow, 22 August 1991. (Ukrinform)

Right: CPU leader Stanislav Hurenko attempts to defend his party during the historic extraordinary session of parliament on 24 August 1991. (Ukrinform)

Below: Kravchuk votes in the referendum on independence, 1 December 1991. (Photo by Serhii Spasokukotsky)

The creation of new national armed forces begins. (Photo by Serhii Spasokukotsky)

Presidents Kravchuk and Yeltsin attempt to patch up Ukrainian-Russian relations in Dagomys, 23 June 1992. Ivan Plyushch (*front row, left*) and (*back row, from left to right*) Yevhen Marchuk, Volodymyr Lanovy, Anatolii Zlenko and Kostyantyn Morozov look on. (Ukrinform)

Left: Changing the pilot: President Kravchuk hands over to Leonid Kuchma, July 1994. (Ukrinform)

Below: President Kuchma and Chairman of the Verkhovna Rada Oleksandr Moroz after the signing of the law on the adoption of Ukraine's new constitution, 12 July 1996. Volodymyr Horbulin, Dmytro Tabachnyk (*from far right to left, respectively*) and Pavlo Lazarenko (*partly hidden behind Kuchma*) look on. (Ukrinform)

with the historic meeting in Rome, Ukraine's Council of Religious Affairs announced that Ukrainian Catholics 'may enjoy all rights which are provided by the law for religious associations in the Ukrainian SSR'. This fell short of full legalization of the Ukrainian Catholic Church and its leaders pointed out that the announcement made no mention of condemning the forcible liquidation of their Church in 1946 or of returning its confiscated property.

The concession, nevertheless, had opened the way for the eventual full legalization of the Ukrainian Catholic Church. It also encouraged Ukrainian Catholics to take over more of their former churches from the Russian Orthodox Church. During December and January, about 370 parishes in Western Ukraine were reclaimed and scores of local Russian Orthodox priests switched their allegiance. By the end of 1989, only four out of nineteen of Lviv's functioning churches remained in the hands of the Russian Orthodox Church. At the same time, the UAOC also continued to win over parishes from the Russian Orthodox Church.[34]

As more and more local Russian Orthodox priests abandoned their Church, and the UAOC began to loom as a new threat, Ukrainian Catholics were taking matters into their own hands by reclaiming churches that had been taken away from them in 1946. Russian Orthodox representatives protested that the 'Uniates' were using 'illegal' methods and 'force' to seize property, and talks between the Moscow Patriarchate and the Vatican were suspended. The 'competition' between the Ukrainian Catholics and the UAOC also soon began to develop into bitter rivalry.[35]

Meanwhile, Rukh and its allies continued to push forward. During October Yavorivsky travelled to the United States as a representative of Ukraine's democratic forces and met with leading American political figures and leaders of the Ukrainian community. He was successful in obtaining support for Rukh's efforts on behalf

---

[34] See Bociurkiw, 'The Ukrainian Catholic Church'; Roman Solchanyk, 'Ukrainian Catholics in the USSR: Toward Legalization', *Report on the USSR*, no. 50 (15 December 1989), and Frank E. Sysyn, 'The Third Rebirth of the Ukrainian Autocephalous Orthodox Church and the Religious Situation in Ukraine, 1989-1991', in Stephen K. Batalden (ed.), *Seeking God: The Recovery of Religious Identity in Orthodox Russia, Ukraine and Georgia*, DeKalb, IL, 1993, pp. 198-9.

[35] See the article by S. Pakholiv in *Postup*, no. 2, January 1990, and the interview with the leaders of the UAOC in *Postup*, no. 4, March 1990.

of children who had suffered as a result of the Chornobyl disaster. At home, patriotic activists finally succeeded in obtaining permission for the bodies of Stus, Lytvyn and Tykhy to be reburied in their homeland. On 19 November, thousands, many carrying national flags, turned out in Kyiv for the funeral procession and to pay their last respects to Ukraine's most recent national martyrs.

Preparations now began in earnest for the parliamentary and local elections. The continually changing political climate and the confidence which it was giving the democratic opposition was evident at the inaugural conference in Kyiv on 28 and 29 October of the 'Green World' Association at which it was decided to move towards the formation of a Ukrainian 'Green party'. But it soon became apparent that for all of Ivashko's calls for dialogue and cooperation with the democratic opposition, the CPU leadership was up to its old tricks. Drach pointed this out in November in an open letter to Ivashko in which he protested against the CPU's harassment of Rukh activists, its attempts to prevent the formation of new branches of Rukh, and the distorted picture of the Popular Movement still being presented in the official press.[36]

As the nomination stage of the elections opened on 3 November, the authorities continued to drag their feet with the registration of Rukh; Memorial had also still not been registered. In this way these organizations were blocked from nominating candidates. Furthermore, the formation of the local electoral commissions was left to the regional authorities, the 'majority of which were in the hands of arch-conservative elements' determined to keep the democrats out.[37] For instance, the Ukrainian Language Society, which had been registered in May, was forced to complain publicly to the Central Election Commission that some of the electoral commissions were refusing to register its nominees.[38] As Drach had emphasized in his letter to Ivashko, all this was forcing Rukh and its allies 'to adopt an appropriate position and to choose appropriate tactics'.

[36] *Viche*, no. 11, 1989, p. 3.

[37] See Peter J. Potichnyj, *Elections in Ukraine*, Berichte des Bundesinstituts für ostwissenschaftliche und internationale Studien, Cologne, no. 36 (April), 1990, pp. 3-5.

[38] See the open letter from the deputy head of the Ukrainian Language Society, I. Yushchuk, to the head of the Central Election Commission, Vitalii Boyko, in *Literaturna Ukraina*, 14 December 1989.

The election campaigns were launched against the background of revolutionary developments in Eastern and Central Europe where communist regimes were crumbling and the Iron Curtain was being dismantled. In October, in Hungary, the ruling Hungarian Socialist Workers' Party had relinquished its claim to a leading role, transformed itself into a social democratic party (the Hungarian Socialist Party), and was preparing for free multi-party elections. That same month, mass protests erupted in East Germany which led to the removal of Erich Honecker and the opening on 19 November of the GDR's borders, including the Berlin Wall. The following day, Bulgaria's Communist leader of thirty-five years, Todor Zhivkov was finally ousted. And in Czechoslovakia, the brutal suppression of a student demonstration on 17 November triggered off the largest protests for twenty years which within three weeks were to topple the Communist government. In Moscow itself, there was a huge alternative demonstration on 7 November on the anniversary of the Bolshevik revolution.

On 12 November, the Republican Deputies' Club announced that it would support candidates in the elections who upheld the following four principles: the need for a new Union treaty, the repeal of Article 6 of the Soviet Ukrainian constitution (corresponding to Article 6 of the Soviet constitution and recognizing the leading role of the Party), acceptance of different forms of ownership, and that the republic's laws should be brought into line with international human rights norms.[39] The following day, a member of the Republican Deputies' Club, Serhii Ryabchenko from Kyiv, proposed in the USSR Supreme Soviet that an open debate be held on Article 6 of the Soviet constitution. 'Article 6 inspires no confidence among the people but rather the suspicion that the Party seeks to hang on to power no matter what', he argued. Gorbachev countered that this was an attempt 'under the cover of criticism to debase the role of the Party', and the proposal was narrowly defeated by just three votes.[40]

On 18 November, the consolidation of the republic's democratic forces reached a new peak when representatives of forty-three independent organizations met in Kyiv and formed a coalition for the elections. The 'Democratic Bloc', as it called itself, included

---

[39] Haran, *To Kill the Dragon*, pp. 73–4.
[40] Reuter, 13 November 1989.

among other organizations, Rukh, the Ukrainian Language Society, Memorial, the Green World Association, the UHU, and the Strike Committees of Donetsk, Mykolaiv and the Lviv region. The new coalition issued an election manifesto, which Pavlychko described as a condensed version of Rukh's programme.[41] It had six main planks: genuine economic and political sovereignty for Ukraine; political pluralism and a multi-party system; a mixed economy; a new republican constitution guaranteeing internationally recognized human and civil rights; Ukrainian national renewal and free cultural development for the republic's national minorities; and full religious freedom, including the legalization of the Ukrainian Catholic Church and UAOC. All was summarized in the slogan: 'Freedom, Prosperity and Justice'. The coalition declared that it was 'entering the election campaign under the slogan of uniting all citizens of Ukraine, regardless of their nationality, party affiliation, religious convictions and social standing, on the basis of democracy and humanism'.[42]

The CPU's response was not long in coming and was delivered at a plenum of its Central Committee held on 29 November to discuss the CPU's election platform. With the Czechoslovak Communist government having just resigned, the mood seemed fairly sombre. Unlike the Communist Party of Lithuania, which had sought to establish a *modus vivendi* with Lithuanian national democratic forces and was at this time being pressured by the Gorbachev leadership not to set a precedent by declaring its independence from the CPSU, the CPU made no attempt to meet the Democratic Bloc halfway and treated the Democratic Bloc's manifesto as a declaration of war.

Ivashko dispensed with his more liberal tone and reverted to Shcherbytsky's style. He warned that the CPU's political opponents were uniting and resorting to 'blatant lies' and 'provocations'; they had even revived the 'counter-revolutionary slogan of "Soviets without Communists"'. Rukh was increasingly becoming 'a cover for anti-Socialist formation' and calls for Ukraine's 'secession from the mighty Soviet Union' and the restoration of private ownership were growing. The Party, he acknowledged, had never had to 'conduct elections in such a complex social and political situation . . . of real

---

[41] Radio Kyiv, 14 December 1989.

[42] See *Viche*, no. 11, November 1989, and *Vilne Slovo*, no. 7, January 1990.

political competition'; the very 'existence of the Socialist order' was at stake. Reiterating that there could be no substitute for the Communist Party, and that it alone was capable of heading the process of restructuring, the Ukrainian Party leader affirmed that 'our flag was and remains the red one'. The plenum also heard calls from hard-liners, such as Kyiv city's Party boss Korniyenko, for a tightening of controls over the media.

There were, however, some indications of differences within the CPU. Reporting on the discussion of the CPU's election platform, Hurenko revealed that representatives from 'the city of Kyiv and the Transcarpathian, Lviv and some other *oblasts*' had wanted to address the following issues: Article 6 of the Constitution, the creation of a multi-party system, the use of national symbols and the CPU's position on the Ukrainian Catholic Church.[43] *Radyanska Ukraina* of 30 November also noted that this and the previous Central Committee plenums had been conducted in Ukrainian.

On 2 December *Radyanska Ukraina* published on its front page a joint appeal from several labour collectives calling for the formation of a 'Union of Toilers of Ukraine for Restructuring'. Although the CPU was not mentioned directly, it was clear from the document and the prominence given to it that this purported initiative from below was in fact an officially sponsored attempt to create an Interfront-type organization as a counter-weight to Rukh and the Democratic Bloc.

The following day, the CPU's Election Platform was unveiled. A year or so earlier, it would have seemed very progressive and in some respects it even seemed to borrow from Rukh's original draft programme. But in the current conditions, it came across as a belated attempt to adapt to an agenda that in fact was being set partly in Moscow and partly by Rukh and the democratic opposition at home. An accompanying appeal to the republic's voters sought to justify the Communist Party's leading role and continued rule, claiming that it was 'the guarantor of restructuring', and that 'realistically' only it was capable of 'representing the interests of all classes and social groups, consolidating society, and safeguarding civic peace'.[44]

As the elections approached, the growing discontent in the

---

[43] *Radyanska Ukraina*, 1 December 1989.

[44] *Ibid.*, 3 December 1989.

republic with deteriorating social and economic conditions and the Party's preservation of its power and privileges erupted in a series of localized mass protests which forced the replacement in quick .succession of no less than eight regional Party bosses. Fortunately, unlike in Romania, where the Ceausescu regime had just been toppled in a bloody revolution, the unrest did not assume violent forms. On 5 January, Radio Moscow announced that the Party leaders of the Chernivsti and Kharkiv regions had been dismissed. The very next day, protests began in Chernihiv after a Party vehicle which was involved in a crash was discovered to be carrying luxury food and drink for local officials. Although Rukh had been relatively weak in this area, it managed within a few days to take control of the demonstrations and, after Kravchuk arrived to defuse the situation, to force a major shake-up of the region's Party leadership.[45] During the following month, the first secretaries of the Donetsk, Ivano-Frankivsk, Transcarpathian, Voroshylovhrad and Khmelnytsky regions were also replaced, as well as the entire Bureau of the Party committee of Kremenchuk.

Paradoxically, the high level of social discontent did not necessarily work in favour of the Democratic Bloc. Many people seemed to have little confidence in the electoral process. General disenchantment with the way *perestroika* was proceeding, the powerful hold which local officials and directors of factories and collective farms still had over the local populations in many regions, and the fact that the authorities were up to their old tricks in the electoral commissions, only reinforced the view that voting would not make a difference.

At the beginning of the new year, however, Rukh managed to raise spirits in many quarters by the success of its action to mark the anniversary of the proclamation of the unification of Ukraine in one united, independent, state on 22 January 1919. The date had additional significance for Ukrainian patriots, for precisely one year earlier, the Central Rada had declared Ukraine's independence. In its boldest and most ambitious undertaking so far, Rukh's leadership called on the inhabitants of Ukraine to express their support for the idea of a united, sovereign and democratic Ukraine by forming, on

---

[45] See Vitalii Hak's account of what occurred in Chernihiv in *Literaturna Ukraina*, 18 January 1990.

Sunday, 21 January, a 500-kilometre-long human chain, a 'Ukrainian Wave', from Kyiv to Lviv. The idea was borrowed from the example which the Balts had set the previous August on the fiftieth anniversary of the Molotov-Ribbentrop Pact. Rukh's action implicitly rejected the official Soviet line on Ukraine's modern history and the underlying aims seem to have been to legitimate both the brief period of independence and Ukraine's national symbols.

Faced with this test of strength and the prospect of widespread confrontation, the CPU leadership gave way. On 19 January, Kravchuk admitted in *Radyanska Ukraina* that the period 1918-19 had indeed been treated in a 'one-sided' and distorted manner and stated that the fact that the attempt to unite Ukraine in 1919 had been made by a 'bourgeois' government should not detract from its significance. He also indicated that the authorities would not attempt to prevent the 'Ukrainian Wave' and would be publishing more objective historical material about Ukraine's modern history. In fact, the appearance of a two-part article by Dzyuba in the same Party newspaper on 17 and 18 January seemed to confirm that the CPU was ready to remove the remaining blank spots. Its theme was the retrieval of Ukraine's suppressed historical and cultural heritage and overcoming the national inferiority complex which Dzyuba argued had been deliberately fostered. And on the same day as the interview with Kravchuk appeared, *Radyanska Ukraina* carried the beginning of a lengthy two-part article which, though still rather tendentious, included the texts of the various declarations of autonomy and independence made by the Ukrainian Central Rada in 1917-18.

This test of both the influence of Rukh and the strength of national feeling turned into a triumph that went beyond the expectations of the organizers. Rukh's leaders claimed that up to 3 million people took part in the action, while the authorities conceded that at least 450,000 had been involved. Not only was the human chain from Kyiv, via Zhytomyr, Rivne and Ternopil, to Lviv, largely completed; in the west, it was extended in a loop from Lviv to Ivano-Frankivsk. As had been requested by the organizers, most of the participants carried blue and yellow flags or other national symbols. Many of the republic's non-Ukrainian inhabitants were also reported to have lent their support. Huge meetings were held later in the day in central and Western Ukraine. In Kyiv itself, an estimated 100,000 people gathered in St Sofia's Square, where

Ukrainian independence had been proclaimed seventy-two years earlier, and approved a resolution that 22 January be made a national holiday in Ukraine. There were also smaller meetings in Kharkiv, Donetsk, Zaporizhzhya and Odesa, and recently formed Ukrainian organizations in Moscow, Riga and Vilnius, as well as Ukrainian communities in the West, also manifested their solidarity.[46]

Ironically, this massive peaceful display of the revived national spirit of the USSR's largest non-Russian nation passed largely unreported outside Ukraine. In the Western press, the 'Ukrainian Wave' was overshadowed by events in the Transcaucasus (a state of emergency had just been imposed by Soviet troops in parts of Azerbaijan after an escalation of the Armenian-Azerbaijani conflict). In the Soviet Union itself, the central media provided minimal coverage: only on 30 January did Soviet central television show a glimpse of the human chain in Kyiv and Ivano-Frankivsk. The day before, however, Soviet central television devoted almost an hour and a half to a film attacking Rukh's deputy leader Konev for allegedly letting down the electorate of Dniprodzerzhynsk by siding with 'Ukrainian nationalists'. Once again, then, *glasnost* was forgotten and the Ukrainian public had to rely for information on Radio Liberty's extensive on-the-spot reports from its stringers and interviews with the organizers of the 'Ukrainian Wave'.[47]

Elated by its success, Ukraine's national democratic movement stepped up its pre-election campaign and adopted a more radical anti-Communist and anti-imperial tone. On 25 January some 10,000 people attended a rally in Lviv to protest Moscow's military intervention in Azerbaijan and to express support for democratic candidates in the forthcoming elections. Pre-election rallies were held throughout the republic on 10 and 11 February, the one in Kyiv being attended by over 50,000 supporters of the Democratic Bloc.

The CPU fought back with a combination of deviousness and ostensibly conciliatory actions. Democratic candidates were besmirched as extremists and in numerous cases the electoral commissions

---

[46] See the coverage of the 'Ukrainian Wave' in *Radyanska Ukraina*, 23 January 1990; in the monthly newspaper of the Ukrainian Language Society, *Slovo*, February, 1990, and, in the first issue of Rukh's newspaper *Narodna hazeta*, February, 1990.

[47] See Bohdan Nahaylo, 'Human-Chain Demonstration in Ukraine: A Triumph for 'Rukh'', *Report on the USSR*, no. 2 (2 February 1990).

manipulated the rules to block their registration. The leaders of the Ukrainian Language Society and the Green World Association, Pavlychko and Shcherbak, protested to the Presidium of the Ukrainian Supreme Soviet about these irregularities.[48] Furthermore, following the success of the 'Ukrainian Wave', rumours were generated that Rukh and the 'nationalists' were about to launch pogroms against Jews and other non-Ukrainians. During February, leaders of Rukh and the Democratic Bloc were compelled to condemn these 'provocations' publicly and to re-emphasize the need for ethnic unity and harmony.[49]

Towards the end of January and in the early part of February, the authorities finally registered Memorial and Rukh, but only when it was too late for them to nominate candidates. All in all, despite continuing protests about the obstructive behaviour of many of the electoral commissions, candidates from the Democratic Bloc were registered in only 45% of the 450 electoral constituencies.[50] According to the Central Electoral Commission, of the more than 3,000 candidates who were registered, only 12.7% were non-Party members.[51]

The CPU Central Committee made another belated concession designed to win support for the CPU: it adopted a resolution, which was published on 7 February, acknowledging that the famine of 1932-3 in Ukraine was the result 'of the criminal course pursued by Stalin and his closest entourage (Molotov, Kaganovich) toward the peasantry'. Also, during January and February, *Radyanska Ukraina* began publishing material promoting the far from Marxist idea of creating a mystic 'Ukrainian spiritual republic' which the controversial writer and former political prisoner Oles Berdnyk was advocating as a means of filling the 'spiritual void' and stimulating Ukrainian cultural revival. In the first of these items, Berdnyk stressed he had recently been received by Ivashko and that the latter fully supported

---

[48] *Literaturna Ukraina*, 8 February 1990.

[49] Haran, *To Kill the Dragon*, pp. 81-4. See also the statement addressed to the citizens of Ukraine on this subject by Rukh's leaders Drach, Yavorivsky and Mykhailo Horyn, in *Vilne slovo*, no. 9, 1990.

[50] This figure was provided by Serhii Odarych, the deputy head of Rukh's election committee. AFP, 21 March 1990.

[51] *Radyanska Ukraina*, 23 February 1990.

'the idea of all-Ukrainian unity and the mobilization of cultural and spiritual forces'.[52]

In the religious sphere, too, certain adjustments were made. At the end of January, the local authorities handed back the Cathedral of the Resurrection in Ivano-Frankivsk to the Ukrainian Catholics. On 31 January, Metropolitan Filaret appeared on Soviet central television to protest this action on behalf of the Synod of the Russian Orthodox Church. Faced with the growing challenge in Ukraine from the Ukrainian Catholics and the UAOC, and no longer having the backing that it used to have on this issue from the Kremlin, the leadership of the Russian Orthodox Church was, however, finally forced to make a major concession to resurgent national feeling. On 3 February, it was announced in the press that the Synod of the Russian Orthodox Church had decided to rename the Ukrainian and Belarusian Exarchates of the Russian Orthodox Church as the Ukrainian Orthodox Church and Belarusian Orthodox Church respectively and grant them a certain measure of autonomy in order that 'church life' in the two republics would correspond more to 'the national religious traditions' of the Ukrainian and Belarusian peoples.

Dissension in the Party ranks

In the final weeks before the elections, however, political developments in Moscow, the Baltic republics and Eastern Europe, resonated in Kyiv and this appears to have stimulated further ferment within the Ukrainian Communist establishment. By now, the Lithuanian Communist Party had asserted its independence, and in Czechoslovakia, Alexander Dubcek, the Party leader during the Prague Spring, had become chairman of the Czechoslovak parliament and the dissident playwright and former political prisoner Vaclav Havel the country's president. Furthermore, signs, of a split in the CPSU were also appearing. In Moscow, on 21 January, more than 450 reformist members of the CPSU from various parts of the USSR met to form an intra-party faction seeking the transformation of the Communist Party into 'a genuinely democratic parliamentary party operating under a multi-party system' and market reforms. Known as 'the Democratic Platform', this group also had supporters in Ukraine who proceeded to organize.

---

[52] *Ibid.*, 12 January and 11 February 1989.

Soon afterwards, on the eve of a crucial plenum of the CPSU Central Committee, tens of thousands staged the largest pro-democracy rally yet seen in Moscow. At the plenum on 5 February, Gorbachev finally conceded that the Communist Party should give up its constitutionally guaranteed monopoly on power and instead compete for power in democratic elections. On the other hand, he proposed that a presidential form of government be created. The Soviet leader also signalled that the Kremlin was now prepared to acknowledge the need for a new Union treaty. The first to criticize Gorbachev's speech and the new Party Platform which he had proposed for the forthcoming Twenty-eighth Party Congress was a representative of the conservative wing of the CPU, Korniyenko. He urged the Soviet leader to use the 'most radical' means to restore order and save the Socialist state 'before it was too late'. The Communist Party, he argued, had to preserve if not a 'leading', then a 'special' role for itself in society.[53] Despite the criticism from the hard-liners, the Platform advocated by Gorbachev was adopted.[54]

Against this tumultuous background, the issue of Ukrainian sovereignty was rapidly moving to the top of the political agenda. The emphasis on the need to achieve sovereignty was evident at a session of the Verkhovna Rada devoted to environmental issues, which opened on 17 February and at which, incidentally, Shcherbytsky's death was announced. For instance, Ivan Plyushch, the head of the Kyiv region's administration, argued that it was time to 'fill the notions of sovereignty and independence with real substance, that is, build our relations on the basis of mutual expediency and choice in a free Union of states'. The session also heard outspoken criticism of the diktat of the central ministries and calls for the closure of the Chornobyl nuclear power plant. In a display of its new assertiveness, the Ukrainian legislature voted to send an appeal to the Soviet Defence Minister Dmitrii Yazov calling for the suspension of the building of a military radar station in the Transcarpathian region until experts had examined the consequences for the environment.[55] A few days later, Yazov agreed to comply with this request.[56]

---

[53] *Ibid.*, 7 February 1990.

[54] *Ibid.*, 14 February 1990.

[55] *Ibid.*, 18, 20, 21, 22 and 23 February, 1990.

[56] *Ibid.*, 25 February 1990.

On the same day as the Verkhovna Rada was convening, supporters of the 'Democratic Platform' in Kyiv formed a coordinating council of local 'progressive' Party clubs and organizations from Kyiv University and various institutes and factories. Among the members were Salii and Karpenko. Similar groups were being formed in other cities.[57]

Meanwhile, the leadership of the Ukrainian Komsomol, which was struggling to hold the organization together and redefine its role, moved closer still towards the positions held by the democratic opposition. At a plenum of the Komsomol's Central Committee on 19 February, its leadership explicitly criticized the Central Committee of the CPU for responding too slowly to 'sharply acute current problems', including 'the question of Ukraine's remaining within the USSR, and of its state, political and economic system in the future'. The plenum came out in support of political pluralism, cooperation in the elections 'with all democratic forces', and the broadest possible political and economic sovereignty for Ukraine on the basis of a new Union treaty. Two important resolutions were adopted. The first 'on the Sovereignty of the Ukrainian SSR', urged the new parliament to make the declaration of the state sovereignty of Ukraine a priority and, echoing much of what was in Rukh's programme, set out in considerable detail some of the principles that needed to be included in it. The other expressed toleration for the use of national symbols. Kravchuk participated in the plenum and in his speech declared: 'I support the position of the Komsomol concerning the sovereignty of our republic.'[58]

The emerging divisions within the CPU leadership between, on the one hand, moderates, reformists and proponents of broad sovereignty, and on the other, conservatives, hard-liners and defenders of the empire, surfaced at the CPU Central Committee plenum convened on 22 February to discuss the situation on the eve of the elections. Ivashko set the tone by warning the participants that the Party's opponents were effectively presenting it with an ultimatum: 'If we do not make a choice between the GDR and Czechoslovak variants, the "Romanian variant" cannot be ruled out.' The CPU would not give in to fear, he asserted, and, with the help of the security forces, would ensure that order was maintained.

---

[57] Haran, *To Kill the Dragon*, pp. 91–2.
[58] *Molod Ukrainy*, 22 and 24 February 1990.

Yelchenko and quite a few other hard-liners, however, called for the restoration of order and discipline not only in the republic but within the CPU as well. The Party had become plagued with divisions between 'rightist and leftist positions, capitulationism, membership in unofficial organizations with a negative political, profile, [and] apathy', he complained, and it was time to purge the ranks. Another speaker, a Party official from the Voroshylovhrad region, declared that Drach, Pavlychko, Yeltsin and Afanasev had no right to call themselves Communists and also attacked Kravchuk for his political evolution and liberal stance.

One of the reformists, the pro-Rector of the Kyiv Polytechnical Institute, M. Rodionov, criticized the calls made 'in many of the speeches for the use of force, because we have ended up under some sort of siege'. Together with Leonid Kuchma, the general director of the 'Pivdenmash' rocket building complex in Dnipropetrovsk, he argued that the CPU and CPSU had lagged behind developments and instead of leading had in fact been pushed along from below. Kravchuk, too, rejected what he described as 'the nostalgia for the stern hand'. The people had grown tired, he said, and what was needed was to win back their confidence.

Several of the speakers, including Kravchuk, stated that the CPU should seek greater autonomy and Rodionov even went as far as to suggest that the CPSU should be transformed into 'a union of independent national parties'. Ivashko himself in his concluding remarks said that the CPU needed to emphasize that 'in its policies it upholds the interests of Ukraine'. Rodionov, Kuchma and Kravchuk went the furthest in calling for the practical realization of Ukraine's sovereignty on the basis of a new Union treaty. As Kravchuk put it, although Ukraine was part of the Soviet federation, 'we have to be masters in our own land'.

One of the factors which seemed to have convinced some of the Ukrainian Communists of the need to take fuller responsibility for affairs in their republic and broaden its sovereignty was disillusionment with Moscow generally, and the Gorbachev leadership in particular, for getting the Soviet Union into such a mess. This theme figured quite prominently at the plenum. Kachura, for example, blamed the Gorbachev leadership for the grave 'political, economic, and ideological crisis' in which the USSR found itself, arguing that the Kremlin's policies had been poorly thought out, inconsistent and belated. The old economic structure had been ruined and was no longer functioning and the very survival of the Soviet state was in question. For those who felt themselves 'responsible for the fate of the republic, for the life and welfare of the people of Ukraine', there was only one way out: the consolidation of all the 'healthy forces' in the republic from both the CPU and the opposition. The Dnipropetrovsk region Party boss, M. Zadoya, used a different argument. The central authorities in Moscow were not in a position to restore order in Ukraine; therefore, the republic had to become sovereign so that its leaders could do the job themselves.[59] Ukraine's Communist leaders also could not help but notice that the demand for the sovereignty of the Russian Federation was growing, with radicals such as Yeltsin, conservative Russian Communists and Russian nationalists all beginning to press for it.

But there were other new developments, too, which alarmed particularly the leaders of the Soviet Union's democratic and national movements. The creation of a strong Soviet presidency, in the absence of a new constitution defining the division of powers, was potentially dangerous for the cause of democracy and the devolution of power from the centre. At the same time, a new law was being prepared on secession which left no doubt that it was intended to make it as difficult as possible for those republics which wanted to leave the USSR to do so. Moreover, on 24 February the Council of the USSR Supreme Soviet approved a bill regulating the declaration of a state of emergency, the provisions of which allowed the USSR Supreme Soviet to impose this measure without the consent of the legislature of the republic concerned.

In some republics, the elections to the republican legislatures were held a week before those in Ukraine and provided encouraging results for the Democratic Bloc. They resulted in a resounding victory for Sajudis in Lithuania, and the defeat of the Communist Party of Moldova by the Moldovan Popular Front. What was also encouraging for Rukh and its allies was that Russia's fast-growing democratic movement was campaigning hard and seemed poised to do well in the elections to the Supreme Soviet of the RSFSR.

---

[59] *Radyanska Ukraina*, 24, 25, 27 and 28 February 1990. The maverick Kuchma urged that 'the first decree of our Renewed Verkhovna Rada should be a decree on the full economic and political sovereignty of Ukraine as a state.' See Yurii Lukakonov, *Tretii prezydent: Politychnyi Portret Leonida Kuchmy* [The Third President: A Political Portrait of Leonid Kuchma], Kyiv, 1996, 17-19.

In the final days before the elections the political polarization in Ukraine grew. On 25 February, the last Sunday before the elections, according to official figures 126 demonstrations involving 300,000 people took place throughout the republic at which the authorities were accused of rigging the electoral process, and genuine democracy was demanded.[60] Pro-democracy rallies were also held that day in Moscow and many other cities in the USSR. Three days later, however, *Radyanska Ukraina* reported that the Union of Toilers of Ukraine for Socialist Restructuring had just held its inaugural congress in Kyiv.

The parliamentary elections become a watershed

On 4 March, almost 85% of the voters turned out to cast their ballots for the 2,888 candidates who were competing for 450 seats. Deputies were elected in roughly a quarter of the constituencies and the run-offs were scheduled for a fortnight later. The initial results indicated that the Democratic Bloc had done very well where it had been able to nominate candidates, winning 43 of the 112 decided seats, and that the national democrats were headed for a landslide victory in Western Ukraine and making a strong showing in Kyiv. Among the representatives of the democratic opposition who were elected were: Drach, Yavorivsky, Chornovil, Mykhailo and Bohdan Horyn, Lukyanenko, Yukhnovsky and Khmara. As for the CPU leaders, Ivashko and Yelchenko were forced into the second round; Kravchuk, Hurenko, Matvienko, Kachura and Masol were elected; and Pohrebnyak and Kryuchkov were among those who lost.[61]

The results spurred some of Rukh's euphoric leaders into issuing a call, without even waiting for the second round of voting, for the transformation of the Popular Movement into a political party committed to achieving Ukrainian independence. On 6 March, the day the appeal was launched, Drach told a Western correspondent that during the election campaign

....people asked us why we did not form a party . . . We finally told ourselves that we should make up our minds and form a

[60] *Washington Times*, 27 February 1990.

[61] *Radyanska Ukraina*, 13 March 1990. For further details, see Potichnyj, *Elections in Ukraine*.

party for the national, social and spiritual renaissance of Ukraine.
. . Our party will stand for the independence of Ukraine, for
its political and social sovereignty. And at this stage the only
way to achieve it is to leave the Soviet Union.[62]

Two days later, *Literaturna Ukraina* published the appeal signed
by twenty-two activists. They included leaders of Rukh and the
UHU, and Communists and non-Communists alike. Among them
were: Drach, Yavorivsky, Pavlychko, Mykhailo Horyn,
Lukyanenko, Konev, Badzo, Donchyk and Holovaty. The statement called for a multi-party system, blamed the CPSU for the
ills that had befallen the Ukrainian nation under its rule, and
rejected the 'imperial Moloch', which the authors said was being
disguised as a renewed federation. They proposed that Rukh be
transformed into a political party uniting all those who wanted
to achieve in a democratic and peaceful manner 'the real and
lasting independence of Ukraine'. They also called on the CPU
to follow the example which Brazauskas and the Lithuanian Communist Party had set and transform itself into an independent,
democratic, leftist party.

The appeal was another milestone, both as regards the development of a multiparty system in Ukraine, and the shift towards the
open embracement of the cause of Ukrainian independence by the
democratic opposition. In fact, the Green World Association, the
UHU and the Ukrainian Christian Democratic Front had all recently announced their intention to become political parties, and
Literaturna Ukraina of 8 March also published material about preparations by an initiative group in Lviv to form a Ukrainian Peasant
Democratic party.

Nevertheless, the proposal about Rukh's future caused a certain
amount of confusion and concern within the Democratic Bloc and
there was strong opposition from those who wanted the Popular
Movement to remain an umbrella organization. It also enabled the
Party apparatus to play up warnings about 'separatists' and
'extremists', especially as on 11 March the Lithuanian Supreme
Soviet, now controlled by national democrats, voted to declare
Lithuania's independence.

Despite the new questions concerning Rukh's direction, the
Democratic Bloc did well again in the run-off elections, the voter

---

[62] Reuter, 6 March 1990.

turnout in which was a little lower – 78.8%. Among the democrats and reformists elected were Holovaty, Oles Shevchenko, Yemets, Tanyuk, Salii and Kotyk. Ivashko and Yelchenko also got in.[63] Altogether the Democratic Bloc won about 110 seats, ten of the successful candidates being former political prisoners. A further thirty or so of the deputies elected turned out to be potential allies of the democrats, so that the democratic opposition in the new parliament made up between a quarter and a third of the lawmakers. The Democratic Bloc achieved similar successes in the elections to the local councils, the national democrats winning control in the Lviv, Ivano-Frankivsk and Ternopil regions, and capturing half of the seats in the Kyiv city council.

The election results provided a fairly good picture of the balance of political forces in the republic. The Democratic Bloc won resounding victories in Western Ukraine and Kyiv, winning all 24 parliamentary seats in the Lviv region and 18 out of 22 in the Ukrainian capital. In Kharkiv the Democratic Bloc won 9 of the 28 seats, and in the Donetsk region 9 out of 45. Generally, the Democratic Bloc did better in the bigger cities than in the rural areas. In fact, its poorest performance was in the rural areas of southern and eastern Ukraine. The Democratic Bloc won seats in twenty of Ukraine's twenty-five regions, failing to secure representation in the Voroshylovhrad, Zaporizhzhya, Mykolaiv, Kherson, and, rather surprisingly, Chernivsti regions, as well as the city of Sevastopol – the main base of the Black Sea Fleet.

As for the ethnic composition of the 442 deputies who had been elected by 18 March, 331 were Ukrainians, 99 Russians, 5 Belarusians, 4 Jews, 1 Armenian, 1 Bulgarian and 1 German. Party functionaries captured at least 97 seats, directors of state and collective farms 33, while directors of industrial enterprises also won a significant number.[64]

The results confirmed that Western Ukraine and Kyiv remained the centres of the national revival but that the pressure for change was also considerable in the cities of Eastern Ukraine, where social and economic considerations dominated. Rukh and the national democrats had made little headway in the more industrialized and Russified regions on the left bank of the Dnipro, and outside of

---

[63] *Radyanska Ukraina*, 24 March 1990.
[64] See Potichnyj, *Elections in Ukraine*, pp. 24–7 and 31.

Western Ukraine their influence in the villages was still weak. Nevertheless, considering the difficulties and obstacles it had faced, Rukh and its allies in the Democratic Bloc, had done remarkably well. The CPU's monopoly, though not its hold on power, had been broken and the political struggle for democracy and sovereignty elevated to a new plane.

Meanwhile, in the Russian Federation, democratic forces had also done well in the elections. Candidates representing the new 'Democratic Russia' Bloc swept to victory in Moscow and Leningrad and captured about a quarter of all the seats to the new RSFSR Congress of People's Deputies. The radical reformers Gavriil Popov and Anatolii Sobchak were subsequently elected to head the city councils in Moscow and Leningrad, respectively. Yeltsin, who after the death of Sakharov in December became the uncrowned leader of the Russian reformist opposition, also won comfortably in Sverdlovsk. When then, on 13 March, the USSR Congress of People's Deputies finally took the historic decision to abolish the Communist Party's constitutional monopoly on power, it was simply acknowledging the new political realities which the elections to the republican legislatures had confirmed. On the same day the Congress elected Gorbachev as president of the USSR, though not without problems: the radical deputies were split over whether to support the creation of an executive president and almost 200 deputies did not vote for the Soviet leader. In short, the elections had drastically altered the political set-up in the USSR and the forces for democracy and republican sovereignty were continuing to set the political agenda.

10

THE NEW PARLIAMENTARY POLITICS
AND THE DEBATE OVER SOVEREIGNTY

New battle lines are drawn

The dust from the election battle was not given a chance to settle for the continuing struggle between the CPU and the democratic forces immediately manifested itself over new issues. On 20 March Rukh's Secretariat applied for permission to hold a rally in Kyiv in support of Lithuania's declaration of independence. The authorities refused and the Popular Movement decided not only to defy the ban but to hold pro-Lithuanian meetings throughout the republic on the last day of the month.

On 21 March, about 30,000 people in Lviv held a demonstration to express solidarity with Lithuania. By now in this city, and in Western Ukraine generally, the newly elected national democratic deputies to the local councils had begun to make their mark. The town council of Stryi led the way by voting to replace the Soviet Ukrainian flag on the municipal building with a blue and yellow one, an action that was promptly condemned by the regional procurator.[1]

On 24-5 March, the Grand Council of Rukh held a special meeting in the Transcarpathian town of Khust to mark the anniversary of the proclamation of the short-lived independent Carpatho-Ukrainian state in 1939. Attended by some 800 delegates, it saw an intensive discussion about the organization's future. Rukh's leaders had decided not to transform the Popular Movement into a party after all because of the continuing need for an umbrella organization to consolidate the diverse groups and currents within the democratic opposition. Pavlychko nevertheless renewed the call for the formation of a political party having Ukrainian independence as its goal.

[1] Radio Kyiv, 31 March 1990.

He announced that he, Drach and other colleagues had decided to leave the Communist Party and intended to form what he provisionally called 'the Democratic Party of Ukraine'.[2] Yavorivsky had already left the Party earlier in the month.

On 24 March the CPU's Secretariat published a statement declaring that Party members who had signed the recent calls in *Literaturna Ukraina* for the formation of new political parties had thereby 'left the ranks of the CPSU'. Five days later, the press announced that three such errant members, Holovaty, Donchyk and Oleksandr Burakovsky (the leading Jewish representative in Rukh), had been expelled from the Party.

Problems with other dissenters within the CPU were also growing. On 24–5 March, supporters of the Democratic Platform held a conference in Kharkiv and established a coordinating council for reformist Party clubs in the republic. The 109 delegates from twenty-one regions differed, however, on the degree of independence which the CPU should have from the CPSU.[3] Thus, the CPU was now faced not only with the external challenge from Rukh and its allies but also with an internal one from the supporters of the Democratic Platform.

While the issue of Lithuania's declaration of independence was driving the two rival political camps further apart, the situation was further compounded on 25 March when the Estonian Communist Party followed the example that had been set by the Lithuanian Communists and voted to break with the CPSU. Still seeking to prevent the pro-Lithuania demonstrations called by Rukh, the CPU Central Committee issued a strongly worded statement on 28 March branding Rukh's behaviour as 'irresponsible, adventurist and provocative'. It was backed up by instructions from the republic's Council of Ministers to local authorities not to allow the meetings to be held. Two days later, *Pravda* added its voice, warning of the 'activation of nationalist forces in Ukraine', particularly in the western regions.

The religious problem in Western Ukraine was, in the meantime, becoming even more acute. Although hundreds of Ukrainian Catholic and Ukrainian Autocephalous Orthodox communities were seeking official registration, by the spring of 1990 the

[2] *Visnyk RUKHU* (Kyiv), no. 4.
[3] Radio Kyiv, 26 March 1990, and Haran, *To Kill the Dragon*, p. 92.

authorities had recognized only a fraction of them. Tensions, especially between the Russian Orthodox Church and the Ukrainian Catholics were rising, and the attitudes of both the authorities responsible for religious affairs and the Moscow Patriarchate were only aggravating matters. In mid-March, Archbishop Sternyuk walked out of talks being conducted in Kyiv by a recently established quadripartite commission, which included representatives of the Vatican (in which the Ukrainian Catholic hierarchy from outside of Ukraine was represented), the Moscow Patriarchate, the Ukrainian Catholic Church in Ukraine and the Ukrainian Orthodox Church. In the statement subsequently issued by the Ukrainian Catholic bishops in Ukraine, it was explained that the Russian Orthodox side refused to recognize the uncanonical nature of its incorporation of the Ukrainian Catholic Church in 1946 and to recognize the latter as 'a Church, an institution and a juridical body, and not just as a group of Greek Catholics'.[4] Relations between the two sides were further strained when, on 6 April, the Lviv city council voted to return St George's Cathedral to the Ukrainian Catholics.

With Rukh determined not to give in to intimidation and numerous newly elected deputies from the Democratic Bloc also coming out in support of Lithuanian independence, the dispute developed into the first major test of strength after the elections between the CPU and the democratic opposition. On 31 March, Rukh went ahead and held rallies in support of Lithuania in various parts of the republic. In Kyiv an estimated 30,000 people took part and approved a resolution criticizing Gorbachev for 'interfering in the internal affairs of the independent Lithuanian Republic'. There were even bigger meetings in Lviv, Ivano-Frankivsk and Ternopil; only in Chernivsti did the authorities intervene and make arrests. Initially, the authorities sought to prosecute about fifty newly elected deputies, including Drach, Mykhailo Horyn and Oles Shevchenko, for their involvement in the protests, but eventually gave up.[5]

Confronted with this defiance from Rukh and the growing challenges from within the Party, the CPU Central Committee held another plenum on 31 March devoted to the forthcoming Congresses of both the CPU and CPSU. Numerous additional Party officials based in Kyiv and in the regions were also invited to attend. In the

[4] Bociurkiw, 'The Ukrainian Catholic Church', pp. 15-17.
[5] Haran, *To Kill the Dragon*, p. 93.

opening speech, Ivashko sought to restore order and morale by indicating that, regardless of what was happening elsewhere in the Soviet Union and Eastern Europe, the CPU did not intend to retreat any further. It would not give in, he declared, to pressure to 'relinquish its Communist ideals' and 'to deprive it of its "vanguard role"', transform it into a parliamentary [party], or some sort of discussion club, and, ultimately, remove it completely from the political arena'. Denouncing 'extremists' and 'separatists', he also condemned supporters of the Democratic Platform, accusing them of wanting 'to destroy the Party' by splitting it from within. He stressed that 'in multi-party conditions' the CPU had to remain united and tightly disciplined and that there could be no room for factions or split loyalties. The CPU would have to undergo a process of 'renewal' through the cleansing of its ranks and the tightening of internal discipline. Expressing concern about developments in Western Ukraine, where the democratically controlled local and regional councils had begun challenging the authority of local Party structures and the Soviet order generally, and religious conflicts between the Ukrainian Catholics and Orthodox believers, as he put it, were assuming a 'nationalist, anti-Russian, extremist character', the Party leader called on the local Party forces to regroup and hold the line.

Salii responded on behalf of the supporters of the Democratic Platform and did not mince his words. He told the plenum that the 'shadow of Brezhnev' was hanging over the meeting. The calls for a purge of dissenters within the CPU would only drive out the Party's 'intellectual élite', as had happened with such dire consequences in the 1930s. 'The biggest evil today, the biggest extremism', he argued, were 'conservatism and reactionary dogmatism'. It was they, 'not the students or democrats' who were 'ruining the Party from within'. From the official press account, his call for greater openness, discussion and tolerance within the Party was, however, very much the minority viewpoint at the plenum and came under fierce attack from conservatives.[6]

What was even more striking about the plenum than the attention devoted to the issue of the Democratic Platform and internal dissent was the prominence given to the question of Ukraine's sovereignty. Ivashko himself stressed that 'the bitter experience' of

[6] For the speeches at the plenum, see *Radyanska Ukraina*, 3–6 April 1990.

Baltic and East European Communist parties had revealed the dangers of lagging behind political events and failing to influence their development. It appears that by in effect adopting much of what had been in Rukh's programme and presenting the CPU as the champion of Ukraine's political and economic sovereignty, the CPU leadership was trying to outflank its democratic opponents and gain the political initiative. Certainly, by now the idea not only of sovereignty, but of full-fledged independence, had caught on in the republic. The new political self-assertiveness was being manifested more and more openly in such ways as opposition among students and youth groups to the draft and to serving beyond Ukraine's borders, calls for the creation of national military formations, and demands for a separate Ukrainian Olympics Committee and a separate Ukrainian national sports team. Evidently, the CPU was hoping to redirect this feeling into what it considered were safer and acceptable forms.

The plenum adopted a special resolution, 'On the Political and Economic Sovereignty of Ukraine', which stated that the achievement of these two goals 'within a renewed Soviet federation', and on the basis of a new Union treaty, was considered to be 'one of the most important tasks' facing the CPU. In fact, the actual description in the resolution of what sovereignty should entail was reminiscent of the Estonian Declaration of Sovereignty which the CPU leadership had opposed so vehemently almost a year and a half before. Among other things, the resolution affirmed that the people of Ukraine, expressing their will through deputies elected to the republican Supreme Soviet and local councils (what had just occurred in Western Ukraine evidently did not seem to count), should be in control of affairs on Ukrainian territory, that the territorial integrity of the republic should be safeguarded, that Ukraine should have the right to decide which powers to delegate to the federal organs, the priority of republican law over all-Union legislation, and that Ukraine's status in foreign affairs and external representation should be enhanced.[7]

This latter aspect was discussed at the plenum by the head of the CPU Central Committee's Department for Foreign Ties, Anatolii Merkulov, who gave a refreshingly forthright account of the international aspects of Ukraine's sovereignty, thereby revealing how

[7] *Ibid.*, 3 April 1990.

relatively radical some of the advocates of genuine Ukrainian sovereignty within the CPU were becoming. He argued that the 'artificial isolation' of Ukraine from the outside world since the 1920s was one of the reasons for the 'negative phenomena' which had afflicted Ukraine's society and that it was essential to end this isolation and for Ukraine to become a direct participant in international affairs. New laws outlining the rights of Union republics in the external sphere could not be left to Moscow to decide – what was currently being envisaged by the centre, he warned, was more restrictive than the rights which the republics nominally enjoyed in the Stalin era – and Ukraine would have to propose its own concept of its right to conduct its own political and economic external relations. In his view, Merkulov said, Ukraine should be a direct participant in the Helsinki process and European forums dealing with security issues and economic, environmental and humanitarian cooperation. It was important to begin reorganizing and enlarging Ukraine's Ministry of Foreign Affairs so that it could start handling the establishment of direct bilateral relations with foreign states, start examining the possibilities for opening embassies and consulates abroad, and, in the meantime, to ensure that there were official representatives of Ukraine in the USSR's existing missions, embassies and consulates.[8]

In preparation for the CPU's Congress, which was due to open on 19 June, the plenum also adopted the draft of the new programme, or 'programmatic principles' as it preferred to call the document, which was supposed to promote the image of the Party as a progressive organization that was keeping in step with the times and serving the needs of Ukraine and its people. The programme stated that the CPU was committed to building a Socialist society in a sovereign Ukrainian state, based on humane, democratic ideals, social justice, the rule of law and the acceptance of mixed forms of ownership. It did, however, contain two new elements which indicated further concessions to the national movement. One was the emphasis now placed on 'the assertion of national statehood' as a guiding principle for the CPU; the other, the belated recognition of the need to institute republican citizenship. A further noteworthy change was the declaration made in the document that 'We are for the independence of the Communist Party of Ukraine within the

[8] *Ibid.*, 5 April 1990.

CPSU.' It was explained that although this did not mean that the CPU supported the idea of turning the CPSU into a federation, it nevertheless wanted to be fully 'autonomous'.[9]

Reflecting the CPU's increasing emphasis on sovereignty, in the weeks following the plenum more and more material began to appear in the press about economic sovereignty. On 5 April, for instance, *Literaturna Ukraina* published a lengthy interview on this subject with Vitold Fokin, the chairman of the State Planning Committee of the Ukrainian SSR. Even this cautious official, after discussing the complexities which this economic transformation entailed and warning that a transitional period of some five to six years would be needed to carry out the shift from a centrally controlled to a 'sovereign' regulated market economy, maintained that the achievement of 'economic independence' was an 'urgent necessity' and the 'last chance to avoid economic catastrophe'.

The case for economic sovereignty was presented quite thoroughly three weeks later in a round-table discussion published in *Radyanska Ukraina* in which some of the republic's leading economic specialists participated. Several of them stressed that the precondition for economic sovereignty was political sovereignty. Serhii Dorohunstov, the head of the Academy of Science's Council for the Study of Ukraine's Productive Forces, for instance, stated quite bluntly that political realities had to be faced: the 'disintegration of the Soviet Union', as the example of Lithuania showed, had begun and hard decisions had to be made about Ukraine's future. Any discussion of economic sovereignty had to take into account whether Ukraine intended to become independent and break away from the USSR, or remain part of the Soviet federation, as he preferred. Another participant, Rukh's young economic adviser, Oleksandr Savchenko, argued that without the introduction of its own national currency, Ukraine's economic sovereignty would not amount to much.[10] What was missing in these materials, however, was information on the degree of the interconnectedness of the Soviet economy and what the rupturing of ties would mean (though, of course, at this stage, the achievement of sovereignty was seen as a gradual and negotiated process, and 'separatism' was still officially

[9] *Ibid.*, 5 April 1990.
[10] *Ibid.*, 25 April 1990.

treated as an extremist position), and the extent of Ukraine's dependence on Russia for its oil and gas.

After the Central Committee plenum, developments in Western Ukraine caused even more alarm in official Kyiv as local councils began in effect to dismantle Soviet rule in their regions. With city and town councils raising blue and yellow flags, declaring Easter to be a holiday, voting to return churches to the Ukrainian Catholics that had been taken over by the Russian Orthodox Church, depriving the local Party organs of the power they had held, and beginning to move in the direction of establishing elements of a mixed economy, the Party and state apparatus moved to defend its threatened position. One of their first steps was to strip the local councils of control over the militia and the appointment of newspaper and television editors.

After the embarrassment of seeing Chornovil elected on 12 April as head of the Lviv regional council, the Kyiv authorities stepped up the pressure. The regional Party leader Pohrebnyak was replaced by a known hard-liner, Svyatoslav Sekretaryuk. Ironically, though, the abrupt and furtive manner in which Pohrebnyak was removed brought thousands of demonstrators out on to the streets of Lviv – the very same people that had failed to elect him in the last two elections.[11] Just as Gorbachev was imposing an economic blockade on Lithuania, a propaganda campaign was launched against the democratic stronghold in Western Ukraine. On 18 April, the official press published a joint statement by the Ukrainian Party, parliamentary and government leadership expressing concern about the 'dangerous' situation in the west of the republic. In it they claimed that 'destructive' and 'extremist' forces had 'guaranteed' majorities for themselves in the local councils and were now pursuing 'separatist' ambitions by 'illegal' and 'anti-constitutional' means. Attempting to drive a wedge between Western and Eastern Ukrainians, the statement declared that the idea of 'so-called Galician autonomy' was being imposed on Western Ukraine's population. Local Communists, it continued, were·being subjected to 'psychological pressure'. It concluded with the warning that the Ukrainian Party and government leadership would use 'resolute means' to ensure that Soviet laws were observed in the troublesome regions. It is worth noting that in the statement, even though the

[11] AFP, 14 April 1990.

constitutional recognition of the Party's leading role had been abolished, the Central Committee of the CPU still put itself before the Presidium of the Verkhovna Rada and the Council of Ministers.[12]

While attention was being focused on Western Ukraine, events in Kyiv demonstrated that the atmosphere in the Ukrainian capital had also become more radical. On 29 March, the outgoing Ukrainian Supreme Soviet had designated the anniversary of the Chornobyl disaster as a day of mourning. Rukh, the Green World association and other democratic organizations decided to organize their own 'Chornobyl Week' commemorations. These turned into another round of huge political demonstrations. On 22 April – the International Day of the Earth – some 60,000 people, according to Radio Kyiv, attended a public ecological meeting, and later in the day, an estimated 100,000 joined a march through the city. The participants shouted 'Independence!' and 'Down with Communism!', and when part of the column passed Lenin's statue – this was also the anniversary of Lenin's birth – members of the radical Union of Independent Ukrainian Youth (SNUM) laid a wreathe made of barbed wire before it and proceeded to burn Lenin's works.[13] On the actual fourth anniversary of the Chornobyl accident, commemorative meetings were held throughout Ukraine at which political and ecological issues were interwoven. In Kyiv, tens of thousands again turned out for a public rally and a commemorative service conducted by priests of the UAOC.

During 'Chornobyl Week', however, Ukrainian national democrats, and especially the leaders of the Ukrainian Language Society, suffered a setback when, on 24 April, the USSR Supreme Soviet passed a law on languages which threatened once again to undermine the status of the Ukrainian language. Although it gave Union and autonomous republics the right to determine the legal status of languages on their territory, it made Russian the official language of the USSR. With this move and the continuing pressure on Lithuania, Gorbachev effectively destroyed whatever lingering support he may have had among Ukrainian national democrats.

There were more demonstrations on May Day. In Lviv, accord-

---

[12] See *Radyanska Ukraina*, 18 April 1990.

[13] Haran, *To Kill the Dragon*, p. 96. *Radyanska Ukraina* of 25 April published photographs of the protest by SNUM members.

ing to Reuter, 'former political prisoners led tens of thousands of people . . . in a May Day parade which turned into a boisterous demonstration for Ukrainian independence . . . Not a single red flag was in evidence.'[14] In the Ukrainian capital, where the official parade was much smaller than in previous years, for the first time, as Radio Kyiv noted, blue and yellow flags were very much in evidence. Meanwhile, in Moscow too, there was a sensation: during the May Day parade Gorbachev was jeered by pro-democracy demonstrators.

In an interview published in *Pravda* on 3 May, Ivashko sought to keep the focus on Western Ukraine and reiterated the CPU's determination not to lose control of the situation. Accusing Western Ukrainian deputies of 'political extremism', he added that some local Party officials like Pohrebnyak had displayed 'political infantilism' in dealing with the problem. Without elaborating, the Ukrainian Party leader declared that 'all the things which are being done illegally in the western regions will be repealed' and that it would be necessary to apply 'measures of a political and economic charac-ter' against the recalcitrant *oblasts*. It appeared that Western Ukraine was being threatened with the same tough treatment as Lithuania.

Meanwhile, the formation of new political parties and groups was continuing. The largest and potentially most influential of them emerged out of the UHU. At the end of 1989, Chornovil had unsuccessfully urged his colleagues in the UHU to transform their organization into a political party. It was only at the end of April that a congress of the UHU, which at this time had 2,300 members, decided to do so and formed the right of centre Ukrainian Republican Party (URP). Lukyanenko was elected to head the new party, and Khmara and Hryhorii Hrebenyuk from the Donbas were chosen as his deputies. Chornovil could not play a role in it because his new office precluded his belonging to any political party. The URP not only sought independence for Ukraine but also the banning of political organizations whose 'controlling centres' were outside the republic, that is, the CPU, as well as the nationalization of the CPSU's assets in Ukraine.[15]

In Western Ukraine, another small radical nationalist organiza-tion was formed in April. Calling itself 'State Independence for Ukraine,' it was led by Lukyanenko's former partner and also

[14] Reuter, 1 May 1990.
[15] Haran, *To Kill the Dragon*, pp. 96–100.

long-term prisoner Ivan Kandyba, and, like the UNP, it was opposed to working within the Soviet system.[16] And in Kyiv, at the Chornobyl- Day rally, Shcherbak announced the formation of the Green Party of Ukraine. Later, towards the end of May, *Literaturna Ukraina* was to publish the manifesto of the Democratic Party of Ukraine, which Pavlychko, Drach, Yavorivsky, Badzo and others were forming.[17] A Social-Democratic Party of Ukraine also appeared.

Various youth and student organizations, such as SNUM, had also come into existence during the last year. SNUM had been launched as the UHU's organization for youth but had become a magnet for radical nationalist elements which eventually were to split the organization. Its leader Ihor Derkach was a moderate, and was elected in Lviv as deputy to the new parliament.[18] In December 1989 a Ukrainian Students' Union had been formed in Kyiv, while in Lviv, the Student Brotherhood had already been in existence for a year.

Outside of Ukraine, political developments were continuing to move at a faster pace. Estonia and Latvia reasserted their independence on 30 March and 4 May respectively. In Russia, the political ferment was intensifying: Russian Communists were beginning to organize a Russian Communist Party, something which Gorbachev had long opposed, and an ultra-nationalist Republican National Party of Russia was being founded. As in Ukraine, the convening of the newly elected Russian legislature with its sizable democratic opposition was eagerly awaited by the democratic forces.

Parliament becomes the primary battleground

On 15 May, the new Ukrainian parliament convened. A huge crowd was waiting in front of the Verkhovna Rada building to greet the deputies from the Democratic Bloc and many of the placards called for Ukrainian independence. Inside the chamber, a sophisticated new electronic system had been installed to register attendance and show voting results on a huge screen. On that

[16] A.O Bilous, *Politychni obyednannya Ukrainy* [Political Associations of Ukraine], Kyiv, 1993, pp. 46-7.

[17] *Literaturna Ukraina*, 31 May 1990.

[18] For further information on SNUM, see the attack on it by Taras Vasylyshyn in *Radyanska Ukraina*, 25 May 1990.

very first day, the deputies from the Democratic Bloc won a crucial early victory: on their insistence, the Supreme Council agreed that the proceedings would be broadcast live on radio and full recordings shown on television in the evening. Thus, the democratic opposition was able to ensure that representatives of the Party and state apparatus would be forced to account for and defend their positions in public while at the same time the democratic candidates and their views would receive mass public exposure.

Despite this success, the initial outlook did not seem very promising for the democrats. In the elections to the temporary Presidium of the parliament, no representatives from the Democratic Bloc managed to get elected. Even Salii had 239 votes cast against him. Ivan Plyushch, a leading Party official in the Kyiv region, ended up temporarily chairing the sessions. Initially, it appeared therefore that the large Communist bloc would simply outvote and block the opposition. But representatives of the Democratic Bloc soon showed that what they lacked in numbers they were able to make up for by their greater dynamism and purposefulness, better tactics and their eloquence. Plyushch was also to emerge as a rather colourful figure and a moderate, and was to win increasing respect for managing to steer the proceedings through numerous stormy or chaotic moments.

The first days were spent wrangling over organizational matters and the agenda. During this period, deputies also formed numerous factions corresponding to the interests or regions which they represented. The largest of these was the Agrarian bloc, a conservative grouping uniting directors of collective farms and farming industry officials; others included a group of thirty-eight Communist deputies supporting the Democratic Platform, and the 'Independence' faction numbering twenty-one deputies. Although, as was to be expected, some of the initial sharp exchanges dealt with the issues of national symbols (a representative of Rukh demanded that a giant bust of Lenin be removed from the chamber and the Communists countered by proposing that the Soviet Ukrainian flag be displayed), the legalization of the Ukrainian Catholic and Ukrainian Autocephalous Orthodox Churches and the Party's control over the media, the Democratic Bloc's representatives displayed considerable shrewdness by placing their emphasis on economic, social and ecological issues. At the top of their list of priorities, which Holovaty presented on the Democratic Bloc's behalf, were the effects of the Chornobyl disaster, the dismal state of rural life and the general economic and political situation in the republic. These were followed by the abolition of Article 6 of the Ukrainian Constitution and the adoption of a declaration on the state sovereignty of Ukraine. Finally, on 23 May, the agenda was agreed and it included more or less what the Democratic Bloc had proposed.

Two other encouraging events occurred early on as well. Plyushch agreed to a request from the 'Independence' faction to allow a guest from Lithuania to address the Verkhovna Ruda. The Lithuanian deputy conveyed a message of greeting from the 'independent' Baltic state to the people and parliament of Ukraine, which was signed by the head of the Lithuanian parliament and leader of Sajudis, Vytautas Landsbergis. On 22 May, the day on which, since the 1960s, Ukrainian patriots had commemorated the return of Taras Shevchenko's remains to Ukraine for burial, Drach called on the deputies to go to the poet's monument that evening to honour his memory. Many deputies, especially from the Democratic Bloc, did so. Plyushch and Drach laid a wreathe from the Verkhovna Rada; Kravchuk was also present. A large crowd assembled at the monument, many with blue and yellow flags, and a spontaneous public meeting was held at which a number of distinguished Ukrainian visitors from the West also spoke. The mood was upbeat, the main theme was independence, and the overall impression created was that of national unity.[19]

A more sober atmosphere was restored two days later when the chairman of the Council of Ministers, Masol, delivered the Ukrainian government's report on the political, social, economic and ecological situation in the republic. Presenting a gloomy picture of the deepening economic and social crises in Ukraine and the USSR as a whole, he had little to offer in the way of encouraging news. Restructuring had not managed to bring any noticeable improvements to the lot of the working people and 'negative phenomena

[19] Vitalii Karpenko, 'Zaimit svoi mistya' . . . [Take Your Places . . .], *Vitchyzna*, no. 4, April 1991, p. 155; Solomea Pavlychko, *Letters from Kiev*, Edmonton, 1992, pp. 15-17. Both of these works provide illuminating eyewitness accounts of the period: the first by the journalist and deputy Karpenko describes the first session of the new parliament; the second, by Pavlychko's daughter – a young literary scholar and translator with good connections among Ukraine's creative intelligentsia and democratic movement – captures the atmosphere prevailing during this time.

in the economy' were making themselves felt more and more. Blaming the centre for the general mess, he argued that it was essential for the parliament to make a priority the adoption of laws asserting Ukraine's state sovereignty and economic independence.

Although by now, of course, the need for achieving republican sovereignty was no longer questioned, Masol's speech contained the most outspoken condemnation of Moscow's economic policies towards Ukraine yet heard from a Ukrainian Communist leader. Stopping just short of using the word exploitation, he said that for decades the centre had dictated Ukraine's economic 'specialization' within the Union, transforming the Donbas into the 'all-Union stoke-hold', and the republic into 'the granary [sic] of ore, cast iron and steel'. 'We can now say openly', he elaborated, that heavy industry had been massively developed in the republic, often without the prior agreement of the republican government, and with scant regard for local needs or ecological consequences. Until two years before, the republican government had control over only 6 to 7% of industrial output in the republic, though this had now risen to almost 40%. In short, Moscow's policies had 'deformed' the structure of the Ukrainian economy and this made it extremely difficult to shift the emphasis to the consumer and agricultural sectors. The prerequisite for change, Masol argued, was for Ukraine to assert control over its economy and to regulate its relations with the other republics of the USSR on the basis of a new Union treaty, concluded not with the centre, but with other equal sovereign states. 'We need sovereignty, not for sovereignty's sake,' he declared, 'but for the improvement of the life of our people, of their economic, social and spiritual development'.

The opposition was not overly impressed, though, by the fact that the head of the Ukrainian government was now repeating the arguments about the need for sovereignty which Rukh had been making a year ago. Moreover, as far as his approach to economic policy was concerned, Masol came across as a conservative with no fresh ideas of his own. Signalling the Ukrainian government's misgivings about the economic reform plan being proposed that very same day to the USSR Supreme Soviet by Soviet Prime Minister Nikolai Ryzhkov, which envisaged a transition to a 'regulated market economy' and the raising of food prices, Masol warned in his speech against 'market euphoria'. He urged that the changes be carried out cautiously and gradually so as to avoid the 'the possible negative social consequences'. Apart from securing sovereignty, the only way out, he insisted, was to raise productivity by renewing the notion of 'conscientious labour', and by strengthening discipline, organization and order in the workplace.[20]

In the discussion following Masol's report, Ivashko was even more critical of the Soviet government's economic reform plan and indicated that it was threatening to cause a rift between Kyiv and Moscow. He explained that the Central Committee of the CPU recognized that the transition to a 'regulated market economy' was essential, but that it had to be done gradually and carefully, otherwise there was a risk of social explosions. Before raising prices, he insisted, the Soviet government should confer with all the republics and hold a referendum. Chornovil and other democrats also opposed the price rises.[21]

In an early assertion of the republic's rights, the parliament voted to make the acceptance of the raising of prices by Moscow conditional on their having been agreed with the republics and on the creation of a 'compensatory mechanism for the social protection of the population'.[22] Another such example was when, on 11 June, deputies were to decide that clocks in Ukraine should no longer be set to Moscow time, but be moved back one hour.[23]

The next major issue on the agenda was the election of a chairman of the Supreme Council and his deputy. Anticipating that the Communists would nominate Ivashko as their candidate, the Democratic Bloc insisted on the principle that the chairman of the parliament could not at the same time be the leader of a political party. It also decided to propose numerous candidates in order to make full use of the opportunity to present the views of the leaders of the democratic opposition to the public. On 28 May, when the nominations were made, thirteen candidates were proposed, including Ivashko. Hurenko and Karpenko withdrew, and Fokin could not be included because he was not a deputy. The following day, the ten remaining candidates were each allowed half an hour to present their programmes. Seven of them were representative of the national democratic forces (Pavlychko, Drach, Chornovil,

---

[20] *Radyanska Ukraina*, 27 May 1990.

[21] *Ibid.*, 29 May 1990.

[22] *Ibid.*, 30 May 1990.

[23] *Ibid*, 13 June 1990.

Yukhnovsky, Yavorivsky, Lukyanenko and Mykhailo Horyn), two were supporters of the Democratic Platform (Salii and Volodymyr Hrynov, a lecturer in applied mathematics from Kharkiv), and only Ivashko represented the mainstream CPU. Thus, the Ukrainian population had a chance to hear and see for itself what some of the leading figures in Rukh, the former UHU and the Democratic Platform represented. 'Everyone listened in, all of Ukraine sitting by its television set.'[24]

Pavlychko was the first candidate to speak, and gave a good idea of what could be expected from his colleagues. In a powerful and absolutely forthright speech he denounced the Soviet totalitarian and imperial system, blamed the Communist Party for the economic, ecological and spiritual crisis in which Ukraine found itself, and argued that independence, achieved in a peaceful evolutionary manner, was the only way forward. There should be no illusions, he warned: in a revamped Soviet federation, 'steel chains' would be replaced by 'velvet fetters'. Lukyanenko, Horyn and Chornovil spoke in a similar vein and in their speeches provided details about their biographies as dissidents and political prisoners and about the indomitable movement for human and national rights in Ukraine in which they had been active. Chornovil strongly attacked Ivashko and Kravchuk for their hostile attitude towards the victorious democratic forces in Western Ukraine and maintained that the removal of the Communist Party from power should have been the first priority of the new parliament. He also called for the election of a Ukrainian president by direct popular vote in a year's, or a year and a half's, time and announced that he intended to be a candidate if such an election were to be held.

Drach, Yukhnovsky, Yavorivsky and Salii were more moderate in their tone and adopted a more centrist position. Drach welcomed Yeltsin's commitment to securing 'full sovereignty' for the RSFSR and stressed that only through cooperation between Russian and Ukrainian democrats would a 'free Russia' and a 'free Ukraine', existing side by side as good neighbours, be possible. Hrynov, whose mother was Ukrainian but who described himself as a Russian and also delivered his speech in Russian, supported sovereignty, but was in favour of Ukraine signing a new Union treaty with, as he put it, a Russia led by Yeltsin, and the transformation of the USSR into a

---

[24] Pavlychko, *Letters from Kiev*, p. 21.

halfway house between a federation and a confederation. He considered that in the long-term there was a danger that extreme nationalist forces might form an alliance with conservatives from the Party state apparatus and create an authoritarian Ukrainian state. While defending the republic's territorial integrity, Hrynov pointed to the regional differences and called for the reorganization of Ukraine into a federation. Chornovil also supported giving the regions maximum control over local affairs, leading eventually, but not immediately, to some form of a federal arrangement. For his part, Ivashko repeated the main planks in the CPU's Platform and stressed that the Party wanted a 'united, democratic, strong and stable Ukraine' enjoying genuine sovereignty, but, of course, within a revamped Soviet federation.

While these exciting developments were taking place in Kyiv, on 29 May in Moscow an even more dramatic event occurred: Yeltsin, the nominee of the 'Democratic Russia' bloc was elected chairman of the RSFSR Supreme Soviet. His victory not only advanced the cause of democratic reform but was also a boon for the defenders of the rights of the republics. In his election campaign Yeltsin had forcefully attacked the imperial centre and accused it of depriving Russia of its 'spiritual, national and economic' independence. Denouncing the imperial structures, he championed the idea of real sovereignty for Russia and its right to establish its own separate treaties with foreign states and other republics of the USSR. One of Yeltsin's first actions as head of the RSFSR Supreme Soviet was to meet with Landsbergis and propose treaties of cooperation between the RSFSR and the Baltic republics.

In Kyiv, four candidates for the post of the chairman of the Verkhovna Rada were left in the running: Ivashko, Yukhnovsky, Hrynov and Salii. Anticipating Ivashko's victory, most of the Democratic Bloc decided to boycott the voting in protest against the fact that the favourite refused to agree to relinquish his post as first secretary of the CPU if he were elected. Of the 339 deputies who participated in the voting on 4 June, 278 supported Ivashko, 28 Hrynov, 24 Yukhnovsky and 4 Salii. Seeking a working compromise, the Democratic Bloc proposed that Ivashko nominate Yukhnovsky for election as the first deputy head of the Supreme Council. Ivashko, however, ignored this suggestion. This led 113 members of the Democratic Bloc to organize themselves formally into a parliamentary opposition known as the Narodna Rada, or

People's Council, which was also joined by twelve supporters of the Democratic Platform. Yukhnovsky was elected its leader, Pavlychko, Lukyanenko, Yemets and Volodymyr Filenko (a Democratic Platform supporter from Kharkiv) as his deputies, and Tanyuk the bloc's secretary. In its first declaration, dated 6 June, the People's Council warned that if the Communist majority continued to try to maintain 'a mono-party dictatorship in the Verkhovna Rada', the opposition would appeal to the public to call for the dissolution of the legislature and 'for new democratic elections on the basis of political pluralism'.[25] Khmara and several others, however, adopted a more radical position and accused Yukhnovsky and his supporters of 'collaborating' with the Communist regime.

The elections of deputy heads of the Verkhovna Rada proceeded without the participation of most of the People's Council. Plyushch was elected first deputy head and Hrynov became the second deputy head virtually by default (as Yukhnovsky and Yemets from the People's Council withdrew). Although the CPU had secured for itself the commanding positions, the gulf between the Communist majority and the People's Council was widening and threatening to paralyze the Supreme Council. Ivashko and his team therefore evidently decided that some compromises would have to be made to prevent a mass walkout by the opposition. 'Secret negotiations' were held with the leaders of the People's Council as a result of which the opposition managed to secure the chairmanship of almost a third of the twenty-three permanent commissions which the Supreme Council voted to establish, and a reasonable level of representation in them.[26] Among the democrats elected to head commissions were Yukhnovsky (the commission on education and science), Tanyuk (culture and spiritual revival), Yavorivsky (the consequences of the Chornobyl disaster), Yemets (human rights) and Pavlychko (foreign relations). After this arrangement had been sealed, political tempers began to cool and it seemed that a more constructive phase could begin.

In the meantime, though, on 9 June British Prime Minister Margaret Thatcher came to Kyiv as part of her official visit to the Soviet Union. The leaders of the People's Council hoped that her address to the Ukrainian Supreme Council would become the

---

[25] *Literaturna Ukraina*, 14 June 1990.
[26] Pavlychko, *Letters from Kiev*, pp. 22–3.

occasion for the acknowledgement by a leading Western leader of Ukraine's resurgence and that the British guest would express support for the efforts of the republics to achieve genuine sovereignty and to enter into direct relations with foreign states. Her speech, however, turned into an embarrassing setback for the national democrats. Tactfully avoiding giving offence to Gorbachev, she refused to comment on, as she put it, the USSR's 'internal affairs', but at the same time made it quite clear that she was not keen to see the disintegration of the USSR.

Furthermore, when Pavlychko asked her in his best broken English whether Britain planned to open an embassy in Kyiv, she replied that her country did not have embassies in California, Quebec, or in the various Australian states, thereby suggesting that, for all its aspirations to real sovereignty, Ukraine was still viewed in the outside world as a mere region or a province. Later, however, Thatcher was to acknowledge in her memoirs that her visit to Kyiv had quite an impact on her. 'Everywhere I went I found blue and yellow bunting and flags . . . and signs demanding independence', she noted. She 'went away . . . understanding how fundamental the whole question of nationality was becoming and doubtful whether the Soviet Union could – or should – ultimately be kept together'.[27]

Once again, though, the pace of political change in Moscow took many by surprise, including presumably Western leaders and policy makers. Ironically, in his comments to Mrs. Thatcher in the Ukrainian Supreme Council, Pavlychko also expressed disappointment that Britain had not recognized Lithuania's independence and asked the British guest, seemingly rhetorically, what London would do if, say, Russia decided to declare its independence.[28] In fact, on 12 June, the Supreme Soviet of the RSFSR came close to doing precisely that when it approved a Declaration of the State Sovereignty of the RSFSR which asserted the primacy of the republic's laws over Soviet ones, the republic's control over its natural resources and the republic's right to secede from the USSR. A 'sovereign' and assertive Russia led by Yeltsin had now suddenly stood the nationalities problem on its head: Russia's defiance of central control became Gorbachev's main headache as he desperately strove to keep the

[27] Margaret Thatcher, *The Downing Street Years*, London, 1993, pp. 806-7.
[28] *Radyanska Ukraina*, 12 June 1990.

Union intact, and it gave impetus to the trend towards the decentralization and dissolution of the empire.

This became apparent on that very same day, for while the Russian Supreme Soviet was adopting its declaration of sovereignty, Gorbachev convened a meeting of the Council of the Federation in order to push ahead with the preparation of a new Union treaty. Ivashko represented Ukraine and subsequently reported to the Ukrainian parliament that the meeting had not gone smoothly. Gorbachev had pressed for the reconstitution of the USSR into 'a union of sovereign Socialist republics' but representatives of the republics, and especially Yeltsin, had insisted that the revamped Union should have two tiers: on one level, the republics, as sovereign states, would themselves decide which powers to delegate to the centre, and on another level they would establish ties directly among themselves on the basis of bilateral or multilateral agreements. Ivashko himself appears not to have known how to react. He told the Ukrainian parliament that when Gorbachev had called on him to speak, he had replied 'I have no mandate to conduct negotiations' on the future of the Union. The Ukrainian Party leader had got himself off the hook by telling the meeting that Ukraine's parliamentarians had received three draft versions of a declaration of state sovereignty and were still studying them.

With the Council of the Federation having decided to set up a working group to draw up a new Union treaty as a matter of urgency, it was clear from Ivashko's report that the Verkhovna Rada ought not to delay dealing with the issue of defining the scope of the republic's sovereignty. He himself stressed this, adding, unexpectedly, a tantalizing piece of information: in Moscow, he had agreed with Yeltsin that they should meet in the near future to discuss drawing up a treaty between Russia and Ukraine; the Kazakhstani president, Nursultan Nazarbaev, had also proposed that Ukraine and his republic exchange representatives in order to promote closer bilateral relations.[29]

Ironically, the CPU leadership was itself now being confronted with the challenge of dealing with a centrifugal force within Ukraine. In Crimea, where the substantial Ukrainian minority still lacked any basic cultural facilities, pro-Russian forces were expressing their opposition more and more forcefully both to the prospect

[29] *Ibid.*, 15 June 1994.

of any Ukrainization, however distant, and to the mass return of the Crimean Tatars. A group of deputies to the region's Supreme Soviet had taken the lead in calling for the restoration of the peninsula's autonomous status and were urging the local population to support the idea of Crimea once again becoming part of the Russian Federation.[30]

A more immediate problem, however, was that of the renewed activism of the disaffected Donbas miners. On 11-15 June, Donetsk was the venue for an all-Union congress of miners, which, hardly surprisingly, produced numerous radical demands. Despite the fact that about a third of the miners' representatives were members of the Communist Party they voiced their lack of confidence both in the current Soviet Government and in the CPSU as a defender of the rights of the workers, threatened new strikes and voted to create a new independent trade union to represent their interests. Among other things, they also called for the establishment of a genuine multi-party system and the nationalization of the CPSU's property.[31]

On 16 June, the revamped Russian parliament formally abolished the Communist Party's leading role on the territory of the Russian Federation and inaugurated a multi-party system. But one of the main political forces seeking to secure a prominent place for itself in the new political environment with which it was reluctantly having to come to terms with was Russia's disgruntled conservative Communists and their hard-line leaders. It was with considerable foreboding, therefore, that reformist and democratic forces awaited the conference which the Russian Communists had called for 19 June.

The forces regroup

Ivashko's immediate priority, though, was the completion of preparations for the Twenty-eighth Congress of the CPU. Although overshadowed by developments in Moscow, the congress was nevertheless an important occasion for the CPU to take its bearings in the fast-changing political environment, register the prevailing attitudes within the organization, and carry out personnel changes

---

[30] TASS, 17 June 1990.

[31] TASS, 11 June, AFP, 12 June and AP 15 June, 1990; and Haran, *To Kill the Dragon*, p. 114.

in its leadership. As it was, numerous regional Party leaders had been swept away by the earlier tide of social and political protest. On the eve of the CPU congress, two of the stalwarts from the Shcherbytsky era, Yelchenko, and apparently Kachura also, indicated that they did not want to remain in the CPU leadership.[32] Furthermore, Ivashko and Hurenko, who according to Kravchuk were now beginning to run things without consulting their colleagues,[33] appear to have decided that Ivashko would relinquish his post as Party leader and, for the time being at least, concentrate on chairing the Verkhovna Rada, while Hurenko would take over from him as Ukraine's Party boss.

On 19 June, the CPU's Congress got off to a stormy start. Delegates were unhappy about the relatively low-level representation from the CPSU leadership – a deputy head of a Central Committee department – and, implying that at this critical juncture the CPU, with its still impressive membership of 3,241,000, was not being afforded the respect and attention which it deserved, demanded Gorbachev's presence. During the next days, the Soviet leader was to be strongly criticized by conservative delegates who blamed him for the CPSU's difficulties. Furthermore, because of the general uncertainty about what would happen at the conference of Russia's Communists (at which, in fact, Gorbachev was present at that time), and at the forthcoming Twenty-eighth Congress of the CPSU, Ukraine's Communists voted that their own congress should be divided into two phases, the second to be held after the CPSU Congress.

Ivashko himself had quite a rough passage: although his report did not contain anything particularly new, it did not go down very well with conservatives who were unhappy with the general state of affairs and the direction in which things were moving; there was commotion in the hall during the address, and criticism of it during the debates that followed.[34] Even the Party organ, *Radyanska Ukraina*, commented that there was a considerable degree of polarization among the delegates and that at times the reactionary 'spirit of Nina Andreeva' could be felt.[35] Some of the delegates opposed the

[32] Yelchenko submitted his resignation a few days before the congress. Author's interview with Yelchenko.

[33] Valentyn Chemerys, *Prezydent*, Kyiv, 1994, pp. 174–5.

[34] *Radyanska Ukraina*, 22 June 1990.

adoption of a new Party statute which asserted the CPU's autonomy within the CPSU, and there were those, especially from the eastern regions, who were unhappy about the fact that the CPU had embraced the 'separatist' idea of affirming Ukraine's state sovereignty.

From among the CPU leaders, Kravchuk came across both as the most forceful advocate of autonomy for the CPU and state sovereignty for Ukraine, and as a pragmatist. Forced to defend his record as ideological secretary, he opined that the sharpening of the political situation in the republic had begun in May 1988, 'when the polarization of political forces had in fact started'. The Gorbachev leadership's inconsistencies in its political and ideological policies had complicated matters, and social and political discontent continued to be fuelled by the shortages of food, soap and other essentials in the shops. The recent elections in the republic had seen the culmination of the process of political polarization and the CPU now needed to change some of its slogans and review some of its policies and tactics. Although there could be no 'consolidation' of forces with enemies of Socialism and of the Communist Party, there could be 'compromises when it was a matter of the fate of the people, when it concerned the fate of Ukraine'. The idea of state sovereignty, the ideological secretary argued, was 'currently the basis on which the people of Ukraine was coalescing', and on which, by 'maintaining its initiative' in this sphere, the Party could 'win authority for itself from the masses'.

The radicals also made themselves heard. The Democratic Platform was represented by the sociologist Valerii Khmelko, who presented a virtual ultimatum from the reformist wing. He informed the delegates that if the CPSU did not accept a number of cardinal changes promoting democratization both within the Party and in political life generally, the organization faced a split and up to 40% of its membership which supported the ideas of the Democratic Platform would probably leave. He appealed to the moderates in the CPU to ally themselves with the democratically minded reformists and to distance themselves from the 'authoritarian' forces.

The divisions within the CPU were highlighted during the election of the Party leader. No less than nine candidates were nominated, including Hurenko, Ivashko, Kravchuk (by a delegate

[35] *Ibid.*, 21 June 1990.

from the Lviv region), Salii (who was vilified by some of the delegates), and the hard-liners, General Boris Gromov, who had distinguished himself during the war in Afghanistan and was now the commander of the Kyiv military district, and Oleksandr Ruzhytsky, the Party boss in the Cherkassy region. All but Hurenko and Salii declined.

In his election address, Hurenko advocated a cautious and unenthusiastic approach to restructuring: sounding an unusually heterodox note for a supposedly disciplined Communist, and implicitly attacking Gorbachev's reformist team, he declared that he was against any further social 'experiments' prescribed by 'a group of theoreticians and politicians' who had 'assumed the right to announce recipes for social development'. For his part, Salii called on the CPU not to squander its last chance to renew itself through internal democratization and the recognition of the incipient new multi-party and parliamentary political system. Hardly surprisingly, when it came to the vote by secret ballot, Hurenko was elected the new first secretary.

Immediately after the conclusion of the first phase of the congress, a plenum of the new Central Committee of the CPU was held at which Kravchuk was elected second secretary. Among others elected to the new Politburo of the CPU were Ivashko, Masol, Ivan Hrintsov (a secretary of the Central Committee of the CPU specializing in agricultural matters), Valentyn Ostrozhynsky (Party boss of the Ternopil region) and Gromov.

Despite the problems with both the conservative and reformist wings, the former CPU leadership managed to secure from the congress endorsement of the general policy and organizational principles which it had proposed. But clearly, the internal and external problems facing the CPU were considerable and its future increasingly uncertain. Apart from the splits within its ranks, the Party appeared remote from the workers and peasants which it claimed to represent (their relatively low representation among the delegates was a source of some concern at the congress), and to have totally alienated younger cadres in the Komsomol. Regional divisions had also opened up and at the congress Ivashko had to placate Crimea's Communists by holding out the prospect of the restoration of the peninsula's autonomous statehood within Ukraine. Sekretaryuk, speaking on behalf of the Communists in Western Ukraine, where the Party had recently been trounced so thoroughly in the elections, called for a more sensitive and sensible policy towards this region: he condemned both the strong-arm tactics that had been unsuccessfully used against Rukh and the shortsighted threats of an economic blockade against Western Ukraine. On top of all this, the CPU now seemed to be openly at odds with the Soviet Party and state leadership. The overall impression, therefore, was of a drifting listing ship for which state sovereignty was the only realistic dock where essential repairs could be carried out.

Meanwhile, Rukh was also having problems, especially in adjusting to the new political situation after the elections. Its Grand Council met on 23 and 24 June in Kyiv and heard various speakers criticize the lack of coordination between the leadership and the regional sections and organizations representing the disaffected miners in the Donbas, the 'lumpenization' of the movement and the growing intolerance of the 'ultra-radicals' within it, and Rukh's failure to effect and sustain a mass political mobilization of the population. Chernyak and others spoke of the need for a more professional approach and changes in Rukh's orientation, strategy and organization. Drach also openly questioned the need for a new Union treaty and he and other speakers thereby indicated that, even as the proclamation of the state sovereignty of Ukraine was being awaited, Rukh was already embracing the idea of independence for Ukraine. The Grand Council decided to amend Rukh's statutes, to convene a second congress of the Popular Movement and, in the meantime, to prepare for mass celebrations in August in Zaporizhzhya of the 500th anniversary of Ukrainian Cossackdom – an action designed to promote the revival of national memory and pride generally, and to stimulate the development of national consciousness in Eastern Ukraine in particular.[36]

It was made very clear at the meeting of the Grand Council that among the issues continuing to divide the national democratic movement was the festering hostility between the nation's main Christian groups. While Rukh's leaders continued to suspect that the rivalry between both the Ukrainian Orthodox and Ukrainian Catholics, and among the Ukrainian Orthodox themselves, was being fomented by the Communist authorities, the situation attested not only to the lack of a tradition of religious tolerance, but also to

---

[36] Pavlychko, *Letters from Kiev*, pp. 27- 34; Haran, *To Kill the Dragon*, pp. 110-12.

the weakness of democratic culture even in Western Ukraine, which had not been under Soviet rule as long as other regions of Ukraine, and where anti-Communist forces were now in power. On 2 July, several prominent national democrats, including Drach, Lukyanenko, UAOC activist Sverstyuk and staunch Ukrainian Catholic Iryna Kalynets, issued an appeal to Ukraine's Christians calling for religious toleration and an end to the antagonism between Orthodox and Catholics.[37]

Despite the inter-confessional conflicts, the growth and organizational consolidation of both of the two main independent churches – the UAOC and the Ukrainian Catholic Church – continued. On 5 and 6 June, the UAOC held its First Sobor (Council), confidently choosing Kyiv for the venue. The Sobor was preceded by a religious ceremony outside St Sophia's Cathedral and a procession through the streets of the Ukrainian capital. Seven bishops and 547 delegates from the clergy and faithful took part in the Sobor and there were numerous representatives from Ukraine's democratic forces and intellectual élite, including Drach, Holovaty, Oles Shevchenko, Sverstyuk, the art historian Dmytro Stepovyk and the archaeologist Petro Tolochko. The Sobor proclaimed an All-Ukrainian Patriarchate, and elected *in absentia* Metropolitan Mstyslav Skrypnyk, the ninety-two-year-old head of the Ukrainian Orthodox Church in the United States,[38] who had not been given a Soviet visa, as Patriarch of Kyiv and All Ukraine and Metropolitan Bodnarchuk as the Patriarch's *locum tenens*. The Sobor ended on an especially uplifting note: despite the determined opposition of the Russian Orthodox Church, the UAOC was able to hold a service within St Sophi's – the pre-eminent symbol of Ukraine's thousand-year-old Christianity.[39]

---

[37] *Literaturna Ukraina*, 12 July 1990.

[38] Metropolitan Mstyslav Skrypnyk was a living link with Ukraine's hitherto suppressed religious and political past. A nephew of Petlyura, he had fought for Ukrainian independence in 1918-20. As a deputy in the Polish Sejm during the inter-war period, he had defended the rights of Ukrainian Orthodox believers in Volhynia. During the German occupation of Ukraine, he had taken part in efforts to revive the UAOC. After the war he eventually emerged as the leader of Ukrainian Orthodox believers in the West.

[39] The author was in Kyiv at the time and witnessed part of the Sobor. Also, see the reports on the Sobor by Larysa Lokhvytska in *Literaturna Ukraina*, 21 June 1990, and by V. Stelmakh, *Kultura i zhyttya*, 24 June 1990.

Three weeks later, in Rome, the Pope convened the first joint meeting of all the Ukrainian Catholic bishops from both inside Ukraine and the Ukrainian diaspora. Ten bishops from Ukraine and eighteen from outside the homeland participated and the meeting was declared an Extraordinary Synod of the Ukrainian Catholic Church. This deprived the Soviet authorities of an excuse they had used to justify their delay in registering the Ukrainian Catholic Church – namely, that the Vatican had not formally recognized the Ukrainian Catholic clandestinely consecrated bishops.[40]

Many other developments, both conspicuous and less evident, also indicated the continuing process of social and political liberalization and national renewal. New political parties were publishing their manifestos, a host of new independent newspapers and journals were appearing, and more information was being made available about Ukraine's history, culture and the Ukrainian diaspora. Indeed the general impression was one of a nation that had survived a severe winter and was beginning to bloom.[41] 'There are congresses going on everywhere in Ukraine right now,' one observer noted, 'and they're all "founding"'. For instance, on 5 July a quasi-religious patriotic movement headed by the former political prisoner Berdnyk – the Ukrainian Spiritual Republic (sic) – which sought to promote the Ukrainian nation's spiritual renewal, held a much-publicized mass meeting in the Western Ukrainian town of Kolomiya; it drew support from politicians and cultural figures ranging from Lukyanenko to Oliinyk.

Of course, the resurgence of Ukrainian patriotism, in all its different forms, was not the only indicator of changing social

---

[40] See Bociurkiw, 'The Ukrainian Catholic Church', p. 17.

[41] The author was first able to witness this resurgence for himself in June 1990 when, while Director of the Ukrainian Service of Radio Liberty/Radio Free Europe, he visited Ukraine for three weeks at the request of the Ukraina Society. This official body, which for decades had sought to monopolize and control ties with Ukrainians abroad, was now 'restructuring' itself and was anxious to shed its negative image. Although I represented an institution which until recently had been officially branded as an 'enemy voice', I was allowed to travel freely and meet with whoever I wanted. In connection with my visit, permission was also finally given by the Communist authorities for the publication of an interview which I had given several months earlier over the telephone to *Molod Ukrainy*. The newspaper published it on 28 June 1990. A second interview, describing my impressions of what I had encountered in Ukraine, appeared in the Ukraina Society's weekly, *Visti z Ukrainy*, no. 28, July 1990.

attitudes and tastes. The removal of Communist ideological and political controls was allowing very different values to be asserted, and for many people the resulting ideological vacuum or confusion was creating a curiosity in, and a readiness to experiment with, all manner of things which previously had been taboo or officially disapproved of. 'On the whole', the same observer noted, 'mysticism, astrology, palmistry and various types of magic are incredibly popular among us. This is the newest sign of the times, the biggest fad . . . Another is pornography . . . Calendars and crude postcards with half-naked and naked girls are sold everywhere.'[42]

The scope of sovereignty is debated

After the CPU Congress and the meeting of Rukh's Grand Council attention once again shifted to the parliament and the main issue on its agenda – the affirmation of Ukraine's state sovereignty. During the last few days, Uzbekistan and Moldova had become the latest republics to proclaim their sovereignty. In Moscow, the conference of Russia's Communists had transformed itself into the founding congress of the Communist Party of the RSFSR. Although it emerged that this organization was far from monolithic, Gorbachev had come under strong attack at the meeting from hard-liners such as Ligachev but had managed to put a brave face on things and to ride out the storm. Nevertheless, under its elected leader, the arch conservative Ivan Polozkov, the new Russian Communist Party represented a serious threat both to Gorbachev's authority and to the political cohesion within the Soviet multinational state which the CPSU had embodied. In an implicit warning both to Yeltsin and Polozkov about the potential dangers of the Russian Federation continuing to assert its own republican interests and to develop its own republican institutions, the Soviet leader pointed out at the congress: 'The question of a Russian Communist Party has cropped up repeatedly, beginning, so to speak, in Lenin's time. And also the question of Russia and its role . . . To put it briefly, one can say that all of this is connected with the unifying role of the Russian Federation and of the peoples

---

[42] Pavlychko, *Letters from Kiev*, pp. 45–6. On the meeting of the Ukrainian Spiritual Republic in Kolomiya, see *Literaturna Ukraina*, 19 July 1990.

of Russia, with the role they played in the formation of our huge, multinational state.'[43]

Against this background, on 25 June Ivashko proposed proceeding directly to the debate on the declaration of state sovereignty but the deputies insisted that a decision first be made on who would head the Council of Ministers. He therefore proposed Masol but, rather surprisingly, the latter did not receive the requisite number of votes. The same happened when Ivashko nominated Fokin. Both advocated economic sovereignty and a gradual transition to a regulated market economy, with Fokin sounding somewhat less conservative than Masol. Among their most outspoken critics during the debates was Rukh's leading economist, Chernyak, who urged that a government of national salvation should be created.[44]

Unable to secure the election of the CPU's candidates, Ivashko made an unexpectedly bold move to end the impasse: he proposed both Masol and Chernyak. Although the latter was taken by surprise and was given only one night to prepare a speech, he made full use of the opportunity to present an outline of a radical alternative programme aimed at promoting a transition to democracy and a mixed economy. Chernyak also argued that for Ukraine to have real economic sovereignty, it should have its own financial and banking system and its own currency. Only 219 deputies participated in the voting, which was insufficient for a quorum. The People's Council also claimed that, in any case, the votes were being tampered with.

Angered by this accusation, and probably not too happy that one of Rukh's leaders was in the running to become the head of the government, Hurenko sought to reinforce Party discipline among the Communist deputies and called a special meeting of their caucus. Ivashko, too, condemned the behaviour of deputies who were absent without good reason and announced that from now on they would need to seek permission in writing from either him or his deputies if they wanted to be away. After this, on the fourth ballot, Masol was endorsed as the chairman of the Council of Ministers by 229 votes to Chernyak's 134.[45]

---

[43] On this and the emergence of the Russian Communist Party, see John B. Dunlop, *The Rise of Russia and the Fall of the Soviet Empire*, Princeton, NJ, 1993. pp. 18–20.

[44] *Radyanska Ukraina*, 26 and 27 June 1994; Pavlychko, *Letters from Kiev*, pp. 35–6.

[45] *Radyanska Ukraina*, 28 and 29 June 1994; Pavlychko, *Letters from Kiev*, pp. 36–7.

On 28 June, with one eye on the last-minute manoeuvring in Moscow before the CPSU Congress, Ivashko formally opened the discussion about the declaration of state sovereignty. The previous Presidium of the Supreme Council had appointed a working group to prepare a draft and, three weeks earlier, the document had been given to the members of the new parliament. Six other variants had been submitted. They included one which had been prepared jointly by a dissenting member of the working group, Tymchenko, and Holovaty.[46] None of these drafts, however, had been published in the press.

Dorohuntsov introduced the officially prepared variant, which essentially reflected the CPU's line. He acknowledged what Rukh and before it Ukraine's dissidents and political prisoners had claimed all along: 'The republic had formally been proclaimed sovereign, but in fact was deprived of the opportunity to realize a whole series of rights characteristic of a sovereign state.' It was therefore essential, he explained, to adopt a declaration on state sovereignty, although Ukraine's future as a sovereign state was, of course, seen to lie within a revamped Union. Indeed, the draft contained an entire section elaborating the basis on which Ukraine should accede to the new Union treaty. But the conditions which were stipulated differed quite significantly from Gorbachev's general approach to the revamping of the Union. They stressed that only the people of Ukraine and its elected parliament could decide which powers they would be prepared to transfer to the Union, that any decision or act by the Union authorities deemed to encroach on Ukraine's sovereignty would be regarded as invalid, and that the republic would retain the right to leave the Union. Furthermore, Dorohuntsov also announced that the working group had prepared a statement addressed to the other republics proposing that a special conference be convened to draw up the new Union treaty at which each republic would have one vote, the chairmanship would rotate, and decisions would be made on the basis of consensus.

After Dorohuntsov's presentation, the authors of the alternative variants were given the floor. As they were virtually all from the national democratic camp, their proposals were far more radical, and they and their colleagues either opposed, or expressed misgivings about, Ukraine signing a new Union treaty. Indeed, several of them

---

[46] Author's interview with Tymchenko.

argued that the declaration should proclaim not Ukraine's sovereignty but its independence, that the Union Treaty of 1922 had in fact been imposed on Ukraine and was therefore not binding, and that a sovereign Ukrainian republic should not still have to call itself a Soviet and Socialist state. Holovaty and others emphasized that a sovereign Ukraine should have the right to have its own national armed formations, while Viktor Bed, a lawyer from Transcarpathia, expressed a view which was also gaining popularity among the deputies – that Ukraine should become a non-aligned state. Several of the more moderate Communists who spoke at the beginning of the debate, such as the journalist Serhii Pravdenko, also indicated that their understanding of sovereignty went a lot further than the officially proposed version of the declaration.

The CPU's leadership had nonetheless prepared their more disciplined parliamentary forces for the debate. When it came to his turn to speak, Hurenko sought to assert the CPU's official line on the question of state sovereignty and declared that the majority of Communist deputies supported the idea of Ukraine becoming a sovereign state, but on the understanding that it would remain part of a renewed Soviet federation on the basis of a new Union treaty. He went on to announce that 239 deputies were forming a bloc whose motto would be: 'For a Soviet sovereign Ukraine!'[47]

The heated debate about what sort of sovereignty Ukraine should strive for continued, in full view of the public, for a second day. After almost forty speakers had voiced their views it was evident that the rift between the proponents of either independence, or a confederate arrangement, and the defenders of the idea of a revamped federation and of a new Union treaty was widening, not narrowing, and that the latter remained numerically stronger.

Several of the deputies warned against allowing 'euphoria' to drown out realism. For instance, Viktor Petrov from the Poltava region, emphasized that it was essential 'to tell people that the proclamation of sovereignty is not a panacea'. It was quite possible, he argued, that economically, things would get worse, not better. Already there was a 'great shortage of fuel' and, because of the lack

---

[47] See *Persha Sessiya Verkhovnoi Rady Ukrainskoi RSR: Byuleten no. 53* [First Session of the Supreme Council of the Ukrainian SSR: Bulletin no. 53], Kyiv, 1990. The official report of the proceedings of the Ukrainian parliament will hereafter be referred to as *Parliamentary Bulletin*.

of newsprint, many newspaper were not appearing (Russia was the main source of both fuel and newsprint). Although the important thing was that, having asserted its sovereignty, Ukraine would be in control of its own affairs, economic ties with the other republics would be further complicated. Another indication of the potential problems facing a sovereign Ukraine was provided by a representative from Crimea, Vladimir Terekhov, who called for the federalization of Ukraine and autonomous statehood for his region.

At the end of the second day of debate, Plyushch announced a break until 5 July in order to provide time for the commissions to work on the draft declaration,[48] though the democratic opposition suspected that it was really to allow sixty-three Communist deputies who were delegates to the Twenty-eighth Congress of the CPSU to leave for Moscow. As representatives of the People's Council were subsequently to point out, the parliament was not even formally consulted or notified about the departure, at this crucial moment, of such a large group of deputies and of the chairman of the parliament.

While the 804-strong delegation from the CPU was making its way to the Soviet capital, the USSR's miners decided to call a warning strike on 11 July in protest against the Soviet government's failure to meet its promises of the previous year. They issued a number of far-reaching political demands, including the resignation of the Soviet Government, the nationalization of the CPSU's property and the depoliticization of the security ministries, judiciary and state bodies responsible for administration and economic management. The threat of this major protest was to hang over both the work of the CPSU Congress and of the Ukrainian parliament.

In Moscow, Hurenko was asked by journalists to describe the CPU's position and the general political situation in Ukraine. In his response, the Ukrainian Party leader went out of his way to emphasize that the CPU had embarked on 'a course of increasing' its 'independence' within the CPSU and rejected the view that the recent Congress of the CPU had been 'conservative in its spirit and make-up'. He acknowledged that the 'national element' was figuring more and more prominently in Ukraine's politics but added that the majority of Ukraine's parliamentary deputies believed in 'the development of Socialist Ukraine within a renewed Federation'

[48] *Parliamentary Bulletin*, nos 54 and 55.

Much depended, he said, on what would happen in the other republics.[49] Pressed by a Ukrainian journalist on the confrontation in the Ukrainian parliament between pro-independence and pro-Union forces, Hurenko replied that if a crisis arose, it would be necessary to hold a referendum and let the people of Ukraine decide.[50]

The Congress was to last for two weeks and witness a continuation of the struggle between Gorbachev and the conservatives and the growing assertiveness of radical and pro-democratic elements. At the Congress, Hurenko and Ivashko were give responsibility for important tasks: Hurenko was chosen to head the commission on social and economic matters, and Ivashko was elected chairman of the Congress's editorial commission. But at home, their absence was to cause a political storm.

---

[49] TASS, 3 July 1990.

[50] See Vitalii Portnikov's interview with Hurenko in *Molod Ukrainy*, 30 June 1990.

11

UKRAINE ASSERTS ITS SOVEREIGNTY

The declaration of sovereignty

While the Congress of the CPSU was continuing its work, the Ukrainian parliament reconvened. But before it could resume its work on the declaration of Ukraine's sovereignty it first had to turn its attention to the approaching miners' strike. The opposition was able to capitalize on this and to press home the argument that only after proclaiming the republic's sovereignty would the Ukrainian authorities be in a position to deal with the miners' problems. Rukh's representative, Mykola Porovsky, read out a statement from one of the mines in the Donbas urging the parliament not to delay the declaration any further, and Yemets, speaking in the same vein on behalf of his colleagues in the People's Council, declared the opposition's full support for the miners and their political demands. Seeking to place all the blame for the miners' grievances on Moscow, Masol, too, agreed that the situation made it necessary 'to speed up' the adoption of the proclamation of sovereignty.

This task had been facilitated by the fact that the parliamentary commission on state sovereignty headed by Mykola Shulha, the CPU Central Committee's new secretary for inter-ethnic relations, had spent the last few days preparing a revised draft of the declaration of state sovereignty which incorporated some of the changes and additions that deputies had proposed in their alternative variants and during the debate. It was, as he acknowledged, essentially a cross between the officially proposed draft and the variant which Tymchenko and Holovaty had submitted. Presenting the new 'working draft' to the deputies, Shulha pointed out that among the compromises which it embodied were the following: a change in the name of the document, so that it now read: 'On the state independence [sic] (sovereignty) of Ukraine'; the exclusion of the section on the new Union treaty; and the inclusion of a section on national armed forces.[1] Clearly, while still not fully satisfying the opposition, the new draft had moved considerably closer to what it sought. On the other hand, the concessions infuriated some of the conservatives. Twenty-four hard-liners within Hurenko's bloc, most of whom were representatives of the security ministries, immediately announced the creation of their own group called 'Loyalty to the Homeland'; they attacked the working draft as amounting to a 'camouflaged exit from the Soviet Union'.[2]

The debate about the terms of the declaration of sovereignty was resumed and once again passions flared up. There was strong opposition, for instance, to the idea of Ukraine having its own armed forces, with one deputy asking what the fate of the Soviet Black Sea Fleet would be, considering that the Russian Federation, Ukraine and Georgia could all lay some claim to it. On the other hand, other deputies pointed to the growing opposition in the republic to the use of Ukrainian conscripts in the conflicts in the Transcaucasus and Central Asia. Numerous deputies from the opposition also expressed their frustration with the fact that the deputy chairman of the parliament, Plyushch, was not opening the discussion of the individual sections of the working draft and voting on them. He, in turn, argued that with so many deputies still absent in Moscow this would be premature.

The People's Council therefore went on the offensive. On Friday 6 July, Yemets proposed that in response to the miners' demands parliament adopt a decision requiring the Commission on Human Rights to draft a 'decree on political power', that is, on regulating the role of the CPU and other political parties, creating a commission to study the issues connected with the CPSU's property in Ukraine, and insisting that the new Ukrainian government (which Masol was still forming) include a committee on the coal industry, or, in other words, that Ukraine assert its control over the coal industry in the republic.

Later that day, while Plyushch was still stalling on Yemets' proposal Chornovil read out a statement on behalf of the People's Council in which the absent Communist deputies were accused of 'paralyzing the work' of parliament and 'blocking' the adoption of the declaration of state sovereignty. It was impermissible, the state-

---

[1] *Parliamentary Bulletin*, no. 56.

[2] Radio Kyiv, 6 July 1990.

ment declared, that at a time of such political and social tension in the republic, the head of the parliament and the other Communist deputies were putting their 'narrow party interests' above 'the interests of the people of Ukraine'. It went on to call for the immediate recall of all Ukrainian deputies from Moscow. Holovaty twisted the knife even more by asking what kind of state sovereignty Ukraine could expect if the head of the parliament had not been present at any of the sessions at which the declaration had been debated, and what sort of role the CPU would seek to play in a sovereign Ukraine if its leader was telling the CPSU Congress in Moscow that 'tendencies that are dangerous for the CPSU have begun to appear in the workers' movement'.

Bowing to the pressure, Plyushch put the proposal to recall the Communist deputies to a vote: 291 deputies supported it, and 20 opposed it.[3] Clearly, many of the Communist deputies who had remained in Kyiv had also had enough of the delays.

The following Monday, Plyushch opened proceedings by reading a statement from the CPU delegation at the CPSU Congress, signed by Hurenko and Kravchuk, protesting about the way in which the Ukrainian parliament had voted to recall the Communist deputies from Moscow. It claimed that Ukraine's Communists were in fact 'upholding the vital interests' of their republic at the Congress. This only drew more devastating criticism from Holovaty and others, who once again accused Ukraine's Communists of regarding the CPSU Congress as more important than the parliament of their republic and taking their orders from Moscow. With the mood in the parliament becoming angrier by the hour, Plyushch agreed to allow a vote on the proposal that the working draft be accepted as the basis of the declaration of sovereignty and that the document be sent for final clearance by the parliamentary commissions. The proposal was overwhelmingly supported.[4]

Plyushch, however, knew something that only perhaps Hurenko, Kravchuk and a few other leaders of the CPU were privy to – that a major scandal was brewing because Ivashko had decided to relinquish the chairmanship of the Ukrainian parliament and not to return at all. According to Kravchuk, who was dispatched to Kyiv with the task of informing the Communist deputies about this

---

[3] *Parliamentary Bulletin*, no. 58.
[4] *Ibid.*, no. 60.

unexpected development, Plyushch tried to persuade Ivashko to change his mind but failed.[5] The reason for Ivashko's abrupt abandonment of his position in Kyiv was to emerge soon enough: as Kravchuk and Hurenko already knew, he had accepted an invitation from Gorbachev to become his deputy at the head of the foundering CPSU. On 11 July, a stunned parliament heard Plyushch read out a statement from Ivashko, apparently written two days earlier, in which he not only announced his resignation but also rather bitterly accused the deputies who had voted for his recall from Moscow, including, as he stressed, 'over 200 members of the Party', of having in effect expressed their lack of confidence in him. His case was not helped when, on that very same day in Moscow, he was elected to the new position of deputy general secretary of the CPSU: this news gave the closing words of his statement – 'I assure the Ukrainian people that I have done nothing to let it down' – an excruciatingly hollow ring.[6]

The Ukrainian deputies reacted with indignation: the national democrats depicted Ivashko as a Communist opportunist who had put his career before his people and its parliament, and most of the Communists who had elected him head of the parliament felt betrayed. Ivashko's 'desertion' left the Communist majority leaderless, embarrassed and in disarray. It upset the balance of forces in the parliament and provided the opposition with a wonderful opportunity to press forward.

Plyushch postponed discussion of Ivashko's decision and invited Shulha to read out the new working draft, which, as the latter acknowledged, had been hastily and only lightly revised the night before by the Commission on State Sovereignty. The document contained further concessions: it did not refer directly either to the USSR or a new Union treaty, and, while asserting the right of the Ukrainian nation to national self-determination, and the desire of the people of Ukraine to build a democratic society based on the rule of law in which the rights of all citizens and peoples would be guaranteed, it also stated, among other things, that the Ukrainian SSR had 'its own citizenship', control over immigration into the republic, an independent banking system, and 'its own armed forces and state security bodies, subordinated to the Supreme Council of

[5] Chemerys, *Prezydent*, pp. 174–5.
[6] *Parliamentary Bulletin*, no. 61.

the Ukrainian SSR'. In other words, it read as a virtual declaration of independence.

The conservative Communists were not about to give up without a fight and launched a battle over the very title of the document, insisting that the name Ukrainian Soviet Socialist Republic be used. The debate revealed, however, that the Communist majority had split. Only 151 deputies voted for using the name Ukrainian SSR in the title, while 173 voted against. A compromise title was supported by 250 deputies; it omitted the word independence and read: 'Declaration of the State Sovereignty of Ukraine.' Nevertheless, when Chornovil proposed that in the opening section the document proclaim that the name of the Ukrainian SSR was being changed to Republic of Ukraine, only 113 deputies supported him.[7]

Later that dramatic day, the demoralized Communist majority was given even more to think about: a resolution adopted by miners at their protest meeting in Donetsk was read out in the parliament in which they reiterated their call for the nationalization of the CPSU's property, an end to the Communist Party's control of the ministries and agencies responsible for defence, internal security and overseeing the economy, and for the Soviet Government to resign.[8] Moreover, the evening's television news showed an abundance of blue and yellow flags at the miners' protests in the Donbas.[9]

The news from Moscow also reflected the general direction in which things were moving. At the CPSU Congress Gorbachev had eventually managed to come out on top and to push through a number of reforms in the new set of Party rules. Two of them were aimed at preventing any further splitting of the CPSU along national lines: although the principle of federalism was rejected, the republican Communist parties were given more autonomy and republican Party leaders were made ex-officio members of the Politburo. Overall, though, as Yeltsin put it, the Congress only 'papered over the cracks'. On 12 July, he, together with some members of the Democratic Platform, announced that he was leaving the CPSU, thereby highlighting the continuing decline of the Communist Party's power and influence.

For more and more Ukrainian Communists the choice was being

---

[7] *Ibid.*

[8] *Ibid.*, no. 62.

[9] Pavlychko, *Letters From Kiev*, pp. 50–1.

reduced to going with the flow for survival's sake, or continuing to battle against the inexorable current in a battered and leaking vessel. In view of all this, the debate on the individual sections of the working draft proceeded in a more businesslike manner. Although both sides continued to defend their positions, a more constructive spirit crept in, with Kravchuk, Shulha, Matviyenko and Plyushch from among the Communists setting the best example. In fact, in what appeared to be an exercise in damage containment and an attempt to regain some of the initiative, on 12 July Kravchuk read out a statement on behalf of the 'For a Soviet Socialist Ukraine' faction in which he called on deputies to remember that at this historic moment the fate of their republic's future and well-being was being decided and to put the interests of Ukraine before those of their political parties or personal ambitions. Warning of the dangers of growing social tensions and political confrontation in the republic, he appealed to the deputies, miners and the Ukrainian public generally to work together on the basis of moderation, mutual understanding, toleration and trust.[10]

The main sticking points during the remainder of the debate were whether citizens of Ukraine should have a single citizenship of the Ukrainian SSR or also remain citizens of the USSR, how the republic should safeguard its defence and security, and the new Union treaty. On the first issue, a compromise was eventually reached, thanks to Kravchuk, whereby citizens of Ukraine were also guaranteed the right to retain Soviet citizenship. The second question proved more difficult to resolve, but here too an agreement was successfully worked out, and it turned out to be more radical and far-reaching in its implications than could have been anticipated. After considerable debate, the principle promoted by the national democrats that a sovereign Ukraine should have the right to its own military and security forces was endorsed by a vote of 230 to 113. This, in fact, was the first challenge of this kind to Moscow in the military-security sphere from any of the non-Russian republics. The deputies also agreed that Ukrainian conscripts should not serve outside the republic without the permission of the Ukrainian parliament. But there was an even greater surprise. During the debate, Drach added another proposal which reflected both the anti-nuclear sentiment in the republic which the Chornobyl disaster

[10] *Parliamentary Bulletin*, no. 64.

had produced and the fact that nuclear weapons and the estimated 1 million or so Soviet troops deployed on Ukraine's territory were associated with Moscow's military and imperial might and that Kyiv had no say in the matter. It entailed Ukraine proclaiming its intention 'to become a neutral state that does not participate in military blocs and that adheres to the three non-nuclear principles: not to maintain, produce or acquire nuclear weapons'. This precept was supported by 238 of the deputies, with 100 voting against.

Towards the end of the debate and voting on the individual sections, which was concluded remarkably quickly in just three days on the evening of 13 July, the conservative Communist forces managed to ensure that a reference to the new Union treaty would be included in the declaration after all. They successfully insisted that the following sentence was added to the final section dealing with international relations: "The principles of the Declaration of the Sovereignty of Ukraine are used for concluding a Union treaty.' Even so, the official transcripts of the proceedings record an unidentified deputy as attempting to call his Communist colleagues to their senses by accusing them of voting 'for the secession of Ukraine from the Soviet Union', and proposing sarcastically that the title of the document be changed to 'Declaration on Secession from the Union'.[11]

Although a vote could have been taken that Friday evening, Plyushch decided to wait for the weekend before asking the Ukrainian parliament to make its historic decision. On Sunday, the democratic forces held a huge demonstration in Kyiv at which calls were made for protests and civil disobedience if the Verkhovna Rada delayed declaring Ukraine's state sovereignty. The following morning, on 16 July, the moment of truth arrived and the overwhelming support which the declaration of sovereignty received astounded even the optimists: 355 deputies voted for the declaration, four against, and one abstained.[12] After decades of being submerged, Ukraine had finally regained its voice and reasserted its desire to be recognized as a state in its own right.

---

[11] The deputy was identified elsewhere as Oleksandr Bandurka from Kharkiv. *Holos*, no. 13 (24), 22 July 1990. For details of the debate, see *Parliamentary Bulletin*, nos 61-6.

[12] *Parliamentary Bulletin*, no. 67.

The adoption of the Declaration was greeted with jubilation and the parliament further underscored the significance of its decision by voting that henceforth 16 July would be observed as a state holiday. For the moment, democrats and Communists united in celebrating what was after all one of the most important events and turning points in Ukrainian history. For the patriotic forces, however, the Declaration represented the first major step towards independence, while for the CPU leadership the document was a means for holding on to power while broadening Ukraine's autonomy within a revamped Soviet system. Nevertheless, the symbolic and psychological value of the document seemed to more than compensate for the flaws and compromises which it contained. The Declaration boosted national dignity and pride, strengthened the sense of a broader Ukrainian republican identity and citizenship and, while signalling a decisive break with the imperial and authoritarian past, also opened the way forward to a more promising future, however interpreted. In the Ukrainian capital, for example, the Kyiv City Council voted on 20 July to raise the blue and yellow flag outside the city hall, and four days later tens of thousands of people gathered to witness and celebrate the event.[13]

With official Moscow, preoccupied with the outbreak of further inter-ethnic violence in the Transcaucasus and Central Asia, muting its reaction, the immediate effect of the Declaration remained unclear. Ukraine was still part of the Soviet Union, albeit an enfeebled one, and, despite their rhetoric, even the most radical of Ukrainian politicians recognized that the realization of Ukraine's sovereignty would be a gradual and complex process. In many respects, therefore, the Declaration was an idealistic statement of intention, which for the time being, at least, seemed more a case of wishful thinking than a blueprint for Ukraine's attainment of independence. Here, perhaps, also lies the key to understanding the behaviour of the conservative Communists who voted for the Declaration. As Shulha had reminded the deputies during the debate on the section dealing with republican citizenship, the document was only a declaration and did not have the force of law.[14] What

---

[13] See the report and photographs in *Molod Ukrainy*, 26 July 1990, and *Kultura i zhyttya*, 29 July 1990.

[14] Rather courageously, Chornovil was later to acknowledge in an interview: 'We proclaimed sovereignty – it's very moving: we cried, we embraced one another,

was needed, then, was a whole series of new laws and a new constitution which would permit the principles enshrined in the Declaration to be translated into practice.

More progress amid renewed confrontation

Once emotions in the parliament had subsided, Pavlychko sought on behalf of the opposition to ascertain how the republic's leadership intended to proceed concerning the new Union treaty. According to Radio Kyiv, the general feeling among the deputies seemed to be that until a new Ukrainian constitution was drafted 'such a treaty was premature'.[15]

Political realities, however, once again soon soured the atmosphere. Many members of the opposition hoped that the parliament would now be able to adopt a decree on power which would formally end the CPU's privileged role and thereby bring Ukraine's political life into step with the times. Instead, the next items of business were the structure of the new Ukrainian government and the election of a successor to Ivashko. In other words, without having reviewed and adjusted the existing political system to reflect the profound changes that had taken place, the deputies were called on to approve an essentially conservative proposal from Masol to establish government structures which more or less followed the old cumbersome Soviet model and to choose, in conditions when the CPU's leading role was still enshrined in the republic's constitution, who would lead the new sovereign but still formally Soviet and Socialist Ukrainian state.

Masol's proposals came under heavy fire and were accepted only after he himself agreed with much of the criticism and assured deputies that the new governmental structures would be only temporary to cover a 'transitional period'.[16] When it came to filling the vacant post of the chairman of the parliament, no less than twenty-seven candidates, including among others from the Communist camp Hurenko, Kravchuk, Plyushch and Mykola Fomenko, the head of the parliament's secretariat, were proposed. Most simply took advantage of the opportunity to deliver programmatic speeches

---

but everyone knew that these were just words.' *Literaturna Ukraina*, 4 October 1990.

[15] Radio Kyiv, 18 July 1990.

[16] *Radyanska Ukraina*, 18 and 20 July 1990.

before withdrawing their candidacies. The Union treaty was the dominant theme, with the Communist representatives defending the idea, and the opposition's spokesmen opposing it. Khmara, Larysa Skoryk, Holovaty, Yemets, Ivan Zayets and other representatives of the opposition also called for the prompt adoption of a decree on power. Eventually, two main contenders were left – Yukhnovsky from the People's Council, and Kravchuk from the CPU. The first round of voting produced no outright winner, but the 224 votes which Kravchuk secured, as compared with the 140 which Yukhnovsky obtained, indicated that the old division between the Communist majority and the opposition remained and that no upset could be expected. Yukhnovsky withdrew from the race and many of the People's Council boycotted the second ballot. On 23 July, Kravchuk easily defeated the remaining candidate, Boris Mokin, obtaining the now symbolic number of 239 votes.

Although Kravchuk called on the parliament to put confrontation behind it and usher in a period of constructive work, his affirmation in his speeches of the Soviet system and of Ukraine's 'Socialist choice', as well as his support for a new Union treaty, left the opposition convinced that the CPU's most capable politician would continue to put his party's interests first. Responding on behalf of the People's Council, Pavlychko declared that in the circumstances the democratic bloc would continue to regard itself as an opposition and that it would take no responsibility for the actions of the new head of the parliament.[17]

Under Kravchuk's new stewardship the debate on the adoption of a decree on power continued to be avoided. The new head of the parliament told a press conference after his election that he doubted whether deputies would manage to agree on such a document before the closure of the current session. He also revealed why by going on to insist that any documents of such major significance, including a new republican constitution, would have to recognize three key factors: 'that Ukraine is a democratic state, that Ukraine is a Soviet state, and that Ukraine is a Socialist state.'[18] He remained just as categorical on the question of the Union treaty. When asked soon afterwards by a visiting Bavarian parliamentary delegation whether Ukraine's Declaration of Sovereignty would

[17] Radio Kyiv, 23 July 1990.
[18] *Radyanska Ukraina*, 26 July 1990.

lead to 'the destruction of the Soviet Union', Kravchuk told journalists he had replied 'No. Because our position is one of support for the Union treaty and we consider that it is necessary.'[19]

Despite the new tensions, the parliament did manage to make several important decisions during what turned out to be the final days of the current session. On 30 July, it defied the Gorbachev leadership and the Soviet top brass by voting to recall all Ukrainians serving in the Soviet security forces in areas of conflict in other parts of the USSR. An elated Drach told Reuter that he saw this as the first step towards the creation of a Ukrainian army.[20] Two days later, the parliament passed a bill calling on the Ukrainian government to work out a new energy programme which would entail the closure of the Chornobyl power station and the reduction of the use of nuclear power altogether. Declaring the whole republic an ecological disaster zone because of the 1986 Chornobyl nuclear accident, it also proposed a programme of additional urgent measures to deal with the after-effects of the disaster, including the evacuation of more people from areas contaminated by nuclear radiation. A government committee on Chornobyl was to be set up and a first deputy prime minister with specific responsibility for Chornobyl issues appointed. Responding to the continuing public opposition to the nuclear energy industry and ecological sensitivities, the parliament also decided to impose a moratorium on the construction of both new nuclear power stations and military radar stations in the republic.[21]

The Verkhovna Rada's attention then shifted to bolstering the Declaration of State Sovereignty with a law on the republic's economic sovereignty. The draft proposed by the government and introduced on its behalf by the newly appointed deputy chairman of the Council of Ministers and head of the State Committee on the Economy, Fokin, had been in preparation for a long time. Specialists from different regions had worked on it and no less than twelve alternative variants had been taken into account. For all its importance, though, the document was short on details and barely elaborated the principles which had been enshrined in the Declaration: in fact, it itself had a declarative ring to it. After a relatively

---

[19] *Ibid.*, 27 July 1990.

[20] Reuter, 30 July 1990.

[21] Reuter, 1 August 1990, and Radio Kyiv, 1 and 2 August 1990.

brief debate, the draft was endorsed and on 3 August the parliament passed the 'Law on the Economic Independence of the Ukrainian SSR'. It was hailed as another triumph for the reformers for it not only asserted Ukraine's sovereignty in the economic sphere – how this was to be implemented was practically left unsaid – but also appeared to set Ukraine on a gradual course towards market relations, albeit in the form of a 'regulated market economy'.[22]

This was to be the last achievement of the first session of the new parliament for that same day agreement once again gave way to confrontation between the Communist majority and the democratic opposition. The atmosphere was inflamed by exchanges over the dismantling of monuments of Lenin that had begun in Western Ukraine. As a result, the Communist majority rejected the selection of Zhulynsky (who, incidentally, had not left the Communist Party) for the post of minister of culture even though he was the only well-known representative from the democratic camp nominated to serve in the new government.

After this, Kravchuk appears to have miscalculated by unexpectedly proposing the formation of a commission packed with Communist regional Party bosses to prepare a draft of a new republican constitution. The opposition greeted this transparent move to secure a political advantage for the Communists with scorn and the proposal had to be shelved. On this discordant note, Kravchuk formally closed the session.

Seeking to gloss over the new impasse, Kravchuk emphasized that, despite the 'complex conditions' which had characterized its work, the first session of the new parliament had succeeded in adopting close to 150 legislative acts and resolutions, including the Declaration of the State Sovereignty of Ukraine and the law on economic independence, and that the most constructive period had been during the last three weeks.[23] Representatives of the opposition also acknowledged, as Chornovil put it, that considering the make-up of the parliament, it had been possible to pass a number of essential laws, not to mention adopt the Declaration, which in the circumstances had been 'one of the wonders of the twentieth century'.[24]

---

[22] *Radyanska Ukraina*, 4 August 1990. For the text of the law, see *Radyanska Ukraina*, 8 August 1990.

[23] *Ibid.*, 5 August 1990.

[24] Radio Kyiv, 10 August 1990.

For its part, the People's Council issued a protest in the form of an appeal addressed to the deputies and the citizens of Ukraine. It pointed out that the session had been closed before the agenda had been completed and before numerous important issues, such as the decree on power, the preparation of a new constitution, the transition to market relations and inauguration of new economic relations with the other republics had been dealt with. It also warned that agitation for the new Union treaty was also being stepped up 'in the corridors' of both the Ukrainian and the Soviet parliaments. The opposition therefore proposed that the summer recess be shortened, that parliament resume its work by 3 September, and that in the meantime work on preparing new legislation be continued by the parliamentary commissions.[25]

While both camps took advantage of the summer break to review the situation and prepare for what was promising to be perhaps an even more difficult second session of the parliament, there were a number of brighter notes that helped raise spirits. During the first week of August, hundreds of thousands of people from all over Ukraine participated in the Days of Cossack Glory in the Zaporizhzhya and Dnipropetrovsk regions. The festival, which was attended by Kravchuk and Plyushch, was a great success and for a few days it seemed to unite the Ukrainian nation in a celebration of its identity and traditions.[26] Later that month, Kyiv hosted the first gathering of its leading scholars from both inside Ukraine and the diaspora. The First Congress of the International Association of Ukrainianists symbolized the breaking down of the barriers that had artificially separated Ukrainians from one another for so long and the irrepressible spirit that had sustained Ukrainian scholarship through persecution and exile. Ukrainian television viewers were also shown the state choir of Ukraine 'Veriovka' performing a specially orchestrated version of the long-banned Ukrainian national anthem at the gala concert in Kyiv's opera house for the participants of the congress. Furthermore, the republican media presented interviews with many of the guests from the diaspora who until only recently had been officially labelled as enemies.[27]

There were also encouraging developments connected with

[25] *Literaturna Ukraina*, 16 August 1990.

[26] See *ibid.*, 9 and 16 August 1990.

[27] The author was present at the Congress.

Ukraine's foreign relations. Eleven representatives of the People's Council, including Rukh's leader, Drach, and the URP's leader, Lukyanenko, met in Moscow on 29 August with members of the 'Democratic Russia' parliamentary bloc and broke new ground. They signed a 'Declaration on the Principles of Inter-state Relations between Ukraine and the RSFSR based on the Declarations of State Sovereignty', which asserted that the Ukrainian and Russian peoples now finally had 'a real chance to open a new chapter in the history of their relations'. Describing the Soviet Union as a 'unitary empire' which was experiencing 'a deep systemic crisis', the signatories declared that the democratic forces in both Russia and Ukraine were committed to 'building democratic independent states' and establishing harmonious bilateral relations between them based on the recognition of the principles affirmed in their respective declarations of sovereignty. They were: the unconditional recognition of one another as subjects of international law; 'the sovereign equality' of both states; 'non-interference in each other's internal affairs and the renunciation of the use of force or economic and other forms of pressure'; the inviolability of existing state borders between the Ukrainian SSR and the RSFSR and the renunciation of any territorial claims; the safeguarding of the political, economic, ethnic and cultural rights of Russians living in Ukraine and vice versa; the desirability of mutually beneficial cooperation in various fields; and the regulation of disputes in the spirit of friendship. The Declaration went on to describe 'the careful dismantling' of the Union structures, 'assertion of the statehood of the republics and transition to a commonwealth of independent states' as 'the main problem of the present period'. The eleven Russian signatories included three members of the Presidium of the Supreme Soviet of the RSFSR – Sergei Kovalev, Sergei Shakhrai and Vladimir Lukin – as well as the historian Afanasev.[28]

On the official level, too, there were the first signs that Ukraine did indeed intend to formulate and pursue an independent foreign policy. This was the main message of a press conference given on 2 August by the newly appointed Ukrainian foreign minister, Anatolii Zlenko, and the chairman of the parliamentary foreign relations commission, Pavlychko. They explained that the initial focus would be on establishing direct ties with 'immediate neighbours' and

---

[28] The text was published in *Literaturna Ukraina*, 6 September 1990.

developing links with states which had large Ukrainian communities, such as the USA and Canada. Clearly, Ukraine's first priority was to secure recognition of its sovereignty, borders and territorial integrity from its neighbours and from the international community generally and to ensure that its links with the large Ukrainian diaspora remained open. Pavlychko also indicated that in the next stage, Ukraine would seek to participate 'directly' and as 'an equal partner' in the 'European process', in other words, that sovereign Ukraine was seeking recognition as a European state and that it wanted to participate independently in European forums and structures.[29]

Hungary proved to be an understanding and supportive neighbour and took the lead in facilitating Ukraine's new opening up to its neighbours and Europe. A Hungarian invitation to Zlenko to pay an official visit to Budapest provided Ukraine with the first opportunity to test its newly declared sovereignty in the area of foreign relations. The visit, on 24 August, was crowned by Hungarian President Arpad Goncz's acceptance of an invitation to visit Kyiv and Ukraine's Transcarpathian region, where some 150,000 Hungarians live. On 27 September, he became the first foreign head of state to visit Kyiv since Ukraine's Declaration of Sovereignty. During his stay in Kyiv, both sides agreed to a major upgrading of bilateral relations, to work towards the establishment of full diplomatic relations in coordination with Moscow and to formalize their respect for the rights of national minorities.[30]

As for the Union treaty, the evolution of Kravchuk's views on this highly sensitive issue was also noteworthy, though at the time the significance of this may not have been readily appreciated. After attending a joint meeting in Moscow in early September of the Presidential Council and the Federation Council at which the Union treaty was discussed, Kravchuk revealed in an interview for Ukrainian television that there had been 'sharp' and 'uncompromising' exchanges and that the representatives of the republics had rejected a draft prepared by the Soviet government which sought to preserve the status quo. Asked to elaborate his own

[29] *Ibid.*, 9 August 1990. See also John A. Marcum, 'The New Ukraine: Changes of Flags in Kyiv', *Christian Science Monitor*, 28 September 1990.

[30] See Alfred Reisch, 'Hungary and Ukraine Agree to Upgrade Bilateral Relations', *Report on Eastern Europe*, vol. 44 (2 November 1990), pp. 6-12.

position on the question, Kravchuk declared that the existing 'unitary state' should be replaced by 'a Union of free, independent, sovereign, socialist, states-republics', and that the sovereign republics themselves, not the centre, should be responsible for the process of creating the new entity. In the interview, Kravchuk also sought to assure his critics in the national democratic camp that he recognized that Ukraine had made its choice to embark 'on the road to sovereignty, on the road to independence' and that he was not doing anything 'behind the back' of deputies to undermine this decision.[31] Such statements, of course, did not help his image among the hard-liners within the CPU.

During the last part of September, though, the issue of the Union treaty was temporarily overshadowed by a new controversy which forced Russians and non-Russians alike to think even harder about their relations and how they saw their future. It was generated by the publication in the Soviet press of Alexander Solzhenitsyn's essay 'How Shall We Reconstitute Russia?' in which he advocated the dissolution of the Soviet Union and the creation of a 'Russian Union', or greater Russia, which would incorporate Ukraine, Belarus and northern Kazakhstan. The essay caused outrage in all three republics and in the capital of Kazakhstan there were even demonstrations against the Russian writer. Oliinyk, who had since been appointed deputy head of the Council of Nationalities and was regarded by many of his former Ukrainian colleagues as having 'sold out' to Gorbachev and 'the centre', declared in the Soviet parliament on 25 September that Solzhenitsyn had insulted the Ukrainians and other peoples and had fanned anti-Russian feeling. When pressed in the parliament by a deputy from Kazakhstan to state his view on the matter, Gorbachev was forced to acknowledge that the essay was inflammatory and to distance himself from it.[32]

The Ukrainian October near-revolution

With the opposition feeling itself blocked in the parliament, lacking representation in Masol's essentially Communist government, and

---

[31] *Radyanska Ukraina*, 12 September 1990.

[32] Soviet television, 25 September 1990. The text of Oliinyk's speech, together with a rejoinder to Solzhenitsyn from the historian Raisa Ivanchenko, were published in *Literaturna Ukraina*, 11 October 1990.

fearing that the CPU's leaders would exploit the Declaration of
Sovereignty as 'a scrap of paper' to be used for their own political
ends, the stage was set for an intensification of the political struggle
outside of parliament and an escalation of tensions. As before,
the anti-Communist forces recognized that the only way in which
they could weaken the Communist hold on the levers of power
was through united action and the mobilization of mass support.
Their leaders had seen how effective worker protests and strike
committees could be, and were also well aware that the deteriorating
economic conditions and shortages of staples in the shops were
continuing to fuel social discontent. If in Western Ukraine
nationalism was still the driving force, in Eastern Ukraine social
and economic factors had galvanized the miners and other workers.
Political activity and defiance in both parts of the republic was
directed against the Communist Party and Moscow, and expressed
in support for maximal sovereignty and, increasingly, independence.
The resulting continuing radicalization and polarization of politics
could also be seen in the evolution of both Rukh and the various
workers' strike committees. Thus, the situation was seen by some
of the more militant leaders of the opposition's forces as ripe for
a decisive push.

Both sides busied themselves preparing for the next session of
parliament, which it had since been decided to convene on 1
October. Seeking to pre-empt the opposition, the CPU made the
first move through its control of the Presidium of the legislature.
On 11 September, the Presidium, chaired by Kravchuk, met to
prepare a provisional agenda for the next session. There was no
mention of the decree on power and instead the Presidium seemed
to be more concerned in trying to pressure numerous city councils,
mainly in Western Ukraine, to reverse their decisions to allow the
removal of statues of Lenin. But what angered the opposition the
most was the decision of the Presidium to impose a ban on
demonstrations and public meetings within a one kilometre radius
of the parliament building.[33]

The People's Council protested against this 'crude violation of
the democratic rights of citizens' and urged the public to
demonstrate outside the parliament on the first day of the new
session.[34] This appeal appeared to be reinforced when on 15 Sep-

---

[33] *Radyanska Ukraina*, 13 September 1990.

tember representatives of strike committees from all over Ukraine decided to call a one-day warning strike on 1 October. In fact, it was to transpire that the more moderate elements within Rukh's leadership were not convinced that strikes at a time of growing economic difficulties were the most appropriate form of political struggle. Likewise, in Western Ukraine, it seemed to make little sense to hold strikes when in fact the first ones to feel the damage would be the democratic authorities.

The Kyiv branch of the Ukrainian Students' Union went further and announced that its members would pitch tents on Kyiv's central October Revolution Square – the opposition had renamed it Independence Square – and start a hunger strike. The students' demands included the nationalization of the CPU's and Komsomol's property and the calling of new parliamentary elections in the spring of 1991.[35]

On 28 September, the CPU Central Committee held a plenum at which Hurenko left no doubt as to how the CPU's leadership interpreted what was happening. He claimed that the opposition had thrown off its 'camouflage' and was seeking to take power by unconstitutional means, including violent ones. This, he argued, was what was behind the mass anti-Communist protests and campaign of civil disobedience which had been planned to coincide with the opening of the next session of the parliament. Significantly, he also referred to 'emissaries' from the Democratic Russia bloc, which he said had also been 'stirring up' things in the republic.[36] At this plenum, Kravchuk wisely relinquished his post as second secretary of the CPU.

On the eve of the protests, the Presidium of the parliament issued an appeal addressed to the citizens of the republic which called for political moderation and unity in the cause of the practical realization of the Declaration of State Sovereignty. Referring to the serious economic and social problems in Ukarine, and growing political unrest, 'disregard for laws', and efforts 'to resolve political problems by unconstitutional means', the Presidium described the situation as 'alarming and dangerous'. It acknowledged that there was widespread dissatisfaction with the slowness in which the Declara-

---

[34] *Literaturna Ukraina*, 27 September 1990.

[35] Haran, *To Kill the Dragon*, p. 125.

[36] *Radyanska Ukraina*, 30 September 1990.

tion of Sovereignty was being implemented and falling living standards, and it sought to assure the public that it was doing, and would continue to do, its best to 'stabilize the political and economic situation . . . [and] build a sovereign Ukrainian state based on the rule of law'. Signalling an important concession designed to reduce tensions, the Presidium also announced in the appeal that it had decided that it would be 'premature' for the republic to sign a new Union treaty before a new Ukrainian constitution had been adopted.

On the other hand, the Presidium also emphasized that it had instructed the security forces to ensure that law and order were maintained.[37] The head of the Kyiv City Administration of the Ministry of Internal Affairs, General Valentyn Nedryhailo, who was responsible for the capital's police force, also appeared on television and announced that a demonstration called by the opposition for Sunday, 30 September, had been authorized by the city council, but that the protest planned for 1 October outside the parliament building had not been permitted. Nervousness gripped the capital as rumours spread about military vehicles being stationed on the outskirts of the city.

All the same, on 30 September, over 100,000 people demonstrated in Kyiv in what was the largest protest yet seen in the Ukrainian capital. Its stated purpose was to oppose the Union treaty and express support for independence, but leaders of the opposition forces also used the occasion to issue an appeal calling on all of the republic's political parties and associations to take part in a 'round-table' with representatives from industry, agriculture, science and learning to find ways out of Ukraine's crisis and to set up a government of national salvation. After a public meeting, the protesters marched through the centre of the capital, many of them demanding the resignation of Kravchuk and Masol, and some calling for the parliament to be dissolved and for new elections.[38]

The same slogans were heard the following day when tens of thousands defied the Presidium's ban and gathered to demonstrate outside the parliament. The authorities decided not to risk aggravating the situation by attempting to prevent the protest. Instead, the

---

[37] *Radyanska Ukraina*, 28 September 1990.

[38] Pavlychko, *Letters from Kiev*, pp. 75-9. The appeal, which was endorsed by the public meeting, was published in *Literaturna Ukraina*, 4 October 1990.

demonstrators were kept some distance away from the parliament by a strong police cordon.

The tensions outside the parliament were reflected inside the chamber. The second session opened with scuffles after some of the more radical members of the opposition attempted to bring a large blue and yellow flag on their shoulders into the chamber. Kravchuk subsequently did not help matters by stating that there could not be any 'consolidation' between the majority and the opposition in the parliament, only 'compromises', and by calling on the deputies to endorse the Presidium's ban on protests near the building, which the majority promptly did. The atmosphere was further aggravated when Konev, now also representing a newly created Association of Democratic Councils of Ukraine, and Tanyuk the People's Council, delivered statements calling for, among other things, the resignation of Masol and Kravchuk. The Communist majority, however, simply blocked their demand.[39]

By the evening it became apparent that the strike action throughout the republic had not been particularly successful and this allowed the central Soviet media to announce that the attempt to organize a Ukrainian general strike had failed.[40] Chornovil was later even to describe it as having been 'a major political blunder' and a setback for the opposition.[41] Certainly, though impressive, the protest actions had not been as massive and effective as the opposition had hoped and failed to alter the political balance.

What was to save the day for the opposition and eventually to break the political deadlock, though, was the students' hunger strike. It began on 2 October and unexpectedly was to provide a new impetus to the opposition's faltering protest campaign. The students, having created a mini-Tiananmen Square in the heart of Kyiv, put forward five basic demands: the resignation of Masol, a law stipulating that Ukrainians do their military service only on the territory of the republic, rejection of the idea of a new Union treaty, nationalization of the CPU's property and the holding of new elections to the parliament on a multi-party basis. That same day, the first clashes between protesters and the police took place and, with additional

---

[39] Radio Kyiv, 1 October 1990, and Haran, *To Kill the Dragon*, pp. 128-9.

[40] TASS, 1 October 1990.

[41] He gave this assessment later in the month at Rukh's Second Congress. See *Suchasnist*, January 1991, p. 44.

units of riot police being brought in to strengthen the cordon around the parliament, the situation grew more and more volatile.[42]

In the parliament, the atmosphere remained strained but the session was at least able to begin its work. Among its first decisions was to reject the government's proposals for stabilizing the economic situation in the republic, which only served to undermine Masol's position even more. A delegation was also sent to meet with the student hunger-strikers and Yemets managed to persuade the deputies to set up a commission to examine the violent incidents outside the parliament building. As for foreign relations, the parliament endorsed a statement read out by Pavlychko welcoming the reunification of Germany and expressing Kyiv's desire for closer bilateral ties with Bonn. Also, as Radio Moscow reported on 8 October, Kravchuk received a parliamentary delegation from the Russian Federation to discuss the establishment of a bilateral parliamentary commission to promote ties between the neighbouring sovereign republics.

Nevertheless, when, on 8 October, it came to the crucial issues of giving the Declaration of State Sovereignty constitutional force, and of removing Article 6 on the leading role of the Party from the Ukrainian Constitution, the proposals failed to pass. The sense of renewed deadlock was reinforced during the next day when the majority seemed to backtrack on the parliament's earlier decision that Ukrainian soldiers should perform their military service on the territory of their republic, and decided that a special delegation should be sent to discuss the question in Moscow. Indignant and disheartened, representatives from the opposition were left declaring that all this was proof that the Communist majority indeed viewed the Declaration of the State Sovereignty as merely a scrap of paper. As one of them, Yevhen Hryniv from Lviv, told Radio Kyiv, the very deputies who had voted for the Declaration were now 'not keeping either to the letter or the spirit of this document'. On top of this, on 10 October, when the students were nine days into their hunger strike, the majority once again blocked a vote on confidence in Masol's government.[43]

During the first half of October, however, the students' protest had gradually begun to capture the attention of the entire republic

---

[42] Pavlychko, *Letters from Kiev*, pp. 82-3.
[43] Radio Kyiv, 3, 8, 9 and 10 October 1990.

and was now drawing support from students in other cities and radical deputies, eight of whom joined the hunger strike on 10 October. Oles Honchar had announced that he was leaving the Communist Party because of the 'behaviour of the group of 239' and especially their reaction to the students' hunger strike. There was also considerable support for the students from other cultural figures and from the democrats among the members of the Kyiv City Council. Furthermore, General Nedryhailo also demonstrated considerable understanding and professionalism: he met with the student hunger-strikers early on and sought to reassure them that they too would be protected by the police against any possible 'provocations' or heavy-handed attempts to disperse them.

After a large demonstration on 10 October outside the republican television centre, the deputies who had joined the students' protest were allowed to read their statements on the air. Two days later, students throughout the republic held a strike and thousands of them demonstrated in Kyiv in support of their colleagues. The protests continued. Every day in the capital thousands of people turned out to demonstrate in support of the students' demands and the militia sought to keep the protesters from breaking through to the parliament. With hard-line deputies calling for tough measures to 'restore order', tension grew and the threat of the imposition of a state of emergency hung in the air. On 16 October, there was another huge student demonstration in Kyiv. One of the students' leaders, Oles Donii, was invited by the opposition to address the parliament and that evening he and his colleagues were also allowed to present their case on television. They called on students throughout the republic to occupy their places of learning and to begin an indefinite strike. That same evening some of the students protesters in Kyiv moved their tents to almost outside the parliament building, while others occupied the main building of Kyiv University and raised a blue and yellow flag over it.

The situation had become extremely perilous, and the danger of a clash or provocation leading to bloodshed, and perhaps a general crackdown by the security forces, seemed greater than ever. Moderates on both sides worked to get reason and moderation to prevail but the hard-liners on both sides remained set against any compromises. On the one hand, radical leaders of the opposition such as Khmara urged the students not to budge on anything and even to go as far as demanding the dissolution of the CPU, while conservative Communist deputies, as for example Vitalii Reva from Crimea, called for the imposition of a state of emergency in the capital and for the protesters to be dispersed by force. What was particularly discouraging for the Communist hard-liners was that all this time, while the more official Soviet central media increasingly depicted the events in Ukraine as nationalism run wild and the students as 'extremists' who were being manipulated by 'political adventurers', the Gorbachev leadership, preoccupied with 'the war of laws' between the centre and the sovereign Union republics, the declarations of sovereignty which were now also being made by autonomous republics within the Russian Federation, and trying to secure support for its compromise economic reform programme, did not intervene.

With the Communist majority beginning to waver, and the opposition threatening to walk out, the parliament decided to establish a bipartisan conciliatory committee headed by Plyushch to seek a solution to the crisis. On Wednesday 17 October, shortly after many workers from the huge and traditionally pro-Communist 'Arsenal' factory in Kyiv had come out in support of the students, the Communist authorities finally yielded. After more than two weeks of confrontation, the parliament agreed, on the recommendation of the conciliatory committee, to accept the students' demands. Masol was sacrificed.[44] It was also agreed that a referendum would be held on public confidence in the parliament which could pave the way for new elections; that a commission would be set up to discuss nationalization of the Party's and Komsomol's property; that Ukrainian citizens would not be made to serve outside their republic; and that Ukraine would not sign the Union treaty before a new republican constitution had been adopted.[45]

There was a general sigh of relief in the republic for the near-revolutionary situation had been the closest that Ukraine had come to large-scale political violence and even civil war breaking out. For the more moderately minded politicians it had underscored the need

[44] Kravchuk later revealed that Masol was removed by a decision of the CPU Central Committee after the decision was first agreed with Gorbachev and Ryzhkov. Radio Ukraine, 7 July 1994.

[45] On the student protests, see *Literaturna Ukraina*, 11 and 18 October 1990; *Ukraina*, no. 48, 2 December 1990, pp. 1–3; and Haran, *To Kill the Dragon*, pp. 129–30, 132–5. The atmosphere in these fateful days is conveyed in Pavlychko, *Letters from Kiev*, pp. 79–96.

for a greater sense of responsibility, gradualism, compromise and cooperation rather than confrontation. But for the hard-liners on both sides, the students' victory had not resolved the fundamental issues and the political struggle had still to be decided.

While the students and their supporters were celebrating, the CPU's Politburo met to discuss the crisis in which the Party found itself. The records of the closed meeting show that Hurenko openly admitted that the CPU had lost an important battle and that it would have been wiser to reach a compromise with the student protesters before they had managed to mobilize mass public support. He expressed concern that there were increasing signs of 'nervousness', 'uncertainty' and internal discord within the ranks of the CPU. Defending Kravchuk, he called on his colleagues to 'cease this total distrust' of the head of the parliament. 'We put him there', he reminded them, 'so let's support him'. He agreed though that Plyushch 'was pushing against us', but cautioned against trying to vote him out of his position as deputy head of the parliament.

Kravchuk's comments at this meeting reveal him as the crafty politician that he was, and the way his mind worked. He advised his colleagues to allow someone not identified with the CPU leadership, even Yukhnovsky or some other representative of the opposition, to take responsibility for the government. The transition to market relations would be unpopular, he argued, there would be unemployment and living standards would continue to fall, and of course the reputation of whoever was trying to deal with these problems would suffer. Did the CPU want to risk taking all the blame by placing a leading Communist at the head of the government again, who in any case would be immediately confronted with mass protests? In traditional style, the Politburo decided to respond to the challenge from the increasingly militant national democratic forces by calling for a closing of ranks and a tightening of discipline within the Communist caucus in the parliament.[46]

Within the next few days, the Communist majority in the parliament, while still resisting calls to give the Declaration of State Sovereignty the status of a constitutional law, finally agreed to make a number of key changes to the existing republican constitution. The most important of these was the removal of Article 6, though this had more symbolic significance than anything else, for the

---

[46] Lytvyn, *Political Arena*, pp. 249–55.

USSR Supreme Soviet had already passed a law on 9 October granting equal status to all political parties, and recognition of the supremacy of the republican legislation on the territory of Ukraine. The latter change happened to coincide with a law passed by the USSR Supreme Soviet, also on 24 October, reasserting the primacy of all-Union laws over republican ones. Because neither the centre nor the republics were able to win the continuing 'war of laws', such decisions had a symbolic value rather than anything else. Other noteworthy changes were: the republic's General Procurator was to be appointed by, and be responsible to, the Ukrainian parliament; that military service performed by Ukrainian citizens was to be regulated by the Ukrainian parliament; and a compromise decision requiring judges to suspend their membership in a political party or movement while they were in office.[47]

Inspired by the victory over the CPU which the opposition thought had cleared the way for movement forward, Rukh decided at its Second Congress, held in Kyiv on 25-8 October, to come out unequivocally for independence and step up its struggle against the CPU. Drach delivered one of the best speeches in his life and was re-elected head of the movement; Mykhailo Horyn was chosen as his deputy. Kravchuk did not attend the Congress, but his deputy Plyushch did, and he endeared himself to the delegates by declaring his support for a 'sovereign and independent' Ukraine and urging Rukh to act as a 'consolidating centre for democratic forces'.

Quite a few of the speakers, however, were candid about the real state of things, about how much still needed to be done, and they sought to dispel any sense of complacency. Lukyanenko, for example, who had advocated moderation during the student protests, reminded delegates that even if the demonstrators had stormed the police lines, they would probably have been shot and the troops waiting on the outskirts of Kyiv brought in to ensure 'the triumph of reaction'. Assuming the protesters had even won in the capital, he asked, could they really have relied on support from the rest of the republic. He thought not, because, in his view, Rukh, and the URP for that matter, still needed time to broaden their support, especially in the south and east of Ukraine, and in the villages. In order to become sufficiently strong to dislodge the 'partocracy', which he described as the rule of the Party administrative apparatus

---

[47] Radio Kyiv, 24 October 1990, and Haran *To Kill the Dragon*, p. 136.

in alliance with the army and security forces, Rukh and its partners had to avoid a situation where force could be used against them.

Chornovil was more critical about the way in which Rukh's organization and activities were developing and he advocated a more resolute strategy aimed at achieving political power by peaceful means and state-building. He supported campaigning for the dissolution of the parliament and for new elections and the idea of a popularly elected president of the republic; he also reiterated his views on the need for some sort of a federal set-up in Ukraine to neutralize separatist tendencies, such as in Crimea, where the Communist-dominated regional council had stepped up its pressure for the restoration of the peninsula's autonomous status. Prophetically, as it later transpired, Chornovil also warned that the opposition needed to be prepared for a possible 'counter-revolutionary coup' by reactionary forces, and to have plans for a general strike and a campaign of civil disobedience prepared in reserve.[48]

One of the highlights of the Congress was the presence at the opening of the head of the UAOC, Patriarch Mstyslav, who had recently finally been allowed by the Soviet authorities to travel to Ukraine. The joy was marred, however, by the fact that despite protests from Rukh's leaders and representatives of the Kyiv City Council, the Moscow Patriarchate and the Ukrainian Orthodox Church went ahead with a visit to Kyiv by Patriarch Aleksii II. On the final day of the Congress, therefore, many of the participants in the Rukh Congress joined members of the UAOC in a demonstration outside St. Sophia's Cathedral to protest against the visit of the Russian Orthodox Patriarch. In fact, the protesters' aim appeared to be to prevent him from entering St Sophia's and to reinforce the campaign for the transferal of the Cathedral to the UAOC. There were ugly scenes and once again the official media did not waste the opportunity depict Rukh and the UAOC as extremists.[49]

Both within Rukh and outside it, there were, of course, more radical and uncompromising groups and politicians than the movement's mainstream. Khmara, for example, had urged the Rukh Congress to ban Communists from its ranks and he, and other militants, such as his colleague in the radical wing of the URP

[48] The main speeches delivered at the Congress were published in *Suchasnist*, January 1991.
[49] The author was an observer at both the Congress and the protest.

Roman Koval, made no secret of their desire to destabilize the political situation in the republic, because for them stabilization meant the perpetuation of the political status quo. Disappointed by the way in which the students' protest had ended, some of these organizations and individuals promptly sought to form an alliance to continue their 'uncompromising' political struggle. They included the Inter-Party Assembly, which had been formed in the summer as a coalition of small, radical, nationalist organizations and which was headed by Yurii Shukhevych, the son of the commander in chief of the UPA, Taras Chuprynka, alias Roman Shukhevych. Its members did not believe that there was any sense in trying to work within the system and they criticized Rukh and the People's Council for doing so. Instead, the Inter-Party Assembly advocated a mass campaign of collecting signatures from people ready to declare themselves citizens of a Ukrainian People's Republic and, when a sufficient number had been gathered, to convene a Ukrainian National Congress to replace the Communist-dominated Supreme Soviet.[50]

New moderate political parties and movements were also developing or being formed, though. For instance, the Organization of the Mothers of Soldiers of Ukraine – a group campaigning for Ukrainian recruits to do their military service on the territory of the republic and against bullying and other cruel practices in the Soviet army – had held its founding congress in Zaporizhzhya on 8 and 9 September; later that month, the Party of the Greens of Ukraine had convened its first congress; and in October the Democratic Party of Ukraine (DPU) unveiled its programme. Another group whose plans were attracting attention were the twenty-eight deputies belonging to the Democratic Platform who, after the Declaration of State Sovereignty, had announced that they were leaving the CPU. At the beginning of December they were to hold the founding congress of the Party for the Democratic Revival of Ukraine (PDRU), whose leaders included Filenko, Hrynov, Yemets, Khmelko and Popovych. All these parties supported independence.

The dramatic Ukrainian 'October' came to a close with the democratic forces confident that, thanks to the students' hunger strike, they had achieved a further hard-won victory. The

---

[50] Haran, *To Kill the Dragon*, pp. 135-6.

breakthrough appeared to have demonstrated that while the CPU could certainly still affect the pace of change, it could not control events through its majority in the parliament or alter the general direction in which things were moving. The mass protests in the capital, which it seemed had taken the republic to the very brink, had reduced the prospect of Ukraine's signing a new Union treaty in the near future and instead had sharpened the focus on the issues of the dismantling of Communist rule and the achievement of independence. When, at the end of the month, the parliament formed a Constitutional Commission charged with drawing up a document which would outline the 'concept', or fundamental principles, of a new republican constitution, the opportunity for effecting a decisive break with the past seemed to be at hand.

But there was also an unexpected development at the very end of the month which brought home the seriousness of the economic crisis in which the republic found itself and which for a time was to divert attention away from issues such as the Union treaty. Just as the parliament began the process of endorsing a successor to Masol – both the majority's and the opposition's initial nominees, Volodymyr Slyednov and Volodymyr Pylypchuk respectively, failed to get enough votes – the acting head of the government, Fokin, proposed the immediate introduction of a republican system of non-transferable coupons for up to 70% of the roubles earned each month by Ukrainian citizens. Arguing that such a move was necessary to protect the Ukrainian consumer sector from buyers from other republics, he depicted it as a temporary step 'until the creation of a separate Ukrainian currency'. Though taken aback by the secrecy with which this measure had been prepared, the deputies voted to implement it from 1 November.

The CPU counter-attacks

Dissatisfaction with the way things were going was widespread not only within the CPSU but was also becoming increasingly apparent among the Soviet officer corps and the secret police. Gorbachev was coming under increasing criticism, and rumours of a possible military coup abounded. In Ukraine, too, even as the democratic forces were celebrating an important victory, reactionary elements were preparing to strike back.

A fortnight after their triumph, Kyiv's students came out with a new challenge to the CPU: they called for the traditional military parade in the capital on the anniversary of the Bolshevik revolution to be cancelled. Both sides dug their heels in and the danger of a potential clash, this time possibly involving the armed forces, grew. Fortunately, the Kyiv City Council proposed a compromise: the military parade would be moved from Kyiv's main avenue, Khreshchatyk, to a square in another part of the city, and the students would also be allowed to hold their own demonstration elsewhere in the capital. The more radical youth remained determined to prevent the military parade but on the night of 6 November the riot police drove them from the square where the parade was to take place.

The following morning, Khmara and a group of his colleagues appear to have been lured into a trap set by the security forces. After a woman had approached the radical deputy in an underpass claiming that she had just been assaulted, he and his friends seized the suspect and attempted to detain and search him. The man, who did not identify himself, resisted. He turned out to be armed with a gun and to be carrying the documents of a police colonel. The entire incident was secretly filmed by the police. A few days later, film of Khmara and his colleagues 'assaulting' the plain-clothes police officer – a certain Colonel Hryhoryev – was shown on republican and central Soviet television. It was evident enough to the opposition that the 'partocracy' was seeking to discredit it and to take revenge for the events of the previous month. By striking at the radical wing, the Communist authorities were evidently also hoping to provoke the militants and to split the opposition.

There were more signs that hard-line forces were launching a counter-attack. At the military parade, General Gromov, still a member of the CPU Politburo, declared: 'We will pronounce a decisive "No!" to all extremists, nationalists, separatists . . . We will not yield . . . we will defend the gains of the revolution ... the greatest event of the twentieth century.'[51] Moreover, on 11 November, *Radyanska Ukraina* published a lengthy appeal addressed to the Presidium of the parliament from the hard-line former Party boss of the Odesa region, Kryuchkov, who was still a deputy in the USSR Supreme Soviet, in which he criticized the Presidium for having put off the decision about joining a new Union treaty. What was particularly striking about this statement, though, was Kryuchkov's

[51] Pavlychko, *Letters from Kiev*, pp. 109.

attack against Kravchuk, whom he accused of helping 'those who strive to prevent the signing of a new Union treaty [and] to destroy the union of Soviet republics'.

When, on the following day, the parliament resumed its work, pro-Communist demonstrators from the Odesa, Mykolaiv and Kherson regions in the south were bussed in, despite the continuing ban on protests in the vicinity; they picketed the parliament building with Soviet flags and placards supporting the signing of a new Union treaty. They were joined by protesting police officers who called for a new law on the militia, the enforcement of law and order and the disciplining of radical deputies who had participated in recent 'disturbances'. Subsequently, *Radyanska Ukraina* was to publish another appeal, this time from some of the demonstrators from the southern regions, calling for among other things, the parliament to revoke its concessions to the students and to establish a bicameral republican legislature which would have a Council of Nationalities in which 'millions of citizens of a non-Ukrainian nationality should be represented'.[52]

The demonstrations staged by the Soviet loyalists from Ukraine's southern regions appeared to represent both a renewed effort to mobilize a broad Interfront movement and an implicit warning that if the republic continued on the road towards independence its unity and territorial integrity would be threatened. Recent events in neighbouring Moldova had graphically demonstrated these dangers. There, the Moldovan resurgence had alarmed the republic's national minorities, and conservative Communists had played on the fears of forcible Romanization and Moldova's possible reunification with Romania; in the late summer, secessionist movements of Russians and Russified Ukrainians on the left bank of the Dniester and the Gagauz in the south had proclaimed their own break-away 'Soviet Socialist Republics' and asked Moscow to recognize them as 'republics within the structure of the USSR'. At the beginning of November, the first major clashes between the Moldovan authorities and a Russian paramilitary detachment had resulted in several deaths.

In Ukraine, potential problems with centrifugal tendencies existed in the Donbas, where attempts were being made to found an Interfront; in the Odesa region, where a former adviser to the breakaway Dniester Republic, Oleksii Surylov, was promoting the

[52] *Radyanska Ukraina*, 13 November 1990.

idea of Novorossiya, or New Russia, encompassing the self-proclaimed Dniester Republic, the Odesa, Mykolaiv and Kherson regions, and Crimea; and in Transcarpathia, where the Society of Carpathian Ruthenians maintained that the Ruthenians were a nation distinct from the Ukrainians and was campaigning for regional autonomy. But the problem was most acute in Crimea. Here orthodox Communist politicians and pro-Russian forces had combined to defend the status quo by seeking, on the one hand, to block Ukrainian influences, and on the other, to keep the Crimean Tatars, more and more of whom were returning to the peninsula, in check. After the Declaration of Ukraine's State Sovereignty and the Ukrainian parliament's postponement of its decision concerning the Union treaty, both the leadership of the Crimean Party organization and the regional soviet had stepped up the campaign for regional self-determination and the restoration of Crimea's autonomy.[53]

On the same day that the Ukrainian parliament reconvened after the holiday for the celebrations of the Bolshevik revolution, the Crimean regional soviet held an extraordinary session devoted to the issues of Crimea's status and the new Union treaty. With the majority of Crimean deputies backing the idea of calling a local referendum on Crimea's self-determination, the seriousness of the situation was demonstrated by the fact that the chairman of the Ukrainian parliament was also present at the session in Simferopol. After listening to a barrage of complaints and allegations about Ukrainian nationalism and separatism and calls for an autonomous Crimea to rejoin the Russian Federation – the session was broadcast live throughout the peninsula – Kravchuk sought to dissuade the Crimean deputies from attempting to break away from Ukraine or calling a local referendum, and to placate them by holding out the prospect of the creation of a Crimean Autonomous Soviet Socialist Republic within the Ukrainian SSR. The growing crisis in relations between Kyiv and Simferopol remained unresolved, however, for the Crimean regional soviet went ahead and issued a declaration calling for the restoration of Crimea's statehood in the form of the Crimean ASSR 'as a subject of the USSR and a party to the Union

---

[53] For an overview of these issues, see Roman Solchanyk, 'The Politics of State Building: Centre-Periphery Relations in Post-Soviet Ukraine', *Europe-Asia Studies*, vol. 46, no. 1 (1994), pp. 47-68.

treaty' and also voted to hold a local referendum on 20 January 1991 on the peninsula's future status.[54]

While the implications of the Crimean soviet's decision, and of Gorbachev being heckled and jeered at a meeting in Moscow with disgruntled military deputies, were being discussed in Kyiv, on 14 November the Ukrainian parliament was able to agree on a successor to Masol. The compromise choice for the new head of the government was Fokin who, while hardly a bold reformer, seemed ready to cooperate with the opposition and to defend the republic's sovereignty.[55] Despite this display of cooperation, later that same day the majority, including Kravchuk and Plyushch, ignored the protests of the opposition and voted to strip Khmara of his parliamentary immunity.

On 16 November, on the eve of the announcement by the Soviet leader of yet another reorganization of the Soviet state and government structures, and as if responding to Kryuchkov, Kravchuk vented his frustration and anger with Gorbachev and the centre for the deepening crisis in which the Union found itself. He told a meeting of veterans in Kyiv that the central authorities had 'split the country, let the levers [of power] out of their hands, [and] the mass media'. They were now seeking a way of restoring order and looking for scapegoats. Either they faced up to the responsibility of dealing with the tasks before them, or they should have the courage to admit: 'we can't'. 'It was not us in Ukraine who began' the 'destruction of Soviet society', he declared, and 'we will never stir up the people' to destroy the Soviet system. 'But if the central power continues to relinquish the levers, as it is doing now, we will assume the responsibility ourselves.'[56]

Whether or not the Khmara case was meant to demonstrate this 'resolve', and what precisely Kravchuk himself thought on the matter, remains uncertain. But on the following day, as excitement was being generated by the news of Yeltsin's imminent visit to Kyiv, the deputy was arrested in the parliament building on the recommendation of the republican General Procurator. Members

---

[54] See the reports on the session in *Radyanska Ukraina*, 14 November 1990, and *Molod Ukrainy*, 15 November 1990.

[55] Fokin had elaborated his views for the opposition in a lengthy interview in *Literaturna Ukraina*, 4 October 1990.

[56] Radio Kyiv, 16 November 1990.

of the opposition were outraged: even if they did not agree with Khmara's militancy, they were appalled by the way that a fellow deputy had been treated and by the precedent which was being set.

On top of this, on 21 November, the majority also pushed through changes in the voting procedure whereby in the case of the opposition refusing to cast their ballots, only half of the total number of deputies would suffice to constitute a quorum, and decisions could be approved by a majority of those participating. Indicating the feelings of the his colleagues, Chornovil issued a statement declaring that he refused to be reduced to a mere 'statistic' by the 'reactionary parliamentary majority' while it continued its 'betrayal of Ukraine and the destruction of its economy', and that in protest he was returning to his constituency.[57]

With demonstrations against Khmara's arrest beginning in the capital and the prospect of the mass arrival in Kyiv of his supporters from Western Ukraine, the situation once again became very tense. Fearing the worst, moderates in the People's Council successfully appealed to Western Ukrainians to stay away so as not to aggravate matters. Apart from organizing further demonstrations in the capital and continuing to protest in the parliament itself, there was little that the opposition could do for the moment to blunt the CPU's counter-offensive.

External relations and Russia

The overall picture though was not entirely gloomy. While the confrontation between the competing political forces continued, Ukraine was making further significant strides in asserting its sovereignty in foreign policy. In mid-October, during the height of the student protests, the Polish Foreign Minister Krzysztof Skubiszewsi had visited Kyiv and placed the links which had been forged by Ukrainian and Polish democrats on a new footing. He signed a Ukrainian-Polish declaration of friendship and good-neighbourly relations in which the two 'sovereign states' recognized each other's sovereignty and existing borders. A few days later, Ukraine and Belarus signed bilateral agreements promoting closer ties and cooperation between their two 'sovereign states'.

In the first half of the following month, while preparations were

[57] *Molod Ukrainy*, 21 November 1990.

apparently being made behind the scenes for a visit to Kyiv by Yeltsin and the signing of a Ukrainian-Russian treaty, Ukraine formally asserted its claim to direct participation in the Helsinki process. First, Foreign Minister Zlenko addressed a letter to his French counterpart, Roland Dumas, requesting that Ukraine be allowed to participate directly in a forthcoming summit of the Conference on Security and Cooperation in Europe (CSCE) in Paris. After the Soviet Foreign Ministry refused to recognize Ukraine's claim to separate representation, Zlenko and his colleagues demonstratively withdrew from the Soviet delegation. Then, in what was probably his first real foray into international affairs, Kravchuk addressed an appeal presenting the Ukrainian case to the participants of the meeting in Paris. The message was delivered by Pavlychko, his deputy in the parliamentary commission on foreign relations, Bohdan Horyn, and Drach who, together with the Baltic and Armenian representatives also seeking separate representation for their republics, carried on lobbying in Paris.

Kravchuk's appeal defied Moscow not only because it challenged the centre's right to speak on behalf of Ukraine and the other republics but also because it rejected the traditional image of Ukraine as a mere province of Russia. 'Ukraine is a large European state and its history and culture are an integral part of European civilization,' the appeal declared. Moreover, the fact that leading democrats were publicizing an appeal signed by their political adversary, Kravchuk, at a major European forum, also underscored the extent to which national Communist elements within the CPU were making common cause with the more moderate figures within the opposition – from whom they were bitterly divided on other issues – in defending Ukraine's sovereignty and wanting to see their republic take its place in the international community of states.[58]

Meanwhile, while Gorbachev was finalizing the preparation of the new Union treaty, Ukraine, like the Russian Federation, was also seeking to develop direct horizontal ties with the other sovereign Union republics. Clearly, for Ukraine, the regularization of bilateral relations with the Russian Federation was crucial and the fact that Yeltsin and his democratic supporters were in power in

---

[58] On the first stages of Ukraine's new sovereign foreign policy, see the author's 'Ukraine is Claiming its Rightful Place in Europe', *Wall Street Journal* (European edition), 30 November 1990.

Russia and were themselves challenging the imperial centre offered a unique window of opportunity. Yeltsin might not have had much time for the nationalities question in the past but his continuing political struggle as the leader of the sovereign Russian Federation with Gorbachev and the centre had led him to come out against the continuation of empire and in support of the transformation of the USSR into a loose voluntary union of sovereign states. At the same time, following the Declaration of Ukraine's State Sovereignty, the continuing paralysis of power in Moscow, and the slow but steady emergence of a national Communist tendency within the CPU, Kravchuk, Ukraine's still Communist leader, who in the past would have viewed Yeltsin as a renegade, had been left with little choice but to do business with him. Furthermore, both leaders were aware of the need for cooperation and understanding between them in facing up to Gorbachev's determination to preserve as much as he could of the old Union; in view of the possibility that the Soviet leader might try to impose a Union treaty on the republics by, for instance, having it approved by the conservative Soviet parliament, this was becoming a matter of some urgency.

There was one other important factor for Kravchuk and the leaders of the other non-Russian republics to reckon with. As the centre's authority continued to decline, the RSFSR seemed poised to fill the power vacuum. After meeting alone with Gorbachev for the first time since the end of August on 11 November, Yeltsin revealed that the Soviet leader had been urging the RSFSR to sign a new Union treaty first and settle all other issues later. For his part, Yeltsin had proposed the creation of a coalition government which would be 'an extraordinary anti-crisis committee, formed on the basis of equal rights, from representatives of the Union republics', with the RSFSR naming the key ministers. He had also insisted on agreements covering the division of functions and property between the central government and the RSFSR. As far as the non-Russian republics were concerned, a deal between Gorbachev and Yeltsin could ultimately cut both ways. For instance, and fortunately in this case for official Kyiv, Yeltsin revealed that he and Gorbachev had discussed the situation in Crimea and had agreed not to apply any pressure on Ukraine as 'experience' showed that outside interference would only have a destabilizing effect.[59] In fact, however,

---

[59] See the accounts of the meeting between Gorbachev and Yeltsin by Vitalii

the prospect of a deal between Gorbachev and Yeltsin receded when, on 16 November, the Soviet leader addressed the USSR Supreme Soviet and asked for the third time that year to be granted fresh powers.

On 19 November, while Gorbachev was attending the opening of the CSCE summit in Paris and warning that any efforts to dismantle the Soviet Union would unleash 'militant nationalism and reckless separatism', which would lead to the 'Balkanization' or 'Lebanization' of entire regions and undermine Europe's stability, Yeltsin carried out his historic official visit to Ukraine. In the event, the results probably surpassed the expectations of even the most optimistic of his Ukrainian hosts.

Greeting the Russian delegation, Kravchuk stressed the 'enormous significance' of the treaty which the two sovereign republics were about to sign. He also noted that Ukraine wanted to see the USSR transformed into a union of sovereign states and that it was important that the Soviet parliament officially recognize the sovereignty which the republics had proclaimed so that the centre would not be able to disregard this fact in the new Union treaty. Yeltsin responded with the following words of reassurance:

> We think that after the signing of our treaty, it will be easier for us. It's still possible for the centre to apply pressure on Ukraine and Russia. But it's not possible to apply pressure on the 200 million people of two great republics. On our part, there will be no retreat from sovereignty.[60]

In his subsequent address to the Ukrainian parliament, the Russian leader called for the opening of a new chapter in the history of the relations between the two neighbouring Slavic peoples. Alluding to their troubled past, he acknowledged:

> We are only just beginning to examine our history systematically and objectively. But already it's clear that it's considerably more complex and not as straightforward as it had earlier seemed. . . . We understand that in the history of our two peoples there were not only shining pages but also much that was bitter and unjust.

Portnikov in *Molod Ukrainy*, 14 November 1990, and in Morrison, *Boris Yeltsin*, pp. 200-1.

[60] *Radyanska Ukraina*, 20 November 1990.

After referring to some of the darker moments which the two peoples had experienced during the Soviet period, and the colossal human price which they had paid as a result of ending up 'in a totalitarian state', Yeltsin stated that the realization of the need to change direction, however belated, called for the 'revival of our republics' and the establishment of 'normal' healthy relations between them.

In proposing the basis for a qualitatively new Russian–Ukrainian relationship, the Russian leader reiterated most of the principles which the Russian and Ukrainian democrats had affirmed several months earlier in their joint declaration. The first was that relations between the two republics should be based on equality. Significantly, in stating this, Yeltsin went out of his way to renounce any imperial role for Russia. 'I categorically reject the allegation that Russia is now claiming some special role,' he declared, adding:

> Russia does not aspire to become the centre of some sort of new empire, to obtain advantages in comparison with the other republics. Russia understands better than others the harmfulness of that role, inasmuch as it was Russia which for a long time performed precisely that role. What did it gain from this? Did Russians become free as a result? Wealthy? Happy? You yourselves know the truth, [for] history has taught us: a people that rules over others cannot be fortunate. . . . We are categorical opponents of a unitary state.

The other principles Yeltsin listed were: that relations between Ukraine and Russia should be those between 'sovereign states'; no interference in each other's internal affairs; good-neighbourliness; the exclusion of the use of force, blackmail and pressure against each other; and, that Russian–Ukrainian relations 'should have their own logic' and not be 'dependent on the Union treaty'.

Speaking quite forthrightly, the Russian leader told the Ukrainian deputies that the days when the centre could impose its *diktat* on the republics 'were over', and that now that the republics had asserted their sovereignty there would be 'no going back'. But the centre was 'fiercely resisting' the attempts of the sovereign republics to establish horizontal ties and the curtailing of its old 'monopolistic' powers. The Soviet president was rushing ahead with new plans, without consulting the republics, to shore up the centre's power by switching to a presidential system of government. There could be no illusions: the time for decisions had arrived and they could not be put off. In view of these challenges and new opportunities, Yeltsin said that the conclusion of a treaty between Russia and Ukraine was 'a very timely step' and he expressed the hope that it would usher in the 'most important, most interesting and most meaningful' period of their mutual relations.[61]

Later that day, Yeltsin and Kravchuk signed a formal broad-ranging treaty between their two republics in which all of the above principles were enshrined. Most importantly, the two republics recognized each other's sovereignty, territorial integrity 'within their currently existing borders within the confines of the USSR', the civil liberties and cultural rights of the national minorities living on their respective territories, and agreed to foster cooperation in the economic, defence, foreign policy, ecological and other spheres, and to exchange representatives. The treaty, which hardly referred to the USSR and completely ignored the Union treaty and the centre, was to remain in force for ten years.[62] The two leaders also signed a joint declaration in which they called on the central authorities and the Soviet parliament to recognize the sovereignty of the republics and the rights of each people to self-determination. Stopping short of describing the USSR as an empire, they described the declarations of sovereignty adopted by the republics as reflecting new political realities and being aimed at 'the assertion of the real sovereignty of the republics and the liquidation of totalitarian structures which have outlived themselves'.[63]

At the press conference which followed, Yeltsin again stressed the historic significance of this move to place Russian-Ukrainian relations on a new footing. Earlier in the day, the Russian leader had symbolically presented Kravchuk with a copy of the Pereyaslav Agreement which had been discovered in the Russian archives. He noted, however, that unlike in 1654, the present treaty had been concluded on the basis of the equality of the two states and as such was the first of its kind in the long history of the relations between the two peoples. To underscore that this was a turning point, the treaty had been signed in Kyiv and not in Moscow. Responding to journalists' questions, he said, among other things: that the new Union treaty had to take into account the sovereignty of the

[61] *Molod Ukrainy*, 2 December 1990.
[62] *Radyanska Ukraina*, 21 November 1990.
[63] *Ibid.*, 21 November 1990.

republics and had to be a treaty of sovereign states; that the idea of a treaty between the three Slavic peoples of the USSR was being floated (by Belarus) and that this was something which it would be hard for the centre to struggle with; and that he viewed Crimea as an internal Ukrainian affair. As in his speech to the Ukrainian parliament, Yeltsin also noted that in some respects Ukraine had gone further than the Russian Federation in asserting its sovereignty – he cited the examples of foreign policy and the decision that Ukrainian recruits should serve on the territory of their republic – and added that the Russian Federation would have 'to catch up'. Summarizing what had just been achieved in Kyiv, he concluded his remarks with the words: 'We will fight together!'[64]

Apart from its historic significance, then, the conclusion of the Russian-Ukrainian treaty provided a great boost to both Yeltsin and Kravchuk at a very tricky moment when conservative forces were on the offensive and the USSR Congress of the People's Deputies, scheduled to convene again in December, was preparing to discuss Gorbachev's proposals for a new Union treaty and giving him more executive powers. But no sooner had Yeltsin returned to Moscow than it became evident that the treaty would not be greeted as enthusiastically in Russia as in Ukraine and that the potential problems in Russian-Ukrainian relations had in fact only been temporarily glossed over.

In Kyiv, the treaty produced a brief display of unity within Ukraine's divided parliament and on 22 November the deputies voted unanimously for its ratification. But even in Ukraine, it was made apparent that not everyone welcomed the breakthrough in Russian-Ukrainian relations and the demonstration of cooperation and solidarity between Kravchuk and Yeltsin. The Russian leader's address to the Ukrainian parliament was 'blocked' from being broadcast live in the republic and from being covered by all-Union television. This led the People's Council to issue a statement protesting against the 'informational discrimination' against Yeltsin and calling for an apology to be made to the Russian Federation. Journalists also noticed that Hurenko was not present at the talks between the Ukrainian and Russian delegations – the Ukrainian delegation had, however, included leaders of the opposition – and, at the press conference, had even asked Yeltsin about this.

---

[64] *Ibid.*, and *Robitnycha hazeta* and *Molod Ukrainy*, 21 November 1990.

In Moscow, also on 22 November, the first attempt to ratify the treaty failed. Some Russian deputies insisted that the problem of Crimea would first have to be resolved, while others argued that the agreement went against the idea of a new Union treaty. Complaints were also voiced that Yeltsin had not kept deputies informed about the Russian-Ukrainian treaty negotiations. The following day, though, after 'energetic pressure' from Yeltsin, the Russian parliament ratified the treaty; 140 deputies voted for its ratification, 6 against, and 40 abstained.

A Moscow-based Ukrainian journalist who interviewed a cross-section of Russian deputies at the time reported that there was considerable concern among them not only about the Crimean issue but also about the broader question of Russia's borders with Ukraine and other republics and, in the event of the dissolution of the USSR, what would happen to the Russians who would end up in the new independent non-Russian states. As Colonel General Dmitrii Volkogonov put it, if it had been made clear in the treaty that Ukraine intended to remain united with Russia in some form of a Slavic union or under a new Union treaty, there would be no 'territorial questions' and the Russian Supreme Soviet would have ratified the treaty unanimously. But 'if Ukraine is not with us in a union', the issue of borders and territory was likely to arise. The journalist also observed that the Russian parliament was generally poorly informed about the situation in Ukraine because, as seen from Moscow, the turbulent republic remained 'a total blank spot'.[65]

The signing of the Russian-Ukrainian treaty did not ease the strained political situation in Ukraine. The acrimonious confrontation between the Communist forces and their adversaries continued and, despite more protests, Khmara remained in prison. Nevertheless, during the following weeks the parliament was able to carry out some constructive work and Ukraine signed agreements with other Union republics. Events in Moscow, however, were to cast a shadow over Ukraine's efforts to assert its sovereignty.

---

[65] Vitalii Portnikov, reporting in *Molod Ukrainy*, 24 November 1990.

12

ZIG-ZAGGING TOWARDS INDEPENDENCE

Ukraine rejects Gorbachev's draft Union treaty

On 23 November, Gorbachev presented the draft of the new Union treaty. Describing the nationalities problem as 'the central issue of domestic policy', he again played on fears of bloodshed and anarchy and depicted the proposed treaty as virtually a last-ditch effort to prevent disintegration. By now, though, the Baltic republics and Georgia had made it clear that they would not sign, and Moldova and Armenia had also expressed their misgivings. Nevertheless, the Soviet leader declared that he was convinced that even in the Baltic republics 'most people' were 'in favour of preserving the Union' and accused their 'separatist leaders' of being afraid to agree to hold referendums on the issue of independence.[1]

As expected, the draft of the Union treaty fell well short of what the republics were seeking. It proposed a federation with a centre which would still have substantial powers and there was no mention of the right to secession. There were, however, three controversial changes. First, the status of the autonomous republics was to be upgraded: the new Union treaty would recognize them as sovereign states and as co-signatories. For Ukraine, this concession to the autonomous republics threatened to complicate its problems with Crimea further. Second, the role of the Council of the Federation was to be enhanced from a consultative to a policy- and decision-making body. And, third, the word 'Socialist' in the name Union of Soviet Socialist Republics was to be replaced by 'Sovereign'. As the prominent deputy from the 'Democratic Russia' bloc, Galina Starovoitova, put it, the draft was simply a 'cosmetic renewal' of the 1922 Union treaty. Yeltsin's deputy, Ruslan Khasbulatov was even

[1] TASS, 23 November 1990.

more direct. 'This Union treaty is a big coffin for all of us to lie in', he declared.

The Soviet leadership appeared to spare no effort to promote the Union treaty and to intimidate supporters of independence in the Baltic republics and elsewhere. Ominously, Soviet Defence Minister Dmitrii Yazov and other military leaders began making tough statements about the need to protect the army's and the country's unity; by the end of November they and Gorbachev were threatening to use force in order to protect the rights of Soviet servicemen and military installations in the Baltic republics and elsewhere. On 27 November, the Chief of the General Staff of the Soviet Armed Forces, General Mikhail Moiseev, addressed the Ukrainian parliament and criticized the decision requiring Ukrainian conscripts to serve in their own republic. As an observer noted, 'for some reason, he referred to the Red Army throughout as the "Russian army". Even the Communist "Group of 239" smarted at his speech.' Kravchuk told him firmly but politely that 'We are not about to revoke our decisions'.[2]

The following day, Gorbachev appealed to the Russians not to get carried away with the idea of sovereignty at the expense of the preservation of the Union and what it represented for Russia. Speaking to a gathering of cultural workers in the Kremlin, he rejected the idea that the USSR was an empire. He maintained that 'this state has been formed over a thousand years' and that it had 'formed as a multinational state'. The Russians, he said:

> Bear a special responsibility, whether they like it or not; that is how it has been, that is how it is – they are the backbone. If there is no Russia, there is no Union. And without the Union, Russia is not the same.[3]

A few days later, in a further direct challenge to the sovereignty of the republics, Gorbachev issued a presidential decree which rejected the right of the republics to form their own armed forces and declared null and void republican laws stipulating that conscripts perform military service in their own republic. In another apparent concession to the hard-liners and generals, he replaced his relatively liberal minister of internal affairs, Vadim Bakatin, with the former

[2] Pavlychko, *Letters from Kiev*, p. 126, and *Robitnycha hazeta*, 29 November 1990.

[3] Soviet television, 28 November 1990.

Latvian KGB chief Boris Pugo and appointed Gromov as deputy minister.

Whether Gorbachev was placating the military and his numerous conservative critics or actually considering some form of a general crackdown, he was clearly shifting to the right. More and more calls were heard from hard-liners demanding implicitly or explicitly that a state of emergency to be declared throughout the USSR in order to restore order and preserve the Union. Indeed, on 5 December Yeltsin felt compelled to warn the military that its intervention in politics would lead to catastrophe and a civil war.

Whatever hopes or plans the hard-liners in Ukraine may have had, for their offensive clearly fitted into a broader pattern, the Ukrainian parliament and government did not waver. In fact, during this uncertain time, Ukraine signed treaties with, among others, the republics which were in the forefront of the drive for independence – the three Baltic republics and Georgia. Furthermore, the parliament did not allow itself to be pressured into debating the draft Union treaty. Its deputy chairman, Hrynov, explained that both the majority and the opposition agreed that the draft was incompatible with Ukraine's Declaration of State Sovereignty.[4] At a meeting on 30 November with deputies from Ukraine to the USSR Congress of People's Deputies, Kravchuk reiterated the Ukrainian parliament's position that a decision on the Union treaty would not be made until after a new republican constitution had been approved. At this meeting it was also agreed that a republican referendum should be held on the question of the Union treaty.[5]

When, on 13 December, the CPU held the second part of its Twenty-eighth Congress, Hurenko, though critical of the Gorbachev leadership's record, declared that the 'stabilization' of the situation in the country was the 'order of the day' and expressed support for the Soviet president's 'programme'. He also underscored that the CPU Central Committee was 'firmly' behind the idea of the Union treaty, though it considered that the present draft needed 'further work'. Hurenko's speech contained more than the usual invective against Rukh and its allies, the Ukrainian Party boss claiming that 'under the umbrella of Rukh' there had 'taken place the legalization of nationalism in its most extreme manifestations'.

---

[4] Radio Kyiv, 9 December 1990.
[5] *Robitnycha hazeta*, 2 December 1990.

He also revived the theme heard earlier in the year that the 'anti-Communist forces' and local authorities in Western Ukraine had gone beyond the law by seeking 'to change the very character of the social order' and spread their 'Galician messianism' and the 'Lviv variant' to other regions of the republic. Western Ukrainian 'national radicalism', he said, was in fact only stimulating 'separatist tendencies' within Ukraine itself. It was the 'nationalist and anti-Communist groups', the Ukrainian Party leader claimed, who were the main danger to Ukraine's sovereignty and territorial integrity.

With Hurenko himself revealing that during 1990 over a quarter of a million members had left the Ukrainian Party's ranks, at the Congress some attempts were made to improve its faltering image. At this belated stage, the Congress adopted a resolution condemning the crimes of the Stalin era and totalitarianism. With it being pointed out that there were already fifteen political parties in Ukraine (in fact the new Party for the Democratic Revival of Ukraine had just held its founding Congress and the Democratic Party of Ukraine was just about to), the CPU claimed for itself the role of a party of 'national understanding' as well as guarantor of stability and social justice. The Congress, however, rejected the idea of the depoliticization and 'de-particization' of the state and economic structures. Moreover, the fact that Kravchuk and Fokin also addressed the Congress, with the former once again emphasizing his loyalty to the Party and the 'Socialist choice', only reinforced the impression the CPU still saw itself as a ruling party. The Congress also adopted statutes for the CPU which, on the one hand, asserted the Party's organizational independence, and, on the other, left it as a constituent part of the CPSU.[6]

When the USSR Congress of People's Deputies convened on 17 December, Gorbachev reiterated his appeal for more powers to hold the country together. Yeltsin and others opposed this, arguing that it would result in dictatorship. Gorbachev also surprised many by calling for an all-Union referendum on the future of the USSR and the new Union treaty. Yeltsin dismissed this proposal as a 'waste of time', while the Baltic republics called on the Congress to recognize their independence. On the other hand, a group of fifty-three Soviet officials and deputies at the Congress, ranging from the Moscow

[6] *Ibid.*, TASS, 13 and 14 December; and *Molod Ukrainy*, 15 December 1990.

Patriarch to General Moiseev, urged Gorbachev to declare a state of emergency and to rule by decree in troublesome areas.

On 19 December, with the leaders of the Communist majority now insisting that it had become 'essential' to begin discussing Ukraine's position on the Union treaty 'immediately', the Ukrainian parliament turned its attention to this cardinal issue. But the charged atmosphere in Moscow appears to have brought home the need for a compromise among supporters and opponents of the idea of a Union treaty. The representatives of the parliamentary Commission on Inter-Republican and International Relations and of the Ukrainian government both rejected the variant of the Union treaty proposed by Gorbachev. From the democrats' camp, Yukhnovsky proposed an alternative draft which allowed for a transitional period for the transferal of key powers from the centre to the sovereign republics. Similarly, Mykhailo Horyn also came out in favour of a temporary Union treaty which would allow for the orderly dissolution of the USSR. An additional and noteworthy alternative variant was proposed by Volodymyr Vasylenko, the co-author with several other legal specialists of a draft treaty for the creation of a Commonwealth of [Independent] States. It was this concept, as Radio Kyiv noted, which most deputies seemed to support.[7] Meanwhile, at the Congress of People's Deputies, a group of over forty deputies from Ukraine, including Korotych, issued a statement asserting that it was up to the Ukrainian parliament and the people of Ukraine, not the Congress, to decide what Union treaty, if any, Ukraine would join. 'Not a "renewed" centralized federation, but a commonwealth of sovereign states – that is our position', they declared.[8]

In Moscow, the drama continued. There was a shock on 20 December when, in his address to the Congress of People's Deputies, Soviet Foreign Minister Eduard Shevardnadze warned that dictatorship was taking hold in the USSR and announced his resignation. This, however, only seemed to encourage the conservatives. The Congress supported Gorbachev's plan to hold a referen-

[7] Radio Kyiv and *Robitnycha hazeta*, 20 December 1990. The draft treaty for the creation of a Commonwealth of (Independent) States was published in *Literaturna Ukraina* on 20 December 1990.

[8] *Literaturna Ukraina*, 27 December 1990. See also the statement issued by the secretariat of the parliamentary majority urging support for the Union treaty and that Ukraine's position be discussed without delay, in *Radyanska Ukraina*, 21 December 1990.

dum on the Union treaty. Even more worrying for the Union republics was that the Congress voted in principle to support the proposed draft Union treaty and, however, that the revamped federation of 'sovereign and equal' republics should retain the name Union of Soviet Socialist Republics.

The supporters of genuine sovereignty for the republics and dismantling of the empire, who were clearly in the minority in this conservative body, fought back. On 25 December, Eduard Kozin, an ethnic Russian deputy from the Sumy region in Eastern Ukraine, tabled a motion on behalf of the Interregional group calling on the deputies to vote by name on the formal recognition of the declarations of sovereignty and independence which the republics had made 'as the result of their free self-determination'. But when the proposal was put to the vote it was defeated by 933 votes to 419, with 266 abstentions.

The subsequent details of how individual deputies had voted provided a clearer idea of where people actually stood. It turned out that 49 deputies from Ukraine voted for recognizing the sovereignty of the republics, and 121 against, among them, the Ukrainian Party leader Hurenko, his deputy Hryhorii Kharchenko and the CPU's ideological secretary Ostrozhynsky, as well as Ivashko, Masol, Yelchenko, Oliinyk and Paton. A number of prominent Russian democrats or liberal figures also voted against (e.g. Sobchak, Zaslavskaya), or abstained (e.g. Sergei Stankevich).[9]

On the following day, before the implications of the stand which the leaders of the CPU had taken in the voting could be assessed, the second session of the Ukrainian parliament concluded its work. Having been able to pass a law on the militia and agree on a budget for 1991, it finished on a brighter note befitting the approaching Christmas season: the deputies voted to make Christmas, (celebrated according to the Orthodox calendar on 7 January), Easter and the Feast of the Holy Trinity public holidays.

In Moscow, the Congress of People's Deputies ended with the majority agreeing to the expansion of Gorbachev's presidential powers and the election of his candidate, Gennadii Yanaev, to the newly created position of deputy president. With his position apparently strengthened as a result of his shift rightward, the Soviet president declared in his televised New Year's message that 1991

---

[9] See the list in *Literaturna Ukraina*, 17 January 1991.

would be the decisive year during which 'the fate' of the USSR would be sealed.

Sovereignty Communists versus imperial Communists

In actual fact, from the centre's perspective, the general situation in the Union was continuing to deteriorate. At the end of 1990 it was not even clear if the Soviet government would have a sufficient budget for the next year. The Russian Federation had announced that it would drastically reduce its contribution to the Union budget and Gorbachev was again forced to work out a compromise with Yeltsin. In Georgia and Moldova, ethnic minorities were defying the titular nation and appealing for support from the centre. And in the Baltic republics, defenders of the empire and their military supporters were also urging Gorbachev to intervene and restore order.

In Ukraine, the New Year and Christmas holidays were over-shadowed by the unabating social and political tensions. While the Ukrainian government was preoccupied with dealing with problems connected with unregulated and soaring prices – described by Krav-chuk as 'blatant banditism in the economy' – and the threat of new strikes in the Donbas, the offensive of the hard-line forces continued. Towards the end of December, Pavlychko was again accused in the press of having been a member of the post-war Ukrainian anti-Soviet resistance movement, and in Western Ukraine a recently erected monument to the nationalist leader Bandera was blown up. On 8 January, the student leader Donii was arrested after an old-style search of his apartment and the confiscation of 'incriminating' literature, and two days later Khmara was formerly charged with no less than seven alleged offences.

The 'critical' new year opened on a tragic and disturbing note. With the Western states preoccupied with forcing Iraq to end its occupation of Kuwait, Gorbachev stepped up his pressure against the Baltic republics and other recalcitrant areas. On the Orthodox Christmas Day, he caused alarm by announcing that paratroopers would be used to enforce the draft in the Baltic republics, Armenia, Georgia, Moldova and Western Ukraine. But it soon became clear that in the Baltic republics, at any rate, there was a more sinister aspect to the deployment of airborne troops.

On 10 January, the Soviet president accused Lithuania's leaders of 'gross breaches of, and departures from', the Soviet constitution and of seeking 'to re-establish a bourgeois system that contradicted the interests of the people'. Either Lithuania followed Soviet law, he warned, or presidential rule from Moscow would be imposed. The following day, a surreptitious and self-proclaimed pro-Moscow 'Lithuanian National Salvation Committee' announced that it was taking control of the republic and Soviet troops seized a number of key buildings in Vilnius. On the morning of 13 January, Soviet soldiers backed by tanks attacked the television and radio centre in the Lithuanian capital killing fourteen people. Thousands of Lithuanian citizens formed a human barricade around their parliament and protests against what appeared to be the beginning of a classic Soviet-style military intervention began pouring in from all over the Soviet Union and the outside world.

Ukraine's democratic forces also promptly demonstrated their solidarity with the Lithuanians. On 13 January, Rukh's leader, Drach, sent a message of support to them and on the same day Radio Rossiya announced that Ukrainian blue and yellow flags had been visible at the protests in Moscow. Demonstrations were hurriedly organized in Kyiv, Lviv, Kharkiv and other cities.

The crackdown in Vilnius exposed the widening division in the CPU's ranks between Communists who were determined to defend the sovereignty of Ukraine, even if it meant defying the centre, and those for whom the preservation of the Union and of the CPSU remained the priority. It was demonstrated by the different positions taken by the Presidium of the Ukrainian parliament and the CPU Central Committee as regards the events in Lithuania. On 14 January, the Presidium adopted a statement which, considering the fact that the majority of this body were Communists, was surprisingly forthright – though not as radical as a similar statement issued a few days earlier by Yeltsin – in its condemnation of the methods that the centre was resorting to in attempting to subdue the indomitable Balts. It stated that the Presidium considered 'inadmissible the use of military force on the territory of any republic in order to resolve internal political or inter-ethnic conflicts without the approval of a republic's legitimate organs of government'.[10]

What was also striking about the Presidium's reaction was the principled position adopted by its chairman, Kravchuk. Already on

[10] Haran, *To Kill the Dragon*, p. 158.

12 January, after attending a meeting of the revamped Council of the Federation at which Yeltsin and other republican leaders had opposed the use of heavy-handed methods in the Baltic states, he told journalists in Moscow that he was against the use of force in Lithuania and that he considered its parliament to be the legitimate representative of the will of the Lithuanian people. He also stressed that he did not consider that draft evasion and the general situation in Western Ukraine warranted intervention by the military.[11] He was even more outspoken after the Presidium adopted its statement, telling Radio Kyiv on 15 January – the same day that *Radyanska Ukraina* published another broadside from Kryuchkov, this time effectively justifying the military actions in Lithuania – that Lithuania like Ukraine was a sovereign republic and that external interference in their affairs was impermissible, that the use of military force had to be condemned and human rights protected.

By contrast, Hurenko was to declare on 22 January, after the crisis in the Baltic republics had escalated, that the CPU's Secretariat considered that the 'dramatic events' were being exploited by 'Lithuanian, Latvian, Ukrainian and other national-chauvinists' to fan 'anti-Communist hysteria' and encourage attacks on the Soviet army. He denounced the slogan 'Today – Lithuania, tomorrow – Ukraine' as 'provocative'.[12]

During these tense days, there were other signs suggesting that a realignment of forces was taking place. Significantly, the parliament's new organ, the daily *Holos Ukrainy*, finally published the texts of the Russian-Ukrainian treaty and of Yeltsin's address to the Ukrainian parliament. Furthermore, Kravchuk also came out in defence of Pavlychko and Donii was released.

As the protests against the military actions in Vilnius mounted, Gorbachev denied responsibility for the bloodshed but, even if hard-line elements were indeed trying to force his hand, refused to call the Soviet military to order. Moreover, he unsuccessfully sought to suspend the law on freedom of the press and, after the appearance of a pro-Moscow Latvian 'Salvation Committee', failed to take steps to prevent the repetition of violence in Latvia. Yeltsin headed the spontaneous opposition to the crackdown. He infuriated Gorbachev and the military leaders by travelling to Tallinn and signing a joint

[11] *Molod Ukrainy*, 15 January 1991.
[12] Ukrinform-TASS, 22 January 1991.

statement of protest with the Baltic leaders. Moreover, he also appealed to Russian soldiers stationed in the Baltic republics not to use their arms against civilians and announced that the Russian Federation would have to consider creating a separate Russian army to defend its sovereignty. On 21 January, the Russian leader declared that it was imperative to 'stop the Union leadership's slide toward reaction' and for the republics to maintain a united front against the centre. In this connection, he returned to the idea of a treaty between Russia, Ukraine, Belarus and, this time, also Kazakhstan, as the best line of resistance.[13]

Nevertheless, on 20 January, the day on which about 100,000 people demonstrated in Moscow against the Gorbachev leadership, Soviet troops seized the Lativan Ministry of Internal Affairs, killing and injuring more civilians in the process. After this, Gorbachev either lost his nerve or realized that the opposition to the hard-line course of preserving the crumbling empire was too great. The pressure on the Baltic republics was reduced and the blame for what had happened placed on military units which had supposedly over-reacted and taken matters into their own hands.

The tragic events in the Baltic republics further increased the political polarization of society and aggravated relations between the centre and the sovereign republics. Conservatives and hard-liners felt betrayed by Gorbachev's retreat, while democrats and opponents of empire were outraged by the bloodshed and the Soviet leader's refusal to accept responsibility for what had occurred. In Ukraine, the use of force in the Baltic republics precipitated the crystallization of two divergent tendencies within the CPU – the 'sovereignty Communists', exemplified by Kravchuk, and the 'imperial Communists' led by Hurenko, as the two groups were now to be dubbed.

Seemingly undeterred by Gorbachev's new vacillation, on the eve of the new session of the Ukrainian parliament, at which both the all-Union referendum and the preparation of a new Ukrainian constitution were expected to be discussed, the imperial Communists appeared determined to secure the political initiative for themselves even if meant taking on Kravchuk and the sovereignty Communists publicly. The opening salvo was fired on 24 January, when the CPU's deputy leader, Kharchenko, announced at a press

---

[13] See Morrison, *Yeltsin*, pp. 217-27.

conference that the CPU Politburo had examined the draft, and as yet unpublished, concept of Ukraine's new constitution being prepared by the parliamentary Constitutional Commission, which was headed by Kravchuk, and had serious reservations about it. The working draft apparently did not reflect 'clearly' enough the 'Socialist choice of the people of Ukraine' and proposed dismantling the Soviet system and transforming Ukraine into a presidential and 'bourgeois' republic. Consequently, Kharchenko explained, the Central Committee of the CPU had decided to invite a group of specialists to prepare an alternative variant which was being submitted to the parliament.[14]

Kravchuk seems to have waited until his first official trip abroad as Ukraine's leader to deliver an implicit response. Addressing the Forty-seventh session of the UN Commission on Human Rights in Geneva in early February, he stressed the republic's determination to break with its totalitarian past. He declared:

> Frankly speaking, in our past our legislation also reflected international human rights standards. But their genuine exercise has become possible only now – now that we have set ourselves in earnest the task of building a state governed by the rule of law, effecting a true division of powers, and setting up an independent judiciary. This is not an easy task to fulfill. But we have embarked on this road and we will stay the course.[15]

Surprisingly, though, this important programmatic statement by the head of the Ukrainian parliament does not seem to have been reported by the Ukrainian media.

There was one other crucial issue facing the Ukrainian parliament – the status of Crimea. On 20 January, the local authorities in the peninsula had conducted their referendum in defiance of official Kyiv and the Crimean Tatar minority. The delicacy of the Crimean question and the powerlessness, unwillingness or inability of the leaders of the sovereign Ukrainian state to tackle it had been reflected in official Kyiv's passivity and reluctance even to challenge the constitutionality of the Crimean referendum. Not surprisingly, therefore, the Communist authorities in Crimea had secured an

---

[14] Radio Kyiv, 24 January, and *Radyanska Ukraina*, 29 January 1991.

[15] 'Statement by L.M. Kravchuk, President of the Supreme Soviet of the Ukrainian SSR at the Forty-seventh Session of the UN Commission on Human Rights', *Press Bulletin*, Permanent Mission of the Ukrainian SSR, Geneva, 6 February 1991.

overwhelming vote in favour of the re-establishment of the Crimean Autonomous Soviet Socialist Republic 'as a subject of the USSR and a party to the Union treaty': 81.4% of the eligible voters participated, of whom 93.3% gave their endorsement. The result threatened Ukraine's territorial integrity and further complicated its position as regards the Union treaty.

Kravchuk steers an independent course

With Gorbachev determined to go ahead with the referendum on the future of the USSR – the USSR Supreme Soviet had on 16 January agreed that it would be held on 17 March – and the continuing fear of a possible attempted coup by disgruntled hard-liners, democratic and anti-imperial forces made new efforts to form a united front. Ukrainian democrats, most notably from the PDRU and DPU, played a prominent role in this respect. On 26-7 January representatives of forty-six democratic political parties and movements from ten Union republics, including 'Democratic Russia', Rukh, Sajudis and the Belarusian Popular Front, met in Kharkiv for the inaugural conference of the Congress of Democratic Forces. The majority of the organizations represented at the conference agreed that the main aim of the new coalition would be 'the peaceful liquidation of the totalitarian regime, the dismantling in a civilized way of imperial structures, the creation of sovereign democratic states' and the establishment of a 'Commonwealth of Independent States'. One of the leaders of the PDRU and chairman of the Ukrainian parliamentary Commission on Human Rights, Oleksandr Yemets, was elected interim head of the Congress' Consultative Council.[16]

A fresh attempt was also made to unite Ukraine's democratic forces. A coalition named 'Sovereign Democratic Ukraine', which included Rukh and the main democratic parties and organizations, was cobbled together. Its first action was to create a coordinating committee, 'Referendum – Sovereign Ukraine', to oversee the preparations for the referendum. Yemets was also elected to head this committee.[17]

---

[16] For the programmatic documents adopted by the Congress, see *Literaturna Ukraina*, 7 February 1991.

[17] Radio Kyiv, 26 January and 14 February 1991.

There was also another significant movement towards consolidation, but on a regional basis, which, because of the precedent it was setting, proved highly controversial. On 8 February, Soviet television aired a report from the Transcarpathian region where representatives of the three regional councils of Western Ukraine had agreed to coordinate their activities and to convene a joint assembly. According to the head of the Lviv regional council, Chornovil, the decision had been based on the need for closer coordination in the economic sphere, the region's opposition to Ukraine's signing a new Union treaty and the 'slanderous' disinformation about the situation in Western Ukraine which he claimed the central and republican Party-controlled media were continuing to spread. The first meeting of the 'Galician Assembly', as it was called, was held in Lviv on 16 February. Although the Assembly was to go out of its way to affirm its commitment to the territorial unity of the Ukrainian state, its creation provided ammunition for those intent on playing up the differences between Western and Eastern Ukraine and was seen as a boon to centrifugal tendencies in Ukraine.

The crucial question, however, was how the rift between the sovereignty Communists and the imperial Communists would affect the alignment of forces within the parliament. On 11 February, though, the third session of the parliament got off to a relatively quiet and constructive start; with Kravchuk travelling to attend the World Economic Forum in Davos, Switzerland, the more sensitive issues were left until his return.

For the time being, attention was focused on another event – a conference organized in Kyiv by the People's Council, Rukh and other democratic organizations on Ukraine's security and the creation of a national army. The conference, whose participants ranged from the deputy head of the parliament, Hrynov, to the radical nationalist Shukhevych, issued appeals addressed to non-Ukrainians serving in the huge Soviet armed forces on Ukraine's territory (which were thought by some speakers to constitute up to 70% of the military personnel) and to the Ukrainian parliament. Asserting Ukraine's right to create its own 'depoliticized', professional army consisting of citizens of all ethnic backgrounds, the conference supported the creation of similar national armies in the other sovereign republics and the right of Soviet military personnel to move to their home republics if they chose and serve there. It also urged the Ukrainian parliament to restore the Ukrainian Ministry of Defence and begin creating national armed forces and the conversion of military-industrial enterprises.[18]

For Ukraine's rival political forces, the approaching all-Union referendum was, however, of paramount concern and they concentrated on launching their respective campaigns. On 4 February, the People's Council and Rukh held a press conference at which their representatives denounced the referendum as 'unconstitutional', arguing that it represented an attempt by the centre to appeal over the heads of the leaders and parliaments of the Union republics – the subjects of the Union – directly to the population. It was for Ukraine, they argued, not the centre, to decide whether the republic should be independent or not. The following day, the Central Committee of the CPU issued an appeal reiterating its support for the idea of a Union treaty, expressing its readiness to accept the variant proposed by Gorbachev as its basis and urging the population of Ukraine to vote for a 'Sovereign Socialist Ukraine in a Renewed Union'.[19]

For his part, Kravchuk declared after his return from Switzerland that he was preparing his own alternative variant of a Union treaty. He again insisted that the new formation would have to be a genuine 'union of sovereign states' with 'a clear delineation of powers between the Union and the republics'. No one had 'the right to interfere in Ukraine's affairs', and if the republic were to give the centre 'any kinds of rights', this did not mean 'that it is forever'. He also announced that Shulha was in Moscow participating in the revision of the draft of the Union treaty which Gorbachev had proposed.[20]

On 12, February Kravchuk successfully steered the parliament through a stormy debate about the status of Crimea and persuaded the majority to agree to the restoration of Crimean autonomy 'within the borders of the Ukrainian SSR'. The opponents, who included many of the opposition, argued that the Crimean referendum had been illegal and should not be recognized. Kravchuk, however, maintained that to ignore the wishes of the bulk of the

[18] *Ibid.*, 3 and 4 February 1991. On 28 February, the Ukrainian parliament was to establish a new commission on the internal and external security of Ukraine headed by Vasyl Durdynets.

[19] Ukrinform-TASS and Radio Kyiv, 4 and 5 February 1991.

[20] Radio Kyiv 11 February, and *Komsolskoe znamya*, 13 February 1991.

peninsula's population would undermine 'peace and understanding in Ukraine'. He expressed his confidence that the leaders of Crimea would abide by the Ukrainian constitution and not discriminate against any of the peninsula's national minorities, adding that in any case the Ukrainian parliament retained the right 'to correct' them if they violated the republic's laws. The head of the Ukrainian parliament was helped by the fact that the head of the Crimean regional soviet, Bagrov, sought to reassure the Ukrainian parliament that he and his colleagues were not questioning the peninsula's status as part of Ukraine.[21]

For the moment the Crimean crisis seemed to have been defused and the parliament shifted its attention to the highly charged issue of the all-Union referendum. Voters were to be asked to answer yes or no to the question: 'Do you consider necessary the preservation of the Union of Soviet Socialist Republics as a renewed federation of equal sovereign republics in which the rights and freedoms of an individual of any nationality will be fully guaranteed?'

By now, though, Gorbachev's gamble was backfiring on him. The three Baltic republics, Georgia and Armenia had already refused to participate in the referendum, Moldova seemed poised to join them and the Russian parliament had decided to add its own question tó the all-Union one. Moreover, on 9 February the Lithuanians had called Gorbachev's bluff by holding their own poll in which the overwhelming majority of the republic's eligible voters had come out in support of independence. Furthermore, while Hurenko on 4 February addressing the Central Committee of the CPSU in Moscow had urged the centre to pursue a firmer and more consistent policy in defence of the Union,[22] representatives of the Russian Federation, Ukraine, Belarus and Kazakhstan had met in the Soviet capital to coordinate their approach toward the Union treaty.[23]

Once again the rift between the sovereignty Communists and the imperial Communists was evident. The Presidium of the parliament criticized the wording of the official referendum question and proposed that a second question be asked alongside it: 'Do you consider it necessary that the Union of Soviet Socialist Republics

---

[21] Radio Kyiv, 12 and 13 February 1991.

[22] TASS, 4 February 1991.

[23] Radio Kyiv, 5 February 1991.

become a Union of Soviet sovereign states in which each people will decide its own fate?' Defenders of the CPU's line presented their own resolution insisting that voters be asked only the question formulated by the centre. The opposition remained resolutely opposed to the referendum. Neither of the two resolutions gathered enough support and, although the Group of 239 had clearly split, it appeared that there would be deadlock.

Kravchuk, however, proposed a compromise which in one masterful stroke pulled the rug from under the feet of the imperial Communists, turned the tables on the centre, placated the opposition and boosted his reputation as the defender of the republic's sovereignty. He argued that a Union was necessary, but one built on entirely new principles. Although the centre should have consulted the Union republics about the text of the question in its referendum, he recommended that the Ukrainian parliament 'rise above' this problem and leave the centre's question as it was. But on the other hand, he told the deputies, 'we cannot continue to remain in the position of servants'. He proposed that the parliament formulate an additional question to be asked in the form of a republican survey during the referendum which would clarify what type of a Union voters in Ukraine would be prepared to join. Therefore, instead of 'disrupting' the referendum, it would be 'conducted in such a way that our rights are charted and that we are not drawn into a war with the [USSR] Supreme Soviet and its powers'. To the dismay of the imperial Communists, Kravchuk's proposal was carried by a resounding 288 votes.[24]

While the parliamentary commissions got to work on the formulation of the additional question, the Constitutional Commission met to review the progress on the drafting of the new constitution. Once again, Kravchuk signalled his independence from the CPU's line. He declared that he was in favour of a compromise between a presidential and parliamentary form of government and a bicameral legislature. It was agreed that the Commission would present its final draft to the parliament in March.[25]

On the following day, 15 February, Kravchuk reiterated his dissenting position on the Union treaty, referendum and other issues at a plenum of the Central Committee of the CPU, thereby making

[24] *Ibid.*, 13 and 14 February 1991.
[25] *Ibid.*, 14 February 1991.

it clear that his role as head of the Ukrainian parliament took precedence over his position as a member of the CPU's Politburo. Significantly, the Ukrainian Party press failed to disclose what he actually said. *Izvestiya*, however, commented cryptically that 'for the first time in recent years' the plenum witnessed 'differences of opinion within the republic's leadership regarding how to solve the present difficulties' and that Hurenko 'did not support L. Kravchuk's proposals'.[26]

In the published version of Hurenko's speech, there was no direct attack against Kravchuk. But it was evident from the Ukrainian Party leader's tone and emphasis that his position differed markedly from the centrist (in the Ukrainian spectrum) and 'national Communist' stance which Kravchuk had adopted. Lashing out again at Rukh and 'extremist groups' in Ukraine, Hurenko conjured up the old-style image of a coordinated conspiracy against the USSR involving anti-Communist and separatist forces in the Baltic and other republics, hostile foreign radio broadcasts and Western 'patrons' providing instructions and financial and technical assistance. He argued that the 'most decisive' sphere of activity was to ensure that what he described as the 'referendum on the preservation of the USSR' produced the required result and paved the way for the signing of the new Union treaty. It was also imperative, he stressed, that the new Ukrainian constitution 'bolstered the Socialist nature of our social order'.

Other speakers joined Hurenko in criticizing the Gorbachev leadership for its lack of resoluteness. Some of them also voiced concern about waning Party discipline, complaining about Communist officials seeking to 'ingratiate' themselves with democrats and that the Communist majority in parliament was too passive. Once again, alarm was expressed about the situation in Western Ukraine and the local Party boss Sekretaryuk protested that the Kyiv authorities were allowing the leaders of the Lviv region to continue with their 'experiment of building anti-Communism in one *oblast*'. Expressing the CPU's anger and impatience with the central leadership, the plenum also addressed an appeal to Gorbachev urging him 'to fulfil his duty before the people, the country [and] future

---

[26] *Izvestiya*, 20 February 1991.

generations' and take emergency measures to 'restore order in the state' and economy.[27]

Clearly, however, the democratic authorities in Western Ukraine had long ceased to pay much attention to the anxiety and indignation which they were continuing to generate within the CPU. Rather, they were avidly following the example which the Baltic republics were continuing to set. In fact, at its first session, the Galician Assembly decided on 18 February that the Lviv, Ternopil and Ivano-Frankivsk regions would add a third question to the all-Union referendum: 'Do you agree that Ukraine should become an independent state which itself decides all questions of internal and foreign policy, [and] safeguards the equal rights of citizens regardless of their national or religious background?' The presence at the session of the deputy head of the Ukrainian parliament, Plyushch, who spoke objectively about the record of the democratic authorities in Western Ukraine, underscored the CPU leadership's lack of control over the 'sovereign Communists'.[28]

Kravchuk was wise enough not to challenge the Galician Assembly's decision. Instead, in the continuing heated debates in the parliament about the all-Union referendum, he condemned the 'nihilism' which the Congress of People's Deputies had shown towards the sovereignty of the Union republics, maintaining that 'to disregard' the declarations of sovereignty was a 'very dangerous policy'. But he also warned against rushing things and rupturing the complex system of economic ties that had developed over the decades. Independence was something, as he put it, 'that we will get to, but we still have a certain way to go'.[29]

On 28 February, the Presidium of the parliament presented the proposed text of the republican survey in which the principle of a loose association of sovereign states superseded the idea of a renewed Soviet federation and in which Ukraine's sovereignty was reasserted. It was worded: 'Do you agree that Ukraine should be part of a union of Soviet sovereign states on the principles of the Declaration of the State Sovereignty of Ukraine?' After a further intense debate, the parliament gave its approval by a convincing margin of 277 to 32.[30]

[27] *Radyanska Ukraina*, 16 and 20 February, and Ukrinform-TASS, 15 February 1991.

[28] Radio Kyiv, 18 February 1991.

[29] *Ibid.*, 20 February 1991.

[30] *Ibid.*, 28 February 1991. See also Roman Solchanyk, 'The Changing Political

The result was a humiliating defeat for the imperial Communists and a personal triumph for Kravchuk. It also attested to the implicit formation of a centrist coalition between the sovereignty Communists and the moderate national democrats who marginalized the militants on both sides of the political divide.

A few days later, Kravchuk's rising popularity as an emergent national leader was demonstrated by the cordial reception which he was given during his visit to Lviv. He, for his part, sounded a conciliatory and statesman-like note and called for unity in the struggle for the realization of Ukraine's sovereignty. It was essential, he argued, not to allow political or regional differences to undermine what would have to be a sustained joint effort 'if the republic was to become a genuinely independent state'.[31]

Ukraine votes for sovereign statehood

As the all-Union referendum approached, the political situation in the USSR seemed to be reaching boiling point. On 19 February, appearing on a Soviet television programme, Yeltsin called for the Soviet president's resignation (Kravchuk dissociated himself from this position); five days later, tens of thousands of Muscovites demonstrated in support of the Russian leader; the parliament of the Russian Federation decided to ask Russian voters if they supported the idea of a popularly elected president of the RSFSR; ethnic conflict smouldered in Georgia's South Ossetian region; on 1 March miners, in the Donbas and other parts of the USSR began new strikes in support of higher wages; and, on 3 March, the inhabitants of Latvia and Estonia also voted overwhelmingly for independence.

Against this turbulent background, on 9 March, the Soviet media published a revised version of the proposed Union treaty which only eight of the fifteen Union republics, including Ukraine, had worked on. With time running out before the referendum, the latter had succeeded in extracting concessions from the centre. These included an acknowledgement of the republican declarations of sovereignty and of the right of the republics to establish their own diplomatic

---

Landscape in Ukraine', *Report on the USSR*, vol. 3, no. 24 (14 June 1991) pp. 20-3.
[31] Radio Kyiv, 4 March; *Molod Ukrainy*, 5 March, and *Radyanska Ukraina*, 6 March 1991.

and other ties with foreign states. Nevertheless, the proposed new Union still retained the essential elements of a federal state, complete with the supremacy of federal laws in a number of key spheres, a common citizenship, a federal budget and federal taxes. Yeltsin rejected it outright, while Kravchuk stated that he had 'reservations about practically every article' in the document.[32]

During the final days before the all-Union referendum, the Gorbachev leadership used every means at its disposal, especially, the central media, to drum up support for a renewed Soviet federation. In a series of emotional appeals, it depicted the referendum as a choice between order, harmony and continued Soviet strength on the one hand, and chaos, bloodshed and disintegration on the other. When it came to the moment of truth, though, the defenders of the Soviet federation managed to achieve only a rather hollow victory and not the convincing triumph which they had hoped for. Although overall about 76% of those who participated in the referendum voted in the affirmative, this was only equivalent to about 58% of the USSR's eligible votes. Six Union republics boycotted the referendum, in several of the remainder the wording of the centre's question was changed, and in Russia and Ukraine support for the preservation of the Union was eclipsed by the voters' more enthusiastic endorsement of the supplementary republican assertions of sovereignty. The strongest support for a renewed federation came from the more backward or politically docile areas – rural Russia, the Central Asian republics, Kazakhstan and Belarus. Embarrassingly for the Gorbachev leadership, barely half of the Muscovites who voted (only 34% of the eligible voters) supported the centre's position, and in Yeltsin's home city of Sverdlovsk almost 70% of the voters opposed it.

In Ukraine, voter turnout was high, with 80.2% of eligible voters participating in the all-Union referendum and 82.2% casting their vote in the republican poll. Some 70.5% of the voters, or 58% of the registered electorate, answered yes to the question posed in the all-Union referendum. But a significantly higher number of those who voted – 80.2% – answered in the affirmative in the republican survey, thereby simultaneously endorsing Ukraine's Declaration of Sovereignty and specifying the terms under which Ukraine would be prepared to join a new Union. Even in Crimea and the eastern

[32] *Holos Ukrainy*, 3 April 1991.

and southern regions, support for Ukraine's sovereignty was given by 83% upwards of those who voted, and only in Crimea did the vote for the preservation of the Union marginally surpass that of the backing for Ukrainian sovereignty (87.6% to 84.7%). Significantly, in the still largely Russified Kyiv, the majority actually rejected Gorbachev's proposal (only 44.6% voted in favour), while 78.2% endorsed the proposition presented in the republican poll. The vote in support of asserting republican sovereignty would have been even higher if many Western Ukrainians had not opposed or boycotted the republican survey in favour of voting for independence. In fact, in Western Ukraine, the majority of voters not only massively rejected the idea of a renewed Soviet federation but also voted overwhelmingly in their regional poll for Ukrainian independence.[33]

With his hand strengthened by the results, Kravchuk seemed to be imbued with new confidence and forcefulness. The republican ballot, he told *The Independent*, had 'put Ukraine on the path of sovereignty and independence' and the results of the all-Union one had 'no meaning' for him. But he was also careful to point out that he remained committed to an evolutionary approach even if this meant distancing himself from his ally in the push for republican sovereignty – Yeltsin. 'I support Yeltsin on sovereignty', he explained, 'but I don't support Yeltsin's moves towards destabilizing the country. We have to avoid all actions that can lead to civil war'.[34]

At his first major press conference after the voting, Kravchuk declared that the people of Ukraine had overwhelmingly made their choice and that there could be no turning back. They had come out in support of full-fledged sovereignty and Ukraine's participation, during what he described as a transitory period, in a loose union of sovereign states. The parliamentary leadership, he indicated, was determined to push ahead in this direction: the Presidium of the Ukrainian parliament had appointed a working commission consisting of Yukhnovsky, Shulha and Kotsyuba to elaborate the republic's position on the new Union treaty in accordance with the results of the republican survey, and the Constitutional Commission

---

[33] See the preliminary results provided by Ukrinform in *Robitnycha hazeta*, 20 March 1991. See also Roman Solchanyk, 'The Referendum in Ukraine: Preliminary Results', *Report on the USSR*, vol. 3, no. 13 (29 March 1991), pp. 5–7.

[34] See Susan Viet's interview with Kravchuk in *The Independent*, 23 March 1991.

was preparing to submit its draft concept of the new Ukrainian constitution to the parliament and convene a special conference at which this document and alternative variants could be discussed. In the clearest statement yet of his new credo, the head of the Ukrainian parliament, who at the same press conference pointed out that at the last plenum of the Central Committee of the CPU he had disagreed with the line it was prescribing, urged that the result 'should be the constitution of a new, democratic and free Ukraine enjoying full rights'.[35]

Behind all this there was probably one other new factor which Kravchuk had taken into account – that sooner or later he would present himself as a candidate for the presidency of Ukraine and that he needed to broaden his support. Certainly this was the general trend in the USSR: Gorbachev had assumed the Soviet presidency and Yeltsin, having secured an endorsement from the Russian voters for the idea of a popularly elected president of the Russian Federation, was moving in this direction. When, on 29 March, the Constitutional Commission met again, after 'stormy' debate, it endorsed a draft concept of the new Ukrainian constitution which foresaw the establishment of a unitary presidential republic with a bicameral legislature.[36]

Although after the all-Union referendum and the republican polls Ukraine's imperial Communists sought to put on a brave face, they also saw that the writing was on the wall. Instead of sticking to the hopeless cause of preserving the Soviet federation intact, Hurenko modified his line and at the beginning of April began telling workers in Kyiv that 'of course, some republics, like Georgia and Lithuania will leave the Union'. But he also invoked Gorbachev's claim that it was unthinkable for Ukraine to go its own way and undermine the rump Union. Nevertheless, even the Ukrainian Party boss now stated that he disagreed with the Soviet president on the need for the new Union treaty to be signed 'immediately'.[37]

The results of the republican survey and the appearance of a new political centre in Ukrainian politics seemed to clear the air and usher in a more constructive period in the parliament's work. During the following weeks the parliament was able to pass laws on freedom of

[35] *Holos Ukrainy*, 3 April 1991.
[36] Radio Kyiv, 30 March 1991.
[37] *Robitnycha hazeta*, 5 April 1991.

conscience and religious organizations, protection of the environment, the rehabilitation of victims of political repression, external economic activity, enterprises, banks and banking activity, protection of the consumer, and adopt resolutions on the establishment of a stabilization fund and recognizing different forms of land ownership. On 5 April, Khmara was freed from custody, although preparations for his trial continued. A week later, though, he was to be detained again when he sought to meet with the striking miners in the Donbas.

There was no let-up though in the general economic crisis and miners in Russia and eastern Ukraine were still continuing their strikes. Indeed, throughout the entire spring the seemingly intractable problem of placating Ukraine's disaffected miners, who were supported by democratic forces, was to sap the energy of the Ukrainian leadership. Without being able to improve their economic and living conditions, Kravchuk's appeals to the Donbas miners not to undermine Ukraine's sovereignty through their industrial action had little effect.

In early April, after the Soviet government introduced sharp price increases, the industrial protests spread, especially among Belarusian workers. In Russia, Yeltsin skilfully used the opportunity to boost his popularity. When at the beginning of April, the Russian parliament agreed to the direct election in June of an executive president of Russia, the portents for Gorbachev and the centre became even grimmer.

Laying the foundations of sovereign and democratic statehood

Although Gorbachev had sought to depict the results of the all-Union referendum as a victory which would accelerate the signing of a new Union treaty, in actual fact he was no longer able to paper over the cracks in the Soviet federation. On 19 April, during a visit to Japan, he signalled another shift in the Kremlin's position and his apparent new readiness to face up to political realities and seek a compromise with the Union republics. He announced that on his return to Moscow he would try to hammer out an agreement on the terms of the new Union treaty with the nine republics which had participated in the referendum.

By now, the fifteen Union republics had divided into three clusters. The six republics which had come out for independence

– Lithuania, Latvia, Estonia, Georgia, Armenia and Moldova – had already begun to coordinate their activities. Ukraine belonged to the second informal coalition which was formed by the five largest republics – Russia, Ukraine, Belarus, Kazakhstan and Uzbekistan – who favoured a confederal arrangement and sought a 'union of states' as opposed to a 'union state'. The third cluster was composed of the four remaining republics: Azerbaijan, Kyrgyzstan, Tajikistan and Turkmenistan. Kyrgystan, however, gravitated towards the second group, while Azerbaijan, still reeling from the effects of the prolonged Soviet pacification, remained an unknown factor.

It was perhaps not entirely fortuitous then that Gorbachev's announcement came a day after a consultative meeting in Kyiv of the representatives of the working groups on the Union treaty of the legislatures of the Russian Federation, Ukraine, Belarus, Kazakhstan and Uzbekistan. Convened on the initiative of the Ukrainian parliament, its purpose was to enable the second cluster of republics to work out a common negotiating position on the Union treaty. Among the points they agreed on was that only Union republics should be subjects of the new treaty and that they would henceforth refer to themselves as states; that it was the Union republics which invested their inhabitants with citizenship and not the Union; and, that the centre's prerogatives should be minimized.[38]

On 23 April, with the strikes in different parts of the USSR still continuing and the situation becoming desperate, Gorbachev met in a government *dacha* in Novo Ogarevo outside Moscow with leaders of the nine republics which had participated in the referendum. Kravchuk, however, was absent – he was on an official visit to Germany – and Ukraine was represented by Fokin. In return for a number of major concessions, the Soviet president managed to obtain the agreement of the leaders of the Union republics to work together with him to stabilize the political and economic crisis in the USSR and to end the strikes. The ten signatories of the five-point deal produced by the meeting agreed that the signing of a new Union treaty by the 'sovereign states' was a top priority for overcoming the crisis. Within six months of the new treaty being

[38] Radio Kyiv, 18 April 1994. See also Roman Solchanyk, 'The Draft Union Treaty and the "Big Five"', *Report on the USSR*, vol. 3, no. 18 (3 May 1991), pp. 16-18.

signed, a new Soviet constitution would be adopted and this would be followed by elections to 'the organs of power of the Union'. All the signatories with the exception of the Soviet president recognized the right of the remaining six Union republics to decide independently whether they would sign the new treaty, but they also made it clear that only those who did would get 'most favoured nation' status in the economic sphere. Yeltsin subsequently also revealed that Gorbachev had accepted that autonomous republics would not sign the Union treaty independently but as members of the delegation of the state which they were part of.

Although the 'nine plus one' agreement immediately lent itself to different interpretations by the centre and the Union republics, it was generally hailed as a major breakthrough. It eased the long-standing tensions between the centre and the Union republics, and especially between Gorbachev and Yeltsin. But the more sceptical critics, ranging from nationalists in Western Ukraine to imperial Communists, concluded that the agreement essentially amounted to a pact between Gorbachev and Yeltsin. In return for vague promises about a 'cardinal enhancement of the role of the Union republics', Gorbachev had won support for the unpopular anti-crisis programme of the new Soviet Prime Minister Valentin Pavlov and could once again present himself as the defender of order. On the other hand, 'Gorbachev would from now on be a political hostage not of the hard-liners, but of Yeltsin and his allies in the republics'.[39]

Kravchuk was distinctly cautious about the Novo Ogarevo agreement. He welcomed the fact that finally there was 'agreement that the Union will be a union of sovereign states, that the centre of economic and political life should be transferred to the republics', but noted all the same that 'this statement has no juridical force'.[40]

Rather than concentrate on the new Union treaty, the head of the Ukrainian parliament remained preoccupied with guiding the efforts being made to lay the foundations of Ukraine's sovereign and democratic statehood. Already, on 18 April, the Verkhovna Rada had agreed to a restructuring of the republican government and the

[39] See Morrison, *Yeltsin*, pp. 253-8, and Roman Solchanyk, 'The Gorbachev-Yeltsin Pact and the New Union Treaty', *Report on the USSR*, vol. 3 (10 May 1991), pp. 1-3.

[40] *Nezavisimaya gazeta*, 5 May 1991.

replacement of the Council of Ministers by a Cabinet of Ministers headed by a prime minister. Fokin was endorsed in this position. On the same day, a three-day 'republican scientific-practical conference' on 'The Concept and Principles of a New Constitution of the Ukrainian SSR' had opened in Kyiv. It had seen the expected clash between representatives of the Constitutional Commission and Hurenko and other defenders of the CPU's line. The latter had spoken out against the 'de-ideologization of the constitution' and continued to insist that the new constitution embody the idea of 'the Socialist choice' and make clear that Ukraine intended 'remaining a member of a renewed Union of Soviet Socialist Republics'.[41]

The areas of agreement and disagreement between the parliamentary majority and the opposition were again thrown into relief on 25 April when both camps delivered programmatic statements. The leader of the Communist majority, Oleksandr Moroz, criticized the Soviet government's anti-crisis programme and called on the republican authorities to propose their own variant; he also spoke of the need for 'constructive cooperation' for the purposes of stabilizing the political and economic situation in Ukraine and bolstering the republic's sovereignty. On the other hand, the People's Council called for the proclamation of Ukraine's independence, introduction of a national currency, adoption of a law on republican citizenship, and the 'de-particization' of the security, military and economic institutions on the republic's territory. Not only was an implicit working compromise arrived at, but also the moderates in both factions united to issue a strong rejoinder, proposed by the opposition, to the hard-line and imperial-minded 'Soyuz' (Union) faction in the USSR Congress of People's Deputies which had again called for the imposition of a state of emergency in order to restore order and save the Union. The statement adopted by the Ukrainian parliament condemned Soyuz's appeal as an attempt by extreme conservative forces to turn the clock back and return the USSR to the times of the 'administrative-repressive system'. In it, the Ukrainian parliament let it be known that it was dealing with the republic's problems and that it considered such

[41] Radio Kyiv, 14-17, 22-3 May 1991; Roman Solchanyk, 'Ukraine Considers a New Republican Constitution', *Report on the USSR*, vol. 3, no. 23 (7 June 1991), pp. 23-6.

calls as those of Soyuz to be an impermissible challenge to Ukraine's sovereignty.[42]

That very evening, though, deputies and the Ukrainian public were given something else to think about by the coverage of Kravchuk's visit to Bonn by the Central Soviet television. There had already been frequent complaints about what many in Ukraine considered to be the central media's insensitive or biased handling of Ukrainian topics and, because Ukrainian television did not have any correspondents based abroad, the republic's dependence on central Soviet television's coverage of events in the outside world. Now, at this delicate stage of the tug of war between the old imperial centre and a republic seeking to assert its sovereignty, Soviet television's main evening news programme, Vremya, broadcast a report from Bonn in which its correspondent, Kondratev, mocked the fact that at the meeting with the German president and foreign minister, the Ukrainian side had preferred to use Ukrainian, rather than Russian. He invited viewers to imagine what would happen if a Bavarian delegation came to the USSR and insisted on conducting talks in the 'Bavarian dialect'. Kravchuk was outraged and his immediate reaction showed it. He told Radio Liberty's Ukrainian Service – the very 'enemy voice' which he as an ideological functionary had combated for years – that he had instructed Foreign Minister Zlenko, who was accompanying him, to send a telegram to the Soviet television authorities stressing that 'we will never let such things by, especially lies and insinuations'.[43]

While Ukraine's parliamentary factions were preparing for the next round of the struggle over the constitution, Kravchuk and Fokin were at least given a respite from the industrial unrest plaguing the republic and the USSR at large when the miners decided to end their strikes. Armed with the concessions which Gorbachev had made in Novo Ogarevo, Yeltsin was able to transfer control of the mines in Russia from the centre to the republic (something Ukraine

[42] Radio Kyiv and Ukrinform-TASS, 25 April 1991.

[43] In fact, it was the author who interviewed Kravchuk in Munich about this incident for Radio Liberty. I recall how anxious Kravchuk and members of his delegation were for the interview to be broadcast to Ukraine as soon as possible in order, as they put it, 'to break the centre's monopolistic hold over the information sphere'. After the interview was broadcast, several newspapers in Ukraine published excerpts from it. See, for instance, *Za vilnu Ukrainu* (Lviv), 30 April, and *Literaturna Ukraina*, 9 May 1991.

had already done, at least nominally) and thereby persuade the Russian miners to return to work. In early May, Ukraine's miners also began to return to work after their nine-week-old strike. But the retreat by the Donbas miners had its price. At the beginning of the month, the Ukrainian government and the Council of the Federation of Independent Trade Unions of Ukraine concluded an agreement on social protection: it committed the increasingly hard-strapped Ukrainian authorities to introduce a new minimum living standard, establish wage indexation linked to price rises, and, in case of a worsening of supplies, to undertake to distribute goods.[44]

The battle over the new constitution and the future political profile of the Ukrainian state was resumed on 14 May when, on behalf of the Constitutional Commission, Kravchuk presented its draft concept to the parliament for its consideration. It was supported in principle by the opposition (which insisted that references to Ukraine's joining a new Union be deleted), but drew a protest from Hurenko, who claimed that it had not taken into account the CPU's position and the results of the all-Union referendum. The subsequent heated debates revealed that although the Communist majority may not have been united on all issues, when it came to defending the CPU's cardinal interests, namely preserving the social and political order in Ukraine, and even the name 'the Ukrainian Soviet Socialist Republic', it was still a cohesive enough and powerful force. Indeed, it was thanks in no small measure to Kravchuk's political skills that a vote of no confidence in the work of the Constitutional Commission was averted.

During a pause in the debate, the president of Croatia, Frano Tudjman, paid an official visit to Ukraine. He was probably the first foreign leader to speak openly of the independence which he said both his republic and Ukraine were seeking. Despite the display of mutual solidarity, Kravchuk showed more caution and restricted himself to speaking, in public at any rate, about the analogous quest of the two republics for sovereign statehood within a union of sovereign states.[45]

With the Communist majority threatening to undo the proposals to move ahead with the political transformation of the Ukrainian state, on 23 May Yemets proposed on behalf of the People's Council

[44] Radio Moscow, 1 May 1991.
[45] Radio Kyiv, 20 and 21 May 1991.

that a referendum be held in which the population of Ukraine would choose between the different concepts of the constitution being proposed by the majority and the minority. The deputies decided instead that the Working Commission would 'refine' the draft concept by June and submit it again to the parliament but that the most sensitive questions concerning the name of the state, the state symbols, the system of government and the 'socialist choice' would have to be put to a referendum. Although the struggle over the constitution still remained undecided, Kravchuk and the supporters of change were left with at least some grounds for satisfaction, not least of which being the fact that the idea of direct presidential elections was approved and that the working title of the draft concept was designated 'Constitution of Ukraine'.[46]

The following day, Kravchuk flew to Moscow to take part in negotiations on the new Union treaty which were again held in Novo Ogarevo. According to his legal assistant, Ivan Tymchenko, who accompanied him to the Soviet capital, the leaders of the Union republics and autonomous republics were whisked off from the Kremlin to Novo Ogarevo without their aides but Gorbachev had an entire team of experts to assist him. Tymchenko, however, had prepared a critique of Gorbachev's draft Union treaty for Kravchuk as well as an alternative variant for the latter to work from. This helped the Ukrainian leader to maintain a clear and well-reasoned position and thereby not only to withstand the Soviet leader's pressure to rush ahead with the conclusion of a new Union treaty but also to influence the leaders of some of the other Union republics.[47]

On his return to Kyiv, Kravchuk gave a major interview on Ukrainian television about how the Novo Ogarevo process was progressing and the position which he had adopted. Unlike the upbeat appraisals of the second meeting given by Gorbachev and Yeltsin, who both expressed confidence that an agreed draft Union treaty would be ready by the following month, the Ukrainian leader emphasized that only the principles on which the new treaty should be based were being discussed and that the preparation of an acceptable document still required considerable effort and time.

---

[46] *Ibid.*, 14-17, 22-23 May 1991, and Solchanyk, 'Ukraine Considers a New Republican Constitution'.

[47] Author's interview with Tymchenko.

There was 'still insufficient agreement on many key questions' and it would be 'unrealistic' to attempt to 'rush' things, he maintained. For instance, the issue of the ownership of property needed to be resolved before a new treaty could be considered. Here, indicating the kind of timeframe which he envisioned, Kravchuk recommended that the Ukrainian parliament and government should work out 'by, say, 1 October', the questions connected with establishing the republic's jurisdiction over the resources and assets on its territory. Insisting on a clear delineation of powers between the centre and the republics in the treaty, he also 'categorically opposed' the idea of any spheres of joint jurisdiction.

Kravchuk also revealed that he and some of the other republican leaders had successfully pressed for the 'de-ideologization' of the treaty, and for it to be called the 'Treaty on the Union of Sovereign States'. In fact, the head of the Ukrainian parliament used this occasion to stress publicly once again that, although he remained a member of the Politburo of the CPU, he had to represent the interests of the entire people of Ukraine and not any one political party. He also revealed that preliminary agreement had also been reached that the new union would be open-ended and that not all states would join it at once. Kravchuk said he had opposed participation in the new treaty of existing Soviet institutions, such as the Supreme Soviet of the USSR, and had insisted that only the states joining the new union and the president of the USSR, representing the centre, could be parties to it. He was also able to reassure his Ukrainian audience that Bagrov had stated in Novo Ogarevo that he was confident that the Supreme Soviet of the Crimean Autonomous SSR would agree to Crimea signing the new treaty as part of the delegation of Ukraine.

There was, however, one inconsistent note in the interview: the Ukrainian leader stated that he leaned towards the idea that the 'new formation of sovereign states' should be a 'federative state union' based 'solely on the powers which will be delegated to it'. It is unclear why at this stage he spoke of the future union as a federation rather than a confederation or commonwealth, something which seemed to contradict the outcome of March's republican poll.[48] This only fuelled suspicion and fears on the part of the opponents of a

[48] The interview was published in *Holos Ukrainy* on 29 May 1991.

revamped Union, who had been galvanized by the Novo Ogarevo process and were busy organizing new protests.

A few days later, *Le Monde* published its own interview with the Ukrainian leader in which he provided some indications about his developing political strategy. 'We must first adopt the new constitution next January', he explained, then adopt a law on a multi-party system, after which, in about April or May of 1992, parliamentary and presidential elections could be held in Ukraine. Because of the uncertain political situation and in order 'to defend Ukraine's interests', it might, however, become 'urgently necessary to consolidate the executive' before then by electing 'a strong president by universal suffrage'. 'I hope to be president', Kravchuk confirmed. What would the sovereign Ukrainian state be called, he was asked. 'Ukraine! Without epithets!' he declared. 'And not the Ukrainian Soviet Socialist Republic. Epithets pass, but Ukraine remains.'[49]

The Central authorities, however, continued to maintain the semblance that the new Union treaty was just around the corner. The next meeting in the Novo Ogarevo process was held on 3 June, after which the chairman of the USSR Supreme Soviet, Anatolii Lukyanov, declared that substantial progress had been made and that it had been agreed that the all-Union parliament would retain its powers until the new Union organs were formed.[50] The pressure from the centre for the new Union treaty to be concluded as soon as possible was stepped up after Gorbachev was formally invited on 13 June for talks with the leaders of the 'Group of Seven' (G7) leading industrial states at their forthcoming summit in mid-July in London. Thus, at a third meeting in Novo Ogarevo on 17 June to discuss the Union treaty, which was held two days after Yeltsin was elected president of the Russian Federation, a working draft of the treaty was finally approved and, after being presented to the public the following day by the Soviet president, was sent to the parliaments of the Union republics for their consideration.

Kravchuk, who was preoccupied during this period with crucial parliamentary work connected with laying the foundations of Ukraine's sovereign and democratic statehood, especially working out a compromise on the concept of the new Ukrainian constitution, remained relatively unforthcoming about the new Union

[49] *Le Monde*, 29 May 1991.
[50] TASS, 5 June 1991.

treaty. On 7 June, the Verkhovna Rada had quietly passed a law asserting the republic's jurisdiction over all-Union enterprises and organizations on the republic's territory. A week later, it was announced that the Presidium of the Ukrainian parliament had created a new council of Ukrainian and foreign advisers to advise on constitutional law, privatization, banking and taxation. Among its members was the Geneva-based management specialist Bohdan Hawrylyshyn and the Hungarian-American millionaire financier and philanthropist, George Soros.[51] A few days later, the Ukrainian parliament voted to mark the first anniversary of the adoption of the Declaration of State Sovereignty by designating it as 'Ukraine's Independence Day' and by making it a public holiday.[52]

Kravchuk scored another significant domestic victory when, on 19 June, the Ukrainian parliament approved without much trouble the revised concept of the new Ukrainian constitution. Although it included the reference to the 'Socialist choice' which the majority had insisted on, the document retained most of the democratic and organizational principles and provisions that the Constitutional Commission and the opposition had supported. It envisaged a democratic and unitary presidential republic with a unicameral professional parliament, an independent judiciary and the government consisting of a prime minister nominated by the president and endorsed by the parliament, and a cabinet of ministers.[53]

At this juncture, Kravchuk also informed the parliament that although a new draft of the Union treaty had been submitted to the parliaments of the Union republics, there was still disagreement on the 'structure and organs of power of the new Union' as well as the system of taxation. The Ukrainian leader explained to the *Financial Times* that he had 'initialled the draft treaty so it could be passed to its [Ukraine's] parliament for discussion; there was no commitment to sign it at the end of the day'. He also declared that Ukraine would not sign any such treaty until 'sovereignty is enshrined in the Ukrainian constitution' and that this would take 'until the year-end at least'.[54]

---

[51] Ukrinform-TASS, 7 June, and Radio Kyiv, 13 June 1991.

[52] Radio Kyiv, 18 June 1991.

[53] *Ibid.*, 19 June 1991. The text of the concept was published in *Radyanska Ukraina*, 3 July 1991.

[54] See Chrystia Freeland's report about Kravchuk in the *Financial Times*, 20 June 1991.

In the meantime, Ukraine's national democratic forces were stepping up their campaign against the new Union treaty but were unable to overcome their own internal rivalries and to cement a genuinely solid coalition. At the beginning of June, for instance, the URP held its second congress. It saw unpleasant exchanges between moderates and radicals and Khmara's militancy and brusqueness apparently caused Chornovil to have a heart attack.[55]

Ukraine sticks to its chosen path

Against the background of widespread protests organized by Rukh and its allies against the signing of a new Union treaty, and with the Union of Ukrainian Students threatening to begin a new protest hunger strike outside the legislature building, on 27 June the Verkhovna Rada discussed the draft which had emerged from the Novo Ogarevo process. By now, however, the parliaments of seven of the nine Union republics which had participated in the negotiations with the centre had approved the draft, thus intensifying the pressure on the Ukrainian and Russian parliaments to make up their minds.

Although the ardent exchanges in the Ukrainian parliament again brought into sharp relief the polarization on this issue, it emerged that even Hurenko and other supporters of the Union treaty had reservations about the draft. Deputies were concerned that the prospective new 'Union of Soviet Sovereign States' was envisaged as a *'sovereign federative democratic state'* [author's emphasis], which would be a subject of international law. This, and the division of powers proposed in the draft appeared to undermine Ukraine's sovereignty.

Kravchuk, who during an interval went outside to reassure demonstrators that the parliament would not make any hasty decision, was instrumental in producing a compromise intended to buy more time. He reiterated that the people of Ukraine had indicated in the republican poll that they wanted to live in a union of sovereign states but noted that the proposed draft treaty still contained numerous provisions which were unacceptable for Ukraine and would require further work. Somewhat unexpectedly, no less than 345 deputies voted to postpone taking any decision on the

[55] Haran, *To Kill the Dragon*, pp. 177–8.

draft until it had been studied more closely and brought into line with Ukraine's Declaration of Sovereignty. They decided to give the parliamentary commissions until 1 September to prepare their comments and changes, after which a parliamentary working group would by 15 September complete the work and submit a revised draft to the new session of the parliament.[56]

This emphatic decision by the Ukrainian parliament to put the interests of the republic first upset Gorbachev's hopes to have a Union treaty signed before mid-July and, suddenly and dramatically, brought home what Kravchuk had already indicated, that it was unlikely that Ukraine would be prepared to sign a new Union treaty in the foreseeable future. When, in early July, the Russian parliament approved in principle the draft Union treaty, Ukraine remained the only Union republic which had participated in the Novo Ogarevo process still to be biding its time.

During the first week of July, which saw the final days of the work of the second session of the parliament, issues connected with enhancing Ukraine's sovereignty continued to dominate. The deputies approved a broad republican anti-crisis programme prepared by Fokin's government and adopted legislation creating the institution of a popularly elected executive president. The presidential election was scheduled for 1 December 1991. Within days the URP was to nominate Lukyanenko as its candidate and by the end of the month some of the more radical elements within Rukh's leadership, as well as the Coordinating Council of the Galician Council, were to propose Chornovil.

On 5 July, Gorbachev unexpectedly held a meeting in Kyiv with German Chancellor Helmet Kohl. This angered many of the Ukrainian deputies who, in view of the fact that the Soviet president had not informed the Ukrainian parliament and government in advance, considered that he had shown total disregard for Ukraine's sovereignty. Pavlychko, the head of the parliamentary foreign relations commission told the parliament that it 'ought to draw serious lessons' from what had happened and strive to ensure that 'the – for the time being – Union president and foreign politicians

---

[56] Radio Kyiv, 27 and 28 June 1991; Ukrinform-TASS, 27 June 1991; and, *Literaturna Ukraina*, 4 July 1991. See also Roman Solchanyk, 'Ukraine and the Union Treaty', *Reports on the USSR*, vol. 3, no. 30 (26 July 1991), pp. 22-4.

take into account our Declaration of the State Sovereignty of
Ukraine and our desire to head towards the complete independence
of the Ukrainian state.'[57]

The events of the next few weeks were to demonstrate, though,
that this still remained a case of easier said than done. The first
anniversary of Ukraine's Declaration of Sovereignty was officially
celebrated with considerable pride and fanfare. Kravchuk, with one
eye no doubt on the forthcoming presidential contest, took up the
mantle of national leader and statesman. Speaking at a ceremonial
meeting on 13 July, he pointed out that Ukraine had already had
two chances during its history 'to renew its statehood' – during
Khmelnytsky's 'War of Liberation' in the middle of the seventeenth
century and 'after the revolution of 1917 – but for various reasons
these had failed. 'Right now, we have another, and it seems a
realistic, opportunity to make our dream come true', he declared.

> Our generation bears on its shoulders the burden of tasks which
> our ancestors were unable to complete and of responsibility
> before our successors. We will be worthy of this responsibility
> and not retreat before any challenges. Let us unite our forces
> in the historic work for the glory of Ukraine and the well-being
> and flourishing of its people.

Reviewing what had been achieved during the past year, Kravchuk noted that during a relatively short, but complex, period
considerable progress had been made towards establishing Ukraine
as a democratic state based on the rule of law, the division of powers
between the legislative, executive and judicial branches, a multi-
party system and respect for the rights of national minorities. He
pointed out that during the past year the Ukrainian parliament had
'adopted 220 legal acts, including 46 laws, relating to the 'constitutional foundations' of Ukraine's statehood', 'democracy',
'economic independence' and 'the transition to a market economy'.
In the sphere of foreign relations, 'a profound rethinking' and
reorientation of Ukraine's foreign policy had taken place and
produced 'positive results' in the form of bilateral treaties with other
states, particularly its neighbours, Russia, Belarus, Poland and Hungary, visits to Kyiv by foreign leaders, the opening in Kyiv of foreign

[57] Radio Kyiv, 6 July 1991.

consulates and visits to Hungary, Switzerland and Germany by the head of the Ukrainian parliament.[58]

Kravchuk's claims about the progress which democracy was making in Ukraine were marred, however, when on 18 July Khmara was detained yet again. This time he was brutally seized from his hotel room in central Kyiv by riot police in full view of foreign journalists and democratic deputies. Kravchuk's role, if any, in this incident remains unknown, but it is not inconceivable that the continuing political farce with Khmara was now being used by hard-liners as a way not only of getting even with the radical deputy but of complicating matters for Kravchuk and maintaining political tensions.

During the second half of July, as Yeltsin and leaders of other Union republics prepared to sign the new Union treaty and worked out further compromises with Gorbachev, Ukraine continued to stand its ground. The Russian leader, who on 20 July had taken the bold step of 'depoliticizing' Russia's state agencies by banning all political party activity within them, managed to extract further concessions from Gorbachev over taxation powers. Unlike Kravchuk, Yeltsin and Nazarbaev apparently felt that they had secured enough concessions from the centre and that, given the continuing economic difficulties and rumblings among the conservatives and hard-liners, there was no point in delaying the signing of the Union treaty any further.

On 23 July, a group of militant defenders of the empire, including General Valentin Varennikov, Commander-in-Chief of Ground Forces, and Colonel General Boris Gromov, issued an unambiguous warning in the conservative *Sovetskaya Rossiya*: they advocated a military coup to prevent the disintegration of the Union. Ukraine's hard-liners also made their feeling known. Towards the end of July, speaking at a plenum of the Central Committee of the CPSU, Hurenko's deputy, Kharchenko, warned that 'In our conditions, feelings of national separatism, or so called national communism, pose a special danger'.[59] Soon afterwards, the Secretariat of the CPU sent a letter to the Central Committee of the Russian Communist Party stating that Ukraine's Communists and workers condemned

---

[58] *Holos Ukrainy*, 14 July 1991.

[59] Haran, *To Kill the Dragon*, pp. 180 and 185.

Yeltsin's ban on the activity of political parties within Russia's state structures and organizations.

A hastily arranged US-Soviet summit meeting in Moscow at the end of July temporarily detracted attention away from the Union treaty. The news that US President George Bush would also visit Kyiv on his way home from Moscow was greeted in Ukraine as a major boost for the republic's sovereignty. Bush also met briefly in Moscow with Yeltsin and Nazarbaev, but his unexpected arrival in Kyiv seemed to bestow international recognition on the republic's assertion of its sovereignty and to hold out the exciting prospect of direct bilateral ties with the world's most powerful state.

Leaders of the Ukraine's democratic forces, however, remembered their disappointment with the position which British Prime Minister Margaret Thatcher had taken a year earlier, and noting that the American president's programme did not include any meetings with the leaders of the opposition, kept their expectations at a modest level. Drach, for instance, told a press conference on the eve of the visit that Bush appeared to be 'hypnotized by Gorbachev'. 'We welcome George Bush as president of the democratic state – the USA,' he explained, 'but we do not accept him as Moscow's agitator for the Union treaty'.[60]

On 1 August, the American president was welcomed by thousands of enthusiastic Ukrainians waving flowers, blue and yellow and American flags, and placards declaring support for Ukrainian independence or opposition to the Union treaty. In his welcoming remarks, Kravchuk told his guest that Ukraine had embarked on 'the path towards democracy, a market economy and sovereignty' and, by pursuing a gradualist approach, was attempting to safeguard peace, stability and ethnic harmony on its territory. He expressed confidence that 'the USA, which adopted the Declaration of Independence, which was one of the first to declare before the entire world the ideals of liberty, equality and fraternity, knows the value of real sovereignty and will understand our desire for freedom for the people of Ukraine'. The Ukrainian leader also said that he hoped that the visit would pave the way for the establishment of direct relations and economic ties between the United States and Ukraine.[61]

[60] Radio Kyiv, 1 August 1991.
[61] *Ibid.*

In his celebrated 'Chicken Kyiv' speech (as the American press subsequently dubbed it) to the Ukrainian parliament on 1 August, President Bush declared that the United States would not try to 'choose between winners and losers in political competitions . . . between republics and the centre' or 'meddle in your internal affairs'. Nevertheless, he proceeded to urge Ukraine to back the Soviet president's efforts to hold the Soviet state together. 'The nine plus one agreement', he argued, 'holds forth the hope that republics will combine greater autonomy with greater voluntary interaction – political, social, cultural and economic – rather than pursuing the hopeless [the original text used 'suicidal' instead of 'hopeless'] course of isolation'. He also issued a stern warning, the first part of which might indeed have rankled Communist diehards in the chamber, but the second part of which seemed inappropriate and insensitive considering the efforts which both the Ukrainian leadership and the democratic opposition had made to avoid ethnic discord in the republic. 'Americans will not support those who seek independence in order to replace a far-off tyranny with a local despotism', he stated. 'They will not aid those who promote a suicidal nationalism based upon ethnic hatred.' Stating that Washington appreciated 'the new realities of life in the USSR' and wanted 'good relations – improved relations with the Republics', the American president, who had just signed a major US-Soviet treaty limiting strategic weapons (START) in Moscow, left no doubt who his administration would continue to give priority to: 'We will maintain the strongest possible relationship with the Soviet Government of President Gorbachev.'[62]

Unlike many others, Kravchuk did not publicly express any disappointment with the Bush visit. Instead, speaking at Kyiv airport after the American president's departure, he said that the lesson to be drawn was that Ukraine had to define more clearly the parameters of its sovereignty and insist that the precondition for its participation in the new Union be the recognition of its rights as a sovereign state, including its right to be 'the subject of international law'. He explained somewhat obliquely that foreign leaders, including President Bush, had all told him that as soon as 'you [that is, Ukraine] dot all your i's and decide who you are and where you are going – we will immediately enter into normal international relations with

---

[62] 'Text of Remarks by the President in Address to the Supreme Soviet of the Ukrainian Soviet Socialist Republic', Kyiv, 1 August 1991.

you'. Kravchuk also announced that the American president had invited him to visit the United States and that he had accepted.[63]

Later that same day, Gorbachev announced on Soviet television that the Russian Federation, Kazakhstan and Uzbekistan would sign the new Union treaty on 20 August, with other republics following later. But on 6 August, Plyushch, who had been Ukraine's 'observer' at the latest round of negotiations in Novo Ogarevo at the end of July, challenged Gorbachev's claims that all the main issues connected with the new Union treaty had now been resolved. In an interview on Ukrainian television, he also indicated that Ukraine had been criticized for its stand by the leaders of Kazakhstan and Uzbekistan, saying they had accused the republic of trying to safeguard its higher standard of living at the expense of the Central Asian states.[64]

Yeltsin was later to reveal in his memoirs about this period that after the Ukrainian parliament postponed its decision on the Union treaty, he, Gorbachev and Nazarbaev in fact held unofficial and confidential meetings to discuss the Union treaty and other 'urgent issues'. At their private consultations in Novo Ogarevo on 29 July, Yeltsin had urged the Soviet president to remove the heads of the KGB and Soviet armed forces, Vladimir Kryuchkov and Dmitry Yazov, and to replace the unpopular Soviet prime minister, Pavlov, with Nazarbaev. According to Yeltsin, Gorbachev had agreed that Kryuchkov, Pugo and Pavlov would be replaced after the signing of the Union treaty. From this account, it would appear that Yeltsin and Gorbachev had been drawing closer to one another while Kravchuk, because of his position on the Union treaty, had maintained his distance. It was now not just a question of a pact between the Soviet and Russian leaders: a powerful new triumvirate, or 'threesome', as Yeltsin referred to it, was forming behind the scenes and assuming responsibility for the fate of the Union.[65]

With Yeltsin publicly defending his decision to sign the new Union treaty from criticism from the likes of democrats such as Sakharov's widow, Yelena Bonner, and Afanasev, Ukraine's leaders remained united in their determination to defend the republic's sovereign statehood. In mid-August, Kravchuk met with Gor-

---

[63] Radio Kyiv, 2 August 1991.

[64] *Ibid.*, 6 July 1991.

[65] Boris Yeltsin, *The Struggle for Russia*, New York, 1994, pp. 38-9.

bachev while the two were on holiday in Crimea and, as the Ukrainian leader later recounted, ended up explaining yet again to the Soviet leader that his sovereign republic still found the terms of the new Union treaty to be unacceptable. Nevertheless, perhaps because of his tacit understanding with Yeltsin and Nazarbaev, the Soviet president had seemed quite confident and had implicitly challenged Kravchuk's right to speak on behalf of all of Ukraine, reminding him that Hurenko and the Central Committee of the CPU were for the Union treaty.[66] With a week to go before the signing of the Union treaty, though, the resolute position of Ukraine's leaders was confirmed by Hrynov, who informed journalists that 'Neither Fokin, Kravchuk, nor I are ready to say on what terms we will, and if we will, sign the Union treaty. But the fact that today it contradicts our Declaration about our sovereignty is incontrovertible.'[67]

Certainly, in mid-August 1991, it seemed that Ukraine's sovereignty and preparations for the republican presidential elections were of greater concern than joining any revamped rump Union. The building blocks for Ukraine's statehood were being put in place one by one. For instance, even in the sensitive defence and security spheres things were also moving forward: the parliamentary commission on the internal and external security of Ukraine had been transformed into a commission on defence and state security; the republic's new minister for the military industry and conversion, Viktor Antonov, had let it be known that Ukraine was getting ready to take over the defence industry on its territory; at the end of July, Rukh convened a meeting in Kyiv of supporters of the creation of a national army, which became the founding congress of a new patriotic pressure group – the Union of Officers of Ukraine,[68] and, public discussion about the future of the Soviet nuclear weapons deployed on the territory of sovereign Ukraine was also beginning.[69]

---

[66] See Kravchuk's description of his last meeting with Gorbachev in the first part of the long interview which he gave to the chief editor of *Kievskie novosti*, Sergei Kichigin. It was serialized under the heading 'Poslednie dni imperii . . . pervye gody nadezhdy' [The Last Days of the Empire ... the First Days of Hope], *Kievskie vedomosti*, 23 April 1994.

[67] 'Vesti', Russian television, 15 August 1991.

[68] For a useful account of the initial efforts in support of the creation of a national army, see A.M. Rusnachenko, *Na shlyakhu do natsionalnoi armii (1989-1991)* [On the Path to a National Army (1989-1991)], Kyiv, 1992.

Furthermore, the parliament was preparing a republican law on citizenship (the draft of which the ever vigilant Heorhii Kryuchkov attacked in the pages of *Radyanska Ukraina* on 16 August), the government was contemplating introducing a national currency, a republican customs system was being established, and the Ukrainian foreign ministry was continuing to assert the republic's new sovereignty in foreign affairs. Thus, regardless of whatever Gorbachev, or for that matter Yeltsin also, might have thought about the prospects for a new looser Union, Ukraine appeared to be set on a course towards independence.

[69] For example, on 7 August Radio Kyiv aired a discussion on this theme with the publicist and representative of the Green Party, Serhii Hrabovsky.

13

INDEPENDENCE AND THE DISSOLUTION OF THE U.S.S.R.

'Mortal danger': Ukraine and the attempted coup in Moscow

On the very eve of the signing of the new Union treaty the hard-liners within the Soviet leadership attempted to seize power. Gorbachev, who was vacationing in Crimea, was placed under house arrest and isolated. On the morning of Monday, 19 August 1991, the official media in Moscow announced that the Soviet president was unable 'for reasons of health, to carry out his duties' and that his deputy, Yanayev, was assuming presidential responsibilities. They also announced that a state of emergency was being introduced in certain parts of the USSR for six months and that the country would be governed by an eight-man State Committee for the State Emergency in the USSR (better known in the USSR by its Russian acronym as the GKChP – for *Gosudarstvenniy komitet po chrezvychainomu polozheniyu v SSSR*), headed by Yanayev. The plotters, or 'putschists' as they were dubbed, included the powerful heads of the Soviet security and defence ministries, KGB chief Kryuchkov, Defence Minister Yazov, Minister of Internal Affairs Pugo, as well as Soviet Prime Minister Pavlov and Chairman of the USSR Supreme Soviet Lukyanov, who was not formally a member of the GKChP.

During the dramatic few days before the attempted coup was foiled by the Russian democratic forces loyal to President Boris Yeltsin, the fragility of the sovereignty of the republics was exposed and the fate of the peoples of the USSR hung in the balance. The action was largely restricted to Moscow where, as the putschists were sending in tanks and troops, Yeltsin called on the population to defend democracy and assumed the leadership of the resistance. The reaction to the attempted coup was varied: only the leaders of the Baltic and Moldovan republics promptly condemned it, while most, including Kravchuk and Nazarbaev, appear to have preferred to wait and see who would come out on top in Moscow.

Once the coup had failed, Kravchuk, Hurenko, Deputy Prime Minister Masyk, and other leading Ukrainian Communist figures who were accused of having sat on the fence or supported the putschists, sought to vindicate themselves. In view of some of the enduring inconsistencies and gaps in the accounts of what occurred, it still remains unclear what was covered up and what degree of *ex post facto* embellishment there was.[1] One thing is certain, though: during the crucial first two days, Kravchuk and his fellow sovereignty Communists did not display the courage and resoluteness which they had showed at the beginning of the year when Lithuania had been threatened, and it was left to the republic's democratic forces to manifest solidarity with Yeltsin and Russia's defenders of democracy.

Kravchuk and Hurenko were both to claim that they learned about the attempted coup in the early morning of 19 August. Kravchuk was to tell the Verkhovna Rada on 24 August that he had been awoken by a telephone call from the Commander of the Kyiv Military District, General Chechevatov, whereas later he would say that it was the Ukrainian Party leader who had informed him of what had transpired. Hurenko claimed that he had learned about the developments in Moscow from announcements on the radio; but, after the failure of the coup, it was revealed from documents discovered at the Party's offices in Lviv that, already on 18 August, the Secretariat of the Central Committee of the CPSU had issued instructions to Party leaders at the republican and regional levels calling for active support for the GKChP.

At nine o'clock on 19 August, Kravchuk, Hurenko and Masyk (Fokin was away on holiday) met in Kravchuk's office with the

[1]. The main published sources on what occurred in Ukraine during the attempted coup in Moscow are: the extensive collection of documents compiled by Les Tanyuk, *Khronika oporu* [Chronicle of Resistance], Kyiv, 1991; the official transcript of the debate at the extraordinary session of the parliament on 24 August 1991, in *Pozacherhova Sessiya Verkhovnoi Rady Ukrainskoi RSR Dvanadtsyatoho Sklykannya, Byuleten No. 1 and No. 2*, [Extraordinary Session of the Supreme Council of the Ukrainian SSR of the Twelfth Sitting, Bulletin nos 1 and 2], Kyiv, 1991, hereafter referred to as *Extraordinary Session*, no. 1 and no. 2; Kravchuk's recollections in Chemerys, *Prezydent*, pp. 204-14, and in his interview with Kichigin in *Kievskie novosti*, 30 April and 9 July 1994; Lytvyn, *Political Arena*, pp. 269-74; and *Nezavisimost*, 25 September 1992.

GKChP's representative who had been dispatched to Ukraine, General Varennikov, who was accompanied by Chechevatov and another general. Varennikov, a tough, imperial-minded, military leader, had formerly commanded the Transcarpathian Military District and been a member of the Central Committee of the CPU. What was actually said and decided at this meeting is uncertain for differing accounts emerged. The fact remains, though, that Varennikov cabled the GKChP informing it that Kravchuk and Masyk had initially 'reacted negatively' to what he had to tell them – Hurenko 'kept silent' – and had insisted that it was up to the Ukrainian parliament to decide if it was necessary to declare a state of emergency anywhere on the territory of the republic. The general had been 'forced to charge the atmosphere somewhat' in order 'to bring home to the comrades' that the GKChP's emergency measures were 'already in force' and that the Ukrainian authorities were expected to comply. He reported that eventually 'Kravchuk and the other comrades agreed with the proposals [which Varennikov had made on behalf of the GKChP, including, it seems, to consider imposing a state of emergency in Western Ukraine]' and would 'shortly take measures in this spirit'.[2]

Kravchuk and Masyk were subsequently to explain that they had sought to defend Ukraine's sovereignty and had challenged the competence of the GKChP on the republic's territory. On being confronted, however, with the threat of military intervention, they had been guided by the desire to prevent tanks from being sent in and blood being split. That same day, 'in connection with the appeal to the Soviet people [sic]' by the GKChP, Masyk created two governmental bodies: a 'temporary commission' headed by the republican minister for defence, national security and emergency situations, Yevhen Marchuk, which was given broad if vague powers to oversee the maintenance of public order and internal security; and, a team of eight members of the Presidium of the Cabinet of Ministers who were given responsibility for ensuring order and the smooth running of the economy in various regions of the republic. One of their tasks – 'the strengthening of control over the activity of the mass media and use of technology for disseminating information prescribed for these officials – sounded very much

[2] Extracts from Varennikov's message were published in *Nezavisimost*, 25 September 1992.

like the imposition of censorship that the GKChP had called for.[3] Democrats were later to accuse Masyk of having in effect begun to collaborate with the putschists by setting up an 'unconstitutional body'; he was to reply that the temporary commission headed by Marchuk was in fact conceived of as a reserve republican leadership in case he and Kravchuk were 'taken away' and that its establishment had been approved by the Presidium of the parliament.[4]

According to Yukhnovsky, when, soon after the meeting with Varennikov, anxious leaders of the opposition met with Kravchuk, the Ukrainian leader had simply told them that the situation in the republic was calm and that the public should be urged to maintain this state. Masyk, however, was to state a few days later that at precisely this time a 'war of nerves' had begun: military helicopters hovered overhead and a Soviet special forces unit was flown in from Brest and stood poised on the outskirts of Kyiv to seize government buildings.[5]

At four in the afternoon, Kravchuk addressed the Ukrainian population on television and radio. By this time in Moscow, as Western radio broadcasts were informing listeners in the USSR, Yeltsin had addressed supporters from atop a tank: he had denounced the coup, appealed for a general strike and declared that he was assuming control of Soviet forces deployed on the territory of the Russian Federation. By contrast, Kravchuk called on the Ukrainian population to remain 'calm', show 'self- restraint' and carry on with their work as normal. He stressed that a state of emergency had not been declared in Ukraine and that its government and parliament were functioning. Evading any direct assessment of what was going on in the Soviet capital, he sought to create the impression that the republic's leaders still did not have a clear picture of what had happened and maintained that it was impermissible 'to be hasty' in such 'extraordinarily serious political matters'. An evaluation of the situation, he said, would be made in due course by the Presidium of the Supreme Council and the parliament itself. Nevertheless,

---

[3] See in Tanyuk, *Chronicle of Resistance*, pp. 129-32.

[4] Masyk's interview in *Vechirnyi Kyiv* of 26 August 1991, reproduced in Tanyuk, *Chronicle of Resistance*, pp. 133-7.

[5] *Ibid.* The author has not managed to find any evidence supporting Masyk's claim that Soviet military helicopters did indeed made a threatening appearance over Kyiv.

Kravchuk did hint that something unconstitutional and sinister was going on and stressed the need for the law, constitutional norms, democracy and the republic's sovereignty to be respected. In the most forthright part of his speech, he appealed to the population to avoid confrontation and to do everything possible to avoid 'destabilizing the situation'. 'Our position is one of prudence,' he declared. 'We should act in such a way that no innocent blood is split'.[6]

Leaders of Ukraine's democratic forces were disappointed by Kravchuk's apparent prevarication and refused to remain passive. Despite the ban on strikes, demonstrations and public meetings which the GKChP had announced, Rukh, using the building of the Writers' Union as the temporary headquarters of Ukrainian resistance to the GKChP, issued a statement at midday signed by Drach condemning the attempted coup. It called for opposition in the form of a republican strike and asserted 'the right of the people of Ukraine' to an independent and democratic state. Other democratic political parties and organizations also began issuing similar statements. By the end of the day, the main democratic forces were forming a coalition which expressed solidarity with Yeltsin and called for an all-Ukrainian strike and civil disobedience. Beyond Kyiv, the Lviv regional council was the first major body to come out against the putschists.[7]

Yukhnovsky was to tell the Ukrainian parliament that when the Presidium of the Ukrainian parliament met in the evening of 19 August, Kravchuk did not clarify his position and argued that only after the USSR Congress of People's Deputies had convened and offered its evaluation would it be possible to say if what had taken place was an attempted coup or not. What is also curious is that Kravchuk apparently did not inform the Presidium about what he would later describe as Varennikov's blatant threats.[8]

Caught between the Presidium's Communist majority, representatives of which seem either to have implicitly supported the GKChP or been reluctant to come out against it, and its forceful democratic minority, which was urging him to take a stand on the side of Yeltsin and convene an emergency session of the parliament, Kravchuk stalled. Avoiding expressing support for Yeltsin, he told

---

[6] The text is reproduced in Tanyuk, *Chronicle of Resistance*, pp. 102-4.
[7] See *Ibid.*, pp. 182-97.
[8] Author's interview with Mykola Shulha, Yalta, 22 September 1995.

representatives of the opposition that 'Ukraine will go its own way'. The only problem, though, was, as the opposition well knew, that in such a situation Ukraine's sovereignty was in jeopardy and the republic's fate was being decided not in Kyiv but in Moscow.

In the meantime, Hurenko called a meeting of the CPU's leadership and stressed the need for the Communist majority in the parliament and its Presidium to remain disciplined and to follow the new line.[9] That same day, the CPU's Secretariat issued secret instructions to regional Party committees throughout the republic. It called on them to support the GKChP and to try to maintain 'calm', 'order' and 'discipline'. Demonstrations and strikes were not to be permitted, nor the appearance of material in the mass media which could 'destabilize the situation'. According to the document, the 'key question' of the day was 'the preservation of the Union of Soviet Socialist Republics' and 'all activity aimed at undermining the Union' and 'manifestations of regional egoism [sic]' had to be curtailed.[10] The following day, however, Hurenko was to present a sanitized version of the CPU's position to journalists: in a statement given to the press, he declared that the Ukrainian Party was adhering to the line which Kravchuk had enunciated on television.[11]

The following day, as the tension in Moscow mounted, the Presidium continued its meeting without reaching agreement. At about two o'clock in the afternoon, seven members of its democratic opposition issued their own statement condemning the attempted coup and expressing solidarity with Yeltsin. They were: Yukhnovsky, Yemets, Tanyuk, Yavorivsky, Pavlychko, Hrynov and Volodymyr Pylypchuk. Kravchuk did not permit their appeal to be read at the meeting of the Presidium and the republic's officially controlled media, which were dutifully publishing the GKChP's documents, avoided mentioning it.[12]

Meanwhile, Ukraine's democratic forces had united in a coalition calling itself 'Independent Democratic Ukraine' and issued a statement declaring that 'all of Ukraine's democratic parties and public

---

[9] *Ibid.*

[10] Tanyuk, *Chronicle of Resistance*, pp. 166-8. The document was first published by Tanyuk in *Vechirnyi Kyiv* on 26 August 1991, and *Literaturna Ukraina* reproduced on 29 August 1991.

[11] Ukrinform-TASS, 20 August 1991.

[12] Tanyuk, *Chronicle of Resistance*, pp. 118-21.

organizations' condemned the 'attempted *coup d'état* ' as an attempt to 'stop the process of democratization', 'restore the unlimited dictatorship of the CPSU' and 'preserve the empire'. It noted that the Baltic republics, Moldova and Georgia had already opposed the GKChP and that in Moscow units of the Soviet security forces had gone over to the side of Yeltsin. In Ukraine, the statement added, the democratic forces were also calling for resistance to the 'putschists' committee' but the Communist majority in the Presidium of the parliament was implicitly siding with the GKChP by blocking condemnation of it. The democratic forces were therefore issuing an ultimatum: either the Presidium acknowledged that the GKChP was an 'unconstitutional body' whose orders had no force on Ukraine's territory and convened an emergency session of parliament, or the coalition would appeal to the population to unite around the Presidium's democratic faction. The statement also appealed to military personnel stationed in Ukraine not to obey the GKChP and urged the population to support a republican strike beginning at noon the following day.[13] That same day, leaders of the Donbas strike committees urged Kravchuk to convene an extraordinary session of the Ukrainian parliament, warning that the 'passivity' of the Presidium towards 'the *coup d'état* that is taking place' and the detention of the Soviet president 'on the territory of Soviet Ukraine', would compromise it 'for ever'.[14]

In the evening, as spontaneous demonstrations continued on Kyiv's Khreshchatyk, the majority of the Presidium finally agreed on a tame compromise statement by a vote of fifteen to ten which merely echoed what Kravchuk had already declared. It failed to pass any judgement on the legality of the GKChP and instead left this matter to be decided by the Ukrainian parliament after the USSR Congress of People's Deputies had taken a position. The furthest it went was to state that until the Ukrainian parliament made its ruling the GKChP's orders had no juridical force on the republic's territory. Rather ambiguously, though, the document affirmed that the Soviet and republican constitutions, and laws 'adopted in accordance with them', remained in force, which the opposition considered as contradicting the Declaration of Sovereignty. The latter also objected to an appeal to the public to 'refrain from strikes, meetings

[13] *Ibid.*, pp. 198–9 and 202.
[14] *Ibid.*, p. 223.

and demonstrations'. Not surprisingly, therefore, the representatives of the opposition rejected the statement. On the other side, Shulha and two other representatives of the majority considered that the statement went too far and also did not endorse it.[15]

By now Nazarbaev had denounced the attempted coup and called for Gorbachev to be allowed to confirm personally if he was unable to carry out his presidential duties. President Bush had also telephoned Yeltsin and expressed his support for Gorbachev. This, and the actions of the democratic forces within the republic, were increasing the pressure on Kravchuk to clarify his position. When he appeared again on Ukrainian television later that evening, he did indeed sound a little bolder: he expressed doubt about Gorbachev's sudden incapacitation, mentioning that he had recently seen him in good health in Crimea, and said that he would insist that the Soviet president be invited to be present at an extraordinary session of the USSR Supreme Soviet which had been scheduled for 26 August.

Nevertheless, the Ukrainian leader still seems to have wanted to hedge his bets. He suggested, as he had done in an interview shown the evening before on central Soviet television – and which he was subsequently to claim had been censored and distorted – that matters could not go on as before in the Soviet Union and that the present situation had not arisen by chance. Gorbachev, he noted, was also to blame for the 'misfortune' which had overtaken the country. What was curious, however, is that Kravchuk now suggested that the USSR Congress of People's Deputies should have taken decisive action earlier and that the USSR Supreme Soviet could still redeem the Soviet legislature and restore faith in democracy and legality. His emphasis on the role of this conservative institution, which he himself had only recently criticized for having rejected the sovereignty of the republics, and whose head, Lukyanov, had on 20 August denounced the Union treaty as going too far in its concessions to the Union republics, did indeed sound odd coming

---

[15] Shulha insists that this did not mean that the three supported the GKChP, as the democratic opposition was later to claim. Rather, he explains, they were anxious to avoid precipitating any intervention by Soviet troops which they believed were ready to strike. Shulha also claims that Kravchuk did not share with the Presidium all the information at his disposal and that the democratic opposition was better informed about how events were developing than the Communist majority. Hrynov, for example, apparently maintained good telephone contact with Yeltsin's associate, Gennadii Burbulis. Author's interview with Shulha.

from a sovereignty Communist. Even more ambiguous was Kravchuk's comment that the GKChP had 'already made quite a few mistakes', but that this was 'normal because it is a new formation; it has not found itself yet'. 'Can this be corrected,' he asked, replying: 'I think it can and that this should be done by an extraordinary session of the [USSR] Supreme Soviet'.[16]

What was particularly compromising, and what Kravchuk himself would tell the Ukrainian parliament on 24 August was his 'one mistake' during the attempted coup, was that he still refused to convene an emergency session of the Ukrainian parliament. During the night of 20-1 August, as reports were reaching Kyiv of shooting in Moscow and what appeared to be the storming of Yeltsin's headquarters in Moscow's White House, the Ukrainian leader continued to reject the appeals of the democratic faction within the Ukrainian parliament's Presidium to come out in support of the Russian democrats.

The following morning, with the opposition intensifying its pressure for the parliament to be convened, Kravchuk still insisted that the signatures of 150 deputies first be obtained. But as the day continued and there were more and more indications that the attempted coup had failed, Kravchuk rapidly changed his tune. In the presence of Yukhnovsky and Yemets, he telephoned Lukyanov and demanded that Gorbachev be present at the extraordinary session of the USSR Supreme Soviet. Later, he had a telephone conversation with Gorbachev, who after all, as the democratic forces had kept pointing out, but the Ukrainian leader had preferred not to mention, had been detained on the territory of 'sovereign' Ukraine. That evening, appearing yet again on Ukrainian television, Kravchuk sought to capitalize on these two conversations, describing the first as an 'ultimatum' delivered to Lukyanov from 'a leader of such a large state as Ukraine', and utilizing the second as evidence of the Ukrainian leader's purported support for a president who he now acknowledged had been 'arrested' by the 'so-called Emergency Committee' which had 'deviated' from democracy and the 'constitutional and legal process.'

---

[16] Kravchuk's extemporaneous explanation that the GKChP was a new body which had not yet 'found itself' was omitted from the version of the interview published two days later in *Radyanska Ukraina*. See Roman Solchanyk, 'Ukraine: Kravchuk's Role', *Report on the USSR*, vol. 3, no. 6 (6 September 1991), p. 48.

In the meantime, thousands of demonstrators continued to protest against the GKChP in central Kyiv and blue and yellow flags continued to be visible among the pro-Yeltsin demonstrators in Moscow.[17] At a large protest rally in the Ukrainian capital, Pavlychko read out a statement, which was 'unanimously endorsed', calling for the Presidium of the Ukrainian parliament to assert control over Soviet military units stationed in the republic, for the parliament to appeal to the outside world for recognition of Ukraine as an independent state and condemning the leadership of the CPU for having abandoned not only the people which it claimed to represent but also its general secretary.[18]

Only on 22 August, after the 150 signatures had been gathered, the Russian parliament had held an emergency session, Yeltsin had emerged victorious and Gorbachev had returned to Moscow, did Kravchuk finally agree to convene an extraordinary session of the Ukrainian parliament – in two days' time. At a press conference, which for some reason he gave that same day only to foreign journalists, he sought to portray himself as an opponent of the attempted coup from the very start and an ally of Yeltsin, who had been thanked by Gorbachev for his support. As for the future, unlike Nazarbaev, the Ukrainian leader reiterated his previous position that there was no need to rush the conclusion of the new Union treaty and ventured that what was needed was a transitional Soviet government consisting of about nine people (the leaders of the republics still prepared to form a Union?). The republic's democratic forces had demanded that, in view of the vulnerability of Ukraine's sovereignty which the attempted coup had exposed, the parliament should assert control over the military forces stationed on Ukrainian territory, but Kravchuk declared that this was 'out of the question', though the creation of a national guard was another matter. Asked if he would now leave the Communist Party, he replied that 'One shouldn't blame the entire Party for what happened', only the leaders who had not 'declared their position during this terrible time'.[19]

As the day continued: in Moscow, an angry crowd gathered

---

[17] On the anti-GKChP demonstrations in Kyiv, see *Kultura i zhyttya*, 24 August 1991. On the participation of Ukrainians in the pro-Yeltsin protests in Moscow, see *Literaturna Ukraina*, 29 August 1991.

[18] For the text, see Tanyuk, *Chronicle of Resistance*, p. 211.

[19] *Molod Ukrainy*, 24 August 1991.

outside the KGB headquarters and toppled the statue of the founder of the Soviet secret police – Feliks Dzerzhinsky; in Estonia and Lithuania the Communist Party was banned; and, in Kazakhstan, Nazarbaev announced his resignation from both the Politburo and the Central Committee of the CPSU and issued a decree on departization.

With the Communist Party totally discredited by the abortive coup, it is not difficult to imagine the alarm and demoralization which must have gripped its leaders, not least in Ukraine. On 22 August, the CPU's Politburo issued a statement condemning 'the adventuristic anti-state plot' and, seeking to distance itself from the putschists, criticized the CPSU Central Committee (Ivashko was still officially the Soviet Party's deputy leader) for failing to provide a timely assessment of the coup.[20] Speaking at a press conference, Hurenko even paid tribute to Yeltsin's 'civic courage'.[21] But these rather pathetic attempts to stave off impending disaster only encouraged the more militant anti-Communist forces to seek to expose the CPU's complicity in order to drive it from the political arena. The following morning, the democratic authorities in the Lviv region headed by Chornovil led the way by suspending the CPU's activities, sealing Party buildings and beginning an investigation of Party documents issued during the attempted coup.

Kravchuk's connections with the CPU leadership during and immediately after the attempted coup remain obscure. His apparent reluctance in the first days after the abortive coup to condemn the role of Hurenko and the CPU leadership nevertheless raises questions about his position. Much later, long after incriminating evidence against the CPU's leadership had been unearthed, Kravchuk would claim that Hurenko and his associates had distrusted him and, although he remained a member of the CPU's Politburo, had not kept him fully informed about the Ukrainian Party's activities in support of the GKChP. Kravchuk would also imply that from the very outset he had resisted Hurenko's attempts to reassert the CPU's control over the republic in the name of the GKChP by refusing to meet him and Varennikov at the CPU's headquarters instead of in his office. On 27 August, Kravchuk was also to announce that he had written a statement announcing his resignation

[20] Radio Kyiv, 22 August 1991.
[21] *Pravda Ukrainy*, 23 August 1991.

from the Party immediately after his meeting with Varennikov on 19 August. But if he did, it seems that he must have kept this document in his drawer.[22] In fact, it later become known that on 22 August Kravchuk participated in a meeting of the CPU's Politburo; it is unlikely that if he had been perceived as a 'renegade' at this time he would have been allowed to participate.[23]

Ukraine declares independence

For Ukraine's democratic force, the collapse of the attempted coup brought elation and relief. Despite the display of unity represented by the formation of 'Independent Democratic Ukraine', it had been unclear how successful this coalition's call for a general strike would have been and how effectively the opposition could have resisted if a state of emergency or military rule had in fact been imposed. Certainly, as one observer noted, the crowds of protesters in Kyiv had been relatively small compared to the demonstrations in Moscow or even Leningrad.[24] Fortunately, the strength and efficacy of the coalition had not had to be put to the test, the defenders of the empire and the old order had shot their bolt, and paradoxically, after three dramatic days of danger and uncertainty, for the defenders of democracy and republican sovereignty the putschists' debacle had turned into a godsend.

While the Ukrainian parliament prepared for its extraordinary session, there were more democratic developments in Moscow and some of the other republics which invariably influenced the atmosphere in Kyiv. On 23 August, Kravchuk flew to the Soviet capital to attend a closed meeting of the republican leaders convened by the Soviet president. Perhaps still not fully aware of the extent to which his power and that of the centre had been weakened, Gorbachev evidently remained determined to push ahead with the conclusion of the new Union treaty. Yeltsin, for one, immediately let it be known though that in light of what had occurred the document would have to be revised. Later that day, the Russian

---

[22] The document is reproduced in Chemerys, *Prezydent*, p. 213.

[23] Lytvyn summarizes the protocol of the meeting, chaired by Hurenko, which he discovered in the Central State Archive of Public Associations in Kyiv in his *Political Arena*, p. 272.

[24] Haran, *To Kill the Dragon*, p. 189.

leader also publicly demonstrated the revolutionary political transformation which the failed coup had precipitated – the collapse of
the Soviet Communist system and the dissolution of the Soviet
empire. Flaunting his increased authority as Russia's victorious
leader, Yeltsin first humiliated the Soviet president, who was still
reluctant to condemn the CPSU outright, in front of the Russian
parliament and television cameras, and then, ignoring Gorbachev's
objections, proceeded to sign an edict suspending the activities of
the Russian Communist Party pending the investigation of its role
during the attempted coup. That same day, while Communist Party
offices were being sealed in Moscow and Leningrad, the white, red
and blue flag of pre-1917 Russia was hoisted above Yeltsin's
headquarters in the Kremlin, symbolically overshadowing the Soviet
flag still flying nearby over President Gorbachev's office.

Against this tumultuous background, Kravchuk returned home
to face the music. Knowing full well that the parliamentary opposition would be after his blood and that his political future was at stake,
he prepared for what was probably going to be the most challenging
day of his life. Formally, the extraordinary session of the Ukrainian
parliament, the proceedings of which were broadcast live on
republican radio and television, had only one item on the agenda:
the political situation in Ukraine and how to protect the republic
from possible military or state coups in the future. Some preparatory
work had been carried out by a working group appointed by the
Presidium and headed by Plyushch, which consisted of members of
both the majority and opposition. It was also proposed by the
Presidium that the debate would be preceded by reports from the
chairman of the parliament and from the leaders of the majority and
opposition.

Kravchuk defended himself by maintaining that in very
dangerous and unpredictable conditions, with the military on alert
and the picture of what was happening in Moscow remaining
unclear, he and his colleagues in the Presidium, which were themselves divided, 'did everything in order that a state of emergency not
be introduced [in Ukraine], that people were not crushed, that there
were no victims and that innocent blood was not spilt'. With his
speech being interrupted by shouts and jeers from the chamber, the
embattled speaker acknowledged that from the vantage point of
hindsight the Presidium's statement about the attempted coup had
been too feeble and come too late, but then played his trump card.

Referring to a record of the meeting with General Varennikov, which he said his close colleague Masyk had made, for the first time he mentioned sensational details about what had purportedly occurred behind the closed doors of his office.

Kravchuk claimed that Varennikov had called on the Ukrainian leaders to support the GKChP and to consider imposing a state of emergency in Western Ukraine and Kyiv. The general had threatened the use of military force in the event of their failing to support the putschists. In a telephone call made to Kravchuk during the meeting, the chief of the KGB, Kryuchkov, had reinforced this ultimatum. The head of the Ukrainian parliament said he had responded by declaring that the GKChP was unconstitutional and that Ukraine would continue to abide by its own laws and constitution and to uphold its sovereignty. Failing to explain why he had not informed other members of the Presidium about this and not shown the same resoluteness in public, Kravchuk declared not very persuasively: 'I categorically reject all accusations about indecision, procrastination and not defining my personal position'.

The Ukrainian leader emphasized that the attempted coup had revealed the limited nature of the republic's sovereignty and that new laws would have to be passed, and 'more decisive and concrete steps' taken, to broaden it. Because of what had occurred, it was also necessary to review Ukraine's position as regards the Union treaty. 'Ukraine can only join the kind of Union,' he now declared, 'participation in which would exclude the possibility of encroachments by anyone on our state sovereignty'.

What specific remedies and proposals did the Ukrainian leader come out with? First, he argued that as head of the Ukrainian parliament he did not have sufficient authority to take decisions on his own and to issue edicts, and that the recent events had underscored the need temporarily to increase the powers of his office so that he could fulfil the role of head of state until a president was elected. The attempted coup had also 'revealed the complete vulnerability' of the republic 'to external and internal adventurism' and the lack of a mechanism for protecting Ukraine against such threats. Kravchuk therefore proposed the creation of a Defence Council which would be responsible for safeguarding the sovereignty of the republic, the creation of a national guard and the adoption of laws regulating the status of the Soviet troops deployed on Ukraine's territory. Furthermore, the KGB and MVD in Ukraine had to be fully subordinated to Ukraine's head of state and could cooperate with, but not belong to, any all-Union structures. Kravchuk's only reference to the future of the CPU was an acknowledgement that the time had come to 'decide on the departization' of these two security ministries.

In view of what had occurred and the radical changes still taking place in Moscow, this was hardly a bold or particularly convincing performance. Consequently, the head of the parliament was subjected to intense questioning and criticism by indignant or incredulous deputies. Holovaty brought up the secret instructions which the CPU leadership had sent out and Masyk's creation of an 'unconstitutional' and implicitly pro-GKChP commission. Seemingly taken aback, Kravchuk announced that on the previous day, on learning about the secret instructions issued by the CPSU's Secretariat from Nazarbaev's public statements, he had resigned from the CPSU's Central Committee and, on his return to Kyiv, had informed Hurenko that he was unable to remain a member of the CPU's Politburo. Pressed by Hrynov and other deputies to put to the vote a proposal to seal the CPU's offices, Kravchuk instead proposed establishing a commission to investigate who had collaborated with the GKChP. After Hurenko was prevented from speaking because of the jeering, Plyushch, who was chairing at that moment, sought to defuse the situation by announcing a break.

After the deputies resumed the debate, it was clear that the People's Council had regained the initiative and was determined to capitalize on the situation to the maximum. On behalf of the opposition, Pavlychko called on the parliament not to get carried away by emotions but to concentrate on three critical issues which he and his colleagues believed had to be decided that day, namely, the proclamation of Ukraine's independence, that the Presidium of the parliament take control over all military units deployed on the republic's territory, and the complete departization of Ukraine's state structures. Hurenko responded by protesting against what he claimed were attempts to turn the session into a 'Lynch court'. He complained that in four regions the CPU offices had already been 'illegally seized' and appealed to the parliament not to go along with the democrats' *diktat*, which he compared to a virtual *coup d'état*. But at this stage, no one was prepared to back him.

Kravchuk had to face even more embarrassing questions about his role. When a deputy confronted him with the fact that Lukyanov had apparently told a group of Ukrainian parliamentarians in Moscow that Kravchuk had informed him that a state of emergency would be introduced in Western Ukraine, Crimea and perhaps even Kyiv, the chairman of the parliament lost his composure and branded the Russian politician a liar and a criminal. Struggling to stay afloat, on the one hand, he sought to convince deputies that, 'They were terrible days and nights; you cannot even imagine what it was like', and on the other, on being pressed to clarify his position, clutched at two of the proposals which Pavlychko had made – independence and departization. He also switched to a more populist and patriotic tone, declaring his faith in 'my people and its own strength'.

At this stage a new element was also introduced into the debate which brought out the unease of many of the Ukrainian parliamentarians about what was happening in Moscow and helped Kravchuk to get off the hook. The news arriving from the Soviet capital raised concern that the Russian authorities were unilaterally taking over the centre's structures, including the KGB. Yeltsin was placing his people in key positions and the Russian government had taken over the all-Union economic and communications ministries. One angry deputy, Valerii Batalov, asked rhetorically whether Ukraine had any need of a Union in which all the key positions would be held by Russians. Kravchuk seized at the opportunity to redeem himself and replied that he too had been 'distressed and even annoyed' by the 'demands that only Russians be appointed'. He warned that although 'democracy had been saved by Russia and Yeltsin', the victory had produced a 'very dangerous' wave of 'drunken democracy' and recommended that the deputies support the declaration of independence.

Now that independence had been placed on the agenda, some of the tension was removed and the deputies heard the reports from the leaders of the majority and opposition. Unlike Hurenko, the leader of the majority, Moroz, delivered a reasonably constructive and conciliatory speech which also contained a few surprises. He condemned what he described as the putschists' attempt to use the CPSU in carrying out their *coup d'état*, but also emphasized that he had protested to Gorbachev as far back as February 1989 that the Party was not developing in the direction of democracy and in the spirit of restructuring. Citing Nazarbaev's example of the previous day of calling on the Communist Party of Kazakhstan to break with the CPSU, Moroz declared that if the next plenum of the CPU's

Central Committee did not 'find the courage' to do likewise, he would take upon himself 'the responsibility for organizing a Ukrainian Communist Party'. He went on to propose that while asserting Ukraine's 'unchanging course towards independence', the parliament should approve, without delay, a number of measures which were essential for bolstering the republic's sovereignty, the most important of which he argued were the creation of a national army and the introduction of a national currency.

Moroz's speech brought the majority closer to the opposition but it conspicuously avoided the question of departization and the fate of the CPU. This issue was taken up very forthrightly by Yukhnovsky, who delivered an outspoken speech strongly condemning the role both of Kravchuk and the CPU. The leader of the opposition presented a chronological record of the events between 19-21 August which directly challenged Kravchuk's account and suggested that the collaboration with the GKChP by the CPU's leaders in Kyiv and in the regions had been more substantial than Kravchuk and others made out. Moving on to the new situation after the failure of the coup, he maintained that: 'In fact, the Union no longer exists as a state. The republics are *de facto* independent states; they should take power fully into their own hands. Russia is doing so.' The question was: 'How are we to do this in Ukraine?'

Yukhnovsky argued that it was not enough simply to declare Ukraine's independence without ensuring the triumph of democracy through the 'decommunization' of the republic. Otherwise, the independent but still 'Communist' Ukraine would be hostile to Yeltsin's 'democratic' Russia and would be recognized only by 'Saddam [Hussein] and other dictators'. Yukhnovsky therefore made the following proposals, which he said he had prepared himself, thereby suggesting that they had not been cleared in advance with the People's Council: that the parliament declare Ukraine an independent and democratic state and that this decision be endorsed by a referendum (this was the first time the declaration of independence was linked to a referendum, and subsequently Yukhnovsky was to be criticized by other democratic leaders for having introduced this idea); that the activity of the Communist Party on Ukraine's territory be stopped, but that all Party functionaries who did not support the coup retain their current level of earnings and be found new jobs; that the Presidium of the parliament resign and a new Presidium be elected; and that all activity promoting 'violence, discord and enmity' be banned in Ukraine. Like several other representatives from the opposition, Yukhnovsky also brought up Khmara's case, which he maintained had been 'fabricated by the CPU and KGB', and called for the deputy's immediate release.

After another debate, during which Yavorivsky read out a proposed version of the declaration of independence and Crimea's representative Bagrov urged the deputies not to rush into voting for independence – 'it means leaving the Soviet Union' he stressed – Kravchuk announced a further break, giving the deputies an hour to try and settle their differences. During it, the People's Council met in the cinema room on the third floor of the legislature building while the majority met downstairs in what was essentially an emergency session. The opposition recognized the need to reach out to the moderate Communists and Pavlychko therefore hastily revised the draft declaration of independence in such a way that the wording deliberately avoided antagonizing the Communists. Yukhnovsky's idea of making the declaration conditional on endorsement in a republican referendum was also accepted.

The despondent Communist majority felt betrayed by the 'centre' and realized that Gorbachev's authority had dissipated. It also felt threatened by the strong anti-Communist backlash in Russia. Hurenko was acting in his typically arrogant and stand-offish manner befitting a Party leader of the old days and Moroz's statement had highlighted the rifts among the Communist leadership. The Communist deputies wanted somehow to save their party and preserve as much unity as they could, but also wished to avoid triggering a social explosion which would release anti-Communist passions. While they were 'groping for a way out', as one participant put it, Pavlychko, Yavorivsky and other representatives of the People's Council arrived and appealed to the majority to unite with the opposition in supporting the declaration of independence. Their argument ran along the lines that: 'we were all once Communists under Moscow, but now a point of no return has been reached and independence is the only way forward. Let's unite around independence.' The overtures from the People's Council turned out to be the lifeline that the majority had been seeking and the Communist deputies eagerly grabbed at it. Suddenly, despair gave way to hope and a new enthusiasm. 'We were like blind kittens who had found a way out', the same witness recalled.[25] In the excitement, agreement was also reached on the departization of the republican Procuracy, MVD, KGB and all military forces stationed in Ukraine.

At shortly before six o'clock in the evening, Kravchuk read out the revised Declaration of Independence:

> In view of the mortal danger surrounding Ukraine in connection with the state coup in the USSR on 19 August 1991,
> – continuing the thousand-year tradition of state-building in Ukraine,
> – based on the right of a nation of self-determination in accordance with the Charter of the United Nations and other international legal documents, and,
> – realizing the Declaration of the State Sovereignty of Ukraine, the Supreme Council solemnly declares the independence of Ukraine and the creation of an independent Ukrainian state – Ukraine. The territory of Ukraine is indivisible and inviolable, From this day forward, on the territory of Ukraine only the Constitution and laws of Ukraine are valid. This act becomes effective at the moment of its approval.

The Declaration, which was to be put to a republican referendum on 1 December, was overwhelmingly approved by 346 votes in favour, 1 against (Albert Korneev, an ethnic Russian deputy representing a constituency in the Donbas) and 3 abstentions. Thus, seventy-three years after the Ukrainian Central Rada had first proclaimed an independent Ukrainian state, and after seven decades of Soviet rule, Ukraine had again affirmed its desire for independent statehood. This time there was no imminent danger of invasion as in January 1918, for the 'mortal danger' had passed with the defeat of the defenders of the Soviet empire; the Ukrainian national democratic movement was significantly stronger and more developed in 1991 than in 1918 and had been able over the last few years to lay the groundwork for statehood based on a civic rather than ethnic basis; and, the decision to proclaim independence seemed to reflect unity and mass support. Just how prepared Ukraine actually was for independence and how broad the support was would still have to be seen.

---

[25] Author's interview with Shulha.

Immediate problems: The CPU, Russian reactions and national security

While the crowds outside the parliament began to celebrate, the deputies pressed on with other important business. The most important issue was the fate of the Communist Party. In accordance with the agreement reached between the opposition and the majority, the departization of the republican Procuracy, KGB and MVD was approved without problems (by 331 for, 10 against and 5 abstentions). Many of the Communists seemed to have felt that this was a sufficient enough concession and that they should not give way any further. A subsequent motion to depoliticize state structures, enterprises and organizations failed, with only 217 deputies supporting it, 84 voting against and 13 abstaining. This only incensed the opposition and increased calls for the banning of the Communist Party. As the debate continued, a group of twenty deputies announced their resignation from the Communist Party. But even this did not prevent the blockage of Hrynov's motion to seal government and Party offices in order to prevent evidence about collaboration with the putschists from being destroyed.

During the final hour of its work, the parliament voted to place all military units stationed in Ukraine under its control, to re-establish a republican Ministry of Defence and to proceed with the creation of republican armed forces. Kravchuk, who had salvaged his authority by backing independence, also managed to persuade the deputies to agree to the extension of his powers until the election of a president. Drawing on all his old skills, he reciprocated by supporting a request from the opposition that the Ukrainian national flag be displayed in the chamber. After Chornovil pointed out that a blue and yellow flag with which 'Ukrainians had stood on the barricades by the White House' was now flying amid the crowds outside the parliament building, Kravchuk forestalled opponents by declaring that this 'memorable flag' had indeed 'won the right to be in this chamber'.

In the euphoria of it all, even the general dismay over the way in which Russia was taking over the structures of the centre temporarily receded and the Verkhovna Rada voted to convey a message of goodwill to Ukraine's northern neighbour. It approved a statement addressed to Russia's parliament and president expressing recognition of their 'heroic actions in defence of freedom and democracy during the *putsch'* and affirming Ukraine's commitment to the principles enshrined in the Russo-Ukrainian treaty of November 1990. Kravchuk adeptly sidestepped the contentious issues concerning the establishment of a commission to investigate who had supported the putschists and the Khmara case by deferring them to the parliamentary commissions. With this, the ambiguous figure who in the morning had begun the proceedings fearing for his political life, but after almost twelve momentous hours had emerged as acting head of an independent Ukrainian state, brought the historic extraordinary session to a close.

While celebrations were continuing that evening it was announced on Soviet television that Gorbachev was resigning as general secretary of the CPSU, nationalizing Party property and banning Party activity in government organizations and the security forces. In other words, the main agent of the Soviet empire's cohesion – the Communist Party – had itself imploded. It also became known that President Yeltsin had issued a decree recognizing the independence of Latvia and Estonia.

The following day, the Belarusian parliament declared the independence of Belarus and voted to suspend the activities of the Belarusian Communist Party. In Kyiv, with its Communist majority stunned by what was happening, the Presidium of the Ukrainian parliament decided to confiscate the CPU's buildings and freeze its assets until the commission which for almost a year had been examining the question of the nationalization of the Party's property had concluded its work. It also announced what amounted to an amnesty for political prisoners, that is, for Khmara, his colleagues and others detained during the recent struggles between the Communist and anti-Communist forces. The leadership of the Kyiv City Council went further and sealed off all the Party offices in the Ukrainian capital, including the Central Committee building outside of which thousands of people had gathered to express their support for this action.[26]

On 26 August, with more evidence of the CPU's complicity in the attempted coup emerging, the Presidium of the Ukrainian parliament decided to 'temporarily suspend the Party's activities. It also recognized the independence of the three Baltic states. For its

[26] *Literaturna Ukraina*, 29 August 1991.

part, the leadership of the Kyiv City Council voted to dismantle the giant Lenin monument in the capital's central October Revolution Square (where the previous autumn student protesters had pitched their tents) and to rename the latter Independence Square. That same day, the CPU Central Committee hurriedly held its last plenum. Behind the scenes, Kravchuk agreed not to sign the Presidium's decree until the plenum had finished its business. The plenum declared the CPU's complete independence and nominated a group of deputies to represent the Party's interests until it could resume its activities.[27] On the following day, Kravchuk would claim that he had resigned from the CPU back on 19 August.

Meanwhile, the reaction in Moscow to Ukraine's declaration of independence, even among democratic circles, was hardly encouraging. In quick succession, on 26 and 27 August, President Yeltsin's press secretary, Pavel Voshanov, and the mayors of Leningrad and Moscow, Sobchak and Popov, either raised the issue of reviewing Russia's borders with Ukraine or, like Gorbachev, expressed anxiety about the implications of Ukrainian independence for the Union. The Soviet president even threatened to resign if the republics did not agree to sign the Union treaty. But it was Voshanov's statement which caused the most damage: his assertion that Russia reserved the right to review its borders with all neighbours that decided to leave the Soviet Union, with the exception of the Baltic states, generated resentment and unease not only in Ukraine, but also especially in Kazakhstan, and dented Yeltsin's reputation.[28]

Kravchuk was quick to respond and told journalists on 27 August that 'Territorial claims are dangerous things.' He also took the opportunity to declare that Ukraine would not consider the issue of the revised Union treaty until after its referendum on independence.[29] That same day in Moscow, Lviv's Bratun protested in his speech to the USSR Supreme Soviet 'about the anti-Ukrainian and anti-republics hysteria concerning the review of borders'. He reminded the deputies that the Western Ukrainians, who were still being described by some speakers as 'extremists' and the source of

[27] Lytvyn, *Political Arena*, p. 273.

[28] For further details, see Roman Solchanyk, 'Ukraine and Russia: Before and after the Coup', *Report on the USSR*, no. 39 (27 September 1991), pp. 13–17.

[29] AP, 27 August, and AFP, 29 August 1991.

Ukrainian 'nationalism', had rallied to the support of Russian democracy, also referring in his speech to the provisions of the Russo-Ukrainian treaty. Reflecting the new spirit in Ukraine, he declared: 'We will not give up our independence. Remember that. And to speak today of a new Union treaty is obsolete. The empire is not to be!'[30]

Now that the USSR was clearly in a state of dissolution, and Ukraine intended to assert control over the military units based on its territory, an important new issue appeared: the fate not only of the Soviet armed forces but also of the huge Soviet nuclear arsenal, significant parts of which were to be found outside of Russia in Ukraine, Kazakhstan and Belarus. There was alarm both in Moscow and in the West. As far as Ukraine was concerned, though, the republic had pledged to become a nuclear-free state and no one was advocating a different position. Besides, even the number of nuclear weapons in Ukraine was still a military secret and few people seemed to have any idea of the costs and technical difficulties that their retention, removal or destruction would involve. Ukraine's official position during these days, as expressed by its ambassador to the United Nations, Hennadii Udovenko, and by Kravchuk himself, was that their country did not want to own nuclear weapons. Rukh's leaders concurred but also made clear their unhappiness with the idea of Russia remaining a nuclear power.

In Moscow, there did not seem to be a clear line on how to deal with problem of potential 'loose nukes'. Russia's Vice-President Alexander Rutskoi came out with a rather odd argument linking the nuclear arsenal with the need to preserve some form of Union. He warned on 26 August that if Russia alone were to keep nuclear weapons, it 'would mean the rebirth of the Russian empire. To avoid this happening a Union treaty must be signed.' On 28 August, however, Yeltsin announced that 'In view of the fact that Ukraine has declared itself a nuclear-free republic, its nuclear weapons will be moved to the Russian Federation.' It is unclear if he had consulted with the Ukrainian leadership before making this statement.[31]

With the implications of Ukraine's declaration of independence becoming apparent and strains developing in Russian – Ukrainian

---

[30] Soviet television, 27 August 1991.

[31] See Bohdan Nahaylo, 'The Shaping of Ukrainian Attitudes towards Nuclear Arms', *RFE/RL Research Report*, vol. 2, no. 8 (19 February 1993), pp. 21–45.

relations, on the morning of 28 August Sobchak proposed that the USSR Supreme Soviet send a delegation for talks with the Ukrainian parliament. 'Our main aim', he told the Soviet deputies, 'is not to allow the uncontrolled disintegration of the Soviet power structures. Today this is a far more important question than all the talk about the Party.'[32] That afternoon, also in full view of the television cameras, the deputy chairman of the USSR Supreme Soviet, Ivan Laptev, added to the drama by suddenly announcing that, in connection with 'an emergency situation', a delegation from the RSFSR headed by Vice-President Rutskoi, and also including Yeltsin's adviser Sergei Stankevich, and the economist Grigorii Yavlinsky, was already on its way to Kyiv. He requested that approval be given for a delegation from the USSR Supreme Soviet to be sent also. The confused deputies agreed and a group led by Sobchak also hurriedly departed for Ukraine.

News of the impending arrival in Kyiv of the two delegations from Moscow caused anxiety in the Ukrainian capital and many thousands instantly responded to calls from Rukh's leaders to 'greet' the unexpected visitors. Both at Kyiv's Boryspil Airport and at the Ukrainian parliament building, the delegations encountered huge demonstrations in support of Ukrainian independence. Initial attempts by Rutskoi and Sobchak to appeal to a sense of Slavic unity competely fell through and only drew shouts of 'Independence!' and 'Ukraine without Moscow!' Passions began to subside only after it became clearer that the Russian delegation had not arrived with threats but was seeking to clear the air and, in Rutskoi's words, to 'stabilize relations' between the two countries during this transitional period.

The Ukrainian delegation was headed by Kravchuk and included among others, Masyk, Yukhnovsky, Pavlychko and Yemets. Sobchak's delegation from the USSR Supreme Soviet acted as observers. The outcome after nine hours of intense negotiations was a joint Ukrainian-Russian comminiqué, signed by Kravchuk and Rutskoi, which in many ways was a prototype of the arrangement on which the Commonwealth of Independent States would be based. It recognized the 'inalienable right' of Ukraine and Russia to 'state independence' and reaffirmed the validity of the bilateral treaty signed in November 1990, emphasizing especially the provision

[32] Soviet television, 28 August 1991.

dealing with mutual recognition of one another's territorial integrity. Both sides pledged cooperation to avoid 'the uncontrolled disintegration' of what was described for the first time in an official document as 'the former Soviet Union'. In the interests of security and of avoiding economic dislocation, the two sides declared that they considered it 'necessary to create temporary inter-state structures that interested states – subjects of the former USSR, regardless of their current status – could join on the basis of representational parity'. The communiqué also acknowledged 'the special significance of military-strategic problems'. The two sides agreed 'not to adopt unilateral decisions' in this sphere and on the need for 'a reform of the armed forces of the USSR and the creation of a system of collective security'. The document also affirmed the adherence of both states 'to commitments by the USSR in international relations', including arms control agreements, and significantly, emphasized their readiness to deal with matters stemming from previously made international commitments through direct negotiations with 'members of the international community'. Finally, the two states agreed to exchange 'empowered envoys'.[33]

At a press conference held at the end of the talks in the early hours of 29 August, Kravchuk expressed his satisfaction with what had been achieved. He stressed that by referring for the first time to 'the former USSR', the two sides had recognized the new political reality, that the communiqué effectively recognized Ukraine's declaration of independence, and that the negotiations would stop the recent wave of anti-Russian feeling.[34] Later that day, seemingly chastened by his experience in Kyiv, Sobchak reported back to the USSR Supreme Soviet that 'Ukraine, like other republics, has firmly taken the path towards genuine independence, genuine freedom, the formation of its own statehood, and no one can force it to diverge from this path.'[35]

Gorbachev, however, continued to suggest that if Ukraine left the Union the republic would split along ethnic lines and, therefore, despite its declaration of independence, would sign the revised Union treaty. He told a Ukrainian journalist:

There can be no Union without Ukraine, I feel, and no Ukraine

[33] *Molod Ukrainy*, 30 August 1991.
[34] *Ibid.*
[35] TASS, 29 August 91.

without the Union. These Slavic states, Russia and Ukraine, were the axis along which, for centuries, events turned and a huge multinational state developed. That is the way it will remain. I am convinced of it.[36]

As soon as relations with Russia had been patched up and the Russian delegation had left Kyiv, the Ukrainian leadership moved ahead with consolidating the republic's independence. Security issues were at the top of the agenda and on 29 August, the Presidium of the parliament met with the commanders of the Soviet military forces stationed in Ukraine to discuss questions connected with the creation of a Ukrainian Ministry of Defence and national armed forces. The challenges facing the Ukrainian leadership were daunting: the huge military force deployed on Ukraine's territory was now estimated to be anywhere between 1.2 million and 1.5 million strong. Moreover, the majority of the officers were Russian and, as it was later to be confirmed, Ukrainians constituted under half of the military personnel.

While the discussion with the generals continued, the Presidium was pushed by the enormous public pressure being generated by the disclosures about the role of the CPU during the attempted coup to take another decisive step – to ban, on 30 August, the Party and nationalize its property. The Communist Party had in any case been placed in an untenable position the day before when the USSR Supreme Soviet had voted to suspend its activities throughout the USSR and to freeze its assets. Ironically then, Ukraine – where the Party had managed to retain its grip on power for longer than in many other republics – was the first after the Baltic republics to ban outright the Communist Party on its territory. While there were protests from some of the Communist deputies about the 'undemocratic' and 'illegal' nature of this move, by and large the bulk of the Communist rank and file who had not broken with the discredited Party reluctantly accepted the verdict.[37] At least, as Yukhnovsky had proposed, there were no purges and former Communist officials retained their positions.

---

[36] *Molod Ukrainy*, 30 August 1995.

[37] On 4 September, Fedir Panasyuk submitted a motion on behalf of ninety Communist deputies calling for a repeal of the ban on the CPU. When it came to vote, however, only fifty-four deputies supported it. Radio Kyiv, 5 September 1991.

In the space of a dramatic week then, Ukraine had declared its independence, seemingly laid the basis for normal bilateral relations with Russia, banned the Communist Party and begun creating a national army. When, on 4 September the Communist majority in the parliament voted to dissolve itself and deputies agreed that the blue and yellow flag should be raised over the legislature building, it only underscored that a new chapter in the history of Ukraine had begun. The hopes raised by the break with the past and the determination to make a success of independence were to grow over the following months as Ukraine's decisive referendum approached and the Soviet Union continued to disintegrate.

14

THE REALIZATION OF INDEPENDENCE
AND INTERNATIONAL RECOGNITION

Consolidating independence

Before the Ukrainian parliament formally resumed its work after the summer recess, Kravchuk made a brief visit on 2 September 1991 to Moscow to attend the opening of the Congress of USSR People's Deputies. By now various other republics had also declared their independence and Gorbachev had to agree to more concessions in order to persuade them to sign a new Union treaty. Kravchuk put his signature to an agreement signed by Gorbachev and the leaders of ten republics which, according to the explanation that the Ukrainian leader presented to his parliament, called for the preparation and signing of a treaty on a 'union of sovereign states', but by states 'which wanted a treaty', and on their terms. In his address to the Congress and at a press conference in Moscow, the Ukrainian leader made it clear that Ukraine was going to wait until after the results of its referendum were known before considering any new Union treaty, and then only if the proposed new Union was a confederation.[1] But the mere fact that he had signed such a document, which also called for the creation of an economic community of the republics,[2] got some of the national democrats worried about what he was up to.

On 3 September, the Ukrainian parliament demonstrated that it was serious about taking charge of defence and security matters by endorsing the appointment of a minister of defence. He was forty-seven-year-old Major-General Kostyantyn Morozov, a Russian, who was the commander of the air forces deployed in Ukraine. He was instructed to draw up plans for the creation of a republican guard

[1] Radio Kyiv, 3 September 1991.
[2] Published in *Izvestiya*, 2 September 1991.

and a national army. To forestall the removal of military equipment from the republic, during the next few days the parliament's Presidium forbade the redeployment of troops within Ukraine without permission of the Ukrainian authorities, and the withdrawal from the republic of weapons and military property. It also issued a decree on Ukraine assuming control over the MVD and border troops stationed on its territory.[3] Interestingly, Soviet television announced on 10 September that a division of KGB special forces based in Kharkiv had requested the Ukrainian government to be included in the republic's republican guard.

While the planning and preparations for the creation of national armed forces proceeded, and the debate about what to do with the nuclear weapons on Ukraine's territory intensified, the parliament continued with its important work of preparing or adopting new legislation on a range of subjects connected with state-building. For example, it began finalizing the draft law on citizenship and, on 24 September, abolished the old republican KGB structure and created in its place a new National Security Service responsible, until the election of the president, to the head of parliament.

There was also considerable activity in the sphere of foreign relations. During September, Foreign Minister Zlenko undertook an official visit to Poland and, among others, French, Canadian and American officials visited Kyiv. A Ukrainian parliamentary delegation travelled to Chisinau and its talks with Moldovan parliamentarians helped pave the way for regularizing relations with another of Ukraine's neighbours. This was an important step because of potential border disputes between the two states and because 600,000 Ukrainians constituted Moldova's largest national minority, and some of them had been caught up in the conflict between Chisinau and the breakaway Transdniester enclave.

But the most significant development in the external sphere was Kravchuk's visit at the end of September to North America, and his brief stopover in France on the way back. The trip provided a splendid opportunity to win greater international recognition and support for Ukraine. It began with a successful three-day official visit to Canada, included a meeting with President Bush in Washington and culminated with the Ukrainian leader's address to the UN General Assembly on 30 September. Kravchuk used the latter

---

[3] Ukrinform-TASS, 10 September 1991.

occasion to introduce independent Ukraine to an organization of which, paradoxically, it had been a founding member but in which, for over forty-five years, it had not been able to speak with its own voice. Ukraine, he told the delegates, was committed to democracy, international cooperation and disarmament. It had no territorial claims on any of its neighbours and did not recognize any claims to its own territory. He affirmed that in accordance with its Declaration of State Sovereignty, Ukraine did not seek to possess nuclear weapons and intended to join the Non-Proliferation Treaty as a non-nuclear state. The Ukrainian leader also let it be known, however, that Ukraine was no longer prepared to leave disarmament issues to Moscow, explaining that his country wanted to become 'directly involved in the disarmament negotiating process'.[4]

Having also met with France's President Mitterrand on the return leg, Kravchuk returned home evidently imbued with new confidence and determination to uphold Ukraine's interests. He told a news conference on 4 October that 'we cannot agree to one republic taking over all the nuclear weapons. We cannot disregard our security'. For the time being, he called for a dual key system of control over the nuclear arms on Ukraine's territory, which would provide a mechanism for Kyiv to veto any use of them; he also reiterated Ukraine's wish to have its own seat at all future negotiations on nuclear disarmament.[5]

With domestic attention within Ukraine beginning to focus more and more on the approaching referendum and presidential election, from now on official Kyiv began to manifest more and more its lack of interest in being drawn into any new Union structures and that Ukraine was preoccupied with state-building and preparing the ground for recognition as a full-fledged independent country. On 7 October, for instance, Soviet Constitution Day was not observed in the republic. On the following day, the Verkhovna Rada finally adopted a law on citizenship which was non-discriminating and granted citizenship to everyone resident in Ukraine at the time. Three days later, the parliament agreed on the wording of the question to be asked in the referendum: 'Do you endorse the Act of the Declaration of Ukrainian Independence?' This cleared the

[4] For the text of his speech, see *The Ukrainian Weekly*, 6 October 1991.
[5] Reuter, 4 October 1991.

way for the launch of an official campaign to secure a yes vote in the referendum.

Also on 11 October, deputies gave their backing to a 'Concept of Defence and the Building of the Armed Forces of Ukraine' as the basis for a draft law on this subject which was published in the press five days later. It affirmed Ukraine's intention 'gradually' to become a neutral and non-nuclear state, to build its own armed forces from Soviet conventional troops based in Ukraine, on the basis of 'reasonable sufficiency' and numbering about 420,000 personnel (in other words, that they should be no larger than 0.9% of the population), and that strategic forces on Ukraine's territory would remain under the unified control of a system of collective strategic defence. One other noteworthy measure connected with ensuring the security of the new state and decided on that same day was the extension of Article 62 of the Ukrainian Criminal Code to prohibit activity aimed at undermining the territorial integrity of Ukraine. The penalties provided for up to three years' imprisonment for individuals found guilty of this offence and seven for repeated offenders or members of organized groups.[6]

In Moscow, preparations were hurriedly being made for the signing of a treaty establishing an economic community and rather tactlessly Gorbachev was at pains to link it with a renewed political Union. Speaking on Soviet television on 12 October about what he described as plans to create 'a Union state' with 'a new centre', he went out of his way to emphasize that Ukraine was 'an irreplaceable factor in the building of our Union'. Revealing the extent to which he misunderstood the mood in Ukraine, he declared: 'I cannot think of a Union without Ukraine. I cannot think of it and I cannot imagine it. I think that they understand this in Ukraine as well.' After all, he argued yet again, had not the voters in the March referendum come out in favour of the Union.[7]

In fact, the Ukrainian leadership could take heart from the results of the polls being carried out to provide an indication of how Ukraine's voters were likely to cast their ballots in the approaching referendum. For instance, on 15 October Radio Kyiv announced that a poll conducted by the Association of Sociologists in Ukraine

[6] Radio Kyiv, 11 October 1991.

[7] See Roman Solchanyk, 'Ukraine, the Kremlin and the Russian White House', *Report on the USSR*, no. 44 (1 November 1991), p. 14.

estimated that almost 87% of the voters would cast their ballot in favour of independence. Displaying a quiet confidence and sticking determinedly to its principled position, therefore, the Ukrainian leadership and parliament resisted the new pressure emanating from Moscow. On 17 October, the very eve of the signing of the economic pact, Ukraine snubbed the old centre: Kravchuk announced that Ukraine was not prepared to sign the agreement and stayed away from the signing ceremony, sending Fokin and Plyushch as observers. This did not mean that Ukraine had no interest in the pact and it indicated that it would continue negotiations to secure some fundamental adjustments to the arrangement which would make it closer, as Kravchuk and other Ukrainian representatives put it, to the model of the European Economic Community.

When the revamped USSR Supreme Soviet opened on 21 October, Ukrainian representatives were conspicuously absent. This prompted Gorbachev, Yeltsin and the leaders of seven other republics to appeal to the Ukrainian parliament to participate in the preparation of a new Union treaty. But the Ukrainian parliament was adamant and the extent of its concessionary response was to send a group of observers to the upper chamber of the USSR Supreme Soviet, the Council of the Republics.

This unrequited 'wooing' of Ukraine, however, was taking place against the background of rising tensions connected with the reaction to Ukraine's moves to establish its own armed forces and the uncertainty over the fate of the Soviet nuclear arsenal on Ukrainian territory. In fact, as the Ukrainian leadership was discovering, some 15% of the USSR's nuclear weapons were deployed in Ukraine, including about 3,000 tactical nuclear arms and 176 ICBMs inter-(continental ballistic missiles, that is, strategic nuclear weapons), with 1,240 warheads. This made Ukraine potentially the world's third largest nuclear state, with a nuclear arsenal larger than those of the United Kingdom, France and China combined. The huge costs and considerable dangers connected with eliminating these weapons – Ukraine did not have the technical facilities to dismantle the nuclear warheads – were also becoming more apparent. As for the former Soviet conventional forces stationed in Ukraine, while the number of actual military personnel based in the republic turned out to be a few hundred thousands less than initially thought even with a more realistic strength of some 750,000, this force constituted the second largest army in Europe after Russia's, and was larger than the British and French forces combined. Moreover, because Ukraine was one of the major Soviet staging areas against the West, the troops stationed in the republic were well equipped with tanks, armoured vehicles, artillery, helicopters and aircraft and reasonably well trained.

Hardly surprisingly, Ukraine's moves to build its own armed forces drew a particularly irate response from the Soviet military. The impression formed in Kyiv was that Moscow was deliberately playing on Western fears of Ukraine wanting to establish itself as a nuclear power and planning to build a huge army that would upset the military balance in Europe. Indeed, the military issue, and especially that of nuclear arms, increasingly began to complicate Ukraine's burgeoning foreign relations as the latter found itself under increasing pressure to leave the nuclear weapons on its territory under Moscow's sole control or to transfer them to Russia.

Matters were not helped when on 20 October *Moskovskie novosti* published a sensational report claiming that Yeltsin had discussed with his military advisers the possibility of a pre-emptive nuclear strike against Ukraine. The Russian president's rather clumsy response – 'Totally absurd. I discussed this question with military officials; technically it is absolutely impossible' – was hardly reassuring.[8]

On the next day, 21 October, addressing the USSR Supreme Soviet and aiming specifically at Ukraine, Gorbachev warned against the 'nationalization' of Soviet armed forces deployed in the republics, describing such moves as dangerous and irresponsible. Ignoring Ukraine's Declaration of Independence, he also threatened to annul such legislation as anti-constitutional. Undeterred, on the following day, the Ukrainian parliament approved a package of laws covering the creation of a Ukrainian army, navy, air force, national guard and border troops, as well as a law on Ukraine's state borders.[9] In his report to the parliament Defence Minister Morozov emphasized that the creation of the armed forces would be carried out gradually in cooperation and agreement with the Soviet General Staff and USSR Defence Ministry.

---

[8] *Moskovskie novosti*, 20 October 1991; and *Nezavisimaya gazeta*, 24 October 1991. See also John Lloyd and Chrystia Freeland, 'Ukraine Accuses Yeltsin of Nuclear Strike Threat', *Financial Times*, 25 October 1991.

[9] Radio Kyiv, 22 October 1991.

On top of the furor caused by the article in *Moskovskie novosti* and Gorbachev's threats, official Kyiv was especially irritated when TASS issued what *The Times* described as 'heavily distorted' reports about the debate in the Ukrainian parliament, suggesting that Ukraine had voted to 'nationalize' the strategic nuclear missile force on its territory. These 'erroneous' reports, as Reuters called them, increased alarm in the West.[10] Ukrainian officials protested against what the deputy chairman of the Ukrainian parliament Hrynov claimed was 'disinformation'. 'We are being depicted as a state that wants to blackmail the world,' he declared. 'These allegations are groundless.'[11] But the damage had been done and on 24 October the Ukrainian parliament felt compelled to adopt a statement clarifying Ukraine's position. It reaffirmed Ukraine's commitment to becoming a non-nuclear state as soon as was feasible; but it also insisted that, until the nuclear weapons based on Ukraine's territory were destroyed (rather than handed over to Russia), Ukraine should exercise some form of joint control over them for the purpose of ensuring their non-use.[12] Ukraine's leaders, who by now had also realized how expensive and complicated the elimination of nuclear weapons on their territory would be, appealed for Western financial and technical assistance to destroy them.

In view of all these latest developments, it was hardly surprising that the Ukraine parliament remained intransigent. On 25 October, by an overwhelming vote, it adopted a resolution declaring that it considered it inappropriate for Ukraine to participate in any inter-republican structure that could lead to its inclusion in another state.[13]

The presidential and referendum campaigns

By now the presidential election was getting into full swing. More than ninety hopefuls initially sought to collect the 100,000 signatures required by law by 20 October for their registration as candidates. Eventually, only seven managed to achieve this and one of them – Oleksander Tkachenko, the minister of agriculture – subsequently

---

[10] Robert Seely, 'Ukraine Denies Plan to "Nationalize" Missiles', *The Times*, and Reuter, 24 October 1991.

[11] Seely, 'Ukraine Denies . . .'

[12] Radio Kyiv, 25 October, and *Silski visti*, 26 October 1991.

[13] Ukrinform-TASS, 25 October 1991.

withdrew from the contest in favour of Kravchuk. Significantly, all of the final six candidates supported independence, democracy and moving towards a market economy. For weeks they travelled the length and breadth of the republic promoting these ideas. The Ukrainian media, enjoying the greater freedom that came after the Communist débâcle in August, also focused on the candidates and their platforms.

Apart from Kravchuk, the other presidential contenders were former political prisoners Chornovil and Lukyanenko, leading democratic figures Yukhnovsky and Hrynov, and the least known of them – Leopold Taburyansky, a Russian-speaking engineer and deputy from Dnipropetrovsk, who was a supporter of private enterprise and the leader of the small Ukrainian People's Party. As the initial polls indicated, Kravchuk was the clear favourite, maintaining a comfortable lead over his nearest rival, Chornovil. Although he was preoccupied with the affairs of state, Kravchuk had the distinct advantage of support from the 'official' establishment and former partocracy, complete with the former Communist-controlled media, which were now in the process of a changeover to a pro-independence mode. He also gained from the fact that the democratic camp failed to rally around a single candidate, thereby weakening its prospects and only exposing the growing divisions within it. Chornovil, for instance, who was nominated by the Galician Assembly, managed to win endorsement from Rukh's Grand Council, yet quite a few of Rukh's leaders, including Drach, Mykhailo Horyn and Porovsky, came out for Lukyanenko, while the idiosyncratic militant, Khmara, backed Taburyansky.

Because of the pro-independence orientation of all the candidates, the presidential campaign undoubtedly played a considerable role in shaping attitudes for the forthcoming referendum. With so much depending on the outcome of the referendum, the Ukrainian authorities threw the full weight of the fledgling independent state behind the campaign to persuade voters, especially in the south and east, to vote for independence. While the former Communist structures and their organs now extolled the virtues of independence, the patriotic and democratic forces also endeavoured to ensure that the referendum, which by no means all of them had welcomed, would finally clinch their country's freedom. Moreover, the largely negative or even hostile coverage which developments in Ukraine received during this period in the central 'Soviet' media, and the strong criticism of the republic's stance from Gorbachev and various Russian political and military leaders, seems to have irritated the Ukrainian population and worked to the advantage of the advocates of independence.

There were a number of regions, though, where problems arose. Of course, the outcome of the voting in Crimea was not something the Ukrainian leadership could feel comfortable about. In fact, on 22 November an extraordinary session of the Crimean parliament adopted a controversial referendum law which appeared to open the way for a future local poll on secession from Ukraine. Meanwhile, in the Transcarpathian region, where the Ruthenian movement for autonomy had been growing, the regional council decided to hold a local referendum on this issue simultaneously with the republican one. After some bargaining, Kravchuk was able to persuade the council to revise its question and to replace a reference to autonomy with the words: 'the status of a special self-governing administrative territory.' Also in Transcarpathia, in the Beregovo district, where Hungarians form a compact majority, the district council decided to hold a local poll on the formation of a Hungarian autonomous district.[14] The Chernivtsi regional council also decided to pose its own question to voters on 1 December asking them if they wanted a special economic status for their region.

There were other problems which complicated relations with its two south-western neighbours. A few days before the referendum, the Romanian parliament renewed Bucharest's claims to territory that had been annexed from Romania by the Soviet Union as a result of the Molotov-Ribbentrop Pact. The territorial dispute predated the Nazi-Soviet agreement and in 1918–20 Ukrainians had protested against what they considered to be Romania's annexation of ethnically Ukrainian districts in Bessarabia and Bukovyna. After the assertion of their republic's sovereignty, the Ukrainian authorities had rejected Romania's territorial claims. On 28 November, however, the Romanian parliament challenged Ukraine's right to conduct a referendum in what it described as 'Romanian territories' in parts of the Chernivsti and Odesa regions.

---

[14] See Roman Solchanyk, 'Centrifugal Movements in Ukraine on the Eve of the Independence Referendum', *Report on the USSR*, vol. 3, no. 48 (29 November 1991), pp. 8-12, and his 'The Politics of State Building'.

Consequently, Zlenko cancelled an official visit to Romania which had been scheduled for the following day.[15]

Meanwhile, in adjacent Moldova, where the Moldovan Popular Front had initially also revived territorial claims against Ukraine, the conflict with the self-proclaimed and staunchly pro-Union 'Dniester (or Transdniester) Republic' was intensifying. The latter was backed by ultra-nationalist forces in Russia and the presence of the Soviet 14th Army in the breakaway region raised the possibility of more direct Russian involvement.

The 'Dniester Republic' occupied territory on the left bank of the River Dniester ('Transdniestra') which before 1940 had administratively been part of Soviet Ukraine; although Russians had flooded in during the post-war period as industry was developed, both Moldovans and Ukrainians still outnumbered them, constituting about 40% and 28% respectively of the enclave's roughly 600,000-strong population. Deprived until very recently of basic cultural facilities (the Moldovan government had sought to allay fears of forcible Romanization and had adopted a liberal policy towards Moldova's national minorities) the Ukrainian population in Moldova had been heavily Russified and the first Ukrainian cultural societies were just appearing. On the Ukrainian side of the border, too, there were sizable 'Romanian' and 'Moldovan' minorities – the rather artificial distinction between the two groups had been officially fostered during the Soviet period – which in 1989 numbered 325,000 and 135,000 respectively.[16] On the eve of Ukraine's referendum, the leaders of a Romanian cultural society in Chernivtsi announced that they expected that some Romanians in the region would respond to the Romanian parliament's resolution on the border issue by boycotting the poll.[17]

As the referendum approached, Kravchuk, the Ukrainian parliament and the national democratic forces did their best to promote unity and to reassure the national minorities that not only would their rights be fully respected in the new Ukraine but also that they

---

[15] TASS, 28 and 29 November, and Radio Kyiv, 29 November, 1991.

[16] On Ukrainian-Moldovan relations, see the author's 'Ukraine and Moldova: The View from Kiev', *RFE/RL Research Report*, vol. 1, no. 18 (1 May 1992), pp. 39-45, and 'Moldovan Conflict Creates new Dilemmas for Ukraine', *REF/RL Research Report*, vol. 1, no. 20 (15 May 1992), pp, 1-8.

[17] AFP, 30 November 1991.

could consider it as their home. The liberal citizenship law certainly helped in this respect. Furthermore, the fact that a Russian, Fokin, continued to head the government, that the new minister of defence was also a Russian, and that another Russian, Hrynov, was running for president, was an encouraging sign for Ukraine's massive Russian population and showed that far from being squeezed out, Russians were helping to build the new Ukrainian state.

Ukraine's second largest minority, the Jews, many of whom had emigrated from Ukraine as from other parts of the USSR in recent years and were continuing to do so, could also witness reassuring changes for the better. For a week beginning on 29 September, the Ukrainian government officially sponsored the commemoration of the fiftieth anniversary of the Nazi massacre of Jews and others at Babyi Yar on the outskirts of Kyiv. Kyiv's main streets were hung with commemorative banners and a special exhibition was mounted along the Khreshchatyk. Kravchuk himself participated in a memorial meeting and delivered a historic statement designed to open a brighter chapter in the often troubled history of relations between the Ukrainian and Jewish peoples by accepting a share of the guilt and offering a formal apology. He declared:

> Babyi Yar was a genocide and not only the Nazis are to blame for it. Part of the blame lies with those who didn't prevent them from carrying it out, so part is ours and we think it only natural to apologize before the Jewish people. . . . We do not accept the ideological concept of the former [Communist] Ukraine that neglected human rights, hid the truth about Babyi Yar, hid the truth of the number killed there and the fact that most were of Jewish origin.

Anti-Semitism, he continued, would not be tolerated in the new Ukraine, stressing: 'We are building statehood for all nationalities living on this land.'[18]

The same democratic spirit was reflected in a Declaration of the Rights of the Nationalities of Ukraine adopted by the parliament at the beginning of November which affirmed, among other things, that 'discrimination on ethnic grounds is proscribed and punishable by the law', that the Ukrainian state guaranteed the national minorities the right to develop their cultural life freely, and that it

---

[18] See the reports by Chrystia Freeland in the *Financial Times* and Susan Viets in *The Independent*, 7 October 1991.

assumed 'responsibility for creating the proper conditions for the development' of their national languages and cultures.[19] Furthermore, on 17-18 November the Ukrainian authorities and Rukh jointly convened a Congress of National Minorities in Odesa. Not surprisingly, the Congress issued an appeal calling on the republic's national minorities to support Ukrainian independence and contribute to building the new state.[20]

Closer still to the referendum, the authorities also managed to convene in Kyiv an unprecedented conference of all the republic's main religious denominations, sixteen of which were represented, most by their leaders. Kravchuk also participated. The gathering on 18–19 November provided a poignant reminder that although the Orthodox and Catholic churches predominated in Ukraine, there were also Protestant, Jewish and Muslim believers. In view of the persistence of religious discord and rivalry in the republic, the Congress served as a useful attempt to promote conciliation and reduce tensions. It also gave the participants an opportunity to press the government to improve shortcomings in the legislation pertaining to religious believers and to return religious buildings still not restored to them.

A prominent role was played by Metropolitan Filaret, who was close to Kravchuk, and who by now had become a supporter of Ukrainian independence. In fact, he was heading efforts by the Ukrainian Orthodox Church, or at least a part of its hierarchy, to obtain autocephaly, or canonical independence, from the Moscow Patriarchate. This 'evolution' had of course brought the Ukrainian Orthodox Church closer to the position of the Ukrainian Autocephalous Orthodox Church and the possibility of a merger of the two Orthodox churches was already being talked about.[21]

However important the efforts to win over Ukraine's national minorities were – the main churches, perhaps with the exception of some believers within the Ukrainian Orthodox Church, were ardent supporters of independence and did not need really need persuading – probably the crucial factors determining the voting in the referendum as far as the critical mass of Russians and Russified Ukrainians in the south and east were concerned were socio-

---

[19] *Pravovi dzherela Ukrainy*, no. 1, 1994, pp. 8–9.

[20] Radio Kyiv, 18 and 19 November 1991.

[21] *Ibid.*, 20 November 1991.

economic considerations. But these, too, were working in favour of independence. After years of watching Moscow make a mess of economic reform and feeling the consequences of the economic crisis and disorder, and having witnessed the decline and continuing dissolution of the Soviet Union, there seemed to be very little reason to place hopes on a reconstituted Union and a revitalized centre. Instead, the belief that social and economic prospects would be better in an independent Ukraine, promoted by Ukrainian national democrats and now Ukraine's government, too, had taken hold. External experts had also reinforced this view by giving a high rating to Ukraine's economic potential.[22]

In reality, serious problems were looming on the horizon for the Ukrainian economy. Ukrainian-Russian relations were being strained by the increasingly frequent non-fulfilment of supply agreements (oil, gas and timber from Russia to Ukraine and grain, sugar, heavy machinery and construction materials going the other way) and the production stoppages and recriminations which this brought. Furthermore, the Russian government was planning to liberalize prices and to raise the price of its fuel exports and this threatened to hit the Ukrainian economy very hard.

Fokin's government had also decided, as an interim step, to introduce a system of multi-use coupons for purchasing food and consumer goods. The decision to use a surrogate currency alongside the rouble was precipitated by the growing shortage of roubles in Ukraine and the need to protect the Ukrainian market, especially in food supplies. Russia controlled the rouble printing presses and the distribution of cash. Having a higher rate of inflation, and itself facing a shortage of roubles, Russia had been raising salaries, while in Ukraine, where prices and wages were relatively more stable, the government had serious difficulties paying even the existing wages.[23]

The Ukrainian parliament had recently voted to close down the Chornobyl nuclear power plant in 1993. It was unclear at this stage, though, how Ukraine, already so dependent on Russia for fuel, would manage to secure alternative sources of energy. And of

[22] For example, a special report published by the Deutsche Bank in October 1990 had given Ukraine the highest rating of all the Soviet republics. See Jurgen Corbet and Andreas Gummich, *The Soviet Union at the Crossroads: Facts and Figures on the Soviet Republics*, Frankfurt, 1990.

[23] Chrystia Freeland, 'Economists Plot Go-It-Alone Strategy for the Ukraine', *Financial Times*, 27 September 1991.

course, the intractable problems of the Donbas and the consequences of the Chornobyl disaster remained and continued to drain resources.

Towards an orderly separation from the Union

Despite the renewed friction between Kyiv and Moscow, Kravchuk and other Ukrainian leaders seem to have gone out of their way to prevent an open rift with Russia on the eve of the referendum. Indeed, it was to the credit of the Ukrainian politicians running for the presidency that they did not seek to fan anti-Russian sentiment as a means of increasing their votes. Kravchuk himself was to stress throughout the preparations for the referendum and the presidential elections how important it was for both Ukraine and Russia to remain on good terms with one another. Choosing not to capitalize on the disclosures in the Moscow press about Yeltsin's alleged discussion of the possibility of a nuclear strike against Ukraine, he dismissed the reports as 'a crude provocation' designed to set the Ukrainians and Russians against one another.

Fortunately for Ukraine, and the other non-Russian former Union republics, since Yeltsin had emerged the victor in Moscow after the failed coup attempt, a group of young and radical anti-Communist figures had become his closet advisers and were gradually to fill key positions in his 'administration'. They included the philosopher Gennadii Burbulis (whose father was Lithuanian and mother Russian), the economist Yegor Gaidar, Sergei Shakhrai and Russia's new foreign minister, Andrei Kozyrev. These Russian 'Young Turks' also constituted what could be termed an 'anti-imperial' party. Opposed to the old centre, they wanted to strengthen the statehood of a democratic Russia, to move in the direction of a market economy and for Russia to assume the rights and obligations of the USSR. They also believed that Russia's relations with the other Union republics should be altered accordingly, that is, that Russia should stop subsidizing them and instead begin conducting business with them on the basis of bilateral agreements.[24]

---

[24] See Alexander Rahr, 'Russia's "Young Turks" in Power', *Report on the USSR*, vol. 3, no. 47 (22 November 1991), pp. 20-3.

Consequently, the lines of communication between Kyiv and Moscow remained open and towards the end of October the two sides agreed to try and work out their problems in a new round of talks, this time in Moscow. First the foreign and defence ministers of both countries met and cleared the air by reaching agreement on a broad range of issues of mutual concern and formalizing the bilateral accord which had been announced in the Ukrainian–Russian communiqué of 29 August. Furthermore, in a wide-ranging protocol signed on 30 October by Zlenko and his Russian counterpart, Kozyrev, the two sides reiterated that the nuclear weapons on Ukrainian territory should be controlled and dismantled by a central authority accountable to all republics.[25] The following day, however, Zlenko issued a statement emphasizing once again that Ukraine wanted the nuclear weapons on its territory to be destroyed, not just moved, and that it also wanted 'full guarantees' that the weapons would not be used before they were destroyed.

Over the next few days further progress in the bilateral talks was made, enabling Morozov to announce on 4 November that Russia had agreed to the creation of Ukrainian armed forces. Two days later, Presidents Kravchuk and Yeltsin signed a communiqué which, while referring to the need for a collective security system with unified strategic forces, acknowledged the right of Ukraine and Russia to set up their own armed forces and once again recognized the existing borders of the two states. Rounding off the series of accords, that same day the two neighbours also signed a trade and economic cooperation agreement for 1992 which seemed to provide Ukraine with a breathing space.[26]

There was almost a hitch, though. While the bilateral talks were under way in Moscow, the Ukrainian parliament reacted with concern to news from Moscow that Kravchuk and Fokin had apparently agreed, without first consulting it, to sign the treaty establishing an economic community which eight republics and Gorbachev had concluded the previous month. It also led some deputies to accuse Yeltsin's government of having begun to use economic and trade levers to 'blackmail' Ukraine.

Fokin responded by confirming that since the economic treaty

---

[25] Ukrinform-TASS and Radio Rossii, 30 October 1991.

[26] Radio Kyiv, 6 November 1991, and Chapter 3 in Clark, *An Empire's New Clothes*.

had been signed, Ukraine had indeed begun experiencing 'complications' as regards the honouring of existing supply contracts between Ukrainian enterprises and their partners in the republics which had formed the new economic community. Ukraine, he argued, could not afford to divorce itself completely from the new arrangement for inter-republican economic cooperation and it was wiser to try and work out compromises. If, for instance, Russia started charging world prices for fuel, then either Ukraine would find itself in the red *vis-à-vis* its northern neighbour or would have to increase substantially the amount of grain, meat, sugar and other products it was delivering to it in exchange. The prime minister was able, however, to reassure the deputies that the treaty had already been amended to take into account some of Ukraine's reservations and that Kyiv would continue to insist on a large number of additional changes on 'matters of principle'. On behalf of the Ukrainian government he proposed, therefore, that for the time being Ukraine initial the treaty subject to its ratification by the parliament. His arguments persuaded the majority of the deputies and on 6 November he initialled the treaty.[27]

But the distrust of the residual centre was so strong and the fear of Ukraine being dragged into a new Union so great that a week later Fokin was reduced to threatening to resign if the deputies blocked Ukraine's adherence to the economic treaty. He was also very forthright in his depiction of what awaited Ukraine if it were to sever its ties with the republics which had signed the agreement: unemployment in the republic would rapidly soar and within months reach about 3 million, and production would fall by 25%. He also reminded the deputies that Ukraine had a negative balance of trade, and that if Russia and other republics moved closer to using world prices in trade the republic would sink into debt.[28]

With confidence growing in Ukrainian political circles that the referendum would produce a decisive endorsement of independence – Kravchuk even expressed the hope that the percentage of voters supporting independence would surpass 85% – Ukrainian leaders continued to work towards an orderly withdrawal from the old Union. The message which was to come across very clearly from official Kyiv during the last month before the referendum was that

[27] *Ibid.*

[28] *Ibid.*, 13 November 1991.

Ukraine had no interest in being part of any political Union but was seeking the most appropriate terms for itself to remain connected to the other republics in some form of loose partnership for economic and other forms of mutually beneficial cooperation. At the same time, Ukraine's Foreign Ministry was actively continuing the diplomatic groundwork for Ukraine's formal international recognition.

When on 14 November Gorbachev called a meeting in Novo Ogarevo to finalize the latest variant of the proposed Union treaty, Ukraine boycotted it. The representatives of seven states, including Russia, which did participate ended up having a heated debate with Gorbachev about whether the new association of states would still be a single state, and the latter threatened to resign if it was not. Eventually, they agreed in principle on a compromise – that the new 'Union of Sovereign States' would be a 'confederative democratic *state*' (author's emphasis).[29] Kravchuk publicly dismissed the meeting, declaring that the Novo Ogarevo process had no future and that it would be better to try and follow the example of the European Community.[30] The following month, he would reveal that around this time he began proposing to Yeltsin and to the chairman of the Belarusian parliament, Stanislau Shushkevich, that they should meet and try and find their own solution for dispensing with the Union and building cooperation among themselves on a new basis.[31]

Some kind of transitional arrangement was clearly essential. On 22 November, Kravchuk pointed out that the Russian government's decision to liberalize prices, 'taken without agreeing it first with the other former Union republics', was 'rather convincing evidence that the treaty on economic cooperation' had been stillborn.[32] Furthermore, on the following day, Fokin complained that Ukraine was being pressured by Russia and the G7 states to agree to pay part of the Soviet foreign debt without knowing how

[29] See Ann Sheehy, 'The Union Treaty: A Further Setback', *Report on the USSR*, vol. 3, no. 49 (6 December 1991), pp. 1-4.

[30] Soviet television, 15 November 1991.

[31] See Kravchuk's interview in *Paris Match*, 26 December 1991, p. 58, and with Kichigin, *Kievskie novosti*, 23 April 1994.

[32] See Kravchuk's speech in *Demokratychna Ukraina* [the new name of Radyanska Ukraina], 26 November 1991.

large the debt was and how it and Soviet assets would be divided up among the former Union republics.[33]

The Ukrainian leader also stayed away from the next meeting at Novo Ogarevo on 25 November. At the beginning of it, Gorbachev, evidently hoping to seal the agreement there and then, announced to the press that the participants had convened to initial the document. But his attempt to force the issue was resisted by the leaders of the republics, who were still not happy with the terms of the arrangement and, as Yeltsin later acknowledged, sceptical about the value of the whole exercise because of Ukraine's absence. Yeltsin has provided a description of the fiasco and its significance:

> When Gorbachev ultimately tried to insist on his own formulation and we unanimously rejected it, he lost his patience, jumped up from the table, and ran out of the meeting room . . . we suddenly realized that it was over. We were meeting here for the last time. The Novo Ogarevo saga had drawn to a close. There was no more progress in that direction and never would be. We would have to seek and conceive of something else.

The official sanitized version stated that the draft treaty was being returned for further consideration by the parliaments of the republics.[34]

This time, Kravchuk was even more scathing about Gorbachev's obsession with preserving the Union when even those republican leaders who had supported the idea had now also accepted that it was time for something else. Commenting on Gorbachev's readiness to describe the new Union as confederative as long as it remained a union state – for instance, the final draft of the Union treaty retained the concept of a popularly elected president – the Ukrainian leader told *Izvestia*:

> Yes, they are now saying: let's create a confederation. And then they add: but we are for a single state. What is this? A confederation and a single state are incompatible and mutually exclusive. When will we stop deceiving our own people? Half-

---

[33] Radio Kyiv, 24 November 1991.

[34] Yeltsin, *The Struggle for Russia*, pp. 110–11. See also the accounts of the last two meetings in Novo Ogarevo in Jack F. Matlock, Jr., *Autopsy on an Empire: The American Ambassador's Account of the Collapse of the Soviet Union*, New York, 1995, pp. 624–9.

hearted measures, vagueness, matters left unsaid, endless attempts to evade the tough questions – how long can this go on? I don't want to participate in this deception.[35]

In fact it did not continue for much longer. But before the result of the Ukrainian referendum produced what Yeltsin described as 'the final blow to Gorbachev's protracted attempt to save the crumbling Soviet Union',[36] there was one other noteworthy last-minute development. On the eve of the referendum, while still pressing the Ukrainian leadership on the issue of nuclear weapons, the Bush administration shifted its position and announced that it would recognize Ukraine's independence if the voters endorsed it. This was encouraging news for official Kyiv which had already received assurances from Canada and Hungary that recognition would be forthcoming if the referendum went as expected. But for Gorbachev it was tantamount to a stab in the back and he virtually accused Washington of interfering in the USSR's 'internal affairs'.[37] Moreover, the Soviet media reported that in a telephone conversation with President Bush on 30 November Gorbachev sought to impress on the White House that he would not interpret a vote for Ukrainian independence as a vote for secession from the Union. Interestingly, that same day, Yeltsin also declared on Soviet television that he could not imagine a Union without Ukraine. He added: 'I have always said that I am for a Union.'[38]

As for Kravchuk, clearly expecting a huge triumph in the referendum and victory in the presidential election, on 22 November he delivered a programmatic speech at a meeting of the Ukrainian parliament to mark the 125th anniversary of the birth of Hrushevsky. Hailing him as Ukraine's first president and without so much as mentioning the Soviet state, the chairman of the Ukrainian parliament stressed that the leaders of the new independent Ukraine saw themselves as continuing the unfinished work of Hrushevsky and his generation.[39]

---

[35] *Izvestiya*, 26 November.

[36] Yeltsin, *The Struggle for Russia*, p. 111.

[37] Gerald Nadler, 'Ukraine Poised to Bolt from the USSR', *The Washington Times*, 1 December 1991.

[38] TASS, 1 December 1991.

[39] *Demokratychna Ukraina*, 26 December 1991.

Ukraine confirms its historic choice

When it came to the crucial vote, the result astonished even the greatest optimists. No fewer than 84.1% of the eligible voters, or almost 32 million people, cast their ballot and Ukrainians and non-Ukrainians alike throughout the republic came out over-whelmingly for independence. An astounding 90.3% of the voters gave their endorsement to the Declaration of Independence which the Ukrainian parliament had adopted three months earlier. The gamble had paid off handsomely.

According to the final results published on 5 December, the vote for independence in the key industrialized but Russified regions was: in Donetsk, 83.9%; in Dnipropetrovsk, 90.3%; in Zaporizhzhya, 90.6%; in Kharkiv, 86.3%; and in Luhansk, 83.3%. In the southern regions, support for independence was also very high: in Odesa, 85.3%; in Mykolaiv, 89.4%; and in Kherson, 90.1%. Even in Crimea, 54.1% of the voters backed independence. In the western and central regions and in the capital support for independence was 90% and upwards.[40] Significantly, two-thirds of the Soviet military personnel stationed in Ukraine apparently cast their ballot for independence.[41] Remarkably then, as *The Times* of 3 December put it, Ukraine's referendum turned out to be 'a model of peaceful change'.

In the presidential contest, Kravchuk won convincingly, obtain-ing an impressive 61.5% of the votes. Chornovil came second with a respectable 23.2% of the votes, and Lukyanenko was third with 4.4%. What was the secret of Kravchuk's success? It was not simply that he had had the weighty support of the former 'partocracy's' apparatus behind him. As Drach conceded, Kravchuk was seen by 'the silent majority of Ukrainians' as 'a stabilizing factor'; in the opinion of another Rukh leader, Mykhailo Horyn, Kravchuk 'appeared to be a centrist' and thereby appealed to the cautious streak in voters.[42] But perhaps the most important factor was that by now

---

[40] *Ibid.*, 5 December 1991. In the local referendums, 78% of the voters in the Transcarpathian region, 89.3% in the Chernivtsi region, and 81.4% in the Beregovo district came out in support of greater local autonomy. In several villages in the Chernivtsi region, Romanians were reported to have boycotted the referendum. *Demokratychna Ukraina*, 4 and 5 December 1991.

[41] Radio Kyiv, 6 December 1991.

[42] AP, 3 December 1991.

Kravchuk, the former Party ideologist turned champion of Ukraine's sovereignty, had become identified with the building of Ukrainian statehood and the quest for independence.

An elated Kravchuk told journalists: 'A new Ukraine has been born. A great historical event has occurred which will not only change the history of Ukraine, but the history of the world.'[43] What he meant was poignantly summed up in one sentence by the *Independent*: 'The birth of Ukraine marks the death of the Soviet Union.'[44] There was still one figure, though, who refused to recognize this – Gorbachev. Despite the choice which Ukraine's population had made, he persisted with his efforts to promote a new Union and to express the hope that Ukraine could still be persuaded to join it. In fact, in his congratulatory message to Kravchuk, he expressed his hope for 'close cooperation and mutual understanding in common efforts to fulfil democratic changes and form the Union of Sovereign States'.[45]

Kravchuk, however, made it abundantly clear that after the referendum's resounding verdict he was no longer interested even in a confederation. What he was after was some kind of arrangement with Russia and Belarus for the purposes of cushioning the Ukrainian economy during this complex transitional period. On 2 December he told journalists that he would be shortly going to Minsk to discuss the creation of 'a new type of economic community'.[46]

Once the provisional results of the referendum had been announced, on 2 December Poland became the first state to accord formal recognition of Ukraine's independence. It was followed by Hungary, and Canada was the first Western country to confirm that it would shortly extend diplomatic recognition. Both Russia and the United States also signalled that they were ready to recognize Ukraine's independence, but, implicitly in the case of the Russian Federation, and explicitly in the case of the United States, on condition that independent Ukraine abided by nuclear disarmament pacts and respected human rights. In fact, the White House imme-

[43] John-Thor Dahlburg, 'More than 90 Percent of Ukrainians Vote for Independence', *Los Angeles Times*, 3 December 1991.

[44] *The Independent*, 2 December 1991.

[45] TASS, 3 and 4 December 1991.

[46] Reuter, 2 December 1991.

diately dispatched a senior emissary to Kyiv to discuss these issues and to prepare the ground for a visit to Kyiv by the US Secretary of State James Baker.[47]

In a statement by President Yeltsin read out on Russian television on 3 December, Russia recognized the 'independence of Ukraine in accordance with the democratic self-determination of its people'. It also declared its readiness to develop bilateral relations on the basis of the principles upheld in the Russo-Ukrainian treaty of November 1990 and the communiqué of November 1991. The statement added that the example of Ukrainian-Russian inter-state relations 'could and should' serve as a model for bilateral relations for 'the republics of the old Union' and open the way for the formation of a 'commonwealth of sovereign states'.[48]

But as the former US Ambassador in Moscow, Jack F. Matlock, Jr., has pointed out, 'the Russian action was more than just generosity forced by necessity'. Since August, Ukraine's surge towards independence had created quite a dilemma for Yeltsin's government. Kozyrev had told the ambassador shortly after the Ukrainian parliament had declared the republic's independence that 'This is a big political issue at home', and had asked 'What can we do?' On being advised to be 'gracious' and not to treat Ukraine 'like Gorbachev did the Baltics' because Russia and Ukraine needed to cooperate in many areas, Kozyrev had agreed. According to Matlock, Kozyrev had 'added, grimacing as if in pain, "But don't think it isn't hard – or that a lot of people won't be upset."' What followed, as Matlock noted, also

> fitted the game plan Yeltsin seems to have been following since at least the middle of November: to use Ukraine's refusal to enter the union as an excuse for breaking his long-standing promise not to be the initiator of the union's collapse. Now, he could argue that Ukraine, not Russia, had brought the Soviet Union to an end.[49]

On 5 December, at a special ceremonial meeting for Kravchuk's inauguration as president, the Ukrainian parliament formerly renounced the Union Treaty of 1922 and adopted a statement to

[47] See Nahaylo, 'The Shaping of Ukrainian Attitudes', p. 30.
[48] TASS, 3 December 1991.
[49] Matlock, *Autopsy on an Empire*, p. 633.

this effect addressed to 'the parliaments and peoples of the world'. It called on the international community to show understanding for the desire 'of one of Europe's most populous peoples to revive its statehood, which had been destroyed not just once' and to support Ukraine's commitment to building an 'independent, democratic' state. The deputy chairman of the parliament, Plyushch, who was elected to take over from Kravchuk as its speaker, aptly summed up the historic significance of the occasion: 'A European state has appeared on the map of the world, and its name is Ukraine.'

Significantly, one of the guests at the ceremonial meeting was Russia's recently appointed representative in Ukraine, Leonid Smolyakov. He read out a message from President Yeltsin congratulating Kravchuk on his election and 'confirming' that now that 'a new level' of bilateral relations had begun.'from 1 December', Russia would be 'firmly committed to the dynamic development of all-round relations' between the two states 'on the basis of agreed upon principles'.

This official statement was reassuring for the newly independent state, for not only Gorbachev, but quite a few Russian leaders who were opposed to the break-up of the Soviet Union, were expressing a very different view. Sobchak, for instance, was warning of forced Ukrainization of Ukraine's Russian population and conjuring up apocalyptic images of a nuclear clash between Russia and Ukraine, provoked by a territorial dispute. Referring to another troubled relationship which had caused international concern, he suggested that Ukraine and Russia were like Serbia and Croatia, except that they were armed with nuclear weapons.[50] Moreover, precisely at this time, there was renewed talk in Moscow about the danger of a military-backed coup, with suspicion focusing increasingly on Yeltsin's disgruntled deputy, Rutskoi.[51]

In his inaugural speech, President Kravchuk described the outcome of the referendum as a 'great historic victory', declaring that Ukraine had finally 'risen from its knees'. After the long years of 'oppression and destruction', during which the historical memory and language of the Ukrainian people had been attacked and its 'thousand-year-old experience of state-building distorted', the na-

---

[50] See the interview with Sobchak in *Figaro*, 4 December 1991.
[51] *The Washington Post*, 6 December 1991.

tion had 'democratically and unambivalently expressed its will' and chosen independent statehood.

The president reiterated Ukraine's commitment to democracy, 'deep and consistent economic reform', peace and nuclear disarmament. While continuing its broad-ranging state-building work at home, he declared, Ukraine would pursue an active foreign policy aimed at securing the country's direct participation in European structures, developing wide-ranging bilateral relations, especially with European and North American states, and 'maintaining good relations with all the republics of the former Union, especially Russia'.[52]

Later on, speaking to reporters, Kravchuk stated that, after living 'all this time in a giant totalitarian imperial state', Ukraine had finally freed itself, and reiterated that Ukraine would not join Gorbachev's proposed new Union treaty. He acknowledged, however, that it was not possible, nor indeed desirable, to rupture all the ties which had developed within the old Union. Answering questions about his forthcoming meeting in Minsk on 7 December with Yeltsin and Shushkevich, the Ukrainian president informed journalists that economic cooperation would be the chief topic, but that the three leaders also intended to have a 'brainstorming' session on political issues and that he was going prepared with 'concrete proposals'.[53]

Ukraine and the creation of the CIS

An official visit to Belarus by Yeltsin provided the opportunity which Kravchuk had sought for a meeting outside Moscow of the leaders of the three Slavic republics. In fact, Shushkevich had phoned Kravchuk and invited him for joint consultations.[54] But the three leaders had different agendas, for Yeltsin and Shushkevich still preferred to salvage the idea of a renewed Union, though they realized that this depended on Ukraine's being won over. Before leaving for Belarus, Yeltsin met with Gorbachev

---

[52] *Demokratychna Ukraina*, 7 December 1991.

[53] Radio Kyiv, 5 December 1991.

[54] On the meeting of the three Slavic leaders in Belarus and the creation of the CIS, see Kravchuk's account in his interview with Kichigin in *Kievskie vedomosti*, 23 and 27 April 1994; with Chemerys in *Prezydent*, pp. 265-75; and for Russian television, shown on 11 February 1992. For Yeltsin's account, see his *The Struggle for Russia*, pp. 111-16.

and, at the latter's request, apparently agreed to try one more time to persuade Ukraine to sign the new Union treaty. On his arrival in Minsk, the Russian president declared before television cameras that if Ukraine agreed to participate, a Union treaty could still be signed, but 'if Ukraine wishes to be a fully independent state, that is, if it does not sign this political treaty, then we will have to look for new variants'.[55] Indirect pressure on Ukraine was also applied by the old centre: it look the form of an announcement by Gorbachev's press spokesman that on 9 December the Soviet leader expected to meet with Kravchuk, Yeltsin and Nazarbaev in Moscow.[56]

Kravchuk was later to acknowledge that he went to Minsk not knowing how the meeting would go but expecting that the issue of the Union treaty would be brought up. On his arrival he discovered that the venue for the consultations had been changed and that they would be held in a government hunting lodge at the Belovezhkaya Pushcha (White Tower Forest) near Brest. The secrecy surrounding the meeting and the fact that Yeltsin had brought senior figures from his government added to the drama. His team consisted of the new first deputy head of the Russian government, Burbulis, the deputy head, Gaidar, State Councillor Shakhrai and the president's aide, Viktor Ilyushin; Belarus was represented by Shushkevich and the Belarusian prime minister, Vyacheslau Kebich, and Kravchuk was accompanied by Fokin.

The meeting began with Yeltsin posing the crucial question on behalf of Gorbachev: on what terms would Ukraine agree to sign the Union treaty? Kravchuk's response was quite categorical: the referendum had irrevocably changed the situation and Ukraine would not join any new Union. According to his account, he then described in considerable detail the results of the voting in the various regions, prompting Yeltsin to ask: 'What, even the Donbas voted "yes"?'[57] With Kravchuk having reiterated his country's choice, Yeltsin acknowledged that without Ukraine the Union treaty was a non-starter. The discussion shifted, therefore, to finding an alternative arrangement which would dispense with the old

---

[55] See Roman Solchanyk, 'Kravchuk Defines Ukrainian-CIS Relations', *RFE/RL Research Report*, vol. 1, no. 11 (13 March 1991), p. 7.

[56] Reuter, 5 December 1991.

[57] See Kravchuk's interview with Kichigin, *Kievskie vedomosti*, 23 April 1994.

Union and its centre and accommodate all three states. Kravchuk presented his ideas on a loose association modelled on the European Community, while for the Russian side, Burbulis, whom the Ukrainian leader later described as having been the 'ideologue' in Yeltsin's team, also made some proposals. It turned out that the positions of the two delegations were not that far apart, and with the Belarusian leaders going along with their Russian and Ukrainian guests in agreeing that the idea of the Union was now well and truly obsolete, within a few hours a compromise was worked out.

The leaders of the three Slavic states agreed to form a loose non-state association open to all former Soviet republics, as well as other states, which they called the Commonwealth of Independent States (CIS). Working through the night, they produced three documents, which they signed in Minsk on 8 December: a declaration announcing the formation of the new entity, an agreement outlining the principles on which the CIS would be based, and a statement on the coordination of economic policy. The agreement on the creation of the CIS declared that 'the USSR, as subject of international law and geographical reality, is ceasing to exist'. It also contained provisions, presented more as statements of intention and subject to further negotiations and agreements, addressing the most serious issues resulting from the break-up of the Soviet empire, including: respect for human rights and protection of national minorities, recognition of the territorial integrity and inviolability of the borders of member states, the preservation 'under joint command [of] a common military-strategic space, including single control over nuclear weapons' and cooperation in the economic, cultural, environmental, foreign and migration policy spheres.[58]

Having announced their momentous decision to declare the USSR defunct, the three leaders braced themselves for the unpredictable reaction from Gorbachev, from their own parliaments and from the leaders of the other republics. They had already informed the American and Soviet presidents by telephone from Belovezhkaya Pushcha and Yeltsin was delegated to brief the incensed Gorbachev in more detail on his return to Moscow. Rather late in their meeting, Yeltsin, Kravchuk and Shushkevich had decided to invite Nazarbaev to join them but had failed to reach

[58] For an English translation of the text of the agreement, see *RFE/RL Research Report*, vol. 1, no. 2 (10 January 1992) pp. 4–5.

him. He was now in Moscow and angered by what he saw as a snub. The leaders of the Central Asian republics also suspected that they were being abandoned by the architects of a new Slavonic union.

Kravchuk decided not to go on to Moscow and flew home to face a public and parliament anxious to hear from their president what exactly he had committed his newly independent state to. Although publicly he ruled out the possibility of Gorbachev resorting to force to hold the Union together, in a later account he was to admit that, because it was uncertain how the centre would respond to the Belovezhsky agreement, special security precautions were taken just in case: details of his return flight were kept secret and his home outside of Kyiv was placed under guard by a detachment of *spetsnaz* – élite special forces.[59]

On 9 December, the Ukrainian president held a press conference in Kyiv in which he was at pains to point out that the new commonwealth had nothing in common with the old Union and that Ukraine was not sacrificing any of its sovereignty by joining it. The CIS, he explained, would have no centre, only coordinating mechanisms. At a time when problems connected with the dissolution of the USSR were becoming 'exceptionally complicated' and the old Union centre was trying to 'return to the old structures', the new arrangement offered prospects for cooperation on a democratic basis between interested independent states. He also stressed that the CIS stemmed from Ukraine's 'decisive' refusal to join a new Union, and left no doubt that Russia and Belarus would have preferred a closer association.[60]

On the following day, Kravchuk addressed the Ukrainian parliament. In addition to the explanations which he had offered to the press, he stressed that the CIS represented an attempt by the three Slavic states both to 'dot the i's' as far as the attempts to restore the old Union were concerned, and, at the same time, to 'halt the spontaneous disintegration' of what was left of the USSR. As if appealing to the crypto-Communist majority, the Ukrainian leader argued that the break-up of the Soviet Union had in fact begun when *perestroika* had been launched and 'the authors' of this collapse were known well enough. He blamed Gorbachev for the destruction of the Soviet economy, inter-ethnic bloodshed and the growing

---

[59] Kravchuk's interview with Kichigin, *Kievskie vedomosti*, 27 April 1991.
[60] Radio Kyiv, 9 December 1991.

number of refugees. The old centre which had caused the problems had proved incapable of dealing with them and was still complicating matters by trying to renew the old methods. The disintegration of the former Soviet Union was not only resulting in economic dislocation, but also 'reactionary forces' were threatening to exploit problems in order to foment confrontation between peoples. The agreement about the formation of the CIS had therefore been aimed at 'stabilizing the situation'.[61]

Although Kravchuk managed to win over the majority of the deputies, the parliament ratified the agreement creating the CIS with quite a few provisos. These included a reaffirmation of Ukraine's independence, emphatic opposition to the 'transformation' of the CIS into 'a state formation with its own organs of power and administration', and even that the word commonwealth be written with a small c and not a capital.[62]

From the very outset, then, the CIS proved to be an uneasy compromise and its was evident almost immediately that Ukraine and Russia had very different views about its significance and prospects. For Ukraine it represented a 'civilized form of divorce' from the old imperial set-up, an interim arrangement providing an orderly framework and procedures for the liquidation of the Soviet Union and for managing some of the complex problems left over in the economic and military spheres. The pride and sensitivities connected with Ukraine's newly achieved independence were undoubtedly significant in influencing perceptions of the CIS. In an interview given to the *Financial Times* on 16 December 1991, Kravchuk put it as follows:

> The empire which endured for 337 years [from the Pereyaslav treaty] no longer exists, and Ukraine is the author of its destruction . . . For me this is a source of great personal pride . . . Right now we must monitor the situation very carefully so that no one tries to stand above anyone else . . . If there is any effort to do this, then the commonwealth will fall apart because Ukraine will never agree to be subordinated.[63]

For Russia, however, the CIS represented at best a means of

[61] *Robitnycha hazeta*, 13 December 1991.

[62] *Ibid.*, 25 December 1991.

[63] Chrystia Freeland, 'Chess Player Moves to a Bigger Board', *Financial Times*, 17 December 1991.

discarding Gorbachev and the old Union centre and, while continuing to assert Russia's authority, the establishment of a new basis for integration and movement towards a more close-knit organization. As Yeltsin put it:

> The Belovezhsky agreement, as it seemed to me then, was needed more than anything to reinforce the centripetal tendency in the disintegrating Union and to stimulate the treaty process [sic] . . . I want to emphasize once again: at that moment, the Commonwealth of Independent States . . . was the only possible preservation of an integrated geographical region . . . I was convinced that Russia needed to get rid of its imperial mission; nevertheless, Russia needed a stronger, harder policy, even forceful at some stage, in order not to lose its significance and authority altogether and to institute reforms.[64]

For many Russians, however, the Belovezhsky agreement creating the CIS and thereby shedding the remnants of the Soviet empire was tantamount to an act of betrayal. As Ambassador Matlock noted, 'not only the unreconstructed imperialists' and 'former Communist *apparatchiks*' opposed the agreement, but also 'respected democrats', such as Sobchak, Popov, 'Nikolai Travkin of the Democratic Party, and most of the leaders of the Movement for Democratic Reforms'.[65] Significantly, within a few days of the ratification of the CIS agreement by the Russian, Ukrainian and Belarusian parliaments, even Burbulis was publicly expressing his doubts about whether the creation of a commonwealth had been the right decision and suggesting that the arrangement was a 'liberal illusion that can lead either to a federation or to war'.[66]

The agreement on the establishment of the CIS notwithstanding, the potential for disagreement and confrontation between Ukraine and Russia remained. It was exposed again in the second half of December as Russia and Ukraine asserted their claims to the assets of the former Union and Russia unilaterally took over what the other former Union republics considered to be their joint property, ranging from Soviet embassies abroad to Soviet central television. While challenging Russia's claim to be the sole legal successor of the USSR, Ukraine also moved ahead with the creation of its armed

---

[64] Yeltsin, *The Struggle for Russia*, p. 114.

[65] Matlock, *Autopsy on an Empire*, p. 639.

[66] Radio Moscow, 12 December 1991.

forces and on 13 December Kravchuk declared himself their Commander-in-Chief.

It was at this point that a new serious source of friction emerged which was to strain bilateral relations for years to come – the issue of the ownership of the Soviet Black Sea Fleet. Having a long coastline, Ukraine considered that it required a navy to protect its shores and its shipping. It sought to apply the same principles in creating a navy on the basis of the 380-vessel Black Sea Fleet based in Crimea as it was doing in creating an army and air force from Soviet military units stationed on its territory. In light of Ukraine's considerable contribution to the Soviet navy, in terms of revenue, shipbuilding and sailors, official Kyiv considered its claim to what after all was the smallest of the USSR's four fleets, and accounted for only about 10% of the entire Soviet navy, reasonable enough. For Russia, apart from its military significance, the Black Sea Fleet was a matter of tradition and prestige and, moreover, was identified with the future of Sevastopol and the Crimean peninsular generally.

At the subsequent CIS meetings in Alma-Ata on 21 December, at which eight other former Union republics joined the new association (Georgia stayed out), and in Minsk on 30 December, the strains between Ukraine and Russia became more obvious. Ukraine continued to oppose any moves which would make the commonwealth resemble a state and vetoed the idea of a charter for the CIS, of a CIS citizenship and of joint guarding of the commonwealth's external borders. It also successfully defended the right of members to have their own conventional forces.[67] Thus, during the very first weeks of the realization and recognition of Ukraine's independence, the stage for the protracted tug-of-war between Ukraine and Russia, which was to be a hallmark of the CIS, was set.

The existence of the new CIS framework nevertheless facilitated the conclusion of important compromise agreements dealing with the future of the Soviet military and its nuclear arsenal. In the second half of December, after a visit to Kyiv by US Secretary of State James Baker and negotiations with the Russians, Ukraine agreed that it would ship all of the warheads from the tactical nuclear missiles

---

[67] See Ann Sheehy, 'Commonwealth of Independent States: An Uneasy Compromise', *RFE/RL Research Report*, vol. 1, no. 2 (10 January 1992), pp. 1–4; and Roman Solchanyk, 'The CIS and the Republics: Ukraine', *RFE/RL Research Report*, vol. 1, no. 7 (14 February 1992), pp. 1–5.

deployed on its territory to Russia for destruction by 1 July 1992 and that it would eliminate the remaining strategic nuclear weapons by the end of 1994. This undertaking was given without prior debate in the parliament, though, and the deputies were not to forget this. Moreover, this decision also appears to have been based on the belief that Western aid for the destruction of the ICBMs on Ukraine's territory would be forthcoming, and that it would speed up international recognition both of Ukraine's independence and its right to have conventional armed forces for its defence. In fact, despite frantic efforts by the former Soviet top brass to promote the idea of a 'unified' CIS army, at the CIS summit in Minsk at the end of the year, the right of the member states to create their own armed forces was acknowledged.

On 25 December 1991, Gorbachev appeared on the former Soviet central television channel to announce his resignation. That night in the Kremlin, the Soviet flag was lowered for the last time. Meanwhile, Yeltsin issued decrees asserting the Russian Federation's control over most of the remaining central structures and more foreign countries announced their recognition of the independent states which had emerged as the result of the dissolution of the Soviet Union. Thus, the USSR formally ceased to exist. On the following day, President Bush announced that the United State would recognize the independence of Russia, Ukraine and several other of the former Union republics.

A few days later, in his televised New Year's message, President Kravchuk greeted the citizens of independent Ukraine with words of reflection on the historic significance of what had occurred during the last year and on the challenges that lay ahead. Ukraine, he emphasized, could pride itself on having changed the course of history by having played a key role in both bringing an end to the Soviet 'totalitarian super-empire' and 'stopping the uncontrolled, chaotic disintegration' of this 'gigantic, moribund' entity and directing the process of dissolution into 'the channel of civilized relations'. As 'the initiator and a co-founder' of the CIS, it had, in fact, made a major contribution to world history. By achieving independence, the president continued, Ukraine had moved from one epoch into another. Having finally been able to take charge of its own affairs, it would now itself be responsible for its own destiny. This meant that there was no place for euphoria and complacency, for freedom and independence needed to be bolstered by economic well-being, order and understanding. The president thanked the population of Ukraine for its patience and perseverance at, what he acknowledged, was, a difficult time of growing social hardships, empty shop shelves, long queues and a rising crime rate. Alluding to even tougher times ahead, he called for unity, tolerance, conscientious work and for all sections of society to pull their weight for the common good. 'We have laid the foundations of the future Ukraine', Kravchuk told the Ukrainian public, 'and how it turns out will depend on every one of us'.[68]

[68] Radio Kyiv, 1 January 1992.

15

THE FIRST YEARS OF INDEPENDENCE

Domestic politics: a promising start falters

Although the rapidity of the disintegration of the Soviet Union, accelerated by the failed coup attempt in Moscow in August 1991, took everyone by surprise, it seemed that Ukraine had managed to capitalize on the situation and launch a twofold revolution: national, in the sense of emancipation from Moscow's rule, and democratic, in the sense of the de-Sovietization of the political system and the economy, and democratic state-building. The achievement of independence and international recognition crowned the first stage of Ukraine's resurgence; the continuation with democratic and economic reforms appeared to augur well for the successful progression of the second stage.

On the eve of the presidential elections, Kravchuk had acknowledged the desirability of holding new parliamentary elections to give a boost to democratic reform. He had pledged that if he won he would urge the Ukrainian parliament to adopt a new law on multi-party elections and a new constitution and then dissolve itself so that new elections could be held. The newly elected president kept his word: on 27 December 1991 he submitted a draft law on elections to the parliament and called on it to publish the proposed draft of Ukraine's new constitution.[1] The parliament, however, demonstrated that it was in no hurry to cut short its existence and ignored Kravchuk's call for new elections. This was an important missed chance for the fledgling state to clear the political decks and start off on a genuinely democratic footing.

Political parties in the full Western sense had not yet appeared and a functioning multi-party system still remained a future prospect. Kravchuk seems to have hoped that after the referendum he would be able to harness the support of Rukh and its allies and make them

[1] Radio Kyiv, 27 December 1991.

432

part of a broader social base. But as always, he seemed to want to have it both ways and to continue relying on his old team as well. During the presidential election campaign he had stressed that he was against 'purges' and drastic changes of personnel; he had argued that the old system was at fault and not individual officials. He continued, therefore, to support Fokin even though after the referendum the democratic opposition in the parliament began to press for his replacement by a bolder economic reformer.

Early in 1992, new political realignments within the democratic camp began to undermine its loose unity. First, the People's Council disintegrated as a new bloc emerged – the 'New Ukraine' group formed by some fifty liberals and moderate leftists committed to radical economic reform, including Yemets, Hrynov, Filenko and Shcherbak. This group broke new ground by announcing that it would form a shadow cabinet and the mere threat seems to have had an effect. In March, in what appeared to be an attempt to deflect growing criticism of his reluctance to ditch Fokin, Kravchuk appointed the candidate of New Ukraine, Volodymyr Lanovy, as minister for economics and deputy prime minister.

Outside the parliament, the democratic forces split over the issue of whether or not to give their political support to the president – he had, after all, only recently been their ideological adversary and many still distrusted him. Chornovil led the opposition within Rukh to the national democrats becoming too closely identified with the presidential administration and advocated adopting a position of 'constructive opposition' to it. Like many other democrats, he believed that independent Ukraine was being ruled and run by a 'party of power' made up of representatives of the old Communist *nomenklatura*, or partocracy, who had simply made an opportunistic switch in their allegiance from Moscow to Kyiv. At the beginning of March 1992, he argued at the third Rukh Congress that most of the map of Ukraine should still be coloured red because the old Communist structures and personnel were still largely in place and would not be removed if the democrats did not actively oppose them.

On the other hand, Drach, Pavlychko, the Horyns (Mykhailo and Bohdan) and various other democratic leaders considered that, during this formative period when the country's independence needed to be firmly consolidated and friction with Russia remained a source of serious concern, Kravchuk, as the embodiment of

Ukrainian statehood, should be given not only a fair chance to get on with his duties, but also solid political backing. They were also more ready to allow for the ideological evolution of the former Communists, many of them having been Communists themselves. In August, some of these more moderate figures were to form the Congress of National Democratic Forces (KNDS) which broadly supported the president. The ensuing divisions within, and subsequent fragmentation of, the democratic forces were, however, to deprive the reform process of impetus.

In the meantime, former Communists were beginning to regroup and to reassert themselves. After the banning of the CPU, some of Ukraine's left-wing forces had formed the Socialist Party of Ukraine (SPU) led by Oleksandr Moroz. It claimed a membership of over 30,000. In February 1992, the SPU was joined by an agrarian ally, the Peasant Party of Ukraine (PPU), which was founded by collective farm directors and forces opposed to the privatization of the land and radical reform of agriculture. In April, the two parties created a leftist coalition. But many other former Communists, especially in the eastern regions, still preferred to bide their time.

After the achievement of Ukraine's independence, forces in Crimea and the Donbas which were opposed to the Ukrainian national movement and Ukrainization and intent on asserting the 'Russianness' of these regions also gradually stepped up their activity. In Crimea, the Republican Movement of Crimea (RDK), led by Yurii Meshkov, spearheaded a campaign for a local referendum on Crimea's independence; in Eastern Ukraine supporters of the local Interfront movements were to unite in June 1992 in an interregional coalition called the Civic Congress. It was to campaign for regional autonomy, for Russian to be made a state language in the eastern regions, for dual citizenship between Ukraine and Russia, for closer relations between the two countries, and for Ukraine's closer integration in the CIS.[2]

Initially, the new president enjoyed considerable confidence and political support. In order, as he argued, to promote reform more effectively and to circumvent conservative structures, he sought to strengthen the executive branch of government and was successful in broadening his powers. At the end of February, he created an

---

[2] Andrew Wilson, 'The Growing Challenge to Kiev from the Donbas', *RFE/RL Research Report*, vol. 2, no. 33, (20 August), pp.8-13.

advisory council called the State Duma, in which he included Yukhnovsky, Yemets and Zhulynsky, but gave responsibility for economic planning to a conservative, Oleksandr Yemelyanov, thereby suggesting that he was of two minds about proceeding with market reforms. Kravchuk also managed to persuade parliament to agree to the establishment of a system of presidential prefects, or plenipotentiaries, in all of the regions of the country as well as in Kyiv and Sevastopol. But in the months to come these moves were to fuel suspicion that the president was simply out to strengthen the presidential system at the expense of the parliament and the local councils.

In the economic sphere, the first year of independence began with unpleasant complications. At the beginning of January, Russia went ahead and freed prices. Ukraine, which together with Belarus had sought to persuade Russia to delay this move, was poorly prepared to deal with the disruptive economic consequences. On 8 January, the Ukrainian government introduced a new form of money, the karbovanets-coupon, which became the only legal tender in state shops. A week later, while Ukraine and Russia were at loggerheads over the ownership of the Black Sea Fleet, Kravchuk accused Russia of 'irresponsibility' and 'interference' in Ukraine's affairs, claiming it had left Kyiv with no option but to raise prices because it did not 'print or issue roubles'.

Ukraine also began to feel the energy squeeze. The republic was consuming about 65 million tons of petroleum and oil-related products per year of which 10 million tons were produced in Ukraine and most of the remainder supplied from Russia at prices which were still well below world level. Both Ukraine and Russia had been experiencing difficulties with oil production and Russia was drastically reducing deliveries to its neighbour. At the end of February, while Russia was contemplating raising its fuel prices, Ukraine's other chief supplier of natural gas, Turkmenistan, suddenly raised its prices very sharply. After talks failed to produce a compromise, Turkmenistan cut off supplies and Ukraine retaliated by stopping the delivery of food.

Apart from exports in the form of foodstuffs and industrial and consumer products, Ukraine had a few other bargaining chips in its negotiations with Turkmenistan and Russia about fuel supplies. Oil and natural gas from Russia, and natural gas from Turkmenistan, were supplied to European countries by pipelines which crossed

Ukraine's territory and therefore tariffs for the transit of the fuels were involved. Furthermore, the large-diameter pipes used by the Soviet fuel industry were produced in Ukraine and, like the former USSR's oil, their price was still much lower than similar pipes being produced outside of the CIS. In addition to this, Ukrainian technicians and workers played an important role in Russia's fuel industries; the 1989 census had registered 260,000 Ukrainians in the oil-producing Tyumen region in western Siberia (the majority of whom had moved there between 1979 and 1989 and over two-thirds of whom named Ukrainian as their mother tongue).[3] Nevertheless, before Kyiv and Ashgabat eventually worked out a deal, Ukraine experienced what being a hostage in an energy trap entailed. The Ukrainian leadership began to look around in earnest for new sources of fuel and turned hopefully to, among others, Iran and Kuwait. In March, Fokin also travelled to western Siberia to try and arrange direct deals with Russian oil and gas producing enterprises.[4]

Although by early March Kravchuk was proposing to the parliament that it declare a 'state of economic emergency' for the remainder of 1992, there were also some hopeful developments. During the spring the parliament adopted several economic laws which, at the time, were hailed as amounting to the burial of Soviet Socialism in Ukraine. They included laws on the privatization of large and small enterprises, on foreign investment, and a land code dealing with the privatization of land. Ukraine also agreed on terms to join the International Monetary Fund (IMF) and was also admitted to the World Bank. By the middle of the year, when the government finally won parliament's approval for the budget for 1992, Ukraine seemed poised to move out of the rouble zone and, if a stabilization fund was obtained from the IMF, to introduce a national currency – the hryvnya.

There was progress, too, in other spheres. In June 1992 the Constitutional Commission submitted the draft of a new constitution to the parliament which proposed a compromise between

---

[3] F.D. Zastavny, *Skhidna Ukrainska Diaspora* [The Eastern Ukrainian Diaspora], (1992, Lviv), pp. 83–91.

[4] See Oles M. Smolansky's illuminating study of this crucial aspect of independent Ukraine's economic and security predicament, 'Ukraine's Quest for Independence: The Fuel Factor', *Europe-Asia Studies*, vol. 47, no. 1 (1995), pp. 67–74.

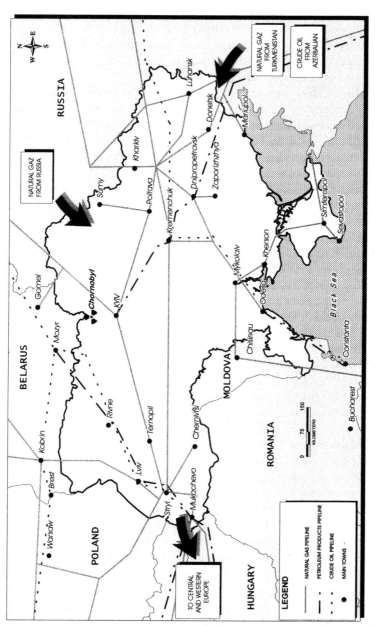

MAIN OIL AND GAS PIPELINES

presidential and parliamentary forms of rule. This seemed to offer a timely opportunity to stave off looming problems over the absence of an up-to-date division of powers. That same month the parliament passed laws establishing a Constitutional Court and guaranteeing the rights of national minorities.

Abroad, too, independent Ukraine sought to demonstrate its commitment to the democratic rule of law. In February 1992 it gained admission to the CSCE process when President Kravchuk signed the Helsinki Final Act in the Finnish capital and by the summer was signalling its desire to become a member of the Council of Europe and to sign the European Human Rights Convention.

After this 'peak', however, the reform process in Ukraine – both in the political and economic spheres – began to peter out. Who or what blocked reform, whether there was a loss of political will to push forward in the spirit of the pledges that were made on the eve of the referendum, and whether domestic developments were influenced more by 'subjective' or 'objective' factors, are some of the key questions which historians of this period will need to address.

Some tentative answers can, however, be proposed. The onerous legacy of the past was of course a factor. After centuries of imperial and totalitarian rule, Ukraine was handicapped by the lack of democratic experience and of a developed democratic political culture, a shortage of cadres trained in the new democratic ways and Western economic know-how, provincialism, the survival of old structures staffed by former Communists intent on preserving their old privileges and influence, and widespread political cynicism and corruption. This, against the background of the crippling economic problems and tensions with Russia, made the building of a new democratic state a daunting task.[5]

As the economic difficulties mounted and the need for decisiveness in moving forward with market reforms increased, the fear of the restive Donbas and of explosions of social discontent seemed to have remained uppermost in the minds of many Ukrainian politicians. In fact, the need to provide some kind of social safety net, as well as the growing struggle for control over decision making between the parliament, which had got used to acting as a combined

[5] For a perceptive and stimulating discussion of the problems and challenges facing the independent Ukrainian state, see Alexander J. Motyl, *Dilemmas of Independence: Ukraine after Totalitarianism*, New York, 1993.

legislature and executive, and the presidential apparatus and the government, emerged as obstacles to bold reform.

The pace of economic reform was to remain disappointingly slow. The government's decision at the beginning of July to free food prices drew protests and Kravchuk appears to have got cold feet. When, a week later, Lanovy announced his resignation claiming that old Soviet-style views and 'economic inertia' were gaining ground and that reforms were being blocked, Kravchuk replaced him with a conservative, Valentyn Symonenko. The Fokin government failed to control inflation and the devaluation of the Ukrainian quasi-currency and instead pursued fiscal and monetary policies which in the circumstances suggested not only mismanagement but also irresponsibility.[6]

The lack of a clear sense of direction and leadership as regards reform was to exacerbate Ukraine's internal problems and increase social discontent. In these conditions, the pro-Communist forces within and outside the parliament gradually began to reassert themselves. The same process, for somewhat different reasons (anger about the way in which the USSR and what it represented had been 'destroyed' from within, and opposition to Gaidar's reforms) was also evident in Russia where the diehard Communists, such as Gennadii Zyuganov, formed a common front against the Yeltsin administration with ultra-nationalists, such as Vladimir Zhirinovsky and Sergei Baburin. The growing strength of these 'red-brown' forces in Russia which were nostalgic for the old Union was to embolden the more hard-line Communists in Ukraine who, after the fiasco of the attempted coup in Moscow, had kept a low profile.

Developments in Russia were also to have an influence on Ukraine in another way. Certainly, Ukraine's deepening economic crisis was compounded by the country's energy dependence on Russia and its growing trade deficit. But Ukrainian politicians were also watching Russia's difficult experience with the 'shock therapy' approach to economic reform inaugurated by Gaidar's team. What they witnessed dampened the enthusiasm for radical and rapid economic change. More and more of them, democrats unhappy with Fokin included, came to reject the shock therapy approach as

[6] On Ukraine's economic problems during its first year of independence, see Simon Johnson and Oleg Ustenko, 'Ukraine on the Brink of Hyperinflation', *REF/RL Research Report* vol. 1, no. 50, (18 December 1992), pp. 51-59.

inappropriate for Ukraine's conditions and instead sought a gradual and cautious transition towards a mixed economy. Consequently, during the course of the next year or two, economic reformers such as Lanovy and Viktor Pynzenyk, who advocated a bold and decisive push in the direction of a market economy, became popular in the West but were to become effectively marginalized at home.

Early foreign and security policy challenges

One of independent Ukraine's priorities was to ensure, as rapidly as was feasible, that it would have the capacity to defend its sovereignty. It was generally believed that one of the main reasons why Ukraine had been unable to sustain independence in the period 1917–20 was because its Socialist leaders had neglected to create adequate armed forces. After the reminder in August 1991 of how precarious Ukraine's sovereignty was, Kravchuk and the former national Communists were in full agreement with the national democrats that the 'mistake' of the founders of the Ukrainian People's Republic should not be repeated. Consequently, the determination and speed with which the Ukrainian authorities continued to press ahead with the creation of national armed forces surprised, and initially startled, the former Soviet top brass, Russian politicians unable to come to terms with Ukrainian independence, and some Western states.

Having reached agreement with Russia and the United States on the fate of the nuclear weapons based in Ukraine and secured general recognition within the CIS framework of its right to create national armed forces, during the first half of January 1992 Kyiv asserted its control over all of the former Soviet military units stationed in Ukraine, except strategic forces. Former Soviet servicemen serving on Ukrainian territory were offered the opportunity to take an oath of allegiance to 'the people of Ukraine' and relatively lucrative terms. Those who did not wish to serve were free to leave for other states. Within the first three months, some 480,000 officers and servicemen were to take the oath of loyalty to Ukraine and some 40,000 who refused were sent to other parts of the CIS.

In Russia, these Ukrainian moves generally met with little understanding, shock and indignation, the situation being aggravated by Kyiv's claims to the Black Sea Fleet. The speaker of the Russian parliament, Ruslan Khasbulatov, declared that Russia would not allow another state to seize 'its' armies and fleets, while Sobchak claimed that the new Ukrainian armed forces would constitute 'a landmine under the future of all mankind'. Yeltsin, who at the end of December had suggested that Russia might agree to divide the Fleet, stated on 9 January that it 'was, is and will remain Russia's'.[7]

Two weeks later, on 22 January, Moscow's *Komsomolskaya pravda* published excerpts from a letter Khasbulatov from the head of the Russian parliament's Committee on Foreign Affairs and External Economic Ties, Vladimir Lukin, which revealed both the problems which Ukraine's independence was posing for Russian policy makers and what their reactions were. Lukin advised the head of the Russian parliament that Ukraine was planning 'to sever completely [its] special relations with Russia, including in the military-political sphere', and that in asserting a neutral stance it in fact intended to follow the lead of other East European states and move westward 'without us'. As a response to Ukraine's claims to the Black Sea Fleet and Kyiv's independent course generally, he recommended that Russia play the Crimean card and apply economic leverage. The following day, tensions between the two states were further exacerbated when the Russian parliament challenged the legal validity of the transfer in 1954 of Crimea to Ukraine. Kravchuk responded to these Russian actions by condemning what he called Russia's 'imperial disease'.[8]

Despite the deterioration of Ukrainian-Russian relations, Ukraine continued transferring tactical nuclear missiles to Russia. In mid-March, however, when over half of them had been handed over, Kravchuk temporarily suspended the process, complaining that Ukraine needed to be certain that the weapons were actually being destroyed. By now, the Ukrainian parliament was also beginning to have serious doubts about the wisdom of handing over nuclear arms to a potential adversary and there was growing concern that Western states did not really understand Ukraine's security concerns.

After a flurry of diplomatic activity involving the Bush ad-

[7] See Stephen Foye, 'CIS: Kiev and Moscow Clash over Armed Forces', *RFE/RL Research Report* no. 3 (17 January 1992), pp. 1-3.

[8] On this, and for a comprehensive discussion of the Ukrainian-Russian relationship in the first years after independence, see Roman Solchanyk, 'Russia, Ukraine, and the Imperial legacy', *Post-Soviet Affairs* vol. 9, no. 4 (October-December 1993), pp. 337-65.

ministration, some of the problems were resolved. In April, on the eve of an official visit to Washington by Kravchuk, Ukraine agreed to resume the transfer of tactical nuclear weapons to Russia. A satisfied Kravchuk explained that having viewed Ukraine 'as being in the orbit of Russia's foreign policy', Washington had now adopted 'a constructive line' towards Ukraine. In fact, during the Ukrainian leader's trip to the United States in early May, President Bush announced that Washington would be upgrading its bilateral relations with Kyiv. For his part, the Ukrainian president was able to confirm that Ukraine had completed the transfer of tactical nuclear weapons to Russia well ahead of schedule. But he also introduced a new note, which would now figure prominently in Ukrainian diplomacy: he emphasized that Ukraine had in fact agreed to carry out unilateral nuclear disarmament but that it feared nuclear blackmail and pressure from the nuclear power to its north and would seek security guarantees from the West. Although he failed to secure the latter, Kravchuk managed to obtain recognition of Ukraine's right to be a party to the START-1 treaty and pledges of American assistance for Kyiv's nuclear disarmament efforts.

After further negotiations, Ukraine joined Russia, Belarus and Kazakhstan on 23 May in signing a protocol in Lisbon formally committing them to ratifying the START treaty in 'accordance with their constitutional practices'. While undertaking to eliminate all nuclear weapons located on its territory within the seven-year period provided for in the treaty, Ukraine appended two supplementary documents in which it insisted on guarantees 'of its national security' and 'reliable international control' over the fate of nuclear warheads being transferred to Russia for destruction.[9]

This breakthrough, and the fact that in March Ukraine had been admitted along with other ex-Soviet states to the newly formed NATO-sponsored North Atlantic Cooperation Council, while in May it had joined the North Atlantic Assembly, strengthened the Ukrainian leadership's sense of confidence in defending the country's interests.

At a CIS summit meeting in Tashkent in early May, the commonwealth's members agreed on how to divide up the USSR's conventional forces in accordance with the limitations contained in the 1990 treaty on reducing Conventional Forces in Europe (CFE)

---

[9] Nahaylo, 'The Shaping of Ukrainian Attitudes . . .', pp.31-7.

which Gorbachev had signed on behalf of the USSR. Ukraine seems to have done quite well out of the deal, being allocated about 27% of the share-out, compared to Russia's 54% and Belarus's 12%, which included 4,080 tanks, 5,050 armoured vehicles, 4,040 artillery pieces, 1,090 combat aircraft and 330 attack helicopters. During the next few weeks, Ukraine joined seven other former Soviet republics in formally adhering to the CFE treaty. According to the agreement, the maximum troop levels were fixed at 450,000 for Ukraine and 1,450,000 for Russia (in its European regions).[10]

Despite this progress, relations between Moscow and Kyiv remained strained, especially over the issues of the Black Sea Fleet and Crimea. Various Russian politicians, including Rutskoi, Stankevich and Sobchak, expressed their support for the Russian secessionist forces in the peninsula and asserted Russia's claims to the territory. In March, a group of Ukrainian radical nationalists led by Khmara also arrived in Crimea and inflamed the situation with their demonstrations. Meanwhile, tens of thousands of Crimean Tatars were continuing to return to Crimea from Central Asia and, finding the local authorities unhelpful or openly hostile, were not only demanding equal political, social and economic rights, but also seizing land and establishing compact squatter settlements. During March, over 1,000 Crimean Tatar representatives went to Kyiv and attempted to draw attention to their plight, but the militia forcibly broke up their peaceful protests. All this complicated the already difficult work which Kyiv and Simferopol were engaged in to delineate powers between Ukraine and the autonomous Crimean state. At the end of March, the Crimean and Ukrainian parliamentary delegations managed to reach an agreement on the terms of an arrangement, but the arrival of Rutskoi and Stankevich in Crimea on Yeltsin's behalf, and a subsequent Russian-Ukrainian 'war of decrees' over the ownership of the Black Sea Fleet, undermined it. The Ukrainian parliament responded by watering down the terms of the power-sharing agreement and a crisis developed.

In early May, the Crimean parliament unexpectedly declared the independence of the peninsula pending its endorsement in a local referendum. The Ukrainian parliament rejected the proclamation as unconstitutional and invalid. After a tense fortnight, the Crimean parliament backed down and eventually settled for concessions made

---

[10] *Frankfurter Allgemeine Zeitung*, 27 May 1992, and *Washington Post*, 7 July 1992.

by the Ukrainian parliament in a law 'On the Delineation of Power Between the Organs of State Rule of Ukraine and the Republic of Crimea' which broadened the republic's autonomous status as a constituent part of Ukraine. In return, the Crimean parliament annulled the declaration of independence and placed a moratorium on the referendum.

With Russian politicians continuing to encourage the separatists in Crimea and the Ukrainian parliament insisting that the autonomous republic bring its constitution and laws into line with those of Ukraine, the compromise reached between Kyiv and Simferopol was to remain a precarious one. On 21 May, for instance, at a delicate moment in the standoff between Kyiv and Simferopol, the Russian parliament voted to declare the transfer of Crimea to Ukraine illegal and invalid.[11] A few days later, the Russian press reported that Baburin, a leading figure in the red-brown anti-Yeltsin opposition, had threatened the Ukrainian ambassador in Moscow that 'either Ukraine reunites with Russia or there will be war'.[12]

The escalation of the conflict in Moldova, which too involved a Russian factor, also posed an early foreign policy challenge for independent Ukraine. With refugees pouring into the Odesa region, and armed Russian Cossack volunteers making their way to the 'Dniester Republic', Kyiv was anxious to contain the conflict and in March sealed Ukraine's border with Moldova. The situation was further complicated in early April by Yeltsin's announcement that Russia was taking over the former Soviet 14th Army based in Transdniestria, which had not concealed where its sympathies lay, and by Rutskoi's visit to the capital of the 'Dniester Republic', Tiraspol, and the strong support which he expressed for the breakaway 'Russian' enclave only days after similar provocative behaviour in Crimea.

The common opposition of Moldova, Romania and Ukraine to a Russian military involvement or continuing presence in Transdniestria led to the shelving of territorial disputes, which permitted the gradual normalization of relations between Kyiv and

---

[11] On the developments concerning Crimea, see Solchanyk, 'The Politics of State Building', pp. 53-7, and Viacheslav Pikhovshek, 'Will the Crimean Crisis Explode?' in Maria Drohobycky (ed.), *Crimea: Dynamics, Challenges, and Prospects*, (Lanham, MD, 1995), pp. 39-65.

[12] *Izvestiya*, 26 May 1992.

Bucharest. Indeed, in April Moldova and Romania jointly supported the idea of establishing a Ukrainian peace-keeping force in the conflict zone, a proposal which Kyiv found too risky to take up. By June, Ukraine was offering to mediate and calling for the 'Dniester Republic' to be given the status of an autonomous republic within Moldova, with the right to decide its own fate if the latter chose to merge with Romania.[13]

On 23 June, Kravchuk and Yeltsin met in Dagomys and managed, rather unexpectedly, to patch up bilateral relations. Ten days later, they met again in Yalta and continued the process. At their two Crimean summit meetings the two presidents signed several accords which they described as marking a turnaround in Russian–Ukrainian relations. They agreed, among other things, to establish joint Russian–Ukrainian control over the Black Sea Fleet for an interim period of three years during which the issue of ownership was to be decided, that Ukraine was entitled to 16.3% of former Soviet assets abroad, that the Russian–Ukrainian border would remain open and without a visa-system (though customs posts were to be gradually established), that the two countries would move to settle their trade accounts on the basis of world prices, that the leaders of the two countries would continue to have regular summit meetings, and that a new, comprehensive bilateral 'political' treaty, based on the principles established in the Russian–Ukrainian treaty of November 1990 and subsequent bilateral agreements, would be prepared on good-neighbourly relations.[14]

These Russian–Ukrainian agreements indicated that both leaders wanted to avoid deepening the rift between their two countries and were prepared to search for compromises. Nevertheless, although Yeltsin himself was to studiously refrain from meddling in the Crimean issue – to his credit, he treated it as an internal problem of Ukraine – the continuing inflammatory statements by other Russian politicians which challenged Ukraine's independence and territorial integrity, and criticized its attitude towards the CIS, were nevertheless to reinforce Ukraine's sense of insecurity. This was to be reflected in the Ukrainian parliament's toughening of its position on the issue of nuclear arms.

[13] See Nahaylo, 'Moldovan Conflict . . .', and Radio Kyiv, 22 June 1992.

[14] For the text of the Russian-Ukrainian agreement signed in Dagomys, see *Polityka i chas*, nos 7-8 (July-August 1992), pp.21-2.

However, the papering-over of differences between Russia and Ukraine, at least at the presidential level, did not mean that Kravchuk was prepared to soften his line on the CIS. At the various CIS summits during the first half of 1992, Ukraine, together with Moldova, Turkmenistan and Azerbaijan, had refused to join a CIS collective security pact, sign various documents on joint armed forces and to support the idea of a CIS inter-parliamentary assembly. In Dagomys, Kravchuk told journalists that Ukraine was not out to wreck the CIS, 'as it is being presented'.[15] He emphasized, nevertheless, that although in Kyiv's view a better-working CIS was desirable, this was one thing, and the transformation of the CIS into a supra-national entity, another. After the very next CIS summit, held in Moscow on 6 July, he reiterated: 'We insist that . . . the CIS is neither a state nor the subject of international law.' The Ukrainian president was to continue opposing moves towards greater integration and the idea of a CIS Charter.

In fact, for all the economic and military threads still binding it to the East, as Kravchuk's trips to Washington, Paris, Bonn, Brussels and Helsinki indicated, independent Ukraine's orientation was clearly pro-Western. But while realism told Ukraine's leaders that they could only look longingly at the European Community from afar, they entertained hopes of forging a closer relationship with some of their immediate neighbours to the west, especially the Visegrad Triangle, consisting of Hungary, Poland and Czechoslovakia, and the broader Central European Initiative (of which the latter three were members), and using these groups as a bridge to the West. Consequently, Kyiv continued to cultivate ties with Budapest, Warsaw and Prague.[16]

Independent Ukraine's active foreign policy and search for trading partners reached in other directions as well, as President Kravchuk's visits to India and Iran in the spring, and to China in October, demonstrated. Closer to home, Ukraine also established good working relations with its neighbour across the Black Sea – Turkey. In June, President Kravchuk was among the signatories in

[15] ITAR-TASS, 23 June 1992.

[16] See Bohdan Nahaylo, 'Ukraine and the Visegrad Triangle', *RFE/RL Research Report*, vol. 1, no. 23 (5 June 1992), pp. 28–9; and Stephen R. Burant,'Foreign Policy and National Identity: A Comparison of Ukraine and Belarus', *Europe-Asia Studies*, vol. 47, no. 7 (1995, pp. 1127–39).

Istanbul of a Black Sea Region Cooperation Treaty.

During the summer of 1992, Ukraine also sent a battalion of 'blue-helmets' to serve with the UN peace-keeping forces in Bosnia. This support for the UN's operations in former Yugoslavia was seen by Kyiv as an opportunity to boost Ukraine's international reputation and to provide its new army with practical experience. It contrasted with the reluctance to be involved in Russian-led peace-keeping initiatives in the CIS area. Ukraine also conformed with the sanctions imposed by the UN Security Council in May of that year against rump Yugoslavia, which cost the country dearly in terms of the loss and disruption of trade on the Danube.

Thus, during the initial period after independence, Ukraine's activity in the external sphere was rather more successful than in the domestic arena. During the first nine months or so of 1992, Ukraine secured further diplomatic recognition, and representation in the CSCE and other international and regional organizations and financial institutions, developed bilateral ties with a host of countries and participated directly in important international disarmament treaties which regulated its military and quasi-nuclear status. Some of the initial problems with Russia also seemed to have eased.

Courting disaster

At the end of September, the impatience with Fokin's hesitant approach to dealing with Ukraine's economic crisis had become so pervasive that, despite Kravchuk's continuing efforts to support the prime minister, the parliament brought down the government. Kravchuk's preferred candidate, Symonenko, did not obtain enough support and on 13 October, as students demonstrated again outside the parliament, the president proposed fifty-four-year-old Leonid Kuchma to head the new government. A technocrat, he was backed by New Ukraine and some of the industrial lobby as well as Plyushch. The parliament approved his nomination by a large majority. The fall of the Fokin government shifted power away from president to parliament, and the appointment of Kuchma meant that Kravchuk no longer had a close ally as head of government.

Although Kuchma, the former director of the world's largest rocket factory in Dnipropetrovsk, was the product of the Soviet military-industrial complex, he had apparently become convinced of the virtues of the free market and stressed that there could be no going back to the old system. Describing the situation in Ukraine as not an 'economic crisis . . . but an economic catastrophe', he declared that his goal was to 'transform the post-Socialist economy into a market economy', through 'evolutionary' reform which avoided shock therapy and relied on a combination of 'administrative and market methods'. The new prime minister called for a reduction in the budget deficit (Fokin's government had issued cheap credits to the state sector, increasing the budget deficit and inflation) and the country's high corporate taxation, the restoration of economic links with Russia and other former Soviet republics and the expansion of ties with the West, the decentralization of powers to the regions, and an anti-corruption campaign to reduce the large-scale theft of Ukraine's property and revenues.[17]

The new prime minister lost no time in asserting his authority. After successfully insisting that the State Duma be dissolved, he proceeded to form what appeared to be a coalition government in all but name. It included representatives from the democratic and reformist camps, such as Yukhnovsky, who became first deputy prime minister, Pynzenyk, deputy prime minister responsible for economic reform, and Zhulynsky, deputy prime minister responsible for humanitarian affairs. Although Zlenko and Morozov remained at their posts in the foreign and defence ministries, Kuchma also made it clear that the new government would pursue a more pragmatic approach towards nuclear disarmament.

The following month, Kuchma persuaded the parliament to grant him extraordinary powers for six months to deal with the collapsing economy. Ukraine also effectively left the rouble zone and the karbovanets became its interim currency. With the new prime minister determined to press ahead with stabilization measures and a campaign against official corruption, it seemed that Ukraine was finally setting off on the road to recovery. But, after what appeared to be a promising new start, things soon went badly wrong.

An immediate priority was to ease the country's fuel shortage. Although Ukraine and Turkmenistan had patched up their differences in September, Russia was reducing deliveries of oil to the CIS countries and in November Yeltsin declared that states which had

[17] On Kuchma and his views, see Chrystia Freeland's interview with him, *Financial Times*, 21 December 1991.

left the rouble zone should pay Russia in hard currency. This move coincided with Ukraine's opposition at CIS summits in Bishkek and Moscow in late 1992 to the adoption of a CIS Charter and growing external pressure on Kyiv to ratify the START-1 agreement, and was therefore perceived by Kyiv as a Russian attempt to use fuel as a weapon. In January 1993 Kuchma made his second trip to Moscow since being appointed prime minister but failed to bring home good news: his Russian counterpart, Viktor Chernomyrdin, confirmed that Russia would supply significantly less oil and natural gas in 1993 than in the previous year. The quota was fixed in mid-January 1993 at a Russian-Ukrainian summit meeting in Moscow, at which Russia undertook to supply only 20 million tons of the 45 million tons of oil which Ukraine had requested. The following month, though, Kuchma complained that Russia was not delivering the fuel it had promised and was trying to 'paralyze' Ukraine. When, later that same month, Moscow disregarded recent agreements and announced that it would charge Ukraine world prices for natural gas, Kyiv retaliated by raising the transit tariff for Russian gas to more than double the world price.

The Ukrainian government desperately continued trying to secure additional sources of fuel. Yukhnovsky and Kuchma made trips to Kazakhstan and Central Asia and achieved modest successes. There were further negotiations with Iran, but the failure to move forward with the implementation of agreements reached the previous year, including an ambitious project for the construction of gas pipelines to carry Iranian gas to Europe via Azerbaijan and Ukraine, indicated that the costs and political and technical difficulties were too great. With no other viable alternatives for the time being to the problematic supplies from Russia, Ukraine agreed in early March at a meeting of CIS heads of government in Surgut to join the other CIS countries in helping the Russian Federation develop its oil and gas reserves. By the following month, Kuchma was left reminding the Ukrainian parliament of the harsh realities: that the Ukrainian economy remained dependent on Russian energy, that Russian-Ukrainian relations were 'determined by political factors', and that because Russia would be raising its fuel prices, Ukraine's economic situation would worsen.[18]

While in January Kuchma described Russian-Ukrainian relations

---

[18] Smolansky, 'Ukraine's Quest . . .', pp. 72-81.

as his government's 'biggest headache', the fuel crisis and Russia's economic pressure formed only the backdrop to the prime minister's other problems. Despite his appeals to the population for under-standing and support, when the government embarked on a stabilization programme ending subsidies on most agricultural and industrial goods, raising prices of food, transport and municipal services, and stepping up the fight against corruption, there was the predictable negative political and social reaction. By February 1993, miners in the Donbas and transport workers in Kyiv were on strike. Moreover, pro-Communist forces, pressing for the ban on the CPU to be lifted, exploited the aggravated social discontent, especially in the industrialized eastern and southern regions, to organize opposi-tion not only to the government's emergency measures but also, increasingly, to the pro-Western and market-oriented course adopted by independent Ukraine.

So 1993 was to see a resurgence of leftist and neo-Communist forces which were opposed to Western-style reforms and favoured re-establishing closer ties with Russia, or even restoring the Union. Depicting themselves as the defenders of the social and economic rights of the workers and farmers, the leftist leaders argued that the principles of social protection and social justice ruled out any radical reform. Their allies included the 'red directors' – the powerful conservative bosses of large enterprises who wanted to preserve their influence and privileges and who in December 1992 had founded the Labour Party of Ukraine (LPU) in Donetsk.

In the meantime, the democratic forces were increasingly plagued by disunity and the inability to mobilize sufficient popular support. During the latter part of 1992, Rukh, which after its internal split was now dominated by Chornovil – Kravchuk's staunch critic-and New Ukraine had launched a campaign to gather 3 million signa-tures required by law to initiate a referendum on early parliamentary elections. They had failed, though. Attempts at the beginning of 1993 to unite the fragmented democratic forces into a new coalition were only partly successful. Furthermore, the national democratic organizations were still finding it hard to extend their activity to the Russified eastern and southern regions. At the same time, though, frustration with the political and economic situation was resulting in the greater prominence in western and central Ukraine of radical-right groups, most notably the relatively small but well-disciplined Ukrainian People's Self-Defence (UNSO) – the paramilitary arm of the UNA.[19]

As social opposition to Kuchma's policy grew, conservative elements within the parliament, presidential apparatus and government itself hindered the stabilization and reform strategy. The prime minister was especially handicapped by his failure to secure control over the National Bank of Ukraine and the emission of credit. When, at the end of March, the National Bank extended fresh credits to industry and agriculture, the progress that had been made in recent months was undermined. The following month, Russia raised its oil and gas prices, which sent prices soaring in Ukraine. This in turn produced demands for more state subsidies.

Kuchma's economic measures brought him into conflict not only with the conservative majority in parliament but also with Kravchuk, who seemed to resent the emergency powers which Kuchma had been given. The obstacles facing Kuchma's team and the intensification of the struggle for control over economic policy was attested to in March, when Yukhnovsky left his post, and again in April, when Pynzenyk lost his portfolio to a conservative. In May, the parliament refused to prolong the government's extraordinary powers and Kuchma offered his resignation. The parliament rejected it, however, leaving him a lame duck prime minister.

In fact, this problem was only part of a three-way struggle for power between the parliament, president and government. During the late spring and summer of 1993 it resulted in political gridlock and saw Ukraine move to the brink of hyper-inflation. At the heart of the malaise was the lack of a precise division of powers, the struggle over which had delayed the adoption of a new constitution. In fact, now that the prime minister had been deprived of his temporary power to rule by decree, there continued to be a shift away from the presidential system which Kravchuk had sought to establish, towards a parliamentary one in which the president was being reduced to little more than a ceremonial figurehead.[20] The main beneficiary of this process was the speaker of the parliament,

[19] See the author's article on the emergence of the radical right in Ukraine in *RFE/RL Research Report* vol. 3, no. 16 (22 April 1994), pp. 42-9.

[20] See Ihor Markov, 'The Role of the President in the Ukrainian Political System', *RFE/RL Research Report* vol. 2, no. 48 (3 December 1993), pp. 3-5.

Plyushch, who was becoming an increasingly influential political figure.

At least the political struggle in Kyiv did not turn as ugly as the growing confrontation in Moscow between Yeltsin and his supporters on the one hand, and the Russian parliament led by Khasbulatov, and its red-brown supporters, including Rutskoi, on the other. The continuing activation and regrouping of Ukraine's Communist forces and sympathizers, nevertheless, brought home the fact that forces from the past were still very much intent on playing a decisive role in the future. In March 1993, Ukraine's Communists had organized a conference in the Donbas. After the Presidium of the Ukrainian parliament effectively lifted, on 14 May, the ban on the CPU, Hurenko quickly organized a meeting in Donetsk at which the revival of the CPU was announced. Petro Symonenko, a former local Communist official was elected to head it (Hurenko had resigned as a deputy at the end of 1992 and did not attempt to play any further role in the revived CPU), and the leadership also included the deputies Oliinyk and Kotsyuba.

By now, both Kuchma and Kravchuk had in their own different ways acknowledged that Ukraine's dire economic situation necessitated a more accommodating attitude towards both Russia and the CIS. Their subsequent actions in this respect were to be criticized by opponents of a more pragmatic approach. In May, at a CIS summit in Moscow, Ukraine signed a joint declaration of intent to deepen economic integration. At the beginning of the following month, as Russia was preparing to suspend oil deliveries to Ukraine because of Kyiv's inability to pay off its mounting debt, Kuchma told the parliament that it was unrealistic to expect that Russia would agree to leave Sevastopol and he proposed that Ukraine lease the naval base in Sevastopol to it. Among those who opposed this was the minister of defence, Morozov. Two weeks later, Kravchuk and Yeltsin met in Moscow and concluded an agreement on the equal division of the Black Sea Fleet. From the provisions it was clear that the Russian part of the fleet would be stationed in Sevastopol and possibly elsewhere in Crimea on terms still to be agreed upon. That same month, Kuchma met with Chernomyrdin in Kyiv and agreed on the quotas of oil and gas which Russia would supply to Ukraine over the next six months at prices which would increase incrementally and reach the world level at the end of the year. The following month, with Ukraine still struggling to pay for the fuel and Russia halting deliveries yet again, Kuchma was to initial an agreement with Russia and Belarus on closer economic integration.

Meanwhile, in June, the miners went on strike again and this time came out with political demands, including administrative autonomy for the Donbas. The Donetsk and Luhansk regional councils backed their call for regional autonomy and the latter also voted to make Russian a state language in its region alongside Ukrainian. Kravchuk saw his chance to reassert his authority and on 16 June issued a decree announcing that he was assuming personal control of the government and of a new committee to fight corruption. This led to another threat of resignation from Kuchma, and deputy parliamentary speaker Hrynov expressed his solidarity with the prime minister by stepping down. After five days, Kravchuk rescinded his decree and the political stalemate continued.

Had it not been for the miners' political ultimatum to official Kyiv that it hold referendums on public confidence in both the parliament and the president, it seems that the latter two would have continued squabbling without calling early elections to break the deadlock. Parliament reluctantly agreed to the miners' demands and scheduled the polls for 26 September. In August, however, after doubts were expressed about the legality of the referendums and concern was voiced about the precedents they would set (especially for Crimea and the Donbas), the parliament cancelled them. Only after railway workers in southern Ukraine went on strike at the beginning of September and Rukh had threatened to call an all-Ukrainian strike did the parliament finally agree to early elections. Kravchuk, too, gambled on shortening his term voluntarily by two years. Parliamentary elections were therefore scheduled for 27 March 1994, and presidential elections for 26 June 1994.

In the meantime, Kyiv's position *vis-à-vis* Moscow as regards Ukraine's fuel predicament was becoming 'untenable'. According to the author of a study of this problem, the Ukrainian administration had by now 'exhausted most of its options'. But

> Kyiv still had some valuable assets that Moscow desired, including part-ownership of the Black Sea Fleet, the naval shore installations and support facilities, situated mainly in Crimea, and enterprises engaged in the transport and processing of fuel. The first step in the process of abandoning assets was taken in August, when

Ukraine offered Russia a small section of the oil pipeline situated on Ukrainian territory, as well as a 45% share in four of its six major refineries.[21]

Because the Ukrainian leadership was reluctant to reveal the full implications of the country's energy crunch, Kravchuk got himself into a political mess at a summit meeting on 3 September with Yeltsin in Massandra, outside of Yalta, when he apparently yielded more ground. The Russian and Western media reported that the Ukrainian president had agreed to sell Ukraine's share of the Black Sea Fleet to Russia to offset the country's debts and initial claims made by the Russian side suggested that he had also undertaken to hand over to Russia the nuclear warheads still left in Ukraine in return for nuclear fuel for atomic power stations. Although Kravchuk subsequently denied that a deal of this sort had been made in Massandra, the fact that he even considered selling off part or all of Ukraine's share of the Black Sea Fleet, and that his position was criticized by other members of the Ukrainian delegation at the summit, namely Morozov (who resigned in October) and first deputy prime minister Valerii Shmarov, undermined confidence in him even among his dwindling supporters.[22]

Kuchma had remained an embattled and controversial figure. His insistence on the need for improving economic relations with Russia, and readiness to reach compromises to this end, provided his opponents with ammunition. On 27 August Pynzenyk resigned, leaving the prime minister isolated within the government. When the parliament rejected further emergency measures which he was proposing, on 9 September Kuchma again submitted his resignation. This time the parliament accepted it.'

With the economic situation so abysmal, and the amount of manouvering and improvisation which Ukraine's internal and external situation demanded, it was difficult to assess Kuchma's efforts in terms of success or failure. For many he became an easy scapegoat; for others, despite his inconsistencies, he represented a thwarted pragmatic reformer who had at least tried to take hold to the controls and to pull Ukraine out of its tailspin.

Kuchma's departure provided Kravchuk with a chance to regain

---

[21] Smolansky, 'Ukraine's Quest . . .', pp. 84-5.

[22] See Bohdan Nahaylo, 'The Massandra Summit: Questions and Implications', *RFE/RL Research Report*, vol. 2, no. 37 (17 September 1993).

some lost ground and to boost his flagging popularity but he was to squander it. First, though, at the next CIS summit held in Moscow on 24 September, the president agreed to Ukraine's associate membership in the new CIS economic union. A few days later he assumed responsibility for forming and directing a new government. He appointed a highly conservative caretaker Cabinet of Ministers which did not contain a single identifiable reformer. It was headed by Yukhym Zvyahilsky, the former mayor of Donetsk, with Valentyn Landyk, another politician from the Donbas who like Zvyahilsky was associated with the LPU, as his deputy.

Ironically, in early October 1993, just as President Yeltsin's tanks were shelling the Russian White House, in which Rutskoi, Khasbulatov and their Communist and ultra-nationalist supporters had their headquarters, the CPU was officially registered again in Ukraine. Claiming the support of 128,000 members and some ninety deputies, it became the country's largest political party. Later that same month, the conservative majority in the parliament demonstrated its residual conservatism by passing an electoral law designed to perpetuate the status quo and discourage the development of political parties.

In addition to all this, in early October the first serious clashes occurred between Crimean Tatars and police seeking to evict them from squatter settlements. These incidents, and the Crimean Tatar protests which followed, revealed that, under the leadership of their elected council, or Mejlis, headed by the former long-standing political prisoner, Mustafa Cemiloglu (Dzhemilev), the 200,000 or so Crimean Tatars who had by now returned to Crimea from their places of exile in Central Asia were well organized. In order to prevent the unrest from spreading, Kyiv was forced to intervene and order the release of detained Crimean Tatar activists. Although it continued to pour funds into Crimea for the integration of the Crimean Tatars – the latter, who lacked any political representation in the regional parliament and government, complained that the money was being misused, or siphoned off, by the Crimean authorities – the Ukrainian leadership remained reluctant to recognize the Mejlis as the official representative organ of the Crimean Tatar people.[23]

[23] See Nadir Bekirov, 'The Crimean Tatar Movement and Ukrainian Strategy in the Crimea: A Chronology of Defeat', *Demos* (Kyiv), vol. II, no. 2 (September

Security dilemmas

Hopes that the Russian-Ukrainian accommodation reached at the summit meetings in Dagomys and Yalta in the summer of 1992 would be followed by a new bilateral treaty were soon dashed when, within weeks, the Ukrainian press disclosed details of a draft treaty drawn up by the Russian Foreign Ministry. These revealed that Moscow was in effect proposing that the two states form a confederation, entailing a closer political, economic and military association and providing for the stationing of Russian troops on Ukrainian territory. Strong objections were immediately voiced in Ukraine and Foreign Minister Zlenko declared that a confederation of any sort was 'totally out of the question'.[24]

Meanwhile, the Russian press had disclosed details of the debates going on in Moscow about the future course of Russia's foreign policy generally and towards the other members of the CIS specifically, and this also gave Ukrainian leaders plenty to think about. As it was, Russian politicians had begun referring to the newly independent states as 'the near abroad', which itself rankled with the sensitive non-Russians. For Kyiv, the line being advocated towards Russia's neighbours by the chairman of the Russian Supreme Soviet's Committee for Foreign Affairs and Foreign Economic Relations, Evgenii Abartsumov, was particularly unsettling. He maintained that 'the Russian Federation's foreign policy must be base on a doctrine that proclaims the entire geopolitical space of the former [Soviet] Union a sphere of its vital interests (along the lines of the US "Monroe Doctrine" in Latin America).' It was necessary, he argued, for Moscow to secure 'from the world community understanding and recognition of Russia's special interests in this space ... [and of its] role of political and military guarantor of stability throughout the former space of the USSR'.[25]

During the second half of 1992, the debate in the Ukrainian

1995), pp.18-19. A broader study of the Crimean Tatars and their history is provided by Andrew Wilson in his *The Crimean Tatars: A Situation Report on the Crimean Tatars for International Alert*, London, 1994.

[24] Reuter, 27 August 1992. For the text of the draft treaty proposed by Russia, see *Vechirnii Kyiv*, 21 September 1992.

[25] *Izvestiya*, 7 August 1992. On the debate, see also Susan Crow, 'Competing Blueprints for Russian Foreign Policy', *RFE/RL Research Report*, vol. 1, no. 50 (18 December 1992), pp. 45-50.

parliament and press about what to do about the nuclear weapons still based in Ukraine intensified. To add to the rising concern about safeguarding Ukraine's security, at the beginning of September it became known that the United States had agreed to buy enriched uranium from Russia that was being removed from nuclear warheads. Ukraine, confronted by economic catastrophe, was facing huge costs to carry out nuclear disarmament and at the same time was having to buy nuclear fuel for its atomic reactors from Russia. It had handed over its tactical nuclear weapons to its northern neighbour without any compensation and felt cheated. On being appointed prime minister, Kuchma had reflected this feeling in several outspoken statements. He accused the West of putting pressure on Ukraine to hand over its remaining nuclear warheads to Russia 'without getting anything in exchange', neither guarantees of its security, nor material aid, just 'advice'. 'Our people are not fools,' he declared.[26]

Towards the end of 1992, as external pressure on Ukraine to speed up the ratification of the START-1 treaty mounted, Kravchuk, Kuchma, Yukhnovsky and other Ukrainian leaders left no doubt that Kyiv intended to use the nuclear weapons as a bargaining chip to obtain compensation, financial assistance and security assurances. The Ukrainian president explained that if Ukraine did not stick to this position: 'We will be praised for being peace-loving but no one will help us. Then it will be said that we are a second-rate country and no one will take any notice of us.'[27]

Kyiv's stance soured its relations with Washington, especially in view of the fact that in January 1993 Russia and the United States concluded a bilateral START-2 treaty intended to slash their nuclear arsenals by two-thirds but which was dependent on Ukraine's ratification of the START-1 treaty. Consequently, Ukraine was depicted as holding the new treaty hostage and criticized. Ukrainian leaders countered that it was unreasonable to expect the Ukrainian legislature to rush through the ratification of the START-1 treaty just because this suited other nuclear powers: they noted that it had taken the US Senate over a year to scrutinize the treaty, which was almost 1,000 pages long; the parliament of Ukraine, a country which had not taken part in the negotiations on the drafting of the treaty,

[26] *Washington Post*, 6 November 1992.

[27] Ukrainian television and Reuter, 16 November 1992

had only received the document in late November. The accusation that the Ukrainian parliament, preoccupied with easing the country's economic and social problems, was deliberately holding up the ratification of the START-1 treaty was increasingly resented in Kyiv.

When the Ukrainian and Russian leaders met in Moscow in mid-January 1993, President Yeltsin appeared to go some way towards allaying Ukrainian concerns by announcing that Russia was prepared to guarantee Ukraine's security. But as the Ukrainian Foreign Ministry subsequently pointed out, what Russia was actually proposing did not even meet Ukraine's 'minimal demands', for Moscow was prepared to respect Ukraine's borders only 'within the framework of the CIS'. Subsequent statements made in February and March by President Yeltsin calling for 'special rights' for Russia 'as guarantor of peace and stability' on the territory of the former Soviet Union, and for greater integration of the CIS, as well as Kozyrev's public acknowledgment that he favoured 'confederation, even federation', only increased Ukrainian anxieties about its security and spurred it to try and interest other Central and East European states in setting up some form of a sub-regional security arrangement.[28]

In November 1992, while receiving the commander of NATO and US forces in Europe, General John Shalikashvili, Kravchuk had alluded to the shortcomings of the existing security structures in Europe and the difficulties which Ukraine was beginning to experience as a result of its location between NATO, and countries which wanted to align themselves with this military bloc, and Russia. 'We must find a formula to guarantee the security of the former states of the Soviet Union, Europe, and the world at large . . . not just two superpowers,' he had told him.[29]

At the end of February, while on an official visit to Hungary, Kravchuk turned for support to the Visegrad group. He was encouraged by the fact that earlier that month, the foreign ministers of Hungary, Poland and Ukraine had signed an agreement in Debrecen, Hungary, about the creation of a Carpathian Euroregion, a project which had been in preparation since the previous

---

[28] See Roman Solchanyk, 'Ukraine's Search for Security', *RFE/RL Research Report*, vol. 2, no. 21 (21 May 1993), pp. 1-6
[29] Reuter, 19 November 1992.

summer. Ukraine was to be represented in this cross-border cooperation arrangement by its Transcarpathian region. As one observer noted, 'For Ukraine, the undertaking took on a significance that outweighed the modest nature of its activities.'[30]

The Ukrainian president proposed the idea of a 'zone of stability and security' in Central and Eastern Europe which foresaw closer cooperation between states in the sub-region, collective consultations on security issues and the promotion of confidence-building and conflict prevention measures. Although Kravchuk and other Ukrainian officials emphasized that the zone would not be a military alliance, and that the initiative was not aimed against Russia but was designed to fill the security vacuum left in the area between the NATO bloc and Russia by the dissolution of the Warsaw Pact, only Hungary showed any real interest in it. But like Poland, the Czech Republic and Slovakia, Hungary too was looking westward and was more interested in further integration in existing European structures than participating in a nebulous sub-regional arrangement which some had immediately interpreted as a 'cordon sanitaire' or buffer against Russia and which would antagonize Moscow.

The lack of enthusiasm for Ukraine's initiative, which was to be underscored in May during a visit to Kyiv by Poland's president, Lech Walesa, as well as the fact that in April the Belarusian parliament voted that Belarus should join the CIS collective security pact (which was opposed by Shushkevich and was to lead to his resignation), increased Ukraine's sense of isolation. It was therefore perhaps not surprising that at the end of April the hardening of attitudes towards the nuclear weapons issue was demonstrated when 162 deputies from across the political spectrum addressed a statement to Kravchuk and Plyushch condemning external pressure on the country and calling for Ukraine to declare itself a nuclear state. They also urged the parliament to confirm Ukraine's right to ownership of the nuclear arms on its territory – Kyiv did not have operational control over the weapons and this was seen as a way of asserting its claim to the material value of the uranium in the warheads that would be dismantled – and only then to proceed with to debate about the ratification of the START-1 treaty.

At this point, having started with a tough line towards Ukraine, Washington's new Clinton Administration apparently decided to

---

[30] Burant, 'Foreign Policy and National Identity', pp. 1129–30.

try using the carrot rather than the stick: in May it sent its ambassador-at-large responsible for the CIS, Strobe Talbott, to placate the Ukrainian leadership. He offered Kyiv 'a new start' in bilateral relations, and held out the prospect of some form of security assurances as well as mediation by Washington in the strained Ukrainian-Russian relationship.[31]

Ukraine's problems with Russia, as well as related ones with Crimea, remained at the centre of Kyiv's security concerns. While the Russian parliament had continued to meddle in the affairs of the peninsula and to encourage the separatist movement, the Yeltsin administration had insisted that Sevastopol be recognized as a Russian naval base. The tensions over the Black Sea Fleet were exacerbated in May when mutinous officers hoisted the pre-1917 Russia naval flag over many of the ships.

Ukraine's economic difficulties and chronic fuel supply problems severely weakened its bargaining position *vis-à-vis* Russia. At a Russian-Ukrainian summit meeting in Moscow on 17 June, Yeltsin and Kravchuk agreed, among other things, that the Black Sea Fleet would be divided equally between their countries, beginning in September, and Moscow appeared to obtain Kyiv's assent to the stationing of units of the Russian navy in Sevastopol and other Ukrainian ports. The decision to split the fleet was denounced in Crimea and Moscow and on 9 July the backlash – Rutskoi, for instance, characterized the agreement as a 'a national and historic tragedy' for Russia – resulted in a politically explosive declaration by the Russian parliament, adopted by 166 to 0, asserting Sevastopol's 'Russian federal status'. Although Yeltsin, who was locked in political conflict with the conservative parliament, declared that he was 'ashamed' by the action of the Russia deputies, the challenge to Ukraine's territorial integrity was taken very seriously by Kyiv. The Ukrainian parliament labelled it 'an aggressive political act' and the country's foreign ministry called on the UN Security Council to condemn it.[32] On 20 July, the Security Council criticized the Russian parliament's declaration as being inconsistent with both the UN Charter and the Russian-Ukrainian

---

[31] *Washington Post*, 11 May 1993. .

[32] See the statement delivered before the UN Security Council on 20 July by Ukraine's deputy foreign minister, Borys Tarasyuk, in *Holos Ukrainy*, 31 July 1993.

treaty of November 1990, and reaffirmed 'in this connection, its commitment to the territorial integrity of Ukraine'.[33]

Although the Russian parliament was to stick to its position on Sevastopol until it was eventually dissolved by Yeltsin in late September, the display of international support for Ukraine was at least reassuring for Kyiv. Furthermore, during the summer, contacts between Kyiv and Washington improved and in July the Ukrainian defence minister travelled to Washington to discuss agreements paving the way for American aid for Ukraine's nuclear disarmament. That same month, a Ukrainian delegation visited NATO headquarters in Brussels and conveyed Ukraine's unease about being caught between the NATO alliance and states which aspired to be linked with it and the security system which Russia was organizing in the CIS region.[34] Another promising development for Ukraine at this time was its acceptance as an associate member of the Central European Initiative.

Ukraine's main source of vulnerability, however, remained its deteriorating economic situation. In May, the Russian Deputy Prime Minister Aleksandr Shokhin had already stated quite openly that participation in the proposed CIS economic union which Ukraine was being drawn into *nolens volens* would 'result in a partial loss of not just economic, but political sovereignty as well'.[35] When Kravchuk and Yeltsin met in Massandra at the beginning of September, even the Russian president seems to have decided that it was time to play Moscow's trump card. Under intense fire at home from the red-brown forces, he needed to bolster his reputation as a defender of Russia's interests. Yeltsin, as the Ukrainian president later recounted, took the Ukrainian side by surprise by presenting it with a virtual ultimatum: either Ukraine repaid its fuel debts or Russia would cut off the energy supplies. A humiliated Kravchuk apparently yielded to what he diplomatically described as 'economic realities', and other members of his delegation preferred to call 'economic diktat', and agreed in principle to the possibility of trading in Ukraine's share of the Black Sea Fleet. The Ukrainian delegation managed, however, to achieve at least one success in Massandra, the

---

[33] For the texts of this and other official statements made at this time, see Drohobycky, *Crimea: Dynamics, Challenges and Prospects*, pp. 215-21.

[34] *Holos Ukrainy*, 2 July 1993.

[35] ITAR-TASS, 18 May 1993.

conclusion of agreements, finally reached after protracted negotiations, on compensation claimed by Ukraine for warhead fissile material transferred to Russia, and on the maintenance and servicing of nuclear missiles situated in Ukraine.[36]

With both side presenting very different interpretations of what had actually been agreed to, the Massandra summit not only deepened the mistrust between Ukraine and Russia but also undermined the special working relationship which Kravchuk and Yeltsin had developed. The Ukrainian president, who had to defend himself at home against charges of capitulation and even betrayal, now proceeded even more cautiously with respect to the CIS economic union and on 24 September brought his country into it as an associate, rather than full, member; the terms of the arrangement still remained to be negotiated.

In the weeks following the meeting in Massandra, the situation in Crimea itself once again became very tense. The Crimean parliament paved the way for the election of a president of the Crimean Republic, and one of the future candidates, the leader of the region's Russian separatists, Meshkov, immediately revived the idea of a local referendum on independence. This only increased the determination of the Crimean Tatars to struggle for their rights and despite Kravchuk's hesitance to back them politically, led them to align themselves more closely with the Ukrainian state. In early October, the Crimean Tatars held mass demonstrations outside the Crimean parliament and eventually, through sheer persistence, won a major temporary concession: they were allowed to have a quota of 14 out of 98 seats in the next Crimean parliament, though only for one term.[37] Over the next few months, however, a series of killings and attacks on political leaders in Crimea, Russian as well as Crimean Tatar, were to keep the atmosphere charged. Because of the pervasiveness of organized crime and corruption in the peninsula, it remained difficult to distinguish politically-motivated acts from purely criminal ones.

The fallout from the Massandra summit inevitably also hardened attitudes in the Ukrainian parliament on the nuclear weapons issue.

---

[36] See John W.R. Leppingwell, 'Negotiations over Nuclear Weapons: The Past as Prologue?', *RFE/RL Research Report*, vol. 3, no. 4 (28 January 1994), pp. 6-8

[37] See Susan Stewart, 'The Tatar Dimension', *RFE/RL Research Report*, vol. 3, no. 19 (13 May 1994), pp. 22-6.

Moreover, on 21 September Russia abrogated the accord on nuclear arms signed in Massandra, and the spectacle, some two weeks later, of fighting in Moscow between Yeltsin's supporters and his opponents made the Ukrainian deputies even more reluctant to agree to immediate nuclear disarmament.

The 'Basic Directions' of Ukraine's foreign policy adopted by the parliament in July, and the country's 'Military Doctrine', which it approved at the end of October, both stated that Ukraine had 'become *the owner of nuclear weapons* [author's emphasis] through historical circumstances' due to the collapse of the USSR, that it still intended to become a non-nuclear state, but that this would depend on 'reliable security guarantees' from the international community. When, after prodding from the United States, including a visit to Kyiv in late October by US Secretary of State Warren Christopher, and pressure from Kravchuk, the parliament finally debated the START-1 treaty on 18 November, the result was a compromise which largely satisfied domestic opinion but vexed the United States, Russia and other concerned states.

The ratification of the treaty was made conditional on numerous provisos, which revealed the extent of Ukraine's security fears. These included long-standing demands for international security guarantees, international assistance for the dismantling of the missiles and compensation for fissile material in the warheads, as well as insistence on a phased de-nuclearization process and rejection of Article V of the Lisbon Protocol requiring Ukraine's adherence to the Treaty on the Non Proliferation of Nuclear Weapons (NPT) as a non-nuclear state. It was the latter conditions which caused the most disquiet in international circles. Here, the parliament contended that the terms of the START-1 treaty covered only Ukraine's older ICBMs – SS-19s (that is, only 36% of the launchers and 42% of the warheads) – and excluded its forty-six multiple-warhead SS-24s.[38]

Washington responded by, on the one hand, implicitly threatening Ukraine with diplomatic ostracism, and, on the other, redoubling its efforts to mediate between Kyiv and Moscow in the search for a deal on nuclear arms that would allay the concerns of the Ukrainian parliament. This took place against a strong showing by anti-democratic forces in Russia's parliamentary elections and the

[38] See Leppingwell, 'Negotiations over Nuclear Weapons', pp. 8–10.

intensification of the debate about NATO's possible expansion eastward. After headway was made during trilateral negotiations in mid-December in Washington and Kravchuk and US Vice President Al Gore met in Budapest, Ukraine announced that as a goodwill gesture it would begin dismantling one third of its SS-24s. A deal based largely on the Massandra agreements was successfully worked out but with the Ukrainian side continuing to insist on some form of security assurances. President Clinton made a brief stopover in Kyiv on 12 January and offered Ukraine membership in the Partnership for Peace Programme, which was to be unveiled at the NATO summit in mid-January, and American help in obtaining assistance from the international financial institutions. On 14 January, a trilateral agreement between the United States, Russia and Ukraine was signed by their leaders in Moscow.

In return for giving up all the nuclear arms on its territory, the trilateral agreement brokered by the United States provided Ukraine with: general security assurances reflecting standard CSCE principles (including the non-use of economic coercion); compensation for fissile material in the form of reactor fuel from Russia (100 tons of enriched uranium in return for the first 200 warheads to be delivered to Russia within ten months) and the prospect of further deliveries over the next twenty years; $175 million in US aid to assist with dismantling the nuclear weapons and promises of additional US economic and technical assistance if Ukraine's nuclear disarmament proceeded successfully. Although there appeared to be no mention of any relief in respect of Ukraine's $2.5 billion debt to Russia or of the question of compensation for the fissile material from the tactical nuclear weapons which had been transferred to Russia, the deal seemed to represent the best that Kyiv could hope for in the circumstances. It also reduced the country's isolation: it opened the way for Ukraine's participation in NATO's Partnership for Peace Programme and enhanced Kyiv's chances of obtaining desperately needed international economic aid.[39]

Despite initial fears that the Ukrainian parliament would still cause problems, on 3 February 1994 it removed its conditions from the ratification of the START-1 treaty. Less than a week later, Ukraine became the first CIS country to sign the Partnership for

---

[39] See John W.R. Leppingwell, 'The Trilateral Agreement on nuclear Weapons', *RFE/RL Research Report*, vol. 3, no. 4 (28 January 1994), pp. 12-20.

Peace framework document. The following month, it was also to become the first CIS country to initial an agreement on partnership and cooperation with the European Union.

On the verge of catastrophe

After assuming control of the government in late September 1993, Kravchuk while evidently trying to placate the Donbas and Eastern Ukraine generally, appeared to shift away from the middle ground towards the neo-Communist forces. With Ukraine's economic situation looking increasingly desperate (the monthly inflation rate in December 1993 reached 91%), winter approaching and energy supplies running out, Kravchuk ruled out any further 'experimentation' with reform until after the elections.

The success of the Trilateral Agreement was overshadowed by the intractable difficulties of paying for fuel deliveries from Russia and Turkmenistan. In November, Shokhin announced that Russia would now insist on 'the conversion of debts into ownership . . . in [certain] enterprises', including the Kremenchuk refinery and the Khartzyzsk pipe-making plant. The situation for Ukraine grew even more catastrophic when, in February, Turkmenistan again stopped deliveries of gas because of Ukraine's failure to pay off its debts and, shortly afterwards, Russia reduced its supply of gas. On the eve of the parliamentary elections, confronted by 'an unusually aggressive Russian stance', the Ukrainian government evidently gave in and agreed to repay the debt for 1993 in money as well as in 'equipment and materials', while the debt incurred in 1994 would be repaid in hard currency and roubles.

> The Russian version of the agreement was more specific. Moscow would receive 'a share in the authorized stocks of the gas transport infrastructure enterprises (51%) and in a number of factories in which Gazprom is interested (51%)'. These included the 'export gas pipeline to Europe, underground storage tanks . . . and Odessa port facilities. Moscow's desire to gain control over the Ukrainian gas supply system was easy to understand: the ability to siphon off Russian gas and to store large amounts of it enabled Kyiv to withstand Moscow's pressure for several weeks at a time.[40]

[40] Smolansky, 'Ukraine's Quest . . .', p. 83.

As the elections drew closer, it was clear that the leftist forces would do well in the eastern and southern regions where they were well represented. When, in January 1994, Meshkov defeated the Crimean parliament's speaker, Bahrov, in the autonomous state's first presidential election, the danger of regional fragmentation and of an intensification of tensions between the Russian-speaking and Ukrainian-speaking areas became even more apparent. Meshkov lost no time in announcing his intention to conduct a local referendum on independence on the same day as the Ukrainian parliamentary elections, to take Crimea back into the rouble zone and to switch locally from Kyiv to Moscow time. In February he defied Kyiv by appointing a Russian citizen, the Moscow-based economist Evgenii Saburov, as the new head of the Crimean government.

Meanwhile, the Donetsk and Luhansk regional councils decided to hold local 'consultative' referenda on the same day as the elections. Voters were to be asked if they agreed that Russian should be recognized as the country's state language along with Ukrainian, that Russian be regarded as the language of administration, education and science in the eastern regions, that Ukraine should become a federation (asked only in the Donetsk region), and that Ukraine should sign the Charter of the CIS and become a full-fledged member of the CIS economic union and Inter-Parliamentary Assembly.

All this indicated that whereas in the years immediately preceding the achievement of independence, Western Ukraine and Kyiv had exerted the main influence on the republic's political life and its evolving political agenda, Eastern Ukraine was now redressing the balance. The prospect of a rift between the Ukrainian-speaking and more pro-Western-oriented western and central regions and the Russophone and more pro-Russian oriented southern and eastern regions was reduced somewhat, though, by the formation of an election bloc, the 'Inter-regional Bloc for Reforms' (IBR), headed by Kuchma and Hrynov. Both of them were primarily Russian-speaking politicians, and their bloc enjoyed the backing of industrial and regional lobbies and was therefore expected to do reasonably well in the eastern and southern regions.

The IBR had essentially a liberal-centrist and pro-market profile but its emphasis on the need to strengthen economic ties with Russia and the CIS divided it from the national democratic forces which formed a coalition led by Lukyanenko called the Democratic

Association Ukraine. Apart from Rukh, the URP and DPU, it also contained, among others, a relatively new party – the Congress of Ukrainian Nationalists (KUN), which saw itself as the direct heir of the Bandera faction of the OUN-B and had adapted to the democratic parliamentary system. To the right of this national democratic bloc were a number of radical nationalist parties, the strongest of which was the UNA-UNSO, and the most extreme of which was the small but vociferous fascist group which had appeared in Lviv called the Social-Nationalist Party of Ukraine. The leftists, though, formed the most formidable group, represented by their main parties, the CPU, SPU and PPU.

As the election campaign gathered momentum and a war of decrees developed between Kyiv and Simferopol, Kravchuk continued to display the indecision and relative passivity which had disappointed so many of his former supporters, thereby creating the impression that he was simply muddling through. In February, he even declared that he would not be standing for re-election as president, which at least one other hopeful, Plyushch, evidently seems to have taken at face value. Underestimating the extent of the growing social dissatisfaction with the mismanagement of the country with which he was directly identified, the president seems to have hoped that voter apathy would prevail – he publicly predicted that voter turnout would be too low for a new parliament to elected – which would enable him to step into the breach and assume extraordinary powers.

In fact, voter turnout in the first round and the run-offs was high – averaging at about 70% – and by the time the new parliament convened on 11 May, 338 of the 450 deputies had been elected of whom only fifty-six had sat in the old parliament; 168 had stood as independents and quite of few of them were representatives of the 'party of power'. Of the remainder, whose party affiliation was known, roughly 25% represented the CPU, 5.9% the PPU, 4.1% the SPU, and 6% Rukh. Among the other parties which were represented, from the centrist parties, there were four deputies from the IBR and four from the PDRU; from the national democrats, eight from the URP, five from the KUN and two from the DPU; from the radical right, three from the UNA-UNSO and two from Khmara's new Ukrainian Conservative Republican Party (UCRP).

Despite the flaws in the election law, independent Ukraine's first parliamentary elections were democratic and took place without major irregularities. Shortly before the elections, though, the head of the secretariat of Rukh, which had now become a political party, and co-chairman of its election committee, Mykhailo Boichyshyn, had mysteriously disappeared and Chornovil and others suspected the hand of the 'party of power'. After the elections there were also claims that Morozov and Hrynov from the democratic camp had been blocked from being elected. In some cases, though, rivals from the national democratic camp challenged one another in the same constituency. For instance, Khmara deliberately stood against Mykhailo Horyn in Lviv and managed to defeat him. Among the other well-known democratic figures who failed to get re-elected was Pavlychko, who refused to stand in a 'safe' constituency and was defeated in Chihirin, while Drach did not seek re-election.

Although the reanimated Communists and their leftist allies had clearly secured a strong position and would constitute the largest bloc, until the independents aligned themselves and more seats had been filled it remained uncertain if they would be able to dominate the parliament. The all-important question was whether the leftist bloc would be united and whether it would obstruct constitutional and economic reform. The first indications were not encouraging: on 18 May, the head of the SPU, Moroz, was elected the new speaker (Plyushch had been tricked by Kravchuk into running for president[41]), defeating the centre's candidate Vasyl Durdynets by 171 votes to 103, and Oleksandr Tkachenko, a leader of the PPU, was chosen as his first deputy. A month later, the parliament endorsed Kravchuk's unexpected last minute nomination before the presidential election of the formerly discredited Masol for prime minister.[42]

The results of the local 'referenda' held in the Donbas and Crimea on the same day as the parliamentary elections only added to Kyiv's problems. After the Ukrainian government had pointed out that regions did not have the constitutional right to conduct binding local referenda, the Donetsk and Luhansk regions changed the name of

---

[41] During his election campaign, Plyushch openly accused Kravchuk of having deceived him after promising to support his candidature. *Kyivskyi visnyk,* 9 June 1994.

[42] On the parliamentary elections, see Marko Bojcun, 'The Ukrainian Parliamentary Elections in March–April 1994', *Europe-Asia Studies,* vol. 47, no. 2 (1995), pp. 229-49; Dominique Arel and Andrew Wilson, 'The Ukrainian Parliamentary Elections', *RFE/RL Research Report* vol. 3, no. 26 (1 July 1994), pp. 6-17; and Chapter 10 of Lytvyn, *Political Arena.*

their opinion polls to 'consultative questions' and went ahead. As was expected, the local population expressed overwhelming support for the propositions concerning the status of the Russian language, the federal idea and closer integration in the CIS. On the same day in Crimea, the majority of the voters supported Meshkov's call for a boycott of the elections to the Ukrainian parliament (12 of the 23 Crimean seats were left vacant) and elected a Crimean parliament in which Meshkov's 'Russia' bloc won 54 out of 98 seats. Furthermore, in the Crimean referendum, which Kyiv rejected as unconstitutional but could hardly fail to take note off, the majority supported greater autonomy for Crimea, dual Ukrainian-Russian citizenship and a broadening of President Meshkov's powers.[43]

After the parliamentary elections and local referenda in Crimea and the Donbas, therefore, the prospects for Ukraine looked even grimmer and there was widespread speculation and concern about the country's chances of survival as an independent state. At the beginning of 1994 the US Central Intelligence Agency had already produced a report warning that Ukraine's economic plight would result in the country's break-up 'along ethnic and geographic lines'[44]. Now, for example, on 7 May 1994, *The Economist* published a lengthy analysis of the situation after the parliamentary elections under the heading 'Ukraine: The Birth and Possible Death of a Country'. The forthcoming presidential elections therefore assumed even greater significance as a potentially decisive moment in the country's short history of independence: they appeared to offer a last chance, as one pessimistic observer put it, 'to step back from the brink of self-destruction'.[45]

Seven candidates were registered, including Kravchuk, who after a rather clumsy display of political brinkmanship finally announced that he was running as late as 29 April. The other main candidates were Kuchma, Plyushch, Moroz and, rather surprisingly, Lanovy. The key issues were the economic crisis and economic reform, relations with Russia and the CIS, devolution of power to the

---

[43] Andrew Wilson, 'The Elections in Crimea', *RFE/RL Research Report*, vol. 3, no. 25 (24 June 1994), pp. 7-19.

[44] 'Daniel Williams and R. Jeffrey Smith, 'U.S. Intelligence Sees Economic Plight Leading to Ukraine Breakup', *Washington Post*, 25 January 1995.

[45] Eugene B. Rumer, 'Eurasia Letter: Will Ukraine Return to Russia?', *Foreign Policy*, no. 96 (Fall 1994), p. 129.

regions and the language issue in the eastern regions. From the outset it was evident that the main fight would be between Kravchuk and Kuchma, who in December 1994 had been elected head of the influential Ukrainian Association of Industrialists and Entrepreneurs and, subsequently, a deputy to the new parliament. Kravchuk's camp sought to discredit Kuchma's record as prime minister and blame him for the country's economic and social woes, while the latter attempted to distance himself from the Communist establishment, from which he had emerged, attacking the 'party of power' and Kravchuk for their mismanagement, conservatism and corruption.

While the presidential election campaign was getting under way, the strained relations between Kyiv and Simferopol resulted in another crisis. It was precipitated by the Crimean parliament's vote on 20 May to restore the Crimean constitution adopted two years earlier when the previous Crimean legislature had attempted to assert the region's independence. Kravchuk and the Ukrainian parliament threatened to impose direct presidential rule on the peninsula and while negotiations went on the situation remained very tense. Appearing on television, Yeltsin warned Kravchuk not to use force, which only drew an angry response from the Ukrainian president, who implicitly accused his Russian counterpart of exacerbating the confrontation and violating diplomatic convention.[46] Despite this, high-ranking delegations from the two feuding countries met in Moscow to continue grappling with the issue of the Black Sea Fleet but failed to get around the stumbling block of Sevastopol's future. With the Yeltsin administration conceding by its subsequent more restrained attitude that the dispute between Kyiv and Simferopol was a Ukrainian internal matter, the international community reiterating its support for Ukraine's territorial integrity, and the Ukrainian presidential election approaching, the crisis eventually petered out without any real resolution of the fundamental issues.[47]

During the final weeks of the presidential campaign, Kravchuk attempted to bolster the declining presidential authority. Although he stressed the need for an executive presidency, he failed to generate a new debate about presidential powers. In fact, he had to experience

---

[46] Reuter, 24 May 1994.

[47] Ustina Markus, 'Crimea Restores 1992 Constitution', *RFE/RL Research Report*, vol. 3, no. 23 (10 June 1994), pp. 9–12.

the humiliation of witnessing the dismantling of the system of presidential representatives which he had established. To replace them, the parliament had agreed that local elections would be held on the same day as the presidential polls in order to elect officials to head regional and city councils.

In the first round of voting at the end of June, Kravchuk obtained 37.68% of the votes, Kuchma 31.25%, Moroz 13.09%, Lanovy a respectable 9.38 (the economic reformer did particularly well in Kyiv, where he won a quarter of all the votes) and Plyushch a disastrous 1.29%. The struggle between the two leading candidates became even more acrimonious. As the gap between them narrowed, the campaign threatened to deepen the division between the Ukrainian-speaking West and the Russian-speaking East which had just been thrown into sharp relief by the parliamentary elections. Kravchuk, having courted the neo-Communist forces and just appointed Masol as prime minister, had done poorly in Eastern Ukraine and now appealed directly to Ukrainian nationalism. At the last minute, he attacked the leftist forces in parliament and sought to project himself as the defender of Ukraine's independence and his rival as a leader who would undermine the country's unity and lead it into the embrace of Russia. For his part, Kuchma placed the emphasis on moving Ukraine away from the 'brink of economic catastrophe' and concentrated on winning the votes of Ukraine's Russophone and more populous eastern and southern regions. 'That's where all the industry and 80% of Ukraine's productive capacity is', he explained to Ukrainian television viewers during a live question and answer session on 3 July, and where 'most factories are standing idle'. During a televised election debate, in the only face-to-face encounter between the two contenders, Kuchma seemed to get to the heart of the matter and to raise his standing. 'You need political will to carry out reforms', he told viewers, 'Believe me, I have the will.'[48]

With Kuchma emphasizing the need for closer economic cooperation with Russia within the CIS and coming across as a supporter of the demands of the eastern regions for greater administrative autonomy and the preservation of the status quo in the linguistic sphere, Western Ukraine and the national democratic forces threw their support behind Kravchuk. A paradoxical situation

[48] Reuter, 8 July 1994

arose: Chornovil, Rukh's leader, and hitherto implacable political opponent of the president, declared that Kuchma could not be supported because 'Russia was banking on him', and came out for Kravchuk;[49] on the other hand, the leadership of the CPU opposed the former Communist Party ideologist, though it also demonstrated its reservations about the reformist Kuchma by leaving it up to party members to decide for themselves whether or not to back him.[50]

Kravchuk appeared to be helped by the fact that after the signing of the Trilateral Agreement on nuclear arms, his international reputation had soared and the international community had shown itself more receptive to Ukraine's requests for economic aid. In June, Kravchuk had signed the EU's first partnership and cooperation agreement with a former Soviet republic and claimed this as a diplomatic victory. Furthermore, on the very eve of the presidential elections, at their summit in Naples, and in what many perceived as a display of support for Kravchuk, the G7 held out the prospect of $4 billion in multilateral financing for Ukraine's economic reforms if Ukraine proceeded with reforms. By contrast, Kuchma was known to be skeptical about Western aid and still thought to hold a tougher position on nuclear disarmament.

Although the contest was closely fought, Kravchuk, enjoying the advantages which being the incumbent afforded him, was expected to have the edge. But the run-off on 10 July produced an upset: Kuchma won 52% of the votes and Kravchuk 45%. The voting showed that the country had indeed split down the middle in its choice: Western and central Ukraine rallied behind Kravchuk, while southern and Eastern Ukraine and Crimea solidly backed Kuchma. Kravchuk who had been depicted by his supporters as virtually the father of Ukraine's independence had been made to pay the price for his subsequent inaction on reform and ineffective leadership at home.[51] His departure, and with him, that of many of the representatives of the party of power, opened a new if uncertain chapter in Ukraine's post-Soviet history.

---

[49] *Nezavisimost*, 6 July 1994.

[50] Radio Ukraine, 4 July 1994. For a useful description of the election battle, see Lukanov, *The Third President*, pp. 66-87

[51] For a thorough discussion of the presidential election and the results, see Dominique Arel and Andrew Wilson, 'Ukraine Under Kuchma: Back to 'Eurasia'?', *RFE/RL Research Report* vol. 3, no. 32 (19 August 1994), pp. 1-12.

16

KUCHMA AT THE HELM

Kuchma's remedial efforts

Subsequent events showed that the dark cloud which hung over Ukraine during the fateful spring and early summer months of 1994 had a silver lining after all. For the time being, Kuchma's victory placated Eastern Ukraine and many in Crimea. However divisive the presidential elections may have been, they had demonstrated that the new state was capable of withstanding considerable internal strains and, at a particularly difficult period, a peaceful transfer of power had been made. Moreover, the new president lost little time in reaching out to Western Ukraine: he began to make it clear that, while wanting to improve economic relations with Russia, he was determined to protect Ukraine's independence. He also dispelled fears that he would make Russian a second state language and demonstratively switched to using Ukrainian while carrying out his official duties. Above all, he sought to demonstrate that he was committed to moving ahead with economic reforms and to fighting crime and corruption. Soon the national democrats and sceptics in Western Ukraine were beginning to give him the benefit of the doubt.

Kuchma brought a new political style and emphasis. At his formal swearing-in on 19 July he declared that 'political romanticism and euphoria associated with a new state need to be replaced with realism, concrete action and pragmatism'. Indicating from the outset that he would seek stronger presidential powers, he announced that 'strict and unpopular measures will have to be taken. We must not yield to the temptation of cosmetic measures, of closing our eyes, of deceiving the nation'. He was just as forthright over foreign policy. He risked alarming supporters of a Western-oriented foreign policy by venturing that 'Ukraine is historically part of the Eurasian economic and cultural space' and that 'the self-isolation of Ukraine' from it had been a 'serious mistake, causing colossal damage' to the

473

country's economy.'[1] But in other statements he qualified this by stating: 'I never said Ukraine was to become part of the Russian empire.' Ukraine's relations with Russia 'are strategic', he explained. 'But they must not be at the expense of other countries East and West.'[2] The country, the president told foreign diplomats in Kyiv on 22 July, could not afford to 'deceive itself' by seeing things in terms of a choice between a Western and an Eastern orientation. The fact was that the country is located at the 'interface' of Europe and Eurasia and, in his view, should therefore 'not be a buffer, but a reliable bridge, a reliable uniting link'.[3]

Kuchma soon had a chance to demonstrate his approach to foreign policy and security issues. Shortly after his election, in his typically frank manner, he had told President Clinton in a telephone conversation that Ukraine had fulfilled the commitments it had undertaken in the first stage of the Trilateral Agreement but that the United States and other countries had so far provided only a 'miserable portion' of the financial assistance which had been promised Ukraine to carry out nuclear disarmament.[4] At the beginning of August, however, he received US Vice President Al Gore and, after being encouraged by him to move ahead with reforms and continue nuclear disarmament, accepted an invitation to visit Washington later in the year. A few days later, he spoke by telephone with Yeltsin and the two presidents agreed to resume work on the stalled Russian-Ukrainian treaty and on a visit to Kyiv in the near future by the Russian leader.

With the stabilization of the economy his top priority, Kuchma's first foreign guest was in fact not the US vice president but the managing director of the IMF, Michel Camdessus. In a clear indication of the difficulties that lay ahead, no sooner had Camdessus announced that the IMF would work with the Ukrainian government on a reform programme than the leftist forces in the Verkhovna Rada demonstrated their strength by voting to suspend privatization. The immediate challenge for Kuchma was how, in view of the pro-Communists' opposition to radical reforms and the fact that the government was headed by Kravchuk's conservative nominee,

[1] Reuter, 19 July, and *Holos Ukrainy*, 21 July, 1994.

[2] Reuter, 21 July 1994.

[3] *Uryadovyi kuryer*, 26 July 1994.

[4] *Ibid.*

Masol, he would install a reform team and initiate reforms.

The new president waited until the parliament recessed for the summer holidays before taking action. With results from the continuing parliamentary by-elections indicating that victories by centrists were eroding the strength of the pro-Communist bloc in parliament, on 8 August he issued two decrees boosting the executive branch's power by taking charge of the government and subordinating regional councils to the presidency. The following month, in a move also designed to placate the regions, he established a Council of the Regions to provide a mechanism for consultations between the central and regional authorities. Its members included the heads of all the regional councils, the city councils of Kyiv and Sevastopol, as well as the deputy prime minister of Crimea.

Kuchma proceeded to isolate Masol, whom he appears to have preferred to leave in place rather than precipitating a showdown with the leftist forces straight away. He quickly put together a relatively young reform team consisting of, among others, Viktor Pynzenyk, first deputy prime minister for economic reform; Roman Shpek, minister of the economy; Ihor Mityukov, deputy prime minister responsible for external finance; and Yurii Yekhanurov, minister of privatization. Viktor Yushchenko, who since the end of 1993 had sought to reduce the issue of money, was kept on as head of the National Bank. Other personnel changes included the replacement of Foreign Minister Zlenko by another veteran diplomat, Hennadii Udovenko; of Morozov's successor, Vitalii Radetsky, by a civilian defence minister, Shmarov; of first deputy prime minister for humanitarian affairs, Zhulynsky, by Ivan Kuras; and the appointment of Marchuk as first deputy prime minister responsible for security.

Apart from Marchuk, two other figures in Kuchma's team were soon to become increasingly influential and prominent. The first was the young historian Dmytro Tabachnyk, who had been Kuchma's press officer while he was prime minister, and whom the president now appointed his chief of staff.[5] The other was Volodymyr Horbulin, who had worked with Kuchma at the Pivdenmash missile-building plant in Dnipropetrovsk and, more

---

[5] Before long, it was being joked: 'Kuchma is president in the administration of "Dima" Tabachnyk.' On Tabachnyk and his role, see Lukanov, *The Third President*, pp. 126-39.

recently, headed Ukraine's National Space Agency. Kuchma made him Secretary of his National Security Council.

Negotiations with the IMF continued throughout the summer and by September an agreement was reached for a $750 million IMF Systemic Transformation Facility (STF). Kuchma's administration agreed to most of the conditions set by the IMF for the loan. They included 'the reunification of the exchange rate and a far-reaching liberalization of prices, domestic trade, and foreign trade. As a consequence of reduced subsidies, the budget deficit was to be reduced from 20% of GDP for 1994 to 10.3% of GDP.'[6] Success, though, remained dependent on Kuchma's ability to win the backing of parliament.

In mid-August, Ukrainian and Russian delegations began working on the draft of the bilateral treaty and, at their first meeting, managed to reach agreement on about 80% of its proposed thirty-six articles. There was no hint of confederation: relations between the two 'friendly, equal and sovereign' states were to be based on 'mutual respect and trust, partnership and cooperation'. Ukraine had introduced new provisions dealing with cooperation in space technology and grappling with the consequences of the Chornobyl disaster and the return and integration of formerly deported peoples. Differences remained, though, on a number of fundamental issues. Ukraine wanted a binding recognition of the inviolability of the existing borders and territorial integrity of the two states, and adamantly opposed dual citizenship. Among other things, it also rejected Russian proposals for mutual assistance in the event of an armed attack by a third party, free transit for persons and goods across the respective territories of the two countries and the restoration, in effect, of a common economic space.[7]

While work on normalizing Russian-Ukrainian relations was being given new impetus, the perennial problems connected with Crimea (which, together with the issue of the Black Sea Fleet, was not mentioned in the draft bilateral treaty) and with paying for fuel imports from Russia nevertheless demanded urgent attention from the new Ukrainian leadership. In August, in a largely symbolic action, the Sevastopol City Council proclaimed the port Russian

---

[6] Anders Åslund, 'Eurasia Letter: Ukraine's Turnaround', *Foreign Policy*, no. 100 (fall 1995), p. 137.

[7] The text of the draft treaty was published in *Vechirnii Kyiv*, 17 September 1994.

territory. Later that month, seeking to improve relations between Kyiv and Simferopol and to ensure that economic reforms in Crimea were synchronized with those in the rest of Ukraine, Kuchma met with both President Meshkov and Sergei Tsekov, leader of the Crimean parliament. That same month, the CSCE, with the approval of Kyiv, decided to send a mission to Ukraine. Among its tasks was to mediate between Kyiv and Simferopol and thereby contribute to conflict prevention and management.

By now though, Crimea's leaders were themselves becoming locked in a constitutional battle between Meshkov's presidential administration, which had brought in specialists such as Saburov from Moscow, and the Crimean parliament headed by Sergei Tsekov. The Crimean president's supporters in the local parliament were also divided. In early September, no doubt to Kyiv's relief, the Crimean parliament trimmed Meshkov's powers and he responded by suspending it and locking deputies out of the legislature building. At this dangerous moment, Kuchma had to warn both sides against the use of force and appointed Marchuk as his mediator. On 15 September, the day on which the Ukrainian parliament rescinded the Sevastopol City Council's decision, the Crimean parliament passed a vote of no confidence in the government which Meshkov had installed, thereby forcing Saburov's resignation.

With his wings clipped, Meshkov backed down, but though his popularity continued to decline, he refused to resign. Kuchma maintained a neutral position but when, in early October, the Crimean parliament confirmed his son-in-law, Anatolii Franchuk, as prime minister of Crimea, his impartiality was placed in doubt. Both the Ukrainian president and parliament continued to insist that the Crimean legislature bring its laws into line with those of Ukraine but Tsekov and his supporters, encouraged by the Russian Duma, still opposed this. In fact, on 23 November, the Russian Duma was to issue a statement declaring that it would not be possible to conclude a Russian-Ukrainian bilateral treaty of friendship and cooperation, nor an accord on the division of the Black Sea Fleet 'without a compromise' in what it referred to as 'the settlement of the Crimean-Ukrainian conflict'.

All this time, despite repeated arrangements for rescheduling payments, Ukraine still could not pay for deliveries of Russian and Turkmen fuel. In August, as Gazprom again threatened to cut off supplies, Kuchma agreed to repay Russia over three months a quarter of a $1.2 billion debt for natural gas, partly by selling shares in Ukrainian oil and gas enterprises. He rejected the idea of privatizing the pipelines running across Ukraine.[8]

As Kuchma prepared to present his economic reform programme to the parliament, he also sought a way of getting around the continuing lack of a new constitution and division of powers, which worked to the advantage of the parliament at the expense of the executive branch. By late September he let it be known that his team was preparing a 'small constitution' that would temporarily delineate powers until a new constitution was adopted. Ukraine, the president argued implicitly, needed to avoid the kind of confrontation between the presidency and the legislature that had been seen in Russia and Crimea. 'I think everyone realizes that conflict between the two branches of power will not be constructive', he declared at the first meeting of the Council of the Regions, 'A decision must be made'. His own preference was for the model offered by France's President Charles de Gaulle and the presidential republic which he had established. 'Until a strong executive branch appears,' Kuchma argued, 'there will be no changes in Ukraine.' He apparently managed to convince the Council of the Regions, for at its inaugural meeting, held in Zaporizhzhya on 24 September, Ukraine's new regional leaders signed a statement supporting his call for a strong executive branch.[9]

Committed to the agreement with the IMF, Kuchma sought to secure additional international aid. The opportunity to press Kyiv's case came at the beginning of October when Ukraine was invited for the first time to attend a G7 meeting being held in Madrid. Shpek represented Ukraine and there was to be a special follow-up G7 conference on 27 October in Winnipeg on aid to Ukraine initiated by Canada. The Kuchma administration recognized the extent to which the question of Western assistance was linked to Ukraine's nuclear disarmament and, in a move to reassure potential donors, at the beginning of October the president submitted a letter to the parliament asking it to agree to Ukraine's joining the NPT as a non-nuclear state. At the same time, he also sent a letter to the leaders of Russia, the United States, Britain and France in which he re-emphasized Ukraine's need for national security guarantees.

[8] Reuter, 16 August and 8 October 1994.
[9] *Ibid.*, 24 September 1994.

To the surprise of many of those who had voted for him in the southern and eastern regions, after his election Kuchma maintained essentially the same detached position towards the CIS as Kravchuk had done. At a CIS summit in Moscow in October he made it clear that would not support the tendency to try and transform the commonwealth into a supranational entity.

On 11 October, the new president delivered his first major programmatic speech to the Verkhovna Rada in which, in very blunt terms, he outlined the seriousness of the country's situation and the stringent emergency reform course he was proposing. Not hesitating to call a spade, he told the deputies:

> It is unpleasant, but we have to admit that Ukraine has not yet achieved real independence. In 1991, it achieved only the attributes of an independent state, but over the last three years it was unable to fill these with real content.

It was imperative, he continued, to 'fend off the threat of national disaster', for the survival of Ukraine as a sovereign state depended on immediate far-reaching economic reforms. 'The exhausting period of transition from a command economy to a market-based, socially oriented economy' could not be 'stretched out in time indefinitely'. Kuchma also warned the population not to expect any quick improvements of their difficult conditions: 'As the state's president, I must declare with all responsibility before the people that we have no real resources at present to raise our people's living standards.'[10]

Many of the more conservative deputies appear to have been taken aback by the forcefulness of the presentation and on 19 October, after a long debate, the parliament gave its backing to the 'main points' of Kuchma's reform programme by an overwhelming margin of 231 to 54. Nevertheless, the debate confirmed that the pro-Communist deputies were opposed to privatization of property and land and, like the speaker, Moroz, were reluctantly supporting the IMF programme because of the need for Western assistance in order to enable the country to cope with its crippling energy debts.[11]

When, shortly afterwards, the government proceeded to free some prices and cut subsidies to producers, protests followed; the leftist

---

[10] As cited by Åslund in 'Ukraine's Turnaround', pp. 134-5.
[11] Reuter, 11 and 19 October 1994.

forces called a special session of the parliament to condemn the price
rises and Moroz threatened to use his 'constitutional right to rescind
government laws'.

Kuchma appealed for calm and reiterated that there was no choice
but to move ahead with economic reforms regardless of how
unpopular they might be. While continuing to issue decrees aimed
at financial stabilization, he sought to raise new loans and reschedule
existing debts to Russia and Turkmenistan. Behind the scenes, the
president persuaded the leaders of Russia, the United States and
Canada that, as Kyiv's largest creditors, Russia and Turkmenistan,
should be invited to the G7 Conference on Ukraine. At the
conference itself, Russian Foreign Minister Kozyrev called for more
international aid to be given to Ukraine, stressing quite openly that
Moscow was interested in this because otherwise Kyiv would not
be able to make payments on its debts to Russia. Kuchma left
Winnipeg with further pledges of support from the G7, including
assistance in persuading Moscow and Ashgabat to reschedule
Ukraine's debts, as well as assurances from US Assistant Secretary of
State Strobe Talbott that Washington was working on a way to
satisfy Kyiv's insistence on additional security guarantees.[12]

At the beginning of November, Kuchma went to Turkmenistan
where, with Washington's help, he was able to secure an agreement
to reschedule Kyiv's energy debt to Ashgabat over a seven-year
period. Two weeks later, as Kuchma was preparing for his official
visit to the United States, during which he was also to address the
UN General Assembly in New York, Ukraine's prospects for
receiving additional Western assistance were given a fillip by the
parliament's almost unanimous agreement to approve the country's
accession to the NPT as a non-nuclear state.

While Kuchma was in Washington, the Clinton Administration
announced that it was stepping up its economic and political support
for Ukraine. In fact, Washington added an additional $200 million
to its assistance package, much of which Kyiv was to use immediately
to pay Russia to keep the gas flowing. Also in November, an IMF
team arrived in Kyiv to begin negotiations on the terms for a much
larger 'stand-by' loan for Ukraine. The one major source of disappointment and difficulty for Kyiv in this respect, though, was the
attitude of some members of the EU (in particular, the United

---

[12] Ukrainian television, 28 and 29 October 1994.

Kingdom, France, Italy and Belgium) which were reluctant to co-finance the IMF's STF agreement and to provide Ukraine with any significant EU assistance.[13] As it was, the EU's protectionism effectively barred many Ukrainian exports (metals, chemicals, textiles and agricultural produce) from the European market. Furthermore, although it had promised only modest assistance for the closure of the Chornobyl atomic station which Kyiv had kept in operation because of Ukraine's energy crisis, the EU also insisted that Ukraine close down the nuclear plant. Among Western European countries which were more favourably disposed towards Ukraine, Germany distinguished itself as the biggest aid donor, though much of it was earmarked to provide housing for former Soviet military personnel withdrawn from Germany.

During his visit to the United States Kuchma made use of the opportunity to keep pressing on the issue of Ukraine's security concerns. The result appears to have been the security memorandum which was signed on 5 December in Budapest at a summit of the Organization of Security and Cooperation in Europe (OSCE, formerly CSCE) by Ukraine and three nuclear states. Under its terms, Russia, the USA and the United Kingdom undertook not to use force against Ukraine, except in self-defence, refrain from applying economic pressure against Ukraine, and, in the event of an attack by a nuclear power on Ukraine, to seek action from the UN Security Council. Washington and Kyiv also established a 'hot line' and two other nuclear states, France and China, also lent their support for Ukraine's security.[14]

In the circumstances, the political assurances contained in the Budapest memorandum were probably as much as Kyiv could realistically hope to obtain in the way of security guarantees and they at least partly placated the Ukrainian deputies who had voted for Ukraine's accession to the NPT. But one other security issue involving East and West was still increasingly worrying Ukraine's policy makers. As the debate about NATO's possible expansion eastward continued, Ukraine's leadership was being forced to think

---

[13] George Soros pointed out in a letter to the *Financial Times* on 2 November 1994 that his own foundation was disbursing more sums to Ukraine than the EU.

[14] F.H. Turchenko, P.P. Panchenko, S.M. Tymchenko, *Novitnya Istoriya Ukrainy: Chastyna Druha, 1945-1995* [Modern History of Ukraine: Part Two, 1945-1995], Kyiv, 1995, p. 286.

about the likely implications. During his visit to Washington, Kuchma cautioned against rushing ahead with NATO's expansion, warning that it could result in the alienation of Russia and a new division of Europe into two armed camps, with a neutral Ukraine caught in between. 'We do not want a situation with two Europes and the border line running across Ukraine', he explained. He also was at pains to point out that Ukraine did not want to come under Moscow's domination again. 'Even in my worst nightmares, I never dream about the restoration of the Soviet Union', he declared. 'There is no road back.'[15]

The struggle over the division of powers

Sooner, rather than later, the persistent president was heading for a showdown with the conservative forces in the parliament. With the government now trying to secure another loan of about $1.5 billion from the IMF, it was evident that a successful outcome would require Ukraine to pursue an even stricter and more painful economic policy. As Kuchma's popularity rose, reaching, according to one poll, a 72% national approval rate in December, and that of the parliament fell (in the same poll it received only a 11.8% approval rating), the leftist bloc in the legislature increasingly resented the new president who had undermined their plans to take Ukraine in a rather different direction. Furthermore, the pro-Communist and pro-Russian forces in the south and east of the country felt let down by Kuchma, but, conversely, in the western and central regions support and respect for him grew.[16]

During the second half of 1994, though, as more seats in the parliament had been filled, the strength of the leftist bloc had in fact been weakened. As a result of the continuing run-offs, a significant centrist grouping had begun to crystallize, which incidentally also included Kravchuk, who was elected in the Ternopil region. Together, the centrists, national democrats and rightists were now able to outnumber the leftist bloc, but the latter was still powerful enough to block economic and political reforms.

The situation at the end of 1994 was that 403 out of 450 seats

---

[15] Reute, 23 November 1994.

[16] See Chrystyna Lapychak, 'Back on Track', *Transition*, vol. 1, no. 3, 15 March 1995, pp. 43-5 and 52.

had been filled.[17] The leftists held about 172 of them, the nebulous centre about 133, the right about 91, and a few deputies remained outside the parliamentary factions and groups as independents. From left to right across the political spectrum, the parliament's main factions and groups in the leftist bloc were the Communists (90 deputies), Socialists (30) and Agrarians (52); the factions making up the centre consisted of the Inter-regional Deputies Group, or MDH, (33), which was the parliamentary faction of the political party formed in December 1994 from the former Inter-regional Bloc for Reforms and led outside the parliament by Hrynov, Nezalezhnist [Independence] (29), Yednist [Unity] (34) and Tsentr [Centre] (37); and three groups made up the right – Reformy [Reforms] (36), Rukh (27), and Derzhavnist [Statehood] (28).[18]

Seizing the political initiative, at the beginning of December, Kuchma moved to resolve what had been described as the 'old Soviet constitutional ambiguity' and 'disorder' resulting from the lack of a precise separation of powers between the executive and legislative branches.[19] He presented to the parliament a draft constitutional bill on the separation of powers and local self-government, which subsequently became known as the Law on Powers. Drawing on the example of the Polish 'small constitution', he proposed the Law on Powers as an interim constitutional arrangement necessitated by the need to push ahead with economic reforms that would clarify the division of executive and legislative powers until the new constitution had been agreed on. The bill was designed to strengthen the presidency at the expense of the parliament and local councils, giving the chief executive powers comparable to those which de Gaulle had secured for the French president. Most importantly, the president would be able to appoint or dismiss a government without the parliament's approval; after consultations with the Supreme and Constitutional Courts, to dissolve the parliament if it repeatedly rejected the budget proposed by the government; and, to directly subordinate local councils to himself.[20]

[17] Because of the continuing low turnout of voters in the constituencies where the seats had still not been filled, it was decided to postpone holding new elections in them for a year.

[18] Based on the reliable study by Artur Bilous, 'Ukraine's Parliament: Who's in Power?', *Demos* (Kyiv) vol. II, no 1 (June 1995), pp. 36–47.

[19] Åslund, 'Ukraine's Turnaround', p. 136.

Predictably, Kuchma's draft constitutional bill was given a hostile reception by the leftist bloc, but there were also many deputies representing the centre and the right who expressed concern that it concentrated too much power in the hands of the president and smacked of authoritarianism. Confronted with stiff opposition, the president offered a concession, proposing that, in certain limited conditions, the parliament would be able to hold a vote of no confidence in the president. But he also warned that he would call a national referendum if the Verkhovna Rada failed to approve the bill and proposed that the Law on Powers be used as the basis of the new constitution. This threat seems at least to have got negotiations under way, for the deputies also knew that in any case constitutional bills had to be passed by a two-thirds majority after their second reading. Eventually, on 28 December, the parliament passed the bill on its first reading but set up a special conciliation committee composed of deputies from all the parliamentary groups and representatives of the president's team to work out compromises for the second reading.

While this work was being carried out, the Ukrainian government, encouraged by a $500 million rehabilitation loan granted by the World Bank in December, continued its negotiations with the IMF for an additional larger loan. Masol appears to have resisted the stringent new budget which this necessitated for 1995 and, eventually, on 1 March, his resignation was announced. Marchuk, who enjoyed an image of toughness and had also been given responsibility for negotiating with Russia on the division of the Black Sea Fleet and the terms of a bilateral treaty, was appointed acting prime minister. Three days later, the Ukrainian government signed an agreement with the IMF for a $1.57 billion loan and pledged to continue with a reform programme that would reduce inflation, already down in February 1995 to about 18% (from a peak of 72.3% the previous November), to 1% by the end of the year, and not to increase the budget deficit running at the time at an estimated 3.3-3.5% of GDP (7.3% according to the Ukrainian definition). Significantly, while the executive board of the IMF waited for the parliament to approve the budget for 1995 before giving final approval for the loan, it also agreed to mediate in Ukraine's talks with Russia about restructuring Kyiv's oil and gas debt to Moscow.[21]

[20] *Holos Ukrainy*, 6 December 1994.

Relations with Russia, which since December had become embroiled in a war against secessionist forces in Chechnya, had remained stable. Moreover, at the end of the year Ukraine had signed a number of trade agreements at a meeting in Moscow of the CIS Council of the Heads of Government. All the same, Yeltsin's visit to Kyiv, and the signing of a Russian-Ukrainian treaty of friendship and cooperation, had not materialized. The unresolved issues connected with the Black Sea Fleet and dual citizenship had held things up as well as perhaps Kuchma's reluctance to support a more integrated CIS. This reluctance was again demonstrated by the display of mutual solidarity during the visit to Kyiv in the second half of January by the President of Turkmenistan, Saparmurat Niyazov, who maintained a similar position towards the CIS as the Ukrainian leadership. He told the Ukrainian parliament that it was in the interests of both countries 'to maintain their sovereignty and full-fledged independence'. All 'attempts to push the CIS towards some sort of union, or pact, or supra-national structure of any kind have some self-seeking aim or interest', he warned.[22]

Eventually, in early February, a Russian-Ukrainian treaty was initialled by senior officials but its signing by the leaders of the two countries continued to be held up. In fact, while visiting the Russian city of Lipetsk, President Yeltsin declared that Russia would not be able to sign the treaty if it did not include provisions for dual citizenship.[23] This statement, and the unresolved issue of who would use Sevastopol as the base for its share of the Black Sea Fleet, set the process back yet again. Soon afterwards, after another CIS summit, held this time in Almaty, a somewhat exasperated Kuchma commented that 'Russia should show the world that it, too, has chosen the path of civilized democratic development' by signing the long-delayed treaty with Ukraine. Responding also to renewed calls in the Russian parliament and elsewhere for the restoration of the Soviet Union, he added that with the conclusion of such a treaty 'speculation' on this question 'could end both in Russia and Ukraine'.[24]

Crimea, where forces were still hoping for the restoration of the Soviet Union or for the peninsula to be transferred to Russia,

---

[21] Reuter, 11 March 1995.

[22] *Ibid.*, 20 January 1995.

[23] *News from Ukraine*, nos 3–5, February 1995.

[24] Reuter, 13 February 1995.

remained a major headache for Kyiv. Although the Crimean leadership had split, and the Crimean parliament's speaker Tsekov had eclipsed President Meshkov, Simferopol had continued to ignore Kyiv's demands that it bring Crimea's constitution into conformity with that of Ukraine and had also demanded dual citizenship for the inhabitants of the peninsula. In January 1995 the Crimean parliament also came into conflict with Kuchma's economic reform efforts by attempting to assert the region's economic autonomy, including control over local privatization.

At this juncture, the Ukrainian leadership appears to have lost patience with the Crimean authorities and, in a rare display of unity between the executive and legislative branches, used the opportunity presented by the internal divisions in Simferopol and Russia's preoccupation in Chechnya to bring Crimea into line. On 17 March, the Verkhovna Rada parliament voted to annual Crimea's constitution and to seek the prosecution of Meshkov for having issued decrees which violated Ukrainian law. At the end of the month, Kuchma brought the Ukrainian parliament's decision into force by presidential decree: it placed Crimea under Kyiv's direct rule, gave the region until mid-May to draw up a constitution acceptable to Kyiv, threatened the Crimean parliament with dissolution and, while Meshkov was facing charges for exceeding his authority, suspended the post of Crimea's president.

Although Moscow stayed out of Kyiv's constitutional dispute with Simferopol, the signing of the Russian-Ukrainian treaty remained elusive. However, thanks to IMF mediation, Ukraine gained a vital breathing space for itself in its complex relations with Russia. The IMF had made a deal on rescheduling the debt Ukraine owed to Russia a prerequisite for further loans to both countries, and on 20 March senior Russian and Ukrainian officials signed two agreements in Kyiv on the rescheduling and restructuring of the more than \$3.5 billion of debt accrued by Ukraine since 1993. Under the terms of the first, Russia agreed to reschedule \$2.5 billion of this amount over thirteen years beginning in 1998 after a three-year period of grace. The second allowed Gazprom to take equity stakes in key Ukrainian industries when they were privatized and foresaw the creation of a joint-stock Russian-Ukrainian company called Gaztransit.[25]

[25] Taras Kuzio, 'After the Shock, the Therapy', *Transition*, vol. 1, no. 13 (28 July 1995), p. 40.

The visit to Kyiv by Russia's First Deputy Prime Minister Oleg Soskovets to finalize the deal on restructuring Ukraine's debts and discuss other outstanding issues failed, however, to resolve the differences over where each country would base its ships from the Black Sea Fleet. This time Kuchma openly acknowledged that talks with Russia were proceeding 'with considerable difficulty' and pointed out that Ukraine was not interested 'in dragging things out'.[26] For his part, Yeltsin was to reiterate in mid-April that Crimea was an internal Ukrainian matter, but also added: 'It will be correct to sign major political documents between Russia and Ukraine only after we are convinced that the relations between Simferopol and Kyiv do not infringe the interest of Crimeans.' The Russian Duma went further and invited Tsekov to address the chamber; seizing the opportunity, he did not hesitate to call for Russian help.[27]

Meanwhile, with the parliamentary conciliation commission still completing its work on the Law on Powers, the Kuchma administration concentrated on getting the budget prepared by the government approved by the parliament and moving forward with reforms. In fact, after accepting Masol's resignation on 4 April, the Verkhovna Rada had passed a motion of no confidence in the government but the president had turned this to his advantage. Having a free hand now to install more reformers, he nevertheless instructed the Cabinet of Ministers to keep working and announced that he would not appoint a new government until the Law on Powers had been passed. He was also helped by the fact that he had managed to split the Agrarian bloc and by the national democrats attacking Moroz and the deputy speaker Tkachenko, who were accused of corruption. On 6 April, with the leftist forces forced on to the defensive, the parliament passed the austere budget for 1995.

By the following week, however, the left had recovered and rallied its forces. On 11 April, it succeeded in blocking a privatization programme submitted by Yekhanurov. The following day, with Kuchma present in the parliament for the resumption of the debate about the Law on Powers, a Communist deputy stepped up the

[26] Reuter, 28 March 1995.
[27] *Ibid.*, 15 April 1995.

counter-attack by accusing the president of heading towards 'un-limited authoritarianism'. The resulting confrontation resulted in Kuchma storming out of the chamber. With the leftists at first delaying proceedings by using the old tactic of the People's Council of refusing to register and thereby making the legislature inquorate, and then supporting the proposal to send the draft Law on Powers back to the conciliation committee for further revisions before a third reading, it looked as if political deadlock had returned.

Kuchma again considered calling a referendum on confidence in his administration if the law was not approved, but he also offered some concessions; he yielded on the most controversial articles which, in certain circumstances, gave the president the right to dissolve the parliament and, correspondingly, the legislature the right to impeach the president. Eventually, on 18 May, after a brief visit to Kyiv by President Clinton had raised spirits, the somewhat watered-down version of the Law on Powers was passed by the parliament by a vote of 219 to 104. But the law could not be implemented without changes to the constitution requiring a two-thirds majority, and this the Communist, and Socialists remained intent on denying the president.

Attempts by moderates to find a way out of the impasse failed and Kuchma decided to risk doing what he had threatened from the outset. On 31 May he announced that he was calling a non-binding referendum of confidence in both the executive and the legislative branches for 28 June. Even the president's supporters in the parliament were taken aback by this move and on the next day voted against his decree; by a vote of 252 to 9 the Verkhovna Rada declared Kuchma's action unconstitutional and prohibited the government from financing the poll. However, the president stood his ground and made it clear that he was determined to go ahead with the referendum.

With Ukraine plunged into its most serious political crisis since independence, Kuchma sought to explain to the public why he appeared to be gambling everything on the showdown with the parliament. 'We have before us an historic decision', he told the residents of Cherkasy on 3 June:

> The question at hand is not about power. It is much broader and deeper – which path should Ukraine take . . . The president has no other alternative but to turn to the chief arbiter – the nation. In today's conditions the country has no opportunities.

We must get through this. God willing we will not turn back to the past.[28]

Fortunately, the dangerous situation did not last long. When the parliament met again on 7 June, it agreed to a compromise which essentially allowed Kuchma to emerge victorious. In return for revoking his contentious confidence poll, the Verkhovna Rada voted by 240 to 81 to approve a so-called 'constitutional agreement' which allowed the president to implement the provisions of the Law on Powers without having to secure the backing of a constitutional majority. The arrangement, which gave the president broader rights to issue decrees (especially economic ones), appoint ministers and subordinate local administrations to his jurisdiction, was to last for a year till June 1996, by which time a new constitution was to be adopted.

As the country heaved a sigh of relief, the compromise was hailed by all the main political actors, with the exception of the Communist leaders. At a special ceremony for signing of the constitutional accord, Kuchma hinted that the country had come dangerously close to 'real conflict' and 'the use of force'. 'We have passed the test for state wisdom and balance, the ability to preserve civil peace and finding a civilized way to resolve all problems', he declared.[29] 'We are all winners, and chiefly the people have won.' He also appealed to the deputies to form a 'constructive majority' in the parliament in support of 'reforming the economy, [and transforming] the political system into a better developed democracy in keeping with the principles of human rights and liberties'.[30] On the same day, Kuchma also announced that he was confirming the acting prime minister Marchuk as the head of the new government.

While this drama was being played out in Kyiv, another struggle over a division of powers had gradually abated. Kuchma and the Ukrainian parliament had persisted with their tougher line towards Simferopol and seemed to have achieved their goal. At the end of May, the Crimean parliament backed down and called off a

---

[28] *Ibid.*, 3 June 1995.

[29] *Ibid.*, 8 June 1995.

[30] Radio Ukraine, 8 June 1995, as cited by Chrystyna Lapychak in 'Showdown Yields Reform', *Transition*, vol. 1, no. 13 (28 July 1995), p. 7. This article charts the tug-of-war between President Kuchma and the Ukrainian parliament and its culmination and temporary resolution.

threatened retaliatory local referendum in support of its annulled 1992 constitution. In June, the Crimean deputies also replaced Tsekov by a more moderate figure, Yevhen Suprunyuk, who was willing to seek accommodation with Kyiv. The Crimean parliament also agreed to work on a draft version of a new constitution acceptable to Kyiv.[31] For the interim period, the Constitutional Agreement confirmed the special status of the Autonomous Republic of Crimea as part of the unitary Ukrainian state.

There was also a hopeful development in Russian-Ukrainian relations. On 9 June, Kuchma and Yeltsin met in Sochi and announced that they had signed an agreement resolving the longstanding dispute over the Black Sea Fleet. True, Yeltsin declared that the controversy had been solved 'once and for all', while Kuchma was more guarded and said that the question had been solved 'in general'. In fact, although quite a few significant details were left vague or still needed to be worked out, at least the basis of a deal had been agreed on: the Fleet would be split, and after trading in most of its share in return for debt relief, Ukraine would end up with 18.3% of the vessels; Russia would have basing rights in Sevastopol on terms still to be negotiated, and Ukraine, too, would use some of the port's facilities.[32]

The summer of 1995 therefore seemed to herald the beginning of a period of economic recovery and political calm. The first signs of economic stabilization were appearing, real incomes were rising, and inflation, now holding steady at just under 5 per cent, was down to manageable levels. Large Western credits had been obtained and Ukraine's debts to Russia and Turkmenistan were rescheduled. In fact, with the exchange rate of the karbovanets-coupon also stabilized, the Kuchma administration hoped to be able introduce the new Ukrainian currency, the hryvnya, in October. In the political sphere, the president had in effect been given emergency powers for one year, and Kyiv's conflict with Simferopol appeared to be defused. Relations with Russia seemed reasonably stable and Presi-

---

[31] See Tor Bukkvoll, 'A Fall from Grace for Crimean Separatists', and Chrystyna Lapychak, 'A Timeline of Crimean Separatism', *Transition*, vol, 1, no. 21 (17 November 1995), pp. 46-9, and 49, respectively. After July, when he was hospitalized with diptheria, Meshkov was to withdraw from political life. The charges against him were eventually dropped.

[32] Reuter, 9 June 1995.

dent Clinton's visit to Kyiv had underscored the new political and economic backing which the United States was giving Ukraine.

Bumpy progress

However, two violent incidents shattered the summer tranquillity and revealed some of the tensions lingering in society. In late June, racketeers killed two Crimean Tatars in a market at Feodosiya, and this, together with the apparent corruption and indifference of the local police, triggered off riots. The protesters attacked enterprises believed to be owned by criminal elements and took the local police chief hostage. Another two Crimean Tatars and a policeman died before order was restored. This first instance since independence of a violent inter-ethnic clash resulting in deaths set off alarm bells in Kyiv. Though strapped for cash, the Ukrainian government was forced to revamp its programme for facilitating the return and integration of the Crimean Tatars and to step up its efforts to combat organized crime and corruption in Crimea. It also appealed to international organizations to provide assistance for the repatriation of the Crimean Tatars.[33]

A second ugly incident occurred a month later in Kyiv itself when, on 19 July, riot police attacked a funeral procession bearing the coffin of the Patriarch of the Ukrainian Orthodox Church of the Kyivan Patriarchate. This Church had been formed in June 1992 after the controversial Metropolitan Filaret had unsuccessfully sought to obtain autocephaly from the Moscow Patriarchate for the Ukrainian Orthodox Church, which split in the process, and been defrocked by the Moscow Patriarchate. Metropolitan Filaret and supporters of autocephaly had then joined with most of the leaders of the Ukrainian Autocephalous Orthodox Church to establish a new 'Ukrainian Orthodox Church of the Kyivan Patriarchate' (UOC-KP). A larger group of bishops within the Ukrainian Orthodox Church, led by Metropolitan Volodymyr Sabodan, remained loyal to the Moscow Patriarchate. Part of the former UAOC also refused to unite with Metropolitan Filaret and elected Dymytrii Yarema of Lviv as its Patriarch. Although Metropolitan

---

[33] In late 1994, the United Nations Development Programme had launched an appeal for international funding for its Crimean Integration and Development Programme, but the response had been rather disappointing.

Filaret remained a powerful figure within the UOC-KP, Metropolitan Volodymyr (Romanyuk), a former political prisoner and UAOC hierarch, was elected in October 1993 to succeed Patriarch Mstyslav who had died a few months earlier.[34]

The mourners, supported by the paramilitary UNSO, sought access to St Sophia's Cathedral to bury their leader there. However, apparently in the hope of preserving its neutrality in relation to the country's three main religious groups who were still bitterly divided – the pro-Kyiv and pro-Moscow Orthodox, and the Ukrainian Catholics – the government had refused permission for Patriarch Volodymyr to be buried in Ukraine's most sacred site, which had remained a religious museum. During the violent confrontation, the deceased patriarch's supporters smashed the asphalt in front of the wall surrounding the cathedral and placed his coffin in a makeshift grave. It was unclear who gave the order for the riot police to be sent in, and recriminations abounded.[35]

The highly delicate nature of the religious issues dividing Ukraine's Christians was attested to by the fact that many months after the incident the Patriarch's body still remained in what was supposed to have been a temporary grave, close to passing traffic. There were further complications in October when, despite his murky past, Metropolitan Filaret was elected Patriarch of the UOC-KP. Four of the Church's leading hierarchs broke away in protest and joined the UAOC, which at the time had about 1,000 parishes. They also announced that the UAOC would be willing to pursue dialogue with the Ukrainian Orthodox Church of the Moscow Patriarchate and were hopeful that the latter would reciprocate.[36]

While the Ukrainian Orthodox remained divided, the Ukrainian Catholic Church was consolidating its organizational structure and preparing for the observance in 1996 of the 400th anniversary of its founding by the Union of Brest. In November, the Vatican issued a special papal missive in this connection, but perhaps the most important development concerning the UCC during this period was

---

[34] Anatolii Kolosha, 'Kyivskyi Patriarkhat: Neprostyi Shlyakh do Yednosti' [The Kyivan Patriarchate: A Complex Route to Unity], *Holos Ukrainy*, 31 July 1993.

[35] The incident and the background to it are described by Chrystyna Lapychak in 'Rifts Among Ukraine's Orthodox Churches Inflame Public Passions', *Transition*, vol. 2, no. 7, (5 April 1996), pp. 6–10.

[36] See *ibid.*

the extension of its structures to central and Eastern Ukraine. Initially, in April 1995, the head of the UCC, Cardinal Lyubachivsky, appointed a visitator for Kyiv and Ukrainian Catholics in Eastern Ukraine, but a year later, in April 1996, it was announced that Bishop Lubomyr Husar, whose secret consecration in 1977 as a bishop for Ukraine by Patriarch Slipy had only just been recognized by the Vatican, was being named exarch of the newly-established Exarchate of Kyiv-Vyshhorod.[37]

Another worrying development during the summer of 1995 was that, even after the signing of the Constitutional Agreement, many of the deputies opposed the attempts by the Procurator General, Vladyslav Datsyuk, to probe into corruption among officials. Two of his investigations had focused on the deputy speaker Tkachenko and the former acting prime minister, Zvyahilsky, who was being accused of embezzling millions of dollars from the state and had since sought refuge in Israel. On 21 June, the parliament voted to dismiss Datstyuk. However, Kuchma stood by him and began another struggle of wills between the president and the Verkhovna Rada.

However, Ukraine's foreign creditors were more concerned by the decision of the president and prime minister to moderate the pace of economic reform. At the end of June, perhaps as an unwritten part of the compromise reached with the parliament, Kuchma indicated that the new government would ease stringent monetary policy and place more emphasis on helping 'priority industries' as well as pensioners and other impoverished social groups. When, a few days later, the president announced the composition of the new government, the name of Pynzenyk, regarded as the chief architect of economic reform, was conspicuously missing.

It had been agreed in the Constitutional Agreement that once the parliament had approved the government's economic programme it would be unable to alter it for a year. Marchuk's team therefore sought to come up with a programme which would keep the economic reform programme generally on track yet partly placate some of the leftist forces and the industrial and agricultural lobbies. In July the new government yielded to pressure from the agricultural sector and violated monetary discipline by agreeing to a credit emission to help finance the purchase of grain by the state.

[37] See *The Ukrainian Weekly*, 31 December 1995 and 7 April 1996.

This, and the uncertainty about government policy, led to a devaluation of the karbovanets by about 10% and a rise in inflation, which in turn aborted plans to introduce the hryvnya.

In August, apparently under pressure from international financial institutions, Kuchma re-appointed Pynzenyk as Vice Prime Minister in charge of economic reforms. Addressing the nation on the fourth anniversary of Ukraine's declaration of independence, he nevertheless indicated that 'corrections' to economic policy were still being worked out. 'We have been trying to follow Western models blindly', he explained. 'We need to look for a Ukrainian model of economic transformation.'[38] To oversee this modification of his reform course, the president was to select cadres from his native Dnipropetrovsk region. In September he appointed Pavlo Lazarenko, head of the Dnipropetrovsk Regional Administration, as First Vice Prime Minister. Having begun his Party career in the agrarian sector, Lazarenko had been associated in recent years with numerous local development projects, including the construction of the Dnipropetrovsk Underground, and had gained the reputation of a progressive administrator.[39]

While the government reviewed its economic strategy, close consultations with the IMF continued. Although it was now clear that Ukraine would not be able to meet all the macroeconomic targets for 1995 previously agreed with the IMF, the latter demonstrated its confidence that Marchuk's government was still continuing in the right direction by releasing, in September, the third tranche of $350 million of the $1.5 billion stabilization package.

Two of the major problems that had been such a huge drain on resources since independence, Chornobyl and the coal-mining industry in the Donbas, continued to pose major difficulties. Although Kuchma had pledged to shut down the Chornobyl nuclear plant by the end of the century, Ukrainian officials reiterated that this could not be achieved without considerable Western assistance, and appealed more urgently to the G-7 and European Union to translate their general offers of help into a concrete financing plan. They also sought external aid to deal with the problems of the costly,

[38] Reuters, 24 August, 1994.
[39] See 'The Reemergence of the Underground as a Factor in Political Struggle', *Research Update* (Ukrainian Centre for Independent Political Research, Kyiv), vol. 2, no. 8 (28 January 1996).

outdated and dangerous mines in the Donbas, many of which the government planned to shut down. In a sign of impending trouble, the country's miners held a one-day strike at the beginning of October to demand that their salaries and pensions be paid on time and that the government provide the coal-mining industry with further subsidies.

Later that month, the Verkhovna Rada approved the government's revised economic reform programme for 1996 by a vote of 234 to 61. Its priorities were to encourage economic growth, speed up privatization, which had been proceeding at a disappointingly slow pace, and revamp the country's energy sector. The government aimed to keep the budget deficit to under 6% of GDP; reduce the inflation rate, which had shot up to 14.2% in September, to an average of about 2.4% in 1996; and, after years of continuous and ruinous decline, to achieve a modest growth of 0.6% in industry and 0.2% in agriculture. Responding to pressure from the industrial lobby and the leftists, the programme also foresaw greater state involvement in the economy. 'World experience . . . teaches us that, in periods economic transformation, the transformation cannot be carried out without decisive state involvement', Marchuk maintained. But the Communist deputies still bitterly opposed the programme. Their leader, Symonenko, told the parliament: 'What we had before was a satanic blitzkrieg. We are now being presented with genocide against our own people'.[40]

In the external sphere, Russian-Ukrainian contacts continued at the official and corporate level but there seemed to no further progress with the bilateral treaty and Yeltsin's visit to Kyiv. Elections to the Russian Duma were scheduled for December, in which Zyuganov's Communist forces and the radical right, both of which wanted to see the restoration of the USSR in a new form, were expected to strengthen their position, and it appeared increasingly unlikely that there would be any further in Russian-Ukrainian relations until after the results were known.

The portents for Ukrainian-Russian relations were unpromising for another reason. On 14 September, President Yeltsin issued a decree outlining Russia's 'Strategic Course' towards the CIS countries. Among other things, the document viewed the CIS as a 'zone' of Russian 'vital interests', asserted Russia's right to use

---

[40] Reuter, 11 October 1995.

'financial, economic, [and] military-political forms of leverage to protect the rights of Russians living in neigbouring states', and defined the overall goal of Russian policy in the CIS as 'the creation of a politically and economically integrated group of states' in which Russia's 'CIS partners should be persistently and consistently guided towards the elaboration of joint positions on international problems and the coordination of activity in the world arena'. The decree was immediately criticized by the Ukrainian Foreign Ministry for ignoring 'norms of international law' and instead promoting 'interference in the internal affairs of the countries of the CIS'.[41] Furthermore, Belarus' continuing moves under President Lukashenka towards integration with Russia and the creation of a customs union between Russia, Belarus and Kazakhstan added to Ukraine's discomfort.

However, Ukraine continued to receive reassurances from NATO that it would not be marginalized in Europe's developing security arrangements. When the British Foreign Secretary Malcolm Rifkind, visited Kyiv in early September, he declared that 'Ukraine's size and strategic position make it one of Europe's pivots'. NATO's expansion would be 'a steady and deliberate, not a rushed process' he explained, adding: 'We recognize the uncertainties felt by those not expecting to join.'[42]

In fact, with President Yeltsin and other Russian representatives warning more and more explicitly that Russia might respond to NATO's enlargement eastward by assembling a new bloc from among the former Soviet republics, Ukraine had in the meantime sought to clarify and cement its relations with the North Atlantic Alliance. These efforts proved successful: in mid-September, Ukraine managed to become only the second state after Russia to secure its own individual cooperation programme based on the formula 'sixteen plus one' (that is, all the member states and a non-member). At the special session of the North Atlantic Council on 14 September in Brussels which effectively upgraded Ukraine's status within the Partnership for Peace Programme by using the 'sixteen plus one formula', Udovenko presented Ukraine's detailed proposals for developing a 'special partnership' with NATO on this basis.[43]

[41] Both documents were published in *Nezavisimost*, 4 October 1995.

[42] Reuter, 4 September 1995.

[43] See F. Stephen Larrabee, 'Ukraine's Balancing Act', *Survival*, vol. 38, no. 2 (Summer 1996), pp. 148-9; Hennadiy Udovenko, 'European Stability and NATO

One foreign policy issue which had seemingly been deferred by mutual consent reappeared during 1995: Ukraine's borders with Romania. It continued to block the signing of a bilateral friendship treaty. During President Clinton's visit to Kyiv in May Ukrainian officials even suggested that Romania should be kept out of NATO until it dropped its territorial claims against Ukraine.[44] During the second half of the year, the dispute increasingly focused on Serpent Island, a tiny rocky protrusion in the Black Sea on which a Soviet (now a Ukrainian) military installation was based. However, what appears to have given the island sudden new importance was the discovery by Ukrainian prospectors of oil and natural gas deposits in the area. In December, Romania suggested that it was considering submitting the dispute to the International Court of Justice in The Hague.

Further afield, Ukraine established better links with a number of Latin American countries, especially Brazil and Argentina, where there are sizeable groups of Ukrainian emigrants and their descendants. For this purpose, at the end of October and beginning of November, President Kuchma made a trip to Brazil, Argentina and Chile. While in Santiago he expressed particular interest in the lessons of Chile's experience with economic stabilization and reforms.[45]

But as far as official Kyiv was concerned Ukraine's most significant success during this period was the decision by the Council of Europe on 26 September to accept it as a member, the first CIS country to be admitted. This was a source of considerable pride for the newly independent country, and Marchuk indicated the symbolic significance attached to it when, on 9 November, at the ceremony in Strasbourg to welcome Ukraine, he declared: 'We were waiting for this historical moment. Another large blank spot has been removed from the map of the new Europe.' The prime minister added that Ukraine viewed its acceptance into the Council of Europe as recognition of the progressive changes which it had already undertaken and as support for its continuing democratic transformation.[46]

Enlargement: Ukraine's Perspective', *NATO Review*, vol. 43, no. 6 (November 1995), pp. 15-16.

[44] *Ibid.*, 16 May 1995

[45] Ukrinform, 1 November 1995.

Although after three attempts by the parliament to oust him, Procurator General Datsyuk was finally forced to resign on 10 October, a bold appointment was made at this time by Marchuk and Kuchma which seemed to underscore the Ukrainian leadership's commitment to pursuing legal, constitutional and political reforms. Serhii Holovaty, the prominent democrat and legal specialist, who had done so much to help the democratic forces both within and outside the parliament, and head of the independent Ukrainian Legal Foundation, was made the new minister of justice. On the other hand, Kuchma's appointment of the procurator of the Dnipropetrovsk region, Hennadii Vorsinov, as the new procurator general only increased rumblings in political circles and the regions about the growing preponderance of 'Dnipropetrovtsi' among the presidential appointees, especially in the presidential administration.

With Lazarenko having now assumed important responsibilities in a Cabinet of Ministers which already included several 'Dnipropetrovtsi' – namely Vice Prime Minister Yevtukhov, Minister of the Cabinet Valerii Pustovoitenko and Defence Minister Shmarov, – rumours soon began to circulate about the beginnings of a political struggle between Kuchma's Dnipropetrovsk clan and Marchuk and his aides from within the country's security apparatus. Indeed, with his popularity riding high, Marchuk had come to be considered by many as a potential presidential candidate, and he himself fuelled speculation about a rift behind the scenes by unexpectedly announcing in late October that he intended to stand as a parliamentary candidate in one of the constituencies which still had not elected a deputy. Many interpreted this as a move by the Prime Minister to ensure a political safety-net for himself in case Kuchma decided to replace him by Lazarenko or someone else. In the next round of elections on 10 December, Marchuk had no problem getting elected in a constituency in the Poltava region.

A few days later, infighting within the president's administration resulted in the resignation of several of his key advisors. The seemingly unbridled political influence of his chief of staff, Tabachnyk, appears to have been the source of considerable dissatisfaction. Kuchma chose another cadre from Dnipropetrovsk, the economist and supporter of market reforms Volodymyr Kuznetsov, to be his new first assistant and head of the presidential advisory team.[47] Thus,

[46] *Ibid.*, 9 November 1995.

while sceptics and opponents of Ukrainian independence had once warned that an independent Ukraine would be largely run by nationalists from Western Ukraine, after four and a half years of independence the country's executive branch was in fact dominated by Dnipropetrovsti, most of them Russian-speaking. Not so long ago, Shcherbytsky's Dnipropetrovsk mafia had sought to keep Ukrainian nationalism in check; now, ironically, a modern Dnipropetrovsk clan linked to Kuchma was defending and developing Ukraine's independent statehood. In other words, within the space of only a few years the political and economic élite of a major industrial centre in Eastern Ukraine, and the country's second largest (after the Odesa region) and second-most populous region (after the Donetsk region) had broken with the stereotype of the Russified East and its indifference or hostility to the Ukrainian movement and was in the forefront of the processes of state-building and national integration.

Meanwhile, new problems arose in Simferopol. First, in October, a row broke out in the Crimean parliament after Russian deputies brought in a Russian tricolour into the chamber and Crimean Tatars demanded that their own sky-blue national standard should also be allowed to stand alongside it. Then, at the beginning of November, ten Crimean Tatar deputies began a hunger strike within the legislature building to protest that the new draft local constitution did not ensure quotas of seats for the Crimean Tatars in the parliament and local councils (over 60,000 who had returned since 1991 had not yet received Ukrainian citizenship and therefore remained politically and economically disenfranchised) and demanding that the Crimean Tatar language be given the same official status in the autonomous republic as Russian and, nominally, Ukrainian. The Crimean parliament yielded to the first demand by agreeing to use a system of proportional representation in the next regional elections which would guarantee Crimean Tatar representation. After ten days, and at the request of the Mejlis, the deputies called off their partly successful protest.

The end of the year brought heightened anxieties about the direction in which Russia was moving and the possible consequences for Ukraine. As expected, the Communists made impressive

[47] See 'Leonid Kuchma is Losing People: A Comment on Recent Resignations in the Presidential Administration', *Research Update*, vol. 2, no. 6 (15 January 1966).

gains in the parliamentary elections: they won 158 out of the 450 seats, that is more than three times the number they had previously held, and twice as many as their nearest competitor, Zhirinovsky's Liberal Democratic Party. Their leader Zyuganov, now seen as the favourite to win the presidential elections in Russia the following June, and his supporters spoke openly of wanting to restore the Soviet Union. Yeltsin was therefore placed under even greater pressure to placate the resurgent 'patriotic' forces' and his replacement of Kozyrev and the departure of other reformers and moderates from his administration did not bode well.

17

SELF-DETERMINATION REFINED

Perseverance

Ukraine entered 1996 with its reform programme appearing to have lost some of its momentum. In early January, the IMF responded by withholding the fourth tranche of the standby loan until the parliament approved a new budget fulfilling reform requirements.[1] At the beginning of the following month, the situation, already made more difficult by an unusually harsh winter, was further exacerbated when the country's miners went on strike. Although the country's energy grid was soon plunged into crisis and Russia severed the joint electricity grid, the Marchuk government stood firm. Eventually, after two weeks, the miners called off their strike without having won any major concessions.

The IMF's action was seen as a temporary hitch and was offset by the prospect of more international economic assistance during 1996. The United States in particular was bolstering its political support for Ukraine with economic and technical aid. In December, during a visit to Kyiv, a member of President Clinton's team noted that in 1996 Ukraine would be the third largest recipient of US aid after Israel and Egypt. Indeed, when at the end of January President Clinton signed the Foreign Assistance Bill for 1996 into law, 'not less than' $225 million were earmarked for Ukraine, which now replaced Russia as the largest recipient of US aid of the countries of the CIS (Russia was to receive 'no more than' $195 million). Also in December, while on a visit to London, Kuchma had obtained a pledge from the European Bank for Reconstruction and Development of assistance worth over $200 million.[2]

While the parliament considered a tight new annual budget,

[1] See Matthew Kaminsky, 'Slow to Reform Ukraine Irks IMF', *Financial Times*, 9 January 1996.

[2] *The Ukrainian Weekly*, 31 December 1995, and 4 February 1996.

Kuchma made a brief visit to Washington, where, apart from being received by US leaders, he also met with the heads of the IMF and World Bank. He was able to announce that the IMF had agreed to expand and release suspended credits as soon as the budget was passed and to begin negotiations about a new three-year loan of between $3 to $4 billion. The country badly needed sufficient loans to enable it to reform the economy and not simply pay Russia and Turkmenistan for fuel imports, he explained.[3] The World Bank also expressed its readiness to consider giving Ukraine further assistance, including help in dealing with the chronic problems of the coal-mining industry.

With the tenth anniversary of the nuclear accident in Chornobyl approaching, Kuchma and other Ukrainian officials also lobbied Western countries to come through with financial aid to help cover the costs of closing down the Chornobyl nuclear plant and providing an alternative source of energy. In December, the G7 states and Ukraine had signed a memorandum envisaging about $2.3 billion in financial aid for this purpose; this fell considerably short of the $4 billion which Ukraine considered was needed to shut down the plant by the year 2000. The replacement of the crumbling sarcophagus covering the plant's destroyed fourth reactor had not been included in the calculations. In fact, just as had earlier been the case with nuclear arms, Ukrainian officials indicated their exasperation that their impoverished country, which was having to allocate some 6% of its budget to clean-up operations, was being pressured to close down the stricken plant according to a timetable proposed from the outside but without a definite financing plan. As a result of Kyiv's insistence on adequate funding, Ukraine was being implicitly, and sometimes explicitly, accused of exaggerating the costs of closing Chornobyl and the damage caused by the accident.[4]

Another huge drain on Ukraine's resources was the defence sector, including both the new armed forces which the country had been creating, and the military-industrial complex, which was badly affected by economic dislocation and undergoing efforts to convert much of it to civilian uses. The replacement of independent

---

[3] Reuter, 24 February 1996.

[4] For example, Horbulin had recently told Reuter: 'I think it is generally supposed that Ukraine is simply begging. We are not begging. Chernobyl is not simply a problem for Ukraine.' Reuter, 15 October 1995.

Ukraine's first minister of defence, Morozov, back in the autumn of 1993, had highlighted some of the difficulties and controversy surrounding these complex issues. Two and a half years later, these problems had become even more pronounced and now it was the current defence minister, Shmarov, a civilian, who was increasingly coming under fire, especially from the national democrats.

The Kuchma leadership's decision to reduce the size of the armed forces from 420,00 to 350,000 by the year 2000 created additional tensions within the military. Furthermore, Shmarov's plan to reorganize the military districts led to friction with the effective number two in the armed forces, the chief of staff, Anatoly Lopata, who tendered his resignation in protest. Details of the differences were leaked to the press.[5] On 12 February, Lopata's objections resulted in his dismissal by the president.[6] The national democrats subsequently stepped up their campaign against Shmarov, accusing him of selling out Ukrainian interests in bilateral deals with the Russian military.[7]

The central domestic issue, though, remained the new constitution, which according to the terms of the Constitutional Agreement, was to be adopted by 8 June 1996. On 11 March, the Constitutional Commission, chaired jointly by Kuchma and Moroz and containing representatives appointed by both the president and the legislature, as well as legal specialists, finally concluded its work on the new draft and eight days later formally submitted it to the Verkhovna Rada. It was clear, however, that although the draft represented a compromise, it remained essentially a working document and that a major political struggle over the details still loomed ahead.

The new draft constitution, which Kuchma declared was 'completely European in its letter and spirit', envisaged Ukraine as a democratic and progressive country possessing what the president described as a 'mixed republican type of government' based on a careful separation of powers in which no one branch of power would be 'supreme', though the president would have considerable powers.[8] Thus, even the name of the parliament was to be changed from the Supreme Council to the National Assembly. The draft

---

[5] See *Vechirnii Kyiv*, 8 February 1996.
[6] Reuter, 12 February 1996.
[7] For details, see *Vechirnii Kyiv*, 8 February 1996.
[8] Ukrinform, 20 March 1996.

proposed that the legislature would become a bi-cameral body, with the lower house, the Chamber of Deputies, consisting of 370 members, and the upper house, the Senate, composed of three representatives each from 'the Crimean Autonomy', the twenty-four administrative regions and the city of Kyiv, and two from Sevastopol. Both the deputies and senators would be directly elected for four years. One of the draft's most controversial features, therefore, was the attempt to placate the regions by giving them institutionalized representation in the revamped political system, though, as critics were apt to claim, seemingly at the expense of the parliament's powers.

Because the proposed new constitution represented a decisive break with the Soviet past, many of the leftists, the more hard line of whom had been encouraged again by the increased political influence of the Russian Communists, were opposed to it. In fact, the Communist faction proposed its own alternative variant of the new constitution, the essence of which was reflected in the desire to restore the name 'Ukrainian Soviet Socialist Republic'. Furthermore, under the influence of the hard left, the draft prepared by the Constitutional Commission had retained elements which Kuchma claimed were populist and impracticable in Ukraine's conditions, such as free housing (for the needy), medical care and secondary and higher education.[9]

Kuchma urged the deputies not to delay the adoption of the new constitution and to facilitate the process by approving the document by a majority vote. He retained the option of calling a referendum on the main principles if the parliament failed to reach agreement. Moroz opposed the idea of a plebiscite but, while making his misgivings about parts of the draft known, did not risk delaying the parliamentary debate on the document for too long: in fact, the parliament's Presidium decided that the debate on the new constitution would begin on 17 April.

Crimea, Moscow and Sevastopol

All this time, Crimea's parliament had been waiting for its Ukrainian counterpart to agree on the details of the new Ukrainian constitution

---

[9] The draft constitution approved by the Constitutional Commission was published in *Uryadovyi Kuryer*, 21 March 1996.

before its own new draft constitution could be harmonized with it. In the meantime, Crimea's prime minister, Franchuk, had been dismissed in early December and a replacement sought. At the end of January, Arkadii Demydenko, the deputy prime minister responsible for industry, was appointed by the Crimean speaker, Suprunyuk, as acting prime minister. Eventually, having received Kyiv's approval, Demydenko was confirmed at the end of February by the Crimean parliament as the new prime minister. He vowed to be 'neither pro-Ukrainian nor pro-Russian' but to defend the economic autonomy of Crimea.[10]

The unveiling of the new draft of the Ukrainian constitution immediately caused problems with the Crimean authorities, though. By referring to Crimea as an 'autonomy', rather than an autonomous republic, and downgrading its constitution to a 'statute', or charter, the draft significantly reduced the region's autonomous powers. The Crimean parliament met in emergency session on 9 March and called on Kyiv to recognize the new Crimean constitution by the end of March. With some of the Crimean deputies also calling for a new local referendum on Crimea's future, Suprunyuk warned of a new confrontation with Kyiv.[11] Senior Ukrainian officials responded that the document prepared by the Constitutional Commission was only a draft, and both Kuchma and Moroz expressed reservations about the articles dealing with Crimea.

The new row between Kyiv and Simferopol threatened to complicate Russian-Ukrainian relations, which in early 1996 entered a particularly delicate phase. Ukrainian officials began voicing their frustration with what they claimed was Russia' s reluctance to demarcate its border with Ukraine. They announced that Ukraine would be taking up the issue of borders at forthcoming CIS meetings and that it rejected the idea being proposed by Russia of 'external' CIS borders and 'internal' ones between the CIS states.

At the beginning of February, after a visit to Kyiv, the tougher new Russian foreign minister, Evgenii Primakov, who had been born in Kyiv and was still remembered in Ukraine for his rigid views on nationalities policy during the Gorbachev era, announced that the repeatedly postponed visit of President Yeltsin to Kyiv would

---

[10] Reuter, 28 February 1996.

[11] *Ibid.*, 11 March 1996.

take place in early April, providing that outstanding issues connected with the Black Sea Fleet were resolved.

The new, even more hardline composition of the Russian Duma and the intensifying political struggle in Russia in preparation for the presidential elections, however, placed in doubt whether Yeltsin would actually agree to sign a Ukrainian-Russian treaty, the terms of which would expose him to fierce attacks from the red-browns at home. In fact, Yeltsin's main political rival for the presidency, Zyuganov, declared during a visit to Kyiv at the end of February as a member of a Russian parliamentary group that 'Ukraine was absolutely sovereign within the former Soviet Union. It was a UN member and had its own Politburo'. Indicating how he saw the future, he added that if he came to power, 'there will be a qualitatively new, powerful international creation which everyone on this planet will have to reckon with'. Zyuganov was demonstratively ignored by the Ukrainian leadership but enthusiastically welcomed by Communist and Socialist deputies.[12]

On 15 March, the State Duma hit out at the Russian president and openly challenged the entire post-Soviet order. It passed a resolution by 250 votes to 98 denouncing the Belovezhky Agreement and declaring null and void the ratification by the previous Russian parliament of the document which had marked the demise of the Soviet Union and the birth of the CIS. Yeltsin immediately condemned the act as unconstitutional and 'scandalous' (the Duma – the lower house of parliament – did not have the authority to annul the decisions taken by the previous full Russian parliament), and claimed that it represented an attempt to disrupt the presidential elections.

Kuchma joined leaders of other former Soviet republics in denouncing the Duma's legally invalid but nevertheless destabilizing action. 'This decision is a real threat not only to neighbouring countries once part of the Soviet Union but for the whole world', he declared in a televised statement which was also shown on Russian television. Russian deputies, he added, had 'laid a mine under the CIS' by in effect saying that 'Russia was leaving' this association, 'not other countries'.[13]

It now seemed almost certain that even if Yeltsin did sign the

[12] *Ibid.*, 26 February 1996.
[13] *Ibid.*, 15 March 1996.

Russian-Ukrainian treaty affirming the principles that had been recognized in the various bilateral agreements since November 1990, the Duma would not agree to ratify it. Ukraine felt even more squeezed between Russia and the emerging military and political bloc which it was creating with Belarus and other CIS members, and NATO and the Central European states which, as Kuchma pointed out after the Duma's condemnation of the break-up of the Soviet Union, would now probably press for their acceptance into the North Atlantic Alliance to be speeded up. In the presence of US Secretary of State Christopher, who while visiting Kyiv at this time went out of his way to condemn the Duma's decision and publicly reaffirm Washington's political support for Ukraine's independence, Kuchma hinted that although his country was not requesting membership of NATO it would have to keep its options open.[14]

While expressing public disapproval of the Duma's action, Yeltsin was at pains to project himself at home as a leader who was promoting deeper integration within the CIS, though in a different way from the Russian legislature. He managed to achieve two successes which boosted his image in this respect. First, Moscow's long-standing emphasis on the 'reintegration' of the CIS countries produced a major breakthrough when, on 23 March, the Belarusian president, Lukashenka, announced that Russia and Belarus had agreed to form a union of their two states and that a treaty paving the way for it would be signed on 2 April. Then, on 29 March, Russia, Belarus and Kazakhstan, who had already formed a customs union, and Kyrgyzstan, which intended to join it, signed an agreement in Moscow on closer cooperation.

The Russian president also began hinting that he might have to postpone his visit to Ukraine yet again because the final terms concerning the basing in Crimea of Russia's portion of the divided Black Sea Fleet had still not been agreed on. During the final week of March, bilateral negotiations continued and, at the end of the month, Marchuk, who had been to Moscow twice in the last fortnight, was still expressing confidence that the conclusion of the Russian-Ukrainian treaty would proceed as planned. Although the

[14] Ukrinform and Reuter, 19 February 1996. Two days later, while visiting Switzerland, Kuchma stated in Geneva that 'In future Ukraine need not necessarily be non-aligned . . . . Ukraine does not see NATO as a threat to its existence and is actively pursuing its cooperation with this alliance . . . the next step could be establishing a special partnership with NATO.' Reuter, 24 March 1996.

Russian and Ukrainian defence ministers, who met at this time at a military base near Lviv, appear to have successfully worked out mutually acceptable agreements, the main working groups, led on the Ukrainian side by Deputy Prime Minister Durdynets, failed to conclude a deal on the terms of the basing of Russia's fleet in Crimea. The sticking point was again Sevastopol: Russia renewed its insistence on exclusive military use of the port, while Ukraine continued to reject this. Although the outstanding issues connected with the Black Sea Fleet had been deliberately excluded from the proposed new Russian-Ukrainian treaty – the actual division of the Fleet had by now got under way – and the Ukrainian side had continued to argue that they should be dealt with separately, the unresolved problem of Sevastopol provided Yeltsin with a pretext not to go to Kyiv.

On the eve of the signing of the Russian-Belarusian integration treaty, Yeltsin called off his visit to Kyiv for the sixth time. His press spokesman explained that 'The president of Russia . . . deems it impossible to sign accords which do not fully meet Russia's interests'.[15] During the next few weeks Yeltsin, Chernomyrdin and other Russian leaders were publicly to renew Russia's claims that Sevastopol be recognized as an exclusively Russian naval base and Defence Minister Grachev ordered the suspension of the transfer to Ukraine of the latter's share of the naval vessels moored in Sevastopol. For their part, Ukraine's officials were to complain that Russia was failing to honour its undertaking to provide nuclear fuel for Ukraine's atomic reactors, and also to step up claims for compensation for the fissile material in the warheads from the tactical nuclear weapons which Kyiv had handed over to Moscow in early 1992. They also pressed Moscow on the issue of the demarcation of the Russian-Ukrainian border, especially in the Black Sea, where new oil and gas reserves had been discovered.

The Chornobyl factor, Marchuk's removal and the constitutional struggle

Whatever disappointment or sense of being affronted might have been felt in Kyiv, it gave way to the acceptance of the fact that, until the presidential contest in Russia was decided, there was

[15] Reuter, 11 April 1996.

unlikely to be any significant progress in Russian–Ukrainian relations. Moreover, of the Russian presidential hopefuls who had declared their candidatures by this time (Yeltsin, Zhyuganov, Zhirinovsky and Gorbachev), Yeltsin was still perceived by official Kyiv as the best of a problematic lot for Ukraine. Thus, in his annual address to the Ukrainian parliament on 2 April, President Kuchma simply commented that 'despite the postponement' of the Russian president's visit to Ukraine, 'the dialogue between the sides is continuing. We hope that the broad-ranging treaty will be concluded.'

In this speech, Kuchma focused his attention on domestic issues, especially the need to adopt the new constitution and to persevere with economic reforms. Both were essential, he argued, to ensure that Ukraine could not be turned back by 'internal [here the president referred to the development of an 'anti-systemic opposition' whose representatives were implacably opposed to Ukrainian statehood and the values associated with it] and external factors' from its chosen path of independent and democratic statehood. Ukraine was already beginning to see some positive results from the efforts to stabilize the economic situation and 1995 would go down as having been 'generally successful' in this respect and the year during which the 'fear of reforms' had finally been overcome. He expressed the hope that the new constitution would 'lay a legal legitimating foundation under a new constructive stage in the development of the country, symbolize the irrevocable assertion of Ukrainian statehood . . . and bear witness to the decisive overcoming of the danger' of Ukraine's returning to totalitarianism and authoritarianism.[16]

Meanwhile, tensions between Kyiv and Simferopol had eased after Kuchma had issued an edict on 15 March which had bolstered Crimea's economic autonomy and the Ukrainian parliament had voted on 4 April to approve most of the new Crimean constitution. The Ukrainian deputies, however, rejected a number of clauses which they considered went too far, such as references to Crimean 'citizenship', the 'Crimean people' and Russian as the peninsula's sole official language. The Crimean Tatars also remained unhappy with the document, maintaining that it did not take their specific concerns into consideration. For the moment, though, the majority

[16] *Ukraina moloda*, 5 April 1996.

of the Crimean deputies accepted this compromise and awaited the outcome of the debate about the new Ukrainian constitution.

In the first half of April, official Kyiv was given another sharp reminder by the IMF that it would have to stick to the agreed strict stabilization course for external financial support to continue. Although the Verkhovna Rada had eventually passed the tight budget for 1996 on 22 March, during the first quarter of the year, when the country had gone without the IMF's financial support, the government exceeded its spending limit and issued too many credits. The IMF responded by cancelling the rest of the standby loan, though it began emergency negotiations with the Ukrainian government on the terms of a new arrangement.

When, in the second half of April, the Ukrainian parliament finally turned its attention to the draft constitution, the opposition to the document was even greater than expected. At first leftist deputies refused to register. But soon it became clear that many of the centrist and right-wing deputies also had misgivings about the document's far-reaching implications. In order to prevent a complete fiasco, the centrist and centre-right factions proposed the creation of a special interim inter-factional conciliation committee to make further revisions to the draft.[17] It took about two weeks before the main leftist factions finally agreed to participate, but only on the condition that each of the twelve registered parliamentary factions would have two representatives on this *ad hoc* body, except for the Communists, who would have six.[18]

This new setback was overshadowed by the commemoration of the tenth anniversary of the Chornobyl disaster. In the weeks before the anniversary, the G7 increased the amount of assistance being pledged to enable Ukraine to close down the Chornobyl nuclear plant to just over $3 billion. At its summit in Moscow on 20 April, at which Kuchma repeated calls for prompt financial help and promised to decommission one of Chornobyl's two working reactors by the end of the year, the G7 also agreed to carry out a feasibility study on replacing the cracked twenty-storey concrete 'sarcophagus'

---

[17] For an 'insider's' account of the struggle to keep the constitutional process going, see the interview with the centrist deputy, Mykhailo Syrota, in *Uryadovyi kuryer*, 3 August 1996.

[18] Ukrinform, 6 May 1996.

encasing the destroyed fourth reactor.[19] No timetable for the disbursement of the funds was agreed on, though.

A few days later, during the solemn commemorations of the anniversary, Kuchma told the country that the Chornobyl nuclear disaster had 'turned Ukraine into an ecological disaster zone. After the Soviet Union fell apart, we were left facing the disaster alone.' For the last ten years, he continued, the country had been living under the 'unbearable burden' of 'the worst nuclear accident in history'. He revealed that since 1991 Ukraine had spent over $3 billion on dealing with the consequences, which was five times more than had been allocated to education, health and culture, combined. At least now, he added, substantial international assistance had finally been pledged to help Ukraine cope with the aftermath.[20]

Statistics about the consequences of the Chornobyl disaster had remained confusing or contentious. According to Ukrainian officials, in Ukraine alone, about 4,300 deaths had been linked directly to the disaster, an estimated 3.6 million people, half of them children, had been affected by the radiation, and hundreds of thousands had suffered ill effects or been displaced. Health officials in both Ukraine and Belarus pointed out that there had been significant increases in thyroid cancer, infant mortality and birth defects.[21]

While hoping that international assistance for dealing with the aftermath of the Chornobyl disaster would now be soon released, during the next weeks, the Ukrainian government successfully completed its latest negotiations with the IMF and secured a $867 million loan which was to be disbursed during the year in monthly tranches. The economic indicators, however, continued to be mixed. On the one hand, inflation had been brought down to 2.4% in April (in May, it was to fall under 1%), exports had risen by 18% during the first quarter of the year, the karbovanets remained stable and the decline in output was slowing. On the other hand, the government had got itself into what the *Financial Times* described as a 'vicious circle of wage arrears [the teachers had just carried out protests about the lateness of their pay], inter-enterprise debt and poor tax collection', all of which threatened to increase the budget deficit.

[19] Reuter 22 April 1996.

[20] Ukrinform and Reuter, 26 April 1996.

[21] Reuter, 22, 26 and 27 April 1996.

Rather unexpectedly, in what appears to have been an attempt to send the right signal to the international financial institutions, on 8 May Kuchma appointed the economic reformer Volodymyr Lanovy as an economic adviser. A week later, the president took it out on the Cabinet of Ministers, accusing it of poor economic management and threatening, in unexpectedly harsh terms, to sack ministers.[22]

The form which Kuchma's abrupt criticism of the work of the Cabinet of Ministers took seemed aimed at the prime minister and made the latter's position untenable. Whatever the hidden tensions between the head of the government and the president's team, Marchuk had stayed out of political controversy and had not openly opposed Kuchma and his policies.[23] On 18 May, however, he broke his silence in a lengthy but still quite guarded newspaper interview. He expressed surprise at the way in which the president had gone about publicly rebuking the Cabinet of Ministers, adding that this was not what he had expected of relations with Kuchma when he had agreed to head the government. Pointing out the extent to which decision-making about personnel appointments, including ministers, had become centralized in the presidential apparatus, the prime minister explained that this had tied his hands and caused problems within the Cabinet of Ministers. He disclosed that he had recently asked the president to remove or censure several of the ministers, adding that if he were given the choice of selecting the Cabinet of Ministers himself he would choose only about a third of the serving ministers.[24]

During the next few days, Marchuk distanced himself still more from the president. Having remained conspicuously reticent on the question of the draft constitution, the prime minister now came out against the idea of deciding things by a referendum, arguing that this would be destabilizing and needlessly wasteful. He also proposed that new parliamentary and presidential elections should be held

[22] Matthew Kaminski, 'Kuchma Takes Tough Stance Over Reforms', *Financial Times*, 15 May 1996.

[23] Some observers argued that a 'quiet war' was being fought out behind the scenes between the Dnipropetrovsk and State Security [Marchuk] teams. See, for example, Ukrainian Centre for Independent Political Research, *Dnipropetrovsk v. Security Service*, Kyiv, 1996.

[24] Evgenii Marchuk: 'Ya soznatelno otoshel ot publichnoi politiki' [I have consciously withdrawn from public politics], *Zerkalo nedeli*, 18 May 1996.

after the adoption of the new constitution, hardly what Kuchma's team wanted to hear. In an address to parliament he also implied that a stringent monetary policy was not a panacea for Ukraine's problems, seemed to argue for a softening of the tough economic programme and called for an overhaul of the cumbersome and inefficient tax system.[25]

While the rift between Kuchma and Marchuk was deepening, the work of the interim constitutional conciliatory commission, though hindered by the obstructive attitude of the Communists and their allies, had progressed. In order to facilitate the adoption of the new constitution, the president agreed to a number of important compromises. The most important of these was his retreat from the principle of a bi-cameral legislature.[26] All the same, when, on 23 May, the *ad hoc* conciliatory committee, headed by the leader of the faction 'Centre', Mykhailo Syrota, submitted the revised draft of the constitution to the parliament, the leftist deputies refused to register and again blocked the proceedings.[27] The centrists and rightists suspected that their political adversaries were deliberately delaying the constitutional debate until the results of the Russian presidential elections were known. Both sides also knew that the Constitutional Agreement was about to expire and that a grave new political crisis could ensue.

Against the background of this deadlock, on 27 May the presidential press office announced a presidential decree sacking Marchuk. The dismissal was carried out rather crudely: there was no recognition of any positive side to the prime minister's record and he was accused of having cared more about his 'political image' rather than the ensuring 'the effective and stable functioning of the government' and repairing the economy.[28] Marchuk, probably saving his ammunition for a later day, exercised self-restraint and refused to be drawn into recriminations. He rejected the purported motives for his dismissal and countered cryptically that the president 'cannot blame the entire economic crisis on one prime minister. The roots of these problems go a lot deeper'.[29]

[25] Reuter, 28 May, 1996.
[26] *Ukraina moloda*, 17 May 1996.
[27] *The Ukrainian Weekly*, 26 May 1996.
[28] Ukrinform, 28 June, and *The Ukrainian Weekly*, 2 June, 1996.
[29] *The Ukrainian Weekly*, 2 June, and Reuter, 28 May, 1996.

As expected, Kuchma replaced Marchuk with Lazarenko. The new prime minister pledged to press on with the reform programme and to concentrate on restructuring industry, accelerating privatization, encouraging foreign investment and solving the wage payment crisis.[30]

While the shock about the manner in which the prime minister had been dismissed was still reverberating in political circles and renewing concern about the extent of presidential powers, the political drama was heightened by developments in the Verkhovna Rada. On 28 May, with the leftists still delaying examination of the draft constitution, the speaker, Moroz, who remained leader of the SPU, came under fierce attack from the centrists and rightists, who accused him of putting his party interests first and blocking the parliament's work. On behalf of 170 deputies, the leader of the 'Reforms' faction, Serhii Sobolev, read out a statement calling for Moroz's removal.[31] The following day, before this motion could be debated, the embattled speaker adjourned the unruly parliament for a week.

The political climate grew increasingly charged as what was widely seen as the last chance approached for the parliament to act before the president resorted to drastic action. Still seeking to appear conciliatory, Kuchma pledged that he would not call a referendum on the new constitution until after it had had its second reading, but there was no certainty that the draft would even reach that stage. With the threat of a divisive referendum hanging over the deputies, and the speaker preoccupied with saving his position, the impasse was temporarily broken: on 4 June the draft constitution got through its first reading quite comfortably by 258 votes to 109. This was still considerably less, though, than the two thirds majority (301 votes) needed for the draft to be adopted on its second reading, which was scheduled to begin two weeks later, just after the Russian presidential elections.

While reformist forces breathed a sigh of relief, opponents of the new constitution made it clear that they intended to challenge many of its provisions. The Crimean parliament also protested that the revised draft, though recognizing Crimea's autonomous status

---

[30] Ukrinform, 29 May 1996.
[31] *Ibid.*

within a unitary Ukrainian state, deprived it of the powers to enact laws and made no mention of a Crimean constitution.[32]

Nevertheless, the president was now armed with the argument that a convincing majority of the parliament had approved the revised draft as the basis for the new constitution. The *ad hoc* conciliatory commission, still headed by Syrota, began working flat out to ensure that the constitutional process was not derailed by the staggering 5,680 additional proposed changes which were now submitted, mainly by the leftists; it worked day and night to ensure that all of these amendments were taken into account before the document was submitted for the second reading.[33]

When the constitutional agreement formally expired, Kuchma maintained that it would remain in force until the new constitution was adopted. Moroz, having succeeded in keeping the question of a vote of confidence in him as speaker off the parliament's agenda, however, saw his chance to reassert himself and declared that the power-sharing arrangement needed to be extended, presumably after difficult and protracted new debates; the existing 1978 constitution of the Ukrainian SSR, with its post-Soviet amendments, was back in force, he declared.[34] Two parliamentary commissions, however, spiked his guns by concluding that the constitutional agreement still remained valid.[35]

Balancing between East and West but gravitating westward

In the meantime, against the background of general concern about the outcome of Russia's presidential election, Ukraine had not only been strengthening its western connections, but actively seeking greater integration within European structures. As a partial response to Ukraine's proposals of the previous September about developing a special partnership between NATO and Ukraine, in mid-April, NATO Secretary-General Javier Solana had visited

---

[32] Reuter, 6 June 1996.

[33] See the interview with Syrota, *Uryadovyi kuryer*, 3 August 1996, and the chronicle of the Fifth Session of the Verkhovna Rada in *Holos Ukrainy*, 2 July 1996.

[34] Interfax-Ukraine, 11 June, UNIAN, ITAR-TASS, 11-12 June, and Ukrinform, 13 June 1996.

[35] Radio Ukraine, 18 June 1996.

Kyiv and announced that the North Atlantic Alliance's Political Committee had decided to broaden cooperation with Ukraine.

A week later, Kuchma visited the Council of Europe's head-quarters in Strasbourg and made use of this opportunity to stress that Ukraine was committed to a policy 'aimed at rapid integration into the European process and increasing its participation in the activities of European and trans-Atlantic organizations and structures'. Making it absolutely clear what Ukraine aspired to, he declared that his country's long-term 'strategic goal' was 'to become a full member of the European Union', and that it in the meantime, while remaining a neutral and non-aligned state, it wanted to 'develop and deepen relations' with both with the EU and NATO and the Western European Union (WEU), the military arm of the European Union. He also announced that Ukraine was not opposed to NATO's expansion eastward as long as it was carried out in a gradual and non-confrontational manner. In this connection, he proposed the creation of a nuclear-free zone in East-Central Europe.[36]

Kyiv also welcomed the timely demonstration by the European Union of its readiness to extend more significant political and economic support. In early May an EU delegation had visited the Ukrainian capital and announced that Ukraine would be given a $260 million loan to help it with its balance of payments problems during 1996 (on condition it continued along the reform path agreed with the IMF), as well as broader access to EU markets.[37] Ukraine's foreign minister, Udovenko, responded by reiterating that his country's 'strategic goal' was 'to attain full membership of the European Union'; he acknowledged, though, that this could only be envisaged at a later stage in Ukraine's development.[38]

High-level contacts between Kyiv and European and NATO structures intensified. Udovenko was invited to a meeting in Rome on 21 May of the EU's ministerial 'Troika' (the current, past and future presidencies) – the foreign ministers of Italy, France and Spain. At this meeting, in connection with the approaching fifth anniversary of Ukraine's independence, the EU issued a special declaration reaffirming 'the fundamental importance of Ukraine's independence, territorial integrity and sovereignty as key elements

[36] *Ibid.*, 24 April 1996.
[37] Monitor, 9 May 1996.
[38] Ukrinform, 8 May 1996.

of security in Europe' and pledging to 'assist the process of the integration of Ukraine into the world economic order, through support for its efforts to meet the requirements for World Trade Organisation membership' and to 'further examine the possibility of recognizing Ukraine's status as an economy in transition'.[39] A few days later, Britain's Ambassador to the WEU John Golden visited Kyiv, his 'only foreign visit', as he explained, during Great Britain's presidency of the WEU.[40]

Ukraine's foreign policy was given another boost at the beginning of June when, just as the country was removing the last nuclear warhead on its territory, it was accepted as a member of the Central European Initiative and President Kuchma was invited to attend a meeting of nine Central and Eastern European presidents in Lancut, southeastern Poland, organized under the auspices of the CEI.[41] Before then, however, Udovenko participated in a conference of NATO foreign ministers in Berlin and Kuchma addressed the WEU's Assembly in Paris. On this occasion he was even more candid about Ukraine's orientation and confirmed that Ukraine was seeking the status of an 'associate partner' of the WEU already enjoyed by other Central and Eastern European states. Ukraine's integration into Europe was not just a question of a 'deeply-pragmatic' choice, he declared, but a matter of time. He explained diplomatically that his country viewed the CIS exclusively as 'a mechanism for the peaceful and democratic resolution of all problems connected with the collapse of the Soviet Union'. On the other hand, he regarded the EU as the organization which would determine the face of the continent in the twenty-first century. Assistance to Ukraine at this decisive period in its history, he continued, was a 'strategic investment in safeguarding European interests'.[42]

In Lacut, on 7 and 8 June, Kuchma did not fail to voice his unease about the imminent presidential elections in Russia and to allude to· the common security problems facing Kyiv and Warsaw. 'If Yeltsin loses', he warned, 'it would be an earthquake, especially for Ukraine, but also for Poland.'[43] By contrast, shortly afterwards, on 10 June,

[39] *Ibid.*, 23 May, and *The Ukrainian Weekly*, 2 June 1996.
[40] Ukrinform, 24 May 1996.
[41] *Ibid.*, 7 and 8 June, 1996.
[42] *Ibid.*, 6 June 1996.
[43] Reuter, 12 June 1996.

Radio Ukraine reported speaker Moroz as playing down the threat of a Zyuganov victory, describing the Communist leader as a 'mature politician and a realist'.

Kuchma had joined other CIS heads of state is expressing support for Yeltsin at a CIS summit in Moscow on 16 May. A week later, Russian Prime Minister Chernomyrdin arrived suddenly in Kyiv, fueling speculation that perhaps, on virtually the eve of the Russian presidential elections, the elusive Russian-Ukrainian treaty might again be within reach. After meeting with Prime Minister Marchuk, however, he left without a single document being signed, the issue of Sevastopol apparently still blocking any last-minute breakthrough.[44]

In the Russian presidential election, after a late recovery, Yeltsin managed to scrape past Zyuganov, with both candidates receiving close to a third of the votes. This meant that a second round of voting had to take place, which was eventually scheduled for 3 July. The surprise impressive showing of Alexandr Lebed, who came in third with almost 15% of the votes, catapulted the outspoken former general, who had made his name as the tough and independently-minded commander of the Russian 14th army in the 'Dniester Republic', into the role of kingmaker. A deal between Yeltsin and Lebed was, or as some observers suspected, had already been, worked out and the Russian president immediately appointed the former officer as the new secretary of the Security Council and ditched several of his closest hardline officials.

While clearly relieved that Yeltsin had taken the lead, the Ukrainian leadership had no illusions about what the new Yeltsin-Lebed alliance was likely to mean for Ukraine. Since his days in the Transdniestrian enclave, Lebed had enhanced his reputation as a staunch defender of Russians living outside of the Russian Federation by becoming a leader of the Congress of Russian Communities, a 'national patriotic' organisation committed to this cause. Although he had been critical about the way in which Moscow had conducted its war in Chechnya, he had run on a platform of restoring order, military pride and Russia's greatness.

Yeltsin and his advisers had continued emphasizing that gradual 'reintegration' was a goal of Russia's foreign policy towards the 'near abroad.' Shortly before the elections, the influential Russian Council

[44] *Ibid.*, 23 May 1996.

on Foreign and Defence Policy, headed by presidential advisor Sergei Karaganov, had issued a draft document on 'The Future of the Post-Soviet Space', entitled 'Will the Union be Reborn?', which focused on the means for promoting the restoration of a Union (first a confederation, then a federation) centered on Russia within the coming decade. The document, which appeared on 23 May in *Nezavisimaya gazeta*, was signed by forty prominent academics, politicians and business people representing 'a broad section of the centrist and liberal Moscow elite'.[45] It described the process of reintegration in terms which had a familiar historic ring as 'a new, absolutely voluntary "gathering of the lands" '. The authors argued that:

> by constructing its relations in different ways, Russia may in the near future create an asymmetric system of mutual obligations, in which Russia will be a center of this system in any event. Despite all the talk about new models – either a CIS or Euro-Asian Union, either confederation or federation, on the territory of the former Soviet Union – a system of Russian regional leadership across the majority of this geopolitical zone is emerging, quietly but positively, whatever the wishes of other participants.[46]

Recognizing that Ukraine's importance and non-compliant attitude posed an awkward problem, the authors proposed, on the one hand, maintaining political cooperation and regular high-level consultations with Kyiv, and on the other, implicitly proposed stepping up economic pressure and penetration which would erode Ukraine's economic sovereignty and make the country increasingly dependent economically on Russia.[47]

Not surprisingly, therefore, less than a week after the inconclusive first round of voting in Moscow, Kuchma was to tell the Ukrainian media quite bluntly that regardless of the outcome of the runoff in Moscow, 'Russian policy towards Ukraine won't change . . . which is why Ukraine should brace itself . . . both politically and economically'.[48] He and other Ukrainian leaders continued to

[45] See Scott Parish, 'Will the Union be Reborn?' *Transition*, vol. 2, no. 15 (26 July 1996), p. 32.

[46] *Ibid.*

[47] See the analysis by Volodymyr Zviglyanich, 'Russia Discusses Plans to Restore the Soviet Union by 2005', *Prism*, vol. II, no. 12, part 4 (14 June 1996).

emphasize Ukraine's desire for a closer 'special' partnership with Western European political and military institutions.

By contrast to the Ukrainian-Russian nexus, Kyiv's ties with Warsaw remained a model of good-neighbourly relations which were being cemented by growing mutual interests, understanding and cooperation. On 25 June, the very day that Yeltsin again floated the idea of a closer union with Ukraine, Kuchma announced during an official visit to Warsaw that his country would not oppose Poland's membership of NATO and reiterated that it was itself interested in eventually joining the EU and its military arm, the WEU; for their part, his Polish hosts undertook to support Kyiv's admission to the Central European Trade Agreement and to continue facilitating the establishment of closer connections with other European institutions. Earlier that month, having invited the Ukrainian leader to Lancut, the new Polish president, Aleksander Kwasniewski, had indicated what the underlying premise of his administration's policy towards Ukraine was, stating: 'The more Ukraine is in Europe, the safer Europe is.'[49]

The struggle for the new constitution is finally won

On 19 June, the Ukrainian parliament was supposed to have begun debating the new constitution in its second reading. Procedural wrangling, however, had resulted in more delays; although the conciliatory commission had managed to incorporate all the major proposed changes into the revised draft, the leftists, abetted in effect by Moroz, insisted that the document be voted on article by article. The main stumbling blocks were still the issues of the state language, state symbols, the degree of Crimea's autonomy and private ownership. It seemed as if the entire process would become bogged down for weeks and that the Communists and their allies remained determined to dilute the key principles on which the national democrats, liberals and economic reformers wanted to build the new Ukrainian state.

One tricky issue on which sufficient agreement had now emerged within the Verkhovna Rada was that of banning foreign military bases on Ukraine's territory. Resenting Russia's adamant claims to

[48] Ukrinform, 24 June 1996.
[49] Reuter, 25 June 1996.

exclusive basing rights in Sevastopol, the parliament voted to include an article on the prohibition of foreign military bases in the draft constitution. The Ukrainian president had appealed to the deputies to take existing political realities into account and not to complicate further the unresolved Ukrainian-Russian dispute over the terms of Russia's use of Sevastopol as its main Black Sea naval base, and was clearly taken aback by the decision.[50]

On 26 June, Kuchma decided not to wait any further and made a courageous, if highly risky, given the prevailing social and economic difficulties, move: he signed a decree calling for a referendum on 25 September on approving the country's first post-Soviet constitution. Although he had threatened to do this all along if the parliament continued to procrastinate, his decision to actually go ahead and gamble everything on a referendum appears to have caught Moroz and the leftists by surprise. The speaker warned that this decision would only deepen the political crisis. Even the centrists and national democrats appear to have been in two minds about the prospect of a potentially divisive plebiscite. As Yavorivsky, the leader of the DPU, put it, the referendum would 'would tear Ukraine apart with an uncertain outcome. It could be tantamount to a vote of confidence in the president.'[51]

But just as a year earlier, during the constitutional crisis over the division of powers, Kuchma's calculated threat of a referendum did the trick. The deputies were also influenced by the fact that the president apparently intended to submit the earlier version of the draft of the constitution which had been presented to the parliament in March and which foresaw considerably stronger presidential powers, rather than the latest one, to the test of public confidence, and by the likelihood that he would also dissolve the legislature. The following day, fired by a greater sense of urgency, the deputies therefore worked non-stop to iron out their differences and to avert a confrontation with the president. They continued their session through the night, with Syrota, a hitherto relatively obscure engineer and member of the DPU from Cherkasy, playing an outstanding role in steering the intense debates over every article in a constructive direction.

The hard left put up a fierce last-ditch fight. On the key issue of

[50] Ukrinform, 24 June 1996.
[51] *Ibid.*, 26 June, and AP, 27 June 1996.

national symbols, the former prime ministers Masol and Marchuk both helped to break the deadlock by arguing in favour of retaining the blue and yellow flag and golden trident. At one point, all the government ministers who were deputies, except Holovaty and Yemets, were absent from the chamber, indicating that the executive branch had given up hope of a breakthrough and was falling back on the referendum. Even the Rukh faction seemed at one stage close to walking out.[52]

Eventually, though, after an all-night session, on the morning of 28 June, the parliament approved a new constitution. Consisting of 161 articles based on the draft proposed by the conciliation committee, it was adopted by a constitutional majority of 315 votes to 36, with 12 abstentions. Spontaneous celebrations, reminiscent of the adoption of the Declaration of State Sovereignty and proclamation of independence, instantly broke out in the legislature, and parliament voted that this date would henceforth be observed as Constitution Day and a public holiday. 'Wisdom has triumphed', the elated president told the deputies. 'This historic event . . . will go down as one of the most significant moments in the annals of the modern history of the Ukrainian state.'[53]

If Kravchuk was associated with the achievement and affirmation of Ukrainian independence, Kuchma had thus secured his place in history as the president who had not only got economic reforms under way, but had also ushered in the country's first post-Soviet constitution. Under Kravchuk's stewardship, Ukraine had chosen independence; under Kuchma, it had finally, and after considerable difficulties, reaffirmed this choice and refined its decision as to the new political and economic system it wanted to build. Just as five years earlier Ukraine had affirmed its desire to be independent, the Ukrainian parliament had now confirmed clearly and unequivocally the country's commitment to democracy, a market economy and a progressive social welfare system. As if amplifying this choice, in various other statements which he was to make during the following weeks, Kuchma also continued emphasizing Ukraine's Western

---

[52] See the retrospective accounts about the adoption of the constitution by Volodymyr Korol in *Holos Ukrainy* and Oleksa Ivashchuk in *Vechirnii Kyiv*, 23 August 1996, and Syrota in *Uryadovyi kuryer*, 3 August 1996.

[53] *The Ukrainian Weekly*, 30 June 1996.

orientation and desire to be integrated as fully and quickly as was feasible in European political, economic and security structures.

The adoption of Ukraine's new post-Soviet constitution marked a turning point in the long-drawn out political struggle between the country's two main rival political tendencies – the neo-Communists, consisting of groups nostalgic for the former Soviet Union and reluctant to move away from what it represented, many of whom were uncomfortable with the very idea of Ukraine's independence, and the emergent liberal centre and moderate right, whose representatives wanted a Western-style democracy and economy and to protect the country's independence.

Apart from its major historic significance as a fundamental law which, by enshrining basic democratic principles and recognizing the right to own private property, including land, confirmed Ukraine's abrogation of its Soviet legacy, the new constitution also represented the culmination of years of effort by Ukraine's national democratic forces in a tactful manner to promote national resurgence, revive national consciousness and restore national pride. The cautious formulation 'the people of Ukraine' was replaced in the preamble by the term 'the Ukrainian people – citizens of Ukraine of all nationalities'. The national symbols adopted by the Ukrainian independence movement before the Soviet period and still evidently reviled by many of the die-hard Communists were finally confirmed as state symbols. Ukrainian was recognized as the country's sole state language, but 'the free development, use and protection of Russian, and other languages of national minorities of Ukraine' was 'guaranteed' (Article 10). The State undertook to promote 'the consolidation and development of the Ukrainian nation, of its historical consciousness, traditions and culture, and also the development of the ethnic, linguistic and religious identity of all indigenous peoples and national minorities of Ukraine' (Article 11). The constitution also described Ukraine as a unitary state (Article 2) but the Autonomous Republic of Crimea was given considerable autonomy, including the right to have its own constitution and legislature (Articles 134 -139).

The new constitution contained a compromise as regards the ban on foreign military bases on Ukrainian territory. The ban (Article 17) was qualified by a 'transitional provision' stating that: 'The use of existing military bases on the territory of Ukraine for the temporary stationing of foreign military formations is possible'

on the basis of a leasing arrangement corresponding to 'the procedure determined by international treaties of Ukraine ratified by the
Verkhovna Rada of Ukraine'.

Although the adoption of the constitution was seen as a major
political victory for the president, in fact the provisions of the
country's new fundamental law diluted the presidential powers that
had been forseen in the draft submitted to the parliament in the
spring. The result was the establishment of a democratic parliamen-
tary-presidential republic, with the Cabinet of Ministers, having
achieved greater powers and autonomy as a distinct executive
branch, emerging as the unexpected real winner.[54] The parliament
had resisted the president's proposal to transform it into a bi-cameral
body, retained considerable powers and ensured that there would
be no early parliamentary elections. The next parliamentary elections were scheduled for March 1998 and the next presidential
elections for the last Sunday of October 1999.

The president retained the right 'to appoint the prime minister
with the consent of more than one-half of the constitutional
composition of the Verkhovna Rada', to appoint the 'power'
(defence and security) and foreign ministers independently of parliament, and to appoint other ministers 'on the submission of' the
prime minister. Without waiting, therefore, for the formal formation of a new government required after the adoption of the new
constitution, Kuchma and Lazarenko continued carrying out personnel changes in the Cabinet of Ministers which they had begun
after Marchuk's replacement. Now the defence minister, Shmarov,
and Vasyl Yevtukhov, the deputy prime minister responsible for fuel
and energy, were replaced. Subsequent criticism of Shmarov from
military and presidential circles suggested that it was not only the
national democrats who were unhappy about his performance. He
was replaced by a military officer, Lieutenant General Oleksandr
Kuzmuk, the commander of the National Guard. The president also
sought to ensure that the new prime minister was approved by
parliament before it adjourned for its summer recess and again
nominated Lazarenko.

---

[54] See the useful analyses by Viktor Desyatnikov in *Kievskie novosti*, 23 August
1996, and Vladimir Seminozhenko, *Kievskie vedomosti*, 2 July 1996.

18

THE STRATEGIC OUTLOOK

The fifth anniversary of independence

With the first fundamental stage of state-building now successfully completed, and no doubt also relieved by Yeltsin's comfortable victory in the runoff, the Ukrainian leadership prepared to celebrate with added aplomb the fifth anniversary of the declaration of independence. But the preparations were marred by the wage backlog and an ensuing new wave of strikes launched at the beginning of July by one of the miners' trade unions, which was supported by about a fifth of the country's more than 200 mines.

The protest action soon took on a more threatening character when some of the more radical miners in the Donbas blocked road and rail lines to demand several months of unpaid wages. Lazarenko, who was overwhelmingly endorsed on 10 July by the parliament as prime minister, declared the crisis in the coal industry as the country's most urgent problem. He and other government officials made it clear that the government was severely stretched to meet the demands for the payment of wage arrears and blamed factories which had not paid for coal deliveries for aggravating the situation. For his part, Kuchma called for emergency economic measures and appealed to Western leaders for soft-term credits to enable the Ukrainian leadership to deal with the crisis.[1]

When, on 15 July, government negotiators headed by First Deputy Prime Minister Durdynets agreed to pay most of the wage arrears by mid-September and the moderate miners' unions had condemned the wildcat strikes still affecting about thirty-six pits, the crisis appeared to have been defused. But the following day, as the prime minister was being driven to Kyiv airport from where he was due to fly to Donetsk, a bomb exploded along the route damaging his car. The identity of those responsible was unknown. Lazarenko

[1] Reuter, 4 and 10 July 1996.

himself ventured that this had been the work of 'criminal structures' opposed to the government's plans to restructure the coal industry and close down unprofitable mines. He also claimed that funds allocated by the government to pay off the wage backlog in the Donbas were being misappropriated.[2]

With the entire country shaken by the bomb outrage, the secretary of the National Security Council, Horbulin, announced that 'elements of a state of emergency' would be introduced. What these measures actually amounted to was a toughening of the Ukrainian leadership's policy in the Donbas: the head of the regional administration of the Donetsk region, Volodymyr Shcherban, who was regarded as a long-standing regional rival of Lazarenko in Eastern Ukraine, and other local officials were replaced and several leaders of the miners' protests who had blocked rail routes were arrested. The crackdown on the militant strike leaders precipitated accusations that Kyiv was violating workers' rights, which in turn drew protests and expressions of concern from international trade union organizations.[3]

In a long newspaper interview, Durdynets attempted to place the developments in the Donbas in a broader context. He explained that because of its difficult social and economic conditions the Donbas had become the country's 'most complex' region and also a major centre of organized crime. He revealed that in recent months the law enforcement agencies had 'liquidated' no less than eleven strong bandit groups responsible for robberies and murders. Corrupt or incompetent mine managers and local officials had also been removed. In an attempt to pull the Donbas's coalmining industry 'out of the abyss', 103 unprofitable or dangerous mines had been slated for closure, about fifty of which the government was planning to close before the end of the year. Durdynets claimed that although the government was well aware of the social consequences of the

---

[2] Ibid., 16 and 17 July 1996.

[3] Among those who protested on behalf of the arrested strike leaders was the Donbas-based Civic Congress, which united former Interfront activists opposed to Ukrainian independence. It appealed for support to the Council of Europe and various international trade unions. UNIAR, 19 August 1996. Concern about alleged 'anti-union repression' in Ukraine was subsequently expressed by, among others, the Chemical, Energy, Mine and General Workers' Union (ICEM) (see its statement, no. 42/1996 of 17 August 1996 and the President of the AFL-CIO, John Sweeney (Ukrinform, 6 September 1996).

closures, and, at a time of continuing economic difficulties and hardship in the country, was seeking to deal with this problem with the help of international assistance, local militants were stirring up the miners in an attempt to force the central authorities to their knees.[4]

The message Kyiv seemed intent on sending was that the government, with international help, was determined to move ahead with its restructuring of the coal industry and that, having paid the miners their arrears out of the central government's almost empty coffers, it would no longer be prepared to bail out the inefficient coal mines in the south-east; furthermore, it would not tolerate actions by militants who broke the law and threatened national security.

Fresh trouble also loomed on the horizon in Crimea where, in mid-August, pro-Russian deputies, led by Tsekov and the Rossiya bloc, narrowly failed to pressure the Crimean parliament to press for greater autonomy than forseen in the Ukrainian constitution and also to oust the Crimean prime minister, Demydenko. There was a sinister twist when, on the night of 24-5 August, just after his return from independence anniversary celebrations in Kyiv, the Crimean speaker, Suprunyuk, was apparently abducted from his home by unknown armed persons; fortunately, though badly beaten up, he eventually managed to escape from them. To add to the complex picture, at the beginning of July, the Crimean Tatars had held their third Kurultai, or national congress, at which the impatience of the more radical groups with the moderate Crimean Tatar leadership had been become apparent.[5]

Despite these problems, perseverance with the state-building and reform processes was beginning to pay off. *The Economist*, which had been a stern observer of Ukraine's often dismal post-independence reform record, now noted that 'reforms begun in 1994 are showing signs of success' and advised investors 'that Ukraine finally deserves a serious look'.[6] This encouraging trend, combined with the adoption of the new constitution and Ukraine's growing ties with Western institutions, as well as the added pride of seeing the country's athletes win twenty-three medals, nine of them gold, at

---

[4] See *Kievskie vedomosti*, 23 August 1996.

[5] See the report by Tatyana Korobova in *Kievskie vedomosti*, 9 July 1996.

[6] 'Ukrainian Finance: Wild, Wild East', *The Economist*, 31 August 1996.

the Olympic games in Atlanta, helped raise spirits during the fifth anniversary of independence.

The official celebrations lasted from Friday 23 August to Monday 26 August. In his anniversary address, President Kuchma opted for a balanced tone, tempering self-congratulation with self-criticism. 'Having started practically from nought, and in conditions which were far from optimal, all the attributes of statehood, from borders to an honours system, [have been created],' he declared. 'The transitional stage of the state's self-determination has been completed', symbolized by the adoption of the new constitution. Ukrainian society had 'received a clear and definitive answer to the question: what are we building and where are we headed?' But much work still lay ahead if the problems accumulated from the previous decades were to be resolved. Ukraine's experience with reforms had exposed the flaws and ugly features inherited from the past, and these, together with the mistakes that had been made, had not allowed Ukraine to achieve more. The president acknowledged: 'Our achievements could have been more substantial and the price of reform considerably lower for people had we been able to foresee at the start of our state-building the entire depth, complexity and multifaceted nature of the problems and to respond properly to them.'[7]

Indicating the Ukrainian leadership's confidence and determination to keep the reform process on track, during the anniversary celebrations it was announced that the interim karbovanets-coupon was finally being replaced with the long-awaited permanent national currency, the hryvnya. The transition was carried out relatively smoothly during the first half of September 1996. By the time the parliament reconvened in mid-September, the government had also managed to complete the draft of the state budget for 1997, which foresaw the first economic growth since independence and a further reduction of inflation.[8] Reform of the tax system was also at the top of the agenda.[9]

Rather impulsively, the Ukrainian president declared very prematurely on 16 September that he would be standing as a

[7] Excerpts translated by the author from the official text of the president's speech delivered in the Ukraina Palace, Kyiv, on 23 August 1996.

[8] Reuter, 13 September 1996.

[9] Ukrinform, 10 September 1996.

candidate in the presidential elections in 1999. This throwing down of the political gauntlet had the effect of encouraging the disparate political groupings within the Verkhovna Rada to begin coalescing around other prospective candidates – Moroz, Marchuk (who now headed the Social Market Economy faction) and Lazarenko. Since the new constitution was adopted, the prime minister was no longer so dependent on the president and therefore was clearly becoming more of a political force to be reckoned with. Although at this expressed disinterest in running for the presidency, it remained to be seen whether he and his team would manage to avoid coming into conflict with a presidential administration in which the powerful figures of Tabachnyk and Horbulin had become used to shaping domestic and foreign policy, and what sort of working relationship he would establish with Moroz and the Verkhovna Rada.

The new constitution had built checks and balances into the political system and inevitably it was going to take some time to see how effectively they would operate. In mid-October progress was achieved when a dispute between the president and the Verkhovna Rada, mainly its left-wing deputies, over the role of the Constitutional Court was resolved and on 18 October sixteen of its eighteen judges were sworn in. Ivan Tymchenko, formerly a legal advisor to both Presidents Kravchuk and Kuchma, was elected chairman.[10]

Less encouraging, however, as far as the independence of the country's media was concerned, was the president's assertion of control over this vital sphere at the expense of the parliament's and government's influence. Eventually, in mid-November, Kuchma was to issue a decree creating a Ministry of Information and appointing a controversial loyal conservative accused of censorship, Zinovy Kulyk, to head it. The new ministry was to be responsible for television and radio broadcasting and the National Information Agency of Ukraine (DINAU), which replaced the former Ukrinform (National News Agency of Ukraine), which had been under the control of the Cabinet of Ministers.[11] Tabachnyk, who was coming under increasing fire in the parliament for alleged misuse of his office and corruption, was believed to have been behind this move, which was widely seen as an attempt to strengthen Kuchma's re-election prospects.

[10] *Ibid.*, 18 and 21 October 1996.
[11] *Ibid.*, 15 November 1996. See also OMRI Daily Digest, 1 November 1996.

The Ukrainian-Russian impasse

At a time when the future political and economic configuration of Europe was being decided, and the dispute between Russia and NATO over the latter's enlargement was intensifying, the main challenge in the external sphere remained the buttressing of Ukraine's balancing position between East and West.[12] The main problem was not NATO's expansion; indeed, the Ukrainian president had made it quite clear that, as long as nuclear missiles were not deployed on the territory of its western neighbours, Kyiv did not object to Poland and the Baltic States becoming members of NATO, and in fact was itself seeking a 'special relationship' with the North Atlantic Alliance and associate membership of the WEU; rather, it was how to remain on good-neighbourly terms with Russia (which did have nuclear arms and was in the process of consolidating its new political, economic and military 'community' with Ukraine's northern neighbour Belarus), while staying out of its economic and political orbit.

Back on 11 June, Kuchma had declared that there had been a significant shift in Europe's view of the role and position of Ukraine and, for its part, Kyiv had clearly defined its 'strategies for integration into Europe'.[13] In speeches and comments delivered during the first half of July in Kyiv and at a East-Central European economics summit in Salzburg, Kuchma continued to expound on Ukraine's goal of achieving fuller integration into European structures and close partnership with NATO. However, he also reminded senior foreign ministry officials that stable relations with Russia were not only a cornerstone of Ukrainian national interests but an essential factor of European and global security. The top priority for Ukraine in the east, he stressed, remained to 'achieve the final normalization of relations' with its northern neighbour through the signing of a bilateral framework treaty.[14]

Yeltsin's victory over Zyuganov, though, did not bring any signs that the Ukrainian-Russian logjam would be broken. In fact, a new complication developed: even before his eventual election triumph, the Russian president had been afflicted by a debilitating heart

---

[12] In late September 1996 Ukraine affirmed its non-aligned status by becoming an observer in the Non-Aligned Movement.

[13] Ukrinform, 11 June 1996.

[14] *Ibid.*, 16 July 1996.

condition and all but vanished from public view; his illness set off a new political struggle in Moscow, leaving it unclear who was, or would be, in control.

Within days of Yeltsin's victory, Kyiv called for the resumption of Ukrainian-Russian negotiations on unresolved issues. When Udovenko met with Primakov, Lebed and Chernomyrdin in Moscow on 1 August, both sides stuck to their respective positions but it was agreed that negotiations about the Black Sea Fleet would continue, as well as bilateral talks on trade and economic relations, and consultations on the demarcation of the Russian-Ukrainian border.

Any hopes that the new talks would, as Udovenko put it, give 'a new boost to Ukrainian-Russian dialogue'[15] were soon dashed, though, by a decree issued by the Russian president on 18 August: despite the free-trade treaty between the two countries, Yeltsin imposed a 20% value-added tax on imports from Ukraine, beginning on 1 September. With 37.7% of Ukraine's total exports during the first half of 1996 having gone to Russia – its largest trading partner[16] – this protectionist measure threatened to seriously damage bilateral trade and hurt the fragile Ukrainian economy just as the country was introducing its own national currency. Furthermore, four days later, Yeltsin appointed Aman Tuleev, a Communist ally of Zyuganov known to favour the restoration of some form of the USSR, as Russia's new minister for cooperation with the CIS countries.[17]

Efforts by Lazarenko and Pynzenyk to persuade the Russian government not to levy the tax on Ukrainian imports succeeded only in achieving a partial deferral of the tariff for a month.[18] Barely restraining himself, Kuchma warned on 7 September that the new

---

[15] Reuter, 1 August 1996.

[16] *New Europe*, 15-21 September 1996.

[17] Monitor, 23 August 1996. When, on 9 September, Tuleev outlined his programme to promote integration processes in the CIS, he called for, among other things, 'merging the member-countries'energy systems into a single CIS energy system through co-ownership arrangements between Russia and the individual countries' and 'massive Russian acquisition of industrial equity in CIS countries to offset debts owed to Russia by those countries'. Monitor, 10 September 1996.

[18] *Ibid.*, 28 August and 3 September 1996. The tariff went into effect on 1 October 1966. Monitor, 2 October 1996.

Russian tax on Ukrainian imports could result in 'economic war' and claimed that it was politically motivated.[19]

A few days later, Russia went ahead and introduced a 10% tax on Ukrainian sugar imports. The atmosphere was further strained by what seemed to be an attempt by leading Russian political figures, while Yeltsin was indisposed, to reopen the issue of the ownership of the Black Sea Fleet and Sevastopol. They included Lebed and Moscow City Mayor Yuri Luzhkov, who declared that Sevastopol could not be considered part of Ukraine. All this prompted Ukraine's security chief, Horbulin, to comment on the eve of a visit to Washington: 'We said that pressure would increase on Ukraine' after the Russian presidential elections.[20]

An unexpected brief visit to Moscow by Kuchma on 28 September for talks with Chernomyrdin, and the latter's agreement to go to Kyiv to continue negotiations, helped clear the air somewhat. But Lebed, whose political reputation had risen even more as a result of his role in negotiating a peace settlement in Chechnya, subsequently publicly reiterated his position on Sevastopol in an open letter published in early October in Russian newspapers in Crimea. His action drew criticism from the Ukrainian Foreign Ministry – Udovenko described it as 'an unfriendly act and tantamount to interference in Ukraine's affairs'[21] – and an official repudiation from Russian Deputy Foreign Minister Sergei Krylov.[22]

With President Yeltsin awaiting a heart operation, the struggle for power in Moscow intensifying, and the attention in Russia shifting away from Chechnya, Kyiv could only expect more trouble of this sort. Defying the Russian president, on 16 October the Russian Duma went ahead and approved a bill (by 370 votes to 5) urging an immediate halt to the division of the Black Sea Fleet. An extremist deputy (Makashov) even called for the imposition of a fuel embargo on Ukraine and claimed that Eastern Ukraine and Crimea were prepared to join Russia.[23] Predictably, the Duma's action outraged the Ukrainian leadership and parliament. In the presence of President Kuchma, the Verkhovna Rada adopted a strongly-

---

[19] *The Ukrainian Weekly*, 15 August 1996.

[20] Reuter, 14 September 1996.

[21] *Ibid.*, 19 October 1996.

[22] See Monitor and OMRI Daily Digest, 14 October, 1996.

[23] OMRI Daily Digest, 17 October 1996.

worded statement which denounced the Duma's bill as 'a gross violation of the most basic norms of international law, an encroachment on Ukraine's sovereignty' and a 'territorial claim against Ukraine', and warned that if the Russian lower house proceeded with making it law, the Ukrainian parliament would demand the immediate removal of Russian forces from Ukrainian territory. Even the Socialist chairman of the Ukrainian parliament, Moroz, who had remained unenthusiastic about Kyiv's growing accentuation of its Western orientation, warned that such actions were undermining bilateral relations and called on Russia to build a naval base on the Russian coast of the Black Sea if it did not want share the facilities in Sevastopol with Ukraine.[24]

Kuchma sought to defuse the situation by asking for a meeting with the hospitalized Russian president. By now the maverick Lebed had increasingly alienated himself from Yeltsin's team and on 17 October was abruptly dismissed by Yeltsin. Perhaps sensing a fleeting new opportunity, Kuchma attempted to clinch a deal with the Russian president before he was operated on and Russia was plunged into even greater uncertainty. The Ukrainian president and Horbulin seem to have gambled on making additional concessions, even in the face of opposition from within the Ukrainian armed forces, for on the eve of Yeltsin's short meeting with Kuchma on 24 October the sudden resignation of Ukraine's three top naval officers was announced.[25]

The two sides did in fact seem to have narrowed their differences significantly, leading Horbulin to comment that they were now 'closer than ever'. Apparently, the Ukrainian side now agreed to lease the naval base in Sevastopol to Russia for twenty years (Russia had reportedly initially insisted on fifty years) and to make do with only one of the port's five bays.[26]

When, however, on 23 October the Russian Duma nevertheless proceeded to pass a law on the suspension of the division of the Black Sea Fleet (by an almost unanimous vote of 331 votes to 1),

[24] Monitor, 18 and 22 October 1996; and 'Verkhovna Rada of Ukraine Denounces Russian State Duma's Anti-Ukrainian Act', Press Release, Permanent Mission of Ukraine, Geneva, 18 October 1996.

[25] Reuter, 23 October, and OMRI Daily Digest, 24 October, 1996.

[26] See Monitor, 25 October, *The Fortnight in Review*, 1 November, and Reuter, 1 November, 1996.

and with Mayor Luzhkov continuing to reiterate his position on Sevastopol, the painstaking work that had been carried out to bring the two sides over the final hurdle in their protracted negotiations over the division of the Black Sea Fleet seemed to have been all for nought.

Initially, though, the meeting between Kuchma and Yeltsin seemed to produce the magical breakthrough. Yeltsin's press spokesman, Sergei Yastrzhembsky, announced that the two presidents had managed to resolve all the problems connected with the Fleet and Sevastopol and that Russian Prime Minister Chernomyrdin would be travelling to Kyiv before the middle of November to sign the relevant agreements. In a televised statement, President Yeltsin also promised that his first official trip after recovering from surgery would be to Ukraine to sign the long-delayed bilateral friendship treaty.[27]

But, as on previous occasions when breakthroughs had been announced in resolving Ukrainian-Russian disputes over the future of the Black Sea Fleet but had proved premature, no specific details were announced and negotiating teams continued their work. Moscow's mayor and other Russian politicians persisted with their claims that Sevastopol was part of Russia and a group of deputies within the Duma announced their intention to introduce a bill on the status of the city. Subsequently, while Yeltsin was recovering from a successful heart operation carried out on 5 November, the negotiations broke down again; indeed, on 6 November the Russian delegation left Kyiv before the closing session of the latest round of talks and a planned dinner. Horbulin was left to comment that both sides had reached the point where no further concessions could be made.[28]

According to Ukraine's first deputy defence minister, Ivan Bizhan, the Russian side remained 'categorically opposed' to Ukraine's naval command being based in Sevastopol, which he said was an internal matter for Ukraine and not for discussion.[29] It also emerged that the Russian side was insisting that the coastal infrastructure at Sevastopol be recognized as Russia's property and therefore not subject to leasing arrangements, and that it had rejected Ukraine's

[27] Reuter, 24 October 1996.

[28] OMRI Daily Digest, 7 November 1996.

[29] Ukrinform, 12 November 1996.

insistence on the removal of Russian ground units which exceeded CFE limits. For its part, Ukraine was proposing to charge rent of between $1.4 and $2.1 billion annually depending on the size of the aggregate land and sea areas to be leased by the Russian fleet and was prepared to deduct the value of the rent from its debts to Russia or energy bills.[30]

Hardly surprisingly, therefore, Chernomyrdin's visit to Kyiv in mid-November did not materialize. Kuchma sought to keep emotions in check and to avoid any drastic actions. During an official visit to Greece in mid-November, he stated that forcing the issue of the Black Sea Fleet would only escalate tensions between Ukraine and Russia. Relations between the two countries were not limited only to this question, he emphasized, and there were a host of economic problems that also needed to be resolved.[31]

The outlook did not look promising. On 13 November, the Duma passed by an overwhelming majority a resolution describing the Transdniester enclave as a 'zone of special strategic interest' for Russia and calling for Russian troops to be permanently stationed there. This action also drew protests and condemnation from the Ukrainian Foreign Ministry and Verkhovna Rada.[32]

Shortly afterwards, the Russian press reproduced a letter from the commander of the Russian Black Sea Fleet, Admiral Viktor Kravchenko, claiming that President Yeltsin had issued a directive 'not to surrender anything in Sevastopol'.[33] Furthermore, the Russian president's foreign policy aide, Dmitrii Ryurikov, publicly expressed the opinion that 'the assertion of Ukrainian statehood to the detriment of close relations with Russia . . . is a temporary phenomenon'.[34] This seemed to reinforce the fundamental complaint – heard so often from Kyiv throughout the last five years –

[30] Monitor, 14 November, and *The Fortnight in Review*, vol. 1, no. 10 (15 November 1996).

[31] *Ibid.*

[32] Monitor, 14 November 1996. On 24 November, the Ukrainian Foreign Ministry criticized this action as challenging Moldova's sovereignty and territorial integrity, violating 'universally recognized international legal principles and OSCE norms', and undermining the joint Moldovan, Russian and Ukrainian attempt to achieve a peaceful resolution to the Transdniestrian conflict. Ukrinform, 25 November 1996.

[33] *Nezavisimaya gazeta*, 14 November 1996.

[34] Monitor, 21 November 1996.

which Udovenko had reiterated the previous month at a CIS meeting in Moscow: 'Ukraine is concerned that that there are constant doubts being raised in Russia about Ukrainian sovereignty and independence.'[35]

Neighbours, friends, partners and antagonists

Developments in Belarus, where the authoritarian behaviour of the pro-Russian president, Lukashenka, who continued to enjoy mass popular support, especially in the rural areas, had led to a conflict with the Belarusian parliament, also posed a problem for Ukraine as well as Belarus' other neighbours. Ukrainian democrats had already been outraged by the fact that that in April the Belarusian authorities had imprisoned seven Ukrainian radical nationalists who had participated in a peaceful anti-Lukashenka demonstration in Minsk and had recently dismissed an appeal against their sentences. With the Belarusian president forcing a showdown with his country's parliament by calling a referendum in order to extend his powers and prolong his term in office, and the threat of destabilization and unrest growing, on 19 November the Ukrainian parliament issued a carefully-worded statement affirming 'non-interference' in Belarus' internal affairs but expressing 'deep concern' about the situation.[36] Furthermore, while Russia sought to mediate directly between the Belarusian president and parliament, the Ukrainian president joined his Polish and Lithuanian counterparts in a joint statement of concern about developments in Belarus.[37]

On 24 November, Lukashenka went ahead with his referendum, which, among others, the OSCE and Council of Europe criticized

[35] Reuter, 19 October 1996. Some external observers saw the impasse in Ukrainian-Russian relations as part of a general hardening trend in Russia's foreign policy. For example, *The Economist* noted that Russia had been 'carving out a tougher yet more pragmatic foreign policy', reflected in its hostility to NATO's planned expansion and the Duma's refusal to ratify the START-2 arms-reduction treaty. 'In the "near abroad" . . . the foreign ministry [and the executive branch] were often content to see the Duma do the bullying'. It surmized that: 'The latest and biggest victim of this crude Russian mood has been Ukraine.' *The Economist*, 23 November 1996.

[36] Reuter, 19 November 1996.

[37] *Ibid.*, and Ukrinform, 21 November 1996.

as undemocratic. After having no problem winning, he proceeded to create a new parliament from the majority of the deputies who had supported him. Russia lost no time in recognizing the results while Ukraine continued to voice its concern along with Poland and Lithuania. In fact, at the beginning of December during the OSCE summit in Lisbon, at which Russia continued to oppose NATO's eastward enlargement and sought to cushion Belarus from direct censure in the final statement, the leaders of Poland, Lithuania and Ukraine held their own mini-summit and, among other things, issued a statement expressing 'grave concern' over developments in neighbouring Belarus and calling for democracy in their region.[38] Kuchma also made use of the occasion to voice Ukraine's enduring security concerns and to affirm once again his country's Western orientation. He also stressed that Ukraine was seeking to formalize good-neighbourly relations with Russia in accordance with OSCE principles.[39]

For Ukraine, there was also one other particularly noteworthy development at the Lisbon OSCE summit. President Kuchma met with Romania's newly elected president, Emil Constantinescu; after their meeting, the Ukrainian leader told the press that a Ukrainian-Romanian friendship treaty would be signed in 1997. For his part, Constantinescu reaffirmed that his country would seek membership of NATO and the EU, and declared that his government wanted good relations with neighbouring countries and to sign a basic treaty with Ukraine similar to the one which it had recently concluded with Hungary. Describing this as a matter of 'overriding importance', he conspicuously made no mention of Romania's territorial differences with Ukraine.[40]

The trilateral Polish-Lithuanian-Ukrainian initiative as regards Belarus underscored the emerging pattern of inter-state relations and alignments in Eastern Europe five years after the referendum on

---

[38] Ukrinform and Reuter, 2 December 1996.

[39] *Vseukrainskie vedomosti*, 4 December 1996.

[40] *Den* (Kyiv), 4 December 1996, and Roland Eggleston, 'OSCE Summit: Romania Seeks Basic Treaty with Ukraine', RFE/RL News Report, 2 December 1996. Coincidentally, the following day, the Moldovan parliament ratified the friendship and cooperation treaty with Ukraine that had been signed in October 1992. The Ukrainian parliament had also only ratified the treaty the previous month, having insisted that border disputes between the two states be settled beforehand. OMRI Daily Digest, 5 December 1996.

Ukraine's independence, the final dissolution of the Soviet Union and the creation of the CIS. For Ukraine, Russia and Belarus were part of an evolving Eurasian bloc, to which it was still attached, whether it liked it or not, by strong economic cords, while Poland had become its main gateway to the West and undisguised strategic partner. This was graphically illustrated by two statements made by the Polish and Russian leaders during the first week of December. Addressing the Assembly of the WEU in Paris on 4 December, Poland's President Kwasniewski declared that 'the position of Ukraine' was a 'crucial issue of the European security architecture'. He recalled that in June President Kuchma had 'made a strong statement of his country's European aspirations', stressing that 'declarations of this kind must be built into our thinking on future security in Europe'. He added that 'strategic partnerships between various Euro-Atlantic institutions and Russia, as well as Ukraine' will be of key importance.[41] By contrast, the following day, President Yeltsin made a renewed call for closer ties within the CIS and accelerated integration. Defending the creation of the CIS, he explained that: 'The Soviet Union had become obsolete. We had to save what it was still possible to save.'[42]

---

[41] Statement by H.E. Mr. Alexander Kwasniewski, President of the Republic of Poland, at the Assembly of the Western European Union, Paris, 4 December 1996.

[42] Reuter, 6 December 1996. Interestingly, that same week, another 'architect' of the Belovezhsky Agreement establishing the CIS, Burbulis, gave a somewhat different assessment of this event. 'The Soviet Union had already disappeared . . . We were recognising formally the reality in which we were all living since the August coup [1991] . . . . disintegration had become irreversible . . . . We found a formula which ensured that the breakup of the Soviet Union took place with the minimum of losses and upheavals.' Burbulis confirmed, according to Reuter, that 'Yeltsin agreed to this only after Kravchuk, buoyed by a 90 per cent referendum vote in Ukraine in favour of complete independence, ruled out other options such as confederation'. Yeltsin's former aide also now felt though that the Russian side had made some blunders as regards Ukraine. 'It was our mistake that at the time we did not record Sevastopol, the Black Sea Fleet and Crimea as problems to be negotiated separately', he explained. He also acknowledged that Yeltsin's team had not anticipated that Ukraine would move so quickly to assert its control over Soviet troops on its territory. 'We believed there would be joint armed forces for a period of five or seven years.' See John Morrison, 'Russian Architect of 1991 CIS Pact Admits Regrets', Reuter, 6 December 1996. Another of the Russian team at the Belovezhkaya Pushcha, Sergei Shakhrai, shared his broadly similar views about why the CIS had been created in an interview published in *Den* on 10 December 1996. Five years later, however, Gorbachev was still continuing to call for a 'new

On 28 November, President Yeltsin vetoed the Duma's bill on halting the partitioning of the Black Sea Fleet. Kuchma responded by calling for the issue of the Black Sea Fleet to be separated from the Ukrainian-Russian treaty, the signing of which he argued remained a priority. 'It is impossible to find a solution today which would satisfy both sides on the question of the division of the fleet', he acknowledged. [43]

These moves were overtaken a week later, though, by another provocative action by the Russian legislature, this time by the upper house – the Council of the Federation. On 6 December, it approved by 110 to 14 a non-binding resolution proposed by Luzhkov demanding that Ukraine hand over Sevastopol, claiming that 'unilateral actions by the Ukrainian side aimed at tearing away from Russia a part of its territory (Sevastopol) are not only illegal under international law but also directly damage Russia's security'. The Federation Council also approved a document to set up a commission to prepare a draft law on the status of Sevastopol. [44] Among the few Russian politicians who publicly condemned this action was former prime minister Yegor Gaidar (who accused Luzhkov of 'electioneering'), the governor of Belgorod *oblast*, which borders on Ukraine, Yevgenii Savchenko, and the ethnic Russian mayor of Sevastopol itself, Viktor Semenov. [45]

Horbulin was the first to respond for the Ukrainian side. He told journalists: 'This is a crude piece of interference in the life of a neighbouring country. . . . [The Federation Council's] position is not just unrestrained but simply aggressive. . . . This will lead to a sharp worsening in Russian-Ukrainian relations.' He also stressed that despite Kuchma's meeting with Chernomyrdin at the Lisbon OSCE summit, 'from now on it will be difficult to achieve anything'. [46] Horbulin and other Ukrainian officials had also let it be known in recent weeks that in view of the continuing Russian claims to Sevastopol, Ukraine was considering raising the issue before the UN Security Council and also reviewing its position on seeking

---

voluntary union' of the former Soviet republics. Reuter, 16 December 1996.

[43] Russian Public Television, 30 November 1996.

[44] Reuter, 5 December 1996.

[45] OMRI Daily Digest, 9 December, Monitor and UNIAN, 6 December, 1996.

[46] Reuter and UNIAN, 6 December 1996.

membership of NATO.[47]

The Verkhovna Rada was quick to respond. Moroz declared the Federation Council's action had 'aggravated the situation to the very limit'.[48] The Ukrainian parliament immediately adopted a declaration denouncing the 'territorial claim and violation of Ukrainian sovereignty' as 'a deliberate attempt to undermine European security', and voted by 227 votes to 38 to begin debating a bill on the withdrawal of Russian forces from Ukrainian territory.[49] The Ukrainian leadership nevertheless sought to prevent the situation from escalating further. Foreign Minister Udovenko declared that Kyiv would not break off its 'negotiating process' with Moscow and Moroz appealed to the Verkhovna Rada to refrain from demanding the withdrawal of foreign troops from Ukrainian territory which could lead to 'dangerous consequences'.[50]

The Ukrainian leadership was reassured by the strong expressions of implicit support which their country received both at the Lisbon OSCE summit and at a meeting of NATO foreign ministers held in Brussels on 10 December. At the latter meeting, Udovenko reiterated Ukraine's security concerns and reaffirmed his country's desire, 'as part of . . . [the] Central-East European region', to become 'an inalienable part' of the 'future European security architechture'. The foreign minister presented Ukraine's position as follows:

> Within the context of the NATO enlargement it is important not to permit the revival of some kind of 'spheres of influence' or 'zones of special interests', that would inevitably bring us back to the division of Europe. . . . It is important for us now, in particular taking into account recent Russian Duma's decisions on the so-called Russian status of Sevastopol. . . . Ukraine considers establishment of a special partnership with NATO as one of the main conditions for ensuring its national interests in the context of NATO enlargement, a guarantee against a new division of Europe and creation of a grey zone of security in Central and Eastern Europe. Good neighbourly relations – as the most important security principle – should remain in the focus of our future activities. In particular, within the context of NATO enlargement, it should become the major

[47] Monitor, 27 November, and Reuter 6 December, 1996.
[48] Reuter, 6 December 1996.
[49] Radio Ukraine and Interfax, 6 December 1996.
[50] ITAR-TASS, 6 December and UNIAN, 7 December, 1996.

criterion and prerequisite for all countries without exception wishing to join the Alliance. Cooperation Partners have to conclude with all their neighbours bilateral agreements, which include clear-cut provisions on good-neighbourly relations, respect of the rights of persons belonging to national minorities, and, of course, on absence of territorial claims and recognition of existing borders.[51]

Despite continuing Russian opposition to NATO's enlargement, the ministerial meeting decided that the Alliance would hold a summit in Madrid in July 1997 at which new members would be invited to join. It also announced that the NATO would not deploy nuclear weapons on the territory of new members from Eastern and Central Europe. The meeting also addressed relations with Ukraine. The final communiqué stated that NATO intended to strengthen 'cooperative relationships with all Partners, including building a strong security partnership with Russia and a distinctive relationship with Ukraine'. In it, the NATO ministers declared:

> We continue to support Ukraine as it develops as a democratic nation and a market economy. The maintenance of Ukraine's independence, territorial integrity and sovereignty is a crucial factor for stability and security in Europe. Ukraine's development of a strong, enduring relationship with NATO is an important aspect of the emerging European security architecture. . . . We are committed to the development in coming months, through high level and other consultations, of a distinctive and effective NATO-Ukraine relationship, which could be formalized, possibly by the time of the Summit, building on the document on enhanced NATO-Ukraine relations agreed in September 1995, and taking into account recent Ukrainian proposals.[52]

While attention had been focused on the impasse in Ukrainian-Russian relations, Kyiv had also been busy developing closer cooperation with several of the CIS states which were also not enthusiastic about Moscow's efforts to promote greater integration in the CIS. For instance, on 15 September, the Ukrainian and

[51] Statement by His Excellency Hennadiy Udovenko, Minister for Foreign Affairs of Ukraine, at the Meeting of the North Atlantic Cooperation Council, Brussesls, 11 December 1996.

[52] Final Communiqué, Ministerial Meeting of the North Atlantic Council Held at NATO Headquarters, Brussels, on 10 December 1995.

Uzbekistani foreign ministers had signed an agreement in Tashkent on coordinating their policies towards CIS issues, leading Udovenko to announce that the two states had agreed to oppose the continued Russian chairmanship of the CIS Council of Heads of State and would be jointly proposing that Yeltsin be succeeded as chairman by either the presidents of Turkmenistan or Azerbaijan.[53] Further more, Ukraine had recently also concluded military assistance agreements with Uzbekistan, Georgia and Turkmenistan.

The search for alternative sources of fuel remained a major preoccupation. During the summer of 1996, for example, Ukrainian experts had conducted negotiations with the Turkish authorities about the possible construction of an oil pipeline from Ceyhan to Samsun, and, reportedly, also with Iraqi officials about the shipping of Iraqi oil to Ukraine via the Turkish terminal of Iskanderon.[54] Back in September 1995, Ukrainian, Turkmen and Iranian officials had agreed in Ashgabat on a triangular deal wherein Ukraine would pay off its debts to Turkmenistan for natural gas by delivering rails to Iran for the building of its Meshkheds-Serakhs railway – part of the planned international 'North-South transport corridor' designed to open up access to the Persian Gulf for some of the CIS countries.[55] In late June 1996, the first meeting of an ensuing Ukrainian-Iranian-Turkmen intergovernmental committee on trade and economic relations and investment cooperation had been held in Kyiv.[56] Meanwhile, the construction of a new oil terminal in Odesa, begun in 1994, had been plagued by financing problems; nevertheless, at the end of 1996 a project to build a new oil terminal south of Odesa at Kherson was also being promoted and funding sought from the European Bank for Reconstruction and Development.[57]

In the first half of November, Lazarenko visited Georgia, where he signed an agreement on the opening of a 'Eurasian transport corridor' stretching from Turkmenistan and Azerbaijan via Georgia, and from the Georgian Black Sea port of Poti by sea to Odesa. On his return to Kyiv, the prime minister also announced that Ukraine and Georgia were conducting negotiations about the construction

---

[53] Monitor, 17 September 1996.

[54] See Alexander Pivovarov's article in *Kommersant Daily*, 17 August 1996.

[55] Monitor, 14 September 1995.

[56] Ukrinform, 28 June 1996.

[57] Reuter, 28 October 1996.

of an 850-kilometre pipeline from Baku to Poti to transport Caspian oil to the Black Sea across Georgian territory.[58] The following month, he travelled to Uzbekistan where he concluded a number of agreements dealing with, among other things, the supply of Uzbekistani natural gas.[59] Visits by President Kuchma to Israel (during which he addressed the Knesset and also met with Palestinian leader Yasser Arafat) and Turkey in late November, and South Korea in mid-December, as well as by other officials at this time to China and the United Arab Emirates, attested to Ukraine's continuing broad-ranging efforts to develop and diversify its economic and trade links.

After his visit to Ankara, Kuchma confirmed that Ukraine and Turkey intended to go ahead with the construction of an oil pipeline from Ceyhan to Samsun.[60] On 16 December, Ukrainian, Georgia and Azerbaijani officials also agreed at a meeting in Odesa to create a sea transportation corridor from Ukraine (Odesa, Ilichivsk), to Georgia (Poti), connected by overland routes to a sea-link from Azerbaijan (Baku) to Turkmenistan (Krasnovodsk), which would form the western extension of a new Euro-Asian trade route linking Central Asia with the Black Sea.[61]

Whether coincidentally or not, the vulnerability of the proposed new sea-link between Georgia and Ukraine had, however, been graphically demonstrated by the arrest in early December by Russian border guard vessels patrolling Georgian territorial waters of a Ukrainian ship near Batumi. This incident, which drew protests from Ukraine and even stronger ones from Georgia, was another blow to relations between Kyiv and Moscow. Once again, though, the Ukrainian leadership exercised restraint. Kuchma continued to express the hope that 'good will, political wisdom and simple common sense' would prevail and that once President Yeltsin had recovered from his heart operation he would find it in himself to come to Kyiv to sign the long-stalled friendship treaty and thereby

---

[58] *Ibid.*, 8 and 11 November 1996. See also Monitor, 6 November 1996.

[59] Monitor, 9 December 1996.

[60] *Den*, 4 December 1996.

[61] Ukrinform, 17 December 1996. On the plans for the new Eurasian trade corridor, see Bruce Clark, 'In Marco Polo's Footsteps', *Financial Times*, 19 December 1996.

remove the 'cold spirit of alienation and mistrust' threatening bilateral relations.[62]

In the meantime, the renewed 'interest' in Moscow in Sevastopol's status seemed to have an instant resonance in Crimea. In the first half of October, the speaker of the Crimean parliament, Suprunyuk, who was criticized for being too pro-Ukrainian, was removed by a vote of no confidence and a moderate pro-Russian deputy, Vasilii Kiselev, elected to replace him. But as local observers pointed out, the political struggle in Crimea seemed increasingly to reflect a scarcely concealed struggle between rival economic clans or mafias for control of the peninsula's resources, rather than a battle over Crimea's relationship with Ukraine.[63] Nevertheless, the more militant pro-Russian forces remained active. For instance, at the end of November, a conference was held in Sevastopol at which complaints about alleged discrimination against Russians in Crimea were voiced and an appeal addressed to the Russian parliament calling for support. The gathering transformed itself into the founded meeting of a 'Russian Duma of Sevastopol'.[64]

Meanwhile, in the Donbas, the sentencing of the first two strike leaders to be tried for disturbing public order, who were given sentences of three and two and a half years respectively, had threatened to produce new protests. In the second half of November, however, the Verkhovna Rada decided to declare an amnesty for all the fourteen strike leaders who had been detained or imprisoned. The pro-Russian organizations in the Donbas, such as the Civic Congress of Ukraine, the Party of Slavonic Unity, the Union of Peace-loving Forces and the Inter-movement also kept up their separatist agitation. For example, the Civic Congress distributed leaflets arguing that there was no common language or interests between Western and Eastern Ukraine and condemning what were described as official efforts to integrate the two and thereby prevent the Donbas from achieving a union with Russia.[65] As in Crimea, on

---

[62] Reuter, 14 December 1996. Horbulin, however, commented that the incident 'leads to the sad conclusion that if the Georgians can do nothing about the Russian military in their own port, then we will have to think very hard about Sevastopol'. Reuter, 12 December 1996.

[63] See for example Ron Popeski's report: 'Ukraine's separatist Crimea plunges into clan warfare', Reuter, 7 October 1996.

[64] UNIAN and *Flag Rodiny*, 30 November 1996.

[65] *Donetskii Kryazh*, no. 43, 1996.

29 November, a meeting was convened in Donetsk at which local trade union and political leaders condemned, on the one hand, the government's economic policies and called for President Kuchma's resignation, and on the other, defended the local dominance of the Russian language and denounced the activities of the Ukrainian Orthodox Church – Kyiv Patriarchate. At the meeting, the Donetsk regional council of trade unions proposed the founding of a public and political bloc – 'Working Donbas' – to promote the 'revival' and 'interests' of the region.[66]

But all this was overshadowed by the professionally-executed assassination on 3 November of a leading businessman from Donetsk and deputy in the Verkhovna Rada, Yevhen Shcherban, together with his wife and one other person in Donetsk airport, which had sent a shudder of revulsion through the country and once again fixed attention on the rampant growth of organized crime and corruption. Moreover, the fact that after the unsuccessful attempt on Lazarenko's life Shcherban's brother Volodymyr had been removed as the head of the Donetsk regional administration, and that the Shcherbans had become closely allied with Marchuk, set off all sorts of speculation.[67]

And, of course, all this time, the Ukrainian government was still continuing to grapple with its huge wage payment crisis, with arrears amounting in mid-October to an estimated $1.7 billion. Little relief was to be gained from reports about similar difficulties and hardships in Russia, Belarus, Kazakhstan and other CIS countries. In mid-October the Verkhovna Rada approved a three-year economic programme prepared by the government designed to accelerate market reform and structural change. It foresaw growth in industrial output during 1997, tax reforms and a further reduction of inflation, but also continuing state support for key industries and the agro-industrial sector. Lazarenko was able to promise workers only gradual relief in monthly installments from the hardships caused by wage arrears and appealed for more patience until production got going again.[68]

---

[66] UNIAN, 30 December, and Monitor, 2 December, 1996.

[67] See Oleg Varfolomeyev, 'Businessman's Murder Impacts on Ukrainian Politics', *Analytical Brief*, OMRI, Prague, vol. 1, no. 462 (14 November 1996).

[68] Reuter, 15 October 1996. For a useful discussion of the programme, see Ben Slay, 'Ukraine's Economic Program – More Muddling Through?', *Analytical Brief*, OMRI, vol. 1, no. 395 (17 October 1996).

Soon afterwards, the Ukrainian prime minister warned the country of worse to come, announcing that the government would be drastically raising duties on food imports in order to protect domestic food producers. By early December, though, the first signs of a rift between the prime minister and the president began to appear as Kuchma criticized the government for seeking to reduce social benefits and accused it of 'inefficiency' and 'lack of responsibility'.[69] There was a further surprise when, on 11 December, the president suddenly sacked his embattled chief of staff, Tabachnyk, thereby removing a figure who until now been his gatekeeper and his close and influential lieutenant. With the departure of Tabachnyk, who had also been Kuchma's presidential election campaign manager, questions immediately arose about how the increasingly isolated president would manage.[70]

The fifth year of Ukraine's independence drew to a close with the Ukrainian parliament and government struggling to agree on an another austerity budget for 1997, the president still seeking to delineate his powers *vis à vis* the parliament and government, one of Chornobyl's remaining two reactors having been shut down but no alternative source of energy for the approaching winter found to replace it, and negotiations continuing with foreign donors and creditors about the level and terms of foreign financing for its reform programme. In fact, in a strong demonstration of support, on 17 December, representatives of donor countries and international financial institutions pledged, at a meeting in Washington, broad financial assistance for Ukraine of over $5 billion over the next three years, providing the country stuck to its economic reform course.[71] Thus, despite the continuing difficulties with Russia, Ukraine's political independence seemed secure, but given the country's continuing difficulties in making ends meet and securing sufficient energy, it rested on a delicate new dependence on Western and Eastern credits and loans.

---

[69] OMRI Daily Digest, 5 December 1996.

[70] Matthew Kaminski, 'Embattled Kuchma Sacks Aide', *Financial Times*, 12 December 1996.

[71] Reuter, 17 December 1996.

Achievements and challenges

After five years of independence, numerous other problems and challenges lay ahead. The economic recession and dismantling of Soviet structures had left Ukraine's science, education, culture and press, not to mention social and health services, exposed to the vagaries of inflation and market forces. The cultural renaissance that many had hoped independence would usher in had been less than vibrant, and the Ukrainian language found itself under renewed pressure; many Ukrainian publications had been forced to fold and Russian-language newspapers and books (many of them published in Russia) had increasingly flooded the market.[72] The regional and religious divisions in society, though gradually becoming less pronounced, persisted, and the ecological and demographic situation was hardly encouraging. Most of all, the continuing economic and social hardships and uncertain future, on the one hand, and corruption, crime and political confrontation hindering the reform of the political and economic system, on the other, had resulted in social exhaustion and widespread apathy.

Nevertheless, with every month and year that passed, Ukraine's independence was being consolidated, and the building of a new state, however run-down it might have appeared as result of the difficult political and economic conditions and squandered time, had continued. Judged by the pace of change in some of its former Soviet bloc neighbours to the west, Ukraine's progress had been disappointingly slow, but compared, more fittingly, to the record of most of the independent states which had emerged as a result of the collapse of the Soviet Union, including Russia, it could claim some distinction.

Despite all of its problems, Ukraine had managed to preserve peace and stability on its territory – which was no mean achievement considering the conflicts and bloodshed which had afflicted many

---

[72] Indeed, in early December, President Kuchma instructed the government to draft a revised version of the Law on Languages with the aim of bolstering the Ukrainian language especially in the sphere of publications and education (Radio Ukraine, 7 December 1996). Typically, a meeting on 4 December chaired by Deputy Prime Minister Kuras to examine the implementation of the state programme for the development of the Ukrainian language in the Kharkiv region had revealed that only 23% of classes in the local junior schools were taught in Ukrainian and less than 8% in institutes of higher learning (Ukrinform, 5 December 1996).

of the other CIS countries – and avoided allowing differences with neighbours to get out of hand. While engaged simultaneously in quasi-decolonization, state-building, fundamental political and economic transformation, demilitarization and the conversion of a huge military-industrial sector to peaceful uses, it had sought to forge a sense of statehood built on modern democratic notions of political citizenship rather than ethnicity, and to base its external relations on openness and good-neighbourliness.

Determined to uphold its independence in the face of strong integrative pressures being generated within the CIS by Russia, and opposed to any new division of Europe into two political and military blocs, Ukraine's sovereignty and neutrality had become a key element in the new European security architecture. As Henry Kissinger put it in the summer of 1996: 'The long-term stakes are high. If Ukraine were to share the fate of Belarus and return to Russian satellite status, tremors would be felt all over Europe. A militarization of diplomacy would be nearly inevitable.'[73] This seemed to have registered with most of the leading Western states: after the caution and skepticism with which they generally responded to Ukraine's push for independence, led by the United States, they had increasingly embraced the country, helping it with internal economic and political stabilization and to anchor itself in Western institutions. This had come after a better understanding of Ukraine's security concerns and recognition that it did not in fact harbour ambitions of becoming a nuclear power. Because of geopolitical and economic realities, though, Ukraine seemed destined to remain a Janus, looking, whatever its actual preferences, east and west simultaneously and continuing the difficult balancing act.

For all the immense difficulties facing it, after five years of independence, Ukraine was recovering and strengthening its own sense of history, pride and identity; furthermore, its leadership was striving to move it towards a better future in which the potential and wealth of this large country would be put to better use. A new generation was growing up in a sovereign and by and large free country, and the hope was that it would be able to shed some of the complexes and neuroses of its parents.

Viewed from a historical perspective, Ukraine's national renewal and resurgent political assertiveness during the dramatic decade since

[73] Henry A. Kissinger, 'Beware: A Threat Abroad', *Newsweek*, 17 June 1996.

the apocalyptic visions of doom and gloom were released together with the deadly radiation by the exploding reactor in Chornobyl had indeed been remarkable. For all the mass rallies, political confrontation, strikes and heated emotions, it had been a singularly peaceful and self-restraining revolution, though not exactly a velvet one. The result was paradoxical: the new Ukraine was not what many patriots had hoped for; but then, it was also not what the opponents of Ukrainian nationalism had feared.

But five years after achieving independence, Ukraine was still not out of the woods: numerous economic, social, political and security problems were the trees that blotted out the light. The future was still full of imponderables. How soon would Ukraine be able to reverse the economic decline and begin raising productivity and living standards? Would the Ukrainian political élite manage to overcome regional, business or ideological interests, safeguard national unity and work jointly for the national good? Would the friction between the different branches of government be reduced, could the parliamentarians agree on a new election law opening up the system to modern political parties, and would the political system be able to combat crime and corruption? Would Ukraine manage to keep the centrifugal tendencies in the Donbas and Crimea in check and to accommodate regional pressures? How would the integration of the country proceed: was Ukraine destined to become an Eastern European variant of Belgium divided into two distinct linguistic communities? Relations with Russia and the West still needed to be formalized, but what form would this take? Would Ukraine's significance decline as Central and Eastern European states were absorbed into Euro-Atlantic structures and be sacrificed as a part of a new implicit division of Europe? Or would its importance as a bridge, indeed even a potential drawbridge, between East and West, remain? Was Ukraine destined to keep looking nervously over its shoulder at its northern neighbour and to remain exposed to the vicissitudes of Russian domestic politics, or would its gradual integration into European structures provide the security and stability it was seeking?

All these future uncertainties notwithstanding, though, the Ukrainian resurgence at the end of the twentieth century was indeed something of a miracle, and even 'believers' have had problems coming to terms with it. A country, one of Europe's largest at that, which had been partitioned for most of its history and until only recently had seemed condemned never to reappear again on the map of Europe as an independent state, has emerged from historical and political oblivion and assumed responsibility for its own future. Despite fears and all sorts of gloomy predictions, the country has held together and stood its ground. Undoubtedly, the road Ukraine has embarked on has proved more painful and difficult than many had expected, or were prepared for, and more challenges and dangers still lie ahead. Recalling, however, W.B. Yeats's description of Ireland's experience 80 years earlier, Ukraine was certainly not the first 'terrible beauty' to be born; left only to regret that history had not been a kinder midwife in those years to their country as well, the builders of the new Ukraine nevertheless took pride in this late European child.

POSTSCRIPT

During the late spring and summer of 1997 Ukraine concluded a number of major agreements. It seemingly settled its long-standing dispute with Russia over the fate of the Black Sea Fleet and its basing in Sevastopol, and saw at the end of May the long-awaited visit to Kyiv by President Yeltsin and the signature of a Ukrainian-Russian treaty of friendship and cooperation. It also finally concluded a similar treaty with Romania, and Presidents Kuchma and Kwasniewski signed a document on Ukrainian-Polish historic reconciliation. In July Ukraine signed a special partnership agreement with NATO. In September, Ukraine's international reputation was given a major boost when Foreign Minister Udovenko was elected president of the UN General Assembly.

Domestically, though, progress with the political and economic reform efforts continued to be slow: battles over powers between the president and the parliament were renewed, and the left continued its blocking tactics. In the middle of 1997 Kuchma replaced prime minister Lazarenko, who was accused of corruption and illegal dealings, with a close political ally, Valerii Pustovoitenko, thereby confirming the split within the ranks of the 'Dnipropetrovtsi'. Holovaty, Durdynets and Kuras were among the ministers who did not reappear in the new Cabinet of Ministers.

In late August 1997 the IMF approved a $542 million stand-by loan but deferred consideration of a longer and larger $2.5 to $3 billion credit. The IMF's assessment of the situation, as reported by Reuter on 25 August 1997, put it succinctly: 'While Ukraine has made great strides, formidable challenges remain as domestic consensus on the nature of reform is sought, particularly as parliamentary elections approach.'

With new parliamentary elections scheduled for March 1988, leftist deputies opposed the adoption of a new election law proposing a mixed majoritarian-proportional representation system. Kuchma's calls for a one-year delay of the parliamentary elections were unsuccessful. The new election law was finally adopted in late

September 1997 after which the country's political forces focused on preparing their election campaigns.

The president's supporters formed the People's Democratic Party (PDP) led by Pustovoitenko; Lazarenko created his own 'social democratic' Hromada (Community) party, and Marchuk and Kravchuk joined forces in the centre-right United Social Democratic Party of Ukraine. Because of political rivalry and distrust, Rukh, still led by Chornovil, and other national democratic and rightist parties were unable to form an effective electoral coalition. The reinvigorated Communist Party led by Petro Symonenko, which with a membership of 140,000 was the country's largest and best organised political party, however, prepared to reap the benefits of the new election law which favoured larger parties. Meanwhile, Moroz, still defiantly wearing two hats – that of parliamentary speaker and leader of the Socialist Party of Ukraine – exploited the increasingly ugly recriminations between Kuchma and Lazarenko and, while backing calls for the president's impeachment, sought to boost parliament's and his own standing.

The elections resulted in a leftward swing and an even more politically polarized parliament. Ironically, it was the Communists who experienced a resurgence, winning over a quarter of the seats (123) and emerging as by far the largest single party in the new 450-strong parliament. Together with their neo-Communist allies they could control about one-third of the votes. Rukh obtained 46 seats, the PDP 28, Hromada 23, the Green Party, an impressive 19, and the United Social Democratic Party, 16.

The political stalemate in the new parliament, accompanied by more miners' protests and social discontent, was demonstrated by the protracted process during the summer weeks of electing a new speaker. Moroz, Symonenko, Kravchuk, Plyushch and quite a few other compromise candidates failed, often by just a few votes, to be elected before, finally, after about twenty attempts, the conservative leftist agrarian, Oleksandr Tkachenko, obtained the requisite number of votes. Control over the parliamentary commissions (renamed 'committees') was divided up among the parties represented in the legislature, with Moroz (agrarian policy), Marchuk (social policy and labour), Oliinyk (foreign relations), Udovenko (human rights, national minorities and inter-religious relations) and Tanyuk (culture) emerging among the new heads. Others included the Communists, Hurenko, whose return to political life was rewarded by his party with the chairmanship of the committee on economic policy, and Hryhorii Kryuchkov, who was given stewardship over the committee on defence and security.

The results of the 1998 parliamentary election and the appointment of the new parliament's officials confirmed that Ukrainian society continued to be pulled in opposite directions: forward and backwards, westward and eastward. Just as President Kuchma and his team were coming under mounting pressure from the IMF and western states to move ahead with economic reforms and to overcome the external frustration with the sluggish pace of change and rampant corruption, the Communists and their allies had taken control of key committees within the parliament. Furthermore, although Ukraine's most pro-Western diplomat, Borys Tarasyuk, has been recently been appointed by Kuchma to replace Udovenko as foreign minister (the latter had become a deputy from Rukh), the Communist leader Symonenko was publicly in league with Russian and Belarusian colleagues who wanted to restore the former Union, and Kryuchkov, was voicing his aversion to NATO.

After seven years of independence, having secured for itself conducive external relations, but still plagued by its internal economic malaise and political divisions, Ukraine was still in the throes of systemic transition and did not seem adequately prepared to face the challenges of the twenty-first century. At almost the end of the twentieth century, as Russia and other former Soviet states also struggled to come to terms with their changed status and the vagaries of political and economic transformation, the fate of the second Ukrainian resurgence in modern times hung in the balance.

SELECT BIBLIOGRAPHY

Works on Ukrainian History

Hrushevsky, Michael, *A History of Ukraine*, New Haven, 1941.
Hunczak, Taras (ed.), *The Ukraine, 1917-21: A Study in Revolution*, Cambridge, MA, 1977.
Joukovsky, Arkady, *Histoire de L'Ukraine*, Paris, 1993.
Kamm, Michael F., *Kiev: A Portrait, 1800-1917*, Princeton, 1993.
Kappeler, Andreas, *Kleine Geschichte der Ukraine*, Munich, 1994.
Luckyj, George S.N., *Between Gogol' and Sevcenko: Polarity in the Literary Ukraine: 1798-1847*, Munich, 1971.
Magocsi, Robert Paul, *Ukraine: A Historical Atlas*, Toronto, 1985.
Magocsi, Paul Robert, *A History of Ukraine*, Toronto, Buffalo, London, 1996.
Prymak, Thomas M., *Mykhailo Hrushevsky: The Politics of National Culture*, Toronto, 1987.
Rudnytsky, Ivan L., *Essays in Modern Ukrainian History*, Edmonton, 1987.
Saunders, David, *The Russian Impact on Russian Culture 1750-1850*, Edmonton, 1985.
Subtelny, Orest, *Ukraine: A History*, Toronto, 1988.
Szporluk, Roman, *Ukraine: A Brief History*, Detroit, 1979.

Works on the Nationalities Question in the Soviet Union

Carrère d'Encause, Hélène, *L'Empire éclaté*, Paris, 1978.
Conquest, Robert (ed.), *The Last Empire: Nationality and the Soviet Future*, Stanford, 1986.
Hajda, Lubomyr, and Mark Bessinger, *The Nationalities Factor in Soviet Politics and Society*, Boulder, CO, 1990.
Nahaylo, Bohdan, and Victor Swoboda, *Soviet Disunion: A History of the Nationalities Problem in the USSR*, London and New York, 1990.
Pipes, Richard, *The Formation of the Soviet Union: Communism and Nationalism, 1917-1923*, Cambridge, MA, rev. edn 1964.
Simon, Gerhard, *Nationalism and Policy Toward the Nationalities in the Soviet Union. From Totalitarian Dictatorship to Post-Stalin Society*, Boulder, CO, 1991.

Works on Ukraine under Soviet Rule

Bilas, Ivan, *Represyvno-Karalna Systema v Ukraini 1917-1953* [The Repressive-Punitive System in Ukraine, 1917-53], 2 vols, Kyiv, 1994.

555

Conquest, Robert, *The Harvest of Sorrow: Soviet Collectivization and the Terror-Famine*, London, 1986.

Dmytryshyn, Basil, *Moscow and the Ukraine 1918-1953: A Study of Russian Bolshevik Nationality Policy*, New York, 1956.

Krawchenko, Bohdan, *Social Change and National Consciousness in Twentieth-Century Ukraine*, London, 1985.

Liber, George, *Soviet Nationality Policy, Urban Growth, and Identity Change in the Ukrainian SSR 1923-1934*, Cambridge, 1992.

Mace, James E., *Communism and the Dilemmas of National Liberation: National Communism in Soviet Ukraine 1918-1933*, Cambridge, MA, 1983.

Sullivant, Robert S., *Soviet Politics and the Ukraine, 1917- 1957*, New York and London, 1962.

Turchenko, F.H., *Novitnya Istoriya Ukrainy, Chastyna Persha, (1917-1945 rr.)* [Modern History of Ukraine, Part One, 1917- 1945], Kyiv, 1994.

Works on Ukraine, 1945-85

Badzo, Iurii, 'An Open Letter to the Presidium of the Supreme Soviet of the USSR and the Central Committee of the CPSU', Part 1 and Part 2, *Journal of Ukrainian Studies* (Toronto), nos 17 (summer 1984) and 18 (winter 1984), respectively.

Baran, V.K, *Ukraina pislya Stalina* [Ukraine after Stalin], Lviv, 1992.

Bihun, Yaroslav (ed.), *Boomerang: The Works of Valentyn Moroz*, Baltimore and Paris, 1974.

Bilinsky, Yaroslav, *The Second Soviet Republic: The Ukraine After World War II*, New Brunswick, NJ, 1964.

Bilinsky, Yaroslav, 'Shcherbytsky, Ukraine and Kremlin Politics', *Problems of Communism*, XXXII (July-August 1983).

Browne, Michael (ed.), *Ferment in the Ukraine*, London and Basingstoke, 1971.

Chornovil, Vyacheslav, *The Chornovil Papers*, New York, 1968.

Dzyuba, Ivan, *Internationalism or Russification? A Study in the Soviet Nationalities Problem*, London, 1968.

Hodnett, Grey, 'The Views of Petro Shelest', *Annals of the Ukrainian Academy of Arts and Sciences in the United States*, vol. 1, nos 37-8 (1978-80).

Kasyanov, Heorhii, *Nezhodni: ukrainska intelihentsiya v rusi oporu 1960-80-kh rokiv* [Dissenters: the Ukrainian Intelligentsia in the Opposition Movement of the 1960s-1980s], Kyiv, 1995.

Kolasky, John, *Two Years in Soviet Ukraine*, Toronto, 1970, p. 206.

Koropecky, I.S. (ed.), *The Ukraine Within the USSR: An Economic Balance Sheet*, New York, 1977.

Koval, Vitalii, *'Sobor' i navkolo Soboru* ['Sobor' and Around Sobor] Kyiv, 1989.

Krawchenko, Bohdan (ed.), *Ukraine After Shelest*, Edmonton, 1983.

Lewytzkyi, Borys, *Politics and Society in Soviet Ukraine: 1953-1980*, Edmonton, 1984.

Potichnyj, Peter J., *Ukraine in the Seventies*, Oakville, Ont., 1975.

Verba, Lesya, and Bohdan Yasen, *The Human Rights Movement in Ukraine: Documents of the Ukrainian Helsinki Group 1976-1980*, Baltimore, 1980.

Works dealing with the Final Years of the USSR and Post-Soviet Period

Carrère d'Encausse, Hélène, *The End of the Soviet Empire: The Triumph of the Nations*, New York, 1993.

Clark, Bruce, *An Empire's New Clothes*, London, 1995.

Corbet, Jurgen, and Andreas Gummich, *The Soviet Union at the Crossroads: Facts and Figures on the Soviet Republics*, Frankfurt, 1990.

Dawisha, Karen, and Bruce Parrot, *Russia and the New States of Eurasia: The Politics of Upheaval*, Cambridge, 1994.

Diuk, Nadia, and Adrian Karatnycky, *New Nations Rising: The Fall of the Soviets and the Challenge of Independence*, New York, 1993.

Dunlop, John B., *The Rise of Russia and Fall of the Soviet Empire*, Princeton, 1993.

Kolstoe, Paul, *Russians in the Former Soviet Republics*, London, 1995.

Matlock, Jack F., Jr, *Autopsy on an Empire: The American Ambassador's Account of the Collapse of the Soviet Union*, New York, 1995.

Morrison, John, *Boris Yeltsin: From Bolshevik to Democrat*, London, 1991.

Muiznieks, Nils, R., 'The Influence of the Baltic Popular Movements on the Process of Soviet Disintegration', *Europe-Asia Studies*, vol. 47, no. 1 (1995).

Smith, Graham, *The Nationalities Question in the Post-Soviet States*, London and New York, 1996.

Trapans, Jan Arveds (ed.), *Toward Independence: The Baltic Popular Movements*, Boulder, CO, 1991.

Yeltsin, Boris, *The Struggle for Russia*, New York, 1994.

Yergin, Daniel, and Thane Gustafson, *Russia 2000 And What it Means for the World*, New York, 1995.

Ukraine, 1985-95

Alexandrova, Olga, *Von einer Soujetrepublik zu einem europäischen Staat: Anfänge der Ausenpolitik der Ukraine*, Berichte des Bundesinstituts für ostwissenschaftliche und internationale Studien, no. 14 (1992), Cologne.

——,*Perzeptionen der auswärtigen Sicherheit in der Ukraine*, Berichte des Bundesinstituts für ostwissenschaftliche und internationale Studien, no. 40 (1993), Cologne.

Arel, Dominique, 'Language Politics in Independent Ukraine: Towards One or Two State Languages?', *Nationalities Papers*, vol. 23, no. 3 (1995).

Åslund, Anders, 'Eurasia Letter: Ukraine's Turnaround', *Foreign Policy*, no. 100 (Fall 1995).

Bahry, Romana M. (ed.), *Echoes of Glasnost in Soviet Ukraine*, Toronto, 1989.

Bilous, A.O., *Politychni obyednannya Ukrainy* [Political Associations of Ukraine], Kyiv, 1993.

Bilous, Artur, 'Ukraine's Parliament: Who's in Power?', *Demos* (Kyiv), vol. II, no. 1 (June 1995).

Boiko, O.D., *Ukraina 1991-1995: Tini Mynuloho chy Kontury Maibutnoho (Narysy z novit istorii)* [Ukraine 1991-1995: Shadows of the Past or Contours of the Future (Essays on Recent History)], Kyiv, 1996.

Bociurkiw, Bohdan, 'The Ukrainian Catholic Church in the USSR under Gorbachev', *Problems of Communism*, no. 6 (November-December 1990).

Bojcun, Marko, 'The Ukrainian Parliamentary Elections in March-April 1994', *Europe-Asia Studies*, vol. 47, no. 2 (1995).

Bremmer, Ian, 'The Politics of Ethnicity: Russians in the New Ukraine', *Europe-Asia Studies*, vol. 46, no. 2 (1994).

Brzezinski, Ian J., 'Polish-Ukrainian Relations: Europe's Neglected Strategic Axis', *Survival*, vol. 35, no. 3 (Autumn 1993).

Burant, Stephen R., 'Foreign Policy and National Identity: A Comparison of Ukraine and Belarus', *Europe-Asia Studies*, vol. 47, no. 7.

Chemerys, Valentyn, *Prezydent*, Kyiv, 1994.

Council of Europe, Parliamentary Assembly, *Report on the Application by Ukraine for Membership of the Council of Europe* (Rapporteur: Mr Masseret, France, Socialist Group), ADOC7370, Strasbourg, 7 September 1995.

Drohobycky, Maria, 'Ukraine and its Ethnic Minorities: An Overview' in Maria Drohobycky (ed.), *Managing Ethnic Tension in the Post-Soviet Space*, Washington, DC, 1995.

Garnett, Sherman W., 'The Ukrainian Question and the Future of Russia', *Politychna Dumka* [Political Thought] (Kyiv), no. 4 (1994).

Haran, O.V., *Ukraina Bahatopartiina: Prohramni dokumenty novykh partii* [Multi-party Ukraine: Programmatical Documents of the New Parties], Kyiv, 1991.

——,*Ubyty Drakona: Z istorii Rukhu ta novykh partii na Ukraini*, [To Kill the Dragon: From the History of Rukh and New Parties in Ukraine], Kyiv, 1993.

Haynes, Viktor, and Marko Bojcun, *The Chernobyl Disaster*, London, 1988.

Hesli, Vicki L. 'Public Support for the Devolution of Power in Ukraine: Regional Patterns', *Europe-Asia Studies*, vol. 47, no. 1 (1995).

Holovaty, Serhiy, 'Ukraine: A View From Within', *Journal of Democracy*, vol. 4, no. 3 (July 1993).

Hrabovskyj, Serhiy and Leonid Shklar, 'The Journey from Colony to Independept State: An Assessment from a Five Year Perspective', *Politics and the Times* (Kyiv), no. 1, October–December 1995.

Instytut Natsionalnykh Vidnosyn i Politolohii NAN Ukrainy (Institute for National Relations and Political Science of the National Academy of Sciences of Ukraine), *Ukraina i Rossiya v Novom Geopoliticheskom Prostranstve* [Ukraine and Russia in the New Geopolitical Space], Kyiv, 1995.

Ivanychuk, Roman, *Blahoslovy dushe moya, Hospoda . . .* [Bless, My Soul, Lord . . .], Lviv, 1993.

Kaminsky, Anatol, *Na perekhidnomu etapi: 'Hlasnist', 'perebudova' i 'demokratyzatsiya' na Ukraini* [In a Transitional Stage: 'Glasnost', 'Restructuring', and Democratization in Ukraine], Munich, 1990.

Karpenko, Vitalii, 'Zaimit svoi mistya . . . [Take Your Places. . .]', *Vitchyzna*, no. 4 (April 1991).

Kincade, William H., and Natalie Melnyczuk, 'Eurasia Letter: Unneighborly Neighbors', *Foreign Policy*, no. 94 (Spring 1994).

Krawchenko, Bohdan, 'Ukraine: The Politics of Independence' in Ray Taras and Ian Bremmer (eds), *Nation and Politics in the Soviet Successor States*, Cambridge, 1993.

——(ed.), *Dissent in Ukraine Under Gorbachev*, London, 1989.

Kuzio, Taras, *Ukraine: The Unfinished Revolution*, London, 1992.

——, and Andrew Wilson, *Ukraine: Perestroika to Independence*, Edmonton and Toronto, 1994.

Lapychak, Chrystyna, 'Ukraine's Troubled Birth', *Current History*, October 1993.

——, 'Ukraine: 1995 in Review', in *Building Democracy, 1995*, OMRI Annual Survey of Central, Eastern and Southeastern Europe and the Former Soviet Union, London, 1996.

Lester, Jeremy, 'Russian Political Attitudes to Ukrainian Independence', *The Journal of Communist Studies and Transition Politics*, vol. 10, no. 2 (June 1994).

Lukanov, Yurii, *Tretii Prezydent: Politychnyi Portret Leonida Kuchmy* [The Third President: A Political Portrait of Leonid Kuchma], Kyiv, 1996.

Lytvyn, Volodymr, *Politychna Arena Ukrainy: Diiovi osoby ta vykonavtsi* [The Political Arena of Ukraine: The Cast and Performers], Kyiv, 1994.

Marples, David R., *Chernobyl and Nuclear Power in the USSR*, New York, 1986.

——, *The Social Impact of the Chernobyl Disaster*, New York, 1988.

——, *Ukraine Under Perestroika: Ecology, Economics and the Workers' Revolt*, New York, 1991.

Masol, Vitalii, *Upushchenyi Shans* [The Missed Chance], Kyiv, 1993.

Morrison, John, 'Ukraine's First Year of Independence', Royal Institute of International Affairs Briefing Paper, 1992.

——, 'Pereyslav and After: The Russian-Ukrainian Relationship', *International Affairs*, vol. 69, no. 4, October 1993.

Mearsheimer, John J., 'The Case for a Ukrainian Nuclear Deterrent', *Foreign Affairs*, vol. 72, no. 3, summer 1993.

Miller, Steven E., 'The Case Against a Ukrainian Nuclear Deterrent', *Foreign Affairs*, vol. 72, no. 3, summer 1993.

Motyl, Alexander J., *Dilemmas of Independence: Ukraine after Totalitarianism*, New York, 1993.

Nahaylo, Bohdan, *The New Ukraine*, London, 1992.

Oliinyk, Borys, *Dva roky v Kremli* (Two Years in the Kremlin), Kyiv, 1992.

Pavlychko, Solomea, *Letters from Kyiv*, Edmonton, 1992.

Potichnyj, Peter J., *Elections in Ukraine*, Berichte des Bundesinstituts für ostwissenschaftliche und internationale Studien, no. 36 (1990), Cologne.

Rumer, Eugene B., 'Eurasia Letter: Will Ukraine Return to Russia?', *Foreign Policy*, no. 96 (Fall 1994).

Rusnachenko, A.M., *Na shlyakhu do natsionalnoi armii (1989- 1991)* [On the Path to a National Army (1989-1991)], Kyiv, 1992.

Rusnachenko, Anatolii, *Probudzennya: Robitnychyi rukh na Ukraini v 1989 –1993 rokakh* [Reawakening: The Workers' Movement in Ukraine in 1989-1993], 2 vols, Kyiv, 1995.

Ryabchuk, Mykola, 'Civil Society and National Emancipation: The Ukrainian Case', in Zbigniew Rau (ed.), *The Reemergence of Civil Society in Eastern Europe and the Soviet Union*, Boulder, CO, 1991.

——, 'Vid "Malorosii" do "Indoyevropy": Stereotyp "Narodu" v Ukrainskii Suspilnii Svidomosti ta Hromadskii Dumtsi' [From 'Little Russia' to 'Indo-Europe': The Sterotype of the 'People' in Ukrainian Social Consciousness and Public Thought], *Politolohichni chytannya* [Politological Readings], Kyiv, no. 2 (1994).

Salii, Ivan, *Ya povertayus* [I am Returning], Kyiv, 1993.

Smolansky, Oles M., 'Ukraine's Quest for Independence: The Fuel Factor', *Europe-Asia Studies*, vol. 47, no. 1 (1995).

Solchanyk, Roman (ed.), *Ukraine: From Chernobyl' to Sovereignty: A Collection of Interviews*, London, 1992.

——, 'Ukraine, The (Former) Center, Russia and "Russia"', *Studies in Comparative Communism*, XXV, no. 1 (March 1992).

——, 'Russia, Ukraine, and the Imperial Legacy', *Post-Soviet Affairs*, vol. 9, no. 4 (October–December 1993).

——, 'The Politics of State Building: Centre–Periphery Relations in Post-Soviet Ukraine', *Europe–Asia Studies*, vol. 46, no. 1 (1994).

Sysyn, Frank E., 'The Third Rebirth of the Ukrainian Autocephalous Orthodox Church and the Religious Situation in Ukraine, 1989-1991', in Stephen K. Batalden (ed.), *Seeking God: The Recovery of Religious Identity in Orthodox Russia, Ukraine and Georgia*, DeKalb, IL, 1993.

Syvokin, Hryhorii, *Avtorytet. Literatura i krytyka v chas perebudovy: Statti, ese, informatsiya* [Authority. Literature and Criticism in the Time of Restructuring: Articles, Essays, Information], Kyiv, 1989.

Szporluk, Roman, 'National Reawakening: Ukraine and Belorrussia', in Uri Ra'anan (ed.), *The Soviet Empire: The Challenge of National and Democratic Movements*, Lexington and Toronto, 1990.

Tabachnyk, Dmytro, Interview with Petro Shelest, *Kyiv*, no. 10, 1989.

——, 'Apostol zasyoyu' [Apostle of Stagnation], *Vitchyzna*, nos 9, 10 and 11 (1992).

Tanyuk, Les, *Khronika oporu* [Chronicle of Resistance], Kyiv, 1991.

Turchenko, F.H., P.P. Panchenko, and S.M. Tymchenko, *Novitnya Istoriya Ukrainy: Chastyna Druha, 1945-1995 roky* [Modern History of Ukraine: Part Two, 1945-1995], Kyiv, 1995.

Umbach, Frank, *Russia and the Problems of Ukraine's Cohesion: Results of a Fact-Finding Mission*, Berichte des Bundesinstituts für ostwissenschaftliche und internationale Studien, Cologne, 1994.

UNDP, *Ukraine Human Development Report, 1995*, Kyiv, 1995.

Vrublevsky, Vitalii, *Vladimir Shcherbytsky: pravda i vymysly*, Kyiv, 1993.

Wilson, Andrew, 'Ukraine', in *Eastern Europe and the Commonwealth of Independent States 1994*, 2nd edn, London, 1994.

Wilson, Andrew, *Ukrainian Nationalism in the 1990s – A Minority Faith*, Cambridge, 1997.

Crimea and the Crimean Tatars

Bekirov, Nadir, 'The Crimean Tatar Movement & Ukrainian Strategy in the Crimea: A Chronology of Defeat', *Demos* (Kyiv), vol. II, no. 2 (September 1995).

Drohobycky, Maria (ed.), *Crimea: Dynamics, Challenges, and Prospects*, Lanham, MD, 1995.

Kuzio, Taras, *Russia-Crimea-Ukraine: Triangle of Conflict*, London, 1994.

Marples, David R., and F. Duke David, 'Ukraine, Russia and the Question of Crimea', *Nationalities Papers*, vol. 23, no. 2 (June 1995) pp. 261-89.

Sheehy, Ann and Bohdan Nahaylo, *The Crimean Tatars, Volga Germans and Meskhetians: Soviet Treatment of Some National Minorities*, 3rd ed, London, 1980.

Ukrainian Center for Independent Political Research, *The Crimea: Chronicle of Separatism (1992-1995)*, Kyiv, 1996.

INDEX

Abartsumov, Evgenii, 456
Academy of Sciences, Ukrainian, 120
Academy of Sciences, of the Ukrainian SSR,
    48n., 58, 82, 97, 107, 175, 179, 265
Academy of Sciences, USSR, 196
Action Group for the Release of Political
    Prisoners, 92
administrative-command system, 51, 116, 182,
    191, 196, 357
Afanasev, Yurii, 99, 195, 196, 253, 305, 370
Afghanistan, 44-5, 73, 195, 196, 228, 282
Agrarian bloc, 270, 483, 487
agriculture, 47, 50, 173, 209n., 272, 451,
    450, 493
Aitmatov, Chingiz: 40n, 66; and *The Day
    Lasts More than a Hundred Years,* 66
Aleksii II, Patriarch, 317, 336
Alma-Ata (Amaty), 68, 120, 429
Altai, 81
Alymov, Aleksandr, 58
Amosov, Mykola, 184
Anarchists, 9
Andreeva, Nina, 126, 138, 280
Andropov, Yurii, 45-6, 47
Andrusovo, Treaty of, 4
Annexation or Reunification?, 31
anti-Semitism, 7, 9, 410
Antonov, Viktor, 371
Arafat, Yasser, 543
Argentina, 497
Argumenty i fakty, 166, 229
Armenia and Armenians, 103, 108, 109, 123,
    126, 132, 136, 145, 146, 160, 195, 217,
    218, 248, 325, 332, 338, 346, 355
army, *see* national army; military
Arsenal Factory, Kyiv, 314
Ashgabat, 436, 480, 542
Association of Democratic Councils of Uk-
    raine, 311
Atlanta Olympics, 527-8
Atmoda, 203
Austria: 6, 17; development of Ukrainian
    national movement under Austrian rule,
    7-8;
Austria-Hungary, collapse of, 8

Azerbaijan, Azerbaijanis, 108, 109, 136, 146,
    215, 248, 355, 446, 449, 542, 543

Baburin, Sergei, 349, 444
Babyi Yar, 410
Badzo, Yurii: 41, 92, 204, 256, 269; and *The
    Right to Live,* 41
Bagrov, Mykola, 232-3, 346, 361, 390, 466
Bakatin, Vadim, 333
Baker, James, 421, 429
Baklanov, Grigorii, 138
Baku, 543
Baltakis, Algimantis, 157
Baltic republics/states, Balts, 74, 84, 135,
    147, 152, 153, 156, 170, 189, 192, 196,
    200, 210-11, 212, 236, 250, 263, 275,
    325, 332, 333, 334, 338, 346, 348, 349,
    394, 398, 421; protests on anniversary of
    Molotov-Ribbentrop Pact, 84, 212; in
    forefront of campaign for broadening
    republics' rights, 103, 108, 136; popular
    fronts in, 128-9, 132, 141, 152-3, 156,
    157, 171, 184-5, 186, 190, 212, 215;
    assistance to other national-democratic
    movements, 203, 215; Baltic Communist
    Parties contrasted with CPU, 206; Baltic
    proposals for economic autonomy ap-
    proved by USSR Congress of Peoples'
    Deputies, 209-10, 228, 210; human chain,
    212, 247; 'Interfronts' and 'Intermove-
    ments' in, 215; Ukrainians in, 217, 248;
    Gorbachev and use of military force in,
    338-41; and attempted coup in Moscow,
    373, 379; and NATO, 530
Baltic Sea coast, 4
Bandera, Stepan, 14, 23, 338, 467
banking system, 295
Baruzdin, Sergei, 57n.,
Batalov, Valerii, 388
Batih, Mykhailo, 190
Batumi, 543
Bavaria, 358
Bazilevsky, Volodymyr, 111
BBC World Service, 123
Bed, Viktor, 289

563

and results of elections to USSR Congress of People's Deputies, 184; nationalities policy 'Platform', 211-12; Central Committee attacks Baltic popular fronts, 215; Central Committee plenum on nationalities question, 225; Shcherbytsky and Chebrikov retired from Politburo, 225; motion to debate leading role of Party in USSR Supreme Soviet narrowly defeated, 243; formation of the 'Democratic Platform', 250; Gorbachev yields on monopoly of power and Union treaty issues at Central Committee plenum of 5 February 1990; 251; Twenty-eighth Congress of, 280, 288, 290-1, 292, 293, 294, 295, 296; issue of property of, 293, 296; Central Committee plenum, late July 1991, 367; and attempted coup in Moscow, 374, 383, offices sealed in Moscow and Leningrad, 385; Communist Party of Kazakhstan breaks away from 385; Gorbachev resigns as general secretary, announces nationalization of Party property and ban on Party activity in government structures and security forces, 393; Belarusian parliament suspends Party's activities, 393; Ukrainian parliament bans activities of CPU, 398

Communist Party of Ukraine (CPU): unsuccessful attempt to create independent Ukrainian Bolshevik party, 10; establishment of, 9; national composition in early years, 9; 'national Communist' current, 10; 'internationalist' current, 9; Ukrainization policies of national Communists during 1920s, 11-12; 'national deviationism', 12; purged by Stalin, 13; Khrushchev sent to head it, 13; combats Ukrainian 'bourgeois nationalism', 18; Kaganovich temporarily replaces Khrushchev as its chief, 18; during Khrushchev era, 20, 25-6; Shelest becomes its leader, 26; autonomous tendency under Shelest, 26-8, 30, 32-3; growth of, and Ukrainization of its leadership, under Shelest, 31; tensions within, 31, 33-8; Central Committee plenum of 29 March 1968, 36; Shelest's position comes under pressure, 37-8; Shelest's removal, 38; purge of 'national communists', 38-9; Shcherbytsky becomes Party leader, 38; Central Committee resolution on national question, 95-6; January 1988 Central Committee plenum at which Shcherbytsky is criticized,

104-7; hardline position of at Nineteenth Party Conference, 136; Central Committee plenum of 10 October 1988, 150-3; attempts to improve ideological work, 153-4; supports Russian Orthodox Church in order to weaken Ukrainian Catholics, 154-5; Central Committee plenum of 12 December 1988, 164; Ivashko elected second secretary, 164; concessions in language sphere, 165-6; tactics and strategy used against Rukh, 178, 179, 181-2, 202; preparation for elections to USSR Congress of People's Deputies and obstruction of democratic candidates, 183; results of elections to USSR Congress of People's Deputies breach its monopoly on power, 184; CPU plenum of 6 April 1989 takes stock of political situation after initial elections to USSR Congress of People's Deputies, 186; Central Committee plenum of 16 May 1989, 191-2; leaders express alarm to Moscow over situation in Ukraine, 210-11; forced to make more concessions to Ukrainian national movement, 215; tactics as regards Rukh's inaugural congress, 215-16; Communist supporters of Rukh, 218; CPU's reaction to Rukh's inaugural congress, 223-4; Gorbachev attends Central Committee plenum at which Shcherbytsky is replaced, 226; praise for Shcherbytsky, 226; Ivashko elected Shcherbytsky's successor, 228; Central Committee plenum, October 1989, 231-3; splits in CPU leadership emerge, 231; Hurenko elected second secretary, 233; Kravchuk becomes ideological secretary, 233; Central Committee plenum, 29 November 1989, 244-5; CPU's election platform, 245; Central Committee plenums begin to be conducted in Ukrainian, 245; social protests result in replacement of eight regional Party bosses, 246; pre-parliamentary election campaign and tactics against democratic opposition, 248-50; Central Committee resolution acknowledging famine of 1933 was a Stalinist crime, 249; growing ferment within, 251-2; hardliners urge firmness from Gorbachev, 251, 253-4; Democratic Platform group formed in Kyiv, 252; leadership implicitly criticized by Ukrainian Komsomol for conservatism, 252; Central Committee plenum of 22 February 1990 sees widening split between hardliners and

4; appeal by national democrats for end to religious antagonisms, 284; religious holidays introduced by the Verkhovna Rada, 337; Verkhovna Rada adopts laws on freedom of conscience and religious organizations, 353-4; conference of religious denominations, 411; splits and rivalry among Ukrainian Orthodox, 491-2
religious freedom, 142, 172, 198, 230, 244, 353-4, 411
Remnick, David, 231
Republican Deputies' Club, 213-14, 220, 234, 243
Republican Movement of Crimea (RDK), 434
Republican National Party (Russia), 269
restitution of cultural treasures, 114, 190
Reva, Vitalii, 314
revisionism, 21, 32, 54
Revolutionary Ukrainian Party (RUP), 6
Rifkind, Malcolm, 496
Riga, 203, 212, 248
Right-Bank Ukraine: 4; Polish-rule over 5-6; popular rebellions against Polish oppression, crushed with Russian help, 5-6; aborption after disintegration of Poland by Austria and Russia, 6; residual Polish influence in, 6
Rivne, 195, 247
Rivne region, 218
Robitnycha hazata, 106, 187
Rodionov, M., 253
Romania, Romanians: 48; seizure of ethnically Ukrainian areas in Bukovyna and Bessarabia by, 9, 408; restrictions on Ukrainian minority during inter-war period, 13-14; OUN activity in Bukovyna, 14; territorial losses stemming from Molotov-Ribbentrop Pact, 14, 408; creation of Moldovan SSR, 14; ally of Nazi Germany, 15; occupation of south-western Ukraine, establishment of 'Transnistria' and suppression of Ukrainian national movement, 15; forced by USSR to give up Northern Bukovyna and Southern Bessarabia, 17; Ukrainian minority in, 24; collapse of Ceausescu regime, 246, 252; Romanian national minority in Ukraine, 409, 419n.; territorial claims on Ukraine, 408-9, 497, 537; Ukrainian-Romanian relations, 408-09, 444-5, 497, 537, 551; and NATO, 497, 537; and Serpent Island, 497

Romanticism, 6
Romanov, Grigorii, 47, 52
Romanyuk, Patriarch Volodymyr, 492
Rome, 516
Rossiya bloc (Crimea), 527
Rossiya Molodaya (Young Russia), 206-7
Rostov region, miners' strike committee, 212-13
rouble, rouble zone, 435, 448, 449
Rozenko, Petro, 45
RSFSR (Russian Socialist Federated Soviet Republic): 57; millennium of Christianization of Kyivan Rus officially depicted as marking 1,000 years of Russian statehood, 65; and issue of attributes of statehood and sovereignty, 211, 254, 274, 275; 1990 election results in, 258; organisation of a Russian Communist Party, 269, 279, 280, 286; Ukraine's dependence on Russian fuel, 266, 289-90, 412-13; Declaration of State Sovereignty, 277; abolishes leading role of Communist Party, 279; and Black Sea Fleet, 278, 293, 306; main source of newsprint for Ukraine, 289-90; Declaration on the Principles of Inter-State Relations with Ukraine, 305; and Crimea, 322; relations with Ukrainian SSR, 325-31, 421, 422, 423; bilateral treaty with Ukrainian SSR, 325; and Union Treaty, 325, 326-27, 328, 329, 330-1, 346, 355; and Soviet federal budget, 338; creation of republican armed forces, 341; and referendum on future of the USSR, 351; institutes office of popularly elected executive president, 350, 354; parliament approves draft Union treaty, 370; pre-1917 Russian flag raised over Kremlin, 385; takes over Union institutions, 388, 392, 430; reactions to Ukraine's declaration of independence, 395-6; and issue of loose nukes, 395; sends delegation sent to Kyiv, 396-7; Ukrainian-Russian communique, 396-97, 421; recognizes independence of Ukraine, 421; economic difficulties, 412; emergence of anti-imperial 'Young Turks', 413; liberalizes prices, 416; and demise of USSR, 423-6, 427-9, 430, *see also* Russia
RSFSR Congress of People's Deputies, 258
RSFSR Congress of Writers, 56-7
RSFSR Supreme Soviet, 254, 275, 277, 305, 350, 354
RSFSR Writers Union, 138
Ruban, Petro, 54